Empire and Aftermath

HARVARD EAST ASIAN MONOGRAPHS
84

Yoshida Shigeru, 1878-1967, as a young diplomat (ca. 1907) and elder statesman (1964)

EMPIRE AND AFTERMATH

Yoshida Shigeru and the Japanese Experience, 1878–1954

J. W. DOWER

Published by COUNCIL ON EAST ASIAN STUDIES, HARVARD UNIVERSITY *and distributed by* HARVARD UNIVERSITY PRESS, *Cambridge (Massachusetts) and London* 1988

This book is dedicated

with love and gratitude

to my parents and aunt

Second printing 1988
Printed in the United States of America

The Council on East Asian Studies at Harvard University publishes a monograph series and, through the Fairbank Center for East Asian Research, administers research projects designed to further scholarly understanding of China, Japan, Korea, Vietnam, Inner Asia, and adjacent areas.

Library of Congress Cataloging in Publication Data

Dower, John W.
Empire and Aftermath: Yoshida Shigeru and the
Japanese Experience, 1878–1954
(Harvard East Asian monographs ; 84)
Bibliography: p.
Includes index.
1. Yoshida, Shigeru, 1878–1967. 2. Japan–
Foreign relations–20th century. 3. Japan–Politics
and government–20th century. 4. Prime ministers–
Japan–Biography. I. Harvard University. Council on
East Asian Studies. II. Title. III. Series
DS890.Y6D68 952.03'3'0924 [B] 79-17810
ISBN 0-674-25126-1

Contents

Acknowledgments

The personal debts incurred in preparing this manuscript are extensive, and it is a pleasure to acknowledge them and express gratitude here. The study began as a doctoral dissertation on "Yoshida Shigeru and the Great Empire of Japan, 1878–1945," accepted for the joint degree in History and Far Eastern Languages at Harvard in 1972. Professors Albert M. Craig and Edwin O. Reischauer were the readers of the dissertation, and they and their colleagues in Japanese studies at Harvard—Professors Howard Hibbett, Donald H. Shively, and Ezra Vogel—have been generous in supporting the project over an unexpectedly long period. Dr. Hata Ikuhiko and his colleagues in the "Postwar Financial History" project of the Japanese Ministry of Finance made it possible to have access to a rich collection of materials during research in Japan in 1972–1973. During this same period, Sasaki Zennosuke of the Yoshida International Education Promotion Foundation permitted use of the foundation's clippings concerning Yoshida, and Professor Inoki Masamichi and Nishimura Kumao kindly shared their thoughts on Yoshida. In 1975–1976, Professors Imazu Akira and Matsuo Takayoshi provided fine hospitality in Kyoto, and made it possible to use the library facilities of Kyoto University. Professor Fujii Jōji painstakingly transcribed hundreds of pages of Yoshida's letters into legible Japanese.

At an early stage in this research, Colonel Frank Kowalski permitted access to the original draft of his illuminating memoir on early Japanese rearmament, and over the years the following good acquaintances have shared materials and information on many of the subjects discussed here: Professor Gordon M. Berger, Professor Herbert P. Bix, William S. Borden, Charles P. Divine, Professor Charles S. Maier, Dr. Joe B. Moore, Professor Dick Kazuyuki Nanto, Ōkubo Genji, Professor Howard Schonberger, Professor Mark Selden, Kim Carpenter Stege, and Professor William Wray. As editor of the manuscript, Florence Trefethen offered many thoughtful and valuable suggestions. Harvard's Council on East Asian Studies, under whose auspices the book is appearing, generously permitted me to resuscitate an old affiliation with publishing and do the design and typography myself. In this task, David Horne of Horne Associates provided good and patient advice over long distances. I am grateful also to Katherine Frost Bruner for assistance in preparing the index. The frontispiece photograph of Yoshida at the very beginning of his diplomatic career is reprinted from the album *Yoshida Shigeru* (Asahi Shimbunsha, 1967) with the permission of Yoshioka Senzō; that depicting Yoshida wearing the imperial decorations bestowed upon him in 1964 was provided courtesy of the *Asahi Shimbun.*

My greatest debt is to my wife, Yasuko, with whom I reviewed some of the most difficult Japanese materials.

Funding was received from a number of sources over the course of almost a decade, beginning with graduate support from the Charles H. Smith bequest at Harvard, and from the U.S. government under the Title VI program. Support directed more specifically to the present study was received from the National Endowment for the Humanities, the Japan Foundation, the Graduate School of the University of Wisconsin, the East Asian Research Center at Harvard, and the Social Science Research Council. Without this, the project would have been impossible.

Finally, it is a pleasure indeed to acknowledge the numerous libraries, archives, and collections through which materials were obtained, and to thank the librarians and resource personnel involved. In Japan, these include the Ministry of Finance, which has assembled an outstanding collection of Japanese and English materials on the occupation in conjunction with its multi-volume project on postwar financial history; the National Diet Library (where Yoshida's prewar letters are maintained among the papers of his father-in-law, Makino Nobuaki [Shinken]); the Yoshida International Education Promotion Foundation (which maintains biographical materials on Yoshida, including tear-sheets from four years of reminiscences which appeared in the internal monthly newsletter of former Japanese diplomats, *Kasekikai Kaihō*); the National Planning Agency (for records of the Economic Stabilization Board); and the various decentralized libraries of Kyoto University.

In the United States, materials were obtained from the East Asian collection of the Harvard-Yenching Institute; Harvard's Houghton Library (the Joseph Grew papers); the John Foster Dulles collections at Princeton University; the Joseph M. Dodge papers at the Detroit Public Library; the oral-history materials on occupied Japan at Columbia University's Butler Library; the archives of the Supreme Commander for the Allied Powers, Japan, maintained under the National Archives in Suitland, Maryland; the Library of Congress (especially for microfilms of the captured archives of the Japanese Foreign Ministry for 1927–1928 and 1936–1938); the Center for Research Libraries in Chicago; and the libraries of the University of Wisconsin, Madison. The Public Records Office in London provided access to valuable Foreign Office records, pertaining especially to Yoshida's activities as ambassador to Great Britain from 1936 to 1938.

Yoshida & the 1980s: A Preface to the Paperback Edition

Empire and Aftermath was researched and written over a period of almost ten years, beginning in the late 1960s. It took longer than expected, led to subthemes unanticipated at the outset (especially concerning Japan's road to war and the war years themselves), and required more pages than planned. Looking back now, however, it is fair to say that a few large concerns lay behind the original selection of topic and persisted to the end. Readers must judge for themselves how clearly these emerge from the welter of detail, but four such concerns seem worth commenting on retrospectively as the book enters a new printing.

Uppermost in my mind was the need to break down the conventional historical compartments of "prewar," "wartime," and "postwar" Japan. It was still fashionable in the 1960s and 1970s to speak of post-1945 Japan as the "new" Japan. And, where legacies from the past were emphasized, it was often the positive prewar tradition of "Taishō democracy" that received greatest attention.

Without rejecting either the radical nature of many postsurrender changes or the importance of prewar democratic traditions, it seemed clear that the conservative political legacy linking prewar and postwar Japan deserved greater emphasis. And what better figure through whom to demonstrate this than Yoshida Shigeru, the proud old conservative who was unquestionably the preeminent political figure of postwar Japan? In a phrase I found felicitous, immediately after the war Prince Konoe Fumimaro described Yoshida as exemplifying "the consciousness of the era of Imperial Japan," and doubted he had a political future. He was right about Yoshida's politics but dead wrong about his future, and that is where the fascination of the subject lies. Yoshida bridged the decades from the turn of the century into the 1950s as successfully and colorfully as anyone, and he was more than just a representative figure. As the head of five cabinets between 1946 and 1954, he guided as well as reflected the trends of his time.

Since *Empire and Aftermath* was published, Western scholarship on modern Japan has, in fact, laid down a fairly steady barrage against the old chronological compartments. Detailed studies of labor and management, of the bureaucracy and policy-making structure, of individual companies and specific industrial sectors, and of economic development in general—all now tend to stress the critical importance of prewar and wartime developments to what happened after 1945. No one can really speak of the "new Japan" any longer without qualifying the flashy phrase with an extended historical discussion emphasizing the dynamic institutional and intellectual legacies of the decades prior to Japan's surrender.[1]

Yoshida seemed an enticing subject for a second reason as well. In his long career, both as prewar diplomat and postwar prime minister, he was preoccupied with Japan's place in the world. And, in his own eyes and the eyes of many observers, he was consistent in promoting a policy that made "diplomatic sense" for Japan. Yoshida thus provided a superb entrée to discussing not only continuities between prewar and postwar foreign policy, but also the symbiosis of international and domestic considerations throughout Japan's modern development.

But what, in fact, did such consistency on Yoshida's part entail? Essentially, two things. First, Yoshida presented himself as a realistic practitioner of power politics based on intimate Japanese relations with Great Britain and the United States. Before the war, in his idealized view, Japan could only find security and breathing space as an imperialist power by operating under the aegis of the *Pax Britannica.* After the war, he sought—and obtained—similar security and room to maneuver within the embrace of the *Pax Americana.* At the same time, Yoshida also enjoyed the reputation of being chary of Japanese military power. Both prewar and postwar, he was a bit of an enigma on this score; but that simply made him all the more interesting as a subject of study.

Both Yoshida's blunt realpolitik and his intriguing strain of resistance to accelerated militarization resonated with contemporaneous issues. *Empire and Aftermath* was begun during the bloodiest years of the war in Indochina, and at a time when Japan experienced the emergence of a vigorous peace movement as well as countervailing pressures (strongly supported by the U.S. government) to revise the Japanese "peace constitution" and rearm rapidly. The writing was punctuated, moreover, by the rude 1971 "Nixon shocks," whereby the United States unexpectedly announced a dramatic volte face in its traditional policy of containment of China—a policy the Japanese since Yoshida's time had acquiesced in faithfully albeit reluctantly—and then, a month later, abruptly devalued the dollar in an effort to undercut Japanese exports. Such circumstances gave immediacy to historical questions concerning Japan's ambiguous relationship with the United States, China, and Southeast Asia and the equally ambiguous thrust of its military policy. Times have changed, but the urgency of these questions remains undiminished.

Part and parcel with these concerns were two final large objectives: to restore the Japanese to English-language histories of Japan's period of occupation (1945–1952), and to assess the legacy of the occupation through someone like Yoshida who stood at the heart of events as Japan made the transition from occupation to restoration of sovereignty. There was a practical spur to these interests, for the declassification of pertinent archival materials was just commencing at that time, while recollections by both Japanese and American participants were becoming more numerous. Yoshida's death in 1967, at the age of eighty-nine, sparked many personal reminiscences on the Japanese side.

Restoring the Japanese to Japanese history meant, in this

instance, offering a corrective to the perception of the occupation period as little more than a top-down U.S. exercise in social engineering. This attitude has been encapsuled in evocative phrases such as "Japan's American interlude" and "MacArthur's Japan," but these are misleading. There was intricate give-and-take between occupiers and occupied, and immense diversity on the Japanese side. Through Yoshida, I hoped to show this in multiple ways. He is the most natural single figure through whom to highlight the role of the Japanese elites in instituting U.S. occupation-period directives, in resisting them, and in pursuing independent policies. He also spent much time skirmishing with other conservatives, exchanging thunderbolts with the political left, and assaying the winds of public opinion on critical issues of democratization and demilitarization. The American occupiers of Japan confronted a complex body politic indeed.

It followed from this that focus on the Japanese side also could help dispel, or at least mitigate, certain tenacious myths concerning Japanese behavior. One could not deal with a public figure as contentious as Yoshida, for example, without revealing the prevalence of disagreement, tension, and outright conflict within this allegedly homogeneous "consensus" society. Indeed, it is integral to my argument that the "Yoshida legacy" and the "legacy of the Yoshida era" are not the same. Where the former refers primarily to conservative trends and the nature of the U.S.-Japan alliance which emerged out of the occupation period, the latter is broader. It also includes democratic and pacifist ideals which survived primarily because they had the support of Yoshida's critics and opponents. Close scrutiny of the Japanese side also explodes the myth of extreme cultural determinism that permeates much contemporary writing about Japan. Of course culture matters; but the "patterns" of postwar Japanese development were most significantly shaped by peculiar historical circumstances, shifting configurations of power, and calculated policy decisions. Basic practices that are closely associated with Japan's postwar accomplishments—such as cooperation within and among groups, and even long-range planning—can be explained quite satisfactorily in practical and historical terms, without recourse to the mythology of unique and immutable cultural traits.

I trust some of this comes through in the text, but a great deal remains to be done on this score. Many other historical studies of individual and institutional Japanese actors in the early postwar years will be necessary before we can really begin to claim to have done the Japanese side justice. In retrospect, moreover, there is obviously a certain danger in such monographic focus on "great men" or major institutions, for this can become misleadingly elitist. It has become much more apparent over the last decade that any rigorous historical understanding of postwar Japan also will require study of participants at the middle echelons of public and private activity, as well as greater appreciation of social currents at the mass level.

My final large concern, assessing the "occupation legacy," ultimately pulled in several directions: toward policy legacies on the one hand and psychological legacies on the other. Both are controversial, and both have recently emerged as integral to current debates concerning where the Japanese nation stands today and may be heading tomorrow.

In 1979, when the book was first published, it was amply clear that Japan was on its way to achieving an economic stature far beyond Yoshida's or anyone else's wildest dreams. I felt at the time that the note of pessimism concerning Japan's "shallow economy" on which the Yoshida era ended, in 1954, was thus an especially valuable reminder of how far and fast Japan traveled between the mid-1950s and mid-1970s. Now, writing in the late 1980s, one can only be doubly taken aback at the speed and scale of Japan's economic growth–and the concommitant decline in the U.S. economic position. In this regard, the vaunted "Yoshida legacy" of concentrating on export-oriented economic expansion under the umbrella of U.S. military protection would appear to have borne incredible fruit.

Yet there is bitter fruit as well, and the legacy of the occupation years and Yoshida era as a whole is still hotly debated in Japan. To main-line conservatives, there is much to be proud of: the country is prosperous and peaceful, no mean accomplishment. The political right in Japan, however, asks not what was gained but what was lost during the critical post-surrender years. Here there is a rising chorus of lament for the humiliation that the very act of being occupied entailed; for the loss of romanticized traditional virtues; for alleged victims of victor's justice; and about legislation, including the liberal peace constitution, that betrays an alien hand. The political left, on the other hand, raises an entirely different question, namely, what was thwarted during the occupation and the years of Yoshida's premiership (and answers: genuine grass-roots democracy and real demilitarization). These points of contention were all clear before Yoshida stepped down as prime minister in 1954, and prosperity has not dampened their volatility.

At the same time, however, there now appears to be general agreement that the manner in which the occupation was terminated and sovereignty restored to Japan imposed an enduring psychological burden on the Japanese people. Whether we speak here of the Yoshida legacy or the legacy of the occupation and Yoshida era, the nub of the problem is clear: in identifying itself so closely with the cold-war *Pax Americana,* militarily and economically, Japan essentially abandoned any pretense at pursuing a genuinely independent foreign policy. What was rationalized at the time as a modest price to pay for security and sovereignty has become, over the ensuing decades, a festering wound to Japanese pride.

As the old colloquialism has it, there is no such thing as a free lunch. The so-called "free ride" in defense outlays, which was a major legacy of the peace settlement Yoshida worked out with the Americans in 1950–1952, had spectacular economic benefits for the Japanese, for ever since then their best brains and wholehearted energies have been focused on the non-militarized marketplace and not dissipated in weapons production. The intangible price paid for this, however, took the form of tacit acceptance by Japanese and Americans alike that, in the game of power politics, Japan's proper place was to be the cold-war follower, the loyal retainer, the adolescent, the pupil, the eternal inferior. It also took the form of thinly disguised racial ridicule of the Japanese as "mere transistor salesmen" (Charles DeGaulle's phrase) or "small and petty bookkeepers" (allegedly Henry Kissinger's scornful private characterization). No econometric model can measure this kind of cost.

In *Empire and Aftermath,* I have addressed the genesis of this psychological dilemma under the borrowed Japanese phrases "subordinate independence" and "dependent independence." These are terms that became popular among both left-wing and right-wing critics of the Yoshida policy in the 1950s, and, in spite of their ideological freight, they still strike me as succinct and accurate. Was subordination unavoidable? To a certain degree, yes—but what that certain degree was at any given point deserves rethinking. It is common knowledge that by 1950 the pressures on the Yoshida government to accede to a cold-war peace settlement were immense, but it is much less well appreciated that by this time the Japanese government possessed a fair amount of bargaining power vis-à-vis the United States, resting in great part upon apocalyptic U.S. reevaluations of Japan's strategic importance in the global balance of power. In what is surely his single most important contribution, Yoshida used this leverage adroitly to resist U.S. pressure for revision of the constitutional "peace clause" and rapid buildup of a huge military establishment (had the Americans had their way, the Japanese military would have been numerically larger by 1953 than it is today). In one of his least impressive performances, on the other hand, Yoshida failed to fight strongly in private for what he publicly declared to be a basic matter of "diplomatic sense," namely, the promotion of constructive ties with the People's Republic of China. Even some of his own trusted lieutenants privately agreed that Yoshida's handling of this latter issue was erratic and in the final analysis obsequious.

As these comments intimate, *Empire and Aftermath* does not fall into the category of hagiography. By and large, I find Yoshida's cantankerous personality and acerbic tongue more attractive than his politics, but I always have assumed that the evidence marshaled concerning his policies may be interpreted differently by others. I see no reasonable grounds for denying, however, that a serious long-term outcome of Yoshida's proudest moment, the peace settlement worked out beginning in 1950, has been the absence of a consciousness of genuine autonomy, the absence of a summons to statesmanship, and the absence of global vision and an appreciation of global responsibilities on the part of Japanese of all classes. For more than three decades, the Tokyo governments that succeeded Yoshida continued to acquiesce in the subordinate role vis-à-vis the United States, even while harboring doubts about the wisdom of U.S. policy (as in the case of the Indochina War, for example). The politicians, bureaucrats, technocrats, and executives who guided Japan's economic renaissance rarely paused to consider that capturing global markets might entail assuming global obligations. Up to the present day, neither side in the U.S.-Japan alliance really has been prepared to think in terms of parity and equality; and, as a consequence, the sudden vogue of "Japan as Number One" sloganeering (which dates from the end of the 1970s and is itself a new form of non-equitable thinking) has found Japanese and non-Japanese alike bewildered about what Japan's new economic leverage really portends, and what the country's global role should be.

There is some merit to the argument that the premiership of Nakasone Yasuhiro from 1982 to 1987 marked the beginning of the end of the Yoshida legacy. Nakasone's ambition and force of personality undoubtedly contributed to this perception, but the real blow to the low-posture neo-mercantilism associated with the "Yoshida school" came from the drastically altered nature of the world economy. By the time of Nakasone's tenure, Japan was no longer engaged in catch-up economics. The country could no longer cry poor as a rationalization for intense economic nationalism. The magnitude of Japan's economic success, to fuse two popular images, finally had made it impossible to continue plucking high global profits from a low posture.

Nakasone's response to Japan's new prosperity and the foreign resentments it engendered was to offer a broad policy agenda that appeared to depart significantly from the mainline conservative policies hitherto loosely associated with the Yoshida legacy. Included in this agenda were visions of a high-tech "information society" unimaginable in Yoshida's day, proposals for sweeping administrative and educational reform, recommendations for unraveling the export-oriented neo-mercantilism on which postwar economic growth rested and restructuring the domestic economy (discouraging savings, increasing consumption, promoting imports, internationalizing domestic financial markets, and so on), and new strategic policies which signaled a more expansive military role for Japan (including violation of the "one percent of GNP" ceiling on military budgets, approval of military technology transfers from Japan to other countries, and renewed calls for revision of the peace constitution). The Nakasone agenda also called, ambiguously, for the cultivation of a new nationalism compatible with Japan's new international role.[2]

Despite such intimations of a new era, however, it is still too soon to ring the death knell for the Yoshida legacy. Much of the Nakasone agenda remained wishful thinking when he stepped down from the premiership, including the critical proposals to "internationalize" Japan's domestic economy. The nexus of conservative political factions, bureaucracy, and big business which emerged by the end of the Yoshida era has become vastly more labyrinthine and diffuse, but still remains formidably entrenched. Japan's strategic policies remain utterly dependent on Washington. Indeed, the Nakasone government's decision to permit Japanese participation in the U.S. Strategic Defense Initiative (the dubious "Star Wars" program) can be best interpreted not as the assumption of new military responsibilities, but rather as a new manifestation of subordination to U.S. strategy. At the same time, however, although certain taboos on military expansion have been violated, popular sentiment continues to hold Japan's leaders to the general policy of "go-slow" remilitarization which always has been one of the most conspicuous legacies of the Yoshida era.

Even the neo-nationalism of contemporary Japan, so well exemplified by Nakasone, conforms to the Yoshida pattern. Both leaders endeavored to reconcile staunch patriotism with pro-American internationalism; and both fell back upon the language and patterns of perception of their formative years. For Yoshida, this was the era of Imperial Japan. For Nakasone, born in 1918, it was the war years themselves, and many of his controversial attempts to promote a new nationalist consciousness actually echo the rhetoric of wartime Japan—references to Japan as Nippon (rather than the blander and more conventional rendering Nihon) and the Japanese people as the "Yamato race," for example, as well as paeans to the unique purity and homogeneity of "one nation, one race" Japan. Even Nakasone's most flamboyant symbolic act, his official visit to Yasukuni Shrine (the centerpiece for wartime veneration of Japanese who died for the Emperor) on the fortieth anniversary of Japan's surrender, was prefigured in a way by Yoshida, who had the news of the peace settlement reported to the imperial ancestors at Ise Shrine.

The conflicting tendencies visible in such developments—the tension between dependence and independence, the pull toward internationalism and more reassuring retreat toward insularity, the simultaneous revelation of feelings of inferiority and superiority—are not peculiar to certain individuals or a certain time. They are not even peculiar to Japan. But they weave through the course of Japan's modern history in conspicuous ways, and make it difficult to predict how Japan will respond to the demands for greater leadership and statesmanship in the new world order that became visible in the 1980s.

* * * * *

Apart from minor corrections, this printing of *Empire and Aftermath* remains unchanged from the original edition. There have been pertinent scholarly studies of twentieth-century Japan and U.S.-Japan relations since the original manuscript was completed, and new primary sources have materialized as well. Nonetheless, it still seems premature to consider undertaking a substantial revision of the text.[3]

Much of the new primary material pertaining to Yoshida per se is anecdotal in ways that serve primarily to reinforce the image of old "One Man" as a character at once shrewd, colorful, erratic, and individualistic—a figure more memorable for the symbolic gesture, the sharp retort, the burst of energy, the fixation on a few key objectives than for any disciplined and sustained attention to the full gamut of policy issues. Letters handwritten in English which came to my attention after the book was written, for example, tend primarily to enhance our appreciation of how gracious and clever Yoshida could be in courting the good will of potential allies on the American side after Japan's surrender. Here we see him, for example, indefatigably sending modest gifts to the wife of General MacArthur—flowers in December 1945 and melons the next June, apples in December 1946, followed by tomatoes in May and peaches in August. As early as December 22, 1945, he also was conveying elaborate presents from the Emperor and Empress to General and Mrs. MacArthur and their young son. There is a nice personal flavor to all this, but this does not alter the basic portrait already drawn.

The most engaging "Yoshida story" that has emerged since the book was published surely is an episode that occurred in January 1951 and involved two things that usually could be counted on to roil Yoshida's blood: rearmament and the political left. Even at this late date, several months after the Chinese entry into the Korean War, Yoshida was still strenuously resisting U.S. pressures for formal Japanese remilitarization (the Yoshida government did not secretely commit itself to a modest rearmament plan until February of that year). To impress the visiting U.S. emissary, John Foster Dulles, with the political difficulty of promoting blatant rearmament, Yoshida secretly dispatched his son-in-law to the head of the left-wing Socialists and another relative to the head of the right-wing Socialists, encouraging both leaders to organize anti-rearmament activities while Dulles was in Tokyo.[4] This was, of course, the very same man who devoted much of his energy as prime minister to breaking labor and the left, and who publicly denounced Japanese critics of the cold-war peace settlement as Communist dupes, fifth columnists, literary sycophants, raving maniacs, and odoriferous fish. On the rearmament issue, the opposition obviously did not really smell so bad.

The most important primary materials of a sustained nature that have appeared since *Empire and Aftermath* was written, however, are generally less flattering to Yoshida. These involve declassified U.S. and British documents pertaining to the early 1950s, and confirm the impression that the Yoshida government fought hard on rearmament but perhaps less vigorously than it might have on other issues which were perceived as compromising Japanese sovereignty. Thus we find Dulles reporting to Washington at one point that "Mr. Yoshida gave the impression that the Japanese were so eager for a treaty that they would be willing to approve almost anything." At another point, the Dulles mission privately acknowledged that the bilateral security treaty was a "one way" agreement, involving "unprecedented rights given to the United States by the Japanese." At the peak of the debate over China policy, the British Foreign Office (which opposed the U.S. containment policy) secretly phrased the issue of subordinate independence in the bluntest possible terms. Japan, it was observed, was assuming "the stigma of being a lackey of the Americans."

Few people would speak so harshly now. The most blatant formal inequalities of the bilateral security arrangements which the Yoshida government agreed to in the early 1950s were removed in 1960, and the vast array of intimate ties that have emerged since then to lock Japan and the United States in a relationship of extraordinary interdependence surely would have gratified the old pro-Anglo-American diplomat. In the last decade, Japan's remarkable economic success has at last brought Japan what Yoshida yearned for but never really lived to see: worldwide respect as a major power.

Yoshida not only would have been delighted by Japan's new image as an economic superpower. He also, it is fair to conjecture, would have taken a certain pleasure in seeing the great nations that once disparaged Japan now grovel a bit. He was, after all, a very proud and power-oriented leader, and much of his career was spent thinking about defeat and victory. One of the thoughts that sustained him in the dark days of Japan's defeat and occupation was the fact, as he expressed it, that history offers examples of losing in war but winning the peace. And in what is certainly the most memorable "Yoshida-ism" that was been exhumed from the archives since *Empire and Aftermath* was published, he found consolation in 1950 in a more vivid and precise historical analogy. "Just as the United States was once a colony of Great Britain but is now the stronger of the two," he responded to those who criticized the unequal nature of the emerging relationship with the United States, "if Japan becomes a colony of the United States, it will also eventually become the stronger."[5]

At first glance, viewed from amidst the economic turmoil of the 1980s, the comment would seem to burnish Yoshida's image as a pithy prophet. Yet, upon closer scrutiny, it is really a sad and sobering vision. To compare Japan to a colonial country on the very eve of the restoration of sovereignty is a stunning acknowledgment of how bittersweet the nature of the peace settlement was to even its Japanese architects. And to dream of Japan becoming one day stronger than the United States was not only a blissful ignoring of the realities of the nuclear age, but also an unwittingly telling commentary on the meaning of success in the world in which we live—a world where one is either stronger or weaker, superior or inferior, and genuine equality or reciprocity is almost impossible to envision. That is not Yoshida's legacy, of course, but rather the legacy of our modern world. And it portends a future of unceasing inequality, insecurity, and conflict.

J. W. D.
March 1988

Introduction

When Yoshida Shigeru died in 1967, at the age of eighty-nine, Japan lost one of its best-known contemporary personalities, and lost a symbol as well. The state recognized the passing of the diminutive and irascible former prime minister with a mammoth and solemn funeral, and the populace recognized that an era of history had come to an end. Actually, two eras had ended. Yoshida's death coincided with the centennial of the Meiji Restoration, the close of Japan's first modern century. And in itself the death wrote the final sentence to the chapter called "postwar," which Yoshida more than any other single Japanese personified.

Wan Man, stubborn and autocratic "One Man," lived nearly a century: Japanese patriot with an English nickname, Anglophile child of Confucianist late Meiji, maverick loyal servant of Taishō and Shōwa, prewar "old liberal" and postwar old guard, conservative doyen of the "new Japan." The impression was both vivid and ambiguous, and thus appropriate to the broader historical experience Yoshida participated in and came to exemplify; and it is this congruence and these apparent paradoxes, more than biography per se, that are the concern of this study. There is nothing very unusual in this approach. The Life and Times of Whomsoever is a well-established genre, and the objective is to weave the personality and the succession of historical moments into a tapestry that can be viewed abstractly as well as concretely: to suggest, more prosaically, historical generalizations and historical problems.

Through Yoshida, for example, it seems possible to break down or at least qualify some of the more simplistic dualities that often emerge in the presentation of Japan's modern experience. To begin with, he was a survivor, conspicuous but hardly solitary, who carved his niche in history when he was in his late sixties and early seventies. Yoshida led five cabinets between 1946 and 1954. The period from 1949 to 1954 is known as the "Yoshida era," and subsequent conservative politics and policies in Japan are frequently assessed in the context of the Yoshida legacy. These accomplishments occurred in the Indian summer of a long career. And they reflected a personal, political, and ideological consistency which, in the larger view, repudiates the conventional easy separation of "pre-surrender" and "post-surrender," or "prewar" and "postwar," or "Imperial" and "democratic" Japan.

Yoshida's career also illustrates the inseparability of international and domestic concerns. This emerges with unusual clarity after 1945, when Japan was subjected to alien occupation. It could be argued that the exceptional nature of these postwar circumstances invalidates any broader generalizations concerning the external-internal dialectic, but in actuality the contrary seems true: the occupation threw such relationships into sharp relief, and can be seen as an almost classic case study of the mesh of international and domestic policy. Yoshida's postwar activity illuminates this—and does so, moreover, against a background of pre-surrender involvement with much the same problem of reconciling internal and external interests.

In the prewar period, Yoshida played two roles, as a diplomat and as a representative of certain vested elite interests. And on occasion he addressed the relationship between domestic concerns and foreign policy directly and bluntly. As the politician who guided Japan from occupation to restoration of sovereignty, he wore two hats more conspicuously, serving concurrently as prime minister and foreign minister until 1952. In the former capacity, he promoted a coherent program of response to and rectification of the "excesses" of early occupation reformism; in baldest terms, he represented big business and central bureaucracy against labor and local community. In the latter capacity, he orchestrated Japan's eventual policies of bilateral alliance with the United States, rearmament, and integration into the global capitalist economy. In his own mind, of course, there was but one large hat. Postwar policies were effected within a framework consistent with prewar preoccupations, and internally consistent as well. And both prewar and postwar, both internationally and domestically, the integrated policy was paternalistic, conservative, counterrevolutionary, and often repressive.

There is a third broad area in which Yoshida can also provide a corrective to conventional dualistic conceptualizations, in this case to the tenacious Kiplingesque dichotomy of East and West. Here one moves not merely from the individual to the "Japanese experience," but from both of these levels to general questions of power, politics, and ideology. The problem is delicate, for it involves shaking the treasured showcase of "particularistic values" to see if more universalistic patterns of behavior and response cannot fall out without breaking. The conclusion is: to a great extent, they can. At one undeniably important level, Yoshida certainly embraced the mystique of "national polity" (*kokutai*), which foreigners and Japanese alike have used to undergird the notion of Japan's uniqueness. From day to day during his active career, however, he performed as a broker of power, a spokesman of interests. His vaunted "individualism," moreover, was both wittingly and unwittingly corrosive. He was frank, testy, and sometimes foul-tongued enough to expose the bare bones of power and ideology, of state and class interests.

These problems are approached only from certain angles in this study, and often only implicitly. Broadly, it is suggested that an important part of Japan's modern experience can be illuminated and placed in larger context by attention to imperialism and by a very dynamic appreciation of contradiction. Such *flexible* concepts help erode the dualities—prewar/postwar, international/domestic, East/West—and they accommodate sub-themes and parallel themes in a meaningful manner. It is impossible to examine Yoshida's career seriously, for example, without addressing numerous other problems which are hardly peculiar to Japan: the persistent interplay of cooperation and conflict at the international and domestic levels, and between these realms; negotiable as opposed to non-negotiable interests; the actual difference between "realism" and "idealism" in affairs of state (and when "realism" becomes irrational and "idealism" realistic); the critical area of congruence between "liberalism" and imperialism; the distinction between tactical and substantive opposition; the relationship between historical consciousness and political activism and policy-making; and the validity (or deceptiveness) of such bedrock structural notions as traditionalism and semi-feudalism as opposed to calculated orthodoxy and bourgeois modernity. As suggested here through Yoshida, such questions often become more comprehensible when the larger problems of imperialism and contradiction are kept in mind. In this same context, it is also possible to gain greater perspective on ideological and rhetorical staples such as "reform," "revolution," "anti-communism," and "conspiracy"—indeed, much of the gamut of common political language.

Throughout this discussion, the mark of "One Man" remains discernible. Yoshida was a source of numerous anecdotes of idiosyncrasy, but it would be incorrect to conclude that such qualities significantly separated him from his class or countrymen or generation in the largest sense, as some stereotypes of Japanese homogeneity and group behavior might suggest. It is more useful to see such individuality as illustrative rather than exceptional—a reminder that Japan, like other nations, has had its fair share of caustic and strong personalities, its constant play of consensus and conflict, its familiar *mélange* of rationality and emotionalism. Yoshida was neither *Jederman* nor an anomaly in his country or in his time. His Anglophile brand of cooperative imperialism, for example, was as fully a part of Japan's modern tradition as the strain of autarkic Pan Asianism he criticized. Like many of his colleagues, he spent much of his career dealing directly with Westerners, learning from them and lecturing to them; when disagreements occurred, these generally reflected clash of interest and analysis rather than any cultural muddle or peculiar personal shortcoming. The task is to give personality its due, to grant Japan its differences, and then to move on to the larger historical insights that can be drawn from the experience of the individual and the nation.

These are issues of more than academic interest. Before he died, Yoshida was being groomed for the Nobel Peace Prize.[1] Since his death, he has been evoked by more conservative Japanese commentators as a stubborn and principled individual—which is attractive—but also as a "realist" worthy of emulation. Such evocations speak to the future as well as the past, for Yoshida dealt with large matters: the desirable structure of the state, and the ideal role of the state in international affairs. His models for both "democracy" and "diplomatic sense" derived from the Meiji and Taishō periods, and reflected the ideals of patriarchal rule and turn-of-the-century practices of cooperative Great-Power imperialism. These were not inflexible models, nor did they prove to be anachronistic when Yoshida personally emerged as a political force after Japan's surrender. Certainly this poses interesting questions. Whether it should be regarded as proof of Yoshida's laudable "realism," as his admirers would have it, or as proof of more subtle and less comforting realities is another matter.

It is true that Yoshida's prewar diplomatic career might have been more successful if he had been more willing to compromise on his convictions. While this can be taken as a measure of integrity, it hardly suffices as a measure of the convictions themselves. In the critical decades of the 1920s and 1930s, Yoshida practiced a *Realpolitik* that was harsh and riddled with double standards. Well before the Manchurian Incident of 1931, he denounced Japan's "passive policy" of "sweet words" concerning China and urged his more conciliatory colleagues to keep in mind both the concrete *practices* of Western imperialism, and the fact that "the past history of Japan has always been that we punish those who behave impolitely to us"; in the 1930s, however, he preached to the Anglo-American powers the "realism" of sweet words and appeasement toward Japan. Although Yoshida opposed Japan's quest for autarky, and consistently argued that global (and thus domestic) stability required close relations with both Asia and the West, his unwavering goal was establishment of Japanese hegemony in Asia (to make China, as the British summarized it, "a vassal State"), and he regarded cooperation with Great Britain and the United States as essential to realizing this. Yoshida's well-known association with the prewar "pro-Anglo-American clique"—and with what later came to be known as the strain of "old liberalism" in Japan—must be seen in this context. First, he was more Anglophile than pro-American. Second, what he most admired in Britain, as well as America to a lesser degree, was the success of these countries in colonial and neo-colonial policy. Third, Yoshida himself reportedly acknowledged that it would be more accurate to see him as belonging to "the clique that makes use of Britain and the United States." And fourth, by the 1930s many British and American officials openly described Yoshida as a determined imperialist whose differences from the Japanese military were essentially tactical.

This last observation was severe, and obscured the pro-Western side of Yoshida's power equation; but it was nonetheless reasonably close to the mark. Yoshida could not conceive of Japan's survival without resolute expansion on the continent. His opposition to prewar militarism was occasionally forthright, but more generally erratic; like any good "realist," he rode the winds of *fait accompli*. Even after Pearl Harbor, his wartime "resistance," although it earned him a brief term in prison, was fascinating as an excursion in elite visions of the apocalypse but farcical as a serious endeavor to end the war.

Coming from the apostles of Britain's empire and America's "Monroe sphere," however, the critique of Yoshida as an imperialist revealed that there was no monopoly on double standards—and it is in such encounters that the larger crisis of the imperialist consciousness and the imperialist system itself is exposed. Yoshida spent a great deal of time in the 1930s explaining Japan's case to the British and Americans: how the vapid idealism of Wilsonian diplomacy had destabilized Japan and Asia by forcing abrogation of the Anglo-Japanese Alliance in 1922, and how the great promise of Meiji-Taishō had been further thwarted by the Depression, by Chinese incompetence and intransigence, and by shortsightedness on the part of the Anglo-American powers concerning Japan's legitimate needs and interests. His "realism" was most fully expressed in 1936 and 1937, when as ambassador to London he prepared a detailed secret plan which he believed could defuse the explosive double-contradiction of the empire: the overt imperialist clash between Japanese expansion and Chinese nationalism; and the capitalist crisis, the inter-imperialist antagonism, between Japan and the Anglo-American powers. The plan was based upon a perception of British as well as Chinese vulnerabilities. It addressed hard facts of money and power, within a traditional framework of Great-Power collusion and trade-off. And although it dismayed the British, it also forced them to acknowledge the dry rot of their own imperium. For many reasons, the secret Yoshida plan proved abortive. The lingering questions are whether there was any other way out of the impasse, short of war, that would not have crippled China, as the Yoshida plan would have done—and whether, even with Western collusion, Yoshida's exercise in power politics would not have proven as quixotic as all other imperialist policies in the face of Chinese resistance.

As the pre-eminent politician of Japan's first postwar decade, Yoshida devoted himself to the tasks of social stabilization, economic recovery, and national reintegration in the international community. He was critical of almost all of the democratic reforms imposed during the early phase of the occupation, and after 1948 enjoyed partial success in "adapting democracy to actual conditions." It was Yoshida who set the pattern for Japan's course of slow but creeping rearmament, and who committed the country to global counterrevolution and integration with the capitalist bloc dominated by the dollar. He operated, of course, under immense pressures, both from the United States and from within Japan. He failed to realize many of his objectives, both in the rectification of occupation "excesses" and in the international posture Japan adopted after 1952. In the overall analysis, however, these facts remain: that the Yoshida era was a major legacy of Japan's American interlude; that under Yoshida, and well before the occupation ended, a new conservative hegemony was consolidated in Japan, resting on the tripod of bureaucracy, big business, and the conservative political parties; and that both the domestic and international settlements were consistent in many fundamental respects with the historical interpretations and political ideals Yoshida had long espoused.

This is not to minimize the great changes that occurred in postwar Japan. On the contrary, change is another theme of this study, but it is not a theme reserved for the post-surrender period alone. Obviously Japan changed enormously during Yoshida's life–and contrary to many orthodox interpretations, it is argued here that the process accelerated dramatically during the "dark valley" of the 1930s and early 1940s. Yoshida perceived this, feared it, and responded to it. Indeed, his perceptions and activities during the occupation and thereafter are comprehensible only when it is recognized, as Yoshida recognized, that change itself–and even potentially revolutionary transformation–was a dynamic link between the prewar and postwar epochs.

Yet at the same time, Yoshida did not find it necessary to bone up on a revised syllabus of political vocabulary in responding to this challenge. Thus, in 1950 he dismissed his critics among the more progressive intelligentsia as "literary sycophants"–but this pejorative from the Chinese classics can already be found in a letter he wrote in 1921, denouncing the dangerous thoughts of an earlier generation of intellectuals and calling for inculcation of an ideological orthodoxy. In a similar manner, he castigated activist postwar unionists as "lawless elements" early in 1947–but this was no more than a set phrase of repression dating back to the peace-preservation laws and the Tanaka Giichi cabinet in the 1920s, a cabinet in which Yoshida had served. It was also rhetoric embedded in the old Western anti-labor tradition, and appealing in new ways to the Americans in the emerging cold-war context–as occupation authorities soon revealed by banning the proposed general strike of 1947, narrowing the purview of the reformist labor laws in 1948 and 1949, and supporting an extensive "Red Purge" of the civil service and union leaders in 1949–1950.

In the pre-surrender period, Yoshida had seized upon a convoluted conspiracy theory to explain much of the domestic crisis and overseas debauchery of the Japanese state, and with slight but ingenious revision he found it convenient to maintain the conspiracy thesis as an explanation of many of Japan's post-surrender dilemmas. The prewar conspirators (radical militarists and "Red fascists") were reincarnated in two especially vivid guises in this Manichean view of the postwar crisis: as a cadre of pink "New Dealer" reformers within the American occupation bureaucracy, and as a claque of communist and fellow-traveling leaders within the ranks of organized labor. Although many individual progressives on both sides were eventually dismissed, purged, or repressed, working-class activism remained to fill much the same role in Yoshida's postwar outlook that "military initiatives" had played in his conspiratorial analysis of the prewar crisis. These analogies were drawn with considerable fervor, and neither their strained logic nor their peculiar national and even personal coloration should obscure the extent to which such reasoning was both revealing and functional. At the deepest level, both prior to and after 1945 the conspiracy theses overlay a real fear of social chaos and class upheaval in Japan. At the most cynical level, this style of scapegoating neatly absolved the established civilian elites from responsibility for both the war and the dismal failure of economic reconstruction in the early postwar period. And at perhaps the most significant practical level, these political equations—in which the distinction between left-wing and right-wing movements was obscured—eventually meshed with some of the broad ideological concepts of the liberal American participants in the cold war, such as totalitarian theory.

The resilient lexicon of political invectives predictably was complemented by a ledger of persistent affirmative values and ideals. "Preservation of the national polity," with all its emperor-centered obscurantism, guided Yoshida prewar and postwar.

Here the United States abetted him by retaining the emperor, and Yoshida actually succeeded in making continuity of the traditional polity a basis for interpreting the new constitution promulgated in 1946. The language Yoshida employed—that "the national polity will not be altered in the slightest degree by the new constitution"—was even ironically reminiscent of the language Itō Hirobumi had employed over a half-century earlier in his famous commentary on the Meiji constitution. Defense of private property proved a durable old staple, and eventually a bond between the anti-reformist Yoshida conservatives and the reformist American liberals. By the end of the occupation, Yoshida was cheerfully singing old imperial tunes with his new American partners: of anti-communism, coexistence and coprosperity, and Japan as the stabilizing power in Asia.

What may be most remarkable about Japan's first postwar decade—and most revealing of the United States as well—is that Yoshida and the conservatives were able to go so far in the "new Japan" without really budging on matters of political outlook and political animus. This can be interpreted in many ways—among them as a lesson in realism perhaps, but also as a further chapter in the problem of imperialism. One of Yoshida's favorite theses was the "pendulum theory" of Japanese history; and the historical epoch he evoked as his ideal touchstone was the era of the Anglo-Japanese Alliance, when Japanese expansion was protected by bilateral entente with the dominant Western power in Asia. From his own perspective, after three decades of crisis and catastrophe, the pendulum turned as he had hoped. In the postwar world, the *Pax Americana* replaced the *Pax Britannica*; and in the U.S.-Japanese alliance of 1952, Yoshida witnessed, as it were, the regeneration of the old imperialist alignment with Great Britain.

As the following pages make clear, this was anything but a simple cycle in the historical process. But it is worth noting, for it informed Yoshida's actions, and it did suggest a pattern and precedent too bold to be ignored. At the same time, several other considerations also should be kept in mind. Throughout his prewar career, Yoshida was more favorably disposed to Great Britain than to the United States; he found the latter deficient in "diplomatic sense." In addition, it was his abiding belief that Japan must maintain close relations with China, whatever the form of government on the continent. And beyond this, his entire prewar experience was an exercise in the tenuous balance of power and interest, cooperation and conflict, among the Great Powers. A second lesson of the Anglo-Japanese Alliance, of course, was that it did not hold.

Although Japan's postwar alliance with the United States was in many respects a personal triumph for Yoshida, it was shot through with tensions and contradictions. The Yoshida government and official Washington disagreed on many critical aspects of the postwar settlement—rearmament, relations with China, and the nature of Japan's reintegration into the global capitalist economy—and when Yoshida left the political scene in late 1954 the alliance was by no means harmonious. This friction, moreover, was mirrored in and inseparable from tensions in the Japanese body politic. That the alliance did survive and Japan did prosper over the ensuing decades is testimony to the durability of the "Yoshida legacy." The tensions also have persisted, however, at both material and psychological levels. And it is here, in retrospect, that the pendulum theory can become an ominous portent for those who evoke the realism of old "One Man."

In the study that follows, the first seven chapters follow Yoshida to the end of World War Two. The frame is chronological, with breaks determined by the juncture of Yoshida's career and critical stages in the unfolding of the imperialist crisis. Chapter Eight is a bridge, a thematic transition from the pre-surrender to post-surrender period; it pivots on the concept of "revolution" as perceived not only by Yoshida and his conservative colleagues, but also by non-Japanese, including the American architects of the occupation. Implicit here is a commentary on the Janus head of political language and a reinterpretation of the significance of World War Two.

The remaining four chapters address the period from 1945 to

1954 and differ to some extent from the organizational structure followed to this point. This reflects the fact that the period is short but Yoshida's role was far more intricate and consequential than before, and the approach differs from earlier chapters in two general respects. There is chronological overlap: the reconsolidation of conservative power, and domestic legacies of the occupation, are surveyed first, before turning to the strands of external economic and strategic policy which in actual practice were interwoven with this domestic settlement. And, ironically but unavoidably, Yoshida's personal activities occasionally become submerged in a more general analysis of postwar developments, for reasons not far to seek: it is often neither possible nor profitable to separate Yoshida from the policies and accomplishments of the cabinets he headed or the interests he endorsed. Even here, however, an attempt has been made to keep Yoshida as close to center stage as seems appropriate—both where his pronouncements can be taken as representative, and where his individual actions were clearly, as in military and strategic policy, of immense consequence.

The analysis rests on available documentation, much of it of a primary and archival nature. All of the major citations in the notes are included in the bibliography, and the key titled "Abbreviations Used in the Notes" can be read as a rough indication of the sources most extensively utilized. An endeavor has been made to let Yoshida and his contemporaries speak quite extensively in their own words. This seems fairer to them than précis, and also will better enable the reader to draw his or her own, and possibly different, interpretations.

ONE

Young Gentleman of Meiji

In a sense, Yoshida Shigeru confronts one with the whole of Japan's modern history—to the extent that this history is seen from the perspective of the elites and decision-makers. His real father and adoptive father were young samurai who made their mark during the tumultuous decades surrounding the Meiji Restoration of 1868. His adoptive mother was the proud progeny of Tokugawa Confucianism. He himself was raised and schooled as a young gentleman of Meiji, and through marriage attained both a personal relationship to the Meiji oligarchs and an entrée to the coterie that hovered close to the throne.

Yoshida entered the diplomatic corps in 1906, at almost the very moment Japan itself assumed a new role as a global power following its victory in the Russo-Japanese War. He was twenty-eight then, and almost thirty-four in 1912 when the Meiji emperor died and the Meiji era came to an end in its forty-fifth year. For three decades, Yoshida participated in his country's imperialist quest for stature and security. He served in both Asia and the West, and retired from his last appointment, as ambassador to London, in 1938—shortly after Japan plunged into the abyss of the "war of annihilation" against China. Throughout the 1930s and early 1940s, Yoshida moved among those better-known men who were deciding matters of war and peace for Japan, and after Pearl Harbor he was prescient in predicting defeat. During the final years of the Pacific War he entertained doomsday visions of revolutionary chaos in war-ravaged Japan, and participated in desultory intrigues to bring a government into power that would sue for peace before the final cataclysm occurred. When Japan surrendered in 1945, Yoshida was approaching his sixty-seventh birthday.

In the decade between surrender and 1954, Yoshida emerged as Japan's most powerful politician and left a name to history. This was a period as dramatic and turbulent as that of the Restoration, beginning with occupation and reformism and ending with restoration of sovereignty, the reconsolidation of conservative elites, and the establishment of new structures of security and overseas expansion. It was also a period in which the Yoshida group addressed many specific policies in the precise and positive context of the Meiji precedent and Meiji legacy. In retrospect, historians can discern a logic in all this, although when Yoshida first appeared on the postwar scene he resembled Lazarus to many. His influence, in any case, carried over into the 1960s and 1970s in the premierships of his protégés, Ikeda Hayato and Satō Eisaku. And when Yoshida died in 1967, Japan lost not only its last elder statesman, but also one of the last truly influential members of the so-called generation of Meiji.

FAMILY TREES

Yoshida was born in Yokosuka near Tokyo on September 22, 1878, shortly after his father had been arrested in Nagasaki for participating in a plot against the government. He was the fifth son among Takeuchi Tsuna's fourteen offspring, and the identity of his real mother remains obscure. She was apparently a geisha, who made her way to the Tokyo area after Takeuchi's imprisonment and gave birth to the child with the aid of Takeuchi's close friend, Yoshida Kenzō. The two men had arranged that Takeuchi's next son would be adopted by Yoshida and his wife, who were childless, and Yoshida Shigeru was handed over to his new parents on October 1, nine days after birth.

It is possible Yoshida never learned who his real mother was, and throughout his life that situation was apparently unpleasant for him to recall. Although his early family register clearly indicates that his mother was "unknown," while he lived the public fiction was maintained that he was born of Takeuchi's real wife; even in later reminiscences on his birth, Yoshida scrupulously avoided mention of his real mother. The actual circumstances were not unknown, however, and have contributed to amateur psychologizing. Yoshida Shigeru's later wife is said to have rationalized her husband's own well-known fondness for the company of geisha by observing that "geisha's sons like geisha"–an intriguing Oedipal suggestion to begin with, and enhanced in Yoshida's case even before his wife's death when he established a long, private, and by all accounts warm relationship with the former Shimbashi geisha Korin (Sakamoto Kiyo). In a different direction, the critic Abe Shinnosuke, one of the most avid of Yoshida's non-admirers, acknowledged Yoshida's fame as a conversationalist but observed that after a while one became aware of a cold and impenetrable detachment; Abe likened this to the personality of a talented geisha. To have been born of such a liaison was not unusual among the upper classes of Meiji Japan, and in Japanese eyes would not have been particularly scandalous. Nonetheless, it was clearly not something in which Yoshida could take pride.[1]

Takeuchi and Yoshida Kenzō were striking products of their day–dynamic and adaptable men of samurai blood who proceeded, in the new era of Meiji, to carve out careers in a manner that had been inconceivable a generation earlier. A native of Kōchi in Tosa, Takeuchi was one of the young samurai of that fief who actively supported the loyalist cause in the Bakumatsu period and thus helped bring about the downfall of the Tokugawa regime. Like many other Tosa activists, he subsequently became disenchanted with the domination of the new Meiji government by ex-samurai from Satsuma and Chōshū (the so-called Sat-Chō clique), and in the late 1870s joined Tosa's Itagaki Taisuke in modern Japan's first political-party movement, the "movement for freedom and people's rights" (*jiyū minken undō*). His arrest just prior to Yoshida's birth was in fact because of complicity in one of the more radical and ambiguous endeavors of this early political opposition—an anti-government conspiracy by the extremist wing of the Risshisha party in 1877, deliberately timed to coincide with the decidedly unliberal Satsuma rebellion led by Saigō Takamori. Takeuchi's role in this conspiracy is vague, but his imprisonment was, in any case, brief. He soon reappeared as one of the leaders of the Jiyutō, the most important of the early Japanese political parties, founded by Itagaki in 1881.[2]

In 1887, during the premiership of Itō Hirobumi, the government issued one of the more notorious of its early peace-preservation laws, the *Hoan Jōrei.* This was designed to break the back of the political opposition, which was attacking the government for its severe deflation policy, its failure to revise Japan's unequal treaties with the Western powers, and its refusal to permit popular participation in deliberations on the promised new constitution and Diet. The new regulations sanctioned the expulsion from Tokyo of persons deemed to be a threat to public tranquility, and Takeuchi was among nearly six-hundred persons actually forced to leave the capital city at this time.[3] Three years later, however, he ran successfully in Japan's first parliamentary election, and he repeated this success in the second election of 1892.

Other than the fact that he reportedly allowed himself to be bought off by Prime Minister Yamagata Aritomo during the first session, Takeuchi does not appear to have distinguished himself as a Diet member.[4] The simple fact of his election reveals that he was a man of means, however, for to qualify as either a candidate or voter it was necessary to pay at least fifteen yen in property taxes; this restricted the electorate to slightly more than one percent of the total population. To his various identities as samurai, loyalist, politician, conspirator, and parliamentarian, Takeuchi also added that of entrepreneur. Even his political mentor, Itagaki, once commented caustically about Takeuchi's "shopkeeper" (*shōnin*) mentality.[5] At the time of his early arrest in Nagasaki, Takeuchi was employed as a manager of the well-known Takashima coal mine, which had been obtained from the government by the Iwasaki (Mitsubishi) family and was notorious for its brutal working conditions.[6] Following the Sino-Japanese War of 1894–

1895, he moved to broader fields. As head of the Seoul-Pusan Railway, he turned his eyes to overseas development and became an early proponent of "management of the continent" (*tairiku keiei*), a vision that was to undergird the development of Japanese imperialism in the coming decades.[7] Here were roots of that economic involvement with continental Asia which was to become a major preoccupation of Yoshida Shigeru himself, in both his pre-1945 and post-1945 careers.

What the son derived from the father is impossible to say, and Yoshida on his own part later ventured little more on this score than the wry observation that both experienced an interlude in prison. Neither Takeuchi nor his family appear to have maintained intimate contact with this superfluous fifth son; in 1887, when Takeuchi's purge from Tokyo coincided with the untimely death of Yoshida Kenzō, it was briefly suggested that the nine-year-old Shigeru accompany Takeuchi and his brood back to Kōchi, but this came to nothing. When Yoshida entered the diplomatic corps, however, Takeuchi gave him one of the family heirlooms, a samurai sword forged by Seki no Kanemitsu, together with this lofty exhortation: "Temptations are great when one enters government; one becomes enticed by worldly desires. As you now become an official, take this sword with you constantly to sever mundane ambition and thus avoid falling into temptation." Close upon this (in time if not spirit), when Yoshida received his first overseas assignment, Takeuchi gave him a letter of introduction to present to his superior abroad and thereby hasten realization of his worldly ambitions. Yoshida treated this with what would later be regarded as a characteristic idiosyncrasy. He did not present the letter until he was being reassigned, and, when asked why, informed his nonplused superior that he simply disliked riding on the influence of one's parent.

It has been suggested that a line of influence can be discerned between Takeuchi's early politics and Yoshida's later "old liberalism," but it is probably closer to the mark simply to note the maverick streak that seems to run through the personalities of both men—a "rebellious" and "outsider" quality Yoshida himself later stressed in reminiscing about his real father. But despite Takeuchi's early sympathies for the Satsuma rebellion and its leader, Saigō Takamori, and despite his associations with Tosa and the early political opposition movement led by Itagaki—or perhaps even because of this, as a rejection of the father who had rejected him—Yoshida expressed little interest in these individuals or their ideals, or in the later party movement of prewar Japan. Instead, he developed a profound respect for and identification with the Meiji oligarchs and that same Sat-Chō clique against which Takeuchi's early political activities had been directed. In his later years he acquired Itō's detached mortuary temple and rebuilt it on the grounds of his estate in Ōiso. Here he maintained photographs of Iwakura Tomomi, Sanjō Sanetomi, Kido Kōin, and Ōkubo Toshimichi—the Restoration architects to whom Itō had also paid devout homage in this private shrine—adding to these photographs of Itō himself and later Saionji Kimmochi. He even held parties on Itō's birthday. It was obviously of little personal significance that it had been under Itō's cabinet that the *Hoan Jōrei* was passed and Yoshida's father driven out of Tokyo in 1887.[8]

Yoshida Shigeru's adoption into the family of Yoshida Kenzō was, in retrospect, the first indication that his guiding star would be capricious but generally benevolent. Instead of being the fifth son of a moderately prosperous family, and an illegitimate son at that, he immediately became the heir of a household of considerable wealth—which he later facetiously referred to as the "Yoshida *zaibatsu*." He came into his inheritance, moreover, at the age of nine. When Yoshida Kenzō died in 1887, around the age of forty, he left his adopted son an estate valued at 500,000 yen, a huge amount by the standards of the day and roughly equivalent to two-billion yen (or five to six-million dollars) at the time Yoshida died.[9] Throughout his life Yoshida Shigeru was a stranger to personal want and real hardship, but this was not the whole of it. In the Yoshida household he was also exposed from childhood to a business atmosphere, and to an environment that was simultaneously Confucian, Anglophile, and internationalist in outlook.

Both parents in the Yoshida household were strong personalities.

Yoshida Kenzō, whose own family origins (and original family name) are obscure, had been one of many young samurai from Fukui who made their way to Nagasaki around the time of the Restoration to study medicine and Western studies. After somehow talking his way aboard an English warship in the late 1860s, he spent two years in England. His friendship with Takeuchi began in Nagasaki, where for a brief period he assisted Takeuchi in managing the Takashima mine. Shortly before Takeuchi's arrest, however, Yoshida Kenzō moved to Yokohama to serve as manager for the British shipping firm Jardine-Matheson & Co. One of Yoshida Shigeru's earliest recollections, he claimed, was of playing in the garden in front of Jardine-Matheson, and in a figurative sense he never strayed far from that domain.

Subsequently, Yoshida Kenzō established his own shipping agency and assisted the new Meiji government in purchasing warships and weapons from the West. Before his early death, he had ventured into journalism, education, and real estate, and in 1884 he settled his small family on a large estate at Ōiso, near Yokohama. The phenomenal opportunities for an aggressive young entrepreneur in this early period of Japan's contact with the West are suggested by the fact that Yoshida Kenzō's fortune was made in a single decade. In his later years, Yoshida Shigeru looked back upon his adoptive father as an exemplar of what Lafcadio Hearn had described as that new class of Japanese whose nationalism took the form of entrepreneurship, and whose commercial competitiveness proved too much for those Western merchants who had attempted to gain an early foothold in the new treaty ports of Japan. Although Yoshida Kenzō's adopted heir later abandoned any thoughts of a business career and claimed he lacked the knack, in his eventual career as a practitioner of international politics, Yoshida Shigeru, like Yoshida Kenzō, laid particular stress upon the establishment of competitive commercial relations and international financial ties, particularly with the West.[10]

Yoshida Kenzō's early death left his young son with apparently few vivid personal recollections. Yoshida Shigeru later mentioned only one of these, that his father had enjoyed hunting and occasionally took Shigeru with him on his outings; but the passion for the kill did not rub off.[11] And thus, abandoned by his real father even before birth, and bereft of his adoptive father at the age of nine, Yoshida's early years became most profoundly influenced by his adoptive mother.

Yoshida Kotoko was the granddaughter of Satō Issai, a well-known Kangaku ("Chinese Learning") scholar who taught at the Shōheikō, the Confucian college of the Bakufu in Edo, from 1841 until his death in 1859. By all accounts she was a woman of strictness, dignity, and impressive self-reliance; her grandson later described her as a true "child of Edo" (*Edokko*), stern and strong-willed (but apparently devoid of the lusty exuberance of the archetypical *Edokko*), and noted also that she was a devout follower of the Jōdo sect of Buddhism.[12] Although even in his later years Yoshida Shigeru remained strikingly guarded in matters of self-analysis, and particularly about his early childhood, he did offer a fleeting glimpse of these formative years and the particular importance of the maternal influence upon him:

> My adoptive mother's name was Kotoko. Since she was born to the family of a Confucian scholar, one would expect the name to have some particular meaning, but I never learned whether this was so. Being raised in a scholar's family, she appears to have taken secret pride in possessing the rudiments of scholarship. Perhaps because of this, she was a proud person [*kigurai no takai hito*; the phrase carries connotations of "conceited"]. But at the same time my adoptive mother often said of me, "This child is a proud child."
>
> It is a strange thing, but perhaps because of being constantly called a proud child, at a certain point I actually did become proud. When I recall my adoptive mother, I feel that it was her influence that made me so. That is probably why, in the eyes of others, I appear to be arrogant (*gōman*), and am thought egoistic (*wagamama*) and referred to as "One-Man" and the like.
>
> On the other hand, however, I can be seen as a person who does not yield to coercion by others, but rather opposes such coercion to the breaking point. This obstinate, or should I say defiant, character may have been inherited from my real father, but at the same time I believe it reflects the strong influence of my adoptive mother. She also often said, "This child doesn't make mistakes." In all probability, this im-

> planted self-respect in me and made me extremely self-confident. And so this too I probably owe to my adoptive mother. Thus, from early youth I was egoistic and greatly troublesome, but having grown old I frequently recall these things of the past to which I remain indebted.[13]

Seen from a distance, the young Shigeru's life seems shrouded with a taut stillness. He was not told he was adopted, and only learned this by chance in adolescence, from an outsider whose intentions appear to have been none too kind; the revelation, Yoshida recalled, left him with an extremely strange feeling. After 1887, when Yoshida Kenzō died and the plan that Shigeru accompany his real father to Kōchi was abandoned, he remained with Yoshida Kotoko as the "young master" of the house. There were servants, and his mother was particularly fond of dogs. During summers, ostensibly for reasons of health, Yoshida Kotoko resided in Hakone or Ikaho, and Shigeru accompanied her on these vacations. The two also made occasional trips to Satō Issai's estate in Sumidagawa, and Yoshida later evoked one shimmering image from these youthful excursions. He recalled his childish delight in visiting Sumidagawa after the heavy summer rains and discovering, in the garden pool of his own home, goldfish and carp that had made their way over from the pools of nearby mansions; he never noticed, he said, that his own fish were simultaneously taking advantage of the flooding to migrate to neighboring places.

Such reminiscence, however, was bittersweet. "After my adoptive father's death, I would return home from school to live alone with my adoptive mother," he later wrote, "and the days and months passed into years, a lonely life in a lonely house." It was a childhood of material comfort, devoid of warmth–and most certainly devoid of that smothering maternal indulgence (*amae*) which contemporary scholars emphasize in the shaping of the "typical" Japanese personality.[14]

BRANCHES OF LEARNING

Patriotism and traditionalism were planted deeply alongside traits of character in these early years, both by Yoshida Kotoko and the nature of the education provided in the schools Yoshida attended. It is intriguing to speculate, but impossible to ascertain, the extent to which the legacy of Satō Issai was conveyed within the Yoshida household by his granddaughter. Yoshida Kotoko often discussed her illustrious forebear with distinguished visitors in Shigeru's presence, and in doing this she was evoking a scholar of considerable intellectual interest and complexity. Although as a teacher at the Bakufu school Satō was theoretically a proponent of the conservative Chu Hsi orthodoxy, in practice he appears to have been attracted to the more individualistic Neo-Confucian tradition exemplified by the Ōyōmei, or Wang Yang-ming, school. As such he was concerned with conscience and personal activism as well as social conservatism—with the samurai spirit exemplified in the concept of *bu*, as well as the scholarly tradition embraced under the rubric of *bun*. His students included some of the great innovators of the Bakumatsu period, such as Sakuma Shōzan, Ōhashi Totsuan, and Yokoi Shōnan; he also engaged in correspondence with Fujita Tōko and Ōshio Heihachirō, one of the truly revolutionary figures of the late Tokugawa, emphasizing to both the public importance of private action. This dynamic variety of intellectual "traditionalism" probably had little direct intellectual influence upon the young Yoshida Shigeru, but it does suggest an interesting kind of mirror which may have been held, unwittingly, by Yoshida Kotoko: one in which the later iconoclasm of the bureaucrat Yoshida Shigeru appears reflected, superimposed, over the earlier iconoclasm of the ostensibly orthodox Confucian teacher Satō.[15]

From the age of nine until his early teens, Yoshida attended a "School of Chinese Learning" (*Kangaku-juku*) in Fujisawa, near Kamakura. Subsequently he was enrolled for four years in an academy in Tokyo, the Nihon Chūgaku in Azabu, run by Sugiura Jūgō, the crown prince's personal teacher of ethics. Yoshida's knowledge of the Chinese classics, and his skill in *kambun* and Chinese poetry, were acquired largely during these years. As an adult, his calligraphy was highly regarded (although to contemporary Japanese it seems often illegible), and he remained emphatic in his respect for classical Chinese thought. To Yoshida, the genius of the Chinese lay in their profound insight into human relations. "For abstract theorizing," he later wrote, "we must learn from the West. But I feel that where our daily lives are concerned, and in matters of intercourse among men, there is nothing we cannot find in the Chinese classics and Chinese poetry." This esteem for the Chinese literary tradition was, of course, typical of Yoshida's generation; as will be seen, it typically also did little to ameliorate the condescension with which he and his compeers viewed the China and the Chinese they actually were called upon to deal with. Beyond this, this early schooling, and the influence of Yoshida Kotoko and Sugiura Jūgō in particular, are commonly cited as the crucible in which Yoshida's loyalism was forged. The depth and importance of this are difficult to exaggerate; loyalism, as much as any other single element, was to define and focus Yoshida's approach to the postwar as well as prewar world.[16]

It is easy to overestimate the extent of the Confucian content of Yoshida's early education, however, and perhaps well to bear in mind that in later life he confessed to a special fondness for samurai stories, traditional popular story-telling (*rakugo*), television detective serials, and Tarzan movies.[17] Although the Fujisawa school in which he received his first formal schooling is generally associated with "Chinese learning," it was actually a more diversified institution than this label implies. Originally named the Kōyojuku, it was founded after the Restoration by a scholar and former samurai from Himeji named Ogasawara Tōyō with the support of a number of his neighbors living around Fujisawa, possibly including Yoshida Kenzō. Ogasawara had died by the time the young Shigeru entered, and the school had also expanded its name to Kōyo-gijuku, adding the character *gi* to signify a relationship with Keiō-gijuku, Fukuzawa Yukichi's pioneer school of Western learning in Tokyo. The headmaster of the Fujisawa school during Yoshida's attendance was probably a Keiō graduate, and another teacher from Keiō came regularly to the Kōyo-gijuku to teach English.[18]

When he was around eighty years old, Yoshida had the startling experience of having someone discover and present him with some of the "Chinese compositions" he had written during those long-ago years, and they were curious academic hybrids indeed—written with brush, marked with the traditional marginal comments of the teacher, and discussing (in one essay called "Paradise") the wisdom of Confucius, Mencius, Tennyson, Fichte, and Samuel Johnson's "Raserasu" in "Happi Barree" (Rasselas in Happy Valley). The papers found were random scraps, but even so they indicate that good patriots learned their priorities at an early age in Yoshida's youth. In an essay entitled "Foundation of the Nation: Urgent Matter," Yoshida, then probably around thirteen years old, took umbrage at the fact that "lately prominent persons are becoming crazy over politics and neglecting industrial development"—an injunction which succinctly encapsules his basic position both while a prewar bureaucrat and during the American occupation of Japan a half century later. Beside this his teacher had stroked in vermillion ink: "Prominent persons put to shame!"[19]

The academy of "Chinese learning" was more than its name implied, but by no means an anomaly for its time. For the sentiment expressed in this fragment from a bygone day nicely captures that cult of the entrepreneur—the vogue of *jitsugyō*—which was germinated in Yoshida Kenzō's generation and had become a strong current in Japanese popular culture by the 1890s. Critics and polemicists such as those associated with the Seikyōsha and Minyūsha groups devoted great energy at the time to castigating politicians and venerating instead the "individualistic" entrepreneur whose industriousness was conducive to the creation of a strong state. This was the era when Samuel Smiles was a best-seller in Japan and Fukuzawa, with his citadel of nascent capitalists at Keiō, was extolling the patriotic virtues of economic man. It was a period of heightened concern over the unequal treaties, and of girding for the first assault against China. And in this respect the watchwords of the day, trumpeted at all levels of society including the voluminous literature directed at youth, are instructive for understanding the later Yoshida. Entrepreneurship and industrialization, commercialism and trade, remained consistent pillars of his outlook throughout his entire life. And simultaneously politics—not to be confused with established elite rule and devoted government service—was at best venal, at worst disruptive to the ultimate goals of the state. Priorities, in this view, were not at issue.[20]

The Fujisawa school is also of interest for the style of life Yoshida experienced there, for it was a rural boarding school, one of whose original purposes was to develop future community leaders among the farmers' sons of the area. The young master enjoyed no special privileges but reportedly shared an eight-mat room with four others when in session, and ate the same rough fare (generally mackerel, rather than the fancier kinds of fish). The school trained young men up to around the age of twenty, and because Yoshida was among the youngest, and perhaps also because he was small in stature, he is said to have suffered some harassment at the hands of older and brawnier classmates. He himself never mentioned these experiences, and throughout his life Yoshida remained reticent about his youth, so it is difficult to evaluate what effect this close and possibly trying contact with persons of a lower social stratum had upon his outlook.

He did establish a close friendship at the boarding school with a farmer's son named Watanabe Kōzō, and this acquaintance lasted throughout Yoshida's life. After Yoshida's death in 1967, Watanabe, then ninety, reminisced about this early period and produced a poem Yoshida had contributed to the school magazine at that time:

> No home to which to return
> And no parents from whom to receive love.
> The heart of this orphan student—
> How pitiful (*aware*) it is.

In later years, Watanabe recounted, he occasionally mentioned this poem to Yoshida when the latter returned to Ōiso on vacation, and Yoshida invariably responded with an expression of distaste.[21] As poetry it was, to be sure, excruciating, and hardly the creative effort one would wish to have recalled. But like his later reflections on life with his adoptive mother, it does offer a rare glimpse behind the hard shell with which Yoshida generally managed to protect his personal feelings. It is another reminder that Yoshida's early years were characterized not merely by wealth, business surroundings, and both traditional and Anglo-Saxon influences, but also by the fact that he did not know his real mother, was unwanted by his real father and left truly fatherless at the age of nine by the death of his adoptive father, had thirteen siblings but grew up as an only child, and had an adoptive mother who was strong and admirable but also correct and distant in her relationship with him. The concept of "family," which carries such a heavy burden in most personal and social histories pertaining to Japan, seems of dubious value when applied to Yoshida; as his youthful poem indicates, he saw himself as bereft of both home and family. Although he did eventually find a structured home of sorts in the Foreign Ministry—and, almost by way of compensation, did avidly embrace the paternalistic idealization of the emperor and imperial family—there is scarcely a period in his life when Yoshida does not seem to stand as a rather isolated figure on however crowded a stage. It is hardly surprising that when he later attained political power he maintained a solitary "one-man" style of operation, however much that ran against the stereotyped image of traditional Japanese political behavior. On the other hand, at one time or another in his life probably every Japanese writes at least one poem about how pitiful (*aware*) life is, and Yoshida emerged with too keen a sense of humor and too fierce a pride to have spent too much time in self-pity. Watanabe himself also offered another vignette: of the young Yoshida riding horseback and practicing archery in the woodlands by Ōiso. And in later life one finds him rather happily cultivating enemies in Tokyo and roses on his country estate.

After the Fujisawa school and later studies with Sugiura Jūgō, Yoshida passed through a disjointed period of the sort that was to recur with fair regularity throughout his career. This first such interlude lasted from his mid-teens until 1897, when he entered the elite Gakushūin, or Peers' School. Prior to this he briefly attended a business school (later to become Hitotsubashi University), in keeping with the assumption that he would carry on the Yoshida family interests along the course his adoptive father had established. Yoshida lasted there for little more than a month before deciding, as he put it, that he was not cut out to handle an abacus—thus abandoning after a few weeks' trial the career role for which, presumedly, he had been adopted. Next he attended a Tokyo middle school for a half year (the Seisoku Chūgaku in Shiba) in order to gain the credits necessary for continuing on to a higher school (*kōtōgakkō*). Then he became ill, and stayed home for approximately a year. When he finally entered the Gakushūin in 1897 at the age of nineteen, he was several years older than his classmates and still without any particular career goal in mind.[22]

Yoshida's years at the Gakushūin coincided with a period of intense nationalism and preoccupation with continental Asia. It was during these latter years of the nineteenth century, and not the early decades of Meiji, that the sovereign was consciously promoted as a semi-divine figure, as seen in the belated use of the mystically resonant word *tennō* to denote the emperor. And it was at this time that emotional slogans such as "Japanism" (*Nippon-shugi*) and "national polity" (*kokutai*) first gained wide currency.[23] Yoshida entered upon his higher education in the wake of the Sino-Japanese War and humiliating Triple Intervention, when national passions were transcending a benign notion of entrepreneurship for the state to embrace a fierce conception of great-power competition for empire. And with China now crushed, concern was directed toward the ambitions of Tzarist Russia in East Asia.

Gakushūin administrators were hardly detached observers of these high-stake games of power and prestige. The aristocratic school had been placed under the management of the Imperial Household Ministry in 1884, with a mission of inculcating a more profound appreciation of the intertwined destinies of the state, the emperor, and the society's chosen few. Courses dealing with military affairs and traditional ethics assumed a large place in the curriculum, and headmasters were often selected from the highest military ranks. The head of the school when Yoshida enrolled was Prince Konoe Atsumaro, father of Konoe Fumimaro, who was then in the process of establishing an attached college for the preparation of future diplomats. Although he himself had studied for six years in Germany and Austria, Konoe's primary interest lay in Asian policy, and under the rubric of "preservation of East Asia" (*Tōa hozen ron*) he was a strong advocate of Asian solidarity against Western encroachment. Konoe founded several organizations dedicated to these goals, among them the East Asia Common Culture Society (Tōa Dōbun Kai) and the Society of Like-Minded Nationals (Kokumin Dōshi Kai). Following the Boxer uprising of 1900 in China, he advocated the total expulsion of Russia from Manchuria, and to this end formed the National League (Kokumin Dōmei Kai) and the Society of Persons of Like Mind Concerning Russia (Tai Ro Dōshi Kai).[24]

Miura Gorō, Konoe's predecessor as headmaster, had been an equally vigorous proponent of continental expansion, and as minister to Korea in 1895 played a central role in arranging the assassination of the Korean queen, a brutal intrigue designed to check Russian influence in Korea and stabilize the Japanese position in the Hermit Kingdom. Courses on "Oriental History" relating directly to such concern had been introduced to the Gakushūin curriculum under Miura; and Suzuki Kantarō, the famous admiral whose cabinet accepted the Potsdam Declaration and terms of Japan's surrender in 1945, lectured to Yoshida and his classmates on military affairs in those days.[25] The final years of Yoshida's education thus took place within the crucible which produced the ideology of the Japanese empire, with all its complex and contradictory ingredients of economic expansionism, military security, chauvinistic mission, and idealistic Pan-Asianism. He belonged to the first Japanese generation deliberately primed for both emperor-centered nationalism and resolute imperialistic expansion.

Yoshida was persuaded to continue on in Konoe's new college for diplomats after completing the normal higher-school course of the Gakushūin, and was in his third year when Konoe died suddenly in 1904, at the age of forty-two, and the program was abandoned. Consequently, in 1905 Yoshida transferred to the political section of the law department of Tokyo Imperial University and took his degree in July of the following year; he was then twenty-eight years old. Among his fellow graduates was Hirota Kōki, whom Yoshida was to assist in forming a cabinet in 1936, and who was hanged as a war criminal after World War Two for decisions made during his tenure as prime minister and later. During this period of attendance at the Gakushūin and Imperial University, Yoshida maintained an undistinguished academic record and a distinguished lifestyle. He kept a private residence in Tokyo and commuted to school on horseback.[26]

Two months after graduating, Yoshida passed the diplomatic and consular examinations of the Foreign Ministry, ranking seventh out of eleven successful candidates. Early in 1907 he was assigned to the Japanese consulate at Mukden, and left Japan's shores for the first time.[27] He had navigated the elite course of a young gentleman of Meiji, and faced what promised to be an equally elitist career, that of the Japanese diplomat-bureaucrat. All that remained to cap the promise at this stage was an auspicious marriage, and in June of 1909 he made exactly such an alliance by marrying Makino Yukiko, the eldest daughter of Makino Nobuaki (Shinken), who later became foreign minister and eventually privy seal and one of the emperor's most intimate confidants.

FRUITS OF MARRIAGE

While Makino's attractiveness as a father-in-law to the young diplomat is obvious, the reverse side of the equation—why Makino chose Yoshida as son-in-law—is far from clear. Yoshida was not an especially promising student; as seen by his performance in the foreign-service examinations of 1906, he did not even rank near the top of his own small group of entering diplomats. Moreover, Makino was the son of Ōkubo Toshimichi, the Satsuma samurai who had emerged as the real strong man of the early Meiji oligarchy by the time of his assassination in 1878. As such, he represented the cream of the new elite in Japan as well as the best blood in the proud and enduring Satsuma tradition. That *han*, place of family origin, did make a difference to Makino comes out clearly in Yoshida's memoirs: "I was, to Count Makino, both his son-in-law and his junior in the Foreign Ministry, and so of course I received special favor (*on*). But until he passed away [in 1949], I was treated as an outsider (*takokumono*). . . . I was not allowed to enter the inner sanctum (*honmaru*). Often, when I presented myself where the Count's relatives were gathered, if talk of their native place came up this was always preceded by [Makino's saying], in every other sentence, 'I hesitate to say this in front of Yoshida, but. . . .'"[28]

By 1909, when the marriage was made, Yoshida also had already acquired a reputation of being high-spirited and somewhat irascible, and if the proud Makino was unaware of this beforehand, his new son-in-law certainly wasted no time in bringing the point home. Yoshida did not even show up at his own wedding reception, but instead had himself hospitalized (allegedly for treatment of "neurosis," but possibly for venereal disease contracted in the rigors of continental service). Makino may simply have admired Yoshida's strong-mindedness and recognized his ideological compatibility with Makino's own views; more probably, Yoshida's major credential was his wealth and ability to guarantee financial security to Makino's daughter. In any case, Yoshida did not distinguish himself as an easy husband; his remarkable behavior at the time of the wedding augured a marital disregard that apparently continued until his wife's death in 1941, and is well known although never documented. In affairs of state, however, father-in-law and son-in-law remained essentially compatible, and in this respect the marriage was of inestimable importance to Yoshida's later activities and outlook.[29]

On the ideological, or perhaps symbolic, level, the relationship with Makino cemented some of the fundamental values and associations which would guide Yoshida throughout his diplomatic and political career. In marrying into Ōkubo's line, for example, he in a sense married into the Restoration, and this was hardly the sort of attachment that would make him amenable after 1945 to views that traced Japan's plunge into the war back to the very nature of the Meiji settlement. The association with Ōkubo is also suggestive as a general point of political categorization and comparison. In the conventional assignment of political labels in Japan, Ōkubo epitomizes the pragmatic, bureaucratic, "realist" strain of the Restoration—in contrast to the more "idealist" thrust of his compeers Saigō (the selfless warrior opposition) and Itagaki (the loyal political-party opposition). Within this framework, most Japanese commentators would agree, Yoshida's own later version of political "realism" falls quite naturally within the Ōkubo tradition.[30] Thus, at the very least, the marital connection with Ōkubo provided a nice metaphor for fusing the personal and political; and to the outside observer, it can serve as a concrete reminder of how proudly Yoshida viewed the accomplishments of the Restoration, and how closely he identified with the "realists" in particular among the Restoration architects.

Makino naturally exemplified these same attachments. Like Yoshida later, he also operated on a level of articulate loyalism, nationalism, and expansionism, combined with avowed friendship with the Anglo-American powers. As education minister shortly before marrying his daughter to Yoshida, he had played a prominent role in promoting moralistic and patriotic indoctrination in the public schools (a cause Yoshida would espouse during the postwar period).[31] He was also a skillful diplomat, who in 1919 spoke for Japan at the Versailles Conference, to which Yoshida accompanied him. Although associated with some of the right-wing organizations that began to flourish in the 1920s, such as the Society to Realize the Way of Heaven on Earth (Gyōchisha) founded by Ōkawa Shūmei in 1924,[32] during the terror of the 1930s Makino was to become one of the prime targets of ultranationalist assassins, one of the "evil men at court," because of his pro-Western sympathies. To a considerable extent, Yoshida's own relationship with the military would become entangled with that of his famous father-in-law during this period; and to a considerable extent also, Yoshida's attitude toward the militarists and nationalists of the 1920s and 1930s was as ambiguous as Makino's.

Perhaps of greatest significance, however, was the fact that through Makino Yoshida established a closeness to the Japanese imperial institution (a "degree of proximity" in Maruyama Masao's phrase)[33] which gave him a personal dimension to his loyalism. Particularly from the 1930s on, he moved not merely in upper-class circles but among the aristocracy and court nobility. The throne, for him as for Makino, was the essence of the Japanese state, and when the holocaust came it was here that some of his greatest concerns were directed.

TWO

"Traditional Diplomacy," 1906–1922

Despite his advantages of money, schooling, and marriage, Yoshida did not enjoy a notably successful diplomatic career. Looking back, the best he himself could find to say about these decades of his prime was that they gave him a knack for understanding China, diplomats, militarists, adventurers (*Shina rōnin*), and politicians.[1] The summing up was wry, but also deceptive, for on at least two occasions—in 1927–1928 and 1936–1937—Yoshida participated in diplomatic undertakings of considerable interest, although he all but ignored these in his reminiscences. Nonetheless, whether notorious or esteemed (like Shidehara Kijūrō), many of Yoshida's peers and colleagues carried greater international reputations into the postwar period. Yoshida's activities took place on the periphery of great events, and outside of certain circles he was not well known even in Japan.

That Yoshida's prewar role was relatively minor, however, does not mean that it is insignificant to the historian. Naturally, it illuminates the personality and later activities of the elderly man who unexpectedly emerged after 1945 as the pre-eminent political figure of twentieth-century Japan. Beyond this, for all of his idiosyncrasies, Yoshida was an exemplary product of his times. He did not decisively influence the course of events for Japan prior to 1945, and in some important instances opposed basic policies. He did, however, participate passionately in Japan's quest for stature and empire, and through his activities it is possible to gain insight not merely into the elite consciousness in prewar Japan, but also into the dynamics and contradictions of Japanese imperialism.

In late 1945, shortly before he committed suicide after being accused of war crimes, Konoe Fumimaro learned that Yoshida was being considered for the post of foreign minister in the Shidehara cabinet. He reportedly expressed his reservations in these words: "I am not behind others in my admiration for Yoshida, but Yoshida's consciousness is the consciousness of the era of 'Imperial Japan,' and I wonder if that can go well in a defeated Japan."[2]

The designation "Imperial Japan" (*Dai Nippon Teikoku*) was a Meiji construct which predated overseas expansion and derived from the governance of the state under the emperor. The ideographs for *teikoku* literally mean "emperor country"; and the constitution of 1889 was formally titled *Dai Nippon Teikoku Kempō.* The phrase can also be rendered "Empire of Japan," and in the twentieth century acquired the further connotation of dominion abroad, in the same sense as "British Empire" (*Dai Ei Teikoku*). There is a further, emotive resonance to the term, however, suggested in the initial ideograph *dai*, or "great," and the closest approximation in English may be "Great Empire of Japan." Konoe surely had both emperor system and external empire in mind in speaking of Yoshida, with all the emotional content this implied for most Japanese of the prewar generation.

At first glance, the comment might seem misdirected, coming as it did from a man who was himself a prince, and who, as head of three cabinets between 1937 and 1941, bore responsibility for initiating the "war of annihilation" against China and proselytizing the "New Order" as a rubric for Japanese hegemony in Asia. Yoshida, after all, was one of the few Japanese bureaucrats who emerged from World War Two with a general reputation as a firm friend of the West, an anti-militarist, a "realist" in international affairs, an "old liberal," and a maverick of sorts in personal behavior. A label such as the "consciousness of the era of Imperial

Japan" carries connotations that are less detached and rational, more emotional and jingoistic, and more culpable.

Yet Konoe knew Yoshida well. His characterization was no less apt than these other images and impressions, and it is in this congruence of superficially contradictory labels that Yoshida's prewar career assumes an interest beyond the life of "one man." Pro-Western sympathies were entirely compatible with imperialist obsessions. Anti-militarism did not necessarily imply opposition to military intervention and aggression, or resistance to the diplomacy of *fait accompli.* "Realism" in foreign affairs readily nourished policies of harshness rather than compromise and conciliation. In domestic affairs, "old liberals" found it easy and appropriate to support the repression of serious dissent.

It would be an error, however, to regard such a complex of attitudes as peculiarly Japanese. One of the further attractions of Yoshida as a subject of study is that one can easily picture him operating in a different national and racial context: strutting with riding crop as a sahib in Imperial India; lecturing and lording over little brown brothers as an American administrator in the Philippines; equating glory with repression as a *colonisateur* in Algeria; venerating the king in London or hailing the chief in Washington; riding with the hounds against the union organizers and radicals and Bonus Marchers of the Western world. Yoshida drew explicit and unsentimental lessons from the West, and was more interested in practices of power than protestations of piety. In this respect, Konoe's observation can be expanded: in reflecting the "consciousness of Imperial Japan," Yoshida embodied many aspects of imperialist (and monarchist) consciousness in general. That such qualities and attitudes did not prevent him from rising to the pinnacle of power after World War Two is again a commentary not only on postwar Japanese politics and society, but also on the international environment, and U.S. policy in particular, which facilitated such survival and continuity.

In his own appraisals of the prewar era, Yoshida drew a clear line of demarcation between "traditional diplomacy" and Japan's later aggressive and disastrous policies. In this scheme, the Sino-Japanese War (1894–1895), Russo-Japanese War (1904–1905), annexation of Korea (1910), occupation of Shantung (1914–1922), Twenty-One Demands (1915), Siberian Intervention (1918–1922), and military deployments to China's Shantung province (1927–1928) had no generic relation to Japan's later militarism. The great watershed was the Manchurian Incident of 1931, but the fatal blow to "traditional diplomacy" occurred a decade prior to this, at the Washington Conference of 1921–1922. Until that time, he argued, Japan's foreign policy had rested upon two principles: maintenance of the Anglo-Japanese Alliance (1902–1922), and determination to resolve Sino-Japanese problems in a "mutually satisfactory" way.[3] When the alliance was abrogated in 1922 and replaced by vague ideals of international cooperation, Japanese diplomacy lost its firm footing and relations with China were disrupted by China's ability to play one imperialist power against the other: "Without the stabilizing influence of the Alliance, our military men saw fit to overrun Manchuria and China; the Second World War started, which was a blow to Britain and reduced China to chaos; and everyone knows what happened to us."[4] Implicit in this breathless compression of one of history's great tragedies was a telling point concerning the precarious balance between cooperation and conflict among the imperialist powers—as well as an historical "lesson" which made Yoshida ripe for bilateral alliance with the United States in the postwar period.

These themes have bearing upon Yoshida's well-known association with the "pro-Anglo-American clique" (*shin-Ei-Bei ha*) within the prewar Foreign Ministry. During the early and formative years of his career, he was himself a participant in the execution of "traditional diplomacy." He attended the peace conference at Versailles as a minor functionary in 1919, and was serving his second assignment to the embassy in London when the Washington Conference and termination of the Anglo-Japanese Alliance took place. The first decade and a half of his professional activities occurred under the aegis of the alliance, and when he looked back upon this nostalgically as the palmy epoch of the empire, he was recalling an arrangement he had experienced personally. The recollection was somewhat romanticized, for even during this period Yoshida was critical of aspects of his government's activities. He believed the empire was not being developed rapidly enough, for want of systematic planning. And he found the China policy of the Ōkuma cabinet (1914–1916) amateurish and disruptive. Still, it was, overall, an era when a Japanese diplomat could hold his head high and look to the future with relative confidence. Nothing symbolized this more vividly than Japan's participation as a great and victorous power in the peacemaking at Versailles—a status enjoyed by virtue of the Anglo-Japanese Alliance, under which Japan had entered World War One and engaged in action against the Germans in China's Shantung province.

This association with the pro-Anglo-American clique, however, requires clarification. Yoshida's prewar career as a whole was not concentrated in the more prestigious "Western track" of diplomatic service. The greater part of his professional endeavors for over three decades was directed toward relations with the Asian continent. He was, if a specialist in anything, a China specialist, and in point of chronology his diplomatic career coincided almost exactly with the establishment, development, and denouement of Japan's Asian empire. Yoshida's first assignment was to the continent, and his activities were interlocked with the treaty system, initiated with the Komura Treaty of December 1905, under which Japan consistently justified its pyramiding "special rights and interests" in China. Yoshida not only matured within the convoluted legalisms of imperialist encroachment on China, but also imbibed the emotional draughts, in his own phrase, of Japan's "special feelings" toward the Asian mainland.[5]

The significance of the Anglo-Japanese Alliance resided in this primary orientation toward Asia, for bilateral alliance with the dominant Western power in the Orient gave Japan security in pursuing its goals across the Sea of Japan. At the same time, Great Britain was also a model for Yoshida. His respect for the country had little to do with political theory (liberalism) or structure (parliamentary government); within England, it was the elite hauteur and rigid class stratification that he experienced and appreciated. But what Yoshida most admired was Britain abroad, the imperium, the global reach and economic heart and legalistic sinews of the lion. He referred, time and again, to "diplomatic sense."[6] This was his most cherished English phrase, and in practice he indicated that it meant skill in power politics, efficiency in empire. Britain in India, or in Egypt, became a point of reference in some of his later proposals for Japan in China. And the prospects of stabilizing the imperialist status quo through *cooperative* gunboat diplomacy continued to attract him even after Britain itself had grown chary of such tactics in Asia.[7]

In this context, identification with the "pro-Anglo-American clique" implied Anglophilism on Yoshida's part. It did not entail comparable respect for the United States. On the contrary, Wilsonian idealism and the largely American pressures that culminated in the Washington Conference rang the death knell for "traditional diplomacy." Yoshida was not anti-American, and in the 1930s, when England's power was draining, he established intimate ties with such Americans as Joseph Grew, the ambassador to Japan. Nonetheless, the Washington Conference remained a lesson in American diplomatic folly that Yoshida never forgot, and throughout his prewar career he regarded the power across the Pacific as wayward and unreliable, out of touch with the realities of the situation in Asia, and lamentably deficient in "diplomatic sense."[8]

In the post-1945 period, such attitudes carried a double legacy. The *Pax Americana* replaced the *Pax Britannica*, and the lessons of "traditional diplomacy" made Yoshida more than willing to enter into a bilateral alliance with the United States. In his own mind, this was the resurrection, metamorphosized, of the Anglo-Japanese Alliance. At the same time, Yoshida continued to believe that Japan could not survive without a close, if no longer primary, relationship with China. And, although less disdainfully, he remained leery of America's hyperbolic diplomatic style. This became a source of most notable friction when the United States forced Japan to participate in the postwar containment of China.[9]

APPRENTICESHIP

Yoshida's diplomatic career began with lack of grace. He was assigned to Tientsin in November 1906, but the order was rescinded and changed to Mukden, owing to the Foreign Ministry's eagle eye. Yoshida was quickly identified as an "impertinent fellow" (*namaiki na yatsu*), and it was decided he would come under more disciplined supervision in Mukden than in Tientsin.[10]

In Mukden, Yoshida participated in negotiations with Russia and China concerning disposition of Manchurian territory occupied by Japan in the wake of the Russo-Japanese War. The task was complicated by a power struggle on the Japanese side between the Kwantung civil government in Port Arthur and the consulate in Mukden, and General Terauchi Masatake was sent from Japan to help resolve these difficulties. When his superior was called back to Japan, it fell upon Yoshida to deal with the formidable Terauchi. His "coolness" impressed this Chōshū protégé of Yamagata Aritomo, he later claimed, and was prelude to a more intimate relationship beginning in 1912. Before that materialized, Yoshida was posted to London (1908–1909) and Rome (1909–1912); the latter appointment began as a honeymoon voyage for the newly-wed young diplomat.[11]

In 1912 Yoshida was transferred to the strategic port of Antung, situated in Manchuria close to the Korean border, where he held a dual position as consul in Antung and secretary to the governor general of Korea, who resided in Seoul. This was his single longest assignment as a diplomat, lasting until late 1916, and Terauchi occupied the post of governor general during this period, before returning to become prime minister of Japan in October 1916.

Historians have regarded Terauchi with distaste. He was one of the outspoken advocates of precipitate war against Russia in 1904; was instrumental in forcing the Korean sovereign to accede to annexation in 1910 (an accomplishment he toasted as the fulfillment of Hideyoshi's dream of continental conquest three centuries earlier); and laid the foundation of Japan's savage colonial rule in Korea by suppressing indigenous opposition during his term as governor general. His premiership was similarly characterized by domestic repression, and his most dramatic contribution to history was a 72,000-man counterrevolutionary army, despatched to Siberia as part of the international intervention which followed the Bolshevik Revolution.[12]

Yoshida appears to have been one of the few persons who was not intimidated by Terauchi, and was probably the only one who has ever characterized the martinet as "loveable." In his memoirs, he praised his superior's "kind heart" and genuine interest in certain favorite subordinates, and related an anecdote about Terauchi and some tiger cubs to illustrate the General's "childlike, loveable" side.[13] Such affinity with and even affection for certain powerful and hard-line military figures was to become a leitmotif in Yoshida's career, even after the Pacific War. He displayed similar compatibility with Tanaka Giichi in the late 1920s; with the "Imperial Way Faction" generals Mazaki Jinzaburō and Obata Toshishirō in the late 1930s and early 1940s; and with the most counterrevolutionary professional soldiers in the post-surrender U.S. occupation force, such as Major General Charles Willoughby and his counter-intelligence staff.[14]

In reminiscing about the Antung period, the tiger cubs and loveable general were the only inhabitants of Korea Yoshida mentioned. A colleague from this time, however, recalled that one of Yoshida's major functions was to adjudicate civil cases at the Antung consulate, almost all of which involved disputes among Koreans. On the basis of this experience, Yoshida drew the stereotype of Koreans as fond of disputation ("two Koreans guarantees three factions"), full of "fighting spirit," and disinclined toward conciliation. He argued that emphasis in Korean schools should be placed on the natural rather than social sciences, and advocated, patronizingly if enigmatically, that the Koreans should be taught that "seeds sown in spring cannot be harvested until autumn."[15] To the end of his life, he regarded the era of Japanese rule over Korea as essentially beneficent, characterized by economic development and elevation of the lives of the Korean people.[16] This attitude also became a consequential legacy to the postwar period, when, as prime minister, Yoshida found the bitter nationalism of Syngman Rhee incomprehensible, a mere confirmation of the intractable national character of the Koreans, and failed to establish relations with the Rhee government.

On a personal level, by the Antung period Yoshida had already adopted the style more commonly associated with his later years—kimono, white *tabi* footwear, walking stick in hand. And he was sedulously honing the irreverent puns that enlivened his conversation throughout his career. There were many deer in the area, he informed one puzzled visitor, and then explained he was referring to the *baka* ("fool," written with ideographs literally meaning horse-deer) variety.[17]

"Fool" remained a favorite Yoshida epithet,[18] and by around 1915 he gave evidence of feeling beleaguered by the species. As a matter of general concern, the empire was developing more slowly and haphazardly than he deemed appropriate. This was compounded by the heavy-handed China policy of the "liberal" Ōkuma government, which came into power in April 1914. In a letter to Makino, Yoshida vented his exasperation at Japan's failure to lay a solid base for expansion on the continent through thorough investigation of local customs, mineral and land resources, transportation, and the like. "Management tends to be governmental and bureaucratic, and the economic side is rather neglected," he complained, "and I think this helps explain why our management of Manchuria has not progressed and developed."[19] He himself devoted a large portion of his time while in Antung to preparing a proposal for a joint Sino-Japanese timber project.[20]

Certain basic strains in Yoshida's consciousness of empire can be discerned in this early period. While accepting both the emotional "special feelings" and formal "special rights and interests" of the Japanese in the northern part of China, he also recognized the limitations of Japanese power and shallowness of the economic base established in the decade since the Russo-Japanese War. Empire-building was laborious, but relentless. "It is my thought," he wrote Makino, "that after we establish our political and economic position in Manchuria, with our power in the area behind Peking, it is necessary to prepare to guide (*shidō*) China sincerely."[21] These ingredients of a successful imperialist program were volatile: a secure political as well as economic base north of the Great Wall of China, a destiny as China's mentor, yet all effected in a spirit of "sincerity," a context of genuine Sino-Japanese cooperation, and a manner that would be endorsed by the great powers of the West. Petty intrigue or precipitous action could only be counterproductive, and in Yoshida's view the Ōkuma cabinet threatened to undermine the entire fragile structure by resorting to two successive ill-conceived policies: the Twenty-One Demands of 1915, followed by a plot to topple the government of Yuan Shih-k'ai through connivance with Japanese soldiers of fortune.

Yoshida's concrete response to the Twenty-One Demands remains shrouded in mystery, but was clearly insubordinate: he attempted to circulate a petition criticizing the Demands among Japanese consuls in Manchuria. This criticism appears to have been directed primarily against the notorious "group five" of the Demands, and to have been an entirely pragmatic response to the global protest that greeted the audacious ultimatum. In later years, Yoshida found occasion to refer to this *tactical* blunder of alienating Western support for Japan's imperialist objectives, but his expression of protest at the time went virtually unnoticed. The Foreign Ministry itself did not learn of it until a year or so later.[22]

Even as the furor over the Twenty-One Demands continued, Yoshida found himself at odds with the Ōkuma government on a new but related issue: the activities of the *Shina rōnin*, Japanese "China adventurers" engaged in espionage and intrigue on the continent. Yoshida was contemptuous of these "drifters" (*furō no yakara*), and characterized their activities as "nothing more than plunder and violence" (*ryakudatsu bōkō*). As consul in Antung he had taken it upon himself to curb them, and believed he was making progress on this score. Around the beginning of 1916, however, he was made aware by Japanese police officials on the continent, among others, that the Ōkuma government had adopted a "hands-off" policy concerning these provocateurs, in the hope that their agitations and conspiracies would help topple the Yuan Shih-k'ai government.

These cabinet intrigues were supported by such prominent liberal ministers as Ozaki Yukio, entailed collusion with segments of the army, and revolved around a so-called "Second Manchuria-Mongolia Independence Plan." They represented precisely the type of meddlesome diddling Yoshida believed to be the antithesis of far-sighted policy, and he lost no time in conveying his concern to both Makino and the foreign minister. In these communications, he noted that the new machinations violated "what I have all these years understood to be the policy of the Imperial Government," and re-emphasized the impossibility of Japanese overseas development without genuine Chinese trust and cooperation: "No matter how we are to deal with Manchuria, if we do not win the people's hearts, then our country's tasks will never be achieved." In a lengthy dispatch, he warned the foreign minister that giving free rein to the "drifters" would destroy friendly trading relations between Chinese and Japanese merchants and deal an immeasurable blow to the overseas economy—not to mention causing the credibility of the Japanese government to "fall to the ground overnight." He was gratified, and somewhat relieved, to find that Terauchi shared these views and, at least for the present, endorsed the wisdom of a "mild" China policy. In a letter probably written in June 1916, Yoshida reported to Makino that he had visited Terauchi in Seoul and heard the latter's China policy in detail. The general also opposed government support of the *Shina rōnin* and instigation of incidents, and agreed that Japan had neither the manpower nor financial ability to detach Manchuria from China or "take the responsibility of China into our hands." Under present circumstances, there was no alternative but to pursue a dignified and trustworthy policy of Sino-Japanese cooperation.[23]

When Terauchi replaced Ōkuma as prime minister in October 1916, Yoshida was recalled to Tokyo and offered the position of private secretary to the new premier. He refused this with typical flippancy, informing Terauchi that "I might be fit to be prime minister, but would not make a suitable private secretary to the prime minister."[24] The offer was naturally dropped, and in December Yoshida was proffered a diplomatic plum—assignment to the embassy in Washington—only to have this snatched away when the Foreign Ministry belatedly became aware of his initiative in opposing the Twenty-One Demands. By Yoshida's own account, only his relationship with Makino saved him from being dismissed from the foreign service for this insubordinate act.[25]

There followed one of those interludes of relative inaction which seemed to recur throughout Yoshida's life, and he was eventually assigned to an insignificant job "outside the mainstream" as head of the Foreign Ministry's archives section in Tokyo in July 1917. The vice foreign minister at this time was Shidehara Kijūrō, and although both men became identified with the pro-Anglo-American clique of the Foreign Ministry, their initial relationship was cold and distant, and remained so until World War Two. Yoshida attributed this to several factors. He spent a good deal of time grumbling about withdrawal of the Washington post, which prompted the austere Shidehara to close his door to him. Another barrier between the two, Yoshida suggested, was Shidehara's superb command of English and his partiality to colleagues who possessed comparable foreign-language skills—which ipso facto excluded Yoshida. Beyond this, there was obviously the friction caused by Yoshida's own brusque personal style.[26] As became more apparent later, the two also did not see eye to eye on foreign policy priorities.

LESSONS OF VERSAILLES

In February 1918, Yoshida was appointed consul in Tientsin, where he became briefly immersed in the Shantung controversy. Japan had laid claim to the territorial rights formerly possessed by Germany in Shantung, and bolstered these claims with a number of secret treaties between 1915 and 1917, involving China itself,

Great Britain, and France. It was China's position that these war spoils had been extracted under duress and were not legitimate. The issue was subsequently resolved in Japan's favor at Versailles, but then revised in favor of China at the Washington Conference—a prime example of the death gasp of "traditional diplomacy."

Before the end of 1918, Yoshida was writing his father-in-law concerning his desire to observe at first hand the "diplomatic war" that would follow World War One, and requesting that Makino use his influence to have Yoshida reassigned to London.[27] This materialized in 1920. Prior to that, he returned to Tokyo in December 1918 to assume a brief assignment in the International Trade Bureau of the Foreign Ministry. The following year he attended the Paris Peace Conference as a personal secretary to Makino, who was second-in-command of the Japanese delegation and the group's real spokesman. This privilege again came as a result of personal importunement. Although Yoshida may have expressed scruples about "riding on the influence of one's father," these did not extend to one's father-in-law.

Yoshida's responsibilities at Versailles were menial—arranging tickets, lodgings, and the like—and, even at that, he performed them so ineptly that Makino did not speak to him during the entire one-month return voyage. It proved, Yoshida later commented, not that he was incompetent, but merely that (like business, and like being a private secretary) he was not cut out for flunky work.[28] Despite this ridiculous situation, the conference made a deep impression on the forty-year-old diplomat, one that, if anything, grew stronger in subsequent years, until it became a retrospective symbol of the high-water mark of the "traditional diplomacy" of Meiji and Taishō. While it is impossible to measure such an impact precisely, Yoshida's subsequent career indicates that the lessons he learned at Versailles were enduring and wide-ranging.

Yoshida's own recollections of the conference were, as usual, impressionistic and anecdotal. He pointed out, for example, that Japan's chief delegate, Saionji Kimmochi, and Clemenceau, the conference chairman, had lived in the same boarding house when

Saionji was a student in Paris, and this personal relationship could not but have helped Japan. Concerning Makino's introduction and defense of the controversial racial-equality clause, Yoshida rejected the interpretation that the Japanese had submitted this as a bargaining counter to enhance their position on the Shantung question. According to him, Makino had become personally involved with the problem of American discrimination against Japanese in California during his term as foreign minister in the Yamamoto cabinet of 1913-1914, and sincerely hoped to put the issue to rest at Versailles.[29] The rejection by the white nations of this simple expression of racial equality naturally had profound repercussions in Asia—repercussions that were particularly subtle because in many cases they were mixed with the generally favorable image the "democracies" gained by their victory in the war. As a result of their disillusionment on this issue, Yoshida wrote, "We gained the impression that the high hopes of a new international order were doomed to disappointment."[30]

Versailles was Yoshida's baptism in big-league diplomacy, and for him it reaffirmed, in positive as well as negative ways, the old rules of the game Woodrow Wilson and the supporters of the League of Nations had hoped to repudiate. He later described the proposed new international order as "a pious experiment in a period of adjustment," and observed that "imperialism had been condemned in principle, but colonial territories other than those of a defeated Germany continued to exist."[31] While other Japanese, such as Shidehara and possibly even Makino, may have been more sanguine about Wilsonian idealism and the possibility of a "new diplomacy" for Asia in the 1920s, Yoshida remained skeptical. As he would argue behind closed doors somewhat later, he concluded that "the national character of the United States is such as to make it not very dependable in diplomacy."[32] The lesson was to stay with the old methods of imperialism, and there were many sides to this.

On the one hand, the racial issue, together with America's failure to support the League of Nations, undermined the appeal of idealism or "internationalism" as a workable diplomatic premise in Yoshida's eyes. He did support Japanese membership in the League and cooperation in a world community, but the failure of Wilson's formulas simply gave negative reinforcement to his faith in the traditional practices of power politics. On the other hand, that faith also received positive reinforcement at Versailles. It was precisely the old style of *Realpolitik* (including bilateral military agreements, secret diplomacy, and concessions under duress) that made possible Japan's success on the Shantung question—that had, indeed, enabled Japan to become, within a generation after the termination of its own unequal treaties with the West, one of the world's "Big Five" (over Germany, Russia, China!), with a delegation of one-hundred-and-fifty ("and that hardly enough," according to Yoshida), seated in the chambers of Louis XIV and helping to divide up the world.[33]

Another young Japanese observer at the peace conference, a man who would bulk large in Yoshida's career, expressed these sentiments bluntly at the time. "Power still governs the world," Konoe Fumimaro wrote in a letter from Versailles; what one saw here was the victors' peace and the "iron principle of power control."[34] There is every indication that Yoshida shared this view. Thereafter he continued to make concrete policy proposals concerning Japan's position on the continent in accordance with the established methods of the diplomacy of imperialism. Balance of power and spheres of influence, condemned by Wilson but endorsed at Versailles, remained touchstones of his vision of Asia even after the initiation of open aggression against China in 1931. As will be seen, at the very moment in 1937 when Japanese and Chinese troops clashed at the Marco Polo Bridge and ignited the Asian continent, Yoshida was in London seeking solutions with pre-Versailles concepts and an old pre-League of Nations imperial partner.

If the Paris Peace Conference confirmed old practices at the time, however, it also laid the ground for a new lesson which Yoshida, three decades later, would find extremely useful: the lesson of the dangers of a punitive peace. After World War Two, when both Japan and the United States began to arrange for a generous peace settlement for Japan, one of the main arguments used against a more restrictive settlement was that the victors' peace at Versailles had merely sown the seeds of future world conflict. In both private and public discussion, beginning in 1950, the Americans and Japanese used the example of Germany and the "lesson of Versailles" to rebut those countries which still regarded Japan as a potential threat to Asia and desired fuller control over its future development. Yoshida utilized this argument, as did the chief American negotiator of the 1951–1952 peace and security treaties, John Foster Dulles, who had also been present at the Versailles conference as a minor functionary. This, however, was the long-range lesson. In the more immediate post-Versailles period, Yoshida was inclined to use the harsh settlement against Germany to support some of his own proposals for Japanese control and occupation on the Asian mainland.[35] History has many uses, particularly for brokers of power.

HOMAGE TO THE FUTURE SOVEREIGN

In May 1920, Yoshida received his second assignment to the London embassy, this time with the rank of first secretary. He remained at this post for two years, during which he experienced one great disappointment, and one brief moment of immense exhilaration. The disappointment lay in having to witness the abrogation of the Anglo-Japanese Alliance, which Yoshida endeavored as best he could to prevent.[36] The euphoria occurred when the crown prince of Japan visited London for the coronation of King George V in 1921, and Yoshida had the opportunity to observe his own future sovereign at close hand.

Yoshida was also given, at this time, the opportunity to present a defense of "Japan's Far Eastern Policy" to the British public. In an article published under a pseudonym in *The Fortnightly Review* in February 1921, he endeavored to explain Japan's pressing needs and honorable objectives, and in the process to expose Chinese and American misrepresentations of Japanese policy. The article represented a vain endeavor to deflect those winds blowing toward the Washington Conference and dismantling of the Anglo-Japanese Alliance.

Yoshida began by emphasizing that Japan's geographical position and increasing population dictated its foreign policy: "The economic problem of Japan's future consists in obtaining from China and Siberia her supplies of food and raw materials and seeking to dispose of her goods in the great market [of the United States] on the east." Traditional policy since the time of Commodore Perry, he continued, "has always been directed toward cultivation of lasting friendly relations with China, Russia and America." Neither the Sino-Japanese nor Russo-Japanese Wars repudiated this tenet. Japan had waged both wars "reluctantly" to remove a menace to Japanese security through Korea, and in the case of Russia had also fought to preserve the ideal of the open door. Both foes had been "temporary enemies," and both wars were quickly followed by resumption of amicable intercourse. While acknowledging that the Japanese had been guilty of "some imprudent and ill-considered actions" in recent years, Yoshida argued that these had been exaggerated and exploited for partisan purposes in a manner that obscured the firm legal basis of Japan's claims on the continent and distorted his country's genuine respect for the integrity of China.

Yoshida passed quickly and lamely over the Twenty-One Demands. If judged by the result, these were an unfortunate event; "Nevertheless, they were originally formulated with the genuine intention of finding a way of liquidating all the outstanding difficulties with China and establishing Sino-Japanese relations on a firm and lasting basis." The bulk of his short article was devoted to an explanation of Japan's position on the still simmering Shantung controversy, and in the course of this he made a telling reference to the double standards of the Western imperialists: if the Chinese argument were accepted, namely, that Japan's claims in Shantung were void because they rested upon an agreement obtained from China by coercion in 1915, "then almost all the agreements made with China by foreign Governments might be the subject of a similar contention." To challenge Japan on Shantung was to challenge the rules of the game, and the potential dire consequences of such a precedent extended even beyond the danger of unraveling the entire foreign treaty structure that had been imposed upon China. The legality of Japan's assumption of former German territorial rights in Shantung had been affirmed in the Treaty of Versailles, and consequently repudiation of these rights would also constitute revision of the terms of the peace settlement, "which would be a grave matter for all the Allies."

Since Japan's claims in Shantung were entirely legal, and since it was the Chinese rather than Japanese side which currently was refusing to negotiate the issue, it followed that clamor over the matter "has been raised solely for the purposes of political party warfare." This was true not only among the political factions in China, but also in the United States, where the Republican Party found the Shantung issue "a convenient stick with which to beat the Democrats." In conclusion, Yoshida combined a Kiplingesque touch of East-is-East-and-West-is-West with a token confession of the great imperialists' classic venal sin in China ("misunderstanding")—and a final barb at the United States:

> The internal politics of China are complicated and difficult for Westerners to understand. . . . If England and Japan had had a clearer understanding in the past with regard to China's gradual evolution and liberal advancement, and if America had not shown sympathy for the South China party, and thus encouraged the continuation of factional strife, much of the present chaos in China might have been obviated.[37]

Dismay over the impending collapse of the Anglo-Japanese Alliance was temporarily allayed by the enthusiastic reception Crown Prince Hirohito received in London during his unprecedented tour of Europe. The occasion provided Yoshida with his first close contact with the man who would become emperor in 1926 and remain on the throne through the remaining four decades of Yoshida's life. It also afforded him a rather uniquely literal opportunity to attain "proximity to the throne." He was sent rushing to Gibraltar to meet the imperial entourage en route and obtain the august corporal measurements in person; these were passed on to London tailors to prepare a wardrobe for the crown prince's public appearances.[38]

Hirohito's visit to London and Europe was recognized as a gamble by high Japanese officials, and was a subject of intense controversy within Japan. His father, the Taishō emperor, was physically infirm and mentally feeble; in fact, almost immediately following the 1921 tour, Emperor Taishō withdrew from all official functions and the crown prince assumed the active role of regent (*sesshō*). Hirohito himself, moreover, had been subjected to a sheltered upbringing, with little contact with the public even in Japan, to say nothing of exposure to Western etiquette and Western eyes. Among the most fevered and ultranationalistic Japanese patriots, it was argued that the future sovereign of the "divine country" would be sullied and tarnished by traveling to "barbarian lands," and that exposure to Western democracy would imperil Japan's very future. One right-wing group actually threatened to block the railroad tracks with human bodies to prevent the crown prince from reaching his point of departure. Even those officials who supported the trip were apprehensive that the twenty-year-old heir apparent might be ill at ease, embarrassed and embarrassing in the glare of Western society. Kanroji Osanaga, Hirohito's intimate companion, recalled: "It was feared that the prince might commit social blunders because of tension or inexperience. And faux pas that would ordinarily be overlooked might have severe repercussions when committed by a crown prince."[39]

This disappointment concerning the Taishō emperor and uncertainty regarding his son must be kept in mind as a backdrop to the unbridled joy with which Yoshida observed, for the first time, the personality and performance of his future sovereign. Yoshida's loyalism and adoration of the throne were planted early, and would remain intact irrespective of the personal qualities of the reigning emperor. At the same time, however, such emotions were capable of being intensified through personal contact and identification. This had occurred in the case of the Meiji emperor, who exerted a personal charisma over those Japanese with whom he came in contact. Meiji's successor, the Taishō emperor, was pitifully lacking in comparable qualities.[40] What Yoshida discovered at this time in Taishō's heir were traits of character and demeanor that were less awesome than those of the Meiji emperor, but impressed him as no less regal, and certainly no less personally attractive. The point is not a complicated one, but merely meant to emphasize that the "loyalism" and "monarchism" which Yoshida later came to personify were buttressed by deep personal respect for Emperor Hirohito, comparable to that which had existed between Emperor Meiji and the Meiji leaders; that there was a further dimension of affection here, kindled by Hirohito's modesty, which was probably lacking between the more carnal and aloof Meiji emperor and his loyal servants; and that these more intimate emotions burst forth, in full bloom, in 1921.

This is made clear in a revealing letter Yoshida sent to Makino in June 1921, in which he began by describing the crown prince's reception as "extraordinary" and his own feelings as "extremely ecstatic."[41] The prince had been received with respectful affection by all levels of British society, high and low, and Yoshida attributed this entirely to "his inborn beautiful characteristics." The essence of Hirohito's attractiveness lay in his "simple and natural naiveté," his almost quintessential embodiment of the "virtue of modesty" (*gokentoku*), combined with an open and unreserved friendliness and poise. Present-day observers familiar with the postwar image of Hirohito as a shy and awkward monarch would probably recognize only a portion of the portrait Yoshida attempted to draw for Makino in 1921, for Yoshida's prince was as regal as he was modest. He greeted the British royal family without any reservations, "as if it were a meeting of relatives," and, although his public speeches were delivered through an interpreter, "the clear and ringing quality of his voice was felt by each and all," and the fact that he spoke without a prepared text left everyone with an impression of his fine memory.[42]

These happy observations led Yoshida, in the same letter, to grim rumination concerning ideology and social order, and the sinister forces that threatened this pristine world of royalty:

socialism, anarchism, "labor-farmerism" (*rōnōshugi*). "These confusions in the Western world of ideology" were causing ideological instability in Japan and becoming increasingly difficult to control in the intellectual world, he wrote, and it was thus essential to defend the imperial household against such threats and turn it into a more positive force for social stabilization and ideological indoctrination. For a person who was often called a "liberal" in prewar Japan, Yoshida's thoughts on this subject were revealing. He advocated that the education of the imperial family be broadened from its present narrow concentration upon Japanese history (*kokugaku rekishi*) to include the scholarship of the West as well as East, and that the imperial household itself send responsible young scholars to Europe and the United States. Unlike the rightists, who flailed against "Western democracy" in general, Yoshida was concerned with the selective and controlled introduction of Western thought in Japan; he desired the imperial household simultaneously to protect itself against the ideological challenges emanating from the West and to serve as a mediating source of "enlightenment" to the public.

The challenge went further, however, and here, having called for larger windows to the West for his sovereign, Yoshida himself turned to Japan's feudal past for inspiration:

> I think it is especially important that modern and scholarly support concerning defense of the national polity (*kokutai*), with the imperial house at its center, be infused into the academic world. The contribution of Hayashi [Razan] and Neo-Confucian scholarship to the three centuries of Tokugawa rule was not slight, and in my view the preparation on the part of Bakufu politicians was quite thorough. But today, under the name of freedom of research and independence of scholarship, scholars who are literary sycophants (*kyokugaku amin*) have appeared and the world of ideology is increasingly confused. In the future, this will become a matter of grave importance. This is the very area in which my concerns lie.

Yoshida's letter concluded with a mundane postscript which rather nicely revealed the class society such indoctrination would hopefully preserve. He apologized for being unable to find a special soap in Paris that Makino had apparently requested.

The ideological orientation this letter revealed surfaced on numerous occasions throughout Yoshida's later career. In 1928, for example, he served in a responsible position in the Tanaka government, under which the first mass arrests of holders of "dangerous thoughts" were carried out. In the 1930s, persons like Makino and, less directly, Yoshida himself, were castigated by ultranationalists for tendering "evil"—that is, pro-Western—advice to the throne. During the Pacific War, as Japan's situation became critical, he came to believe that prolonged war would destroy the country's last defenses against subversive ideologies; much of his opposition to the war rested upon this premise. In the immediate postwar period, his most intense endeavors were devoted to protecting the emperor and reaffirming the immemorial nature of the "national polity." And in 1950, three decades after the above letter to Makino, Yoshida created a mild sensation by publicly attaching the epithet of "literary sycophant" to the president of Tokyo University and other intellectuals who advocated permanent and unarmed neutrality for Japan.[43]

THREE

Managing the Empire, 1922–1930

In March 1922, Yoshida was appointed consul general in Tientsin, then famous, among other attractions, for the sweatshop conditions under which Chinese laborers were employed in Japanese factories. For him, this marked the beginning of a period of intimate involvement in continental affairs which coincided with China's entry into an era of truly historic change and upheaval. The political situation in China was, by any standards, chaotic. Warlord armies trampled the land in maneuvers of dizzying complexity, while "central governments" filtered through Peking as through a sieve. Disorder was furious and seemingly endemic, but beneath this a steady tide was rising which threatened Japan's imperialist ambitions even more than political instability in China: the tide of Chinese nationalism.

Yoshida's immediate response to these developments can be gleaned from letters he sent to Makino around 1923. In these he took a position severely critical of the ostensibly conciliatory "new diplomacy" of the post-Washington Conference period, and the manner in which his own Foreign Ministry appeared to be acquiescing in this. Yoshida was articulating at this time the lessons in power *he* had derived from Versailles, and from the "traditional diplomacy" of Meiji and Taishō. These were lessons which, beginning in 1924, were to place him at odds with the low-posture policies espoused by his erstwhile fellow Anglophile, Shidehara Kijūrō.

His position was fundamentally simple: Japan could not afford to remain a "bystander" to the turbulence in China, viewing events on the continent as a "fire on the opposite bank."[1] At the very beginning of 1923, he acknowledged that Japan's "passive policy" had been successful thus far, but continuation of a neutral stance would merely "invite scorn." "If we just carry on like this," he forecast to Makino, "our success will turn to bubbles." He called for an "active policy," and indicated that this would involve giving aid and assistance to one faction in the internal struggle for unification of China. Yoshida himself was inclined to support Tuan Ch'i-jui.[2]

In a later letter, Yoshida pulled out all stops in denouncing his country's "no-action, no-policy" diplomacy—its reliance on little more than "sweet words" and "cultural enterprises." He attributed anti-Japanese agitation in China to the instigation of "political gangs and devious Chinese merchants," who had succeeded in gaining student approval. And he called for what was to become one of the most overused phrases in his diplomatic lexicon: "strong resolution" by the Japanese government. Yoshida linked anti-Japanese activity in China to discriminatory legislation against Japanese immigration by the United States and Australia, and expressed fear that the sale of Japanese goods to the overseas Chinese community as well as to China proper could be throttled if Japan did not act decisively to suppress the Chinese opposition. This could be accomplished by forcing the Chinese government to mobilize police against anti-Japanese demonstrations and spokesmen. It was necessary to make the then dominant Chihli Clique "learn the fearsomeness of the Japanese reaction" to the anti-Japanese movement—and Yoshida went on to declare that such resolute action by Japan would actually be applauded in the West. Both the United States and Great Britain, he informed Makino, supported Japanese initiatives which would restore order and contribute to the revitalization of foreign prestige in China.[3]

Yoshida had greater opportunity to propagate his "active policy" after 1925, when he left Tientsin to assume one of the most important posts in his prewar career, that of consul general at Mukden. Before leaving Tientsin, however, he added another leaf to what must have been a rather lively personal dossier at the Foreign Ministry, coupling a breach of bureaucratic etiquette with a lofty gesture of bureaucratic disdain:

> At that time a certain Diet member came over from Japan. Early one morning he appeared at my official residence as I was about to leave and announced, "I wish to see the consul general." "The consul general is out," I said. "Really?" he asked in disbelief, whereupon I replied, "If the consul general himself says he is absent, then he is really absent." As a result of this, I came under severe criticism in Tokyo.[4]

Such brusque touches of personal color have attracted many latter-day Japanese commentators on Yoshida. Among his personal acquaintances, especially from within the diplomatic corps, he has proven a rich source of anecdote, and his personality often has garnered more attention than his policies.[5] Yet the policies he proposed in the years following the Washington Conference were as dramatic and consistent as the egoistic indulgences, and far more revealing. Denunciation of "sweet words" and "no action" characterized Yoshida's position throughout the decade prior to the Manchurian Incident. He remained a consistently severe critic of Japan's foreign policy during these years, but a critic on the side of a more resolute, active, and positive policy for "managing the continent." Were his various criticisms and proposals to be presented without attribution, conventional wisdom could easily assign many of them to the jingoists, nationalists, and militarists who denounced "weak-kneed" policies of conciliation, lambasted the "pro-Anglo-American clique," and, as the version goes, prepared the ground for the Manchurian Incident. Yet, at the same time, Yoshida also remained a critic of army intrigues and, in 1930, navy endeavors to overturn the "conciliatory" policy of the Hamaguchi cabinet.

In the name of realism and diplomatic sense, Yoshida walked a thin line between advocacy of force and support of "cooperation," and his personal activities raise a number of questions concerning the categorical dichotomies frequently read into this decade of Japanese history: military versus civilian; ultranationalist versus internationalist; Tanaka diplomacy versus Shidehara diplomacy; Asia clique versus Anglo-American clique; and so on.

"MANAGING MANCHURIA"

Originally, Yoshida had been slated for appointment as minister to Sweden or Norway in 1925. This failed to materialize when the position in Mukden opened and no other suitable candidates seemed available. Shortly after being posted to Tientsin, Yoshida had been promoted to the second rank of the higher civil service, the highest rank not requiring imperial confirmation. He accepted the Mukden assignment with the understanding that he would be advanced to the first rank, but this was frustrated in an ironic turn of events. Since Yoshida had entered the foreign service at the same time as Hirota Kōki, it was decided that the latter should be put up for promotion at the same time. This was done, and Hirota passed. Yoshida, however, was denied the promotion and did not receive it until March 1928. Thereafter Hirota's career outstripped Yoshida's.[6]

From Yoshida's perspective, Mukden was a more critical post than Tientsin. For while the empire was perceived as embracing China as a whole, the heart of the imperium clearly lay in the "Three Eastern Provinces" of Fengtien, Kirin, and Heilungkiang. Collectively the three provinces comprised Manchuria, a designation especially convenient for those who would treat the area as separate and distinct from "China proper." As the key diplomatic representative there, Yoshida's energies were devoted to attempting to protect Japanese commercial interests, bring about a semblance of political and fiscal order in the three provinces, restrain the northern warlord Chang Tso-lin in his quest for power south of the Great Wall, and assert the authority of the Foreign Ministry in the midst of a thicket of competing Japanese organizations and individuals. His task resembled that of a man attempting to keep his eye on a collection of kaleidoscopes constantly forming new configurations both among and within themselves—developments in the Three Eastern Provinces; warlord politics to the south;

Chiang Kai-shek's Northern Expedition; emerging schisms within the Kuomintang; shifting opinions and competing bureaucracies on the Japanese side; the rise and eclipse of Soviet influence and communist power south of the Great Wall; and the responses of the Western powers to all this. It is hardly surprising that Yoshida later looked back on this period as having been a good training ground for the tangle of competing groups and policies he was confronted with in the post-1945 political arena.

Within the Three Eastern Provinces themselves, a large portion of Yoshida's energies from the outset was directed to rectification of alleged treaty violations. These involved such issues as improper taxation of Japanese nationals; "illegal" railway construction by the Chinese; disruption of Japanese commerce by strikes, demonstrations, and boycotts; individual incidents against Japanese nationals or Japanese property; interference in the preparation and distribution of Japanese-controlled Chinese newspapers; and publication of anti-Japanese articles in the Chinese press. On a more general level, he faced the problem of creating a stable political and economic environment. Here Yoshida was confronted with fiscal chaos, caused in large part by indigenous political and military rivalries and the issuance of various currencies. While Chang Tso-lin dominated the political scene by virtue of his powerful Fengtien Army and territorial base in Fengtien province, he was not the only influential warlord north of the Great Wall. Two of Chang's old and loyal comrades, Wu Chun-sheng and Chang Tso-hsiang, controlled their own armies in Heilungkiang and Kirin respectively. Other figures also emerged within the Manchurian politico-military complex as men to be dealt with in their own right, notably Wang Yung-chiang, Chang's fiscal adviser; Yang Yü-t'ing, head of the Mukden arsenal and probably Chang's most brilliant commander; and Mo Te-hui, civil governor of Fengtien and a man with whom Yoshida dealt with particular frequency.[7]

On the Japanese side, Yoshida was compelled to maneuver in a bewildering field which he castigated as "double and triple diplomacy" (*nijū sanjū no gaikō*), marked not only by the overlapping bureaucracies of the Foreign Ministry, Kwantung civil government,

Kwantung Army, and South Manchurian Railway, but also by a variety of other Japanese interests and influences. These included the Army General Staff, quasi-official army adventurers such as Doihara Kenji, and reserve-officer advisers to Chang Tso-lin such as Machino Takema and Matsui Shichirō (a relative of Matsui Iwane, chief of the Intelligence Division of the General Staff). Japanese policy was also subjected to pressure from Japanese business interests, and was strongly influenced by political developments within Japan itself. The Seiyūkai in particular, which was the opposition party for much of this period, used China policy effectively to serve its partisan interests. The complexity of such interrelations was not ameliorated by Yoshida's own abruptness. The necessity of coordinating activities with Kodama Hideo, governor general of the Kwantung Leased Territory, for example, did not prevent him from openly expressing his dislike for Kodama. "If you wish to see a child unworthy of his father," he commonly told Japanese visitors to Mukden, "then go to Port Arthur."[8]

On the international front, Yoshida's position required that he keep abreast of British and American attitudes toward Asia, as well as the vortex of events within China as a whole. From Mukden as from Tientsin, he witnessed at close hand the tragicomedy of warlord politics around Peking, a charade he observed scornfully and characterized as little more than a clash of "bandits," the private vendettas of military cliques.[9] This did not imbue him with respect for the Chinese, and steadily reinforced his concern for Japanese "resolution" in securing and protecting Japan's continental interests, particularly in the Three Eastern Provinces. Yoshida's continental assignments between 1922 and 1928 were also of incalculable significance in shaping his understanding of three intertwined developments which would return, a quarter century later, to become again of great concern to him. He witnessed the rise to power of Chiang Kai-shek, the earliest activities of the Chinese Communist Party, and the first intrigues of the Soviet Union and international communism in China. All three movements vigorously attacked Japanese imperialism, and naturally none gave him comfort. For a time during this period, the Soviet Union also attempted to exert influence on Chang Tso-lin.[10]

One firm mooring in the midst of these turbulent waters was Yoshida's own undeviating faith in the absolute legitimacy and inviolability of Japan's treaty rights in China. In January 1927, he joined the commander of the Kwantung Army and governor general of the Kwantung Leased Territory in emphasizing that Japan's objectives were "to protect and ensure Japan's particularly predominant position and rights in Manchuria and Mongolia,"[11] and he yielded to no one in his devotion to this task. In the mid-1920s, the greatest threat to achievement of this goal appeared to be posed by Chang Tso-lin, the former bandit who had risen to power under the wing of the Japanese Army during and after the Russo-Japanese War. On the one hand, Chang had become critical of certain of the agreements on which Japan's alleged rights rested, and was even deemed responsible for instigating some of the anti-Japanese activity which increased sharply during this period. On the other hand, he had embarked upon a bid for power beyond the Three Eastern Provinces, and his involvement in warlord struggles south of the Great Wall posed a double threat to the Japanese position. Not only did it divert Chang's attention from the pressing internal problems of the Three Eastern Provinces, but it also raised the specter of the civil war to the south spilling over into this area. Should this occur, it would not only strike at the economic heart of the empire, but also, in the important geopolitical dimension of the continental enterprise, weaken Manchuria as a strategic counter to the Soviet Union.[12]

Yoshida was thus eager to enlighten Chang concerning these dire prospects. He did not find his pupil attentive, however, and in the overview of Yoshida's career Chang emerges as one in a long list of individuals who found his "one-man" style intolerable. (In one of the humorous anecdotes in his memoirs, Yoshida recalled that on a certain occasion Chang presented leading Japanese officials with tiger skins, and Yoshida later discovered that the one he received came from the smallest tiger.)[13] The tension between the two men flared openly in 1927, sparked by a dispute involving a

Japanese-run Chinese newspaper. A good example of the propagandist dimension of neo-colonialism, as well as of Japanese extraterritorial rights in Manchuria, the paper was run by two Japanese acquaintances of Yoshida and constituted the major source of public information in the Mukden area. Yoshida used this as a mouthpiece for his own views, and when the paper began to run a series of editorials which were highly critical of events both within and outside the Three Eastern Provinces, Chang struck back by obstructing deliveries and sales and prohibiting the Chinese population from reading the paper (he could not close it because of its extraterritorial status).[14] Such personal tensions contributed to Yoshida's advocacy of an exceptionally hard line where Chang in particular and management of the empire in general were concerned.

Morishima Morito, who replaced Yoshida in Mukden in 1928, recalled that upon arrival at his new post he was confronted with an enormous collection of reports Yoshida had prepared. The most important of these were gathered in several volumes under the collective title "Warnings to Chang," from which Morishima deduced the heart of the Yoshida policy to have been as follows: (1) force Chang to abandon his ambition of moving into central Chinese politics and have him concentrate on management of the Three Eastern Provinces; (2) bring order to the financial chaos of the three provinces, caused by civil strife and overissue of military currencies, by obtaining a loan from Japan; (3) demand, in return for the loan, expanded Japanese rights in Manchuria; and (4) send financial advisers from Japan (Yoshida specifically recommended Ono Giichi, a former vice minister of finance).[15] These were, however, only the bare bones of Yoshida's various proposals. Morishima neglected to mention, for example, the keen attention Yoshida accorded to railway rights, which he correctly saw as a key to overseas exploitation.[16] Looking ahead to Yoshida's postwar career, in any case, it is interesting to observe the predominantly fiscal and economic thrust of these prewar concerns. Although Yoshida abandoned early plans to pursue a business career on the grounds that he had no talent for such matters, his diplomatic career involved him deeply with similar concerns. After

World War Two, while others placed greater emphasis upon activities in the political or social spheres, he continued to give greatest emphasis to economic stability and strengthening the economic sinews of the state through overseas involvement.

In summarizing his predecessor's activities, Morishima evaluated them highly. Had Yoshida's policies been adopted, he concluded, the Manchurian Incident of 1931 might well have been avoided, and thus it was regrettable that Foreign Minister Shidehara had not seen fit to go along with this advice. This was, of course, only one man's opinion. One of Yoshida's greatest opportunities to push his continental policy came after April 1927, when Shidehara's party was voted out of office and the new prime minister, Tanaka Giichi, initiated a reappraisal of policy toward China. At the famous Eastern Conference convened in Tokyo from June 27 to July 7, 1927, and for a number of months thereafter, Yoshida played a role of some small historic significance in the imperialist endeavors of his country. The complex setting in which he acted already has been described in some detail in Western scholarship.[17] By viewing this record from the more exclusive vantage of Yoshida, it is possible to draw a fairly full portrait of his attitude toward Japan's proper role in Asia prior to the Manchurian Incident—and to gain perhaps a more vivid and personalized sense of the imperial, and imperialist, consciousness in prewar Japan.

THE IMPERIAL CONSCIOUSNESS, 1927–1928

The Foreign Ministry archives for 1927–1928 provide the most detailed early insight into Yoshida's view of the empire. As the basis for a brief sketch of the imperial consciousness, these records have several attractions. They were set down prior to the Manchurian Incident, and indeed prior to the assassination of Chang Tso-lin in June 1928, and thus represent a period of Japanese expansion before the element of military initiative and conquest had become a central concern. In addition, the archives make possible a portrait based primarily on the memoranda and dispatches of pressing daily business, rather than later sanitized reminiscences or speeches for public consumption. This conveys a sense of the blunt, operative vocabulary of imperialism, a bluntness reinforced by Yoshida's personal disdain for rhetorical frills. Overall, these records permit several broad observations concerning Yoshida's attitude and mode of operation in this period:

- His disagreements with his colleagues were more tactical than fundamental, although some of his proposed courses of action were so severe that they were rejected by almost all other Japanese officials, both civilian and military.
- He laid particular stress upon the legal framework of overseas expansion and control—the specific treaty rights Japan had wrested from China in the course of some two decades—and warned of the dangers of relying upon "vague notions of Sino-Japanese goodwill," or being taken in by one's own propaganda.
- On numerous occasions, he also warned against becoming sucked into the vortex of internal political rivalries in China by "playing with small conspiracies."
- He justified certain of his proposals concerning Japanese administration, intervention, and repression on the continent by citing Western precedents and examples.
- To a greater extent than some of his colleagues, he recognized that Japan's actions on the continent required the support of the Anglo-American powers; this led him not merely to emphasize Japan's international image, but also to propose that cooperation with the Western imperialists be manifested in *joint* military intervention in China south of the Great Wall.
- His view of the empire was a dynamic one in that he endeavored to use economic linkages (as through loans) and legalistic devices (such as treaty rights) as a lever for the steady enlargement of Japan's position abroad; in addition, he advocated taking advantage of disorder, distress, and misfortune in China to extract further rights and concessions.
- Like the majority of his associates, his attitude toward the Chinese, both for private and public consumption, was condescending and shaped by a pervasive sense of moral righteousness and implicit racial superiority.
- To a greater extent than almost any other Japanese at that time, he endorsed the use of force, threats, and intimidation

to gain compliance with Japanese demands, and proposed military or "police" intervention to suppress anti-Japanese disturbances and protect Japan's "special rights and interests." In fact, it can be argued that Yoshida implicitly advocated taking over northeast China by military force as early as April 1927, more than four years before the Manchurian Incident.

By 1928, Yoshida's "active policy" had provoked riots in Mukden, strong protest from native officials, and criticism from virtually all other Japanese interests involved, including spokesmen for the Kwantung Army, the South Manchurian Railway, and the Kwantung civil government. Early in 1928, he was compelled to resign as consul general in Mukden on the pretext of illness; as the British Foreign Office noted drily some months later, he "was essentially removed from his post by his Govt. as being not quite up to it, so he must be feeling very fed up with China and the Chinese."[18] Within a matter of months, however, Yoshida had rebounded from this personal setback and become one of Prime Minister Tanaka's chief foreign-policy advisers.

Although Yoshida eschewed some of the cant which commonly characterizes the pronouncements of colonial officials, he nonetheless operated fully within the conventional framework of slogans and attitudes under which Japanese expansion took place. Catch phrases such as "coexistence and coprosperity" (*kyōzon kyōei*) and "management of the continent" (*tairiku keiei*) permeate his dispatches, and he was especially zealous in defending Japan's "superior position" (*yūetsu naru chii*) in Manchuria.[19] In his view, "management of Manchuria" was not a static and conservative undertaking, but a dynamic enterprise of empire-*building*, in which existing treaty rights constituted "the foundation for the future development of our power." More specifically, the key to enlargement of this power lay in railroads and fiscal policies. Thus, at one point he emphasized taking optimum advantage of both Japanese-controlled railroads and railroads in which Japanese capital was invested.[20] Elsewhere, as Morishima recounted, he advocated using loans as a wedge for extracting further concessions. In more sanguine moments, he expressed optimism that the disorder in China could prove a blessing in disguise for Japan. If only a cabinet emerged in Japan "which has resolution and the actual ability to carry (*seou*) China" he declared, then "the foundation for the prosperity of the nation may be opened through this opportunity."[21] These were orthodox proposals, fully consistent with the diplomacy of imperialism as it had been introduced to Asia by the Western powers at the turn of the century—and, in his view, still consistent with the realities of the "new diplomacy" of the 1920s.

In his major statement at the Eastern Conference in July 1927, Yoshida dwelt in a rather restrained manner upon the theme of expansion within the formal legal framework of the treaty system:

1. It is convenient for us to maintain the present system and organization of the Three Eastern Provinces *for the time being* [emphasis added]. However, it is not good to place too much weight upon the fate of Chang Tso-lin. While it is all right to support Chang when he has the power to support himself, to support Chang when he lacks such power can only result in "one-hundred harms and no profit." In other words, it is most important to leave the fate of Chang to the power of Chang himself.
2. A policy that endeavors to bring about the development of Manchuria and Mongolia by depending on the good intentions of a Chang Tso-lin or any specific political power is not good. The power of Japan in Manchuria—with Japan possessing various kinds of treaty rights such as leased territories, railroads, ancillary administrative rights, rights of stationing troops, mines, and so on—is not that slight. Our past policy has tended to forget this fact and try so hard to gain the good will of Chang that we have been taken advantage of by Chang Tso-lin and failed to achieve our goals.
3. However, it will not do for us to overdo reliance on our strong position in Manchuria. Keeping thoroughly in mind, first, the fact that the development of Manchuria is to be accomplished within the territory of China and therefore the sovereignty of China must be respected; and second, the future of the popular movement in China, then:

   a) It is important for us to make our demands in every way rational and something which we would not hesitate to announce to the world; and not to repeat a failure such as that of the Twenty-One Demands, which received criticism from other countries for being

> selfish and resulted in our having to give up in Washington [that is, at the Washington Conference] what we gained in China.
>
> b) To achieve this, it is important that we do not depend upon force but rather make China understand that Japanese demands are fair as well as profitable for China—in other words, that they are for the coexistence and coprosperity of Japan and China.
>
> I believe that at this time it is necessary for our government to think carefully and study concrete plans concerning such matters.[22]

Although earlier Yoshida had endorsed Japanese support of Tuan Ch'i-jui, during his Mukden period he frequently reiterated the warning that Japan should avoid partisan involvement in Chinese warlord politics. Such warnings were intended, moreover, primarily as a criticism of support of Chang Tso-lin's ambitions by the Japanese military—before segments of the military reversed course with a vengeance and assassinated the northern warlord—and Yoshida's later antagonistic relationship with the mainstream of the military had origins in the intrigues of this period. In a letter to Makino in mid-1926, Yoshida characterized the embroilment of the Japanese military in Chinese politics as being based upon "half-informed China theories and political theories," and ridiculed the Army's explanations that support of Chang was necessary to prevent the bolshevization of China, or to counter Anglo-American support for other Chinese factions.[23]

His allusions at the Eastern Conference to respect for Chinese sovereignty and avoidance of reliance upon force were considerably more disingenuous. The atmosphere in which Yoshida and his colleagues operated afforded scant place for respect for the Chinese, and the dominant tone was one of exasperation and contempt. Not only did Japan possess superior rights on the continent; in their view, it was obvious that the Japanese as a people possessed superior abilities. The persistent moral sniveling of their memoranda and conversations represents an almost quintessential dimension of the imperialist mentality. They contain so many calls for "sincerity" (*seii*) and Chinese "self-reflection" (*hansei*) that unwary scholars stumbling into this hall of mirrors can easily come away with the impression that the business of empire was little more than a perverse moral crusade. The Chinese were arrogant. They were insincere. They were incapable of solving their own problems, or of recognizing their own best interests. Japan should respond sympathetically to the nationalist movement in China, the Japanese minister to Peking observed, just as one deals with a ward.[24] Japan would be sympathetic and understanding to the reasonable demands of the Chinese people, Shidehara stated in a famous speech in January 1927, and then later explained that "reasonable" meant seeking "coexistence and coprosperity" with Japan, and unreasonable meant threatening Japan's economic interests on the continent.[25] At one time or another, Yoshida himself seems to have played nearly all the possible points and counterpoints of this dreary conceit:

> *Rueful:* "Chang and others have gotten used to us over the years and have forgotten our special relationship."[26]
>
> *Threateningly Rueful:* "The Mukden officials have grown accustomed [to us] and do not realize that we are to be feared."[27]
>
> *Aggrieved:* "That Chang and others say this and that toward us is nothing new. They are selfish. . . ."[28]
>
> *Threateningly Aggrieved:* ". . . relying upon vague notions of Sino-Japanese goodwill rather than upon the exercise of national power. . . . is making Chinese flunkies needlessly haughty."[29]
>
> *Injured:* "I shall count out the various unpardonable outbursts of unjust incidents against us."[30]
>
> *Threateningly Injured:* "If the Mukden officials do not show the fruit of self-reflection concerning their various unpardonable attitudes toward us, then I will personally tell the civil governor that we will stop the Peking-Mukden line from passing through our territory along the Mukden Railway."[31]
>
> *Beneficent (and Dry):* "Taking this opportunity, we urge them to self-reflection and awaken them to the truth of our relationship. Otherwise the Mukden faction will eventually destroy itself, which will not be in their interest either."[32]
>
> *Threateningly Beneficent:* "If we do not force them to adequate self-reflection now, then it will not be to their own benefit either."[33]

Mo Te-hui, governor of Fengtien, was Yoshida's major civilian counterpart on the Chinese side during this period and thus had the privilege of observing Yoshida practice the full scale of imperialistic moralism:

> *Direct:* "I told [Mo] that it is important that he himself show sincerity. . . ."[34]
>
> *Unequivocal:* "I told him that discussion was finished and the point was whether he had exercised self-reflection or not."[35]
>
> *Doubly Unequivocal:* "I gave him some time for self-reflection and also hinted that in case he does not show the fruits of self-reflection then we will not hesitate to take measures to make him self-reflect."[36]

Mo's response, upon reflection, was to cable the Japanese minister in Peking and request, in near despair, that Yoshida be dismissed as consul general in Mukden.[37]

The threat of firm and even militant response which runs through these quotations was not an idle one in Yoshida's mind. His communications contain numerous references to resolution, thoroughness, determination, and force. He was exceptionally quick to advocate the use of police force and even military intervention to defend Japan's position or back up his country's demands, and his statement to the contrary at the Eastern Conference rings hollow in the context of his concrete proposals both before and after that occasion. In an exceptionally revealing memorandum of April 21, 1927—which coincided with the establishment of the Tanaka cabinet—Yoshida clearly indicated both his contempt for treaty stipulations that did not serve Japan's purpose and his easy tolerance of military force to advance these purposes:

> 1. It is desirable that the preservation of peace in Manchuria, whether inside the railway zone or not (*tetsudō fuzokuchi naigai o towazu*), should be entrusted to our forces wherever they can be deployed.
> 2. Such things as strikes instigated by laborers or farmers, or by the Southern Army or the Soviets, or which are provoked by the fall in value of the Mukden currency or stagnation in the financial world, should be vigorously suppressed by our authorities.

3. Our management of Manchuria should be executed by the national power of our country and should not be done by relying on Chang [Tso-lin] or Yang [Yü-t'ing] or Wang [Yung-chiang]. No matter what, we should absolutely exclude playing with small conspiracies.

4. The major concerns in our Manchurian administration should be railway and fiscal policy for the Three Eastern Provinces, seeking the opportunity to implement there the following two measures: working out a substantial plan for the currency system and devising a system whereby the Japanese, Russian, and Chinese railways in the Three Eastern Provinces might be linked up as a single unit.[38]

The sweep of this proposal, as Professor Gavan McCormack has noted, was striking indeed. Yoshida was not merely advocating reliance on the Japanese Army in areas covered by Japan's treaty rights, but also envisioning deployment of the military outside the railway zone, where such rights did not apply. And he came very close to advocating the iron hand of colonialism in an area which was not under formal colonial rule—both in the repression of popular movements and the imposed integration of fiscal, commercial, and administrative policies in the Three Eastern Provinces.[39]

What Yoshida had in mind might be described as a Japanese rendition of the gunboat diplomacy so effectively used by the Western powers in Asia—the threat of force backed by actual willingness to use this, whether against recalcitrant officials or the native populace. It was his insistence upon immediately carrying out a more limited manifestation of this aggressive policy—by denying Chang's Fengtien Army the use of the railways in their retreat north, on the grounds that this would draw the civil war into the Three Eastern Provinces—which eventually separated him from his colleagues and led to his resignation. In 1927 and early 1928, Yoshida was more precipitous than Prime Minister Tanaka himself in the espousal of a "positive policy," and in retrospect his position in these years cannot be neatly detached from that of the military activists who assassinated Chang during his retreat in June 1928, or of the Kwantung Army, which three years later did indeed spill out of the railway zone and leased territory and endeavor to "preserve the peace" throughout the Three Eastern Provinces. Not surprisingly, Yoshida's various postwar reminiscences are conspicuously silent on his actual proposals and activities relating to management of the empire.

The militant reflex was not a passing belligerence confined to the memorandum of April 1927, but ran consistently through Yoshida's proposals during the critical months of mid-1927, and thereafter. Thus in the second week of June he suggested that it might be necessary for the army to take over temporarily both Chinese and Soviet railroads in the northeast, to prohibit the Chinese military from approaching within twenty miles of Tientsin, and even to assume temporary control over the arsenals in Mukden. "In the future," he noted in a classic example of the gunboat *quid pro quo*, "when a person of real power emerges in the Three Eastern Provinces, we will then take measures to hasten the materialization of our demands relating to the development of Manchuria and Mongolia in conjunction with the return of the above-mentioned occupied railways."[40] At the beginning of August, piqued that Mo Te-hui had not responded with proper sincerity to his non-negotiable demands, Yoshida wrote that "to our regret we must take suitable measures to promote his self-reflection"; he informed Tanaka that this might well involve military action. In the same cable he associated Chang Tso-lin with the rising anti-Japanese movement in Manchuria and reiterated his proposal that use of the Peking-Mukden line be denied to the Manchurian warlord.[41] On August 4, convinced the time had come to make a firm show of strength in Manchuria, Yoshida on his own initiative gave notice that the trains would be stopped on August 7, and cabled Tanaka requesting him to make the necessary arrangements.[42] The prime minister rejected this initiative and at this point shifted the negotiations to Peking, a move Yoshida opposed on the grounds that it would focus international attention on the negotiations, place Chang or the central Peking government in a position where they would be even more concerned with maintaining face, and thus greatly hamper the possibility of Chinese acquiescence to Japan's demands.[43] When massive anti-Japanese and anti-imperialist demonstrations erupted on September 4 in Mukden, the very heart of Yoshida's base of operations, he cabled that it would be necessary to use the Japanese police and army against any future such demonstrations. In this he was again overruled by Tanaka, the very personification of Japanese imperialism in the eyes of the demonstrators.[44] Months after the riots, in January 1928, Yoshida deemed it appropriate to inform Mo Te-hui's successor that in September the Japanese had decided it might be necessary to induce "self-reflection" by occupying Chang's Mukden castle if the anti-Japanese demonstrations were repeated.[45]

Although his proposals were generally rejected by other Japanese officials, Yoshida regarded them as fully consistent with policies decided at the Eastern Conference as well as instructions subsequently received from Tanaka. His reasons for believing this are plausible. In his study of the period, Akira Iriye has argued that the decisions made at the Eastern Conference were ambiguous, and Tanaka's subsequent direction of continental policy was vacillating and indecisive.[46] Neither recent scholarship nor the opinions of Yoshida's peers, however, offer any grounds for altering the interpretation that Yoshida chose to handle the situation in a manner more severe and inflexible than most other responsible Japanese officials at the time. Several considerations thus arise in connection with the Yoshida hard line: the grounds on which it was opposed by the Japanese establishment; the manner in which he himself qualified it by reference to a proposed role for the Western powers; and the particular (and particularly fine) distinction he drew between intervention and non-involvement in domestic affairs abroad.

The most interesting internal criticism of Yoshida's position came from Kodama (Port Arthur's "child unworthy of his father" in Yoshida's estimation). In a cable to Tanaka dated August 4 and devoted mainly to Yoshida's proposals, the governor general of Kwantung accused Yoshida of employing double standards by proposing that alleged treaty violations by the Chinese be countered with what amounted to Japanese violation of treaty agreements (prohibition of the use of the Peking-Mukden line by Chang's military forces). He predicted that such policies would provoke anti-Japanese activities, necessitating constant reformulation of responsive policies and possibly leading to military escalation: "If we once assume an intimidating attitude and the effect is negligible, then we will be forced to adopt increasingly severe measures, and this would entail a decision and readiness to push on to the ultimate resort." Kodama also noted a number of purely practical problems involved in the Yoshida proposal, and used a very Yoshida-like argument in suggesting that obstruction of the trains would inconvenience the Western powers and possibly have international repercussions.[47] Honjō Shigeru, commander of the Kwantung Army, cabled Vice Chief of Staff Minami Jirō similarly arguing that it would be precipitous for Japan to make the first resort to forceful measures, and much the same opinion was conveyed to Tokyo by representatives of the South Manchurian Railway.[48]

In responding to Kodama's criticism, Yoshida made immediate reference to Western precedent and current practice. "It is an international custom," he cabled both Tanaka and Kodama, "to take suitable measures of confrontation in dealing with the violation of treaties by other countries. Even now Great Britain is considering the employment of naval power in response to the unfair taxation of the Nanking government." He felt that tactical problems could be avoided and that the Chinese were so beset with internal and external problems that they could not "dare anything bold." "If we overlook their vulnerability now," he concluded, "the solution of Manchurian-Mongolian problems will never be attained. What is essential is to seize the opportunity and carry things forward, and since policy has already been decided at the imperial conference and the arrow has left the bow, I expect, if fortunate, your cooperation and look forward to the fulfillment of our purpose."[49] He followed this with a top-secret cable to Tanaka reiterating Mo Te-hui's "lack of manners" and failure to show sincerity; predicting that if the trains were not stopped, "there will be many such incidents until solution"; and urging the prime minister to issue firm orders along the lines he was proposing to both Kodama and the president of the South Manchurian Railway. Despite criticism from virtually all quarters, he refused to soften his position on the grounds that "the past history of Japan has always been that we punish those who behave impolitely to us."[50]

It has been argued that Japanese policy-makers in the late 1920s tended to regard continental policy in a vacuum, without giving great consideration to coordinated efforts with the Western powers.[51] In Yoshida's case this does not apply too well, although he did give the United States rather short shrift. "The national character of the United States is such as to make it basically not very dependable in diplomacy," he informed Tanaka prior to the Eastern Conference, "and so its agreement or disagreement should not be of great concern."[52] He was more partial throughout this period to the necessity of a "thorough understanding" with Great Britain. At the Eastern Conference itself, he warned of the negative consequences which would result from adoption of a China policy that provoked Western suspicions, and this was more than a mere platitude. In his more private communications during this period, Yoshida addressed the issue of cooperation with the West with startling concreteness: he advocated resolute joint military intervention in China by the imperialist powers.

Yoshida broached this in general terms in his correspondence with Makino, and conveyed his thoughts on the subject to Tanaka in several long cables dated June 9 and 10. In these dispatches, he advanced a concept of intervention in which he endeavored to draw the distinction between petty conspiracy and grand policy. On the one hand, he reiterated his belief that Japan should avoid tying its fortunes to any particular Chinese leader and allow political power on the continent to be decided by Chinese "public opinion." On the other hand, he proposed that if Chang Tso-lin continued to provoke disorder south of the Great Wall, the Japanese government should take the initiative in summoning the great powers and intervening in concert to bring about a cease-fire in

China. The particular advantage of this from Japan's point of view would be to secure the railways, especially the Peking-Mukden line, against military use and thus prevent the war from spreading to the Three Eastern Provinces.[53]

The line between intervention and interference was a fine one, but in Yoshida's view it could be honored. He defended his position to Tanaka in terms of both Japanese and Chinese self-interest, and rested his argument ultimately upon a frank reading of imperialist precedent and a bleak assessment of the history of the Chinese people in the years that had elapsed since the 1911 Revolution and overthrow of the Ch'ing dynasty:

> Recently many of those who discuss China say that they will go along with the legitimate demands of the Chinese people, or that China should be allowed to govern herself. In the early days of the republic, other countries had hopes for the young China and do not seem to have minded the fall of the Ch'ing dynasty, and there is evidence that they even aided the revolutionary movement. For more than a decade since then there has been no end to disturbances, however, and since the appearance of the Republican government in the south the disturbances have increased even further. Incidents such as those at Shanghai, Nanking, and Hankow remind one of the return of the bandits everywhere. Thus I think that, whether the military of the north or south seizes power, there is no difference between them insofar as lack of ability to govern is concerned, and tyrannical government will remain unchanged. Therefore it would be a vain hope to seek the peaceful government of China by placing hope in cooperation between the north and south or by leaving things up to them. I would place faith instead on the good that can be accomplished by other countries actively intervening for the sake of peaceful government in China. Looking at this in the light of China's recent history, there has been no instance in which civil disturbances were settled without the intervention of foreign countries. Moreover, in the present day of international closeness, the internal disturbance of China is not a Chinese matter alone. Other countries in the world receive its ill effects. From the economic point of view of our own country, we should not overlook this. Therefore I desire that the Imperial Government now propose to other countries that, first of all, military cliques and privates cliques [in China] be prohibited. Forcing a cease-fire is, of course, a form of interference in domestic policies, but it is merely an act of self-defense for each coun-

> try's economy. Also, from a humanitarian point of view with regards to the natives of China, there is no other course. . . . Moreover, to whom political power eventually comes would be left entirely up to Chinese public opinion, and when a politician emerges who in all our views is capable of achieving the task of Chinese reunification, other countries will support him and enable him to achieve his task. Therefore such interference is not necessarily bad.[54]

In a supplementary cable to Tanaka, Yoshida elaborated on these thoughts. In the eventuality that the Chinese armies did not obey an international demand for a cease-fire, he offered a list of railway lines and arsenals the foreign powers should seize, and also recommended that they prohibit arms traffic. Such an occupation could be financed by the profits from the occupied railroads. As a precedent for this, Yoshida cited the occupation of the Rhineland. (This was before he had been awakened to the dangers-of-a-punitive-peace interpretation of Versailles. After World War One, the Allies occupied the left bank of the Rhine, with civil administration remaining in German hands—an occupation which the French sought to perpetuate).[55] By almost any standards, this was a bold plan, a contemptuous view of China and its national aspirations, a benign appraisal of the consequences of some eight decades of imperialistic encroachment on China, a generous evaluation of Japan's own righteousness and internal discipline, and a miscalculation of the extent to which the Tanaka cabinet was prepared to make either a major, or a cooperative, military commitment to China.

It was also a misreading of the West, and particularly of the extent to which Great Britain was willing to support decisive foreign intervention in China at this juncture. Yoshida continued to belabor this plan as tenaciously as he worried most of his policy panaceas, and in late March of 1928, shortly after his return from Mukden, he took the occasion of a dinner party given by Makino to convey an updated version of the proposal to Cecil Dormer, an official in the British embassy. Yoshida's proposed area of intervention had altered in the interim, undoubtedly in conjunction with the fluctuations of the civil war in China, but his position had not exactly mellowed: he advocated foreign occupation of Shanghai and the whole of Kiangsu province. Dormer reported the conversation to London as follows:

> I asked him whether Japanese difficulties in Manchuria were on the mend, but he replied that they were becoming worse, and went on to speak of the necessity for close co-operation between Great Britain and Japan. When I remarked that there was already a fair degree of co-operation, and that we, on our side, were keeping the Japanese fully informed of our attitude, as, for instance, in regard to the settlement of the Nanking incident and other questions, he said that that was not enough. That was "negative" co-operation; what was wanted was co-operation in a positive way, and he left me in no doubt that what he was advocating was actual intervention. There was too much mutual suspicion, he said; Japan was afraid to act as she would like owing to her distrust of the British and American attitude. Shanghai was the nerve-centre of the South, and it was from there that all Chinese agitation sprang; the only way to put an end to that agitation and to make the Chinese mend their ways was to occupy not merely the City of Shanghai but the whole province.

Dormer responded by pointing out that "the days for intervention of that nature had passed, that it was wholly at variance with British policy, and that even if it was practicable, which it was not, and was carried out, it would be playing into the hands of Soviet and Chinese propagandists." When he reminded Yoshida of recent incidents in Shanghai and Canton where Japan had failed to cooperate with Britain, Yoshida acknowledged these but countered "that Japan had learned the error of her ways" (the error, presumedly, of Shidehara diplomacy). To his own government, Dormer noted that Yoshizawa Kenkichi, the Japanese minister to China, had made similar suggestions in the past, but he did "not notice their echo in Tokyo." The Far Eastern section of the Foreign Office in London did not take the proposal seriously, beyond expressing some relief that Yoshida "does not cut much ice in Tokio."[56]

On March 16, 1928, Yoshida was appointed minister to Sweden. Instead of assuming the post, he remained in Tokyo and became, on July 24, vice foreign minister under the Tanaka cabinet. During the months that intervened between these two appointments he expended considerable energy in lobbying for the vice-minister's position and attempting to press his policies on the government, and on April 27 he completed a lengthy memorandum which surely represents his seminal expression of "the imperial consciousness" at this point in Japan's history.[57] In this he made a number of frank observations, among them that: (1) since the Restoration, Japan's political and economic well-being had been ultimately dependent upon great "incidents" of an international nature, notably the Sino-Japanese War, the Russo-Japanese War, and the World War; (2) Japan could not survive without an empire from which to derive food and raw materials and to which to sell her manufactured goods; (3) idealistic slogans were irrelevant, as was concern for the feelings of subject peoples—what mattered was power; (4) in seizing the opportunity to expand and consolidate its position on the Asian continent irrespective of the desires of the Chinese, Japan would simply be following the example of Western powers such as Great Britain, France, and the United States in their own colonial or neo-colonial domains; (5) the key to overseas control lay in transportation and financial administration; and (6) Japan's failures in her continental policy hitherto lay primarily in lack of resolution. The memorandum verges on being a small classic of its genre and reads as follows:

PERSONAL OPINIONS ON MANCHURIAN POLICY

During the holy Meiji period, whenever there was financial depression or severe political struggle, there invariably arose momentous incidents involving the outside world, notably the Sino-Japanese and Russo-Japanese wars. In this manner, the financial world came to enjoy a period of flourishing and the political struggle was also naturally eased. While this was a coincidence, there was also present here the wisdom of the great Meiji emperor and the preparedness of the politicians of the day. Afterwards, with the great European war, our people's economy experienced an unprecedented expansion. The territories and domain we obtained after that war, however, were not much at all compared with what the various European countries gained. Moreover, in order to adjust their domestic economies and alleviate unemployment problems, these countries have since then been paying particular attention to their colonial policies and consider the territories obtained from Germany as a result of the war to be still insufficient. Thus Italy, which is most similar to us insofar as the condition of the country is concerned, is still concerned about obtaining colonies in Albania, Asia Minor, North Africa, and also in South America. At such a time, what would happen if China should be drawn close to Europe in her present condition? In spite of the fact that China is called one of the rich sources of the world, it seems that we stand by with our hands in our pockets [lit., "sleeves"], neglecting her and leaving her to tyrannical government by military cliques. With regard to the management of Manchuria and Mongolia, where it is said that the wisdom of the great Meiji emperor particularly lay, not only do we needlessly take account of the feelings of a character like Chang Tso-lin and let this keep us from doing anything, but also for many years we have been laboring to keep him smiling. Although there are those who wish to advance the foundations of our power, we are still in a state of looking this way and that. As a result, this has caused a feeling of doubt among our people in Manchuria; they are in fear of changes in policy or of becoming victims of national policy and thus are unable to develop satisfactorily. Now, with economic expansion and population increase, our people are filled with vitality within but lack the freedom to extend out. No matter how we adjust our internal government and try to promote industry, this narrow island country [lit., "island empire as big as a cat's brow"] will eventually reach a state where it cannot accommodate the pent-up vitality of the people. Thus it is not a coincidence that recently there is depression in the financial world and the domestic political struggle is becoming more severe. As long as the peaceful governing of China, which should be the realm (*tenchi*) of our people's activities, does not materialize—and as long as Manchuria and Mongolia, which are suitable locales for the development of our race, are not opened—it will be difficult to create a foundation for the recovery and prosperity of the financial world, and the political struggle will not be eased. For this reason, there is no alternative but to make the renovation of China and Manchuria policy the urgent task of the moment.

Causes of Deadlock in Past China Policy

1. After the European War, certain thoughts which arose as a response to the war—such as racial self-determination (*minzoku jiketsu*)—were talked about among the people for a while. As it happens, we have paid too much attention to these.

2. We have been too enslaved by such phrases as "Sino-Japanese good will" (*Nisshi shinzen*) and "coexistence and coprosperity."

3. [There has been] disunity regarding China among national organizations.

The causes lie in the above. In essence this is merely to say that we lack political statesmanship (*seijikateki keirin*). China now suffers from many years of its own military disturbances, and other countries are no longer deluded by empty Chinese-style propaganda. Thus we are facing an opportune moment when it should not be difficult to have the Chinese people and other countries listen to us if our China policy is fair and proper. We must not let this opportunity pass in vain. I earnestly desire that the Imperial Government plan with firm resolution to be thoroughgoing in its policy.

Renovation of Manchurian Policy

The essential point of Manchurian policy lies in making Manchuria and Mongolia a place of peaceful residence for both natives and foreigners. Still, if we simply demand this of the government of the present ruler, Chang Tso-lin, it will be difficult to expect our policy to be thoroughgoing. Although I am not saying that we should dare to place the Three Eastern Provinces in our own hand, in actuality it may be necessary to improve the government of the Three Eastern Provinces under our guidance and achieve a record of administration there comparable to that of Great Britain in Egypt. In other words, I desire that we take practical measures sufficient to make the Chang government fully listen to and respect the demands of the Imperial Government insofar as transportation and financial administration are concerned.

1. *Transportation.* Make the Chang government agree to the establishment of several major railway lines originating at the Sea of Japan and Korea and crossing the Three Eastern Provinces. Obtain for ourselves the present position held by British capitalists in that part of the Peking-Mukden line between Shanhaikwan and Mukden, and make the Chinese side come under our leadership. (This can be obtained in exchange for giving up profits from the Kaiping coal mines agreed upon by the British capitalists, as both Mr. Young of the mine, and Major Nathan, desire and have stated.) It would be meaningless, however, to establish new lines that do not contribute to the development of the Japanese people, as is the case with the Taonan-Angangki line as well as that from Taonan to the South Manchurian Railway. On the other hand, in the present situation it is not possible to urge the Chinese to immediately handle the commercial tax, so we should free several square miles along the railroads or around main stations (including along the South Manchurian Railway) and set up Chinese-operated loading areas. With regard to the operation of the railroads themselves, we should possess suitable rights of management, and should perfect transportation connections by unifying the entire Manchuria-Mongolia railroad

system. Next it will be necessary to obtain suitable rights of management insofar as telegraph, telephone, mail, and roads are concerned.

2. *Financial Administration.* Chang's military government has caused confusion in the financial administration of Mukden, and at one point the Mukden currency fell to the 5,000-yuan line. The people's weariness and the decline in their buying power have a great influence upon our trade with Manchuria. Given the annual 70-million yen imbalance in exports over imports in Manchuria, however, it will not be a difficult task to put the Mukden financial administration in order. First [we must] put Mukden silver in order, and thus supervise provincial financial administration. It will be easy to stabilize the basis of Mukden currency and restore the buying power of the provincial peoples.

Furthermore, if we extend this also to Heilungkiang and Kirin provinces, we can anticipate the prosperity of the Three Eastern Provinces. That fiscal adjustment has not taken place up to now is because we lacked resolution and the actual power of enforcement which would be sufficient to make Chang listen to us.

Results of Transportation Development and Adjustment of Financial Administration

It goes without saying that it is we who would profit first of all from cultivating the rich resources of Manchuria, increasing the buying power of the people, and fostering the peaceful residence of natives and foreigners. This is not simply because we have the geographical advantage of being close to Manchuria and Mongolia. Politically, there is our actual power, which we have implanted over the course of many years. Economically, there is our special privilege of a one-third discount in the overland customs tax. As a result of the liberation of Manchuria and Mongolia, it is easy for us to maintain this area as our economic market. The Three Eastern Provinces are five times the size of us [Japan proper], and moreover both Heilungkiang and Kirin provinces are virgin land suitable for rice production.

We desperately need the mineral and timber products of the area. If we rely upon this land for industrial raw materials and food for our populace, and on the other hand distribute our manufactured goods there and make this our economic market, then the Sea of Japan will become our own economic territorial water *(keizaiteki ryōkai)* and that will inevitably bring about the development of that part of Japan which lies along the coast there.

Method of Realizing the Manchurian Policy

The past ills of our Manchurian policy came about, not because the goals of that policy were wrong, but rather because its means and methods of practice were wrong. In relying upon vague notions of Sino-Japanese good will rather than upon the exercise of national power in seeking to execute a national policy aimed at stabilizing our people's livelihood through management of Manchuria and Mongolia, all of us, from top to bottom, have been engaged merely in pleasing the Chinese side and in the end have fallen into a subservient position without being aware of it. What is more, this is making Chinese flunkies needlessly haughty. Of course it is natural to seek the understanding and agreement of the Chinese, but this should be done only after having resolved upon the exercise of national power itself. In planning the development of one's national power upon the territory of another country, I know of no international example where anyone succeeded merely by appealing to the good will of the other side's people or government. Also, in executing a national policy that aims at the advancement of national power, one should not hesitate or scruple because that national power is unpopular with the other side. The India policy of Great Britain is, of course, not what is welcomed with favorable feelings by the Indians. The French do not abandon their national policy because they are unpopular in Algeria. The Americans are abhorred like a serpent in Central America. No native peoples can be expected to welcome intruders with open arms. Thus, it is difficult to understand why we alone are afraid of anti-Japanese feelings among the Chinese while at the same time intending to carry out our China and Manchuria policy. As long as we plan development in China and Manchuria, we must be prepared for anti-Japan [activities]. Moreover, the fact that the anti-Japanese movement of the Chinese is not to be feared is revealed by the examples of the past, while in Manchuria it is clear that the Chinese are in a situation where they would not dare to do this. Is there, then, any need to vacillate in carrying out our policy? In my opinion the military government of Chang Tso-lin will soon fail in various respects, and thus disturbance of peace and order and of the financial world in Manchuria is to be expected. Therefore, as a countermeasure to this at the present time, we must carry out whenever the occasion arises either an increase or dispatch of soldiers in such places as Tientsin, Shanhaikwan, Taonan, Kirin, Linkiang, and Chientao, and prevent military disturbances within the Great Wall from extending into Manchuria. In addition, we must demand of the Chang government that it improve its administration. With regard to administrative improvements, this was already demanded of Chang by the consul general in Mukden under the name of the Imperial Government in April 1925. In September of the same year, the Mukden consul general pointed out the confusion in

> Mukden's provincial financial administration and obtained from Chang at the time an agreement to introduce our adviser on financial administration. In August 1927, based on the above negotiations, the consul general in Mukden urged his further self-reflection concerning the administrative failures of the Mukden provincial government. These facts should provide sufficient grounds on which the Imperial Government can began concrete negotiations with Chang for the improvement of administration from this point on. I firmly believe that there should be no impediment whatsoever to our urging this upon Chang, and once our preparations are completed I anticipate a thoroughgoing policy. Success or failure depends solely upon our resolution as well as upon whether complete cooperation among the various organizations of our government is achieved.[58]

Two months after the Yoshida memo, members of the Japanese Kwantung Army blew up Chang Tso-lin as he was returning by train from Peking to his base in Mukden. Their ultimate goals were not greatly different from those held by Yoshida, and their performance was resolute and sincere by their own standards, and certainly thoroughgoing (*tettei-teki*, another of Yoshida's favorite words) insofar as eliminating the problem of Chang was concerned. But the method was crude, and not what Yoshida or the Tanaka cabinet had in mind. Thereafter Japan moved perceptibly toward increasing influence by "military cliques," analogous to the situation which Yoshida had belittled in China, and increasingly the Japanese government came to be accused by others of that same lack of sincerity and self-reflection and political competence that it was accustomed to charging against China. Yoshida, however, recognized neither the poetic justice of these developments nor the possible contribution of attitudes such as his own to them.

YOSHIDA, TANAKA, AND THE "POSITIVE POLICY"

One of the great debates among historians of modern Japan concerns evaluation of the so-called Shidehara and Tanaka diplomacies in the years between 1924 and 1931. As foreign minister in the Minseitō cabinets, which held power from June 1924 to April 1927, and again from July 1929 to December 1931, Shidehara commonly has been associated with espousal of a moderate and cooperative diplomacy, in which the Western powers were accorded due place and the integrity of China as a whole more or less respected. He embodied the spirit of the Washington Conference. Tanaka, on the other hand, who served as foreign minister as well as prime minister during the tenure of the Seiyūkai cabinet (April 1927 to July 1929), conventionally is associated with a "positive policy" characterized by relative neglect of relations with the Western powers, greater reliance upon force in Asia, and essential denial of China's territorial integrity by treating the Three Eastern Provinces as a separate entity and special Japanese preserve.

In the most Manichean depiction, Shidehara and his diplomacy are taken to exemplify Western, rational, universalistic, bourgeois-liberal values, as opposed to Tanaka's personification of a traditional, irrational, particularistic, and feudalistic outlook. A romanticized Japanese Woodrow Wilson confronts an anachronistic samurai thug—and gets jostled aside, paving the way for the militarism of the 1930s.[59] To a certain degree, this type of stereotyping guided American policy-makers who planned the later occupation of Japan.

An alternative interpretation is characterized by greater charity toward Tanaka, emphasis upon the similarities between the Shidehara and Tanaka diplomacies, and the attempt to deny that these policies bore any meaningful relation to those pursued by Japan after the Manchurian Incident. This was the position Yoshida himself later espoused:

> While not as theoretical as in the case of economic and financial policies, in foreign policy the comparison between Shidehara diplomacy and Tanaka diplomacy was also somewhat understandable, particularly in the case of China policy. The China policy of the Minseitō cabinets advertised itself as non-interference in the domestic policy of China and cooperation with other countries. On the other hand, Tanaka's Seiyūkai cabinet insisted upon an independent foreign policy within limits, emphasizing our country's rights and interests in Manchuria and Mongolia. This much was true.
>
> When it came to how much difference there was in actuality, how-

ever, I think it is fair to say that there was not much fundamental difference at the time; this seems even more apparent in retrospect. In essence, there was only a slight difference in the manner in which they handled the China problem, and even that was not based upon theoretical grounds. Rather, we should recognize that such differences were affected by the domestic political situation at the time of each cabinet as well as by differences and changes in the international scene.

Thus, where "Shidehara diplomacy" was concerned, this by no means disregarded the rights and interests [of Japan] in Manchuria and Mongolia and did not call for abandoning them. And, even though the "Tanaka diplomacy" was said to be independent, this had nothing to do with the military diplomacy of later years which aimed at asserting its own way even at the complete neglect of treaties and agreements already made between ourselves and the Western countries. In fact, such incidents as the blowing up of Chang Tso-lin went totally against the intentions of Prime Minister Tanaka, and it is now widely known how the handling of this case worried and troubled him. Therefore, unless for purposes of propaganda, there is little meaning in describing one as a "soft, weak foreign policy," or the other as a "hard, strong foreign policy."[60]

A third and more radical line of analysis accepts the tactical differences but essential similarities between the Shidehara and Tanaka policies, while arguing that *both* led almost inexorably to the intensified conflict of the 1930s. The common ground of both diplomacies was Japan's inextricable entanglement in the coils of imperialism, and the difference between the so-called "soft" and "hard" or "liberal" and "militarist" approaches was essentially one of timing. Bluntly expressed, this was the difference, as it were, between go-slow imperialism and go-fast imperialism—and neither approach offered an alternative to the eventual catastrophic eruption of the imperialist crisis.[61]

Yoshida was an intimate participant in both of the policies under discussion, and while later he may have chosen to minimize the differences between them, at the time he regarded them as, at least potentially, significantly distinct. Given his Anglophilism and popular association with the "pro-Anglo-American clique" within the Foreign Ministry, the rigid "cultural-values" analysis of these years would predict Yoshida's alignment with the Shidehara policy. In fact, he rested far greater hope in Tanaka's "positive policy"—not because he was a secret samurai, but because both conventional wisdom and the Western example itself indicated that power rather than abstract pieties remained the essence of an effective foreign policy. By Yoshida's own criteria, the hard-line position was, if anything, *more* "rational" and "Western" than Shidehara's.

As seen in his correspondence with Makino in 1923, Yoshida had adopted this position even before Shidehara became foreign minister. The first interlude of the Shidehara diplomacy, from 1924 to 1927, merely confirmed his fear that Japan would fail to transcend the diplomacy of "sweet words," and his lengthy memorandum of April 1928 was an exasperated and thinly disguised attack on the "subservient" Shidehara legacy. Virtually everything Yoshida wrote during the 1920s reflected his own rendition of contemporary criticism of Shidehara's "weak-kneed" policy. Without actually calling for detachment of the Three Eastern Provinces from China, moreover, his consistent proposals for strengthening and expanding Japan's pre-eminent rights and interests in this area skirted perilously close to outright colonialism. A Foreign Ministry colleague from this period recalled that Yoshida was regarded within the ministry as a hard-liner outside the Shidehara mainstream, and did not in practice really treat the Three Eastern Provinces as an integral part of China. Yoshida was said to have expressed the distinction picturesquely: it was all right to wear an apron when dealing with China proper, but Manchuria required formal dress.[62]

Espousal of these views placed Yoshida very close to the jingoistic foreign policy proclaimed by the Seiyūkai and its leading firebrand, Mori Kaku. As parliamentary vice foreign minister of the new Tanaka cabinet, Mori also attended the Eastern Conference in mid-1927, and it was at this time that the two men discovered the compatibility of their views on China policy and formed what came to be called the "Mori-Yoshida combination."[63] Yoshida endeavored, with uncertain success, to persuade Makino to meet Mori, whom he described as one of the "most superior of the young Seiyūkai politicians."[64] And Mori on his part maneuvered, with belated success, to have Yoshida appointed as Tanaka's vice foreign minister; since Tanaka was nominally his own foreign minister, the post was potentially a significant one. It would appear from these relationships that, in a limited way, the hawkish Seiyūkai may have been tentatively promoting Yoshida as a counterfoil to the Minseitō's relationship with Shidehara. And although, unlike Shidehara, Yoshida did not form a close relationship with the party in the prewar years, it is interesting to note that after 1945 he became president of the political lineage that traced back to the Seiyūkai, while Shidehara became president of the party line deriving from the Minseitō.

The vice foreign minister's post fell open in March 1928, shortly after Yoshida was recalled from Mukden, and quickly became a target of internal factional competition. Yoshida lobbied personally for the position, but it appears that Tanaka himself was initially leery of the "Mori-Yoshida combination." The prime minister's own inclination was to cooperate more closely with Chang Tso-lin, while relying on such unofficial Japanese emissaries as Yamamoto Jōtarō, president of the South Manchurian Railway. It was only after Chang's assassination had upset his plans that Tanaka finally agreed, almost two months after the incident, to accept Yoshida.[65] As a token of his success, Yoshida earned the nickname "Self-Invited Vice Minister" (*Oshikake Jikan*).[66]

This appointment coincided with a tide of anti-Japanese activity in China, sparked by the clash of Chinese and Japanese troops in the Tsinan Incident of May 3. Although this was the type of situation that caused proponents of the "positive policy" to breathe fire, neither the Self-Invited Vice Minister nor his most superior political cohort were able to use this to bring about any fundamental policy reformulation. What Yoshida did apparently succeed in doing was to enable many Japanese exporters to stay afloat until the Chinese boycotts of their goods subsided. The boycotts were particularly severe on cotton manufacturers in the Osaka area, and Yoshida was able to persuade the Mitsui interests (specifically Mitsui Bussan) to make extensive temporary purchases of cotton yarn and cloth from these smaller entrepreneurs.[67] His inability to bring about a major readjustment of foreign policy, which was clearly the premise of the "Mori-Yoshida combination," was at least in part attributable to the domestic repercussions of Chang Tso-lin's assassination. Caught between those who demanded severe punishment of the assassins and the army, which opposed this, Tanaka stumbled through the final year of his premiership as a distraught and hobbled man.[68]

Despite the lack of enthusiasm with which he had been appointed, and despite his failure to make any notable contribution to a "positive policy" during the final year of the Tanaka cabinet, Yoshida later recalled this interlude fondly as one of the most pleasant in his entire diplomatic career. He described Tanaka as the easiest superior he ever had, a man who left the initiative to his staff and often signed memoranda drafted by Yoshida without even reading them—what Yoshida characterized as the "Okay? Okay" style (*daijōbu ka? daijōbu desu*). This was a sharp contrast to the meticulous and indefatigable Shidehara, and Yoshida went so far as to say that he "fell in love" (*horekomu*) with this heir to the Chōshū military tradition.[69] Such affection calls to mind the relationship Yoshida had enjoyed more than a decade previously with "loveable" General Terauchi, and may be provocative to those inclined toward psychohistory: was the "orphan child" of long-ago Ōiso finding here, perhaps, stalwart fathers?

Or rather stern realists, cut of the same cloth, who brooked no nonsense in affairs of state in a manner Yoshida deemed appropriate? Both Terauchi and Tanaka were Chōshū protégés of the iron-willed Meiji oligarch Yamagata Aritomo, and both were associated with interventionist foreign policies. Tanaka had joined Terauchi in promoting the Russo-Japanese War and in endorsing Japan's massive contribution to the Siberian Intervention, for example, and as early as World War One had proposed the establishment of a Japanese puppet regime in Manchuria. Between May 1927 and May 1928, his own cabinet dispatched Japanese troops to Shantung on four occasions, the last of which precipitated the Tsinan Incident.[70]

Like Terauchi also, Tanaka did not hesitate to move decisively to repress those "dangerous thoughts" Yoshida himself had long viewed with alarm. On March 15, 1928, the Tanaka cabinet initiated the first mass arrests ever to be carried out under the 1925 Peace Preservation Law, and the following month introduced an amendment to the law whereby a penalty of death or indeterminate punishment could be decreed for organizers or officials of groups advocating, or even proposing to study, any doctrine that contemplated changes in the national polity (*kokutai*). In Tanaka's words, "We intend to control 'dangerous thoughts' in such a way that their holder may abandon them in favor of traditional ideas." When this bill failed to be approved by the Diet, it was enacted as an emergency imperial decree after the Diet had adjourned.[71] Although Yoshida did not participate in these repressions, he surely endorsed them. Nearly two decades after the Tanaka era, as foreign minister during the early months of the Allied occupation of Japan, he endeavored to persuade occupation authorities to at least leave the Peace Preservation Law applicable to the Communist Party. And as the occupation drew to a close in the early 1950s, his own cabinet sponsored new peace-preservation legislation (the Subversive Activities Prevention Law) which was widely criticized as an attempt to resurrect the Peace Preservation Law.

Two stalwart anti-communists associated with the Tanaka cabinet also played notable roles in Yoshida's later career. The better known of these was Hatoyama Ichirō, a leading Seiyūkai politician who served as chief cabinet secretary under Tanaka and as minister of education under the later Inukai cabinet. Under Tanaka, Hatoyama was involved in the revision and implementation of the Peace Preservation Law, while as education minister he lent a ready hand to indoctrination and political purges in the schools. When Hatoyama was himself purged by occupation authorities in 1946, he passed the mantle of presidency of the reconstructed Seiyūkai—and, in the circumstances, the premiership—to Yoshida. The second significant personal connection from these years involved Ueda Shunkichi, Tanaka's personal secretary. Ueda became a key figure in advancing the thesis that guided Yoshida's "anti-war" activities over a decade later: that conspiratorial "Reds" were largely responsible for Japan's disastrous course from the 1930s, and that the ultimate crisis of the Pacific War was that it threatened to shatter the emperor-state ideology and open the floodgates to radical thought and revolutionary upheaval. In 1949–1950, Ueda served as attorney general in the third Yoshida cabinet and helped direct an extensive "Red Purge" of the civil service.[72]

MANEUVERING AGAINST THE NAVY, 1930

Yoshida's retrospective comments on the Shidehara and Tanaka policies ring half-true. The stereotyped invectives he later dismissed as mere propaganda were clichés which by and large he personally believed in deeply at the time—at least insofar as these entailed denigration of the Shidehara diplomacy. Tanaka, Mori Kaku, and the Seiyūkai, to whom Yoshida volunteered his services, certainly characterized their own policy as being substantially different from that of Shidehara and the Minseitō: as "positive" rather than "negative," "strong" rather than "weak-kneed," "autonomous" rather than "conciliatory." And this disesteem and sense of basic difference was reciprocated by the Minseitō, which characterized Shidehara diplomacy as rational, cooperative, progressive, economic-minded, and peaceful—and freely bestowed the antonyms to these virtues upon the Seiyūkai (emotional, unilateral, traditionalistic, defense-oriented, and militaristic). If the Tanaka "positive policy" did not depart substantially from the Shidehara legacy, then to judge by the expressed purposes of Yoshida, Mori Kaku, and others at the time, this reflected failure of execution rather than of intent.

Yoshida's own association with the Seiyūkai, on the other hand, does vitiate those critiques that stress the "traditionalistic" or primarily "defense-oriented" aspects of the Tanaka policy. And when Tanaka was forced to resign in mid-1929 because of his inability to resolve the conflicting pressures concerning disposition of the Chang Tso-lin affair, the fact that the Seiyūkai and Minseitō policies still shared common ground was indicated by Yoshida's continuation as vice foreign minister under Shidehara and the Minseitō. While serving in this capacity, moreover, Yoshida did have an opportunity to affirm his commitment to a critical and controversial Shidehara policy: he supported the cabinet's decision to accept a naval-ratio agreement demanded by the Anglo-American powers and deemed disadvantageous by many responsible Japanese naval officers.

As a superior, Shidehara was a far cry from the "Okay? Okay" school, and his vice minister had little latitude for initiative. Partly because of his family connections, however, Yoshida was enlisted as an intermediary with the emperor's close advisers (such as Makino and Saionji Kimmochi), as well as with certain naval officers, particularly those inclined to be sympathetic to the government's position (such as Vice Admirals Ōsumi Mineo, Nomura Kichisaburō, and Kobayashi Seizō). Some of these latter relationships were to become consequential in Yoshida's later career. For a while during the Pacific War, he endeavored to unseat Prime Minister Tōjō Hideki and have him replaced by Kobayashi, and in the postwar period Nomura became one of Yoshida's key advisers on matters of security and remilitarization.[73]

The crisis of 1930 concerned the forthcoming London Naval Conference and the demand by the United States and Great Britain that Japan agree to limit its tonnage in heavy cruisers to sixty percent that of both the U.S. and British navies. Navy planners led by Admiral Katō Kanji, chief of the Naval General Staff, argued (with considerable justification) that a seventy percent ratio was essential to ensure Japan's security. The issue posed a severe threat to Japan's relations with the Anglo-American powers, and both Makino and Yoshida supported the cabinet and Foreign Ministry on the necessity of accepting the lower ratio.

One of Yoshida's more significant endeavors in this tangled

business entailed an interesting exercise in the manipulation of family relationships and traditional clan loyalties. Makino arranged for Yoshida, his son-in-law, to visit Admiral (and former prime minister) Yamamoto Gombei, his Satsuma clansman, to explain the details of the conference and attempt to persuade the old admiral to swing his weight against Katō. By his own version, however, Yoshida did not feel constrained to tread lightly in this hallowed terrain. He accused the venerable Yamamoto of a "navy-first" bias, and suggested that he pay more attention to his juniors.[74]

While these various backstage activities contributed to the government's ability to carry out its intentions at the London Conference, they also stigmatized Makino as a traitor in the eyes of many ultranationalists and made him a target for assassination in the 1930s. And Yoshida's association with Makino became, in turn, a stigma to him where the militarists were concerned. Thus, while his later general reputation as an "anti-militarist" derived primarily from activities subsequent to the Manchurian Incident, the roots of his conflict with the military were planted in this earlier period: in his criticism of crude army intrigues in China from 1926, and his opposition, along with Makino, to navy opinions in 1930.

In the public debate concerning naval limitations, the political parties supported the Navy General Staff and roasted the prime minister and foreign minister in the Diet for compromising the nation's security. Whatever hopes Yoshida may have rested in Mori Kaku and the Seiyūkai were soon dispelled, and his basic distrust of party politics in general came again to the surface. Harada Kumao recorded in his famous diary at this time that Yoshida expressed concern that the views of the Seiyūkai on foreign affairs bore little relation to reality, and that domestic political squabbles threatened the proper execution of Japanese policy abroad. In December 1930, while still serving as vice foreign minister, Yoshida found further occasion for umbrage in the Seiyūkai's response to the Chientao Incident, in which the Foreign Ministry was resisting pressure from the Government

General in Korea to use Japanese troops to resolve a problem involving mixed populations along the Manchuria-Korea border. With Chinese cooperation, the incident was being settled quietly when Seiyūkai members, led by Mori, demanded information on the handling of the affair. Yoshida put them off on the grounds that this could only lead to publicity and argumentation in which there would be nothing to gain and everything to lose.[75] On yet another occasion, Harada recorded a small luncheon he had arranged with Yoshida, Kido Kōichi, Tani Masayuki, and Minobe Tatsukichi, at which the topic of conversation concerned both the despotism of the military and corruption of the political parties.[76]

Harada's passing references are of interest when one keeps in mind that Yoshida later became, initially against his better judgment, one of the most important party leaders in Japanese history. They serve as a reminder that the "Mori-Yoshida combination" was ephemeral, and that Yoshida's dominant impression of the political parties in these prewar years was one of venality and irresponsibility. Such concrete occasions for disenchantment, along with his own personality and general professional background, help illuminate Yoshida's postwar style as a party president: his cavalier attitude toward the rank-and-file, his siring of a "bureaucratic clique" within the party, and his penchant for secrecy in important matters of state, particularly where these involved foreign relations.

FOUR

Explaining the New Imperialism, 1931–1937

In December 1930 Yoshida was appointed to his first ambassadorship, to Italy. He remained there for two years, and in retrospect had little to say of the interlude beyond recalling that in presenting his credentials to Mussolini he walked across an immense room to where the dictator sat waiting, during the course of which approach he and Il Duce came to dislike each other.[1]

Even while posted in Rome, Yoshida's concerns and energies remained strongly directed to Asian affairs—almost obsessively so after September 1931, when the Manchurian Incident led to international condemnation of Japan and the country's eventual withdrawal from the League of Nations. He personally witnessed some of the early sessions of the League during which Japan came under fire, and, as the acknowledged "China expert" among Japanese ambassadors in Europe, was involved in the early debates concerning Japan's appropriate defense of its actions before the international body.[2] Much of the final year of his ambassadorship was devoted to submission of repeated requests that he be allowed to return to Tokyo to explain his views to the Japanese government in person.[3]

In the months and years following the Manchurian Incident, Yoshida found himself increasingly engaged in one of the more blatantly contradictory tasks that confront the diplomatist. On the one hand, he endeavored to rationalize and justify Japan's actions in Asia to his American and European counterparts. "He visits me at frequent intervals to explain and defend the Japanese case," the British ambassador to Rome reported in April 1932, "and plies me with written propaganda on the subject."[4] After returning to Japan in late 1932, Yoshida continued to work this channel through personal contact with British diplomats in Tokyo, and in 1936 this became a full-time job when he was appointed ambassador to London. During these years, Yoshida also forged closer ties with leading spokesmen for the United States, most notably with Joseph Grew, the U.S. ambassador to Japan from 1932 to 1941. His influence in shaping Grew's understanding of and sympathy for Japan was considerable.

At the same time, however, Yoshida accompanied his apologetics to Westerners with admonitions to his own government. His experience in Asia had convinced him that Japan could not survive without an assertive continental policy, but his experience in Europe, especially during the Rome interlude, led him to conclude that the Japanese government appreciated neither the depth of Western hostility toward Japan's actions nor the extent to which the good will of the Anglo-American powers remained essential to "management of the continent." He entertained no dreams that autarky was a feasible course for Japan, and thus there were two sides to his defense of continued good relations with the West: Japan's imperial position in Asia required Anglo-American endorsement; and the Asian empire alone was insufficient to ensure Japan's security and economic well-being.

Such attitudes placed Yoshida more and more on the defensive vis-à-vis the emerging military and civilian policy-makers who envisioned a self-sufficient Asian empire pivoting on the new puppet state of Manchukuo, which Japan formally recognized in September 1932. But it must be noted that Yoshida himself was not an outspoken critic of Manchukuo, or of the general concerns and objectives that lay behind the Manchurian Incident and detachment of the Three Eastern Provinces from China. He argued consistently during this period that Japan's case in Manchuria was solidly grounded—but poorly executed, and amateurishly presented. Thus he offered mild criticism of the baldness of military takeover north of the Great Wall, and more vigorous criticism of the extension of military activity to areas of China where the Western powers themselves were entrenched. But his most untempered expressions of outrage and disgust were reserved for the ineptitude with which the Japanese government handled these incidents *diplomatically* and before the court of world opinion. Japan's blunders, from this perspective, were largely tactical, and consequently Yoshida retained hope that even Manchukuo did not pose an insurmountable barrier to the restoration of more amicable relations with the Anglo-American powers.

In the years following the Manchurian Incident, Yoshida thus practiced the diplomacy of *fait accompli,* partly because he was powerless to overturn his government's policies, but more generally because he believed that, skillfully handled, the Western powers could be persuaded to acquiesce in those policies. Manchukuo, the bastard progeny of the Manchurian Incident, would then become the legitimate offspring of a restored structure of cooperative imperialism. In dealing with the British and Americans, Yoshida's pressing goal thus was to buy time, to create sufficient understanding of Japan's case among the Westerners so that they would remain conciliatory until matters could be put right and the *revised* situation be adapted to a more normal course of "peaceful diplomacy." To ultranationalists in Japan, such endeavors were taken as proof of Yoshida's treasonous fawning upon the West, but he himself characterized his activities more accurately as an exercise in *Realpolitik.* "To the public I am known as belonging to the 'pro-Anglo-American clique' (*shin Ei-Bei ha*), but that is not so," he is said to have remarked. "It would be more correct to speak of 'the clique that makes use of Britain and the United States' (*Ei-Bei riyō ha*)."[5]

Such *Realpolitik* rested upon more than the assumption that the Anglo-American powers could be persuaded to recognize the legitimacy of Japanese encroachment upon northern China. Yoshida also based his actions upon perceptions of Western self-interest and vulnerability. He believed that Great Britain and the United States could be made to recognize that an uncompromising policy toward Japan threatened (1) to unravel the entire global imperialist structure, (2) to thwart escape from the world depression, (3) to fan the fires of international communism, and (4) to weaken Britain in particular against the rising menace of Nazi Germany. During the first year of his ambassadorship to London, he was encouraged to believe that he was indeed on the verge of working out a concrete agreement that would reflect these premises and ensure the integrity of the new Japanese empire. These hopes were shattered by the China Incident of July 1937 and Japan's initiation of full-scale war against China, although Yoshida remained in London, still endeavoring to buy time, until October 1938.

The failure of these exercises in persuasion and power politics represented what Yoshida would regard as one of the great lost opportunities of the prewar years. Had his own policies of imperialist cooperation been adopted, there may have been no "World War Two," but only a European War. And the Japanese empire might well have survived. Such reasoning belongs to the Cleopatra's-nose school of history, and among other imponderables grossly ignores the rise of nationalism and dynamics of change within China itself. It does, however, help illuminate imperialist relations, and rationalizations, at an advanced stage of crisis and conflict.

From another perspective, Yoshida's activities following the Manchurian Incident also hold a mirror to his postwar role as prime minister during the occupation of Japan. At that time he again became immersed in the task of "buying time" until the Allied Powers recognized the folly of idealism in affairs of state, and retreated from the objective of forcing drastic change upon Japan. Prewar practice may or may not have improved his skills at the task, but this second time around he ultimately did taste sweet fruits of success.

THE MANCHURIAN INCIDENT AND THE LEAGUE OF NATIONS

In dealing directly with Westerners, Yoshida was often cagey and occasionally unintelligible. Generally, however, his points were uncomplicated and he expressed them with frankness. Cecil Dormer, to whom Yoshida had conveyed his proposals for joint intervention in China in 1928, reported to his superiors at that time that "Mr. Yoshida . . . expresses his mind more freely than almost any Japanese whom I have met."[6] This appraisal was repeated by most other Englishmen and Americans with whom Yoshida had relations.

He maintained this frankness in discussing the Manchurian Incident with British officials. Even as international criticism of the incident was at its highest pitch, Yoshida did not hesitate to tell the British ambassador to Rome that, while the follow-up military excursion in Shanghai (January and February 1932) constituted a "grave miscalculation" on Japan's part, "the Japanese case as regards Manchuria is unassailable." The Manchurian Incident and takeover of the Three Eastern Provinces, in his view, had only been "badly presented and handled."[7] Nor did he attempt to qualify this position later. In November 1936, for example, when discussing the possibility of Japan's return to the League of Nations with Anthony Eden, Yoshida explained, as Eden summarized it, "that the difficulty in connexion with the League was that whereas Japan had been ready to collaborate in the early stage, they had soon felt themselves diplomatically at a disadvantage there. Mr. Yoshida feared that the Japanese were not good diplomatists, and did not state their points of view effectively. The Chinese, on the other hand, excelled in these methods."[8]

Frankness operates at various levels of specificity, however, and Yoshida went considerably further in conveying his thoughts to Makino. He was also able here to present these thoughts in the context of the long diatribe against Japanese diplomatic style which had dominated correspondence with his father-in-law since the early 1920s. Thus in March 1932 he criticized the "casual" execution of the attack on Shanghai and indicated, not that this military excursion should have been avoided entirely, but rather that it should have been undertaken only after prior endeavors to convince the Western powers "that the circumstances were unavoidable." Japan "could have obtained what was to be obtained without this much suffering," he exclaimed, and he seemed convinced that the imperialist powers had been alienated by the style rather than substance of the attack on Shanghai: "Since the Manchurian Incident, we have had a state of total non-diplomacy, and whenever the strong countries came to rescue us, we made them lose face without so much as a second thought. Indeed, it has gone to the extent that I can no longer even regard it as sane behavior."[9]

Yoshida acknowledged that recent events seemed to reflect "a certain kind of fascist tendency within the country," and he drew a passing comparison to the Italian situation.[10] In Japan's case, however, Yoshida regarded this trend as the almost inevitable spawn of the country's prior *conciliatory* diplomacy. There can be little doubt as to the particular villain he had in mind. In June 1932, after expressing shock at the May 15 Incident, in which Prime Minister Inukai Tsuyoshi was killed and Makino narrowly escaped assassination, he went on to note that he had sensed rising tensions within Japan prior to the Manchurian Incident and vainly urged Shidehara to come up with a clear Manchurian policy. "Cooperative diplomacy is all right as an ideology," he observed, "but a diplomacy that dampens the people's desire to expand abroad makes others regard it as empty diplomacy, as no-action, no-policy." It was the "unpreparedness" of Japanese diplomacy that laid the ground for the current unrest within Japan, and it followed that stabilization of diplomatic policy would lead to stabilization of the people's mind.[11]

There were essentially four groups of actors in Yoshida's perception of the crisis of mid-1932: the Japanese military, Japanese Foreign Ministry, Anglo-American powers, and smaller countries within the League of Nations (China remained less an actor than a stage to act upon). At this juncture, his wrath seemed drawn irresistibly against the weaker forces: the Foreign Ministry and smaller countries. If Yoshida's position were to be boiled down to a sentence, it could be said that he attributed Japan's misfortunes primarily to flaccid diplomats in Tokyo and puny countries assembled in Geneva.

To prolong for a moment these ungainly images: the flaccid were flaccid because they failed to distinguish between the puny and the strong. Yoshida's personal attendance at sessions of the League of Nations in the wake of the Manchurian Incident evoked nostalgic recollections of Versailles, and drove him to near distraction. At Versailles, he recalled for Makino, Japan was recognized as a great power. Now, at the League of Nations, the country was treated as a defendant, "there was no respect shown for a great power," and this fall in esteem could be attributed to "the maneuvering of the small countries." Yoshida had always regarded membership in the League as a symbol of status and a vehicle for Great-Power politics. Now this had become dubious. "If even the South and Central American and North European countries are to interfere in the Far Eastern problem, then in the end even Japan cannot help but reconsider the benefits of having joined the League of Nations."[12]

The inanity of the Foreign Ministry lay in its failure to recognize the distinction between the "small countries" and Great Powers. The United States and Great Britain were so troubled by the global economic crisis, Yoshida informed Makino, that "they do not have the least intention of starting up anything against us in the Far Eastern problem." On the contrary, they would be more than ready to negotiate a reasonable solution to the Manchurian issue, but the Foreign Ministry had failed to present anything concrete. "The Imperial Government should immediately make a draft proposal and show it to the strong countries, especially Great Britain and the United States, and give them peace of mind," Yoshida declared. This would undercut the "unthoughtful and unreserved activities of the small countries." He seemed confident that a proposal could be drafted which would satisfy the Japanese military as well as the Anglo-American powers. And he indicated that China could be handled by a piece of paper—nothing less, indeed, than the Nine Power Treaty of 1922, which guaranteed China's territorial integrity. The new situation in Manchuria was not necessarily incompatible with the Nine Power Treaty, Yoshida opined. Japan should thus emphasize the treaty to China, and "urge China to carry it out"![13]

In several particulars, Yoshida's views at this time did have a substantial echo in the private chambers of British, if not American, policy-makers. Like Yoshida, majority sentiment within the Foreign Office in London drew a sharp distinction between the attack on Shanghai, which threatened British interests and was unacceptable, and the takeover of Manchuria, where it actually was generally accepted that the Japanese "had a great deal of right on their side" and the Chinese "were almost entirely in the wrong." And like Yoshida again, British diplomats tended to agree, as one officer phrased it, that "modern Chinese have facile tongues while Japanese are notoriously inarticulate."

Britain's inclination to appease Japan in Manchuria, however, was incompatible with its commitment to the League of Nations and its dependence upon the United States. China's victory in the war of words at Geneva (which to the smaller countries was surely based more on substance than style) posed a dilemma: to side with Japan would be to side against the League, and ipso facto weaken the League in European affairs. Beyond this, the U.S. government did not share the Foreign Office's pragmatic pro-Japanese outlook, but rather moved in the contrary direction of Secretary of State Henry Stimson's moralistic "non-recognition" policy; and Britain was neither willing nor able to appease Japan without U.S. support. Not for the last time, the type of traditional Great-Power collusion Yoshida envisioned was thus thwarted not merely by Japan's own "tactical" ineptitude, but also by Europe-related concerns and by disagreement within the Anglo-American camp.[14]

After repeated entreaties, Yoshida was allowed to return to

Tokyo in September 1932, via the overland route through Berlin, Moscow, Siberia, and Port Arthur.[15] Upon his return, his attention was immediately drawn to Japan's impending withdrawal from the League of Nations (effected March 1933) and, despite his reservations concerning the international body, he opposed such precipitous action on the grounds that it made no sense for Japan to deny itself "the sole important right of being able to speak out on various political, diplomatic, and economic problems as one of the great powers."[16] Yoshida appears to have anticipated the later general consensus that Matsuoka Yōsuke, Japan's delegate to the League and later foreign minister, was more or less deranged. Soon after returning, he met with Matsuoka and urged him to allow one of Japan's older statesmen to be the chief Japanese spokesman to the League, arguing that someone of the stature and disposition of Akizuki Satsuo would have a better chance than Matsuoka to restore understanding between Japan and the United States and Great Britain. When Matsuoka abruptly rejected this advice, Yoshida treated him to one of his more acid observations. Before departing for Geneva, he told Matsuoka, "you should go to an insane asylum, douse your head in water, and then leave after you've cooled down a bit."[17]

Even when other nominally pro-Western figures such as Saionji began to equivocate, Yoshida held fast to his pragmatic opposition to withdrawal. When it became known in February 1933 that the army planned an imminent attack in Jehol, for example, he immediately saw this in the international context and opposed it on the grounds that it would complicate the impending confrontation at the League. "The army is saying, 'We must take care of Jehol by such-and-such a date,' as if it were a contract job, but in the face of this grave international situation something like the attack on Jehol is not the sort of problem where we cannot afford to lose a moment," he argued. "In this case we must turn this grave situation about, and either postpone the attack for a while or temporarily cancel it." In the final days before the die was cast, he joined Makino in urging that a solution be sought through a meeting of the *jūshin*, or elder statesmen.[18]

"PENDING APPOINTMENT," 1932–1935

Shortly before departing from Rome, Yoshida wrote his father-in-law: "I know nothing about my future."[19] He was thus taken by surprise when, upon returning to Tokyo, he was offered the ambassadorship to the United States. And, for a zealot of the grasp-the-nettle school, his response appeared most quixotic. He refused the post. Yoshida was supported for the job by Foreign Minister Uchida Yasuya and Vice Foreign Minister Arita Hachirō, as well as Saionji and other high imperial advisers. When Saionji's private secretary, Harada Kumao, visited him to inquire about his refusal, Yoshida merely repeated what he allegedly had told Uchida himself: "that basically I am not the type of man for America, and, although it was improper to say so, I could not become ambassador to America under his policies." Uchida reportedly was dumbfounded, although it is unclear whether the insubordination or lack of careerism impressed him more. Yoshida, on his part, went on to urge that Vice Admiral Nomura be given the prestigious assignment.[20]

Following this episode, Yoshida's career fell into limbo. His status was officially designated as "pending appointment," and he maintained a murky association with a research bureau within the Foreign Ministry. He remained a dangling diplomat until November 1935, when he formally retired from the foreign service after thirty years of relative obscurity. During this final three-year interval, he made two trips abroad on behalf of the Foreign Ministry, regaled Makino with further portents of doom and prescriptions for redemption, and made a niche for himself in the U.S. embassy.

The first of Yoshida's official trips took place in late 1932 and early 1933 at the suggestion of Vice Foreign Minister Shigemitsu Mamoru, and included China as well as Europe and the United States in the itinerary. Among the noteworthy encounters of this journey was Yoshida's contact with Eugene Dooman, who happened to be sailing on the same ship from Paris to Washington. Dooman shortly thereafter became Ambassador Grew's right-hand man in Japan, and subsequently emerged as one of the core members of the State Department's wartime "Japan Crowd." In 1944 and 1945 he was to play a key role in the planning for post-surrender Japan, and in the immediate postwar years he became one of the most effective early advocates of a strong, reconstructed Japan allied with the United States.[21] With the insight of hindsight, Dooman later recalled this early visit by Yoshida to the United States:

> Mr. William R. Castle, who was still the Undersecretary of State in the administration of President Hoover, invited Mr. Yoshida to dinner, and also invited ten or twelve of the leading Senators, particularly those who were members of the Committee on Foreign Relations. I was there also. Now, the picture was Mr. Yoshida alone surrounded by ten or twelve Senators, including Senator Borah. These men took turns in grilling Yoshida on the actions of the Japanese in Manchuria, on their violations of the Nine-Power Treaty, and so on and so on. Now, I had talked to Yoshida on the boat; I had talked to him in Paris; I know that he was in complete opposition to the policies which the militarists had forced the Japanese government into. And yet, as a patriotic Japanese there he was all alone and he defended as best he could the actions of his countrymen—which, as I say, I am convinced he thoroughly disapproved of. But there was the measure of the man, which I saw for the first time. He showed himself then on that occasion as a great man.[22]

Yoshida's second official tour while "pending appointment" was sponsored by Foreign Minister Hirota, his old classmate, and lasted from October 1934 to February 1935.[23] By this time Yoshida's pro-Western activities had become more widely known, and extremists had added him to their list of traitors. On the eve of his departure, the police noted that "with regard to Ambassador Yoshida's present tour abroad, right-wing elements have been laying schemes and there is a plan to assassinate him on the grounds that 'he is going to proclaim Privy Seal Makino's weak-kneed diplomacy (*nanjaku gaikō*) and will lead the country astray.' It is probably not serious, but we are being extremely careful."[24]

The ostensible purpose of Yoshida's trip at this time was to inspect Japanese missions and consulates abroad, and to gather information concerning Western attitudes toward Japanese business practices. Actually, Hirota appears to have given him the dual (and doubly depressing) task of first attempting to influence the naval conversations then taking place in London, and, anticipating the failure of these conversations, to attempt to mollify the suspicion the Western powers could be expected to entertain.[25]

Yoshida continued on to the United States during this trip, visiting Ambassador Saitō Hiroshi and conveying a message from Ambassador Matsudaira Tsuneo in London to the effect that Saitō talked too much. A similar concern with verbiage dominated Yoshida's conversation with Cordell Hull, with the secretary of state delivering an impractical talk on avoiding "unnecessary, untimely and . . . impractical talking in our various countries."[26] Yoshida also met with such individuals as Colonel Edward M. House and Joseph T. Robinson, chairman of the Senate Majority Conference, and once again was invited to dinner at Castle's home. Unlike the occasion at Castle's two years previously, however, this time the dinner guests did not include a Japanophile like Dooman who found patriotism a sufficient measure of greatness. Instead, Yoshida found himself breaking bread with the State Department's most outspoken critic of Japan's continental expansion, Stanley Hornbeck. To Yoshida's great embarrassment, Castle asked him to explain Japan's position to his guests, whereupon Hornbeck proceeded, in Yoshida's phrase, to "attack" this explanation.[27] Neither his country's performance nor his own cut any ice with the man who dominated the State Department's Far Eastern Division, and this also had repercussions later when Hornbeck and the "China Crowd," unimpressed by rationalizations of Japan's accelerated course of empire, took issue with Dooman, Grew, and the "Japan Crowd" and demanded a hard peace and radical restructuring of defeated Japan.

Upon returning to Japan, Yoshida reported his conclusions to Hirota and then visited Ambassador Grew to repeat his observations. Grew cabled these to Washington, and they give a superficial indication of Yoshida's thinking as of early 1935:

> 1. There should be less talk and more constructive action which should be aimed at improving Japan's international relations in a practical way.
> 2. With regard to the question of naval ratios, the Japanese have been consistently basing their demand for parity on the hypothesis of a war with America. Naturally, if such a war should come, Japan would want to win it, but so would America, and if the hypothesis of an eventual war is taken as a basis it is perfectly natural that the United States should not wish to cede parity to Japan. The obvious way out, therefore, is to find some basis for a naval agreement other than the hypothesis of a possible war between Japan and the United States. If the matter is approached along other lines Mr. Yoshida thought that an eventual solution might be found. He did not, however, specify what line of approach he had in mind, if any.
> 3. Mr. Yoshida thinks that the primary and most important policy for Japan to follow at present is to develop improved relations with China on a constructive basis with the cooperation of other Powers. Only thus can mistrust of Japan's intentions be set at rest. He said that he had strongly advocated this policy to Mr. Hirota and had asked that he be allowed to continue his tour of inspection into China so that he might study the situation and make concrete recommendations on his return. He said that Mr. Hirota was considering the matter.[28]

Shortly before this second trip, Yoshida also conveyed his most recent thoughts about both the international and domestic situations to Makino. He speculated that U.S. diplomatic recognition of the Soviet Union (completed November 1933) may have been motivated by a desire to restrain Japan, and expressed fear that the United States and Great Britain would agree on measures "to secure the China market and check Japan's invasion diplomacy." He found the situation within the country bleak—"morale is deteriorating, rumors are rife, there is no trust in authority"—and his proposed antidote reflected a surprising susceptibility to the rhetoric commonly associated with the radical right. Makeshift policies were out of the question. It was now necessary to "remake the world" (*yonaoshi*) and "infuse the spirit of a Shōwa Restoration among high and low." He looked forward to a strong leader who would be capable of carrying out a sincere, frank, and moderate (*onken*) foreign policy—and proposed Yamamoto

Gombei, the old admiral whom he himself had told to listen to his juniors in 1930.[29]

AMBASSADOR GREW AND THE PENDULUM THEORY

That Yoshida took it upon himself to report to the American ambassador on his official tour for the Foreign Ministry highlights one of the more interesting dimensions of his activities after 1932, his personal relationship with Grew. During a period of increasing anti-Americanism, Yoshida remained an open and loyal friend, and more. He served as a liaison between Japanese officials and the American ambassador, thus enabling both sides to avoid the publicity that hounded official visits.[30] Within a few weeks after Hirota had replaced Uchida as foreign minister in September 1933, for example, Yoshida set up a private meeting between the two men, and thereafter functioned as Hirota's key unofficial contact with Grew.[31] Later he performed a similar role between Grew and Konoe.

In addition, Yoshida served as one of Grew's "inside sources" for information on trends and personalities within the Japanese political scene. As Grew reported to Hull in 1934: "While men such as Kabayama [Aisuke, of the House of Peers], Yoshida, Sugimura [Yōtarō, one-time ambassador to Italy] and others speak without authority to commit anyone, they are nevertheless in close and constant touch with and even participate in the councils of those who are in fact shaping the country's policies; when they speak they must be considered as accurately reflecting what has actually occurred during the discussions."[32] During this period, go-betweens such as Kabayama and Yoshida were in fact doubly welcome to Grew because, in his words, "I can often plant ideas in Hirota's mind through them without making diplomatic representations and I find that some of these seeds readily take root."[33]

More significantly, Yoshida helped shape Grew's interpretation of the larger patterns in Japan's historic experience. It was through him and other respected acquaintances such as Makino, Shidehara,

Kabayama, Matsudaira Tsuneo, and Debuchi Katsuji that Grew became enticed by the "pendulum theory" of Japanese development—the view that "Japanese history shows that the country has passed through periodical cycles of intense nationalism attended by anti-foreign sentiment, but these periods have always been followed by other periods of international conciliation and cooperation . . . and there will be a similar outcome in the present situation."[34]

In fact, Yoshida, Makino, and this handful of aristocratic, cosmopolitan Japanese came to exemplify, not merely propound, the potential validity of the pendulum theory for Grew. They were Grew's "moderates" and internationalists, their hour would come, the pendulum would swing their way again—someday. Yoshida and his close relatives and acquaintances were to a large extent the models for Grew's affectionate portrait of the "other" Japanese, the antidote to that negative stereotype of the unregenerate militarist which was on its way to currency. "For me," Grew confided, "there are no finer people in the world than the type of Japanese exemplified by such men as Count Makino, Admiral Saitō, Count Kabayama, Yoshida, Shidehara and a host of others."[35] Some of Grew's most memorable introductions to Japanese culture took place in private with Count Makino and the Yoshidas, and the ambassador's respect for the aging count was profound. "I regard him," he noted in his diary, "as the most distinguished gentleman whom we have known in any nation."[36] Yoshida's wife (Makino's daughter) was Mrs. Grew's most intimate Japanese friend, and when she lay dying of throat cancer in the fall of 1941, it was the Grews who provided Ovaltine, which was all she could eat, and made a vehicle available to Yoshida and his daughter so that they might visit her at the hospital. Grew described her, again in the diary, as "the best that Japan can produce, a great lady and a lovely character."[37]

Grew's response to Yoshida himself was more qualified. He described him as a "pronounced liberal," accepted him without question as "a good friend of the United States and a good friend of mine," and regarded him as "one of the few Japanese to whom one can speak with the utmost frankness."[38] When there was rumor that Yoshida might again be offered the ambassadorship to the United States in the fall of 1934, Grew spoke of this as "an ideal appointment" and expressed regret that it did not materialize.[39] Yet at the same time the ambassador entertained reservations about Yoshida, and made the following observations in May 1936, after Prime Minister Hirota had appointed his now retired ex-classmate ambassador to Great Britain: "I doubt if Yoshida will have anything approaching the prestige and popularity of Matsudaira in London; in the first place he lacks the personal distinction of Matsudaira; secondly his grasp of English and precise phraseology are greatly inferior and it is sometimes difficult to know exactly what he is driving at; and thirdly I doubt if he has the resiliency of mind to understand the directness of the English character. He is however a difficult man to know intimately, largely as a result of his slow and uncertain command of English, and I may perhaps be wrong in my estimate of his abilities."[40]

In later years, Grew's evaluation of Yoshida continued to waver, but this did not diminish the role Yoshida and the "moderates" played in shaping, both by conversation and by personal example, Grew's view of Japan as a great culture and civilization temporarily gone amuck. He did not accept the interpretation, held by colleagues such as Hornbeck and the China Crowd, that Japan's actions in the 1930s derived from structural flaws extending back to the nature of the Meiji state. Like Yoshida and Makino, Grew was a great admirer of the Meiji oligarchs, and the proper course for Japan as he saw it was to return to their brand of statesmanship. This was an important perspective, particularly later when it came to considering how to deal with Japan in the post-surrender period, for it meant that what was necessary was that Japan return to a path embarked upon earlier—not make an entirely new start.

As filtered to Grew through this coterie of high-ranking Japanese acquaintances, moreover, this essential Japan seemed to draw its very life's blood from the Japanese throne. If Makino was a gentleman whose qualities transcended national bounds, he was also one of Japan's most impassioned loyalists:

> After dinner [March 1935] I sat with Count Makino and had an interesting talk, in the course of which he told me of a conversation he had just had with Dubosc, editor of the Paris TEMPS, who has been traveling in Japan. Dubosc apparently told Count Makino that he considered the political situation in Japan as "dangerous" owing to the strife and corruption among the political parties and the risk of military fascism on the one hand and of communism on the other. Makino said to Dubosc (as the former repeated the conversation to me) "When you return to Paris and make your report or write your editorials on the domestic situation in Japan, cut out the word 'danger' from your vocabulary. We have a safeguard in Japan which other countries do not possess in the same degree, namely the Imperial Household. There will never be 'danger' from military fascism or communism or from any other kind of 'ism' simply because the Emperor is supreme and will *always* have the last word." I have never heard the old man speak so emphatically or exhibit so much patriotic emotion; his eyes filled with tears and he had to wipe his glasses. I told him that I completely understood and that during my three years in Japan I had come to understand better every day. . . . The manner in which he talked tonight—his emphasis and emotion—gave a momentary revelation of the intensity of their devotion to the Throne, and I think that the force of that devotion throughout the nation—in spite of all the bickerings and political agitations and even the assassinations—or perhaps because of them—is stronger, much stronger, than foreigners generally appreciate. At any rate, I was greatly impressed tonight by this momentary glimpse into the mind of the usually suave, courteous and eminently gentle Count Makino whom I shall always regard as one of the world's greatest gentlemen.[41]

Makino was wrong, of course. Whatever "ism" it was that seized Japan, the imperial institution proved no safeguard, and it can even be argued that it was the conduit through which disaster came. Nevertheless, belief in the emperor as the ultimate resort, a final redoubt against both "fascism" and "communism," a *real* actor in the unfolding of Japan's destiny, remained an article of faith to the loyalists even after the outbreak of the China and Pacific wars. Yoshida later rested both his wartime and early postwar activities on this premise—even while fearing that the redoubt was fragile and vulnerable. And Grew, with his clubbish propensity to equate high society with the "real" Japan and gourmet dining with democracy, linked it all together like a string of pearls: the emperor; the old count and his honest, "liberal" son-in-law; civilization, moderation, respectability, comfort, internationalism, peace. . . .[42] When the issue of the future of the emperor system arose in the late wartime and early postwar years, the Japanese throne found its foremost American defender in Joseph Grew.[43] Makino's dinner parties and tears had nurtured enduring sympathies.

CABINET-MAKING, 1936

Following his retirement in November 1935, Yoshida proceeded to become involved in political and international situations of greater moment than those that had occupied him as a career professional. What propelled him out of comfortable retirement was insurrection and rebellion, notably the attempted military coup of February 26, 1936. Following this incident, in which Makino again narrowly escaped assassination, the *jūshin* attempted to persuade Konoe, then president of the House of Peers, to assume the premiership. When the prince refused, citing his persistent excuse of poor health, attention turned to Hirota. Konoe relied on Yoshida and the old school tie to persuade Hirota to accept the post, and when this proved successful Yoshida proceeded to become one of Hirota's major advisers in forming the new cabinet.[44]

This was Yoshida's first venture into parliamentary politics, and when the minister designates appeared in the press on March 6, they included Yoshida himself as the proposed foreign minister. It was not to be. Members of the Army General Staff, led by General Terauchi Hisaichi (the army's candidate for war minister) and Major General Yamashita Tomoyuki (later hanged for war crimes in the Philippines in the controversial "Yamashita case"), visited the official residence of the foreign minister on the following day and opposed the candidacies not only of Yoshida but also of Ohara Naoshi (Justice), Shimomura Hiroshi (Education), Nakajima Chikuhei (Commerce and Industry), and Kawasaki Takukichi (Home). In general, the military regarded these individuals as too liberal and sympathetic to Great Britain and the United States. More specifically, Yoshida was still known as much for his relationship to Makino as for his own personal attitudes on such matters as the League of Nations and relations with the Anglo-American powers; Ohara supported Minobe Tatsukichi and his "liberal" interpretation of the emperor as an organ of government in the constitutional debate then raging; Shimomura was an executive in the purportedly progressive *Asahi* newspaper; Nakajima had contributed money to the political parties from his earnings in aircraft construction; and Kawasaki was a prominent member of the Minseitō.[45] Yoshida was replaced as "organizing chairman" of the new Hirota cabinet by Baba Eiichi, president of the Hypothec Bank and a man more amenable to the army, who then emerged as Hirota's vice prime minister as well as finance minister. The foreign minister's portfolio was assumed by Arita Hachirō.[46]

In the long view, the military's rejection of Yoshida proved a blessing in disguise. Hirota was hanged as a war criminal for actions taken during this cabinet and later, and had the Yoshida appointment gone through, he would in all likelihood have been automatically purged in the immediate postwar period for having held a cabinet position at that late date.[47] While the incident might be numbered as yet another intercession by a whimsical guardian angel, Yoshida's own reaction to the course of events was interesting. Grew saw the entire public role which Hirota enabled Yoshida to play as a puzzler—"precisely like waving a red flag at a bull." To him it seemed so obvious that the army would reject Yoshida that he even mused on the possibility of it all being a subtle stratagem on Hirota's part: "some deep-seated purpose in the maneuver, possibly to place squarely on the Army the responsibility for tampering with Hirota's foreign policy."[48] On his own part, however, Yoshida seemed to take the matter lightly. In early April he told Grew that his first plunge into the political circus had been "great fun."[49] And in an intriguing memorandum of a conversation with Yoshida on April 30, Grew noted that, despite his abrupt repudiation by the army, "Mr. Yoshida said that the incident of February 26 was having a favorable and healthy effect in the army, arising largely out of the splendidly strong stand taken by the Emperor. The army was getting tired of the direct actionist element and the dissension within its ranks and a general movement was now on foot to eliminate those elements."[50]

This would seem to be a naive position at best, which gave little cognizance to the political thrust of the military leaders who assumed power after the February 26th Incident, and which at the same time was overly sanguine concerning the independence, wisdom, and intentions of the civilian "moderates" such as Hirota.[51] Indeed, in the decade which followed, February 26 became a major, and curious, turning point in Yoshida's perception of Japan's proper course. Yoshida and the "moderates" gradually came to see the emergence of the army's Tōsei-ha (Control Faction) which occurred in the aftermath of the rebellion as having disastrous rather than stabilizing consequences, and to a certain extent one of their goals became a return to the status quo ante of the February 26th Incident (rather than of the Manchurian Incident). Yoshida, Konoe, and others later were to propose resolving Japan's dilemma by rehabilitating key members of the army's Kōdō-ha (Imperial Way Faction) who had been discredited by the 1936 rebellion, despite the fact that these individuals were deeply implicated in some of the more notorious and militant events of the period between 1931 and 1936. Yoshida's later "anti-militarist" associates, that is, represented and exemplified precisely that "direct actionist element" against which the emperor took the "splendidly strong stand" Yoshida applauded in the April 30 conversation.

After Hirota finally succeeded in creating a cabinet acceptable to the military, he appointed Yoshida ambassador to Great Britain; Yoshida regarded this as essentially a gesture of compensation for the debacle over the foreign minister appointment.[52] Nonetheless, selection of the Anglophile Yoshida at a time when Anglo-Japanese relations were extremely strained, and despite the opposition the appointment was certain to generate among the same circles which had rejected Yoshida as foreign minister, suggests that the new prime minister still hoped to mend his country's relations with the Anglo-Saxon powers. It was not a popular appointment by any means, since various sectors of the bureaucracy, led by the Home Ministry, also opposed it. For a while Hirota contemplated backing down by offering Yoshida an appointment to the House of Peers, and he went so far as to have Harada broach this alternative to Yoshida. Yoshida's response was typically unorthodox. "To me," he informed Saionji's aide, "what matters is the creation of the Hirota cabinet, and from the beginning I've given absolutely no thought to whether I personally become a member of the House or cabinet member or ambassador. To start saying such things now destroys my honor, and it would suit me better if you don't go into such matters. I haven't the slightest thought about wanting to do this or that, and want you to understand this thoroughly."[53]

Yoshida apparently only accepted the ambassadorship when pressured to do so by Matsudaira and others, and on the condition that he be given a more or less free hand in London.[54] Before leaving Japan, he discussed Japan's plight with Grew; and before arriving in Great Britain, he visited the United States to set forth in some detail for Cordell Hull and Norman Davis and others the dynamics of Japanese expansion as he perceived them.

EXPLAINING JAPAN TO AMERICA

In all of his conversations with the Americans, Yoshida reiterated several basic points; one of his trademarks, as should be clear by now, was hammering a few nails solidly. These points were subsequently collated in a memorandum by Stanley Hornbeck which, together with the April 1928 policy paper cited previously and the proposals he was shortly to make in London, helps delineate the parameters of Yoshida's "imperial consciousness" prior to the outbreak of the China War. Yoshida's views naturally were enunciated with an eye to Japan's economic crisis: the hardships of the world depression had been compounded by restrictive tariffs against Japanese exports, particularly textiles, by the Western powers. In brief, he stressed these points to the Americans:

- Japan's population growth made expansion inevitable; the Japanese people were faced with the "absolute necessity for more territory for their existence in anything like a satisfactory way."
- Population pressure plus the general economic situation made it essential for Japan to have secure trade outlets and secure sources of raw materials, especially oil.
- Japan's intentions were confined solely to the "peaceful penetration" of Asia. Talk of war was "utterly foolish." The build-up of Japanese armaments was "not intended for use against any particular country." In short, the West and indeed the world misunderstood Japan; apprehensions of Japanese militarism were delusions.
- As proof of countervailing trends, one could point to the strengthening of "liberal elements" within Japan, as well as the fact that "Army leaders are becoming more moderate in their views."
- Japan was destined to play a "stabilizing role" in the Far East—the implication being not only stabilization of China through various forms of Japanese involvement, but also creation of a bulwark against communism and the Soviet Union.
- In securing the above necessary and peaceful goals, Japan required the "friendship and cooperation of Great Britain and the United States." In particular, it was essential that the United States play the role of an "honest broker" for Japan.

Hornbeck recorded these arguments in fuller detail as follows:

[Washington] June 25, 1936

In Tokyo's despatch No. 1798, April 30, 1936, Ambassador Grew reported as follows:

"On April 30, 1936, Mr. Shigeru Yoshida, recently appointed Japanese Ambassador to Great Britain, called and stated, in the course of our conversation, that the population problem in Japan was becoming increasingly difficult and that foreign countries should realize the seriousness of the situation and endeavor to help Japan in finding an adequate outlet. He said that it was principally a matter of finding outlets for Japan's trade. Upon being asked, he said that it meant peaceful penetration. Again upon being asked, he said that he thought that the 'blue-water school' (i.e., the school advocating expansion to the south) would win out eventually over the 'continental school.' [He then harped for a moment on the well-worn theme of Japan as a 'stabilizing influence' in East Asia.] "[55]

Under date May 20, 1936, Mr. Grew states in his diary that on that day Mr. Yoshida called on him and a conversation was held which covered approximately an hour. In the course of this, Yoshida stated that he was expounding a personal point of view: he said that it was necessary to solve Japan's problem of overpopulation, necessary to find some outlet, as well as important to acquire increased opportunities for obtaining raw materials and especially oil. Grew asked how Japan expected to acquire those things if they already belong to other nations. Yoshida said he hoped that new sources of raw materials and oil could be exploited and possible contacts be made with countries which already possessed such sources. He said that Japan's thought was only one of peaceful penetration and that in developing this peaceful penetration he hoped that the United States might lend its cooperation and play the part of "honest broker." He said that the talk of war with Soviet Russia or with the United States or with Great Britain was utterly foolish and that Japan's aims and efforts were purely pacific. He wished that Japan and the United States together might solve the whole problem of permanent peace in the Pacific area.

Under date June 12, 1936, the Secretary of State made a memorandum of the conversation held between him and Mr. Yoshida on that day. Yoshida said that he was very desirous of promoting better relations and better understanding between his country and the United States. He said that the one big fact which he wanted the American people to recognize was the immense and rapidly growing population of Japan and the absolute necessity for more territory for their existence in anything like a satisfactory way. He referred to the fact that there was misunderstanding and misapprehension on the part of our people in this respect as it related to Japanese movements in and about China; that this also was probably true as to the British; that the Japanese armaments were not intended for war against any particular country, especially us, but that Japanese naval officials were always undertaking to create additional vacancies and additional room for promotion, etc., etc. He expressed an earnest desire for conference, collaboration and, without alliances, such relationships as would work out any questions arising in an amicable and fairly satisfactory way. He expressed his purpose to have a number of conversations with Ambassador Bingham [U.S. Ambassador to London], as well as with the British officials, on these subjects, with the view to the former conversations getting back to the Secretary.... He stated that he would like for the Secretary to remember the difficulties of the businessmen and traders of Japan and the necessity for outside trade.

On June 16, 1936, Mr. Yoshida called on Mr. Norman Davis. According to Mr. Davis' record, in a letter of June 17, Yoshida said that he felt he could talk with Mr. Davis with entire frankness. He had endeavored to explain to the Secretary of State the problem confronting Japan of keeping its growing population employed, but he had not entered into details. The Japanese people do not want to leave home and the most practical solution would be to keep them employed at home by sending their trade abroad. The wiser element in the Army realize that the Army has gone too far. They realize that they have created an impossible situation and are calling upon the diplomats for help. The Army has been surprised to find out how well Russia is prepared. They may need to take a new tack. Japan needs to see to it that no other country join with Russia, and, if possible, to get an alignment with some other power. He had conferred with Army leaders in Tokyo and these leaders feel that in regard to China they should cultivate the friendship and cooperation of Great Britain and the United States. In fact, they want to cultivate friendship with Nanking also. He knew that Great Britain would not make any agreement with Japan without the approval of the United States, but his idea was first to approach the British with a view to ascertaining whether they have any definite opinion as to the best way to deal with the China situation. Then, if it is found possible to reach a tentative meeting of minds conditional upon American approval and cooperation, he would visit Washington on his way back to Tokyo. He is convinced that the United States holds the key to the whole situation. The liberal elements in Japan have been strengthened and the Army leaders are becoming more moderate in their views: the wiser one are getting the upper hand over the wild younger officers. The wiser naval officers realize that they made a mistake in leaving the Naval Conference without an agreement; but they are not as yet speaking out and he did not know whether opinion would change sufficiently during the next few months to make the Government feel justified in signing the Naval Treaty. There could be no ultimate solution to the naval question nor to any of the difficult problems in the Far East without a political foundation. It is essential to establish such a foundation.[56]

Grew did not comment on Yoshida's views. Hull was frankly skeptical and told Yóshida that "the impression among many persons in this country was that Japan sought absolute economic domination, first of eastern Asia, and then, of other portions as she might see fit; that this would mean political as well as military domination in the end; that the upshot of the entire movement would be to exclude countries like the United States from trading with all of those portions of China thus brought under the domination or controlling influence so-called of Japan. . . ." He then went on to deliver a long and well-rehearsed lecture on reciprocal trade agreements.[57]

Hornbeck was predictably more acerbic. He commented that the opinions expressed by Yoshida boiled down to endorsement of the view that Japan must expand; desire to bring about a Japanese-American-British rapprochement which would facilitate such expansion; and affirmation of an upswing in liberal and moderate sentiment in Japan. Yoshida had failed to make any concrete proposals, Hornbeck observed, and his tactics and assertions were unexceptional, merely a "repetition of the method and the affirmations with which we have become familiar on the part of Japanese diplomats." Maxwell Hamilton, assistant chief of the Division of Far Eastern Affairs, was perhaps more willing than Hornbeck to accept Yoshida's genuinely good intentions, but this did not render his conclusions less damaging: "No matter how sincere Yoshida may be, will not his efforts in London serve, as did Matsudaira's, to attract the attention and support of some of the British and thus to throw a partial smoke-screen around Japan's continued aggression in China?"[58]

OPPOSITION TO JAPANESE-GERMAN RAPPROCHEMENT

Yoshida's arrival in Great Britain coincided with Japan's negotiation of the Anti-Comintern Pact with Nazi Germany, a development hardly designed to enhance the new ambassador's prestige in London. The pact was ultimately signed in Berlin in November 1936, but prior to that the Japanese government endeavored to elicit the support of its ambassadors abroad. Pressure to this end was brought to bear on Yoshida during September by the Japanese military attachés in London and Germany, Tatsumi Eiichi and Ōshima Hiroshi respectively. Subsequently Shiratori

Toshio, the "reform bureaucrat" *exemplaire* of the Foreign Ministry, joined those who sought to convince Yoshida that the future lay with Germany.[59]

Yoshida resisted these pressures, and continued to oppose rapprochement with Germany even after the Axis Alliance of 1940. His reasoning was as usual pragmatic. He shared his government's distrust of the Soviet Union and ideological repugnance for communism, but rejected out of hand the argument offered to him in 1936 that the Anti-Comintern Pact had no implications beyond an ideological front against international communism. On the contrary, he argued, its military and political implications were far-reaching. He predicted that the pact posed the danger of Japan being drawn into formal alliance with Germany and thus direct confrontation with Great Britain and the United States; that if war came about, Japan would be sucked into it; and that in all probability Germany would lose such a war.

Tatsumi, the first person assigned to convince Yoshida of the value of the pact (and one of Yoshida's major unofficial advisers on security policy over a decade later, during the occupation of Japan), later recounted his unsuccessful session with the new ambassador in some detail. He "quoted" Yoshida's rebuttal of his arguments as follows:

> First of all, the Japanese military is overestimating the actual military power of Nazi Germany. Having been beaten so badly by the Allied forces in the World War, and having lost in addition all territories abroad, no matter how great the German race may be, Germany could not have recovered in a matter of twenty years to the point of being able to fight on an equal basis against Great Britain, France, and thus the United States. On the other hand, Great Britain and the United States have vast territories and abundant resources throughout the world. In addition, the fundamental political and economic strength they have cultivated over the course of the years is certainly not to be regarded lightly.
>
> The military may say that a pact with the Axis side is merely a matter of ideology, that is, simply preventing communism. But to make such a pact clearly indicates that Japan is siding with the Axis, and in the future this will inevitably develop further into something political

> and military. When that happens, then should the Axis side, which is advancing calling for the destruction of the status quo, cause a war, there is a danger that as the tide moves Japan may fall into a situation of having to fight against Great Britain and the United States.
>
> At present the powers are divided into two camps, but it is absolutely not the time for Japan to seek to join the Axis side. Viewing the present international situation, I think it is wise for Japan to have diplomatic *flexibility*, but if we are to take sides, then I would choose the Anglo-American side over Germany and Italy. I positively believe that this is the road to be taken for the future of Japan.

Tatsumi was overwhelmed by these arguments and cabled his superiors: "Inadequate ability unable to convince." The army then ordered Ōshima (who was later to become lieutenant general and ambassador to Berlin) to fly to London from Berlin to take up the task. Ōshima closeted himself with Yoshida for three unavailing hours, while the dinner got cold, and departed the following day, Tatsumi recalled, "in a terrible mood."[60]

Such calculated appraisal of power realities, guided by nationalism more than any principled concern with "fascism" or "democracy," remained the mainstay of Yoshida's analysis of Japan's proper role vis-à-vis the European powers. This continued even into the war years. In August 1940, a month before the conclusion of the Tripartite Pact, for example, he warned Harada that a German victory still appeared "highly doubtful."[61] At the same time, it still remained necessary to keep one's options open, to maintain "flexibility." As late as 1942, it will be seen that he was urging that Konoe be sent to Switzerland where, depending on how the war progressed, he might be sought out as a peace negotiator by either the Axis or Allied powers.[62]

As Yoshida made clear around the time of the Tripartite Pact, his opposition to rapprochement with Germany, and later Italy, also was based upon concern for the emperor. He feared that alliance among the three countries would place the emperor on the same level as Hitler and Mussolini, which in itself would tend to denigrate the throne. More ominously, it placed the throne in jeopardy should a crisis occur. Hitler and Mussolini were expendable, he told a Foreign Ministry colleague, but Japan should not dare to expose the emperor to such a danger.[63]

In explaining the Anti-Comintern Pact to his British counterparts in 1936, however, Yoshida pursued a line of argumentation almost the opposite to that he had used in private with his own government. Initially, for example, he tendered Foreign Secretary Eden the explanation his own military attaché had unsuccessfully attempted to foist on him, that is, that the agreement "could only have to do with communism, which His Majesty's Government themselves did not favor."[64] In an official capacity, he also appears to have broached the possibility of a non-aggression pact between Great Britain and Japan; according to one account, he even went further to suggest British participation in the Anti-Comintern Pact itself. These proposals seem to have been intended primarily as a graphic indication of the non-hostile intention of the Anti-Comintern Pact insofar as Great Britain was concerned, and were not presented with serious expectation of British acceptance.[65]

Unofficially, in a manner reminiscent of his initiatives in Mukden a decade earlier, Yoshida carried the art of persuasion to such an extreme that it caused consternation among both the British and Japanese. According to Harada, on the eve of the formal announcement of the pact Yoshida bluntly asked the British if they would maintain benevolent neutrality in case of war between Japan and the Soviet Union, while promising that in any dispute between Britain and another country Japan would assist in protecting British rights and interests. The suggestion clearly harked back to the role Japan had played as a protector of British interests in the Far East during World War One. But to make such a comment at that particular time, before the China Incident and Japan's "advance south," simply fanned rumors of an impending Japanese attack on Russia and caused the British ambassador to Tokyo to request clarification.[66]

This problem of misleading or misinterpreted personal initiatives was to plague Yoshida's term in London, but the issue of the Anti-Comintern Pact itself soon receded before two more dominant concerns: the China problem, and the rectification of economic relations between Japan and Great Britain. Yoshida was almost exclusively concerned with these two areas in the period prior to the China Incident of July 1937.

LESSONS IN HISTORY AND POLITICS FOR THE BRITISH

Yoshida's major accomplishment as ambassador to London was the preparation of a secret plan which he believed could simultaneously lead to resolution of the China crisis, restoration of Anglo-Japanese relations, and recovery from the global depression. The plan was relatively detailed and concrete, and is discussed in the following chapter. Since the British were inclined to regard optimists with suspicion during these years, Yoshida's initiatives were received with skepticism in many quarters. To help create a more receptive climate, he thus lectured his British counterparts on matters of history and politics whenever the occasion presented itself, and often when it did not. The secret plan was hatched within a cocoon of commentary concerning Japan and its place in the world.

Several themes wound through this commentary: (1) the pendulum theory and a somewhat subtle notion of "two camps" within Japan; (2) an often reiterated interpretation of Far Eastern history since the Washington Conference, which placed much of the onus for Japan's "failure" in China upon the Chinese themselves, as well as the Western powers; (3) a parallel argument that Soviet-directed communism rather than Japanese militarism lay at the root of unrest in China, *as well as in Japan*, and constituted the major threat to peace and stability in Asia; and (4) the fundamental notion that Anglo-Japanese economic conflict did not derive primarily from the global depression, but rather from the turmoil in China and consequent disruption of Japan's natural and essential market in continental Asia—disruption which had forced Japan to become a vigorous trade rival in the sphere hitherto dominated by the United Kingdom.

Yoshida repeatedly described Japan as divided into two camps at this time, but with a nuance in his definition of these camps.

On the one hand he employed the conventional dichotomy of "militarists" versus "moderates," numbering himself unequivocally among the latter and predicting with unflagging hope the imminent repudiation of the former. The "moderates" were largely Anglophile, led by the emperor, Prince Saionji, and sectors of the diplomatic corps and business community.[67] At the same time, however, Yoshida endeavored to qualify this rigid antithesis by speaking also of "two schools of political inclination, one toward Anglo-Japanese and the other toward Sino-Japanese collaboration"—and by *dis*associating himself from exclusive attachment to either school. Both schools had failed, he argued, precisely because of their partisanship, and "the double failure had brought about skepticism in Japan." Thus Yoshida presented himself to the British as "a firm believer in both schools."[68]

Both versions of the two camps were adaptable to use in support of the pendulum theory, for together they enabled Yoshida to argue not only that the "moderates" were waiting in the wings, but also that there were broader trends within Japan of moderation-in-the-offing. The latter theme was reflected in his expressed belief that the "militarists," who hitherto had been mesmerized by the Asian connection, were gradually coming to recognize, like himself, the necessity of also cultivating cooperative relations with the West.

These distinctions were not always finely and consistently drawn, and in many of his conversations Yoshida tended to dwell more exclusively on the moderates-in-the-wings. Most simply, he called attention to the failures of Japan's China policy, and suggested that popular sentiment in Japan would soon turn against the army and pave the way for the return of more liberal politicians and statesmen. Even this, however, could not occur without Great Britain's assistance, for in the present situation the "moderates" were incapable of reversing the pendulum by themselves. It remained Yoshida's deep conviction during his ambassadorship that clear gestures of good will on the part of Britain would have a most salutary effect on Japanese politics. In the first place, they would encourage the "moderates" themselves, give them heart and renewed hope. In the second place, conciliatory gestures would undercut militarist propaganda, which cast Britain as hostile and fed on fears of Japan's international isolation.

Time and again, Yoshida discerned ideal opportunities for such expression of good will and urged the British to take advantage of them, usually to little avail. A typical exchange occurred in November 1936, for example, when Yoshida suggested to Sir Frederick Leith-Ross of the Treasury that if Britain aided Japan financially, by lowering the interest rate on Japan's long-term sterling debt or raising British credits to Japanese banks, this "would help the moderate element in Japan to control the Military Party." The pungent flavor of British response to the pendulum theory in general was conveyed in the internal comment of one Foreign Office Asian specialist concerning this proposal: "Before lending money to the 'moderates' we should be sure that the military will not find it just as easy to control the moderates with the money as they seem to do the moderates without the money."[69]

Yet Yoshida persisted. In January 1937, he endeavored to turn the conclusion of the Anti-Comintern Pact into a positive opportunity. The agreement had been freely criticized in Japan and thus had shaken the cabinet, he informed Alexander Cadogan, the deputy under secretary of the Foreign Office and a former ambassador to China. "He maintains that during the coming session of the Diet the position of the Japanese Cabinet will be rather precarious and he professes to hope that out of the crisis there may emerge a Government which will be more liberal and more independent of the military party," Cadogan noted, "and he always hints that some vague friendly declaration on our part might help to bring this about and strengthen the more moderate elements in Japan." Cadogan was courteously skeptical of this possibility; the British ambassador to Tokyo simply dismissed it as "nonsense."[70]

The Hayashi Senjūrō cabinet, formed at the beginning of February, did kindle Yoshida's hopes, for the new foreign minister, Satō Naotake, was a surprising choice who was associated with the more moderate group of career diplomats. Foreign Secretary Eden recorded that on February 5 Yoshida had personally informed him that "recent developments were encouraging for the Moderates and he himself was convinced it would not be possible for any government to survive without the support of the Diet. Japan was passing through a difficult transition period and in the meanwhile he much hoped that [Great Britain] would show all possible sympathy and understanding with her in her difficulties."[71] In March, after Satō had spoken publicly of Britain in relatively conciliatory terms, Yoshida attempted to use indirect channels to further impress upon Eden the desirability "at some time or another for some friendly references to Japan to be made publicly by someone in authority" in London. "The effect in Japan would be appreciable and salutary," he told Ashley Clarke: "It was the kind of encouragement which the more liberal minded Japanese and those already inclined towards friendship with England needed. There were people in Japan who liked to claim (in the Diet and in the press) that his (Mr. Yoshida's) mission to England to improve relations had completely failed. He did not believe this himself and there were many people who still hoped and believed that relations with Great Britain could and should be improved. A gesture of the kind that he had indicated would put new heart into these people."[72]

In April, Yoshida renewed the campaign with Cadogan in the context of his own personal initiatives to promote "some kind of agreement to remove tension and misunderstanding in the Far East, and particularly, to promote the economic rehabilitation of China." It was in Britain's interest to do this, he argued, not so much as a response to any concrete change of direction in Japanese policy, but rather as a potential stimulus to such a change. For, as Cadogan summarized the conversation, Yoshida "insisted that the militarists are losing ground in Japan and that it would be very helpful towards getting Japan on the right track if something could be done to induce Japan to revise her policy in China, which had been a failure, and adopt a policy of cooperation which would soon justify itself."[73]

It is apparent from such exchanges that Yoshida's pendulum theory tended to assume the character of a hoped-for self-fulfilling prophesy: if Great Britain demonstrated its own faith in the theory by adopting a more conciliatory attitude toward Japan, *then* political sentiment in Japan would indeed be inclined to swing back in the direction of a more moderate and internationalist policy. This also held true for the other aspect of the two-camps thesis: the argument that there were growing trends toward moderation even among the militarists.

One key to this broader "moderation-in-the-offing" argument was the rise of Soviet power in the Far East. In 1932, Yoshida had informed the British ambassador to Rome that Japan's leaders had concluded "there was now nothing whatever to fear from Russia and that the Japanese Government could, to all intents and purposes, ignore her in any action they wished to take."[74] By 1936, and for sound reasons, this position had been drastically revised. In April, Sir Robert Clive, the British ambassador to Tokyo, reported that Yoshida had visited him prior to his departure for London and emphasized this new appraisal of Russia. "He had recently noticed a very marked and rapid change in attitude, not only among statesmen, but in the Army; and even the younger officers were anxious for 'an alliance or something of the kind' with Great Britain. The reason for this is that the Army now feels that the U.S.S.R.'s improvement and increase in tanks, aeroplanes and armoured cars has made a war with Russia a dangerous adventure and Japan would like 'some allies'."[75] Yoshida continued to emphasize this line prior to Japan's conclusion of the Anti-Comintern Pact. He reiterated it to Clive on May 21, 1936, stressing that "a friend if not an ally was necessary, and Great Britain was the obvious country to be this friend," and repeated it in his first conversation with Eden on July 17, and again in a conversation with Sir Robert Vansittart on September 23.[76]

Interestingly, Yoshida's impressions of this trend were strongly echoed at the time by the British military attaché in Tokyo, Major General F. S. G. Piggott, who on September 17, 1936, submitted a lengthy and controversial memorandum to Ambassador Clive based on allegedly extensive conversations with Japanese military authorities. Fear of Russia on the part of Japan's military "realists," Piggott argued, had indeed begun to reinforce the influence of the traditionally pro-British "sentimentalists," and he emphasized that he had discerned such sentiment not only at the highest levels of military leadership (such as General Araki Sadao and retired general Kawai Misao), but also among influential field officers holding the ranks of colonel and major. Piggott confessed that he had held "considerable doubts on first arrival" concerning these younger officers, but they had "gone out of their way to emphasize the desirability, if not the absolute necessity, of grasping the opportunity that now exists of adjusting Anglo-Japanese relations." Similar sentiments were growing noticeably among the middle and lower classes ("shopkeepers, peasants, priests, servants, porters, artisans, petty officials, labourers, and others"). Piggott also intimated that the major impediment to rectification of relations between the two countries "now lies with British public opinion, rather than with Japanese." In conclusion, he quoted a sailing metaphor used by one of his Japanese military contacts: a "favorable wind" prevailed, and should not be lost.[77]

The Foreign Office regarded this favorable wind as little more than Piggott's own hot air, and its response to its own military attaché suggests the reception given to Yoshida's similar views. One commentator dismissed it all as "a little puerile." Cadogan remarked, "I am quite ready to believe that there exists in Japan a body of opinion sentimentally inclined to friendship with us (just as there still exists in England a reminiscent—and also rather sentimental—feeling for Japan). But unfortunately it is difficult to find a basis on which a real understanding leading to cooperation can be built." Ambassador Clive, who actually withheld Piggott's report from the Foreign Office for over a month, acknowledged the connection between Britain and Russia in Japanese eyes (Britain controlled the strategic raw materials vital to Japan in any war with Russia, as well as critical financial support), but concluded that rapprochement would antagonize the United States and of course Russia, and if interpreted as *desinteressement* in China might further exacerbate the political situation there. "Time being in our favor," he concluded, Britain would do best to remain imprecise toward Japan, but "keep the ball in play."[78]

For the most part, however, Clive left the burden of rebuttal to his commercial counsellor, George Sansom, who concluded that Piggott's optimism was itself largely sentimental, for Japanese and British interests were "in most respects irreconcilable." Sansom did not deny the possibility that the Russian angle might be conducive to an Anglo-Japanese agreement, but rather questioned where such agreement might lead: "The practical considerations are clear and simple. Japan wants to expand. The chief obstacle to her economic expansion is the British Empire. Therefore it would be convenient to make friendly arrangements with the United Kingdom. Japan's expansion may involve her in hostilities, with Russia or with China, or even with ourselves. If she can count on the benevolent neutrality of the United Kingdom her path is easy. If she makes friends with the United Kingdom she is relieved of anxiety as to one possible enemy; she is tolerably sure of supplies of raw materials which are essential for her further expansion; and she has a better prospect of borrowing capital of which she is short."[79]

This interpretation—that the "Russian menace" argument as espoused by Yoshida and Piggott did not represent merely a benign opening for Anglo-Japanese rapprochement, but rather implied a joint anti-Soviet entente which would ultimately act against British interests—was widely shared in the Foreign Office. The April conversation on the subject between Yoshida and Clive, for example, had elicited this response from one Asia hand: "The new friendliness is due to the fact that Japan is afraid of Russia and needs our benevolent neutrality to overcome this obstacle to her expansion. Shall we not merely be next on the menu if we help Japan to beat Russia?"[80]

In tandem with the argument that fear of Russia was encouraging more moderate counsel within the military, Yoshida also took pains to emphasize the popular backlash to be expected as Japan's war expenditures increased. This too was a point emphasized in his first meeting with Eden in July 1936. "The Ambassador believed," Eden recorded, "that with the coming of autumn we should find a steady increase in the authority of those who supported more moderate counsels in his country. The autumn would bring the budget and the increased taxation which the budget would necessitate, which he hoped would have a sobering effect on the less responsible elements." Vansittart was treated to the same argument on September 26, as was Sir Robert Craigie of the Foreign Office on December 4; and even when the anticipated public reaction failed to materialize, Yoshida continued to espouse the "tax burden" argument.[81]

Yoshida doggedly professed to see the imminent swing of the pendulum even after the China Incident in July 1937. The establishment of the Konoe cabinet on June 4, 1937, in which Hirota became foreign minister, undoubtedly struck him as confirmation of his predictions of a moderate upswing in Japan. Neither the fact that the Hirota cabinet had concluded the Anti-Comintern Pact with Nazi Germany, nor the fact that the Konoe cabinet soon thereafter enlarged the China Incident into a "war of annihilation" against China, caused him really to reflect upon the possible *fundamental* fallacy of the liberal-militarist dichotomy. As late as April and May of 1938 he was continuing to argue that Japan had become "war weary," that it "was at the end of its tether," and that "recent Cabinet changes were symptomatic of the recognition that the war was unpopular in Japan."[82] On September 10, 1938, in one of his last acts as ambassador, he protested against the possibility that Britain might support aid to China through the League of Nations, arguing that this would be recognized as an "unfriendly measure" in Japan and undercut the attempt of Foreign Minister Ugaki Kazushige to exert a moderating influence on Japanese policy. "Your friendly attitude will greatly enhance the prospects of a betterment of Anglo-Japanese relations," he wrote to Lord de la Ware, "as it will render General Ugaki's task much easier."[83]

Although the British government did evince increasing interest in Yoshida's "secret plan" prior to the China Incident, and even viewed it with some slight wistfulness thereafter, such interest was practical in origin and not motivated by any strong faith in the pendulum theory. Cadogan captured the general response to these theories early on in the game: "We must remember that Mr. Yoshida was barred from office by the military, and therefore of course has no love for them. But I am afraid the wish is father to the thought when he speaks of the possibility of strengthening the liberal elements in Japan at the expense of the military."[84]

The second dimension of Yoshida's "pedagogic" endeavors in London entailed placing the contemporary global crisis in historical perspective. To a certain extent, this exercise in nationalistic historiography actually contradicted the two-camp thesis, for it could be read as exonerating the "militarists" by treating their actions as more responsive than provocative—responsive to *China's provocations* in particular, and to the disadvantageous hand which recent history had dealt Japan in general. Although the British were not entirely unreceptive to Japan's case, Yoshida's particular version of the post-World War One era impressed them little more than did his pendulum theory. "Mr. Yoshida's sketch of history is a remarkably poor one," one member of the Far Eastern section noted in December 1936, "& does not help us to believe that he is able to face the realities of the situation, in spite of his admission that Japanese policy in China has been an utter failure."[85]

Accurate or not, it is difficult to exaggerate the *political* significance of Yoshida's interpretation of modern Japanese history. Those who make history themselves often do so on the basis of a dubious historical consciousness, and Yoshida *did* make history after 1945. His opposition to the early reforms of the occupation was firmly grounded in much the same "sketch of history" as that he conveyed to the British in the late 1930s.

Yoshida lectured his British counterparts on history both before and after the China Incident, with little apparent concern for revising his interpretation in the light of that cataclysmic event, and with little concern also for the obvious ennui of his listeners. By 1938 the British had reduced it all to a cliché: "It is unnecessary to repeat His Excellency's talk about the days of the old Alliance,"

Lord Hankey wrote to Cadogan in April: "the long story of how it came to an end; the subsequent misfortunes of Japan; the boycott of their goods in China and, indeed, in Manchuria; their search for alternative markets; the closing, or partial closing, to them of many parts of the British Empire; the sharp effect of this on the promotion of anti-British feeling in Japan; and the desirability of getting back on to something approaching our old terms. I listened to all this with mere murmurs of sympathy."[86] And indeed Cadogan had been privileged to receive the long story earlier, in writing, from Yoshida. On December 17, 1936, Yoshida followed a conversation on the subject with a letter devoted entirely to "the present situation in the Far East and the events which have led up to that situation." It read as follows:

> Prior to the Washington Conference Japanese foreign policy was founded on two basic principles. It is unnecessary for me to stress that the first of these was that of unswerving friendship with Great Britain based on the Anglo-Japanese Alliance. The second was the determination to put our relations with China on a more solid footing and to settle the outstanding questions between us in a mutually satisfactory way.
>
> It must be admitted by all concerned that the outcome of the Washington Conference changed the entire picture in the Far East. At the same time I wish to make it clear to you that the Japanese Government consented to the Shantung Agreement and to the abolition of the Anglo-Japanese Alliance in the firm belief that by that consent the establishment of happy relations between Japan, Great Britain, the United States and China might be brought about.
>
> It is a matter of history that this desirable issue did not eventuate. Any joint policy among the Powers interested in Chinese affairs ceased and the Chinese began to pursue the policy of playing off one Power against another. The various boycott movements instituted by the Chinese afford abundant proof of this. When the boycott of Japanese goods began in North China after the signature of the Shantung Agreement, we were unable to obtain the sympathetic help of any of the friendly Powers. Later the boycott movement was directed against the British, Americans, and French, each in their turn; but, owing to the cessation of any co-operation among the Powers, all those who were made to suffer by the boycott movement sought to escape their immediate difficulties by competitive intrigue with the Young Chinese in the various centres involved. The result of this was twofold; firstly, an in-

> crease of internal chaos in China and, secondly, a development of misunderstanding and mistrust between the foreign Powers concerned with regard to their individual activities.
>
> With the increase of chaos Japanese relations with China became more difficult, and at the same time the mutual misunderstandings between Great Britain and Japan were enhanced.
>
> The latter unfortunate situation was not improved by the fact that the continued unrestricted boycott of Japanese goods from the Chinese market forced the Japanese exporter to find markets for his goods elsewhere, thereby bringing about a trade conflict with Great Britain.
>
> You alluded the other day to the apprehension among the British public concerning our China policy, but the Japanese people have equal apprehensions concerning British policy in China and concerning your Trade policy against Japan. I would, however, say that in the eyes of our people our foreign policy in the past is regarded as an utter failure, and it is in the light of their desire to develop a co-operative and constructive policy that I wish you to read this letter.
>
> I am aware that some British people attack the "undue influence" of our so-called Militarists, but Japanese militarists are no more military than those of other nations. It is only when "economic sanctions" become coercive or when the attitude of friendly Powers becomes unsympathetic that people will pay undue heed to the voice of the military. An example of this is clearly seen in the enhancement of the popularity of Mussolini after the "sanctions" discussions at Geneva.
>
> However, as I said to you on Monday, mutual criticisms of each other's past is of no practical value. The wiser course is surely to consider a constructive future policy for the benefit of all concerned.

The letter apparently was not answered, and Cadogan made only one marginal notation where Yoshida had observed that "Japanese militarists are no more military than those of other nations." "No," he wrote, "our complaint is that they are so much more *political*."[87]

China's Machiavellism and masochistic unreasonableness were basic truths to Yoshida. Nothing that happened in the 1930s really caused him to modify the indignation at China's lack of "self-reflection" and "sincerity" which had permeated his views in the 1920s. And nothing in his frame of reference allowed him to recognize the double standards he employed concerning appropriate tactics in foreign affairs. Where Japanese policy toward

China was concerned, he heaped scorn upon conciliation and "sweet words," but where British policy toward Japan was concerned, he touted the wisdom of appeasement and gestures of "good will." What was statesmanship and diplomatic sense for Japan (cooperation and connivance with the great powers; exploitation of weakness and disorder in China; punishment of "those who behave impolitely to us"; manipulation of economic levers) was petty and reprehensible behavior when practiced by China ("playing off one Power against another"; refusal to submit to foreign "impoliteness" of the most humiliating, rapacious, and atrocious sort; resort to the weapon of the boycott). Even after the Konoe cabinet initiated the undeclared "war of annihilation," Yoshida continued to vilify the victim. "It was the old, old story," the secretary of state for dominion affairs wrote Lord Halifax in April 1938. "His Excellency recited once more the Japanese version of the events of the last year in the Far East, from which I gathered that responsibility for the Japanese invasion of China rested solely on the wicked Chinese who were always anxious to be at the throats of the Japanese. The Ambassador even included us amongst those who were at fault, suggesting that if only we had restrained the Chinese the war would not have started. I remarked that I supposed that if we had restrained the Chinese the only result would have been that the Japanese invasion would have been swifter and more far reaching. In the course of the conversation he and I fell foul of each other, in the most friendly spirit, on many historical details."[88]

It is probably a truism that those who preach self-reflection most practice it least, and such Great-Power arrogance remained an abiding part of the consciousness exemplified by Yoshida during these decades. By the latter part of the 1930s, however, this consciousness had come to embrace a further, critical dimension—one that was surprisingly neglected in the December 17 letter to Cadogan. This concerned the responsibility of communism and the Soviet Union for unrest in Asia, and several aspects of Yoshida's version of the Red Peril deserve notice. First, although the anti-communist phobia had been present in his views on China in the 1920s, it was from the mid-1930s, considerably after the 1927 rout of the Comintern in China, that this appears to have become a dominant element in his thinking. And second, in citing the communist menace, Yoshida did not merely allege that the Soviet Union lay behind the anti-Japanese movement in China, but cast the far broader accusation that communist influence was also to a considerable extent responsible *for Japanese militarism itself*; that is, the militarists were, at least in part, communist-inspired. This notion that Japan's militarism was alien to the true Japan, almost un-Japanese—that it was another manifestation of the uncanny hand of communist subversion—was not a mere rhetorical gambit, for it will be seen that such beliefs strongly influenced Yoshida's so-called anti-war activities during the Pacific War. Nor was this incompatible with his passing acknowledgment of "fascist" tendencies in Japan; such seeming contradiction would later become neatly resolved by postulating the existence of "Red fascism."

Yoshida's position on the Soviet Union was not entirely Manichean. On one occasion, for example, he acknowledged to Craigie that the Japanese army had begun to prepare for war against Russia "at a time when Russian power in the Far East was relatively weak"—largely because after abrogation of the Anglo-Japanese Alliance Japan had become isolated, the military had sought to counter this with rearmament, and "it was necessary to have an enemy." Implicitly, then, Yoshida recognized both the spuriousness of some of his government's strategic planning after World War One, and the *defensive* origins of Russia's own military build-up in the Far East in the 1930s.[89]

By 1936, however, he was not concerned with original motives, but rather with the "impregnable" defense the Russians had created in north Asia. And, even more than the hard power of the Soviet Army, he dwelt upon the subtle and corrosive influence of the Communist International. Thus in a meeting with Eden on July 30, 1936, he emphasized, as Eden summarized it, "the very considerable preoccupations of the Japanese Government in respect of communism which existed not only in China, but also in Japan, and was an important element in both countries." "The recent mutinies in Tokyo," Eden was told, in reference to the February 26th Incident, "had been due to Communist influence. It was also important to diminish the Communist influence in China itself." Yoshida then went on to admit that the Japanese government had only recently come to realize that the Russians were far better armed in the Far East than had been anticipated.[90]

Approximately a week later Yoshida dwelt upon the same themes in a more emotional manner during a conversation with an old acquaintance, Sir Francis Lindley, then chairman of the Japan Society of London and formerly ambassador to Japan. Lindley described him as "more earnest than coherent in his observations about the Russian danger," and advised that Yoshida "evidently wished to be taken very seriously." He reported this portion of the conversation to the Foreign Office as follows:

> But the root of our problems, he declared, was not China but Russia. Communism was exercising the mind of the Japanese Govt. far more than was the Chinese question. He had found many younger officers in Manchuria tainted with communistic ideas. And it was a matter of life and death for Japan that these ideas shall not prevail. If China came under Bolshevik influence, it would be the ruin of Japan; and, naturally, our interests in China, [though] far less important to us than were Japan's interests to Japan, would be equally ruined. If we could come to some arrangement with Japan about the Russian menace, he did not for a moment doubt that we could find a satisfactory solution to our differences about China. In fact he was confident that he could get a solution put through.[91]

Some months later, when Cadogan questioned Yoshida's allegations that anti-Japanese activities and incidents in China were part of a Soviet conspiracy, Yoshida responded that these were indeed "directed from Moscow." At a meeting in Moscow that very summer, he said, "a decision was taken and communicated to the Communist Headquarters in China directing a campaign of outrages against Japanese citizens."[92]

The British were not at all immune to the anti-communist sentiment, but they hardly shared Yoshida's analysis of the problem. Where the *overt* Soviet military threat to Japan was concerned, they welcomed rather than empathized with Japanese apprehensions to the extent that the northern threat posed a potential check against further Japanese adventures to the south, where Britain's major interests lay. This was suggested in the Foreign Office response to the Piggott memorandum discussed above, and received frequent explication elsewhere. "We must weigh the consequences very carefully before we do anything to alienate the Soviet Government and weaken her as a counter-poise either against Japan in the Far East, or perhaps still more important, against Germany in Europe" is one typical comment.[93] At the same time, it was felt that to join with Japan against Russia would have only "temporary value" at best, for once having eliminated the Russian problem Japan could be expected to renew her pressures against British interests in China.[94] What Britain desired was neither Japanese nor Russian victory, but rather a continued stalemate between the two Asian powers: "We do not wish to see Russia crush Japan, because that would bring us back to the pre-war Russian menace to India & possibly Europe also, with the new & insidious weapon of Communist agitation in Russia's armoury. I suggest that our policy be to make Japan pay something on account for what she wants, & to remain neutral in her conflict with Russia, meanwhile preparing ourselves to meet our own ordeal later. We might judiciously apply such pressure to either side as appeared possible to prevent either from obtaining a decisive victory."[95]

Where the issue of China and more *covert* Soviet or communist influence was concerned, the British were similarly disinclined to accept Yoshida's analysis. On the contrary, they saw Japan as the greater threat to British interests in China, and with considerable reasonableness turned the Yoshida formula around: rather than Japan's being a bulwark against communism in Asia, as one member of the Far Eastern section observed, "Japanese pressure on China seems more likely to turn that country toward Communism, (or at least Russia) than would be likely if they helped China to become strong and independent."[96] Despite British coolness toward his version of the issue, however, Yoshida persisted in making anti-communism a part of the first draft of his secret plan.

While theories of pendulums, history's harsh hand, and communist conspiracy were integral to Yoshida's outlook, British disagreement on such matters did not preordain a failure of rapprochement between the two countries. For the ultimate touchstone for both was national interest, and the most crucial aspect of Yoshida's endeavors in London lay in his attempt to convince the British that they would profit, not only in China but *globally*, by appeasing Japan. His tactical objectives were traditional: to undercut China's ability to run "squealing to the U.K. and the U.S.A." (Cadogan's summary phrase) by first working out a Great-Power agreement among Japan, Great Britain, and later the United States, and then imposing this on China. As Cadogan interpreted it, "we should lend a hand with the big stick."[97]

The heart of the strategic argument for British acquiescence in this tactic was essentially summarized by Eden, following a conversation in December 1936 in which Yoshida expressed the view that the intensity of Anglo-Japanese commercial rivalry lay at the root of the current alienation between the two countries, and indeed had been the major factor behind Japan's conclusion of the Anti-Comintern Pact. "He fully admitted the intensity of our trade rivalry," Eden noted. "At the same time he felt that this was in a large measure due to the situation in China. Japan had lost a large part of her Chinese market owing to the boycott of Japanese goods in that country and to other causes. If the position in China would be improved and Japanese trade with that country increased, the pressure of her competition in the Dominions and in the Colonies would be correspondingly relaxed."[98] Yoshida frankly acknowledged that this was a barterer's deal. "He would not hide from me," Craigie wrote that same December, "that, of the increase in trade which might be expected to result from a marked improvement in China's economic and political situation, Japan would expect to get the lion's share; but this in turn would automatically reduce the Japanese pressure on British markets and would make a commercial agreement between the two countries far easier."[99]

This, garnished with rhetorical genuflections to territorial integrity, the Open Door, and such, was the pivot of the "Yoshida plans" to be discussed in the following chapter. It seemed dispassionate and logical, but was in fact optimistic, perhaps even sentimental, to the extent that it rejected that fatalistic economic determinism which gripped so many of Yoshida's contemporaries. In August 1936, George Sansom, the great scholar and esteemed financial adviser to the British embassy in Tokyo, had already submitted a bleak, and quite prescient, assessment of Japan's dilemma and the stalemate between the two island empires:

> One is therefore pushed to the conclusion that, if a breakdown of the Japanese economic programme occurs, it is likely to come through difficulties in foreign trade; and here it is significant that it is the British Empire which is felt to be the main obstacle to Japan's overseas commercial expansion and therefore to her legitimate economic and political development. The bearing of this feeling upon the problem of Anglo-Japanese relations is important. Japanese diplomats, and some Japanese in high places who have a sentimental connexion with England, talk of traditional Anglo-Japanese friendship; and that kind of language evokes a pleasant sentimental reaction on our side. But it represents no political reality and the tradition, such as it is, is almost worthless unless it can be nourished by concrete benefits which we are expected to confer. In Japan's international relations to-day, if the Soviet Union figures as the enemy, Great Britain figures as the dangerous rival, conspiring all along the line against Japan. . . . The Government which came into power after the February "incident" is committed to reforms which it obviously cannot carry out, since no Government can overnight make Japan rich in natural resources and find the answer to her diplomatic problems. Consequently, if Mr. Hirota cannot perform an impressive conjuring trick this year, he is likely to be replaced by a more authoritarian Prime Minister with an even more ambitious policy, and a determination to control industry and finance in the interests of that policy. This would not solve all Japan's economic problems, but it might push them into the background by furnishing another "crisis." The crisis might occur in domestic politics or it might take the form of a new adventure on the Asiatic continent. Fundamentally, the position is that

> Japan is a small, poor country determined to expand, and if she cannot expand, she will explode. Her economic expansion seems for the moment to be checked, largely, she supposes, by the British Empire; so that, if she explodes, we shall be in some measure responsible. Anyhow, we shall be blamed.[100]

At year's end, in the very midst of Yoshida's frenetic endeavors to transcend the impasse, Sansom calmly informed his government that "a comprehensive arrangement . . . is likely to be extremely difficult, because our interests are, fundamentally, opposed at every point."[101]

FIVE

The Secret Yoshida-Eden Plan of 1936–1937

As presented by economic analysts such as George Sansom, the prognosis that by the mid-1930s contradictions between British and Japanese objectives were irreconcilable was almost Leninist in its grim certitude. And in retrospect the prediction appears to have been confirmed. The period of Yoshida's ambassadorship in London marked the decisive parting of the ways for the two former allies, the two dominant foreign powers in China.

Although Yoshida looked back on these years as a high point in his prewar career,[1] they were a period of transparent discomfort and failure. As an Oriental in the Occident, he was removed from the milieu in which his high-handed style could be indulged. And while fully cognizant of the diplomatic challenges that confronted him, Yoshida was probably less aware of the personal liabilities he carried to London. He was, simply, not greatly respected as a diplomat by many of his British counterparts. His vita in the February 1936 listing prepared by the British embassy in Tokyo carried little more than the bland and somewhat surprising notation that "Mr. Yoshida does not give the impression of being a man of strong personality, but is amiable and agreeable to talk to. He speaks English and French, but is not very fluent in either language. . . ."[2] In virtually all quarters, he was prejudged as "not of the calibre of his predecessor," Matsudaira Tsuneo.[3]

These personal handicaps were compounded by the succession of incidents and events that occurred in Asia between 1936 and 1938 and tended to substantiate Sansom's gloomy presentiment of inevitable conflict. Domestic politics in Japan appeared to be disintegrating; in the year between his arrival in London and the China Incident, Yoshida was forced to deal with three different cabinets (Hirota, Hayashi, Konoe). Yet instability within Japan seemed counterbalanced by mounting consistency in the pursuit of an aggressive policy in Asia. Separatist movements promoted by Japan in north China; the incident that became a war and then escalated further, in Nanking, to an explosion of murderous frustrations; the aerial attacks on the vessels *Ladybird* and *Panay*, contemptuous punctuation marks in a steady encroachment on Western interests in China—all took place while Yoshida was serving in London, and it was his task to interpret them to the British. Incidents now all but forgotten consumed hours of time and quantities of spleen: Japanese smuggling in north China pinched His Majesty's Government severely, for it denied crucial revenues to the British-administered Chinese Maritime Customs;[4] Japanese police in Formosa broke the jaw of a British naval officer in a rather symbolic incident which pained the entire Foreign Office for months (the Keelung Incident); the British ambassador to Peking was attacked and injured by Japanese aircraft while riding in his auto. While Yoshida preached conciliation and compromise to Great Britain, in many British eyes Japan had virtually presented the Western powers with a "Hands Off China" *diktat* ever since the Amau Doctrine of 1934, and thus all but precluded meaningful cooperation.[5]

Prior to the China Incident, however, and to a lesser extent even thereafter, Yoshida eschewed pessimism of the Sansom mode on several grounds. To begin with, he discerned two contrary lines of thought concerning Japan among British policy-makers—much as he perceived "two schools" within Japan. He informed Malcolm Kennedy at the time that he found "the friends of Japan more friendly and the hostile critics more hostile" than ever before.[6] The same impression was conveyed in a letter to Makino in August

1936, in which Yoshida referred to both "bad currents" and "unexpectedly favorable feelings" regarding Japan. In such figures as Neville Chamberlain, Austen Chamberlain, Sir Samuel Hoare, Sir Horace Wilson, Sir Warren Fisher, R. A. Butler, Sir Francis Lindley, and Sir Robert Craigie, Yoshida found relatively sympathetic souls with whom to lament Britain's great diplomatic blunder of bygone years: abrogation of the Anglo-Japanese Alliance.[7] And beyond this, he firmly believed that these more favorable attitudes rested upon concrete considerations which could be exploited to Japan's advantage. These material considerations were by no means insubstantial.

First, while the crisis of British capitalism had prompted discriminatory tariffs against Japan, aspects of that crisis suggested that Britain might be forced to cooperate with Japan for economic reasons in the imminent future. The Japanese market was extremely important to Britain, just as the United Kingdom bulked large in Japan's export trade, and thus commercial protectionism was double-edged and conceivably negotiable.[8] It was also Yoshida's belief that mounting unemployment in Great Britain, which he observed with keen interest, was forcing British policymakers to recognize the necessity of enlarging their China market, and any such endeavors would require collaboration with Japan.[9]

Second, where China in particular was concerned, the traditional view of cooperative imperialism retained potent appeal to many of Britain's old China hands, who still hoped against hope that, as the British ambassador to Nanking phrased it in late 1936, "China was big enough for both of us."[10] For political and technical as well as financial reasons, moreover, Britain's own schemes for Chinese "reconstruction" would be best served by Japanese participation. This was especially true in the critical area of loans for railroad development, where British officials privately acknowledged that it was "by no means an easy or desirable alternative" to proceed without Japanese cooperation.[11] In addition, Yoshida was gratified to hear a number of Britain's purported China experts describe China as "rotten" and incapable of putting its own house in order. Such views, he hoped, would prevail and persuade policy-makers in London of the mutual benefits to be derived from acceding to Japan's heightened political involvement on the continent.[12]

Third, policy-makers in London were overwhelmingly preoccupied with Europe and the Nazi menace. Yoshida found his most sympathetic listeners within the Neville Chamberlain group, and to the end of his life he defended Chamberlain's appeasement of Hitler as statesmanlike and realistic, given the situation.[13] More germane to his own objectives, it was Yoshida's hope that the German menace would also predispose Britain to appease Japan in Asia in order to free its hand on the home front.

Fourth, and related to the above, Britain's position in Asia, militarily as well as economically, was extremely vulnerable. In a January 1936 memorandum on "The Importance of Anglo-Japanese Friendship," the War Office noted that "events are moving fast in the Far East, and it is clear that we are already faced with the prospect of a gradual loss of our whole commercial position there by peaceful penetration on the part of Japan, and that without a shot being fired. A political agreement with Japan does, however, still appear to offer a chance of saving much of our position, and that too by peaceful means, if we will but seize the opportunity." Peaceful means were in fact all Britain could muster at this juncture. The report acknowledged that, "so long as affairs in Europe remain unsettled, our interests in the Far East, at any rate north of Singapore, are at the mercy of the Japanese. It would seem a reasonable precaution, therefore, to try by every means and even at some cost, to safeguard, by an amicable agreement with Japan, interests which we are unable to protect by military measures."[14]

Yoshida's sensitivity to this situation rendered his own position on Japanese militarism ambivalent and opportunistic. Although Japanese aggression had thus far been detrimental to the Anglo-Japanese relationship, the specter of further aggression might indeed prompt Britain to adopt a more conciliatory policy. Thus in August 1936 Yoshida wrote Makino that he felt as if he were "walking on thin ice," in constant fear that an incident might occur in north China and undercut his position in London.[15] But in April 1937, he was expressing a far more sanguine view of the *threat* of such an eventuality: "If an incident occurs in the Far East, Great Britain may not be able to protect its rights if Japan becomes the enemy. That is why, I think, the British authorities are paying attention to the Anglo-Japanese relationship."[16]

Fifth, although British diplomats as a whole did not agree with the substance of Yoshida's analysis of the Soviet threat–and indeed desired that the Soviet Union be maintained as a counterpoise to both German aggression in Europe and Japanese aggression in Asia[17]–Yoshida nonetheless believed that the fundamental anti-communist animus of his British counterparts could be exploited in working toward Anglo-Japanese rapprochement, especially where China was concerned.

Finally, and more tenuously, Yoshida could find some encouragement in the latent tension within the Anglo-American relationship. The Foreign Office constantly reminded him that the United States would have to be consulted before any decisive Anglo-Japanese agreement might be made, and on the surface Yoshida readily accepted this. It has been seen, however, that Yoshida regarded the United States as fundamentally lacking in "diplomatic sense"[18]–and British diplomats frequently expressed similar vexation. Trans-Atlantic cooperation during this period was riddled with disagreement, and this was directly reflected in policy toward Asia. London was more willing than Washington to give serious consideration to proposals for positive joint action in China, and, like Yoshida, many diplomats in the Foreign Office were inclined to regard the lofty "moral diplomacy" enunciated by the State Department as vacuous, unrealistic, and self-serving.[19]

Yoshida accepted the ambassadorship to London with the understanding that he would be given a relatively free hand by his government. His departure from Japan in May 1936 was accompanied by press accounts, duly noted in England, to the effect that he had consulted with Saionji and representatives of the army and business community "to assure perfect enforcement of Japan's British policy"; that he would devote his attention to

Anglo-Japanese conflicts in China and Japanese trade problems in the Dominions and British colonies; and that while he would have considerable initiative, "any special exchange of documentary instructions" would be avoided, and no formal agreement between the two countries was to be expected in the immediate future. In a personal interview with the press, Yoshida professed to see an upturn in Anglo-Japanese relations, and emphasized the necessity of grounding diplomacy in "well-established facts" rather than "wild flights of imagination." His primary task in London, he explained, would thus be the relatively preliminary one of cleansing a poisoned atmosphere, for "the situation between the two countries has actually not advanced so far yet as to need or permit of the conclusion of any special treaty or agreement." The British-owned *Japan Advertiser*, like the Foreign Office itself, applauded this as "a statement of obvious fact. . . . Mr. Yoshida's task, it can be confidently said, is neither conceivable in Japan or acceptable in Britain as one of negotiating agreements."[20]

The lessons in history and politics Yoshida subsequently attempted to impress upon his high-placed contacts in London represented his endeavor to clear the atmosphere—although frequently, as seen in the preceding chapter, his own "well-established facts" were regarded by his listeners as themselves little more than "wild flights of imagination." At the same time, however, and contrary to his remarks upon departure, Yoshida did succumb to the Lorelei of attempting to bring about a more formal *modus vivendi.* The initiative caught his British counterparts off guard, but Yoshida pursued this so tenaciously that in the final analysis the sum of the first year of his ambassadorship becomes the story of this concerted endeavor. And the endeavor itself, by virtue of its detailed nature, provides an unusually concrete case study of the possibility of imperialist cooperation in a time of genuine crisis.

Shortly after his arrival, Yoshida began a series of confidential conversations with representatives of the Foreign Office (notably Deputy Under Secretary Alexander Cadogan and Foreign Secretary Anthony Eden), as well as with other influential British figures; the talks were clearly directed at providing the basis for a comprehensive resolution of outstanding issues between the two former allies. On October 26, 1936, he submitted the first detailed "Yoshida plan," to which the Foreign Office replied on January 18, after extensive internal study. Five days later Yoshida responded equivocally to this reply, in a manner that infuriated the Foreign Office, and on January 28 he submitted a reconsidered memorandum which failed to mollify the exasperation of the British side. On June 2, 1937, Yoshida presented a revised unofficial draft proposal to the Foreign Office. This represented, in his view, a statement both generalized and specific enough to provide the working basis for formal negotiations; and it remains a moot question whether it would have led to meaningful compromise had the China Incident not occurred on July 7 and forced Britain to cancel the discussions.

Although the initiative throughout was Yoshida's, and at first was met with a heavy measure of scorn, his endeavor was regarded with increasing seriousness by the Foreign Office and later became known as the "secret Yoshida-Eden plan." It eventually involved the Treasury, Colonial Office, Dominions Office, and Board of Trade, as well as a variety of prominent British statesmen whom Yoshida personally recruited as potential supporters. By June 1937 both governments do seem to have come to regard Yoshida's proposals as a potential basis for serious negotiation. On July 28, the Japanese foreign minister announced in the Diet that prior to the outbreak of hostilities in north China, "conversations between Japan and Great Britain with regard to [the] Far Eastern question had made substantial progress."[21] And as late as the latter part of 1939, long after Yoshida had returned to Japan, it was British policy that His Majesty's Government was "ready to resume consideration of [the] Eden-Yoshida project of 1937 for world-wide Anglo-Japanese economic arrangement," in order "to ensure a peace generous to Japan and equitable to China"—or, as the position was relayed by the British ambassador to Stanley Hornbeck, who had not exactly mellowed in his antipathy to appeals for generosity to Japan, simply "a peace equitable both to Japan and China."[22]

HOPE VENTURED: THE FIRST YOSHIDA PLAN

Yoshida broached the desirability of "a definite agreement as to policy" to Eden as early as July 30, 1936, and repeated this to Sir Hugh Knatchbull on the same day. He essayed a general proposal which Knatchbull, soon to depart as ambassador to China, described as "odd" and Eden also found rather curious. Eden summarized it as follows:

> The Ambassador went on to elaborate a somewhat obscure proposal, which he said was entirely his own, that Japan should be charged with the maintenance of law and order in China, while we should be charged with the irrigation of that country, which was an immense task, and which we had special qualifications to carry out. Nothing mattered more to China's prosperity than that the perpetual menace of floods should be met. I asked his Excellency whether it was in his mind that the United States should be included in any understanding that was reached and also what view he thought the Chinese were likely to take of Japan's exercising law and order throughout the country. I should have thought they would quite certainly have said that they would prefer to do this themselves. In reply to my first question, the Ambassador said that he supposed the United States would have to be a party to any agreement that was come to, for otherwise they would not feel content with the situation. He thought that they might also be allotted a role in this task of restoring the prosperity of China. As to law and order, it was really not possible for the Chinese to pretend that they could maintain it themselves. There were now three Governments in China—one in the north, one in the centre and one in the south. He knew that the Chinese said the troubles in the north were due to the Japanese, but this did not alter the fact that the Southern Government was quite incapable of keeping law and order and this was certainly not due to the Japanese, who were not there.[23]

The concept that Japan assume responsibility for "law and order" in China remained implicit in Yoshida's later and more specific proposals. It implied de facto Japanese control in China, and was unpalatable to the British; Yoshida argued this was necessary to gain support of the military party in Japan,[24] although he seemed to find it a happy prospect himself. The irrigation proposal was not emphasized in the first Yoshida plan of October 26, but re-emerged in his later revisions of this plan. It also elicited little enthusiasm in London, possibly because waterworks did not evoke visions of immediate dividends.

The Far Eastern section of the Foreign Office was aware of Yoshida's uneasy relationship with his own government, and thus constantly uncertain as to how consonant his "initiatives" were with official thinking in Tokyo. In September Yoshida indicated that he had received general instructions to work toward an Anglo-Japanese agreement, although as yet no concrete proposals; later he said he had been given virtually *"carte blanche."* Despite this uncertain note, the Foreign Office encouraged him to proceed with his self-described "dream" of formulating a basis on which substantial negotiations might begin.[25] On October 7, for example, Cadogan referred to the July 30 conversation with Eden and asked Yoshida "whether he was yet in a position to suggest any definite proposals or line of action." Yoshida avoided a direct reply, indicating that he wished first "to consult with his own people," and then went on to deliver what Cadogan described as "some rather cryptic remarks" to the effect that Japanese "statesmen" had been incorrect in attempting to negotiate directly with the Chinese government: "no good results had been achieved, and in his opinion it would be better for his Government to consult with other Governments interested and endeavour to agree on a joint line with the Chinese Government." Cadogan did not respond to this, although he later privately condemned it. He did encourage Yoshida on the possibility of joint financial assistance to China for the development of communications, production, and the like.[26]

The "first Yoshida plan" was received by the Foreign Office on October 26 through the irregular channel of the chancellor of the exchequer, a post then held by Neville Chamberlain. This penchant for indirect diplomacy was to prove a constant source of irritation to the Foreign Office, and certainly in this case did not predispose the Far Eastern section to treat him charitably. "The Ambassador has an irresistible desire to discuss policy with everyone except those who are primarily directly concerned with it" was a typical comment on the Yoshida style—and although it is questionable whether England's own ambassadors abroad were more scrupulous in remaining within the formal groove, Yoshida's prestige within the Foreign Office undeniably suffered as a result of this.[27] Despite this inauspicious beginning, the Yoshida memorandum was discussed throughout the British government over the ensuing several months. It read as follows:

Draft Memorandum

(Communicated by the Japanese Ambassador to the Chancellor of the Exchequer.)

(Strictly Confidential)

The Ambassador for Japan has received instructions from Tokyo to approach the British Government with a view to establishing a definite understanding between Japan and Great Britain concerning all matters in which their joint interests are affected.

No specific instructions as to the form of this understanding have been laid down, so that the Ambassador judges that he has full authority to use his own initiative in the matter, and he accordingly puts forward the following suggestions for the consideration of the British Government, the result of which he will communicate to the Japanese Government.

The Ambassador considers the present situation in China not only constitutes the principal source of mutual misunderstanding, but also represents the most vital issue to Japan. He is of the opinion that any agreement between Great Britain and Japan for stabilising this situation will have far-reaching results on other issues outstanding between the two Governments, in addition to securing a stabilising force for peace in the Far East.

The Ambassador is fully aware that there are many difficulties before a satisfactory solution can be arrived at, but he believes that a genuine desire to overcome these difficulties in a spirit of mutual understanding can bring about the desired result, and to this end he submits the following proposals for consideration:—

(*a*) Both countries will undertake to respect in full the territorial rights and sovereignty of China, south of the Great Wall.

(*b*) Both countries will support in its entirety the principle of the "open door" in China, as established by existing treaties, and will respect the integrity of the Chinese Maritime Customs in all treaty ports in China.

(*c*) Both countries will recognize and respect foreign rights and interests in China. It must, however, be pointed out that in recent years foreign rights in China have not been respected in their entirety by the Chinese Government. Specific examples of this are to be found in the trade boycotts, which the Chinese Government have taken no measures to oppose, and in the student agitations, which no effective measures have been taken to check. The Japanese Government feels that this state of affairs is partly due to lack of co-operation between the interested Powers, and it is therefore suggested that when instances occur of failure on the part of the Chinese Government to respect such rights, or in the event of unacceptable attempts being made by the Chinese Government to undermine those rights, or in the event of boycotts against the trade of any country, the British and Japanese Governments should consult together with a view to joint representation on the matter at issue. Similarly, it is suggested that before any action is taken by either Great Britain or Japan to alter or modify the existing treaties concerning China, the matter should be frankly and fully discussed between the two countries.

(*d*) The principle of a stabilised and commercially prosperous China is fully admitted to be a vital necessity to Japan, seeing that a prosperous China affords the natural market for the output of Japanese industry. It cannot be gainsaid, however, that existing conditions in China militate to a dangerous extent against China's recovery to a normal state, and it is therefore suggested that a scheme of active co-operation should be evolved with a view to terminating the recurrent disorders now prevalent in China.

It is felt that the Chinese Government is seriously attempting to restore order and to develop China's resources, but success in this attempt must be dependent upon financial and political assistance from other Powers, which alone can enable China to effect the maintenance of order, steps for flood prevention, and the extension of communications, which are necessary to real reconstruction. It is therefore proposed that there should be frank discussion on the possibility of giving the requisite financial and political aid to the Chinese Government.

In connexion with this financial aid, it is considered that a more rapid and satisfactory conclusion can be arrived at by initial discussion between Great Britain and Japan, and it is therefore suggested that a plan should be evolved before being jointly submitted to China, the United States of America and other interested Powers. It is understood that the possibility of rendering financial aid to China has been explored by Sir Frederick Leith-Ross, and his recommendations on this point could form the basis of such discussion.

(*e*) The Japanese Government feels that one of the prevalent dangers which obstruct the Nanking Government in its attempt to secure order in China is the steady spread of Communist influence by the Soviet Government. It is feared that the British Government fails to realize the danger to all foreign interests in China which will result if the steady extension of this influence is not checked by the Chinese Government. The attention of the British Government is especially drawn to the danger existing in Western China from the Soviet advance in Sinkiang. It is suggested, therefore, that discussions with the Chinese Government should include the question of assistance in checking the spread of communism.

It is recognized, however, that the problem of restoring political order in China must depend upon the military force of the Central Government. Seeing that Japan is the country most vitally interested in the restoration of that order, it is suggested that an arrangement should be come to between the Nanking Government and Japan for the provision by Japan of long-term credits for the arms and ammunition that may be required for the forces of the Central Government. It is also suggested that an adequate number of Japanese military officers should be employed by the Central Government in an advisory capacity.

The Ambassador thinks it right to make it quite clear that this suggestion does not imply any intention to obtain military domination of China. The objects aimed at are twofold; firstly, to ensure that the channel for the importation of arms and ammunition into China should be limited to one country only, so as to obstruct as far as possible the opportunities of independent generals obtaining supplies elsewhere; and secondly, to strengthen the unification of Japanese Government policy in China. At the present moment the non-uniformity of Japanese policy in China is due to the fact that the Foreign Office deals direct with the Central Government at Nanking and army policy is chiefly directed towards North China, while naval policy is directed more towards the South. By the appointment of naval and military officers in an advisory capacity to the Nanking Government the present lack of unification can be avoided.

The Ambassador is of the opinion that the two questions raised in this suggestion should be dealt with by direct negotiations between Japan and China, but if the two countries should fail to come to agreement in the matter, the British Government's sympathetic assistance would be welcomed.

(*f*) One of the principal results of the slow disintegration of China as a world market has been the inability of Japan to find her natural market for her increased industrialisation. A direct consequence of this loss of the Chinese market has been the increased export of Japanese goods to Great Britain and her Colonies in quantities which have caused unfortunate trade controversies. The Japanese Government feels with justice that a fair market should be accorded to the products of Japanese industry, and that trade barriers, such as high tariffs and arbitrary quotas, represent a cause of ill-feeling between the two countries which it is desirable to remove by a mutual understanding of each other's difficulties.

On the premises that the two countries will jointly assist in bringing about the restoration of China's prosperity, it is suggested that Great Britain and Japan should give evidence of their mutual goodwill by discussion of a reasonable quota for Japanese exports. Such a proposal might include the acceptance by the British Government, on their side, of the quantities of textiles and rayon exported by Japan during 1935 as a basis, less a reduction on the Japanese side of 20 per cent. Such an arrangement might be accepted for a period of five years, at the termination of which further negotiations could be reopened as circumstances dictate.

(*g*) It is suggested that if an agreement on these lines can be arrived at, the British Government should use its good offices to obtain similar agreements between the British Dominions and Japan.

(*h*) It is suggested that there should be closer financial relations between the two countries. An exchange of views on the Treasury policies might be considered.

(*i*) It is clear that any agreement on the above lines arrived at between the two countries would result in a similarity of the view of both countries on the naval question, so that in the event of such agreement being arrived at, it might be considered feasible to revive the Naval Conference on the basis of this similarity of view.

It is also suggested that any understanding arrived at might be extended on the lines of a defensive agreement, embodying an understanding of benevolent neutrality on the part of Great Britain in the event of war between Japan and the Soviet, in return for an undertaking by the Japanese Government to protect British possessions and trade routes in the East in the event of Great Britain being involved in a war elsewhere.

(*j*) Similarly, if an agreement on the above lines is arrived at, it is suggested that the Japanese Government might consider co-operation with Great Britain in any plan accepted by the latter for the reconstruction of the League of Nations.[28]

HOPE DISPARAGED: BRITAIN'S RESPONSE AND YOSHIDA'S HUMILIATION

The Foreign Office assumed that the memorandum had been prepared after consultation with Tokyo, although George Sansom ventured the opinion that points (a) through (e) bore Yoshida's personal imprint.[29] Responses to the plan came at several levels: skepticism concerning its practicality as a comprehensive working basis for serious talks; nagging intimations that it nonetheless might be all that Britain really had to go on if it hoped to take any positive action to resolve the Anglo-Japanese impasse; and point-by-point analysis to determine where cooperation might in fact be feasible.

On the broadest level, the internal Foreign Office response was hardly encouraging. "An embarrassing thing to comment upon" was one immediate annotation; "I am afraid I have to add that I have no great faith in the sincerity of this approach" was another.[30] A later commentator culled some prevailing clichés in expressing "fear that when we get behind the screen of pious hopes and unexceptional platitudes, there will be very little that he will be able to offer us (and a great deal that he will be made to demand). However that remains to be seen."[31] Ambassador Clive cabled, "What is required from us is specific and concrete, what is offered to us is vague and abstract"—but he also ventured the hope that the Foreign Office would not discourage Yoshida but rather "keep him in play."[32] And that hope, indeed the very phrase itself, became the watchword of the British response. Britain could not afford to burst the bubble, Cadogan wrote on December 11; "we rather want to keep the Japanese in play, in the hope that Japanese policy *may* undergo a change."[33] There was little alternative, and indeed when Clive turned lukewarm on the matter near the end of the year, his colleagues in London found themselves unexpectedly provoked. "The atmosphere for serious negotiations is certainly not very good," one responded, "but is there any real prospect of improving it without such an attempt as these discussions with M. Yoshida represent?"[34]

From a different perspective, the overall British response can also be seen as a combination of moral righteousness and *Realpolitik*. The former emerged in consistent pronouncements of Britain's respect for Chinese integrity—its opposition to any proposals that might result in the imposition of "foreign control"—and also in asserting that Britain had abandoned the old tactics of joint *démarche*, secret diplomacy, and bilateralism.[35] Yoshida was constantly reminded that any Anglo-Japanese agreement that might result from the talks would be subject to consultation with the United States and China. In the best Confucian tradition, the Foreign Office also indulged in extensive commentary on Japan's lack of "sincerity";[36] in this respect, the British memoranda *about* Yoshida and Japan in the 1930s pose an ironic mirror to the memoranda *by* Yoshida about China a decade earlier. All governments, one can probably conclude, see themselves as embodying "sincerity" and the states with which they are dealing as in need of "self-reflection"; it is an unconscious matter of self-interest, rather than any peculiar cultural value.

The *Realpolitik* of the general British response assumed greater resonance in the context of this moralism, for it involved not only explicit recognition that the Yoshida plan was fundamentally exploitative, but also implicit indications that Britain itself had not entirely forsaken the old attitudes of power politics in China. What had changed most notably was the power Britain could marshal, and the attitudes followed reluctantly. Thus "foreign control" was undesirable in good part because the era of the *Pax Britannica* was waning, and in the prevailing situation such control in China would now be predominantly Japanese. The most optimistic view expressed prior to the October 26 memorandum was that Yoshida "tends to regard China as a passive body on which Japan and Gt. Britain can operate,"[37] but even this did not long survive. The concept of political assistance contained in items (d) and (e) of the Yoshida memorandum was the giveaway in British eyes: "This is the bait which Mr. Yoshida holds out to his own military to induce them to call off aggression in North China and acquiesce in the Gaimusho policy," and, should Britain acquiesce in this, it "would in effect make China a vassal State of Japan."[38] "The kernel of the whole problem," another officer wrote, was "whether there is to be general appeasement & cooperation, which is what we want, or a sort of combine between us & Japan to exploit China, which *at best* is what Japan wants (actually she would like to do all the exploitation with our connivance at the price of a few pickings to us)."[39]

But whether described as "cooperation" or "combine," the British concern was in the final analysis material rather than moral, exemplified in such sacrosanct phrases as "order and prosperity in China for the sake of British trade," and "we are resolved to maintain our rights and protect our interests."[40] "We seek no special advantages ourselves," Cadogan commented, in the classic status-quo phraseology of a power which has already expanded and exploited, and now finds its acquisitions threatened;[41] and to some extent Britain was saying to Japan at this juncture: it is immoral to take from China and ourselves what we ourselves previously took from China. At a somewhat later date, John Brenan of the Foreign Office frankly noted that "the truth of the matter is that we acquired our dominant position in China as the result of our wars with that country in the nineteenth century," and he described that dominant position as consisting not merely of "numerous and valuable commercial enterprises," but also "our privileges of an unusual and extraterritorial nature such as the British hold on the Customs Service, our control over the administration of the Shanghai settlement, our personnel in the railways and the maintenance of our shipping interests along the coasts and waterways of China. That is the meaning which we have attached to the Japanese assurances to respect our rights and interests." And, as Brenan went on to note, even the pro-Anglo-American groups in Japan would not and could not assure this, for to do so would be to repudiate the "national sacrifices" of the 1930s.[42]

Here then were basic contradictions: between Britain's professed opposition to foreign control and its commitment to preservation of its own established levers of control in China; and between the British and Japanese interpretations of cooperation and reciprocity.[43] Beyond this, prior to the China Incident some British observers simply believed that Japan would ultimately fail in its endeavor to dominate China. China, one Foreign Office member wrote in the minutes concerning the October 26 memorandum, "is like an india-rubber ball: you can make an impression on it by squeezing it, but only so long as the pressure is kept up. Does Japan really contemplate with equanimity the prospect of having to exert pressure in this way indefinitely?" The prospect was unlikely, and the conclusion pragmatic: Japan "is not likely ultimately to rule the roost in a degree which will make it worth our while to antagonize the Chinese people with whom we want to trade for the sake of such favours as Japan will allow us."[44] Moralism, unlike special rights and interests, was apparently negotiable–although after the China Incident the latter, threatened with total Japanese eradication, also became less inviolable to the diplomats at Whitehall.[45]

Yoshida met with Eden on November 6 to discuss the October 26 memorandum in general terms and indicated, somewhat enigmatically, that, although he did not actually write it himself, it represented his personal suggestions within a framework of definite instructions from Tokyo. The two men then skimmed the specific points of the proposal. Eden welcomed the territorial integrity and open-door guarantees of items (a) and (b), while taking deliberate care to avoid Yoshida's significant qualifying phrase "south of the Great Wall." Regarding (c), the joint representations item, Eden made clear, in a more genteel way, the Foreign Office view that this implied joint *démarche*, the big stick, and was practically and morally unacceptable; Yoshida took no exception to this, and said he had merely wished to emphasize mutual respect for each other's interests, and particularly to reassure Britain concerning its interests "in the centre of China."

Items (d) and (e), on assistance and anti-communism, were of particular interest to Eden as indeed to the entire Foreign Office, and on this occasion the foreign secretary sought to draw out what Yoshida had in mind by Japanese "political assistance." "Somewhat to my surprise," Eden recorded, Yoshida "explained that this referred to Japanese relations with Chinese generals." With no great clarity, Yoshida indicated he envisioned Japan ceasing to meddle in warlord politics as in the past, and concentrating its political support instead on creation of a strong central government in China. When Eden questioned the practicality of Yoshida's proposal in (e) that China buy its arms exclusively from Japan, Yoshida cheerfully stated that this had been included "to give a certain satisfaction to the military and naval authorities in Japan. China now received her arms from a number of sources, and if relations with Japan were once established on a friendly basis it would be of great assistance to the political element in Japan if this concession could be granted."

Eden then indicated that he would have the relevant departments look into the trade and finance items (f, g, h), and Yoshida in return lamented Japan's "unhappily low" credit rating in London; such discrimination was counterproductive, he argued, for eventually it forced Japan to export more and thus intensified the commercial animosity between the two countries. The final two points of the Yoshida plan concerning naval agreement (i) and the League (j) were mentioned in general terms, for, as Eden indicated, they were fundamentally matters of international rather than bilateral concern.[46]

Eden's remarks indicated the parameters of Foreign Office concern fairly well: to avoid the geographically delimiting "trap" in item (a), the intimations of "exclusive cooperation" and "bullying China" in (c), and the "cloven hoof" of political assistance in (d) and (e).[47] Items (f), (g), and (h) were recognized as more particularly the province of the Treasury, Board of Trade, and Dominions and Colonial offices; (i) and (j) were so remote and platitudinous as to deserve little attention at the present time. By far the keenest interest within the Foreign Office, however, was directed toward the possibility of Anglo-Japanese financial assistance suggested in (d). In British eyes this was the most immediately feasible of the concrete Yoshida proposals, the most in keeping with Britain's own current conception of "cooperation" in China, and the "test of Japanese sincerity."[48] It was "the kernel of the whole problem," the key to breaking the "vicious circle,"[49] and, not surprisingly, the issue was narrowed down to those old sinews of empire with which Yoshida had been preoccupied since the 1920s: railroads. Eden dwelt on this in a second meeting with

Yoshida on December 8,[50] and considerable time and interdepartmental correspondence were devoted to sounding out the possibilities of a joint loan for railroad construction in China. In the course of this, two points became clear: first, for a variety of reasons, Britain would be hard pressed to make such a loan unilaterally, and thus *needed* Japanese cooperation;[51] and second, although Anglo-Japanese conversations were in fact taking place on this matter within the established consortium, the Japanese government was reluctant to commit itself on the railway issue prior to resolution of its stalemated negotiations with the Nanking government.[52]

It was not until approximately December 21 that the Foreign Office definitely decided to prepare a written interim reply to Yoshida's memorandum, and Yoshida was informed on the following day that this would be forthcoming. Prior to this there occurred an unpleasant incident which reveals in an unusually vivid manner some of the raw tensions and personal frustrations of the period. On December 10 the Foreign Office was informed through its embassy in Rome that a recent hostile article in the *Times* had so demoralized Viscount Ishii Kikujirō and other "moderates" then attempting to thwart the signing of the Anti-Comintern Pact between Japan and Germany that they had, in effect, given up the fight. "Unhappily," the embassy reported, "the Japanese Ambassador in London had also thrown in his hand when this article appeared and had said that while some little time ago England had shown that she wished for Japanese friendship, it was clear that His Majesty's Government had become irritated at the slowness of proceedings in Japan and had therefore decided that nothing more could be done. The 'Times' article, he told his Government, revealed the real opinion of His Majesty's Government and of the British public about Japan."

This report originated with the Japanese ambassador to Italy, who also indicated that "he had sent his own Counsellor from Rome to London in order to try to encourage M. Yoshida in his task; the latter was inclined to become downhearted, and when this happened he let things slide." Yoshida's averred despair would certainly have deepened had he seen the immediate response to this communication in London. "He is a very feeble person," one officer wrote; "he is really not much use at his job." And Cadogan, who himself had frequently expressed despair over the possibility of an Anglo-Japanese agreement, was more scathing than fair: "As to Mr. Yoshida, I cannot help saying he is a very unsatisfactory [representative]. He gives us wide berth: he communicates his 'suggestions' to the Chancellor of the Exchequer: he consults all sorts of outside people, but he never comes here. . . . He is not in a position to say what are the views of H.M.G., as he makes no effort to find out."[53]

The first draft reply to the October 26 proposals was prepared on December 21. This was sent to Clive with a covering cable which indicated that the pendulum theory had not been entirely without effect, for Clive was specifically asked if this would "help the moderate elements in the Japanese Government."[54] On January 7 a revised draft incorporating views of the Board of Trade and Colonial and Dominion offices was prepared, with an appended acknowledgment that "the reply is not particularly encouraging, from a Japanese point of view."[55] Between January 13 and 15, the Foreign Office and Treasury engaged in a rather vigorous exchange which revealed, among other things, that Treasury was not entirely clear as to what was north and what south of the Great Wall of China. The exchange also confirmed that Chamberlain, then chancellor of the exchequer, had considerable personal interest in the Yoshida plan, and in the final analysis Treasury's last-minute contributions to the formal response indicate that Yoshida's activities outside the Foreign Office, which so irritated Cadogan, had been natural and reasonable.[56]

The final *aide-mémoire*, personally handed to him by Eden on January 18, caused Yoshida unanticipated anguish. Item (a) deleted reference to the Great Wall and applied respect for China's territorial integrity to non-interference in Chinese administration; item (b) on the Open Door was so phrased as to constitute an attack on Japanese smuggling and a reaffirmation of the Maritime Customs Service; (c) was friendly but noncommital on consultation concerning China, while emphasizing protection of British rights and interests. On the pivotal item (d) concerning financial and political assistance to China, the British expressed "the utmost sympathy" for active cooperation, while emphasizing that this must be in forms totally acceptable to China. The projected railway loan received specific mention, and the onus for failure of cooperation on this was placed clearly on the Japanese. This item concluded with a thinly disguised rebuke to prevailing Japanese policy by emphasizing that "stability in China can only be attained if all the Powers exercise the greatest patience and restraint in the face of the occasional disappointments with which they are bound to be confronted."

On point (e) the British flatly rejected Yoshida's original suggestion that military advisors and arms be supplied to the Central Government exclusively by Japan. While not denying the communist threat in China, this section clearly suggested that Britain did not evaluate it in the same terms as did Japan, that is, as basically political, military, and Moscow-directed. On this point, the Foreign Office actually opposed a stronger statement endorsed by Treasury which explicitly related the communist movement to the economic needs of the peasantry.[57] On the crucial items pertaining to trade, (f) and (g), the British did not foreclose the possibility of negotiating a global allocation of markets. But it would have taken an optimistic Japanese indeed to read any real hope for this in the *aide-mémoire*. The imposition of import quotas on textiles in the Colonies was described as entirely defensive, a response to "excessive and unregulated competition," and it was stated unequivocally that the Japanese had been responsible for the failure in 1934 of prior attempts to resolve this.

Item (h) briefly and perfunctorily expressed willingness to exchange views on financial matters; it went into none of the depressing explanations which had been conveyed to Yoshida at an earlier date concerning why Japan could expect little financial aid or favor from London. On (i) and (j), naval matters and the League, Britain stressed the international nature of such matters and difficulty of linking this with any special Anglo-Japanese agreements. The *aide-mémoire* then concluded with an expression of His Majesty's Government's willingness to collaborate with Yoshida "in seeking to overcome the difficulties that exist in a spirit of mutual understanding."[58]

The expression of avowed willingness to collaborate on which the *aide-mémoire* ended was almost immediately devoured in an unusually contemptuous outburst of disgust with Yoshida by members of the Foreign Office. For to the immense exasperation of the Far Eastern section, Yoshida returned three days later to state that he found the British reply "embarrassing" and desired instead merely a vague and general statement; he pressed once again for assurances which would "encourage his people" at home.[59] Cadogan agreed to do this but was privately irate at "the Ambassador's rather extraordinary manoeuvres." "His Excellency was rather more unintelligible than usual," he wrote in his minutes; in a report to Eden, who was abroad at the time, he reduced this to "He was incoherent." A vague declaration such as Yoshida now requested, he felt, was "a piece of paper which will mean nothing and will not advance matters at all." Vansittart summarized the new situation as "very crooked, and a definite step backward. The Japanese always recede when it comes to practical issues. This shows clearly that they are not at present prepared to deal; but if they wish to resort to this crab-like procedure, we must humour them & keep them in play."[60]

This was, as it turned out, but the beginning of what must rank as Yoshida's most degraded week in the Foreign Office dossiers. On January 23 he returned to submit a revision of his original October 26 memorandum, which he hoped would remove "misunderstandable points." As the Foreign Office was aware, he had previously requested permission to return to Tokyo in the near future to consult with his government in person, and in a handwritten covering note to Cadogan he indicated that he hoped for a British reply which he might use "to show your friendly feeling to a very limited [number of] person[s] in the responsible quarter"; he gave assurance that such a note would never be publicly quoted. Yoshida's revised memorandum of January 23 omitted many of those leading (Yoshida would say misleading) phrases the British had particularly seized upon: the "south of the Wall" phrase in (a); intimations of joint *démarche* in (c); suggestions of exclusive Japanese political and military "assistance" in (d) and (e); and so on. Financial assistance to China was again stressed, with new emphasis on the old "flood prevention" concept and no explicit reference to the railway loan; naval agreements and the League were not specifically mentioned. Greatest space was given to relating the trade crisis to the China problem, and urging consideration of an Anglo-Japanese textile agreement.[61]

Cadogan met again with Yoshida on January 25 and pointed out the seemingly obvious: that the new Yoshida document, like the earlier, was fairly specific. A vague British reply such as Yoshida now indicated he wanted would be impossible in such a case.[62] At this juncture, Yoshida apparently requested that Cadogan himself draft an acceptably vague "Japanese" statement—and as he retired to mull this over, his reputation hit rock bottom. On January 27 Ambassador Clive cabled that "with all respect to the Japanese Ambassador, his statement that [the] document he hopes to obtain would strengthen the chance of a more liberal Government in Japan, is nonsense. . . . I am afraid that Mr. Yoshida is not taken very seriously in Japan and I do not understand his persistent desire to return here nor do I see what he hopes to accomplish." Clive's major source of information was apparently Matsudaira Tsuneo (a fleeting glimpse of backbiting within the "pro-Anglo-American clique"?), and he went on to note two seemingly trivial "blunders" Yoshida had made upon leaving for London which had "much annoyed the Court."[63] The cable seems a normal piece of carping from the rather inflexible Clive, but it triggered an extraordinary series of personal attacks on Yoshida among those members of the Far Eastern section to whom it was circulated: "Mr. Yoshida seems to be an accomplished blunderer"; "It would be quite impossible to negotiate anything serious with M. Yoshida"; "Mr. Yoshida is just plainly no good. We can leave it at that: play him, but don't take him seriously." To which Eden penned: "I agree. . . ."[64]

On the day following this indulgence, Yoshida returned to present Cadogan's prose as his own revised statement—a *reductio ad absurdum* of the desirability of rectifying the China problem, trade crisis, and financial relations of the two countries.[65] "All . . . very futile, and rather ridiculous," Cadogan said, and on Feburary 5 Eden personally handed Yoshida a British reply in the same genre. It was the first meeting between the two since Eden had delivered the original British reply of January 18, and Yoshida was frank and short about his reasons for rejecting that: it had been "too detailed and too truthful about difficulties." He asked Eden "to look at the matter to some extent from the Japanese end. There were many people in Japan who believed that the trade rivalry between our two nations all over the world was now so acute that no return to the previous good relations between us was possible. Mr. Yoshida did not share this view, but if the Japanese Government was to be persuaded of this it was wiser not to set out all the difficulties in the way of negotiations at the outset."[66]

HOPE DENIED: THE SECOND YOSHIDA PLAN

Yoshida's projected return to Japan did not materialize, for at the very moment he was engaged in his awkward *pas de deux* with the Foreign Office, the Hirota cabinet he had helped create less than a year previously collapsed (January 23, 1937). And there followed a temporary, intangible change in atmosphere. The foreign minister in the new Hayashi cabinet was an unexpectedly "moderate" choice, Satō Naotake, until then ambassador to Paris. Satō's pronouncements on Anglo-Japanese relations were well received in London, and his policy toward China was judged to be more conciliatory. Despite Clive's earlier fulminations, that is, the new cabinet seemed to betoken the possible turn of the pendulum; and Satō's presence seems to have imperceptibly diminished the perpetual complaint of Cadogan, Clive, and others that Yoshida did not truly represent his government.[67]

Satō's tenure was short-lived, for the Hayashi cabinet resigned on May 31 and, despite Yoshida's expectations, Satō was not carried on as foreign minister by the succeeding government.[68] Even this, however, did not dampen a hesitant hopefulness within the Foreign Office, for although the British regretted Satō's departure, they concluded that the new cabinet, headed by Konoe and with Hirota as foreign minister, "would not necessarily represent a step backward."[69] This rise in anticipations is obliquely reflected in the fact that from spring to early summer of 1937 derogatory remarks about Yoshida become less frequent in the Foreign Office archives, and by June the British were looking forward to serious Anglo-Japanese negotiations. They did not romanticize the possibility of success, but their pessimism seems to have lost its earlier desperate edge. In April, for example, Cadogan informed Norman Davis of the United States that the Foreign Office was awaiting definite proposals from the Japanese government, and summarized the conversation for the record as follows:

> In the meanwhile it was rather difficult to see what proposals could be made which would materially ease the Anglo-Japanese situation: it was probably almost impossible to devise on paper measures that would give the Japanese the trade advantages that they desired and which it would be possible for us and for our Dominions to grant. The approach to better Anglo-Japanese relations would undoubtedly lie in a change of policy on the part of Japan in regard to China. If Japan could establish better relations with her neighbor and help the latter to develop her market, it was possible that the whole situation might be eased. There was some sign that the Japanese might be beginning to move in this direction, and we could only hope that that movement would gain impetus. Mr. Davis entirely agreed with this view of the situation.[70]

On May 6, the British government acknowledged in the House of Commons that informal talks were under way which might conceivably lead to formal negotiations.[71] By this time public speculation and controversy had already arisen. It was bruited, for example, that the talks represented an attempt "to revive the system of 'spheres of influence' in China." Both Eden and the then foreign minister Satō denied this, but Grew, appraising the situation from Tokyo, remained dubious. Despite the denials of the two countries, he cabled Washington that "the fact remains that the tendency in Japan to regard North China as a special sphere for Japanese exploitation is not only strong but appears to be growing, and Mr. Sato . . . had twice indicated that Japan regards North China as a region which Japan should treat separately from the rest of China. The Japanese apparently are not asking for and do not expect to receive monopolistic economic rights in that region, but are working toward establishing special interests there much as they established special interests in Manchuria prior to 1931. If they are successful in their efforts, the eventual net result, if one can judge by the result in Manchuria, will be much the same as the establishment of an exclusive 'sphere of influence.'"[72] The Chinese made their concern known to both British and American representatives, and received assurance from both that Britain, as ever, had China's best interests firmly in mind.[73] At the end of May, Eden and Chamberlain personally informed the Chinese that the anticipated Yoshida plan would be "based on an agreement with regard to removal of British quotas against Japanese goods and on an agreement with regard to the economic development of China." They assured the Chinese representative that Britain would not consider recognizing any special position for Japan in China, and intimated that one reason for this was that such an agreement would limit their own economic interests there.[74]

To a significant extent, the new and fragile hope for real negotiations rested upon Yoshida's ability to work out with his government an official statement that took into account the exhausting exchanges of January. The British appear to have understood that after Satō became foreign minister, Yoshida communicated both his October 26 memorandum and the original British reply to this to his government.[75] On May 3, Yoshida wrote Cadogan that, "with regard to the Anglo-Japanese Entente under consideration, I have received from Tokio Govt. their views which are in principle on the lines of my ideas." There remained some points of disagreement, however, and thus it would be some time before he would be able to submit these to His Majesty's Government. With inimitable luck, he cabled home a draft plan which he was confident Satō would approve just before learning that the Hayashi cabinet was resigning; and on June 2 he confidentially provided a copy of this draft to the Foreign Office to give them an indication of the type of "definite proposal" in the offing.

The June 2 memorandum was again a largely personal draft, which can appropriately be called the "second Yoshida plan," and it again posed certain problems of phraseology to which the British took exception. These were pointed out to Yoshida, who accepted the corrections with equanimity, and British officers who had recently written off the Japanese ambassador now expressed genuine hopes that his proposals would provide "a favorable send-off to the negotiations."[76] They did not. The June 2 "unofficial draft" was the end of the line insofar as Yoshida's hopes for a definite agreement were concerned. It read as follows:

> Recollecting the cordial relations which existed in the past between Japan and Great Britain, and considering the complicated situation which has arisen in China since the Washington Conference 1921–22, and realizing the inseparable connection between peace in the Far East and the general prosperity of the world, it is deemed of vital importance that the relations between Japan and Great Britain should be adjusted and placed on a more satisfactory footing.
>
> The principal source of discord between Japan and Great Britain is commercial conflict, and though the commercial conflict between the two countries has developed all over the world, its main cause is to be found in China, where the anti-Japanese movement drove Japanese industry out of its natural market and forced it to find an outlet in other parts of the world. The boycott of Japanese goods in China was followed by the general trade depression all over the world, and these two factors working together have brought about the present world-wide conflict between Japanese and British commercial interests. It is, therefore, felt that, if co-operation between Japan and Great Britain can bring about the maintenance of order and increase of prosperity in China, not only will trade competition between Japan and Great Britain be everywhere alleviated, but also the prospect of a general trade recovery will appear from the direction of the Far East.
>
> The chief questions which require frank discussion between the British and Japanese Governments may be summarized under three heads as follows:–

(1) Co-operation between Japan and Great Britain with a view to China's reconstruction as a solid factor in world trade.

With regard to this, it is deemed essential:

(a) That Japan and Great Britain should mutually reiterate their policy of respecting the sovereignty of China and should co-operate for the maintenance of order and the promotion of prosperity in China;

(b) That the Japanese and British Governments should continue as occasion may demand to exchange their frank views on any development, political or economic, which may arise in connection with China.

(2) The question of Anglo-Japanese trade competition.

Recent negotiations with various Dominions have resulted in the conclusion of trade agreements, but the Japanese Government feel that the ground might be explored for a more lasting solution. To this end, it is deemed necessary that the present position of Japanese and British commercial requirements in world trade should be studied jointly, and measures to arrive at a satisfactory solution might be discussed on the following lines:

(a) The British Government might give their consideration to the existing barriers or discrimination against Japanese goods in the British Dominions and Colonies and render any assistance possible in obtaining a basic equality of treatment as each opportunity arises.

(b) With regard to the importation of Japanese goods into the United Kingdom, the Japanese Government propose the establishment of an Anglo-Japanese Joint Trade Committee in London.

(c) With regard to Anglo-Japanese trade conflict in other world markets, the Japanese Government are most anxious to find a mutually satisfactory solution and would welcome a proposal from the British Government.

(3) Closer financial contact between Japan and Great Britain.

With a view to cementing the friendly relations between the two countries and to promoting the long established connection between the Japanese and British financial markets, it is considered desirable that views should be exchanged between the Japanese Financial Commissioner in London and the British Treasury on the financial policies of the two countries and on any other financial questions that may arise.

The Japanese Government take this opportunity to enquire whether financial assistance could be rendered by the British Government in either of the following methods:

(a) Provided that the market prices of Japanese loans permit, the possibility of securing another loan to Japan could be considered, or

(b) Arrangements could be made, through the machinery of the Exports Credits Guarantee Department for the purchase of British goods on long term credits.

Explanatory Remarks on Questions relating to China.

1. The Japanese Government categorically affirm that they have no intention either to sever North China from the Nanking Government or to exclude foreign interests from that region.

The Japanese Government, however, feel fully justified in pointing out that, owing to the territorial contiguity of North China to Manchoukuo, they cannot remain indifferent to any disorder in North China or to any action on the part of the local authorities which is inimical to Japan and Manchoukuo. The Japanese Government realize that the present situation in North China is the direct outcome of the fact that the status of Manchoukuo has not yet been agreed upon by China. It is felt, however, that the existing situation in North China might be relieved ["immediately" appears in the memorandum at this point, but is crossed out] if the British Government could advise the Nanking Government to refrain from any action inimical to Japanese interests in North China and the peaceful development of Manchoukuo.

2. The Japanese Government are anxious to negotiate with China upon all outstanding questions and to establish the relations of the two countries upon an assured foundation.

The Japanese Government are fully prepared to lay before the British Government a frank exposé of their aspirations with regard to the relations between Japan and China. The Japanese Government expect in return the assistance and support of the British Government by friendly counsel to the Chinese Government should occasion arise.

3. With a view to eliminating individual competition in investment in China, it is suggested that the Japanese and British Governments should consult with each other whenever financial aid to China in any form is contemplated by either party.

4. The Japanese Government will support in its entirety the existing organization of the Chinese Maritime Customs.

The Japanese Government realize that as any reconstruction of China must involve financial assistance, it is important that the Chinese Customs organization should be strengthened. The Japanese Government expect that the British Government will co-operate with the Japanese Government in ensuring that Japanese representation in the Chinese Customs Service will be maintained in accordance with the fundamental principles governing foreign representation in that Service.

> 5. The Japanese Government also suggest that the British Government should co-operate with the Japanese Government to secure a modification of the existing Customs tariff, which is regarded as an impediment to trade.
> 6. The Japanese Government affirm their desire for the establishment of a peaceful and prosperous China and welcome the opportunity to discuss any proposals which the British Government may have already considered desirable to effect this purpose.
>
> With a view to promoting the mutual interests of both countries, the Japanese Government undertake to respect in toto all British rights and interests in China and affirm that they have no intention whatever of obstricting [*sic*] British economic development. It is hoped that Great Britain on her part will assist Japan in obtaining the complete cessation of the anti-Japanese boycott or of any other movement which interferes with Japanese interests.[77]

On June 23, the Foreign Ministry informed the American embassy in Tokyo that the Japanese government had approved Yoshida's draft outline, thus implying that future talks in London would have official sanction. From his own limited knowledge of the situation, Grew concluded that the essence of the Japanese negotiating position was "an exchange of a Japanese declaration to refrain from molesting British interests in China for a British assurance to refrain from discriminating against Japanese goods in British markets including probably Dominion markets." He predicted this would be a hard bargain for the British to accept.[78] As late as July 1, however, Cadogan reported he still had not received official notification of a Japanese proposal from Yoshida, and had concluded that, contrary to recent expectations, the new Konoe government might be shifting to a hard-line policy concerning north China.[79] At this moment, on July 7, the China Incident occurred and open Japanese aggression turned southward toward the heart of China and the real nerve centers of Britain's "rights and interests." Yoshida's efforts of a year were swept aside in a day, and the imminently anticipated negotiations became a tiny item in history's cluttered dustbin, a development that might have been.

THE IMPERIAL CONSCIOUSNESS, 1937

Cadogan's apprehensions just prior to the China Incident were not misplaced, for just as Yoshida's proposals seemed about to expand into real negotiations, he found himself unexpectedly at loggerheads with his new foreign minister and prime minister and erstwhile kindred souls, Hirota and Konoe. Whether time and argument would have resolved this clash of opinions on the Japanese side if the China Incident had not occurred is a matter of pure conjecture, as indeed is the question which follows: whether substantive negotiations based on the secret "Yoshida plan" had any chance of success even if the crisis of July 1937 had not occurred.

Viewed from the British side, Yoshida's first year as ambassador to London seems hardly consistent with his later tough, stereotyped image. The iconoclastic "One Man" of Japanese bureaucratic circles was looked down upon as an amiable figure who "does not give the impression of being a man of strong personality." The sharp-tongued, haughty elitist whose Japanese pronouncements were distinguished by their bluntness was described as "incoherent," "unintelligible," "more earnest than coherent" when he turned to English, and at moments emerges as an abject, insecure, and pitiable man; his haughtiness hardly had a chance against the British on their own grounds. The China hand who prided himself upon his "realism," and even in departing for London emphasized the necessity to avoid "wild flights of imagination" and rely on "well-established facts," spent much of his time soliciting vague expressions of good will—and in British eyes belonged among those Japanese whom Sansom and others were wont to call "the sentimentalists." Although Yoshida's most treasured foreign phrase was an English one, "diplomatic sense," the English found him woefully lacking in this himself, a "blunderer" at worst, at best a man to "keep in play." Yoshida did not fare well on Western ground, where he was deprived of the props of class and position and material advantage which supported his more authoritarian proclivities in Japan and China.

It nonetheless would be incorrect to see Yoshida as a weak or particularly "sentimental" figure even at this difficult juncture of his career. For while the British constantly alluded to Yoshida's personal opposition to the "military group" in Japan, and his consequent lack of influence—while Cadogan could even be moved to exclaim, "In some ways it would be more satisfactory to have to do with a fire-eating Major General!"[80]—at the same time it must be noted that the Foreign Office also found Yoshida's concrete "personal" proposals concerning China to be imperialistic, exploitative, and in fundamental respects congruent with the attitudes of the militarists. The summaries of Yoshida's various proposals by British officials make this eminently clear: the "wicked Chinese," the "lion's share," the "vassal State" and "passive body," the "joint *démarche*" and "exclusive agreement." It is undeniable that Yoshida was at odds with his government on basic policies such as the Anti-Comintern Pact and the relative weight to be placed on Anglo-Japanese relations; he was frankly critical of the role of the Kwantung Army, and more inclined than his superiors to solicit Western mediation of the China crisis. But he was also not about to renounce what Japan had gained in continental Asia, whether through the legalistic duplicities of the old imperialism or the *fait accompli* of the new, as in Manchukuo and north China. Patriots, even liberal ones, do not voluntarily disgorge. Both privately and publicly, Yoshida's attitude toward the Chinese remained every bit as condescending and unyielding as it had been in the 1920s.

Despite the impression his London counterparts received of an earnest but somewhat wooly-headed bumbler, Yoshida also was not particularly sentimental toward *them*. He believed Japan needed Britain, but also that she had Britain in a vise, and could squeeze concessions from her by tightening this adroitly. Turned about and seen from the perspective of Yoshida's communications to Tokyo at the time, it could be asked whether it was not the British who were being sentimental in insisting on the preservation of their traditional rights and privileges in China when in fact their power was draining. Yoshida did not address his own government on the same basis that he approached the Foreign Office, that is, by soliciting vague statements of good will. To both sides he did stress his basic thesis that the China problem and crisis in global trade were inseparable, and he did not minimize the difficulties of solution to either government. In an ironic little tableau, however, Yoshida emphasized to Tokyo the internal pressures of British capitalism (erupting in the unemployment problem), which he argued would force the Conservatives to deal on China—while the British, on their part, were simultaneously pointing to the impending crisis of Japanese capitalism (armaments and fiscal instability) as an indication that Britain stood to profit by playing for time.

While Yoshida was attempting to clarify "misunderstandable points" in the first Yoshida plan to the British, his cables to Tokyo indicate that these points had indeed been quite correctly understood by the Foreign Office: Yoshida *did* consistently envision a virtual Japanese protectorate over China based on exclusive arrangements in military aid and Sino-Japanese economic integration. He did not place undue weight on traditional British sentiment or good will toward Japan—or, on the potentially negative side, British pronouncement of moral commitment or similar pieties—but rather argued that rapprochement was possible because of British *practicality*. Its Asian "experts" already recognized that China was weak, "rotten," and unable to produce in matters of power politics; sooner or later His Majesty's Government could be expected to acknowledge the harsh realities of Britain's strategic and economic vulnerability in Asia and the futility of excessive commitment to China.

The record on the Japanese side is fragmentary, but it does include several items which illuminate Yoshida's stand vis-à-vis his own government during the period of the "Yoshida plans." In early January, between the personal nadirs of discouragement marked by the *Times*-article incident and the firm tone of Britain's January 18 *aide-mémoire*, Yoshida conveyed guarded optimism to

Tokyo that "relations between England and Japan are taking a decided turn for the better." He was encouraged, he said, for several reasons: "First the British Government has come to attach great importance to the Anglo-Japanese relationship. Second, there is a strong intention to rely on Anglo-Japanese cooperation in the China problem. Third, they are showing support for the goal of developing Anglo-Japanese commercial relations—here referring not merely to relations between the two countries, but also to trade rivalry in other markets. Fourth and Fifth, they have shown willingness to arrange to respond through a trade conference to the matter of the threat posed by Japan's trade expansion, and the low-interest refunding of Japanese bonds." According to Harada, Prime Minister Hirota was pleased at this report and responded, "If things proceed this way, the general outlook appears excellent."[81] The Hirota cabinet fell within a matter of weeks, however, and the most interesting insights into Yoshida's views are to be found in several lengthy summary dispatches he subsequently sent to the successive statesmen who briefly prowled the corridors at Kasumigaseki prior to the China Incident.

The new cabinet of General Hayashi Senjūrō was established on February 2, and until March 3 Hayashi simultaneously held the post of foreign minister. Yoshida's first extended cable was dispatched to Hayashi in the latter capacity on February 17; it summarized his position on the China-Britain-Japan dilemma and concluded by offering his own plan for solution of the China problem. The memorandum stressed these points: (1) The key to Anglo-Japanese relations lay in adjustment of overall trade interests by creating a prosperous China market, and Japan could most effectively demonstrate its role as the "stabilizing power" in East Asia by contributing to the "realization, maintenance, and advancement of that prosperity." Such development, however, should be accomplished with the understanding and assistance of Great Britain as well as the United States. (2) While Britain undeniably had been greatly concerned over Japanese trade expansion in the past, this concern had recently been somewhat alleviated by the quota system; the rising cost of raw materials, which was slowing Japan's expansion; the effects of the Ottawa trade agreements; and a domestic boom within Great Britain itself. Nonetheless, Britain remained concerned about Japan's actions in China as well as indigenous developments within China. The confused political situation in Europe made the British all the more uneasy about their ability to protect their interests in Asia, and thus they were particularly attentive to Anglo-Japanese relations. (3) The Conservative Party in Great Britain was greatly troubled by the domestic unemployment problem, and "from this point of view it is natural that Britain cannot neglect trade with China and investment [in China]. Thus the stability and prosperity of China cannot but be one great focus for opening up the Anglo-Japanese relationship." (4) From the Japanese point of view, failure to break the impasse in Sino-Japanese relations would hinder Japan in its endeavor to emerge as the stabilizing power in Asia, and would also become "one large obstacle in our relationship with Russia." The Imperial Government's policy of excluding third-party participation in the Sino-Japanese negotiations had not proven effective. ("When we added a little pressure on China, China adopted the strategy of evading our thrust by relying on Britain, the United States, and others.") Thus it followed that China was the key to Anglo-Japanese relations and at the same time Britain was the key to Sino-Japanese relations.[82]

With this general background, Yoshida proceeded to offer Hayashi his own personal "humble views" as a basis for grasping the nettle of the China problem and at the same time bringing about regulation of "the general Japanese-British trade relationship":

> (1) Arrange with China that weapons and military materiel needed by the Chinese military be entirely dependent upon Japan, and replace foreign military advisers or instructors presently employed by the Chinese with Japanese military personnel. On the basis of this plan, guide the strengthening of China's military armament. At the same time, Chiang Kai-shek should be placed in charge of suppressing the anti-Japanese communist movement and maintaining order.
>
> (2) Adequately discuss Sino-Japanese economic relations, and establish reciprocally exclusive cooperation [lit., "special-for-each-other

> cooperation"] concerning tax agreements, development of resources, and development of industry.
> (3) When the Nanking Government agrees to the above-mentioned two items, then the Imperial Government should pursue a consistent policy of assisting Chiang's political power and helping to stabilize his government.
> (4) With regards to water control and transportation in China, utilize the financial power of Japan, Great Britain, (and the United States) and endeavor in this manner to bring about the prosperity of the China market.
> (5) Obtain the understanding of Great Britain concerning the above-mentioned policies, and have Great Britain assist us from the side in the Sino-Japanese negotiations. After having discussed this with Great Britain, then invite the United States also.[83]

This could hardly be regarded as a conciliatory plan from the Chinese point of view, for the five proposals, in order, implied (1) Japanese political and military control in China; (2) special economic privileges to Japan; (3) Japanese intervention in Chinese domestic politics in support of Chiang Kai-shek; (4) increased foreign control of Chinese communications; and (5) Great-Power pressure against the Nanking Government.

Two further general points should be noted concerning these proposals. First, they were issued in the wake of the Sian Incident of December 1936 in China, which had led to the creation of a united front between the Kuomintang and Chinese Communist Party against Japan. In urging Japanese "support" of Chiang Kai-shek, Yoshida was thus not only revising his earlier policies of non-involvement in Chinese domestic politics, but also presumedly attempting to break the united front.[84] And second, although Yoshida opposed the Twenty-One Demands in 1915, his concrete proposals of late 1936 and early 1937 can be seen as an attempt to impose conditions upon China almost identical to some of the "wishes" or "desires" contained in the notorious "group five" of the Twenty-One Demands, which had provoked such outcry at the time that Japan had been forced to abandon them. "Group five" had proposed that China rely on Japanese military, political, and financial advisers; that China obtain its arms from Japan; and that joint Sino-Japanese police control be established in designated areas.[85] These proposals were universally condemned at the time as a blatant infringement of Chinese sovereignty, and Yoshida had opposed them then on the tactical grounds that they provoked Western suspicion of Japan's motives. In the new diplomacy of *fait accompli*, he apparently concluded that their time had come.

When Satō Naotake replaced Hayashi as foreign minister on March 3, Yoshida deemed it necessary to review his position for his new superior. In a cable sent over the course of two days (March 10 and 11), he reviewed most of the basic points made in the communication to Hayashi: the interrelationship between Japanese diplomacy toward China and Great Britain; Britain's preoccupation with Europe and consequent desire to bend over backwards to avoid antagonizing Japan; the importance of the unemployment issue in shaping British attitudes; the importance of the China market and necessity of cooperating with Britain in developing this; Japan's destiny as the "stabilizing power" in Asia; the necessity of a *concrete* plan for Anglo-Japanese cooperation; specific reference to the proposal he had previously made to Hayashi, that Japan support Chiang against the Chinese Communists; and so on.[86] He explained to Satō that one of his influential and like-minded contacts in London was Leith-Ross, Chamberlain's close assistant in the Treasury:

> What always concerns the British government, and particularly the politicians of the Conservative Party, is the unemployment problem, and the places they regard as the primary new markets for British industry are South America and China, particularly the latter. Since his visit to China, however, Leith-Ross argues that the prosperity of China depends upon the improvement of Sino-Japanese relations, and that unless such improvement is envisaged the security of investments in China cannot be anticipated. In my opinion, he has had an influence upon the British government, particularly Neville Chamberlain. Although Chamberlain has his own reasons for his pro-Japanese attitude, his convictions must have been strengthened by Leith-Ross's ideas.
>
> My opinion that tensions relating to Anglo-Japanese trade should be eased by true prosperity in China, and that this prosperity can only be brought about with the cooperation of Great Britain, happens

> to be in accord with Leith-Ross's view, and I think that is why my opinion has come to receive Chamberlain's support.[87]

Yoshida also blithely informed Satō that he felt one of the virtues of his China proposals was that they would eliminate the suspicion that Japan harbored territorial ambitions regarding China, and that he was confident he could gain Britain's "understanding" concerning the line of action he was proposing. In conclusion, he reiterated that the United States should not be excluded from any agreement concerning China, but, in his words, "given the national situation in the United States, which is still in the dark about the China situation, we should first obtain the understanding of Great Britain and after that approach the United States."[88]

British records indicate that between April and June 1937 Yoshida engaged in fairly concrete correspondence with the Foreign Ministry concerning the various memoranda he had been preparing in English; the Japanese record is simply unclear on this. Satō unquestionably encouraged Yoshida to pursue his endeavors, but was replaced as foreign minister by Hirota on June 4, with Yoshida's vaunted political healer Konoe assuming the premiership for the first time. The "second Yoshida plan" of June 2 was in all likelihood the first item concerning Anglo-Japanese relations that Hirota confronted, and sometime in mid-June he conveyed substantial criticism of this to Yoshida. Exactly what this was must be surmised by Yoshida's blunt reply of June 28, which expressed "extreme disappointment" over his old classmate's policy proposals, and then proceeded to list eight specific points of rebuttal:[89]

(1) Japanese diplomatic cables emanating from Tokyo and Nanking misrepresented actual British intentions as Yoshida understood them. In fact, the interest for Anglo-Japanese rapprochement existed before Yoshida arrived in London, and the initiative for some sort of talks had come from the British side. Yoshida stressed that this was not just some vague feeling of friendship on the part of his British acquaintances: "This of course does not derive from their private feelings, but because

they believe that Anglo-Japanese rapprochement is advantageous to British plans."[90]

(2) Britain's current military vulnerability in the Far East was conducive to an Anglo-Japanese deal: "Although the complications of the European situation have caused Great Britain to decide upon a £1.5-billion national defense budget, when one thinks of the difficulties of defending British rights and interests east of India should something happen, then it is common sense that they recall the old times of the Anglo-Japanese Alliance and think of the advantages of Anglo-Japanese cooperation. Thus the true intentions of the British side are extremely clear."[91]

(3) Yoshida then attempted to apply a harsh bit of *Realpolitik* in refutation of those who argued that, contrary to Yoshida's evaluation, British attitudes toward Japan had become irreconcilably hostile: "Among those British officials abroad who can see before their very eyes the overflow of the anti-Japanese tide in China, naturally there will be some who preach the foolishness of approaching Japan with regards to China policy. And on the side of the Chinese Government as well, there will be those who exaggerate the friendly relationship between Britain and China expressly for anti-Japanese purposes. On more than a few occasions, however, I have listened to those Englishmen who regard China as *rotten* or *mysterious* [Yoshida used the English words]. How many knowledgeable British men who are familiar with China's past and present situation are confident that they can seriously trust China? And how many Chinese politicians possess self-confidence in being able to obtain Britain's trust? What is more, it cannot be said even as flattery that China possesses the actual power to be able to contribute to that world peace which Great Britain constantly advocates. It must be said, moreover, that it is only common sense for British politicians to regard Japan as important from the point of view of their own world policy. For these reasons, a new China theory by officials abroad or certain groups of authorities cannot be taken seriously from the political center of the British homeland."[92]

(4) Yoshida, however, did acknowledge substantial criticism and suspicion of Japan in Britain, and argued that to overcome this it would be necessary for Japan "passively to display respect for Chinese sovereignty, and actively [to work for] prosperity and cooperation." Then, apparently as a concession to Hirota's own position, he added that if respect for China's sovereignty were unacceptable, it would be all the more necessary to stress prosperity and cooperation. And he warned Hirota against "using empty phrases, and . . . proposing meaningless cooperation."[93]

(5) He then emphasized that the many Englishmen who were knowledgeable about China were also cognizant of the dangers of extensive involvement in the China quagmire through loans or investment. His argument here seemed intended to assuage in a backhanded manner the fear that British financial involvement in China might develop to Japan's disadvantage: "Increase of investment is increase of danger. There is no necessity for needless envy of British investments. If her investment is large and Great Britain becomes deeply involved with China, then there would be that much more probability of her having to depend upon us. This is why Englishmen of deep experience are not readily receptive to talk of loans to China."[94]

(6) In a section evocative of Grew's comments on "spheres of influence"—and redolent also of the "diplomacy of *fait accompli*" which Yoshida and the moderates allegedly opposed—he turned his attention more specifically to the situation in north China: "The north China situation is merely ancillary to the Manchurian Jehol Incident. If China frankly recognizes the established fact of Jehol and responds to our negotiations concerning its remedy, then it logically follows that the China problem should be solved. Therefore, since China does not respond to remedies in spite of the present situation of Jehol, which exists as an established fact, then it naturally follows that the north China situation is what it is today. Thus we should face Great Britain and others with the attitude that the responsibility rests upon China. On the other hand, the north China situation is also an established fact which has been built up by our efforts

over the past several years, and so we must make use of this situation as one weapon toward China through which to attain our just demands. In short, the north China problem concerns China and is not a problem between Japan and Great Britain. There is only the question of how we should make use of Great Britain in the course of Anglo-Japanese negotiations to break the impasse in Sino-Japanese relations."[95]

(7) and (8) In the final two items in his cable, Yoshida attempted to persuade Hirota to allow him to open negotiations with Great Britain essentially on the basis of the proposal he had previously submitted—presumedly the June 2 memorandum—agreeing, however, to delete the phrase "respect of sovereignty" which had apparently vexed the new foreign minister.[96]

Hirota obviously was not swayed. His reply to Yoshida's June 28 cable is also not available, but in response to it he was shortly treated to a further expression of pique and a short lecture on proper diplomatic practice from his undiplomatic subordinate in London. In an angry dispatch dated July 7 from London—only hours before Chinese and Japanese troops were to begin their fatal skirmish near the Marco Polo Bridge—Yoshida informed his foreign minister that he required further clarification before he could carry out his most recent instructions.[97] As Yoshida explained it, "What Great Britain seeks is not explanations of the intentions of the Imperial Government, but a *definite* (or *concrete*) *proposal* [Yoshida's English] for adjusting the national diplomacy of Japan and Britain." Hirota's instructions, Yoshida stated, on the one hand failed to meet this need and on the other hand proposed an explanation where none was called for: "Insofar as the foreign policy of the Imperial Government is concerned, even when asked, it is appropriate not to reply in certain circumstances. Offering explanations or excuses on our own volition, when not requested to do so, is something which, for the sake of the honor of our country, I would not presume to do."[98] He went on to assert that, as far as he was able to comprehend them, Hirota's proposals assigned little more than a "perfunctory meaning" to the adjustment of Anglo-Japanese diplomacy insofar as China was concerned, and could be handled at a lower level. Should he actually convey Hirota's plan to the British, Yoshida predicted, they would be "astonished that the voice is large but the facts so small." In Yoshida's opinion, the same criticism could be leveled at Hirota's proposals concerning general Anglo-Japanese trade relations which, as he interpreted them, were actually premised upon the assumption that meaningful cooperation between the two countries was impossible.[99]

After in effect refusing to relay Hirota's instructions to the Foreign Office, Yoshida proceeded to expound his basic position once again, in the process adding a few power considerations that had not appeared so explicitly in the previous cables to Hayashi, Satō, and Hirota:

> In my opinion, the impasse in Sino-Japanese relations is to be broken by a proper application of Anglo-Japanese cooperatism (*kyōryokushugi*). Since China lacks funds and is madly running around in a move for loans, we should first cut off her source of money [lit., "the road over which the crops are brought"] and persuade Great Britain to adopt the principle that unless there is an improvement in Sino-Japanese relations she [also] will be unable to respond to a loan for China. According to your cable, however, it is my understanding that for the time being you propose to advance primarily with a policy of economic and cultural affiliation with China, but you do not appear to have any notion of utilizing the Anglo-Japanese relationship. This is where I cannot help but feel disappointment.
>
> Today, as national expenditures increase and annual expenses are doubling, we must double our trade and push it up to the 10-billion [yen] level in order to maintain our national destiny (*kokuun*). And it is impossible to think of the development of our trade amidst hostility, or excluding the British Empire, which occupies one-fourth of the land of the world, and China, which embraces one-fourth of the population of the world. In this situation, in order to handle our relationship with both Britain and China properly, please once again give adequate consideration to my plan.[100]

In conclusion Yoshida seized upon a formality, the fact that Hirota had said his view and Yoshida's actually differed little in "general intention," and requested once again that he be permitted to open negotiations with Great Britain on the basis of his own previously submitted proposals. On that inconclusive note ended Yoshida's last hope for a global imperial arrangement.

REALISM AND MORALISM: A POSTSCRIPT ON THE IMPERIAL CONSCIOUSNESS

Although the Yoshida plans died on July 7, 1937, Britain's initial response to Japan's massive expansion of the China Incident suggests a brief postscript to the issue of "moralism" and "realism." Confronted with the Japanese onslaught, but not yet with the full resiliency of Chinese resistance, Britain appears to have found both its avowed ideals and its traditional "rights and interests" in China negotiable—much as Yoshida had been hoping all along.

Two reports submitted to the Foreign Office by Sir John Brenan and Sir John Pratt in January 1938 suggest this.[101] "It would be foolish not to adopt a realistic attitude toward Japan's undoubted military power and her firm resolve to secure a stronger economic and strategic position in East Asia," Brenan began. "No more than the Germans can the Japanese be indefinitely suppressed." At the same time, he did anticipate prolonged Chinese resistance. Japan should therefore be urged to withdraw its forces from south of the Great Wall, and China on its part urged to recognize Manchukuo and to grant extensive mining, industrial, and railway rights to the Japanese in north China. An international customs administration should be maintained "with tariff amendments in Japan's favour." Shanghai should be demilitarized, as Japan desired, with as large a Chinese participation as possible in a reorganized administration; in a revised international gendarmerie for Shanghai, China would hopefully dominate but "the Japanese, in view of their large local community, would presumedly have to have a substantial share in its composition and command." Foreign extraterritorial privileges might be surrendered to the Chinese, with safeguards, if the Chinese government had not become irreparably damaged.[102]

Sir John Pratt premised his parallel proposals on the assumption that they would be backed by joint Anglo-American naval action in China. "If the British fleet is sent to the Far East," he emphasized, "it will be sent, not for the purpose of imposing sanctions, or of upholding the Covenant, or maintaining world peace, or for any other altruistic purpose, but for the purpose of defending important British interests threatened with destruction." Britain should not, however, be directly concerned with north China. Peace terms should be "generous to Japan" and "fair to China." The crux of the problem was Shanghai, and Japan might be appeased on this through "a self-denying ordinance under which whatever Japan is asked to surrender, Great Britain and America will also surrender." Pratt, like Brenan, acknowledged the extent to which Shanghai embodied the contradictions of the imperialistic position in China: "The traditional aim of British and American policy, enshrined in the Nine-Power Treaty, has been to encourage China to develop into a modern State, but this aim has been to a large extent frustrated by inability to break away from the older tradition of imposing tutelage and protecting foreign interests by armed force." The foreign settlements, extraterritoriality, and the like were now anachronisms—and, moreover, if this system of foreign control were perpetuated, it would inevitably confront the twin evils of Japanese domination and Chinese resistance. "If force can no longer be employed to maintain foreign municipal institutions in Shanghai against Japanese aggression on the one hand or Chinese nationalism on the other, then the only wise course would seem to be to liquidate the whole position when an opportunity for doing so on favourable terms presents itself." Pratt thus proposed a demilitarized Shanghai under Chinese authority, with foreign representation in municipal government.

Apart from the Shanghai nerve center, Pratt advocated that Britain should "use our influence with China, even putting pressure on her, if necessary, to secure satisfaction for Japan on points to which she attaches importance, such as anti-Japanese teaching in school textbooks, tariff rates unfavourable to Japanese trade, etc. . . . As regards North China, it is no part of our business to drive the Japanese beyond the Great Wall, even if we had the force to do so. We might therefore in the first instance leave the Chinese and Japanese to negotiate a settlement of North China, urging Japan to be moderate and urging China to make the fullest possible concessions to Japan in the economic sphere in return for full recognition of China's sovereignty over the five northern provinces." Japanese military evacuation south of the Great Wall was essential. Manchukuo, however, was conceded to Japan, for "the Great Wall is a natural boundary between China and territory that is not really regarded as part of China."[103]

The Foreign Office endorsed these views and incorporated them in a secret memorandum submitted to the United States on February 14 which emphasized the necessity of supporting peace terms which would "not humiliate" Japan—or again, which, "besides being fair to China, should be fair and even generous to Japan." Specifically, the desirability of revising the nature of foreign control over Shanghai was emphasized, along the lines of the Brenan-Pratt proposals, with the city and its environs being demilitarized to a radius of approximately thirty miles—"thus giving effect to one of the *desiderata* to which the Japanese have always attached great importance." In addition, the memorandum proposed "recognition of Manchukuo by China—a measure which would remove one of the irritants that tend to disturb international relations generally—and the grant of special facilities for economic co-operation and the investment of Japanese capital in North China. This might include mining and industrial concessions for Japanese corporations, and some measure of Japanese participation in the management of the Northern Railways."[104] To a very considerable extent, in short, the Foreign Office was at this juncture willing to accede to Japan's demands in north China and to endorse its detachment of Manchuria in return, it was hoped, for a measure of security for its own predominant interests in central and south China and Hong Kong.[105] In the process, however, it was forced to acknowledge the heavy hand with which the foreign powers continued to hold the door "open" in China, and to propose relinquishment of some of the more blatant inequities of the allegedly post-imperialist Washington system.

The American response was delayed until mid-April, and took the form of an unofficial twenty-six page statement drafted largely by Stanley Hornbeck and efflorescent with the familiar phraseology of "moral diplomacy." Hornbeck and his State Department colleagues rejected the various concessions concerning Manchukuo and north China contained in the British proposal, noting that there was little reason to believe China would benefit through such "cooperation." They applauded the interesting suggestions concerning Shanghai, but with the vexing and all too familiar hedge that "the time has not yet arrived for a commitment—such as would be involved in the launching of any particular 'plan'—regarding the future of Shanghai."

Somewhat paradoxically—in the best tradition of the black humor of imperialism—one thus finds the British willing to ameliorate the unequal-treaty system while selling out the Chinese, while the Americans argued that one could jettison neither the Chinese *nor* the apparatus which denied China its full sovereignty and integrity. The American position was quite simply to do little or nothing, although an attempt was made to anticipate such criticism. "Is not the policy which has thus far been pursued and which is now being pursued by the United States," the reply asked rhetorically, "as sound a policy as can be pursued?" And responding directly to the familiar complaint that American policy in the Far East was "unduly 'idealistic' and not closely enough responsive to 'realities'," the memorandum went on to emphasize that "it is our belief that the approach which the Government of the United States makes to the problems involved is in fact definitely and conspicuously *realistic*." The essence of this realism, it was further and redundantly explained, lay in insistence upon adherence to the provisions of the Nine Power Treaty which had emerged from the Washington Conference a decade and a half earlier.

Only in the final paragraph of its lengthy response did the State Department offer a remote, and intriguingly impartial, possibility for joint Anglo-American action in the China crisis—one which suggests that the ultimate touchstone of America's "moral diplomacy" also resided in the unequal treaties. It was noted that American officials were studying the feasibility of "taking action in the nature of 'reprisals' in the commercial & economic field against Japan *or China or both* in connection with the disregard, growing out of the present hostilities, for the rights, the interests and the diplomatic representations of the United States and other countries." [italics added][106]

In keeping with Pratt's advice, the February 14 British proposal had insisted that the terms suggested be presented to the belligerents in the Sino-Japanese conflict in concert with a joint Anglo-American naval demonstration. Since this was explicitly rejected in the U.S. response of mid-April, the plan became stillborn on this account alone. Beyond this, the winds of war had altered somewhat in the intervening two months; as Brenan noted in his minutes to the American reply, "at the time [the original proposal] was written . . . the Japanese were at the height of their military success and China's remarkable recovery in the field had not begun."[107]

The more enduring issues of "realism," rhetoric, and the eye of the beholder of course remained, and this brief postscript to the China Incident suggests that in such matters Britain and Japan may have been, as Yoshida constantly assumed, closer in certain *potential* respects than were Britain and the United States. The British position in the end rested frankly on considerations of real strength; in the blistering glare of dramatically shifting power realities, definitions of national interest withered while moral scruples burned away like celluloid. "History is not lacking in examples of successful conquerors, and conquered states which have remained in subjugation," Brenan observed in his comments on the American reply, and the original proposals "were introduced, not for their intrinsic merit, but because they conceded some of Japan's fundamental aims in the present conflict and might induce the Japanese to keep the peace, at least for some years to come."[108] In this context, moreover, American moralism was hardly respected as purely altruistic by the Foreign Office members engaged in Far Eastern affairs; it was regarded as a luxury permitted only by differing national interests. "The Americans can afford to take a more detached philosophical and long-sighted attitude towards the conflict than we do," it was felt, largely because "their vested interests in China are comparatively small and the home country is isolated geographically from the potential dangers of a Japanese victory."[109]

Cadogan, the senior member in the Far Eastern section, gave the American response even shorter shrift. "A lot of this is awful stuff," he wrote, and, in a phrase which might have been borrowed from Yoshida himself, he concluded: "I have learned to expect nothing of America."[110] Nonetheless, America's refusal to commit itself precluded British action, and this in turn stymied Yoshida's lingering hopes for a solution to the Asian crisis based on Anglo-Japanese rapprochement. And thus the several parties involved—self-avowed realists and peace-lovers all—remained stalemated while China burned.

SIX

Pursuing Rainbows, 1937–1941

Eden reminded me of what I know so well from my frequent contacts with educated cosmopolitan Japanese like Yoshida and his predecessor Matsudaira and others, that no one can accept a statement from this type of Japanese as really representing the attitude of the Japanese Government.[1]

—Bingham, U.S. Ambassador to Great Britain
October 30, 1937

I am astonished by Yoshida's statements.[2]

—Grew, U.S. Ambassador to Japan
November 1, 1937

We have on various occasions tried to ascertain from him whether he has any authority whatever from his Government in putting forward these views, but he always assures us that he has none, and then disappears for a number of weeks during which he airs his personal views to other people. I really do not think that we can pay much attention to what a foreign Ambassador says in his "personal capacity."[3]

—Halifax, British Foreign Secretary
May 7, 1938

Yoshida has so persistently told us that a solution of all our difficulties is "just around the corner" that one suspects him naturally of wishful thinking.[4]

—Craigie, British Ambassador to Japan
March 17, 1939

> With him the wish is father to the thought and better things are always just around the corner.[5]
>
> –Grew
> April 27, 1939

> Then I had a long talk with Yoshida who always predicts the rainbow just around the corner and tonight was no exception.[6]
>
> –Grew
> April 16, 1940

> Yoshida, much as I like him, is difficult to debate with, for he keeps coming back to his original point no matter what one says–compromise, compromise, compromise.[7]
>
> –Grew
> October 24, 1941

> No one could have foreseen this tragic end of our long standing friendly relations, although so many unfortunate events occurred in recent years.[8]
>
> –Yoshida letter to Grew
> December 17, 1941

Even after the China Incident, Yoshida refused to close ranks with the disorderly parade of militarists, Marxists, and bourgeois pessimists who argued that Japan's relations with the West had passed the point of no return. Between 1937 and 1941, he made a number of appearances as a small fisher for peace, and continued to do so after Pearl Harbor–floating his proposals on a troubled sea of events, where they bobbed in and out of sight for a while until some great happening crested and smashed them out of relevance, out of memory. While others worked the deep waters, Yoshida played the shallows, with small hooks and uncertain bait. But although there were more diligent and intense fishermen around him, in the end all had the same luck. Or so it seemed at the time. Only in the post-surrender period did it become apparent that luck in this matter could also be a personal and retroactive affair. Then Yoshida was resurrected to a new career as an old fisher for peace who had not soiled his hands in the process–as had, it was charged, such colleagues and contemporaries as Konoe, Hirota, Shigemitsu, Kido, and Tōgō Shigenori. He was imprisoned for ten weeks in the spring of 1945 for involvement in "anti-war" activities, and it is largely on this incident that his reputation as a war opponent rests. This was, however, only the last of a series of occasions on which Yoshida cast a line for peace—or, at least, for reconciliation with the West.

Yoshida's "peace proposals" between the China Incident and Pearl Harbor are of interest in that they involve what less fatalistic observers have regarded as some of the crucial turning points or lost opportunities of these dismal years. These included most notably the controversial Japanese overtures of late 1937 and the last-ditch "Proposal B" submitted to the United States in November 1941. Between 1942 and 1945, his most interesting activities consisted of participation in some of the anti-Tōjō maneuvers which took place within the Japanese establishment, culminating in the remarkable "Konoe Memorial" of early 1945. On a more personal level, the activities of these years further illuminate the nature of Yoshida's "realism," and of his "opposition" as well. They also throw into sharper focus his position within the prewar elite; his loyalism; his doggedly optimistic interpretation of the dynamics of the Japanese state; his total antipathy to popular and radical movements; his distrust of the Soviet Union; and the occasionally ambiguous twists within his seemingly straightforward ideological orientation.

THE DIPLOMACY OF CONCILIATION, 1937–1938

To both his own government and the British and American officials with whom he was in most frequent contact, Yoshida's propensity for acting on his own initiative was a frequent source of uncertainty and misunderstanding. The problem had arisen in connection with his initiatives in Mukden following the Eastern Conference, and recurred in his representation of the Anti-Comintern Pact to the British nearly a decade later. The secret proposals of 1936–1937 were similarly plagued by the blurring of private and official representations. A lesser instance of the dichotomy between Yoshida's statements and the position of his government occurred in August 1937 when the British ambassador to China, driving from Nanking to Shanghai, was wounded in an attack on his vehicle by Japanese aircraft. While Yoshida immediately expressed regrets, Tokyo lagged behind in handling the case and even then addressed the problem unsatisfactorily in British eyes.[9]

This reputation of being an inaccurate and unreliable diplomatic intermediary shadowed and undercut Yoshida's attempts to check the further disintegration of Japan's relations with the Western powers after July 1937. It was, in brief, never entirely clear to his Anglo-American contacts whether he was speaking officially or unofficially, and this uncertainty operated both to raise false hopes and to obscure possibly meaningful Japanese overtures. According to Kase Toshikazu, one of Yoshida's close acquaintances and a diplomat in London at this time himself, this highly personalized style was among the considerations which led to Yoshida's recall in the autumn of 1938.[10]

History's vagaries and debaucheries often sweeten fruits once deemed hardly palatable. Certainly the drastic turn of events signaled by the China Incident enhanced the attractiveness of the Yoshida plan in British eyes, and within the week Eden met with Yoshida and emphasized "the importance we attached to conversations with [the] Japanese which we had hoped would shortly begin," and his regret that present conditions rendered this impossible.[11] Privately, Yoshida expressed guarded optimism that the China Incident actually could be turned to Japan's advantage. On September 21, he wrote Makino that British officials were less upset by the Japanese attack in north China than by the corollary military action in Shanghai, as well as the outrage against the British ambassador. In a manner very similar to his response to the Manchurian Incident six years earlier, he argued that effective diplomacy could not only rectify the show of force, but also capitalize on it: "If we satisfy [the British government] on the matter of the ambassador incident, and if we handle the postwar situation well, then Anglo-Japanese cooperation is not impossible. And since this incident has made clear the difference between the national power of Japan and China, the authorities can turn this unfortunate situation into a profitable opportunity." At the same time, he feared that the Japanese government would fail to seize this opportunity. "We are playing sort of a double game," he told Makino, and if this continued it would not be possible for him to remain in London.[12]

As the war against China was expanded, however, the proposed terms of the Yoshida plan became increasingly outdated, although the prospects for rapprochement were not necessarily immediately dimmed. Good realists rode the inexorable tides of *fait accompli*, and Yoshida continued to attempt to turn each ebb and flow in the war into an opportune occasion for Anglo-Japanese reconciliation. Initially he assured his British contacts that the Japanese government desired to restrain the fighting in north China,[13] and, despite consistent developments to the contrary, that chimera was never entirely dispelled from his thoughts. Thus on October 29 and 30, 1937—when most of north China had fallen to the Japanese, and Chinese troops were being routed from Shanghai—Yoshida met successively with Eden and Bingham, the U.S. ambassador to London, to discuss the situation and present an argument which was characteristic both in its earnestness and in the confusion it caused. Also characteristic was his generally encouraging appraisal of the trend of opinion in Japan even at this critical juncture.

This unflagging ability to portray Japan's situation and Japan's future in the most optimistic light is worthy of note. No matter how far his country descended into the "dark valley" of conflict abroad and disruption at home, Yoshida remained convinced of both the fundamental soundness of the society and the eventual satisfactory resolution of its dilemma. He was not immune to depression or, as the following chapter indicates, apocalyptic visions, but his confidence—or his *posture* of confidence—was only rarely shattered, and in the postwar period this was to become one of his most striking and effective traits. It stayed him against the initial shock and despair suffered by many of his countrymen in the face of staggering defeat. It enabled him to hold steadfastly to a conservative and non-reformist position, confident that the thrust of new threats to the traditional system—this time by U.S.

occupation personnel—would also be blunted in the long run. And it provided for some Japanese citizens a small, tough, cantankerous personal symbol of hope and confidence in Japan and in the future. This unshakable nationalism permeated his behavior even during these years of disaster, during which, to borrow Grew's phrase, Yoshida continued to see the rainbow just around the corner.

In his conversations with Eden and Bingham, Yoshida sought to resolve the new China crisis by soliciting British and American mediation. Although Japan had refused an invitation to present its case at the forthcoming Nine Power Conference in Brussels, Yoshida reported that his government in fact desired to discuss the problem with representatives of the two powers. He urged, and would continue to urge until Pearl Harbor, that no formal condemnation of Japan be made, arguing that this would only exacerbate the situation by forcing the Japanese government to harden its official position. Instead he advocated a "smoke screen" approach. By this, he explained, he had in mind the creation of a subcommittee at Brussels on which both the United States and England should be represented and with which the Japanese could then conduct informal and unpublicized negotiations, laying the foundation for a future peace conference to resolve the Far Eastern crisis. Japan's official rejection of open international intervention in the China crisis was implicit in its refusal to participate in the Brussels conference, but the extent to which the Japanese government actually desired informal mediation was a matter of less clarity. Eden informed Bingham that he thought the Yoshida proposal worth a try, and Britain would approve such a maneuver if it were supported by the United States. At the same time, however, he made clear his skepticism as to Yoshida's credibility as a spokesman of the true Japanese position.[14]

For an individual who had only recently complained of a "double game" in Tokyo, Yoshida seemed remarkably oblivious to the sea change his own standards of "realistic" diplomatic tactics had undergone in the course of journeying to the Atlantic. A decade earlier, when China was being accused of treaty violations and called upon by Japan to show its "sincerity," he had ridiculed vague notions of good will and preached the necessity of a firm and uncompromising stand, backed up by force. Then, when it had been Chinese rather than Japanese "military cliques" that posed a threat to the vested interests of the imperialists in China, he had argued the desirability of international intervention south of the Great Wall. In the 1930s, however, and particularly after 1937, he became *to the West* an apostle of the "realism" of patience, compromise, and conciliation in international affairs.[15]

To back up his argument that a peace conference was possible in the near future, Yoshida offered both an apologia for the China invasion and a reiteration of his pendulum theory. The Japanese government had found it necessary to send a "punitive expedition" to China, he argued, "on account of Chinese hostility and boycott." They did not intend to hold Shanghai, however, and in fact would not be able to do so because public opinion in Japan had swung decisively against the military. He traced army and navy initiatives both abroad and within Japan itself to the alarm caused by reduction in the military budget around 1930, and acknowledged that hitherto military propaganda concerning external dangers confronting Japan had succeeded in mobilizing the support of the majority of the Japanese public. As originally presented to the Diet by the army and navy chiefs, he continued, the cost of the punitive expedition was to be small and its execution "short and swift." Because it was anticipated that Chinese resistance would be weak, and also because of the necessity of guarding against Soviet intervention, the initial troops dispatched had been both small in number and inferior in quality. When Chinese resistance proved unexpectedly strong, this had "forced the Government to send a larger and stronger army for protection against the Russian menace"; the Soviet Union was apparently a flexible debater's point. This unexpected acceleration, he concluded, had turned public sentiment against the miltary, a reversal in popular support which was greatly strengthened by resentment against the increased taxes necessary to support the military venture.[16] This insertion of popular resentment against economic burdens as a pivot on which the pendulum would swing became, in the years to follow, a pivot on which Yoshida also was to balance a good part of his optimism. Well into 1940 he would continue to inform his Western contacts that the intolerable financial burden caused by military expenditures was about to precipitate an anti-militarist reversal in Japan.[17]

Grew was immediately informed of Yoshida's views, and responded with incredulity. He denied that any responsible Japanese official had seriously proposed discussing termination of Far Eastern hostilities with either of the Anglo-American powers, and interpreted both governmental and popular opinion in Japan as running in a direction almost completely contrary to that described by Yoshida; this was consistent with the position Grew had maintained since July, namely, that Japanese support for the war effort in China was virtually unanimous.[18] On the very day Yoshida was expressing his views to Bingham, in fact, Grew had cabled Washington that "the war spirit in Japan is noticeably growing."[19] On November 1, addressing himself directly to Yoshida's statements, he quoted an editorial from the October 31 edition of the *Asahi*, which he described as "the most moderate Japanese paper," to the effect that "the position of Japan is that it positively wants no armistice until China reconsiders its attitude and is prepared to liquidate its anti-Japanese policy. There is need for the concerned powers to revise their knowledge on this point. Rumors to the effect that Japan desired an armistice derive from prejudiced countries which seek to succor China from the plight into which it has fallen, and the effort by the powers toward peace which is based on these rumors is, so far as Japan is concerned, merely misplaced kindness."

With the exception of certain segments of big business engaged in foreign trade, Grew found "no evidence that . . . there is any substantial section of the population which now holds any such opinion as that described by Yoshida," and he proceeded to state that there had in fact been no substantial tax increase, that there was no unemployment or other hardship worth mentioning, and that the Japanese embroilment on the continent was being presented to the public as a series of uninterrupted victories. He concluded that, in all probability, Yoshida was acting on his own initiative.[20] From this time on, Grew tended to regard Yoshida with a mixture of personal friendliness and mounting professional skepticism. At the same time, however, he joined Craigie in warning against any action at Brussels that might be interpreted by Japan as diplomatic pressure.[21]

Despite Grew's disclaimers, Yoshida continued to interpret the Japanese position in a more positive manner. In mid-November—as Shanghai fell and the Japanese attack on Nanking began—he personally informed Eden that Craigie and Grew had been told, by the vice foreign minister and foreign minister respectively, that "the Japanese Government would be disposed to accept an offer of good offices looking toward peace." Both ambassadors, while acknowledging conversations with the officials named, deemed it necessary to correct this impression that the Japanese government was formally soliciting an offer of good offices. While Craigie and Grew were receptive to the idea of Anglo-American intermediation, they regarded it as essential that any such move be approved by both China and Japan, and it was their impression that, contrary to this, any thoughts the Japanese might have concerning Western mediation involved bringing pressure to bear upon Chiang Kai-shek to enter peace negotiations. Vice Foreign Minister Horiuchi Kensuke had said as much to Craigie when the latter pushed him on this point on November 19, and Grew concluded from this that, despite the impression conveyed to Eden by Yoshida, the time was still not opportune for mediation.[22]

On February 4, 1938—as Japanese troops were advancing down the Yangtze following the rape of Nanking—Yoshida again visited Eden to suggest that an opportunity might occur shortly when an informal British offer of good offices would be appropriate. He acknowledged that he was speaking on his own, without instructions, and volunteered that the failure of his earlier proposal along these lines at the time of the Brussels Conference was due to the fact that the Japanese government had decided at that time to rely on German rather than Anglo-American mediation. He again stressed the severe economic and financial strain of the war on Japan, and informed Eden that the Japanese military had abandoned plans for an attack on south China. When Eden emphasized that Britain would only act in conjunction with the United States in any possible good offices, Yoshida—in Eden's notes—"assented, though without any enthusiasm."[23] Yoshida's informal comments at this time accompanied presentation of two documents to Eden: a copy of Foreign Minister Hirota's policy address to the Diet on January 22, 1938, and an *aide-mémoire* from the Japanese government which Craigie later described as a "very friendly advance."[24] These two ostensible reflections of the Foreign Ministry position were indeed conciliatory, although in the broadest possible terms, concerning "cultivating traditional friendship with Great Britain," and the British cabinet subsequently discussed the February 4 conversation on several occasions and urged the Foreign Office to look further into Yoshida's averred opportunity.[25] As usual, nothing came of this, but the episode does suggest an interlude when both Japan and Britain were simultaneously probing the edges of possible rapprochement; the Brenan and Pratt appeasement proposals, it will be recalled, coalesced at this time in the February 14 memorandum to the United States.

Yoshida persisted in urging British mediation of the China crisis, although somewhat erratically. Thus, on February 15, Baron Tomii Shū of the Japanese embassy called on Leith-Ross at Treasury to broach the possibility of Anglo-Japanese financial cooperation in north China; Tomii at the same time indicated that Yoshida was awaiting Eden's reply to the February 4 conversation.[26] But, as it happened, Eden himself had arranged to meet Yoshida on the same day, and concluded that Yoshida was now offering "no encouragement whatsoever to think that our mediation would be appreciated at this time."[27] Precisely a week later, however, Leith-Ross was personally informed by Yoshida that discreet mediation would indeed be welcomed by the Japanese government, even though they might not be able to say this publicly under the existing circumstances. The British found it all a bit "strange,"[28] although a glimmer of the thinking of the Japanese Anglophiles came through several days later, on February 25, when Cadogan discussed these puzzling mediation proposals with the visiting Viscount Ishii Kikujirō. Ishii, a former foreign minister best known for his part in the 1917 Lansing-Ishii agreement, was another stalwart of the so-called "moderate" camp in Japan, and his response to Cadogan's inquiry provided a nice insight into just how severe and coercive "moderation" could become.

Ishii informed Cadogan that he had no official authorization to invite mediation, but in his own view Anglo-American pressure *on the Chinese* would be appropriate. As Cadogan summarized the argument, China's "situation was desperate and there was no prospect of her being able to carry on the struggle. General Chiang-Kai-Shek, having refused the Japanese terms, was no doubt deterred by considerations of prestige from making any further approach to Japan. What Viscount Ishii thought was that if Great Britain, or perhaps, better still, Great Britain and America, were to urge General Chiang-Kai-Shek to sue for peace, the latter might be able to represent to his people that there was no longer any hope, and that on the advice of two great Powers he was doing the only possible thing." Ishii then concluded with a discourse on recent Japanese history which Cadogan by then, no doubt, could have delivered chapter and verse himself—speaking "for some time on the situation in which Japan found herself, or had found herself during the last 40 years of increasing difficulty, of her need for expansion, for markets and for defense against the spread of Communism."[29]

Yoshida continued his overtures to buy time throughout April and May, compensating for lack of innovation in theme by introducing greater variety in audience: Maurice Hankey of the Cabinet Offices on April 5, for example; Cadogan on April 26; the Secretary of State for Dominion Affairs on April 29; Clive of the Foreign Office on May 1; Leslie Hore-Belisha of the War Office on May 6; and so on.[30] Typically, Yoshida was neither generous to the Chinese nor hesitant in his intimations that "Japan was at the end of its tether."[31] And, also typically, the British found him increasingly unpersuasive. "Mr. Yoshida is very prone to go about saying this kind of thing to everyone he meets and he seeks interviews with all and sundry in order to talk to them in this sense," Foreign Secretary Halifax informed Hore-Belisha on May 7. "We have on various occasions tried to ascertain from him whether he has any authority whatever from his Government in putting forward these views, but he always assures us that he has none, and then disappears for a number of weeks during which he airs his personal views to other people. I really do not think that we can pay much attention to what a foreign Ambassador says in his 'personal capacity.'"[32]

On May 30, Yoshida personally suggested to Halifax that recent cabinet changes in Japan, in which General Ugaki had assumed the foreign minister's portfolio, reflected the unpopularity of the war in Japan, and that the anti-British movement in Japan "should not be taken too seriously," since it existed "largely among certain of the younger people as also in some circles of the cotton manufacturing world whose self-interest supported association with such a movement." He described his government's official policy toward China as resting on three points—respect for China's territorial integrity (which, it will be recalled, Hirota had privately repudiated to Yoshida in July 1937); respect for foreign interests in China; and insistence that the anti-Japanese movement in China be stopped—and added to this his personal opinion that, in Halifax's summary, "special provision would have to be made—whatever this might mean—in regard to the Chinese provinces which bordered on Manchukuo in order to protect the position of the latter from the operation of influences inimical to the regime." "There was, as I expected," Halifax concluded, "nothing very precise or tangible in the suggestions which the Ambassador made."[33]

This final year of Yoshida's ambassadorship was surely one of great personal pain and embarrassment. He was treated courteously but lightly in London, and must have sensed this (after his resignation the British government decided not to present him with the usual perfunctory honors).[34] And yet it is difficult to imagine how a good, patriotic, and isolated imperialist could have acted other than he did—that is, simply to try to keep the ball in play until a time when his country's quest for autarky had been abandoned, or at least tempered. His earnest lectures on recent history were received with obvious impatience by the British, however, who failed to see a similiar fatuousness in the proffered history of their own imperial experience, while his endeavors to explain Japan's case were simply met with counter-statements outlining the British case against Japan,[35] and dismissed by many with that burdened workhorse of the diplomatist's lexicon: charges of insincerity. Beneath the ever-present veneer of civility and propriety, the British tended to regard Yoshida with much the same condescension he himself accorded the Chinese.

His position vis-à-vis his own government was hardly more conducive to self-confidence, for the British at least grasped at some of his straws, while his endeavors similarly to prod Japan's leaders toward a closer reliance upon British mediation ultimately failed completely. Yoshida endeavored to exploit his contacts with the more traditional channels of political influence in Japan, notably the court circles and senior statesmen, to impress his views upon the government. In May, for example, simultaneously with his widely dispersed personal diplomacy in London, he informed Makino and Saionji that the Chamberlain government was eager to assist in the resolution of the China problem and would gladly lend assistance in anything the Japanese might propose. Would it not be good, he concluded almost plaintively, for the Japanese government to "think of something as soon as possible?"—the implication being, wouldn't it be good for Saionji to exert his influence more forcefully in this direction.[36] This assessment was based on the not entirely incorrect assumption that Britain's greatest concern as Japan devastated China was "business as usual," and that Chamberlain was particularly desirous to lend such assistance as would resolve the China crisis before British economic interests there became thoroughly unhinged.[37] As indicated below, Yoshida was overly sanguine as to the extent to which Britain actually was willing and able to compromise its own position as of mid-1938, but his general impression of British willingness to participate in a Far Eastern peace settlement was correct, for on June 21 R. A. Butler, another of Yoshida's acquaintances, did acknowledge before Parliament that Great Britain was willing to mediate the hostilities in China, *singly* or in conjunction with other countries. Butler went on to note, however, that as recently as four days earlier the Japanese foreign minister had publicly rejected third-power mediation, and shortly thereafter a Japanese spokesman specifically rebuffed this open British offer.[38] Again Yoshida appeared to be pursuing rainbows. Had he been doing so all along?

In retrospect: yes. But if Yoshida misplayed the situation in these long and dreary months which followed the China Incident, it was hardly for want of consistency in his own outlook, but rather because that outlook was flawed in key particulars: first, in its overestimation of the extent to which the Anglo-American powers would be willing to reaffirm the traditional policies of capitalist cooperation in Asia in the name of anti-communism and "stabilization," even at the cost of sacrificing some of their established (but secondary in the larger global picture) interests on the continent; second, in its misreading not so much of the so-called Japanese "military cliques," but rather of the civilian leaders who purportedly would undertake to reverse the pendulum; and third, in its self-delusion as to the extent to which the type of "mediation" he himself envisioned represented a plausible and "moderate" alternative, or was even perceived as such by the British themselves. Yoshida's theories, in retrospect, misrepresented the depth of the capitalist crisis, the situation in Japan, the strength of Chinese nationalism, and even his own role itself.

On the more formal diplomatic front, it is possible to argue that, in the months following the China Incident and even up to February or March 1938, the Japanese government did in fact indicate some receptivity to the possibility of third-power mediation. Prior to the October and November 1937 conversations, Yoshida had received communications from Tokyo which indicated general interest in this, and in the view of scholars such as Dorothy Borg, the Yoshida overtures of these months were actually part of an "extraordinarily intense 'peace drive' on the part of the Japanese"—signals the Western powers, and Ambassador Grew in particular, missed because they had misread the complex situation within Japanese ruling circles at the time.[39] Similarly, it has been noted here that in his February 4 meeting with Eden, Yoshida presented two documents, Hirota's Diet speech and an *aide-mémoire*, which were recognized as being exceptionally friendly in their acknowledgment of Britain's legitimate interests in China. From the Japanese record as conveyed in the Harada diary, it would appear that Foreign Minister Hirota took these gestures seriously, for he personally informed Harada at the time that Yoshida had been given instructions to inform the British government that "we will absolutely not do anything to harm British interests. Whether we extend or settle the situation [in China], we intend increasingly to promote friendly relations with Great Britain; thus even if by chance (*manichi*) the state of war should continue and advance further, we of course have no intention of infringing upon British interests, and so desire that Great Britain give careful thought to matters concerning her shipping and residents [in China]." Near the end of February, Hirota apparently followed this up with general instructions that Yoshida meet with Chamberlain and Halifax, the new foreign secretary, and "take the initiative from our side."[40]

Taken at face value, such instances would seem to remove the aspersion of personal quixotism from Yoshida's activities in London and cast them instead as part of one of the best lost chances for a peaceful solution in the Far East following the China Incident. If so, his reputation for private initiative and inaccurate representation was certainly not helpful in getting these signals across. But if the signals existed and the situation within the Japanese government was more complex and potentially flexible than outsiders appreciated, then why did nothing come of this?—for, as evidenced by the Brenan and Pratt plans noted in the preceding chapter, by February 1938 the Foreign Office seemed resigned to the possible necessity of rather exceptional appeasement of

Japan in China. The answer, it would seem, lies partly in the cold water America threw on Britain's proposed conciliation, and partly also in the rapidly changing course of the China War.

But beyond this, and perhaps more persuasively, it might be argued that what a Hirota or a Yoshida said, or even imagined, they might offer was overriden by more relentless circumstances that were only partly of their own making. The new course of empire carried its own momentum for Japan, and with this a constant updating of the status quo ante which inexorably precluded Japanese toleration of a decisive British role in China, or of meaningful Chinese "territorial integrity." And similarly—despite the preoccupation with the Nazi threat in Europe, despite the bleak awareness of military impotence in Asia, and despite the frank acknowledgment in the Brenan and Pratt proposals of the anachronistic, hypocritical, and ultimately self-defeating nature of the entire foreign position in China—Britain's old and beleaguered empire had a heavy and ponderous momentum of its own. In the end, as suggested in the Brenan excerpt below, Britain's leaders found that they too were unable to repudiate or extricate themselves from the tangled skein of their own imperialistic structure in Asia. From this perspective, it becomes a moot question indeed as to whether the type of velvet-glove adjustments Yoshida was advocating bore any meaningful relationship to the stakes involved, the crisis on hand.

Within Japanese policy-making circles, moreover, the very "moderates" in whom Yoshida rested hope were instrumental in expanding the war against China. As James B. Crowley has shown, the crisis of the China Incident actually enabled Prime Minister Konoe to assume broader authority than he would have possessed otherwise, and Konoe and Foreign Minister Hirota wielded meaningful power in this critical period. The months immediately following the incident at the Marco Polo Bridge represented an acid test for the pendulum theory—for that moderate, civilian element of the Japanese elite Yoshida had always pointed to as Japan's true ruling class, its genuinely enlightened statesmen. The validity of that theory, and the accuracy of

Yoshida's representations to the British and Americans in this period, should thus be set against such considerations as the following:

(1) In the final analysis it was Konoe and Hirota who led the hard-liners in Japan, expressed the militant, escalatory rhetoric, and formulated the policies that enabled field commanders in China to expand their aggression.[41] It was their unilateral decision of July 11, 1937 that committed the Japanese government to a "fundamental solution of Sino-Japanese relations" and thus opened the door to the military escalation which followed.[42] In mid-October, just prior to the Yoshida conversations with Eden and Bingham, it was Konoe and Hirota who countered the Army General Staff's opposition to military and political activities in China and threw their support to field commanders who advocated a coordinated series of aggressive campaigns in north and central China.[43] On November 19, only a day or two after Yoshida informed Eden that his government was interested in "an offer of good offices looking toward peace," Konoe and Hirota again overrode the General Staff and supported the capture of Nanking.[44] By the time of Yoshida's conversation with Eden in February 1938, nearly a month had already passed since Konoe and Hirota led the cabinet in severing relations with the Kuomintang and calling for a "war of annihilation" against China. Throughout this period the civilian element headed by Konoe and Hirota, and backed by palace officials such as Kido Kōichi, rejected even the submission of concrete peace terms to the Chinese on the grounds that this might convey an impression of Japanese weakness by indicating a desire for quick termination of hostilities.[45]

(2) Contrary to Yoshida's thesis that economic hardships were turning Japanese public opinion against the China war, during the months in question the leaders of Japanese business and industry not only failed to protest increasing tax burdens, but actually endorsed the position of the Japan-China Business and Industrial Association to the effect that "a military government should be set up not only in North China, but in all China." In keeping with the diplomacy of *fait accompli* followed by the

Konoe government, the business lobby justified its support for conquest of all China by citing the cost in Japanese lives and material incurred since the China Incident. The political parties also supported an uncompromising China policy.[46]

(3) The emperor, Japan's ultimate "safeguard" in the Makino-Yoshida thesis, indirectly gave his personal approval to the Konoe annihilation policy by refusing to give cognizance to the General Staff's peace proposals. When the General Staff sought an audience with the emperor on January 14, 1938, through which they might clarify their case and solicit imperial support, the emperor turned the request down on the grounds, as he later told Konoe, that "I suspected they wanted to overturn what had already been decided." Although Konoe, together with Yoshida, would attempt to solicit imperial intervention for peace seven years later in the famous Konoe Memorial, his attitude toward the General Staff's similar endeavor in 1938 was disdainful. They were, he said, attempting "to use the Emperor as a tool."[47]

Regardless of whether such manifest betrayal of true moderation and decency is explained in terms of personal flaws—as often done with Konoe in particular[48]—or policy dynamics, the "moderates" emerge poorly. For it must be concluded either that virtually all "moderates" were weak, or else that the so-called moderate position itself permitted such easy transition into exploitation abroad and actual warmongering. Yoshida's own role is illuminating here, and would suggest the greater validity of the latter argument in at least two respects: the striking resonance—in vocabulary, perceived goals, and conceit of proper firmness or "realism" in foreign policy—between the "military diplomacy" of the Konoe-Hirota *civilian* claque in 1937–1938 and Yoshida's own posture prior to the Manchurian and China incidents; and the extent to which the self-styled Anglophile critics of Japan's policy in the late 1930s, such as Ishii and again Yoshida, actually gave tacit support to critical aspects of post-China Incident policy.

The rhetoric employed by the Konoe group to justify Japan's aggression, for example, rings like a mindless recitation of the catechism of "sincerity" and "self-reflection," "thoroughness" and "resolution," "prestige" and "punishment," which permeated Yoshida's own earlier pronouncements concerning China policy. Thus, Hirota informed the Diet on September 5, 1937 that "in accordance with the right of self-defense as well as with the cause of righteousness . . . our country is determined to deal a decisive blow, so that [China] may reflect on the error of its ways." Before the same body on the same day, Konoe declared that, "[if] China fails to realize its mistakes and persists in its stubborn resistance, our Empire is fully prepared for protracted hostilities."[49] The Hirota speech of January 22, 1938 which Yoshida tendered to Eden on February 4 was a more leisurely excursion through the familiar enchanted garden of imperial clichés, which for the student of Yoshida vividly evokes the ghostly shades of Chang Tso-lin and Mo Te-hui and the Japanese consulate in Mukden. In this, Hirota condemned the Chinese for their "lack of understanding" of Japan's "true intentions," for being "unrepentent," for "ignoring our magnanimity," for failing "to send a reply that could be regarded in any way as sincere." Nonetheless, rest assured, "the sincerity of our Government and people" would prevail.[50]

One assumes the rhetoric was intoxicating to those who purveyed it, but even if dismissed as propagandistic drivel, the underlying contempt for China—not merely its military capacity and nationalistic will, but its very right to exist autonomously—was unmistakable. And to a certain extent the Konoe-Hirota clash with the General Staff duplicated and enlarged the dispute between Yoshida himself and the Kwantung Army concerning policy in Manchuria in 1927–1928; in both instances, the most aggressive course of action was endorsed by the purported civilian moderates and opposed by responsible military leaders. At the time of the China Incident, the General Staff, led by Generals Tada Shun and Ishiwara Kanji, urged moderation and conciliation toward China on the pragmatic grounds that military priorities demanded preparation for possible war against the Soviet Union, and the China venture would prove a quagmire which diverted energies and resources from this goal. As late as the beginning of 1938, moreover, this position had substantial support in both army and navy circles.[51]

The ultimately decisive counter-position, on the other hand, was well summarized by Harada in his diary entry for January 19, 1938, in which he recorded this gist of a discussion between Konoe and Kido:

> The General Staff's earnest desire for peace is certainly understandable, but since events have come to this point, to be half way through and then take the initiative and put out various conditions showing generosity, with an attitude in every respect like that of a defeated country being dragged along by the other side, as if to say, "How would it be to make peace along these lines?"—this is not an attitude appropriate to a country which has seen successive victories up to now. Indeed, should we do this, others will appraise our state of affairs with the notion that "Japan is quite weak—is she not already facing a crisis?" And then the Japanese exchange rate might fall drastically abroad, or public bonds might drop, and we would be unable to engage in trade, to buy goods even if we wanted to, or a *panic* might occur, and then what would we do? Even if we wish to bring the matter to a close, we must settle it in an appropriate manner. Their way of thinking is indeed curious.[52]

Yet it was largely this elite circle of Konoe, Kido, Makino, and Saionji, pivoting on the court and linked together by Harada's busy web of gossip and message-carrying, upon which Yoshida relied to convey his own messages advocating melioration of the militant diplomacy and greater attentiveness to relations with the West.

In this context of giant steps forward in the conquest of China, Yoshida undeniably did advocate certain more "moderate" solutions. As early as the Shanghai Incident of August 1937 he, Makino, and Matsudaira came under fire from certain pro-expansion forces in Japan for their opposition to this escalation of hostilities,[53] and he took no steps to disguise his Anglophilism in a period when this was an increasingly uncomfortable label to bear in Japan. He also, as he made clear to the British, regarded the severance of relations with Chiang Kai-shek and the Kuomintang in January 1938 as a mistake.[54] In the larger perspective, he consistently opposed the quest for autarky insofar as this, first, ignored the economic necessity of maintaining close relations with the West and, second, was imbued with a strong element of radicalism and "national socialism," as discussed in the following chapters. At the same time, however, like the good Anglophile Ishii, and like the Konoe cabinet itself, he too rode the winds of war, for it is difficult to interpret the "mediation" proposals of the moderates themselves in these months as other than an attempt to offer the Chinese an opportunity for unconditional surrender, as opposed to military annihilation, and to do so in a manner which would simultaneously restore the traditional cooperation of the great powers in *and against* China.

While the "pro-Anglo-American clique" lost no occasion for evoking the "good old days" of the Anglo-Japanese Alliance, moreover, by the late 1930s their vision had far transcended mere nostalgia. At no apparent point did they take substantive issue with either the legitimacy of Manchukuo or the newer economic and strategic goals of incorporating north China in Japan's redefined sphere of influence.[55] In a situation where his own government refused to consider conciliation with China, Yoshida devoted his energies to urging the Anglo-American powers to be conciliatory toward Japan. Thus, while the group exemplified by Yoshida and Ishii sought to turn the clock back to an earlier era of imperialist cooperation, at the same time their envisioned arena of cooperation in continental Asia had been drastically recontoured. They conceded nothing to China's nationalistic aspirations, but on the contrary endorsed the expansion and intensification of neocolonial control; on this account alone, it can be argued that their "realism" was doomed to failure. And in the process they assumed that Britain and the United States must necessarily acquiesce in the redefinition of the Japanese imperium, even at the sacrifice of some of their own traditional "rights and interests" in China. Thus the moderates too played the diplomacy of *fait accompli*, and brandished the inevitable vouchers of the blood debts of war; witting or not, they imbibed the vapors of a new order in Asia. The history lessons with which they so wearied their British counterparts emerge in this light as more than just a plaint at the unjust hand recent decades had dealt to Japan; implicitly they were also the text of a manifest destiny for Japan in Asia, and good realists did not quarrel with destiny.

Destinies thus perceived in terms of the individual state, however, ultimately collided. As analyzed by the Foreign Office's Sir John Brenan, by mid-1938 the core of Yoshida's dilemma lay deeper than his apparent isolation from and lack of influence in Tokyo, *for the position of the Japanese "moderates" and Anglophiles was itself unacceptable to London.* Despite the conciliatory secret proposals of January and February 1938, which Brenan himself had helped draft, Britain in the end concluded that its own position in China was not fundamentally negotiable. This conclusion was undoubtedly influenced by the fact that as the China War entered a period of apparent stalemate, British policy-makers became less awed by the potential of the Japanese military machine. But the larger problem implicit here is especially interesting, since for the Japanese side it formulates in concrete terms the issue of the tacit collaboration of the moderates with the war effort and war goals, and at the same time graphically illustrates the relentlessly unfolding crisis within the imperialist camp. Brenan, in his bluntness, seems somewhat of an Anglo-Saxon Yoshida, and his analysis as of July 1938, almost exactly one year after the China Incident, ran as follows:

> There is no need to attribute conscious dishonesty to those Japanese who assure us that they wish for a resumption of more friendly relations. . . . These people are doubtless sincere in their desire to be on better terms with us, but their ideas of how this shall be brought about and what the terms shall be differ vastly from ours. Apart from the preservation of our numerous and valuable commercial enterprises we want to retain intact our influence in China; our privileges of an unusual and extraterritorial nature such as the British hold on the Customs Service, our control over the administration of the Shanghai settlement, our personnel in the railways and the maintenance of our shipping interests along the coasts and waterways of China. That is the meaning which we have attached to the Japanese assurances to respect our rights and interests. Consciously or not, we are demanding that the Japanese shall put the clock back and restore us to the position we occupied before the outbreak of the hostilities, or as near thereto as may be possible.

> It is, however, becoming increasingly clear that it is beyond the power of [the Foreign Minister] General Ugaki and the "pro-British" section of the government to do anything of the sort, even if they wished to, which of course they do not. We may be sure that the Japanese authorities, even those who are well-disposed towards us, have no intention of foregoing the only reward which they can see for their national sacrifices in this war. Those who distrust the German-Italian connection and wish to retain the good will of the democratic Powers do not mean what we mean by cooperation and respect for foreign interests. They hope that we and the others will accept and recognise Japan's new position on the mainland; that we will abandon Chiang Kai-shek and cooperate with Japan in developing the occupied territory by financing Japanese enterprises. If we do this, they will remove some of the petty irritations, pay off the railway debts, maintain the service of the loans and so on. It would not mean (in their intention) the survival of our larger trading interests in China, but the manner and tempo of their passing would be eased. . . .
>
> The truth of the matter is that we acquired our dominant position in China as the result of our wars with that country in the nineteenth century and we can now only keep it by the same or similiar methods. We must either use force, or otherwise bring sufficient pressure to bear on the Japanese authorities to compel them to relinquish in our favour what they regard as the spoils of victory. We may, without fighting ourselves, be able to apply that pressure if the Japanese are exhausted by a long war with the Chinese, but it is futile to expect that we shall get what we want for the mere asking, or by protests about the infringements of our "rights," or by a more friendly attitude.
>
> . . . there is no prospect of obtaining anything of permanent value by abandoning China and cooperating with Japan—at least, not yet. The "stalemate" policy still offers the best hope for the survival of our influence in China.[56]

Yoshida's London tour ended shortly thereafter, on this note of ominous stalemate. He continued to pass suggestions on to his more charitable and like-minded British friends, and to receive a modicum of encouragement from them. In July 1939, for example, he received through Sir Horace Wilson a reply actually drafted within the Foreign Office acknowledging "that Japan stands in a special relation to China, quite apart from geographical propinquity," and looking forward to a peace settlement "generous to Japan, equitable to China." The reply went on to note frankly that "the last thing we want to see is China and Japan exhausting themselves in futile combat—on purely materialistic grounds alone this would spell disaster for us," and even evinced some resignation to the prospect that, although "there is room for both of us to trade" in China, British interests might be expected to suffer somewhat in any expansion of Sino-Japanese economic relations.[57]

Upon his return to Tokyo, however, Yoshida's activities became directed more toward the United States than toward Great Britain, due both to the shifting focus of the international crisis and his own personal relationship with Ambassador Grew. What is perhaps most interesting in retrospect in surveying the developments of these later years is that the events of late 1937 and early 1938 did not prompt Yoshida to revise his theories of the pendulum and the moderates and the safeguards of the emperor system. For the next several years he continued to predict the imminent upsurge of moderate sentiment in Japan, and even after belatedly acknowledging Konoe's failures in 1941, during the years of the Pacific War he again rested his hopes for Japan's redemption on the tarnished prince. Throughout his entire life, moreover, he never departed from the interpretation that the crisis of the 1930s was to be explained as a departure from the traditional diplomacy of Meiji and Taishō instigated under the irresistible pressure of extremist and conspiratorial militarists.

THE PIPE LINE AND THE PENDULUM, 1939–1940

In September 1938, when it was already known that he would shortly be retiring as ambassador, Yoshida made one of his final official representations to the British government. China had appealed to the League of Nations for economic aid, and Yoshida's task was to make clear to Foreign Secretary Halifax the unfortunate effect British support of this request would have on Japanese public opinion. He emphasized Japan's desire for better relations between the two countries, and ended by expressing his personal hopes that Britain might find it possible to act in such a way as to "impress upon Japanese public opinion the good intentions of

His Majesty's Government with regard to Anglo-Japanese relations." Halifax did not take well to the notion that it was up to Britain to demonstrate good intentions,[58] but until Pearl Harbor Yoshida continued to stress the importance of a conciliatory attitude toward Japan on the part of the Anglo-American powers so as to prevent any conclusive diplomatic rupture. To ensure general continuity with his own approach on the Japanese side, he successfully urged the appointment of Shigemitsu Mamoru as his replacement in London.[59]

Upon his return to Tokyo, Yoshida, now sixty years of age, retired for the second time from the foreign service. He continued to maintain both unofficial and semi-official relations with Grew and Craigie, however, interpreting the Japanese scene to both and constantly urging the necessity for patience, moderation, and positive gestures of good will by the respective governments of the two ambassadors. Thus, at the end of February 1939, Yoshida called on Grew to express the opinion that "if at this juncture the American Government would make some gesture of friendship to Japan it would have tremendous effect." Two days later, to Grew's own surprise, the United States did make such a magnanimous gesture by offering to convey the ashes of Ambassador Saitō, who had died at his post in Washington, back to Japan on an American cruiser. But no "tremendous effect" was forthcoming.[60]

At approximately the same time, Yoshida joined other "moderates" such as Matsudaira, Kabayama, and Harada in urging both Grew and Craigie not to take their planned leaves of absence during the summer months of 1939. As Craigie explained the situation to London, "Yoshida, who, as always, is the most outspoken, says that the main reason for this feeling is that it is impossible for Japan to continue on her present course for more than a few more months and that, when the inevitable reaction comes, it is essential that I should be here to take advantage of it, particularly as Grew will be absent." Ikeda Seihin, former finance minister and the dominant figure within the Mitsui *zaibatsu*, associated himself with the Yoshida group and wrote to Craigie supporting the view that "Japan cannot stand the financial pace for more than a few months longer"—the main basis of Yoshida's optimistic outlook.[61] In April, Grew noted the "thoroughly anti-British" tone of the Japanese press in his diary, but shortly thereafter he recorded a conversation with Yoshida which was "all about the prospect of eventual peace with China which Great Britain must arrange, but very nebulous." Once again, Grew commented on Yoshida's poor command of English, and expressed the increasingly familiar lament that "with him the wish is father to the thought and better things are always just around the corner."[62]

In October of the same year, the summer of the alleged financial crisis having passed with no "inevitable reaction," Grew returned from leave and had dinner at Yoshida's home. Yoshida and Shirasu Jirō (a key personal aide during Yoshida's postwar premierships) urged Grew to convey his impressions of American public opinion concerning Japan directly to the new prime minister, General Abe Nobuyuki, as well as to Konoe, who they indicated had been instrumental in the formation of the Abe cabinet in late August. Grew expressed reluctance to by-pass formal channels of communication through the Foreign Ministry, and the prime minister himself apparently refused to engage in such direct conversations.[63] Instead, during the brief four-and-a-half months of his tenure, Abe used Yoshida as a go-between with Grew. The general impression Grew derived from these exchanges was that the Japanese government was "floundering" with regards to Japanese-American relations.[64]

On April 16, 1940, Grew spent another evening with the Yoshida family and Count Makino, and again the old themes were rehearsed:

> I had a long talk with Yoshida who always predicts the rainbow just around the corner and tonight was no exception. He said that I must under no circumstances leave Japan this spring because an important turn in the situation would come in June and it would be most unwise for both Craigie and myself to be away at that time. His argument is that when the new tax law comes into effect and the exporters, at the beginning of the exporting season, find that their exports are going to

> be drastically limited, the present optimism among the farmers and others owing to the current high prices will depart and the public will demand an end to the China campaign which will affect even the military. Then the United States will rapidly find that her interests in China are to be respected. I said that this, if true, was very good news but considering the fact that Japanese interference with American rights in China is steadily increasing (I told Yoshida of the flood of reports to that effect which cross my desk daily from such places as Tientsin, Peiping, Amoy, Foochow, etc.) I was less optimistic than he as to a sudden and radical improvement in the situation. Yoshida merely repeated what he had said, over and over again, so we did not get very far toward a meeting of minds. My last word was that I could not guarantee the continued patience of the American Government and people forever and that if a change is to come, it had better come soon and effectively.[65]

Yet, if Grew was dubious, he was still attracted to that ever-suspended pendulum that had first been dangled before him by Yoshida and his colleagues some eight years before. He did postpone his projected leave, and in mid-June 1940, he summarized the various viewpoints held by influential Japanese—dividing them primarily into those who sought a deal with the Soviet Union, the pro-German camp, and the pro-Anglo-American moderates. The moderates, he claimed, recognized the impossibility of attempting to create a closed economy in East Asia, and the inevitable failure of the Chinese puppet regime under Wang Ching-wei, and thus supported a generous settlement with Chiang Kai-shek. They realized that Japan's future welfare lay primarily in "good relations and cooperation with the great democratic commercial Powers." To press this position within Japanese ruling circles, however, it was necessary that the democracies assure Japan of economic and financial assistance and cooperation, including credits and, implicitly, non-discrimination in trade arrangements.

"This is the old story that we have heard for many years," Grew acknowledged, "to the effect that just beneath the surface there exists an important body of moderates who only need a little encouragement from abroad to emerge and to gain control from the military and the reactionaries. Such men as Yoshida and Kabayama and others have always predicted the rainbow just around the corner, ever since I came to Japan. But now there is something in it." Grew now felt that the people were becoming "heartily sick of the 'China Incident'," and that the moderates' recognition of the fallacy of Japan's quest for autarky was shared by "most of the world of business, some of the higher and far-sighted military officers and many influential elements both within the Government and out of it." On the basis of his "pipe lines," Grew was inclined to believe that Prime Minister Yonai Mitsumasa, the war and navy ministers, and the foreign minister were all coming around to this view and would welcome encouragement.

Thus Grew's well-known and increasingly controversial advocacy of "constructive conciliation" toward Japan remained closely tied to the line, and "pipe line," (and in the end the pipe dream) represented by Yoshida and the Japanese moderates. Even as China's war dead approached two million, he continued to hope for a chastened but still powerful Japan allied with the Anglo-American powers in Asia.[66] He resented comparison of his position with that of Chamberlain's "appeasement" at Munich,[67] but U.S. public opinion turned increasingly against him, as did events in Japan. The formation of the second Konoe cabinet in July 1940 struck him from the start as retrogressive, and with the famous "green-light" cable of September 12, 1940, even Grew parted company with the "moderates." The question for him was no longer whether the United States should take positive action against Japan, but when.

THE DIPLOMACY OF DESPERATION, 1941

With the signing of the Tripartite Pact among Germany, Italy, and Japan on September 27, 1940, followed two weeks later by creation of the Imperial Rule Assistance Association as part of Konoe's domestic "New Structure," Grew's pessimism grew greater while contact with his Japanese acquaintances diminished. He maintained relations with Yoshida, however, particularly when Yoshida's wife lay dying in the fall of 1941, and in the weeks thereafter up to Pearl Harbor. And he did have recurrent visions of the pendulum, especially when Germany attacked the Soviet Union in June 1941 and overtures were subsequently made by the Japanese side for a meeting between Konoe and Roosevelt. But in general his prognosis remained gloomy, and when Yoshida called upon him in late October 1941 to offer suggestions concerning the Hull-Nomura talks underway in Washington, Grew's response was abrupt:

> He wants us to make a joint declaration with Japan stating that we have no intention of "infiltrating" into Indochina, and, as usual, he said that compromise would be necessary if we were to make progress. I was pretty severe in replying, pointing out that there was no room for compromise and explaining the absurdity of issuing such a joint declaration as he suggested. I gave him a copy of my long letter to Soyeshima of September 1, to read, mark, learn and inwardly digest. Yoshida, much as I like him, is difficult to debate with, for he keeps coming back to his original point no matter what one says—compromise, compromise, compromise.[68]

Yoshida did not give up easily, but visited Grew twice more within the next week. After the third talk, on October 30, Grew noted in his diary that Yoshida "said that hereafter he proposed to work behind the scenes and would not continue to come to see me. A wise decision."[69]

More than a wise decision, this was a desperate last resort. For a figure outside the mainstream, Yoshida maintained an extremely intimate and up-to-the-minute knowledge of decisions being made at the highest level. This derived from a web of contacts with a variety of well-placed individuals. The elite Tokyo Club appears to have been a major meeting place for those who opposed the war policy, and the inner circle with which Yoshida conversed was dominated by peers and high court officials. These included Count Makino and Count Kabayama, Imperial Household Minister Matsudaira Tsuneo, Privy Seal Kido Kōichi, Chief Secretary to the Privy Seal Matsudaira Yasumasa, and Hara Yoshimichi, the president of the Privy Council. Former prime ministers Okada Keisuke (a retired admiral) and Wakatsuki Reijirō, as well as the Mitsui doyen Ikeda Seihin, were also major contacts in the months prior to Pearl Harbor. Through Admiral Kobayashi Seizō, Yoshida kept abreast of trends within the navy and, to some extent, the army as well. The circle also included diplomats such as Shidehara, Satō Naotake, Obata Kunryō, and Tōgō Shigenori.[70]

As a result of such contacts, Yoshida was fully aware of the momentous Imperial Conference held on September 6, at which the emperor gave approval to a plan, "The Essentials for Carrying Out the Empire's Policies," which set a deadline of the first ten days of October for reaching a satisfactory conclusion in the negotiations with the United States. If Washington and Tokyo still remained deadlocked, the plan committed the government to "immediately decide to commence hostilities against the United States, Britain, and the Netherlands."[71] Yoshida's hope in Konoe reached a low point at this time. On September 6, he wrote to Makino that, although the prime minister was pro-American and opposed to war "in his heart," he lacked the courage to stand up for his convictions. This was true also of the foreign minister, Toyoda Teijirō.[72]

On September 17, Yoshida took the liberty of writing Konoe and advising him to resign. The populace was confused as to the nature and meaning of the New Structure, he stated, and domestic discontent was mounting. While acknowledging that he was not privy to the details of the pact with Germany, Yoshida warned that Germany faced a prolonged war, with no good outcome in sight. And he chastised Konoe for failing to settle the China crisis: "As I have often told you, the reason why the China Incident has not been resolved as desired is because [the government] has been counting on Germany and Italy, who are of no help, and has failed to prepare to utilize the power Great Britain and the United States have in China." It was Konoe's "supporters" rather than he himself who were to blame for these problems, Yoshida said, but these so-called supporters were now allowing the prince to become the target of criticism. It was for this reason–that is, implicitly, to protect his reputation–that Konoe should resign, and Yoshida rather drily observed that it would be possible to cite any number of reasons for doing so: diplomatic, military, or economic. Yoshida did not offer any suggestions concerning Konoe's successor as prime minister, and it is unclear whether he had anyone particular in mind.[73]

Konoe did resign almost exactly one month later, on October 18, and with the creation of the Tōjō cabinet a new deadline for war or peace was set. This was the setting in which Yoshida made his several visits to Grew, and he was thus acutely conscious of operating on borrowed time. On October 30, the very day of the third meeting with Grew, the Tōjō government convened the 65th Liaison Conference and concluded that Japan had three alternatives: (1) to avoid war at all costs, and thus "undergo great hardships"—a course which all present, with the exception of Foreign Minister Tōgō, agreed would reduce Japan to a "third-rate country"; (2) to decide on war immediately and settle matters by war; (3) to decide on war but carry on war preparations and diplomacy side by side, seriously seeking a diplomatic solution, with an absolute deadline of November 30.[74] On November 1, in an historic seventeen-hour meeting, the Liaison Conference adopted the third alternative, stipulating that war would be initiated on December 1 if the negotiations with the United States had not been successfully concluded by midnight of the previous day.[75]

Yoshida learned of these meetings almost immediately, and informed Makino that what little optimism he had maintained heretofore was now all but gone.[76] At this juncture there truly seemed no alternative to war other than "compromise, compromise, compromise" on the part of the United States, and in this context Yoshida's specific proposal to Grew several weeks earlier, which had focused on Indochina, turns out to have been of considerably greater significance than the merely private whistle in the dark Grew seemed to have regarded it as at the time: it touched the heart of "Proposal B," the absolutely final proposal Japan would shortly make to the United States. Nor was it mere happenstance that Yoshida focused his attention on Indochina at that time, rather than on China as heretofore. He himself helped draft Proposal B, and must have been working on it during the period in late October when he suddenly began importuning Grew. It was introduced in the decisive November 1 Liaison Conference by Foreign Minister Tōgō.

Tōgō had accepted the post of foreign minister under Tōjō with the understanding that he would be allowed to exert all efforts toward a diplomatic solution of Japan's impasse. At this point, Yoshida and Shidehara submerged old antagonisms to cooperate in advising Tōgō, and they appear to have been the persons primarily responsible for the draft version of Proposal B prepared by the Foreign Ministry.[77] In contributing to Proposal B, it can be said that Yoshida, although by no means one of the influential men deciding Japan's fate in these final months, did participate directly in the last conceivable chance to prevent the Pacific War. As generally recognized by all concerned, Proposal B was offered as a *modus vivendi* to buy time for further negotiations between the United States and Japan, in which the larger issues separating the two countries could be addressed. As such, its specific conditions were directed primarily to the issue of Japan's advance into Indochina, while key points of disagreement—Japanese troops in China, the Tripartite Pact, and nondiscrimination in trade—were left unresolved.[78] The original Foreign Ministry draft submitted to the Liaison Conference on November 1, which is the version with which Yoshida and Shidehara would have been directly involved, read as follows:

> (1) Both Japan and the United States will pledge not to make an armed advance into Southeast Asia and the South Pacific area, except French Indochina.
> (2) The Japanese and American Governments will cooperate with each other so that the procurement of materials they need in the Netherlands East Indies will be assured.
> (3) The United States will promise to supply Japan with one million tons of aviation gasoline.
> Notes: (a) Japan is prepared to move her troops presently in the southern part of French Indochina to the northern part in the event an agreement along these lines is reached. (b) If necessary, those provisions relating to nondiscrimination of commerce and the interpretation and application of the Tripartite Pact that have been proposed before may be added.[79]

This proposal initially met strong opposition from the military representatives present at the November 1 meeting, particularly the chief and vice chief of the Army General Staff, and it was only after Tōgō gave the impression that he might resign and thus bring down the cabinet if the *modus vivendi* were not approved that the conference finally accepted an amended version of Proposal B.[80] The third paragraph was changed to make it clear that Japan sought a return to the status quo ante of July 24 by stating that the two governments would restore trade relations to their status prior to the freezing of assets, and the United States would guarantee Japan the petroleum it needed (the United States had frozen Japanese assets on July 25 and imposed the oil embargo August 1). In addition, a significant change was made by inclusion of a fourth paragraph stating that the United States would not obstruct settlement of the China problem, which meant that America should suspend aid to Chiang Kai-shek.[81] This last condition proved a critical one. According to one standard Western interpretation, by insisting on this, Japan "insisted on war."[82]

Like the controversial Japanese "peace initiatives" in which Yoshida was involved four years earlier following the China Incident, this final Japanese proposal has been subjected to greatly varying interpretations, both by decision-makers then and scholars since. The Japanese leaders took it seriously. Prime Minister Tōjō himself told one of his subordinates in the War Ministry on November 6 that "Proposal B is not an excuse for war. I am praying to the Gods that somehow we will be able to get an agreement with the United States with this proposal."[83] The army, although unenthusiastic about the contents of Proposal B and dubious that it would be accepted, nevertheless committed itself before the emperor, in the Imperial Conference of November 5, to call off the use of force if the negotiations succeeded by midnight of November 30.[84] Foreign Minister Tōgō, who had introduced the proposal in an earnest endeavor to prevent war, was deeply pessimistic as to its chances of acceptance; yet he regarded it as a real concession on Japan's part, and the furthest Japan could be expected to go at that time while still preserving the "honor and self-defense of our Empire."[85]

Tōgō's pessimism was well grounded. Hull, who knew the contents of Proposal B well in advance of its formal presentation to the United States on November 20 (through the *Magic* operation, by which the Japanese code had been broken), and was aware that this was the last card Japan had to play, chose to interpret Proposal B as an ultimatum and rejected it out of hand as demanding "virtually a surrender" on the part of the United States.[86] He also rejected an alternative *modus vivendi* proposal—initiated by Secretary of the Treasury Henry Morgenthau, Jr., drafted by Harry Dexter White, and reworked within the State Department—which coincided with Proposal B in advocating recision of the freezing order and suspension of aid to Chiang while Sino-Japanese negotiations took place. As originally conceived, this U.S. *modus vivendi* was to be presented to the Japanese along with a "Ten Point Note" outlining America's maximum demands for a permanent settlement in the Far East. On November 26, however, after consultation with President Roosevelt, Hull decided to present only the Ten Point Note, the most drastic statement yet of American conditions, as a response to Proposal B.[87] This time, and perhaps with better justification, it was the Japanese who felt they had been presented with an ultimatum, since the ten points included demands for complete Japanese evacuation of China and Indochina as well as abandonment of the Japanese puppet regime under Wang Ching-wei at Nanking, while entirely omitting any suggestion of American interest in a temporary settlement.[88]

For Japan's leaders, the die was cast with this famous "Hull Note" of November 26. Yoshida, however, continued from his position on the periphery to attempt to stem the tide. Despite his pessimism, and contrary to his assertion of October 30, he had persisted in maintaining contact with Grew in the weeks prior to receipt of the Hull Note. In the early part of November he again warned the U.S. ambassador that time was running out, and a breakdown in the Hull-Nomura talks would lead to "drastic and fateful results."[89] During November he also met on several occasions with Craigie, apparently with the hopes of bringing about British support for the Japanese position in Washington. With

Churchill's speech on November 10, however, in which the British prime minister declared that, if war occurred between the United States and Japan, "the British declaration will follow within the hour," it became clear that Great Britain would not play a mediating role. "The impression I received from the speech," Yoshida later wrote, "was that, in order to crush Nazi Germany and bring the war to a speedy end, Great Britain was prepared to do almost anything to draw the United States into war."[90]

At the same time, he continued his endeavors to mobilize effective Japanese opposition to the war policy. In mid-November, he informed Makino that the outlook for the Hull-Nomura talks was still uncertain, and on November 22, two days after Japan's final proposal had been submitted to the United States, he expressed a faint hope that the U.S. mood may have "loosened somewhat." It was his impression that President Roosevelt was more inclined than the State Department to compromise with Japan. Admiral Kobayashi was endeavoring to mobilize opposition to war within the navy, he reported, and had intimated that such sentiments were shared by army generals such as Minami Jirō, Hata Shinroku, and Umezu Yoshijirō.

The situation was clearly desperate, however, and at this juncture Yoshida turned attention to the great loyalist dilemma: how to use the emperor while at the same time protecting him. He discussed this in a letter to Makino which seems written in haste and is not entirely clear. It was important to prevent the emperor from taking a direct role in the debate, he indicated, and necessary to avoid any appearance of confrontation between the emperor and the war advocates. At the same time, Yoshida seemed to hope that the emperor could be indirectly utilized. He suggested that the issue be referred to a conference of the senior statesmen (*jūshin kaigi*), which would presumedly take issue with the government's deadline for war. The matter would then be carried to the level of an Imperial Conference (*gozen kaigi*), at which it might be hoped that Wakatsuki and Hara, by their eloquence, could turn the tide against the military hard-liners in the presence of the emperor. He indicated that an attempt would be made to convey these thoughts to the emperor through Konoe, Kido, and Matsudaira Tsuneo.[91] It was a circuitous and ultimately futile business, which calls to mind the British comment several years earlier concerning "crab-like" procedures.

Through Satō Naotake, who was then serving as an adviser to the Foreign Ministry, Yoshida was shown a copy of the Hull Note shortly after it was received. He immediately brought this to Makino, whose response was revealing. The old statesman reflected on the great accomplishments of the Meiji Restoration, led by men of Satsuma such as Saigō and his own father Ōkubo, and observed that if war occurred between the United States and Japan these achievements would come to naught. As foreign minister, Tōgō, himself of Satsuma background, would bear great responsibility for this and "stand accused before the Throne and the Japanese people. . . . Moreover, it would mean that he had disgraced the work of the men of Satsuma province of which he was a native."[92] On the verge of world war, more than seventy years after the Restoration, the old gentleman still saw the present through the past, and the policy-makers of the present in the context of their old clan loyalties.

Yoshida found these sentiments impressive. He conveyed them to Satō, Shidehara, and Tōgō, and made a last, futile endeavor to influence the course of events by stressing to Tōgō that the Hull Note was prefaced with the notation that the ten points were "tentative and without commitment," merely an "outline of proposed basis for agreement between the United States and Japan." It was his impression that the extremists in the Japanese government had obscured these phrases deliberately in order to intensify hostility toward the United States and thwart further Japanese gestures for reconciliation.[93] This was at best a dubious understanding of the situation. Tōgō's statement in the Imperial Conference of December 1 offered a fair evaluation of the American position, and virtually all scholarly commentaries agree that the Hull Note represented a sudden and drastic hardening of the U.S. negotiating conditions.[94] Nevertheless, this served to reinforce Yoshida's view that the root of Japan's dilemma lay in deliberately provocative actions on the part of "the more reckless elements within the Japanese Army."[95] Grew also sought to convey to the Japanese that the Hull Note was not an ultimatum but merely a basis for future negotiations. He met Yoshida at the Tokyo Club around November 29 and asked him to arrange a meeting with Tōgō. By this time the decision for war had been made, however, and Tōgō refused; he summoned the American ambassador only after Pearl Harbor had been hit, to announce the break-off of relations between Japan and the United States.[96]

Like Yoshida, Tōgō was a great loyalist, a firm defender of the Japanese empire, and an opponent of the resort to large-scale war as a solution to Japan's problems in Asia. But Yoshida did not condone his course of action in the final days before Pearl Harbor. Following receipt of the Hull Note, Yoshida claimed to have proposed an alternative course to Tōgō by suggesting that, if necessary to prevent a declaration of war against the United States, Tōgō should resign as foreign minister and bring down the cabinet. It was an intriguing suggestion, which may have had its inspiration in the effective manner in which Tōgō had used a threat of resignation earlier, on November 1, to gain approval of Proposal B. At best, however, it could have been only a stopgap measure. Yoshida acknowledged that such a gesture might well have led to Tōgō's assassination, but told his colleague that "such a death would be a happy one." In his memoirs, Yoshida looked back on the failure of a really articulate opposition to emerge among Japan's leaders prior to the Pacific War and cast this in a reflective racial light: "It is perhaps a characteristic of the Yamato race not to say things when they need saying, and to be wise after the event."[97]

Ten days after Pearl Harbor, Yoshida wrote this personal note to Grew:

> No one could have foreseen this tragic end of our long standing friendly relations, although so many unfortunate events occurred in recent years. I well remember that you always tell me that to promote the friendship of our two countries is your life work. I know also how hard you worked to prevent the breaking up of the talk in Washington

even till the very last moment. It is a very sad thing that even your unfatigued efforts could not save the peace. But you can rest assured that we will never forget your friendship to our country and to us. Before ending my letter I must add one thing. Whenever I told the progress of our talk in Washington to my wife at her sick bedside during the last summer, she always tried to strain her weakening nerves not to have escaped any words from her ears. She is happy not to have witnessed in her lifetime this tragic end of our good relations.

Please accept my gratitude for your personal friendship and kindness to me and to my family, and I beg to remain,

Yours most sincerely,
SHIGERU YOSHIDA[98]

SEVEN

The "Yoshida Antiwar Group" and the Konoe Memorial, 1942–1945

On April 15, 1945, Yoshida was arrested by the Kempeitai, Japan's military police, and held in custody for forty-five days. The Kempeitai were particularly interested in his involvement in the drafting of the Konoe Memorial, one of the most intriguing documents of Japan's wartime years, but their concern was broader than this. Yoshida was privy to shortwave radio reports on the progress of the war in both Europe and Asia.[1] From an early date, he predicted Japan's defeat and advocated a diplomatic solution,[2] and there coalesced around him a number of more or less like-minded persons who became known to the police by the code name YOHANSEN, an abbreviation for "Yoshida Anti-War" (*Yoshida Hansen*).[3] YOHANSEN was a loose grouping of men who represented a cross-section of Japan's upper classes, and in practical terms the results of its activities were negligible. Nevertheless, it probably had a larger number of participants and longer duration of activity than any other Japanese "peace endeavor" during the war.[4] Thus YOHANSEN can provide the basis for a case study of the nature and limitations of "resistance" in wartime Japan.

The opposition to the war offered by those associated with YOHANSEN was conservative and highly ideological. The primary motivation of most was not simply to bring an end to physical death and destruction—both that which Japan was inflicting upon others and, increasingly, suffering itself. Rather, their concern was the preservation of the traditional Japanese state, and their greatest fear was that prolongation of the war might lead to a revolutionary situation both at home and abroad which would bring about the destruction of that traditional polity. As Japan's war situation worsened, such fear assumed apocalyptic dimensions in the minds of some; the Konoe Memorial, which Yoshida helped polish in February 1945, represents the consummate expression of this view.

This fear of communism and revolution in Japan, and of radical trends in general, was fed from many sources. It tapped deep historic fears; it was nurtured by a surprisingly broad variety of potentially "revolutionary" developments within wartime Japan itself; and it bore striking parallels to interpretations of World War Two which were then being advanced elsewhere throughout the world. Yoshida's activities during the war years thus open a major area of concern, one which suggests significant revision of prevailing stereotypes of the war–of reactionary "fascism," for example, or overriding and ethnocentric "feudal legacies," or a populace cowed into mindless fanaticism and subservience. Such issues and Yoshida's own response to them, moreover, were to burst to the surface in post-surrender Japan, when he himself emerged as the dominant figure in the Japanese political scene. Neither the reforms of the early occupation, the seemingly extraordinary vitality of popular and leftist movements in post-1945 Japan, nor the ultimately successful conservative response to these developments can be understood without an appreciation of the visions, and realities, of "radicalism" in wartime Japan.

THE FLEXIBLE-EMISSARY PROPOSAL OF 1942

Following Pearl Harbor, Yoshida continued to maintain indirect contact with Joseph Grew, who had been placed under house arrest in the American embassy. He wrote Grew on a personal basis several times before the U.S. diplomatic community was repatriated in 1942, and sent food and other favors to the embassy on holidays and special occasions.[5] Although this had no overt political content, it reflected a characteristic measure of integrity and political courage on Yoshida's part. In the long run it also undoubtedly redounded to his credit and helped in maintaining that image of the "other Japanese" which was to play a role in U.S. pre-surrender planning for post-surrender Japan. For Grew, upon his return to the United States, held the post of assistant secretary of state until the Japanese surrender and was the acknowledged leader of the State Department's "Japan Crowd," which advocated a generous settlement with Japan and the post-surrender restoration to leadership of this traditional "moderate" elite.

The fall of Singapore in February 1942 struck Yoshida as providing an opportune moment for Japan to initiate peace negotiations, but he does not appear to have taken any action at that time. He recognized that conquest of Britain's key Asian base gave Japan a commanding position in the Far East, and clearly assumed that the Allies would be receptive to such overtures as "the most effective means of bringing the war to an early end." Privy Seal Kido, while rejoicing at the early Japanese victories, entertained similar thoughts and conveyed them, to no effect, to the emperor.[6] Japanese critics have generally regarded such opinions as little more than an attempt to preserve the fruits of Japan's swift initial victories.[7] And indeed, the turning point in Japan's martial fortunes came shortly thereafter, and only then did the Japanese antiwar movement begin to show some life.

In early June, shortly after the Japanese defeat at Midway, Yoshida approached Konoe with a proposal he had been mulling over for some time. As Yoshida recalled it in his memoirs, Konoe would have been sent to Switzerland (by an overland route through Korea and Manchuria, and thereafter via the Trans-Siberian Railway), where he would reside, attract notice, symbolize Japan's serious desire for peace, and be available as a potential mediator should either Great Britain or Germany suffer serious reverses.[8] As he actually presented it in writing to Konoe at the time, and then on June 11 to Kido, the plan was somewhat more detailed and opportunistic, and provides another glimpse into the difficulty of combining the roles of "realist," loyalist, patriot, and Anglophile. In extremely formal language, Yoshida explained his plan to Konoe (and Kido) as follows:

> The attitude you should assume today toward the imperial family and the nation is to single-mindedly aid the sovereign in suppressing evil and upholding good (*ichi-i kentai seraruru*) in order to build the nation's future by bringing the holy war to a successful conclusion (*seisen o kansui shite*). Thus, at this time, accompanied by an ambassador and minister and three or four diplomatic personnel, you should go to Europe under the guise of observing the situation there and adopt an attitude of not hesitating to accept meetings with leaders or politicians of various countries along the way should they seek you out. You should pass through the Soviet Union and the Axis countries and settle down in a neutral country such as Switzerland which, in terms of communications, is convenient to the countries engaged in war, and maintain for a while this attitude of leisurely observing the situation. In the meantime, those with you can secretly make overtures to the politicians of various countries and arrange for them to approach you. If the war should develop advantageously for Germany, the United States and Great Britain should seek a way out of the impasse through you; on the other hand, if the war should turn against Germany, then Germany should adopt the same attitude. Your past personal history should make both the United States and Germany regard you as their ally (*mikata*), and thus, if our diplomacy takes advantage of your particular situation, it would be sufficient to place us in a leading position insofar as peace is concerned (*wakyoku ni oite ware o shudō no chii ni okashimuru ni tarubeshi*). If there seems no hope for the future after you have remained in Europe for several tens of days, you should return with an indifferent attitude. Should there be something to which hope might be attached, then you should enlist suitable persons (if possible, those who have acquaintances in Europe and America would be appropriate) among our country's civilian and military bureacrats, scholars, and businessmen, and have them prepare a draft for a peace treaty and submit this as a reference to the Imperial Government. At the same time you should have them assume the task of inducing and enlightening other countries for our own benefit (*ware no rieki ni yūdō keihatsu no nin ni atarashime*). Then, when the time comes for world peace, by commission of our Imperial Government, you, as the head plenipotentiary, should lead an accredited delegation to the peace conference, with other members of the retinue joining the accredited delegates and taking care of the clerical work relating to the peace.[9]

Yoshida envisioned himself as one of the persons who would accompany Konoe on this mission. Konoe himself was reportedly somewhat startled by the proposal, but willing to give it a try. At his suggestion Yoshida then presented the plan to Kido, but the privy seal's response was noncommital and the matter died there. In retrospect, after the Japanese defeat and occupation, Yoshida still believed that something might have come of such a mission.[10]

This resting of Japan's peace hopes upon Konoe was one of the striking recurrent phenomena of the decade prior to Japan's surrender in 1945, and Yoshida was but one of many Japanese who continued to believe that a resolution of Japan's dilemma could best be brought about through this moody scion of the high nobility. This sentiment lay behind the "liberal" support given the three disastrous cabinets Konoe headed between 1937 and 1941, and emerged vividly in the desperate Japanese attempts to arrange a meeting between Konoe and Roosevelt in the summer of 1941. It was revived in the closing years of the war, when plans were bruited to send Konoe to the Soviet Union as a formal emissary of the emperor, and throughout the war years the particular group of peace advocates with which Yoshida was associated continued to rely on collaboration with Konoe. Even in the months following the Japanese surrender, until his suicide upon being charged with war crimes, Konoe was to remain a key consultant and symbol to the "moderates"—a complex and puzzling symbol of the tragedy of Imperial Japan.[11]

YOHANSEN: OUTFLANKING THE RIGHT

The opposition group with which Yoshida became associated was an extremely informal configuration of individuals, one to which the word "membership" hardly applies. In the broadest view, the following persons were involved in some of the discussions concerning peace in which Yoshida and the core group of YOHANSEN engaged:[12]

Harada Kumao (b. 1888). Baron; member of the House of Peers;

former employee of the Bank of Japan; long-time private secretary to Prince Saionji until Saionji's death in 1940.

Hatoyama Ichirō (b. 1883). Party politician in the Seiyūkai line, first elected to the House of Representatives in 1915; chief secretary to the Tanaka cabinet, 1927–1929; minister of education, 1931–1934.

Ikeda Seihin (b. 1867). Financier; retired as director of the Mitsui Bank in 1936; in 1937–1939, served as governor of the Bank of Japan, minister of finance, and minister of commerce and industry; member of the House of Peers and Privy Council.

Iwabuchi Tatsuo (b. 1892). Journalist and political critic associated with the *Mainichi* newspaper (previously with the *Yomiuri* and *Kokumin* newspapers).

Kabayama Aisuke (b. 1865). Count; member of the House of Peers; Taishō-period journalist, with later close ties to big business; graduate of Amherst College and active in various international cultural and friendship organizations.

Kobayashi Seizō (b. 1877). Admiral (retired); vice minister of the navy, commander of the joint fleet, and supreme war councillor in the early 1930s; governor general of Formosa in the late 1930s; in 1944 became member of the House of Peers and state minister in the Koiso cabinet.

Kojima Kazuo (b. 1865). Meiji-era journalist; Taishō-period politician, associated with Inukai Tsuyoshi; member of the House of Representatives beginning in 1911 and, from 1932, the House of Peers.

Konoe Fumimaro (b. 1891). Prince in the venerable Fujiwara line; former president of the House of Peers (1933–1937); former president of the Privy Council (1939–1940); three-time prime minister between 1937 and 1941.

Makino Nobuaki (b. 1861). Count and intimate imperial adviser from the early 1920s, serving as imperial household minister (1921–1925) and privy seal (1925–1935); previous bureaucratic service as prefectural governor, minister of education, minister of agriculture and commerce, and foreign minister; son of Ōkubo Toshimichi and father-in-law of Yoshida Shigeru.

Mazaki Jinzaburō (b. 1876). General (reserve); made inspector general of military education in 1934, but removed in 1935 in a factional struggle which contributed to the attempted military coup of 1936; forced into reserve status following the February 26th Incident, although later found not guilty of direct complicity in this incident.

Mazaki Katsuji (b. 1884). Rear admiral (reserve); brother of Mazaki Jinzaburō, with special expertise in Russian and Soviet affairs; forced into reserve status following the February 26th Incident, and subsequently critical of the war with China; elected to the House of Representatives in 1942.

Morioka Jirō (b. 1886). Home Ministry police official with service as police chief and later governor in several prefectures; head of police in Korea, 1929–1931; chief of the Home Ministry's Police Bureau in the early 1930s; high colonial official in Formosa in the late 1930s.

Obata Toshishirō (b. 1885). Lieutenant general (reserve); stationed in Russia during World War One and the early revolutionary period; head of the Army College in the early 1930s; forced into reserve status in the wake of the February 26th Incident.

Suzuki Kantarō (b. 1867). Admiral (retired), baron; former head of the Navy Academy and chief of the Navy General Staff in the late 1920s; severely wounded in the February 26th Incident; grand chamberlain from 1940; vice president of the Privy Council from 1940, and president beginning in 1944; prime minister from April 1945 through Japan's surrender.

Ueda Shunkichi (b. 1890). Former Finance Ministry bureaucrat, with service in Formosa; private secretary to Prime Minister Tanaka, 1927–1929; subsequently engaged in business.

Ugaki Kazushige (b. 1868). General (retired); four times war minister between 1924 and 1931; governor general of Korea, 1931–1936; failed in an attempt to form a cabinet after the collapse of the Hirota cabinet in 1937; briefly foreign minister under Konoe in 1938.

Wakatsuki Reijirō (b. 1866). Baron, bureaucrat, politician; Finance Ministry bureaucrat until 1911, when appointed to the

House of Peers; twice finance minister in the 1910s; home minister, 1924–1926; political party leader in the Minseitō line; prime minister in 1926–1927, and again in 1931; chief Japanese delegate to the 1930 London Naval Conference.

As a whole, in its current and past associations the group represented a fairly complete microcosm of the elites at play in presurrender Japan: court circles, army, navy, business and financial world, bureaucracy, police, colonial administration, diplomatic corps, titled nobility, Privy Council, House of Peers and House of Representatives, political parties, and world of journalism. Through Konoe and Wakatsuki, the group had entrée to the *jūshin*, or senior statesmen, who were generally responsible for recommending a new prime minister. Through their own ranks and personal contacts (with imperial aides such as Kido Kōichi), they eventually obtained access to the emperor himself. With a few exceptions, they might have posed for a portrait of what is sometimes called the Meiji generation. When war began between Japan and the Allied powers, the average age of these men was sixty-three—which, as it happened, was Yoshida's age at the time.

As indicated in the discussion that follows, unanimity did not prevail among these individuals concerning the specific actions through which Japan might extricate itself from the war. In the case of some, even their resolution to bring the war to a swift end was unstable. In general, however, all shared a dissatisfaction with the existing situation, and held the unquestioned assumption that change could only be brought about through proper and peaceful political channels. They did not contemplate active disruption through such tactics as assassination or sabotage, nor did their considerations include the possibility of encouraging any coup entailing force. No thought was given to the possibility of "negative sabotage" in the form of passivity, industrial hoarding, or deliberate inefficiency such as the elites *did* practice in the postwar period of the occupation. And it ran against the very grain of the group to contemplate the possibility of a mass-based resistance movement. Rather, their deliberations and manipulations were directed primarily to obtaining control of the prime minister's and war minister's portfolios, then utilizing these positions to oust the existing military leadership. With this decorous objective in mind, from 1942 through 1945 members of YOHANSEN became associated with a series of endeavors to place certain individuals in these cabinet positions. Their major candidates for the premiership were General Ugaki, Admiral Kobayashi, Admiral Suzuki, and Prince Konoe. None of the plans was successful, although shortly before the surrender Suzuki did become prime minister, independent of the activities of YOHANSEN. Even the ouster of Tōjō in July 1944 occurred with little direct contribution from the Yoshida group.

The key figures in YOHANSEN were Yoshida, Iwabuchi, Ueda, Konoe, Obata, and Mazaki Jinzaburō; Hatoyama also appears to have remained fairly close until the final stages of the war, when he split with the group in a tactical disagreement relating to support of General Ugaki for the premiership.[13] The main lines of analysis advanced by this core group were quite specific, and can be summarized as follows:

- They ascribed Japan's plunge into militarism to the machinations of a "ring" within the army, the Tōsei-ha (Control Faction), and argued that the first step in bringing about peace had to be the wresting of political control from the Tōsei-ha.
- The events of the 1930s were interpreted as part of a conscious plot on the part of the army clique and its supporters—a plot, moreover, which was fundamentally, and for the most part wittingly, communist.
- Overthrow of the Tōsei-ha could only come from within the military itself. As Konoe personally told the emperor in February 1945, "It is impossible for the civilian bureaucrats to suppress the military. We must find and use someone from within the military."[14] This was to be promoted, however, only through orthodox political channels.
- The only military faction capable of replacing the Tōsei-ha and commanding the loyalty of the military forces was, in their view, the Kōdō-ha, that is, the "Imperial Way Faction"

which had been implicated in the abortive February 26th Incident of 1936 and ousted by the Tōsei-ha at that time. Significantly, leading representatives of the discredited Kōdō-ha were also key members of YOHANSEN: Generals Obata and Mazaki, both of whom had been forced into reserve status following the attempted coup d'état of February 26. Both generals figured prominently in the various plans for a political change the Yoshida group considered between 1942 and 1945.

- Replacement of the Tōsei-ha and establishment of peace was deemed urgent because the deteriorating war situation threatened the very fabric of the traditional Japanese state, the *kokutai* or national polity. The core group's actions were consistent with their professed belief that the throne remained Japan's unique and final hope, for in the end—through the Konoe Memorial—they sought to gain the emperor's personal and active support in the campaign to replace the Tōsei-ha. At the same time, however, their evaluation of the devotion with which the Japanese people embraced the *kokutai* tended to be pessimistic, for they envisioned a revolutionary upheaval against the *kokutai* if the war were not terminated quickly.
- This threat was seen in both a domestic and international context, and was based upon a broad and intricate vision of "revolutionary" or "communist" developments in both arenas. Stated differently, the group did not see the primary significance of the Pacific War as being the existing conflict between Japan and the Allied Powers. What was of greater concern was the left-wing, or potentially left-wing, revolutionary tendencies the war had released both within and outside Japan.
- Even during the American air raids over Japan, the group's appraisal of the United States and its probable postwar attitude toward Japan was quite sanguine. In August 1944, Konoe had been informed that the majority of the American populace respected the imperial household and believed that the emperor was basically for peace, and any future change in

Japan would have to be built around the imperial house. Konoe's informant, Kase Toshikazu, went on to predict that America's goals in the postwar era would be demilitarization and democratic government.[15] Konoe advanced this view in his audience with the emperor the following February. Despite its demand for unconditional surrender, and contrary to the opinion of the General Staff, he argued, the United States "will not do such a thing as reform Japan's *kokutai* and remove the imperial house."[16] Many of the general peace plans advocated by individual members of the core group rested on similar assumptions of the willingness of the Allied Powers, especially the United States, to agree to a fairly generous peace for Japan. In the case of Konoe, such trust in the Western powers appears to represent a departure from the critical attitude toward Western imperialism in Asia which had long characterized his views.[17]

Despite their sense of crisis, even key members of YOHANSEN appear to have been unable to marshal firm resolve; they were beset with feelings of ambiguity and futility. As late as April 1944, for example, Konoe informed Prince Higashikuni that he was unsure whether a personnel change would really accomplish anything, or might not even be counterproductive. Perhaps, he ventured, it would be better to let Tōjō continue to bear the onus of responsibility in the world's eye, and thus protect the image of the non-responsibility of the imperial house.[18] Prior to Pearl Harbor, when as prime minister he was in a stronger position actually to try to use the Kōdō-ha to turn the trend of events within the army, Konoe refrained from attempting to do so on the curious grounds that this might have precipitated a military coup and the assassination of Mazaki and Obata, thus depriving the rival military clique of its potential effectiveness.[19] In countering the argument that resurrection of the discredited Kōdō-ha would cause confusion, Konoe at one point responded that the situation was confusing anyway.[20] During the Pacific War, Konoe characterized some of his own proposals as perhaps "wishful thinking."[21] Ueda described his personal scenario for peace as "like a dream."[22] While continually arguing that termination of the war had to be sought through the twin vehicles of the emperor and the Kōdō-ha, the group's members were fully aware that the emperor distrusted the Kōdō-ha generals, and their proposal was thus flawed from the start by internal contradiction.[23] As late as February 1945, Prince Takamatsu indirectly accused the self-described peace advocates of "running around" without a concrete plan.[24] The activities of the group as a whole—flurries of meetings and discussions interspersed with long periods of apparent inactivity—convey an overall impression of lassitude, indirection, incompleteness, and hopelessness.

The fundamental policy associated with YOHANSEN, that of playing the Kōdō-ha against the Tōsei-ha, was bold, ironic, and controversial. It was also an old policy, to the extent that it predated Pearl Harbor. In the late 1930s, Konoe, as prime minister, had contemplated countering the influence of Tōsei-ha advocates of "total war" planning and the creation of a "national defense state" by reinstating key officers of the Kōdō-ha, and this association carried over through the war years. He was a close friend of such leading Kōdō-ha generals as Araki Sadao, Mazaki, and Obata, and apparently sympathized with their strident emphasis upon Japan's unique spiritual qualities, as exemplified in the slogans of *kokutai* and *Yamato damashii* (spirit of Japan).[25] The ambiguity of such sympathy lay in the fact that the ultranationalist terrorists of the 1930s were also inspired by such sentiments.

On the surface, the Kōdō-ha's appeal to certain members of YOHANSEN was understandable, for the clique professed fidelity to the traditional axiom that the military should remain clean of involvement in political or economic affairs—a view the defense-state advocates could not readily avow. Domestically, controls supported by Tōsei-ha members such as Tōjō were subjected to an important interpretative metamorphosis: initially attacked as "fascist" or "National Socialist" by their Kōdō-ha opponents, as time passed and the war was prolonged they became identified with socialism and incipient communism. Insofar as the international situation was concerned, Konoe claimed to see a simple distinction between the two army factions. In his words:

> The ideology of the *Kōdō* generals was exclusively concerned with the Soviet Union. They were, for example, completely opposed to Japan's interference in China or to the advance into Southeast Asia. . . . Consequently, when these officers were removed in the aftermath of the February rebellion, it furnished the Control Faction with an opportunity to alter Japan's foreign policy, a change which later caused the China Incident and the present war.[26]

The analysis was oversimplified and Konoe was being understandably modest concerning his own positive role in turning the China Incident into full-scale war, but it remains true that the Kōdō-ha was commonly associated with "northern aims." In this light, YOHANSEN assumed the cast of being a "wrong-war" opposition group: opposed to the China and Pacific wars, but carrying associations of Japanese military action against the Soviet Union.

Konoe was perhaps the most complex individual associated with the Yoshida group. Certainly he was the most famous among a number of prominent men, and there is no reason to believe that he and Yoshida saw eye to eye on all issues. Konoe appears to have been the more ambiguous, cynical, and, in his way, iconoclastic of the two. He had flirted with socialism in his youth, and became an imperialist even while deriding what Yoshida admired—the classic tactics of Western imperialism in Asia. In the 1930s, Konoe openly expressed sympathy with some of the concerns of the radical nationalists, and claimed that those who regarded the Manchurian Incident and its aftermath as simply a military coup were guilty of "shallow reasoning." He disassociated himself from the "internationalism" of the *genrō* and *jūshin*, and it was during his own premiership that Japan proclaimed a "New Order" for Asia as bulwark against the dual menace of Western imperialism and communism. Konoe operated on a more imaginative level than Yoshida—more potentially "radical," yet at the same time more touched by a black sense of fate. And what he himself touched turned to ashes. By 1941, looking back upon the devastated landscape of his recent past, Konoe had begun to soften his critique of Western imperialism and to become more obsessed with the specter of Red subversion and upheaval in Japan and Asia. This vision led to theories of conspiracy, which helped absolve him of some of the responsibility for his own disastrous policies, and culminated in the nearly catatonic vision of the Konoe Memorial. Although Yoshida came to endorse the same vision, one can imagine that he came to it from a simpler direction.[27]

Konoe's personal opinion as to the type of peace settlement Japan might hope for in the Pacific varied as the war situation changed. Even as the imminent collapse of Japan's ally, Germany, became apparent, however, he appears to have assumed the possibility of a comradely Great-Power settlement. In January 1944, for example, his view was as follows:

(1) Problems of the Pacific should be dealt with by the powers of the Pacific.

(2) A five-power committee consisting of Japan, the Soviet Union, China, the United States, and Great Britain should be organized.

(3) Areas occupied by Japan, as well as various Pacific islands, should be demilitarized.

(4) With the exception of Manchuria, independent countries other than the major nations in the area should be made permanently neutral along the lines of Switzerland. Other areas would be dealt with by the above five-power committee.

(5) The Soviet Union should act as mediator in arranging such a solution.

At the same time, however, Konoe retained reservations that such an arrangement might be too conciliatory on the part of Japan.[28]

While Konoe's relationship with Kōdō-ha spokesmen such as Mazaki and Obata is well known, Yoshida's wartime collaboration with the two generals seems more surprising, since both were implicated in events he had strongly condemned when they occurred. Yoshida did have at least a passing acquaintance with Mazaki prior to the China War, however. In 1936, two weeks before the February 26th Incident, for example, he informed Harada that he had had a long conversation with Mazaki concerning the animosity between the Kōdō-ha stalwart and General Ugaki—an ironic prelude to YOHANSEN's later "Ugaki movement." Yoshida described Mazaki as "quite gentle," a quality he had previously found in Generals Terauchi Masatake and Tanaka Giichi, and when Harada warned him not to let himself be deceived, Yoshida assured him that he "wasn't being fooled."[29]

Yoshida and the generals may well have found each other personally compatible. All three were blunt, outspoken men of considerable personal strength. They shared a profound devotion to the throne. They had suffered similar reverses to their careers at the hands of the Tōsei-ha officers who came to power in the aftermath of the February 26th Incident—Mazaki and Obata being shunted to reserve-officer status, Yoshida having the plum of a long diplomatic career snatched away when the Tōsei-ha overrode his appointment as foreign minister in the Hirota cabinet. It is difficult to ascertain, however, where their politics and geopolitics coincided.

Mazaki, a protégé of General Araki Sadao, had emerged as an idol of radical ultranationalist officers in the mid-1930s and played a central if ambiguous role in some of the most violent incidents of 1935 and 1936. An outspoken critic of the "fascist" policies of the Tōsei-ha, he had given tacit or explicit support to such episodes as the assassination of General Nagata Tetsuzan by Lieutenant Colonel Aizawa Saburō; the turning of the Aizawa trial into a propaganda showpiece for the Kōdō-ha ideal of "national reconstruction"; proposals to assassinate the inspector general of military education as well as Prime Minister Okada Keisuke (who was one of Yoshida's confidential contacts in the months prior to Pearl Harbor); and the February 26th Incident itself (in which Yoshida's father-in-law, Count Makino, narrowly escaped assassination as one of the "evil advisers to the throne"). In the early part of 1935, Mazaki, then inspector general of military education, had lent his voice to the attack on Professor

Minobe Tatsukichi and his "organ theory" of the Japanese state, an attack that was a major landmark in the strengthening of Japan's prewar police state.[30] Mazaki also supported the Kōdō-ha's "northern aims"; and in the early 1930s Obata, who was a protégé of Mazaki and Araki, had made clear that what the group had in mind vis-à-vis the Soviet Union was more than just long-range contingency planning. At the close of 1932 and beginning of 1933—at the very moment Yoshida was attempting to postpone expansion of the Manchurian Incident and keep Japan in the League of Nations—Obata had provoked great controversy in both military and civilian circles by calling for conquest of Jehol followed by a swift campaign against the Soviet army. Yoshida, it will be recalled, had attacked this plan at the time.[31] Throughout the 1930s an immediate preventive war with the Soviet Union was, in Professor Crowley's phrase, Obata's "favorite strategic idea," and it was generally understood that he had the backing of Mazaki and Araki in advocating this.[32]

The third army figure who played an important role in the plans of the Yoshida group had a similarly ambiguous background. Ugaki, a subordinate of Tanaka Giichi, had supported controversial programs of military demobilization in the 1920s; had close relations with both big business and the political parties, notably the Minseitō; by the late 1930s had expressed a sympathetic appreciation of China's nationalistic aspirations; and as foreign minister in the Konoe cabinet had shown desire for rapprochement with Great Britain.[33] At the same time, the deactivation of four army divisions which took place under Ugaki as war minister in 1924 was paralleled by a rationalization of the military which increased its effectiveness. Also, as war minister in 1927, Ugaki had collaborated with the Ministry of Education in introducing military-training programs into the public education system and establishing vocational training which would contribute to the technological development of the military establishment. In this way, he contributed to the blurring of separation between the military and civilian realms. In a manner similar to Mazaki's controversial involvement in the February 26th Incident, Ugaki had played an ambiguous role in the events leading up to the abortive March Incident of 1931. Whatever his later appreciation of Chinese nationalism, he had been among the earliest Japanese leaders to raise alarm at the threat of communism on the continent in the 1920s, to assert a relationship between Japanese concessions to China and Chinese "arrogance," and to call for a reassertion of the prestige of the Japanese empire.[34] While desirous of rapprochement with Great Britain and regretful of the decline of the prestige of the Great Powers in China, he had also lambasted America's "hypocritical humanitarianism."[35] Although an opponent of the Tōsei-ha by the late 1930s—according to Grew's informants, Ugaki had been behind the courageous anti-war speech of Diet member Saitō Takeo in early 1940[36]—in the early 1930s Ugaki had been one of the supporters of Nagata Tetsuzan's thesis that Japan required "total war" capability, a "national defense state," and "total mobilization" of the resources of the nation.[37]

It is not entirely clear when Yoshida began to work closely with Mazaki and Obata. According to Ueda Shunkichi, the three men were brought together by himself and Iwabuchi shortly after Yoshida returned from London. Konoe then joined the group following the collapse of his third cabinet in October 1941.[38] They do not appear to have engaged in serious discussion of political maneuvers until the autumn of 1942, however, at which time Iwabuchi contacted Yoshida through Hatoyama and then drew in other individuals, beginning with Obata, to begin planning for the overthrow of Tōjō.[39] Although less famous and of lower social position than most of the individuals associated with YOHANSEN, Ueda and Iwabuchi played a central role in shaping the thought of the group and were the only two members actually arrested with Yoshida in 1945 for their involvement in these endeavors. Iwabuchi is primarily associated with formulating and reiterating the thesis that Japan's problems since the 1930s were attributable to the Tōsei-ha and could be solved by replacing this military coterie with the Kōdō-ha, while Ueda's main contribution was to add the apocalyptic dimension to the group's fundamental anti-communist outlook, while at the same time reinforcing the conspiracy thesis.

Iwabuchi had established his anti-Tōsei-ha credentials as a journalist as early as March 1936, when the Kempeitai summoned him and demanded that he cease publishing critical articles about both the events surrounding the February 26th Incident and what he had been describing as Tōsei-ha plans for an invasion of China. By September 1936 he had become convinced that China was prepared to wage a long war of attrition against Japan in north China, and in 1937 he unsuccessfully endeavored to persuade Konoe to refuse the premiership and thus place the onus for Japanese aggression squarely on the military. From this early date he continued to advocate purging the Tōsei-ha through the Kōdō-ha. The latter clique, as he saw it, not only constituted the major competing faction within the army, but also shared his own "liberal" values in its avowed principle of military non-involvement in politics, as well as its anti-Soviet and anti-communist ideology. Iwabuchi appears to have been the most dynamic operator within YOHANSEN, the real spark plug of the group, and in the immediate postwar period he exercised a modicum of backstage political influence. He had some say in the selection of Yoshida as foreign minister in October 1945, which marked the old diplomat's postwar political debut, but later became disillusioned by the extremity of Yoshida's conservatism in responding to the occupation reform program.

Like most of the key members of the Yoshida group, Iwabuchi's hopes for peace rested to a considerable degree upon utilizing Konoe. By the latter stages of the Pacific War, his personal "peace plan" reportedly consisted of four major parts:

(1) Carry out an internal army takeover through the Kōdō-ha, and then utilize the Kōdō-ha's influence and prestige to set the basis for peacemaking within the military establishment itself, and especially within the army.

(2) Prior to entering peace negotiations with the enemy, marshal Japan's remaining fighting forces for a last great assault against the enemy, thus preparing an advantageous battlefield situation from which Japan could proceed to dealings at the bargaining table.

(3) Enter peace negotiations by first sending Konoe to Chungking, where he could open negotiations with Chiang Kai-shek and then, through Chiang, seek a peace with Great Britain. If Great Britain proved receptive, the negotiations could then be expanded to the United States either directly or indirectly through Britain.

(4) Maintain as non-negotiable conditions the security of the imperial house as well as of territory presently "owned" by Japan, including Korea and Formosa.[40]

Iwabuchi, in short, believed that the Kōdō-ha was capable of taking over the army, would then opt for peace, and would be successful in gaining adequate support for this option throughout the military establishment. He recognized the relationship between battlefield positions and peace negotiations, but nonetheless assumed that China, Great Britain, and the United States would be so impressed by a last-ditch Japanese offensive that they would be receptive to peace overtures. And despite the unconditional-surrender stipulation advanced by the Allies beginning in late 1943, he had in mind a peace settlement that preserved not only the *kokutai*, but parts of the external empire as well.

Ueda's relationship with Yoshida dated back to the late 1920s, when he had served as personal secretary to Prime Minister Tanaka Giichi. Since Tanaka simultaneously held the foreign minister's portfolio, a considerable part of Ueda's time was spent dealing with Yoshida, who was then vice foreign minister. Their relationship was renewed following Yoshida's return from London, and although Ueda's reputation never approached that of other members of the Yoshida group and he had little personal contact with Konoe, he did play an especially influential role in shaping the group's *Weltanschauung* as it emerged in the Konoe Memorial. During the course of the war, Ueda became obsessed by the possibility of Japan becoming communized through the organizational controls and policies of centralized planning being pushed forward by both the military and bureaucracy. These fears apparently dated back to shortly after the Tōsei-ha strengthened its influence in the wake of the February 26th Incident, and were buttressed when Ueda obtained a copy of an allegedly secret army document from Ayukawa (Aikawa) Yoshisuke, the powerful "new *zaibatsu*" entrepreneur. As Ueda interpreted it, this secret plan revealed that the military intended to transfer to the Japanese homeland itself centralized financial and economic policies developed by the army in and for Manchukuo. The plan, Ueda alleged, was drafted by persons who had studied under communist teachers in Europe, and if actually carried out meant nothing less than the fact that "Japan could not help but become communist in the end."[41] Ueda showed the plan to a number of acquaintances, among them Wakatsuki, Yoshida, and possibly Shidehara, and later prepared a long analysis which developed his apprehensions in detail. The ideas in that statement, together with material drawn from other sources, were later utilized by Konoe (and Yoshida) in drafting the Konoe Memorial. Yoshida's receptivity to Ueda's thesis of a communist conspiracy by the architects of central planning in Manchukuo is not surprising, since as ambassador to London he had informed the British of his own perceptions of the alarming influence of communism within the Japanese army and, specifically, in Manchuria. His appreciation of Ueda's anti-communist vigilance was expressed during the postwar occupation, when Ueda was appointed attorney general in the third Yoshida cabinet and helped direct the McCarthyist "Red Purge" in the bureaucracy.

Shortly after the surrender, Ueda published this summary of the scenario he had envisioned during the final stages of the war:

> The imperial order is given to Konoe. That evening, only War Minister Mazaki and Prime Minister Konoe are sworn in, and without even reappearing from the court they proceed in accordance with a prearranged plan and, following a list prepared ahead of time, fire the leaders in the War Ministry and General Staff Headquarters, and place them all on reserve status. The chief and vice chief of the General Staff, as well as the heads of the Military Service Bureau (Heimukyoku) and Bureau of Military Affairs (Gunmukyoku) in the War Ministry are naturally included, and from them everyone down to the provost marshal is placed on the reserve list. People begin saying, "What's become of Konoe? He received the imperial order and is supposed to have gone to the court, but he hasn't come out yet. What's going on?"—but just then

> the dismissals are completed and Konoe reappears from the court. The following morning they assume command of the First Regiment of the Imperial Guard, surround the homes of the leading officers who have been placed on the reserve list, arrest them and search their homes. Then he clearly announces to the populace why he has taken such drastic action, and also clarifies the situation for the various military units abroad. Once the purge of the army is completed, they move on to the next task. . . .

In Ueda's own phrase, the plan was "like a dream" (*yume monogatari mitai na mono*).[42]

None of the individuals associated with the Yoshida group could be described as being motivated by humanitarian concerns or a commitment to abstract freedoms. Many, on the other hand, had already had their place in the sun and contributed in one way or another to the eclipse and Japan's descent into the "dark valley." This can be suggested by brief sketches of some of the more prominent but peripheral figures associated with YOHANSEN.

Wakatsuki, former prime minister and party president, and since 1934 one of Japan's senior statesmen, had a record of "liberal" political endeavors to his credit. As home minister in the Katō Takaaki cabinet, he had helped push through the universal male suffrage law of 1925. As head of the Japanese delegation to the London Naval Conference in 1930, he had supported, with considered and reasonable reluctance, the government's decision to acquiesce in the 10:6 cruiser ratio. And as prime minister at the time of the Manchurian Incident, he had endeavored zealously but ineffectually to prevent the expansion of Japanese military activities on the continent. On the other hand, as home minister under Katō, Wakatsuki also played an inside role in drafting the 1925 Peace Preservation Law, emphasizing that this was aimed only at the repression of communism, anarchism, and similarly extreme forms of radicalism;[43] in practice, the law became a central instrument of the police state. And until the end of the Pacific War, Wakatsuki wavered between advocacy of ending hostilities before Japan's total defeat and fighting on to the bitter end.[44]

Ikeda Seihin, director of the Mitsui Bank and the key manager of the Mitsui complex, had been singled out as a symbol of decadent bourgeois interests by ultranationalists and earmarked for assassination in 1932; yet in the aftermath of the February 26th Incident it was revealed that he had dispersed funds to an extensive list of rightists including Kita Ikki, Nakano Seigō, Matsui Kuka, Iwata Fumio, Akiyama Teisuke, Akamatsu Katsumarō, Tsukui Tatsuo, and Hashimoto Tetsuma.[45] Along with Generals Mazaki and Obata, he had been one of the early prominent members of Baron Hiranuma Kiichirō's right-wing National Foundation Society (Kokuhonsha), established in 1924 to counter leftist activities in Japan and "nourish and develop the national spirit."[46] For a period during the war he served as minister of commerce and industry under Konoe. Like all members of the Yoshida group, he regarded the "thought problem" as a momentous one, no matter what the outcome of the war. When Yoshida formed his first cabinet in 1946, he intended to make Ikeda his minister of finance, but this was thwarted by occupation authorities.[47]

Even Makino, Grew's "eminent gentleman" and a consistent target of terrorist attacks throughout the 1930s—who died with the complacent observation that "throughout my entire life I have never once done anything which would shame my conscience"[48]—was prone to sympathetic relationships with the ultranationalists. When the rightist philosopher-ideologue Ōkawa Shūmei split with Kita Ikki and formed the Society to Realize the Way of Heaven on Earth (Gyōchisha) in 1924, Makino, who became privy seal the following year, became a "councillor" of the organization, joining other prominent sponsors such as the Kōdō-ha general Araki Sadao.[49] In 1931, in the midst of the consternation caused by the Manchurian Incident, Makino threw his support to the anti-Shidehara political extremists led by Adachi Kenzō and Kuhara Fusanosuke—provoking thereby an ironic historical lesson from Prince Saionji, who reminded the privy seal of the statesmanship of his own father, Ōkubo, who had met a comparable crisis in 1873 by firmly opposing a proposed invasion of Korea.[50] Throughout the 1930s, while militant extremists continued to attack Makino as a symbol of the emperor's evil advisers, Harada and Saionji were simultaneously voicing concern over the old statesman's "gullibility" and tendency to attempt to control the military by consorting with equally dangerous elements.[51]

Of all those associated with the Yoshida group, Hatoyama, by conventional bourgeois standards, might have been expected to offer the most committed and thoroughgoing defense of liberalism. He was the only pure party politician of the group, having been elected to the Diet in every general election from 1915. His father had been a Diet member; his brother was a Diet member and delegate to the League of Nations; and his brother-in-law, Suzuki Kisaburō, was a president of the Seiyūkai. He had taken his degree at Tokyo Imperial University in English law, and his wife from a wealthy and influential family; he was free from material concerns.

If the Yoshida anti-war group represented a microcosm of various elite interests in pre-surrender Japan, however, Hatoyama personally embodied much of the dreary venality of the prewar political parties, and only a few of their virtues. To his credit, in March 1940, despite internal Seiyūkai pressure, he opposed the expulsion of Saitō Takao from the Diet for his anti-military speech; he refused to join the Imperial Rule Assistance Association, and prior to the war participated in an attempt to weaken that organization by cutting its budget; he announced his resignation from active politics prior to Pearl Harbor, and when he decided to run as an independent candidate in 1942, he included in his campaign literature, amidst less praiseworthy pronouncements, a defense of constitutional government.[52]

On the other side of the ledger, as a member of the Seiyūhontō party in the 1920s, Hatoyama opposed universal suffrage on the grounds that it would undermine the traditional family system.[53] Like Ugaki, Yoshida, and Ueda, he was an alumnus of the Tanaka cabinet. As chief cabinet secretary from April 1927 to June 1929, he participated in the decision to amend the Peace Preservation Law to decree death or indeterminate imprisonment for persons advocating or even proposing to study any doctrine that contemplated changes in the national polity. These revisions also denied the right of trial by jury to persons accused under this law (Hatoyama had previously opposed institution of the jury system itself).

As education minister in the Inukai Tsuyoshi and Saitō Makoto cabinets between December 1931 and March 1934, Hatoyama was involved in the notorious Takikawa case, involving the dismissal (under the Peace Preservation Law) of Professor Takikawa Yukitoki from the law faculty of Kyoto Imperial University in May 1933. Takikawa was purged for defending Tolstoy's notion that society is as responsible as the individual criminal for crime, and for criticizing the relegation of Japanese women to an inferior social and legal status. Hatoyama's term as education minister also coincided with extensive purges of primary and normal-school teachers regarded as holding "dangerous thoughts." During this same period, textbooks were revised to conform to prevailing nationalistic ideologies, and students were mobilized for such activities as collecting goods for Japanese soldiers in Manchuria, sending off recruits and greeting returned soldiers, and demonstrating against the League of Nations. Hatoyama resigned as education minister after being charged with "receiving and paying bribes, selling honors, evasion of income taxes, and falsification of stock ownership statements of himself and his wife."

Hatoyama's relationship with Yoshida became close in 1938, when he visited London in the course of a world tour as a special emissary for Prime Minister Konoe; the politician and the ambassador reportedly found their views compatible. Upon returning from this trip, Hatoyama published an ambiguous book entitled *Face of the World* (*Sekai no Kao*) which was recalled from the dustbins in 1946 and used with devastating effect to bring about his purge from postwar political participation. The book contained favorable comments about the efficiency of both German and Italian fascism, among them the discovery of a "striking affinity" between German Naziism and Japanese *bushidō* ("way of the warrior") and the recommendation that, to minimize class conflict, Japan should study and adapt Hitler's methods for control and regimentation of labor. He qualified his endorsement of Hitlerism by noting that, while the adoption of such authoritarianism was understandable, there should be a limit to this. His definition of liberalism, as explained in an election brochure shortly after the war, was succinct: "What is liberty? It can be, I believe, exhaustively covered by the following statement: 'A freedom to do what you should do and not to do what you should not do.'"

In an earlier election pamphlet (April 1942), Hatoyama praised the foreign policy of Tanaka Giichi on the grounds that it had "liquidated the weak-kneed diplomacy toward England and America" of the earlier period. "Today the world policy drafted by the Tanaka Cabinet is steadily being realized," he added—"today" being two months before the battle of Midway. This was more than wartime rhetoric, for Hatoyama had attacked the Shidehara diplomacy while supporting the Manchurian Incident in 1931.[54] As education minister under Inukai, he criticized the previous cabinet (when Shidehara was foreign minister) for having checked the Japanese advance on Chinchow and praised the Inukai government for driving the Manchurian warlord Chang Hsueh-liang out of Chinchow without suffering foreign interference. The lesson, he concluded, was that "the Inukai Cabinet is an independent and strong Government. The Shidehara diplomacy is a subservient and weak-kneed foreign policy."

During his world tour, postwar American investigators found that Hatoyama "promised the Germans economic advantages in China after the British had been driven out; in England he tried to interest the British in loans for the exploitation of China in return for advantages to the British." According to *Sekai no Kao*, Hatoyama learned of the Japanese seizure of Shanghai's Northern Station during this mission abroad and was moved to poetry. He wept with joy, and "with a voice full of tears was singing of victory to the road and to the forest.... What a fine day!" A measure of Hatoyama's political adroitness is suggested by the fact that in the 1942 election he received endorsements from both Tōyama Mitsuru, doyen of the ultranationalist Black Dragon Society, and Ozaki Yukio, Japan's "god of constitutional government," who is often regarded as one of the few consistently idealistic politicians in prewar Japan.

After Japan's surrender, Hatoyama reorganized the old Seiyūkai under the disarming name of Liberal Party (Jiyūtō), and succeeded in winning a plurality in the general election of April 1946. He was purged on the eve of assuming the premiership, and handpicked Yoshida as his successor. Yoshida parlayed this opportunity into the personal power base from which he dominated subsequent conservative politics, and his political demise, like his rise, involved Hatoyama. Following his depurge in 1951, Hatoyama waged a bitter struggle to regain control of the party, and in December 1954 he succeeded Yoshida as premier.

BACKSTAGE POLITICKING, 1942–1945

By autumn of 1942, Yoshida was convinced of Japan's impending defeat and sought to turn this into a hopeful augury for promoting a negotiated peace.[55] The first concrete endeavor by the Yoshida group to prepare for peacemaking took place shortly thereafter, during the closing months of 1942. Largely at Yoshida's instigation, the group decided to urge Ugaki to make a bid for the premiership. Makino, Harada, Konoe, and Iwabuchi supported this proposal from the outset, and at Konoe's suggestion Iwabuchi met with Ugaki on December 20 to broach the possibility of an Ugaki cabinet. Between December 20 and December 31, Iwabuchi, Yoshida, Obata, and Mazaki Jinzaburō each met separately with Ugaki. Kojima, Kobayashi, and possibly Hatoyama also participated in discussions of the Ugaki plan, and Kido recorded that the group was also in contact with Ikeda Seihin.

The general plan proposed to Ugaki seems to have omitted some particulars: it began by assuming Tōjō had already been unseated and Ugaki designated his successor. Ugaki would meet the emperor, be returned to active-duty status, and concurrently assume the positions of prime minister and war minister. Obata would be returned to active status and become vice war minister, while Mazaki would become active "in the field" to marshal the support of Kōdō-ha adherents behind Ugaki and carry out a purge of Tōsei-ha elements within the army. This accomplished, the group would then proceed to concrete plans for the peacemaking.

Although this early Ugaki plan was accompanied by a flurry of secret meetings, many at Yoshida's home, it came quickly to a dead end. While Ugaki seemed receptive to the idea of forming a cabinet, he was unwilling to return to active duty, or to engage in a purge of the Tōsei-ha. In addition, he indicated his personal preference for General Koiso Kuniaki as war minister, rather than himself or either of the two Kōdō-ha generals, Obata and Mazaki, who bulked so large in the YOHANSEN plans. Most initial participants in the Ugaki plan gave up hope in the old soldier almost immediately. With wonted tenacity, however, Yoshida continued to nurse hopes for the plan, but his first endeavor in backstage politicking essentially reached an impasse when he failed, on December 31, to convince the famous "political general" to hew more closely to the YOHANSEN line. Despite the apparent hopelessness of the situation, the Ugaki plan was renewed later by the Yoshida group.[56]

Following the Ugaki fizzle, the group, again largely at Yoshida's suggestion, turned its attention to the possibility of forming a cabinet around Admiral Kobayashi, an acquaintance of Yoshida since England in the early 1920s. This project enjoyed a far longer gestation period than the Ugaki plan, but proved similarly abortive in the end. Konoe was persuaded to throw his support behind Kobayashi around March 1943, and joined Iwabuchi and others in broaching the idea to Kobayashi himself. The plan followed essentially the same line as that proposed previously to Ugaki, including the hiatuses. The Tōjō cabinet would be overthrown and replaced by a Kobayashi cabinet, with Kobayashi simultaneously becoming navy minister. Kobayashi would meet with the emperor and have Obata and Mazaki returned to active status, whereupon the former would be made war minister and Mazaki, if possible, made chief of the General Staff. Obata and Mazaki would then proceed to direct a reform of the army. Yoshida would become foreign minister in the Kobayashi cabinet, and presumedly lead the quest for peace once the military establishment had been brought into line.

A "burn-after-reading" letter from Yoshida to Makino discusses this shift from Ugaki to Kobayashi. Ueda Shunkichi, it is stated, had assumed responsibility for the ideological aspect of the problem, while Yoshida was concentrating on the essential diplomatic side. Since Ugaki was wobbling, the group had turned to Kobayashi. The most urgent task of the moment was to create an advantageous military situation for diplomatic initiative, and this would entail reinforcing the navy to the point where it could inflict severe damage upon the U.S. forces. The problem was to convince the army to support the navy. The letter was redolent with the necessity for "resolution" (*kakugo*).[57]

Kobayashi agreed to lend himself to the plan after being importuned by Konoe, but a year later, when the occasion for pushing the Kobayashi candidacy actually presented itself, Konoe failed to follow this up. When Tōjō was finally brought down in July 1944, Konoe did not even mention Kobayashi's name in the meeting of senior statesmen which convened on July 18 to select a new prime minister. The post went to General Koiso Kuniaki instead, and the Kobayashi plan, never a burning one, flickered out. It was during this long interlude when the Kobayashi plan was being bruited, however, that the Yoshida group decided that it was necessary to prepare a document that clarified the importance of utilizing the Kōdō-ha. Ueda was assigned responsibility for this, as indicated in Yoshida's letter to Makino, and produced the manuscript that later was utilized in drafting the Konoe Memorial. In retrospect, it is difficult to conclude that the failure of this second major proposal by the Yoshida group was of any significance to the cause of an early peace. Kobayashi shortly thereafter became head of the Great Japan Political Association (Dai Nippon Seiji Kai), a pro-war association of Diet members, and proceeded to endorse the sentiments of that group rather than endeavor to lead it toward an anti-war position.[58]

The third stage in YOHANSEN's maneuvers began around October 1944 and again sheds light upon Yoshida's astuteness in selecting dedicated peacemakers. Konoe and Yoshida met with Suzuki Kantarō at Yoshida's home and attempted to convert the old admiral (Yoshida's teacher at the Peers' School four decades earlier) to their cause. They met a swift rebuttal. When Konoe argued that the war had to be brought quickly to a close, Suzuki responded with a speech along the following lines: "The results of war do not become clear unless you fight to the end. And so one should not think frivolously of peace midway. A time when we are in trouble at home is a time when the enemy is also in trouble, and victory will be obtained by the one who endures. We must avoid following the example of Chia Su-tao of the Southern Sung, who invited the destruction of the Sung by making a careless peace with the Mongols."

Konoe was inclined to abandon Suzuki with no further ado, but Yoshida carried on a number of further conversations on his own. Konoe reentered the picture when Yoshida informed him Suzuki was coming around, and a meeting between Suzuki and Mazaki was planned pending the successful outcome of the Konoe-Suzuki conversation. Konoe found the admiral as stubborn as before, however, and on his part Suzuki deemed it expedient to terminate his relationship with the Yoshida group at that point.[59] Nearly a year later, he did emerge as the prime minister who led Japan to surrender, but only after urban devastation, the atomic bombs, and the Soviet declaration of war had been introduced against the example of Chia Su-tao.

THE KONOE MEMORIAL

The failure of the Suzuki plan coincided closely with the Japanese defeat at Leyte in the closing weeks of 1944; together with the campaign in the Marianas, this enabled the Allied forces to threaten Japan directly.[60] A new sense of urgency and desperation gripped not only the Yoshida group, but also a number of other Japanese searching for peace at this time. All these activities were discrete and ineffectual, and even at this late date no attempts to build a broadly based and closely coordinated peace movement were ventured.[61] For the key members of the Yoshida group, the opening weeks of 1945 were devoted to making plans for soliciting the emperor's active support in bringing the war to a close, plans which were to culminate in Koneo's presenting the Konoe Memorial to the emperor on February 14. This was the apogee of YOHANSEN's endeavors, its most enduring entry in the pages of Japan's modern history.

On the first two days of the bitter year of 1945, Iwabuchi, Obata, and Yoshida set in motion the sequence of preparations that was to culminate in the famous memorial. After deciding among themselves that the urgency of the situation required the emperor's direct intervention, they visited Konoe on January 6 and 19, at Hakone and Yugawara, to convince him of the necessity of his personal devotion to this task. There is some indication that the first meeting was inconclusive, but at the January 19 meeting, in any case, Konoe committed himself to the plan. Much of the burden of setting up an imperial audience apparently devolved upon Yoshida. Through the intermediation of Suzuki, Harada, Kido, and Fujita Hisanori, a reserve navy admiral and then grand chamberlain, it was arranged that between February 7 and February 26 the emperor would listen to the opinions not only of Konoe but of all the senior statesmen (*jūshin*).[62]

Konoe's audience was scheduled for February 14, and in the interim he was tormented by a sense of both imminent crisis and futility. The former derived from the mounting expectation of Allied invasion of Japan. By the end of January, Konoe had learned that the army anticipated invasion of Kyushu in June and of Honshu in September, although persons such as Prince Takamatsu were predicting an earlier invasion of the main island.[63] The sense of futility derived from Konoe's dim appraisal of the possibility of actually persuading Emperor Hirohito to take decisive action. According to Kōmura Sakahiko, Konoe's personal secretary, Konoe prepared the draft of his memorial on February 11, and at that time expressed this gloomy view of the isolation and impotence of his sovereign:

> This being the last time I intend to present a memorial, I wish to do so boldly. The problem, however, is to what extent the emperor will listen to the opinions of the *jūshin*. His Majesty shuns listening to opinions other than those of persons of formal responsibility, even from the *jūshin* and members of the imperial family. This is the result of Prince Saionji's education, and in time of peace, when newspapers

> and the like freely criticize politics, that may be all right. But this is extremely troubling in a situation where the press is controlled and only that is reported which supports what the government and high command say. It's as if the emperor is only able to drink distilled water. Thus if I speak decisively, in the end I will probably only offend him.[64]

Konoe arrived at Yoshida's home in Tokyo on the day prior to his audience, and spent the night there discussing and revising the draft he had brought with him with Yoshida, to the satisfaction of both men.[65] On February 14 he was driven to the palace in Yoshida's car for his presentation. There, before the emperor, he conveyed a dire vision of impending revolutionary chaos, of the world turning Red and the Japanese imperial system tottering on the brink of destruction. This thesis represented the ultimate synthesis of views held by core members of YOHANSEN. Certainly it was the most systematic analytical excursion undertaken by the group, and its presentation to the emperor represented their supreme political act.

Exactly when Konoe personally began to subscribe to this analysis is not entirely clear, although his obsession with a "Red movement" within Japan reportedly became pronounced around the time of the Japanese defeat at Guadalcanal in early 1943—a logical point, since it was then that the Tōjō cabinet initiated its final great push to create a centrally coordinated war economy.[66] In January of that year, Konoe wrote to Privy Seal Kido concerning selection of a possible successor to Tōjō, who was ill at the time. He had recently had occasion to see the "reform plan" under consideration by the Tōjō cabinet, Konoe told Kido, and wished to emphasize that this could be understood only in the context of both internal and external developments since the Manchurian Incident. Specifically, the Tōjō plan derived from a "Five Year Production Expansion Plan" prepared for the General Staff in 1936–1937, which had "remained in a corner of the military, gradually becoming radicalized, until today it is no different than the structure of Soviet communism. . . . cleverly becoming realized bit by bit." While early proponents of the plan such as Ishiwara Kanji (a charismatic Kwantung Army officer and architect of the Manchurian Incident) undoubtedly viewed it as essential to the creation of a "high level defense-production state" which would enable Japan to meet its military requirements, an influential minority viewed the situation from a completely antithetical perspective. Rather than see domestic reform as essential for carrying out the war on the continent, according to Konoe, their *object* was radical domestic reform and they saw war as a means to this end. Initially these elements had endeavored to bring about internal renovation in Japan by destroying "those powers which supported the existing condition of the state" through the terroristic incidents of the early and mid-1930s—"but these did not work out well. Thus it became necessary to resort to a greater sacrifice, namely war. To these Reds the question of victory or defeat is no problem. In fact, they desire defeat." For this reason, these subversive elements deliberately expanded the China Incident during the first Konoe cabinet, and willfully frustrated United States-Japan negotiations during the later Konoe cabinets.[67]

In July 1944, as the Tōjō cabinet was actually about to fall, Konoe reiterated these themes in another letter to Kido. "Left-wing elements are lying low all over, waiting to seize the opportunity of impending defeat to incite revolution," he wrote. "Added to this, the majority of those who as so-called right-wingers call for unyielding prosecution of the war and annihilation of the United States and Great Britain are left-wing apostates, and we must weigh their true intentions. It is difficult to imagine what sort of schemes these groups have for taking advantage of the confusion."[68] In the conference of senior statesmen convened on July 18, 1944, to chose a successor to Tōjō, Konoe emphasized that this must be the major consideration in selecting a new prime minister:

> If one is to speak of the extremity of our country today, it lies in the movement toward left-wing revolution. This trend is visible in all conceivable conditions. Defeat is of course terrible, but it is leftist revolution which is as frightening, or more frightening, than defeat. Defeat is temporary and can be redressed, but if we have a leftist revolution, *kokutai* and everything will be gone to the winds. Thus the most pro-

> found attention concerning leftist revolution is necessary. It is not only those who operate openly on the surface who are left-wing. There are in fact many among the bureaucrats and military men who present what seem to be right-wing faces. There are extremely many persons who, even if they do not have that intention, are completely Red in what they do. Thus it is absolutely necessary to have a person [as prime minister] who will wield an axe against this.

Former prime minister Hiranuma said, "I completely agree," and Kido and former prime minister Wakatsuki also expressed agreement. Apparently none of the senior statesmen present took issue with Konoe's assessment.[69]

By the time of the imperial audience of February 1945, Konoe had considerably broadened the context of the alleged communist conspiracy. With the possible exception of the Anglo-American camp, the menace lurked in virtually every direction to which he turned his attention. Internationally it was to be seen in the fruition of Soviet designs to communize the world. Here Konoe drew upon the reports of Ogata Shōji, head of the Foreign Ministry's research bureau, to describe in some detail the first fruits of those communist plans as they were then ripening in both eastern and western Europe; in the Japan Emancipation League operated by the Japanese communist Nosaka Sanzō in Yenan; and in revolutionary resistance movements in both Korea and Formosa.[70] (Interestingly, he did not go on to describe the dramatic relationship between anti-Japanese sentiments and the rapid expansion of left-wing popular movements in both China and southeast Asia, although he was naturally aware of these).

Domestically, Konoe drew upon the Ueda vision of a leftward-careening society. He pointed not only to the revolutionary tinder of a war-weary and impoverished populace, but also to both conspiratorial and unwitting communist trends at the top levels of the military, within the bureaucracy, among the so-called right-wing defenders of the *kokutai*, and even in the imperial family itself. The Iwabuchi thesis of a malevolent military clique manipulating Japan's destiny received its broadest application in the Konoe Memorial. He had been duped in the past, the prince informed the emperor, but now it was all clear: the Manchurian Incident, the China Incident, and the Pacific War had all been perpetuated by a military ring (*ichimi*) as part of a communist plot. The full memorial read as follows:[71]

THE KONOE MEMORIAL

Regrettably, I think that defeat is inevitable. What I shall say is based on this assumption.

Defeat will be a blemish upon our *kokutai*, but public opinion in Great Britain and the United States up to now has not gone so far as change in this *kokutai* (of course there are extremist opinions among some, and it is also difficult to gauge what sort of change may take place in the future). Thus, if it were only a matter of defeat, I think it would not be necessary to be so concerned about the *kokutai*. More than defeat itself, what we must be most concerned about from the standpoint of preserving the *kokutai* is the communist revolution which may accompany defeat.

After careful deliberation, it is my belief that at the present time events both within and outside the country are moving rapidly toward a communist revolution. That is to say, outside the country there are the extraordinary advances of the Soviet Union. Our people have failed to grasp accurately the intentions of the Soviet Union. Since the adoption of the people's-front tactic in 1935, that is, the tactic of two-stage revolution, and particularly since the recent dissolution of the Comintern, there has been a notable tendency to regard the danger of bolshevization (*sekka*) lightly, but to my mind this a superficial and frivolous view. That the Soviet Union has not abandoned its plan to ultimately bolshevize the world is gradually becoming clear by her recent obvious machinations toward various countries of Europe.

In Europe the Soviet Union is trying to establish soviet-style governments in the countries on its borders, and at least pro-Soviet, pro-communist governments in the remaining countries. She is progressing steadily in this task, and at present is encountering success in most instances.

The Tito government in Yugoslavia is the most typical concrete example of this. In Poland she has set up a new government centering around the Polish Exiles League prepared ahead of time in the Soviet Union, without considering the exile government in Great Britain.

When one examines the cease-fire conditions in Rumania, Bulgaria, and Finland, although she stands on the principle of non-intervention in domestic politics, the Soviet Union demands the dissolution of organizations that supported Hitler and in practice makes it impossible for a non-soviet government to survive.

In Iran she demanded the resignation of the cabinet on the grounds that it did not respond to her demands for oil rights. When Sweden proposed opening diplomatic relations with the Soviet Union, the Soviet Union opposed the Swedish government as being pro-Axis and this left no alternative but the resignation of the Swedish foreign minister.

In France, Belgium, and Holland, which are under Anglo-American occupation, a severe struggle is continuing between the governments and the armed resistance groups which were used in the war against Germany; these countries have all met political crises, and those who are leading these armed groups mainly follow the communist line. In Germany as in Poland, she intends to establish a new government centering around the Committee for a Liberated Germany which has already been set up, and this has now created a headache for Great Britain and the United States.

Despite the fact that on the surface her position is one of nonintervention in the domestic affairs of the various European countries, the Soviet Union in this way is actually interfering extensively in domestic affairs and endeavoring to drag domestic politics in a pro-Soviet direction.

Soviet intentions toward the Far East are the same. At the present time the Japan Emancipation League has been organized in Yenan under Okano,[72] who came from Moscow, and is linking up with the Korean Independence Union, the Korean Volunteer Army, the Formosan Vanguard Army, and the like, and making overtures toward Japan.

As I consider the situation in the light of such conditions, there is considerable danger that the Soviet Union will eventually intervene in Japan's domestic affairs (for example, recognition of the Communist Party; participation in the cabinet by communists as was demanded of the DeGaulle and Badoglio governments; abrogation of the Peace Preservation Law and the Anti-Comintern Pact; and so on). Turning to the domestic scene, I see all the conditions necessary to bring about a communist revolution being prepared day by day: the impoverishment of daily life; an increase in the level of labor's voice; a pro-Soviet mood, which is the other side of a rise in hostile feelings toward Great Britain and the United States; the reform movements of a ring within the military; the movement of the so-called "new bureaucrats" who ride on this; and the secret maneuvers of leftist elements who are manipulating this from behind. Of these, that which warrants greatest concern is the reform movement of a ring within the military.

Many young military men seem to believe that our *kokutai* and communism can coexist, and it is my belief that the basic tone of the reform theory within the military also reflects this. [I have heard indirectly that this view is even listened to within the imperial family.] [73] The majority of professional military men come from families below the middle class, and many are in circumstances which make it easy to accept communist allegations; in addition, since they are thoroughly indoctrinated in the concept of *kokutai* through their military education, the communist elements are trying to get hold of them through this theory of the coexistence of *kokutai* and communism.

It has now become apparent that it was a deliberate plot within the military which gave rise to the Manchurian Incident, the China Incident, and, by expanding this, eventually led to the Great East Asian War. It is a well-known fact that at the time of the Manchurian Incident they publicly stated that the aim of the incident lay in domestic reform. At the time of the China Incident it was a central figure of this ring who publicly stated, "It is better for the incident to be prolonged, for if it is solved domestic reform will become impossible."

Although the goal of the reform theory of this ring within the military is not necessarily a communist revolution, the intention of deliberately dragging this toward a communist revolution is held by a segment of the bureaucrats and civilian supporters involved (whether you call it right wing or left wing, the so-called right wing has become communism wearing the garments of *kokutai*), and in my opinion it is not far from wrong to regard the simple, ignorant military men as being manipulated by them.

For the past ten years I have had associations in the several fields of the military, bureaucracy, right wing, and left wing, and this is the conclusion I have reached recently after calm reflection. And when I observe the events of the last ten years in the light [lit., mirror] of this conclusion, I now feel that there are a great many things that fall into place.

During this period I have twice received the imperial order to form a cabinet,[74] but in order to avoid conflict and dissension within the country I was impatient to achieve national unity by accommodating as much as possible the pronouncements of these reform advocates, as a result of which I failed adequately to perceive the intentions hidden behind their pronouncements. This was due entirely to my lack of insight and was indeed inexcusable; it is a matter for which I feel deep responsibility.

Recently, as the war enters a stage of crisis, voices calling for "one-hundred million fighting to the death" have gradually increased in strength. Those who make such pronouncements are the so-called right-wingers, but it is my estimation that the ones who are agitating them from behind are communist elements who ultimately are aiming at the goal of revolution by turning the country into chaos in this manner.

On the one hand we advocate the complete destruction of the United States and Great Britain, while on the other hand the pro-Soviet atmosphere appears to be gradually becoming thicker. There are elements within the military who even preach holding hands with the Soviet Union no matter what sacrifice this entails, and others who are considering cooperation with Yenan.

As I have stated above, both within and outside the country every condition favorable to the advancement of a communist revolution is growing day by day, and should the state of the war become even more disadvantageous hereafter, it is my opinion that these conditions will develop rapidly.

It would be a different matter if there were even a slight hope of breaking free insofar as the future state of the war is concerned, but if we continue under the assumption that defeat is inevitable, to pursue the war further with no prospect of victory will place us completely in the hands of the Communist Party. Thus, from the standpoint of preserving the *kokutai*, I firmly believe that we must work out our method of concluding the war as soon as possible.

The greatest obstacle to conclusion of the war is the existence within the military of that ring which ever since the Manchurian Incident has been pushing things forward until the situation of today. Although they have already lost confidence in their ability to carry out the war, they will nonetheless resist to the end in order to maintain face.

Should we resolve to end the war quickly without wiping out this ring, then there is the danger that the civilian supporters of both the right wing and left wing, who are the counterpart of this ring, may well cause great confusion within the country and make it difficult to achieve this objective. Thus, if we are to terminate the war, as an essential precondition to this we must first wipe out this ring.

If only this ring is wiped out, then the bureaucrats as well as the civilian elements of the right wing and left wing who ride on its coat-tails will be subdued. They do not yet constitute a major force and are merely trying to realize their ambitions by utilizing the military, and thus, if we cut off the root, the branches and leaves will wither as a matter of course.

> Also, although it may be rather wishful thinking, once this ring is wiped out the features of the military will change greatly, and is it not possible that the atmosphere in the United States, Great Britain, and Chungking will then relax? From the beginning the goal of the United States, Great Britain, and Chungking has been the overthrow of the Japanese military clique, and so, if the character of the military changes and its policy is altered, I wonder if they on their part would not reconsider the continuation of the war.
>
> Be that as it may, since wiping out this ring and carrying out the reconstruction of the military are the preconditions and prerequisites for saving Japan from a communist revolution, I entreat your extraordinary and courageous consideration.

The emperor was reportedly surprised by the passion and focus of Konoe's analysis, and apparently intrigued as well, for following the formal presentation he invited Konoe to be seated and discuss the matter further. Konoe recounted this conversation to Iwabuchi, and several years later the latter reconstructed it as follows. General Umezu Yoshijirō had conveyed the views of the Imperial Headquarters to him five days previously, the emperor said, and these were completely at variance with Konoe's interpretation. According to the army, it was American policy to pursue the war to the bitter end, until the *kokutai* had been destroyed and Japan itself desolated. Thus it was out of the question to consider peace with the United States. On the contrary, Umezu stated, Japan could rely only on the Soviet Union and had no alternative but to continue the war, even if it meant the destruction of the homeland. (Iwabuchi placed this in the context of propaganda then current in the Japanese press, calling for deployment of the Japanese military in the central mountain ranges of Japan; arming of the entire population in accordance with the National Mobilization Law; resistance to an American invasion even to the point of reliance upon scorched earth and bamboo spears; and, if necessary, final removal of the emperor to continental Asia and continuation of the war there with the backing of the Soviet Union.)

When the emperor asked his interpretation of this line of thought, Konoe replied:

> I think there is no alternative to making peace with the United States. Even if we surrender unconditionally, I feel that in America's case she would not go so far as to reform Japan's *kokutai* or abolish the imperial house. Japan's territory might decrease to half of what it is at present, but even so, if we can extricate the people from the miserable ravages of war, preserve the *kokutai*, and plan for the security of the imperial house, then we should not avoid unconditional surrender.

The emperor replied, "I agree," and Konoe went on to emphasize that in any case it was essential first to gain control over extremist elements within the military, and to this end the emperor's own decisive judgment was necessary (*heika no goeidan ga hitsuyō da*). When the emperor asked what this implied, Konoe replied that, since civilian bureaucrats could not suppress the military, it was necessary to use someone from within the military itself. To the question of who this should be, he reportedly answered, "I feel there are no alternatives other than Ugaki Kazushige or Mazaki Jinzaburō."[75] At this the emperor remained silent—largely, it has been suggested, because he did not share the Yoshida group's optimistic evaluation of the intentions and capacities of the Kōdō-ha adherents, who a scant nine years earlier had themselves attempted to overthrow the regime.

Konoe's feeling upon leaving the audience was that he had gone as far as a subject could dare in making his case to the emperor, and with little effect. The emperor's obvious antipathy to resurrection of the Kōdō-ha leaders upon whom the Yoshida group rested their hopes, Konoe informed another confidant, meant that "Japan will probably continue on to the very end after all."[76]

INCARCERATION

On April 15, 1945, Yoshida, Ueda, and Iwabuchi were arrested in connection with their role in preparing the Konoe Memorial. In the two months that intervened between Konoe's audience and these arrests, however, the Yoshida group engaged in a final flurry of proposals which deserve brief mention. These took place when the holocaust had come brutally home: the "double kill" of destruction from the sky added to economic strangulation from the sea had been initiated by the Allies in November 1944 with regular and almost unopposed American bombing raids against Japan's cities, reaching a peak of horror on March 10, 1945, when approximately 130 B-29s killed an estimated 100,000 civilians in Tokyo and turned 16 square miles of the heart of the great city to rubble.

Yoshida's political proposals after the American terror intensified involved resurrection of the candidates that YOHANSEN had vainly endorsed during the previous two-and-one-half years. In response to the impending collapse of the Koiso cabinet (which resigned April 5), Yoshida initially threw his support behind Admiral Kobayashi for the premiership. When this move collapsed, in large part because of Kobayashi's reactionary proclivities, the Yoshida group renewed its advocacy of a cabinet headed by Ugaki, with the understanding that Mazaki would come in as war minister. This movement, which was supported by various former members of the now defunct Seiyūkai, collapsed when Ugaki, as previously, opposed the Kōdō-ha general and expressed preference for General Yamashita Tomoyuki as war minister. Instead of pursuing this alternative, Yoshida and Konoe then met at Yoshida's house with Suzuki and apparently decided that Konoe should step in and form his fourth cabinet. Whether Konoe agreed or not seems a matter of dispute. In any case, in a meeting held in the emperor's presence on April 5 to select a new prime minister, Suzuki began by nominating Konoe for the post, but the proposal was not accepted and the mantle of the premiership finally fell on the old admiral himself.[77]

For Yoshida, only one last gesture remained. Shortly after the Suzuki nomination, he was approached by Akizuki Satsuo, a diplomat and distant relative, and informed that the navy was considering secretly transporting someone to Great Britain by submarine, where he might engage in peace negotiations. In Akizuki's opinion, Yoshida was the person best qualified for such a task and, should he perish en route, at least it would be with the comforting knowledge that one could not ask for a better death. Yoshida thought this was rather extraordinary, but visited navy authorities to check it out nonetheless. He met no one with knowledge of such a plan, and was arrested before he could pursue the matter further.[78] Once again, to complete a nearly perfect prewar record, his rainbow had failed to top the horizon.

Yoshida had actually been under surveillance for six years prior to his arrest. The Kempeitai began to investigate the so-called pro-Anglo-American clique seriously in 1939, in connection with leaks of sensitive information to the British and American embassies, and soon narrowed its attention in this area to the *jūshin* and such individuals as Yoshida, Kabayama, Harada, and Ikeda Seihin. By 1941 both Yoshida's Tokyo residence in Kōjimachi and his country estate in Ōiso were under close survey.[79] The outbreak of the Pacific War and repatriation of the Anglo-American diplomatic communities eliminated the problem of intelligence leaks, but by 1943 the Anglo-American faction became a concern to the military police because of its detrimental influence upon popular morale. According to Ōtani Keijirō, the very blunt chief of the Kempeitai in Tokyo from November 1944, the "Red army" concept was an old one but had gained great vogue within political and business circles by the beginning of 1945, and thus became regarded as a serious cancer upon an already vulnerable public spirit. This development, moreover, was clearly linked to the Yoshida-Konoe group, and the military police were thus attentive to the group's position and activities before Konoe actually presented his memorial. In Ōtani's view, the "communization" thesis was wild—he compared it, in retrospect, to McCarthyism in America—and thus doubly pernicious because untrue and demoralizing. In a nice twist, the enforcement arm of the military state thus viewed the Yoshida-Konoe group as *contributing* to declining morale and erosion of the polity. They posed an immense problem, however, because thorough removal of this malignant line of thought would entail arrests at the very highest levels of Japanese society—in itself a potentially unsettling act.[80] Consequently, the police divided suspect members of the Yoshida-Konoe circle into three tiers of increasing sensitivity, of which only the first and

and lowest—Yoshida, Iwabuchi, and Ueda—were actually arrested. They were, it seems obvious, an object lesson to the others.[81]

Ōtani was scornful of those "slip-away liberals" (*nigedashita jiyūshugishatachi*) who bemoaned the miseries of war while themselves maintaining comfortable existences in their villas in such secure and detached retreats as Hakone and Karuizawa, and his account of Yoshida's arrest evoked a concrete image of the continued comfort of the privileged classes even as Japan's cities suffered the direct ravages of war. The police arrived at Yoshida's home in Ōiso around daybreak on April 15 and found themselves in a "separate world," where cherry blossoms dotted the verdure of hills far and near "as in a dream," and the smell of the sea wafted faintly in from a distant shore off which the fishing boats were visible.[82] They were admitted by a maid, and left to wait in the entry for some twenty minutes or more before Yoshida himself appeared. During that interval, it was later learned, Yoshida had hurriedly gathered his private papers and had his consort Korin conceal them in her *obi*; following his instructions, she later burned them. Thus the police group which entered the Ōiso residence immediately after the arresting party had left with Yoshida found virtually no materials of a revealing or incriminating nature. Through spies planted earlier in the Yoshida household as domestic help, however, the army already had obtained a photocopy of Yoshida's own handwritten copy of the Konoe Memorial, which he had made to show to Makino and possibly others.[83]

Yoshida, Ueda, and Iwabuchi were interrogated separately, and charged with four specific offenses on May 2. Three of these fell under Article 99 of the Military Code, which stated that "in time of war or incident, those who spread groundless rumors concerning the military are subject to not more than three years imprisonment." They were (1) dissemination of the contents of the Konoe Memorial; (2) dissemination of anti-war rumors to the effect that the military had already lost confidence and its morale was declining; and (3) malicious allegations that the Kwantung Army was Red and the core of the army was manipulated by a Red faction. The fourth charge fell under Article 4, clause 1, of the Military

Secrets Protection Law, which read: "Those who learn or collect military secrets and transmit these to others are liable to penal servitude for an unlimited period not in any case less than two years." Here the three men were accused of "imparting to others information learned concerning the disposition, armament, activities, etc. of the Kwantung Army." The arrest of civilians under military law was highly irregular, but despite the protest of such persons as Konoe and Tōgō, the Kempeitai refused to release its prisoners immediately.[84]

In the course of their six-year surveillance, the police had drawn a rather sharp profile of Yoshida. He was characterized, or caricaturized, as a supporter of the weak-kneed Shidehara diplomacy and a worshiper of Great Britian (*hai-Eishugisha*), whose antipathy toward the military had been exacerbated when the army denied him the foreign minister's post in 1936. Following his arrest, he was questioned on his relationship with Grew, but without leading to any substantial or damaging revelations. The charge of disseminating military secrets—which presumedly referred to relations with Grew and Craigie as well as discussion within Japanese circles of the various "Red" plans of the military—appears to have been a Red herring. As Ōtani later observed, although in the postwar period Yoshida was credited with having devoted himself to ending the war, he had actually done very little besides talking.[85] Thus, the investigation focused largely upon his perpetuation of "sensational rumors" (*zōgen higo*). A letter he had sent to Kabayama was used to prove he had maligned the military with charges of defeatism,[86] but the bulk of the interrogation focused on the Konoe Memorial. Here the police were concerned not merely with Yoshida's role in the preparation of the document, but also—and to a seemingly greater extent—his dissemination of its contents to others.

According to Ōtani's fairly lengthy account of the episode, Yoshida was initially stubborn and uncooperative, denying any particular knowledge of the memorial until the copy in his own handwriting was shown him, to his great astonishment. He then spoke more readily, and it emerged that on the afternoon following his audience, Konoe had recounted his conversation with the emperor to Yoshida in some detail, emphasizing his own argument that the influence of Grew and other American leaders ensured that America would not destroy the *kokutai*. Yoshida had immediately conveyed this to Makino (who was delighted at Konoe's performance), Ueda, and several others.[87]

Iwabuchi's experience confirmed the military's primary concern with the Konoe Memorial. The Kempeitai displayed a copy when Iwabuchi was first brought to police headquarters, and his interrogators repeatedly made the remark, "Konoe is a Badoglio. We must take care of him." (This comparison to the conservative, monarchist Italian leader who turned against Mussolini in 1943 and received the backing of the Allies became permanently associated with the events surrounding the Konoe Memorial, which is commonly described by Japanese commentators as "Japan's Badoglio Incident"; Ueda himself, for example, later wrote of the affair under this title.) Iwabuchi was also told by a military judge that the main reason for his arrest was his belief that the army was Red; this was clearly the thrust of the Konoe Memorial, and the military was concerned to discover just who had put such ideas in Konoe's head.[88]

Ōtani personally visited Ueda in prison and requested a detailed explanation of the supporting evidence for the communization thesis. He was treated to a twenty-minute discourse on the Kwantung Army, the Concordia Association (Kyōwakai) and developmental policies in Manchukuo, the army's five-year plan for heavy industry, and the socialistic thrust of army plans in general. In rebuttal, Ōtani delivered an analysis of his own in which he argued that these matters were old hat. He acknowledged that the Concordia Association had originally been influenced by the "one-country one-party" concepts of national socialism, and that there had indeed been direct socialist influence on both this group and the early economic policy of Manchukuo, but this had been investigated, exposed, and thwarted by the government as early as 1938. Ueda's "evidence" was thus past history, he charged, and in

Ōtani's own account Ueda accepted this criticism and immediately apologized for his rashness.[89]

Ōtani was hardly an impartial observer, and consequently his retrospective version of the arrests must be viewed with some caution. He did offer two "quotations" from the interrogation report on Yoshida which are unavailable elsewhere—one that rings true, and another that challenges the popular account that Yoshida stubbornly held his ground to the very end. Thus at one point in the investigation Yoshida is quoted as having made this succinct summarization of his basic position:

> No matter what anyone says, Japan is completely incapable of prospering without a close relationship with the United States and Great Britain. Therefore the war against the Anglo-American powers cannot be terminated a day too soon. Even if we lose this war to the two powers, the *kokutai* absolutely will not be destroyed; but, should the country turn Red within, then there will be no alternative to destruction.[90]

According to Ōtani's citation from the final investigative report, however, Yoshida, like Ueda, eventually came to acknowledge his misunderstanding of the situation, and apologized with these words:

> Not having thought the matter through sufficiently, I slandered the military, and for this I offer my sincere apologies. I hope you will excuse me on this point. Henceforth I shall revise my mental attitude, and desire to cooperate as a subject in the execution of this war.[91]

However one may respond to this alleged apology, it is generally acknowledged that, despite his intensive interrogation, Yoshida was well treated during his incarceration. He personally attributed this to the intercession of General Anami Korechika, who had been a neighbor of his in Tokyo. He was permitted to have food sent to him from outside, and the treatment accorded himself and his two colleagues from YOHANSEN provides a picture of the penetration even into jail of the niceties of social hierarchy. As the best blooded and best connected of the three prisoners, Yoshida was placed in a "first-class private cell"; Ueda, of lower status, was provided a "second-class private cell"; while Iwabuchi, a commoner of no official standing, was assigned a small cell with other prisoners. To ensure that Yoshida's food was not poisoned, according to one account, it was first checked by soldiers under the supervision of a Colonel Kurosaki.[92]

After two weeks of confinement in military police headquarters, Yoshida was transferred to a prison in Yoyogi. On May 25 the Yoyogi prison suffered a direct hit in an air raid, and he escaped the conflagration with the assistance of a military guard and spent the evening in the outer garden of the Meiji Shrine. From there he was moved to a prison in Meguro, and when this also was bombed he was transferred to a nearby primary-school building. On June 24, after seventy days of confinement, Yoshida, Ueda, and Iwabuchi were simultaneously released. A week later, Yoshida was summoned back to his last place of confinement to learn—from a lieutenant general who began by observing "There is no greater patriot than Your Excellency" (*Kakka hodo no aikokusha wa nai*)—that the charges against him had been dropped.[93]

It had been an unpleasant interlude, but it was to prove a decidedly helpful bit of biography with which to enter the postwar world. It placed a stamp on his "anti-war" credentials—just as the far longer prewar prison experiences of the communists and holders of "dangerous thoughts" also gave them prestige after they were released to become Yoshida's political foes in the postwar era.

EIGHT

"*Revolution*"

At the time of Japan's surrender, Yoshida was sixty-seven years old and had been in official retirement for seven years. His situation was comfortable, and he does not appear to have been possessed of any gnawing desire to add a final grand chapter to an eventful if peripheral public career. Had Yoshida died at this time, Konoe's frank appraisal might have prompted an apt, and all but unnoticed, epitaph: Here Lies Y.S.—Tenacious, Occasionally Maverick, An Exemplary Product of Imperial Japan. Westerners who had observed the activities of the prewar Japanese "moderates" with a mixture of exasperation and jaundice might have agreed on a different turn of phrase, along the lines of Defender of Empire, Ostensible Friend of the West, Spokesman for the Old Guard and Go-Slow Imperialists.[1] Both his stature in Japan and niche in history at this time were slight, and seemingly destined to remain so. In the heady period of initial post-surrender reformism, Yoshida appeared to belong to a repudiated past. He was, many assumed, an anachronism.

Instead, he left his name upon an era. Yoshida became foreign minister in the Higashikuni and Shidehara cabinets, and then headed five cabinets of his own between May 1946 and December 1954, while leading his party in opposition for the single period from May 1947 to October 1948. His total service of eighty-six months as premier fell only four months short of the record held by Itō Hirobumi, whom he so admired; Itō's record itself was surpassed in 1972 by Yoshida's own protégé, Satō Eisaku, who retired after serving as prime minister for ninty-two months. Yoshida did prove adaptable to the political currents of the postwar world. Or perhaps more accurately stated, postwar trends, particularly in American policy, turned eventually in the direction of Yoshida's own conservative proclivities. His postwar regenesis as a man of political power and influence involved no personal *volte-face*, no sacrifice of basic values and priorities, no belated kindling of progressive ideals. He had staked out his terrain long before and sought to "win the peace" on his own grounds, and in large part he succeeded. Less than five years after the surrender, the "new Japan" became synonymous with the "Yoshida era." And when Yoshida died in 1967, at the age of eighty-nine, his legacy remained pre-eminent. His declining years were spent in rare good humor, and his major regret at the very end was that he was unable to see Mt. Fuji one more time.[2]

This unexpected personal renascence was neither smooth nor easily stereotyped. Although he eventually emerged as America's "man in Japan," Yoshida's first cabinet (May 1946 to May 1947) was roundly castigated in most official American circles as an inept and reactionary disaster, and even in late 1948 there were concerted endeavors within the Government Section of SCAP (Supreme Commander for the Allied Powers) to thwart the formation of a second Yoshida cabinet.[3] While the deflationary fiscal policy imposed by special ambassador Joseph M. Dodge beginning in early 1949 reflected United States commitment to the Japanese conservatives' own priority upon economic rehabilitation, the Yoshida cabinets opposed the Dodge Line on such basic issues as tax scales, funding of local government, unemployment and wage policy, financing of public works, governmental support for small industry, and so forth. In essence, the Yoshida group's disgruntlement over the Dodge route to economic "self-sufficiency" reflected both a partisan eye to domestic politics and basic theoretical disagreement on appropriate economic policy; the Japanese side actually endorsed a more "liberal" and Keynesian policy of deficit spending, while Dodge hewed to the staunch conservatism of severe "disinflation" and a balanced budget. Both before and after the Korean War, Dodge privately accused the Yoshida governments of attempting to "sabotage" his program.

Similarly, the apparent harmony that united Yoshida and John Foster Dulles in the making of the peace and military settlement of 1950–1952 did reflect a convergence of counterrevolutionary interests between the ruling groups of the United States and Japan, but again disagreements on economic and strategic policy (such as Japan's international trade structure, relations with the People's Republic of China, speed of Japanese rearmament, and the scope and stature of U.S. military bases in Japan) persisted beneath such surface amity. America's man-in-Japan, in short, met Washington's needs, but never nestled complacently in its pocket. The United States did not awe him as Great Britain had done during the gaudy years of empire, and the conclusion he had reached decades earlier—that the United States was not entirely trustworthy in matters of "diplomatic sense"—was never entirely repudiated.[4]

Along similar lines, in the domestic arena Yoshida is the most prominent figure associated with reconsolidation of the conservative hegemony—the nexus of big business, bureaucracy, and conservative politicians—which weathered initial occupation reforms and became the open pivot of real power in Japan after 1948. Yet it is misleading to cast him simply as a mainline conservative politician. He scuttled into his future base of political power in 1946 as president of the leading conservative party in a manner that was diffident, oblique, almost crab-like, and initially even balked at the job on the grounds that "strange fellows" would be slapping him on the back and acting familiar.[5] He inherited a party, the old Seiyūkai lineage, with which his prior relationship (during the Tanaka cabinet) had been tenuous at best, and which had been recreated after the surrender essentially as the personal machine of Hatoyama Ichirō. Had Hatoyama not been unexpectedly purged, he rather than Yoshida in all likelihood would have become the dominant political figure of Japan's first postwar decade. As party leader, Yoshida disdained such critical functions as fund raising, and to a notorious degree also showed contempt for his own rank and file. "It is impertinent," he once stated, "for party members to question what the party president does."[6] With much the same gusto, he described the Diet as a zoo and its members as monkies.[7]

While his ostensible base of power lay in the political-party system, in which he had slight interest and no prior experience, in practice Yoshida continued to function in the more familiar roles of bureaucrat and "diplomat." This deserves emphasis. Given Japan's peculiar status as an occupied country, a central task of the Japanese government was "foreign relations" with the occupying powers, notably the United States, and it is not surprising that, following the transitional Higashikuni cabinet, three of the four occupation-era premiers (Shidehara, Yoshida, and Ashida Hitoshi) were former Foreign Ministry officials.

Yoshida's political downfall was a protracted and excruciating one, which lasted from mid-1952 to the end of 1954 and was brought about not by "progressive" political forces, but rather by conservative opponents within the party ranks, bureaucracy, and business community. Conservative politicians did not form a single party until after Yoshida's political demise, and the funding structure that linked *zaibatsu* interests to these politicians was not formalized until then.[8] Yoshida was eventually routed from power by his own ostensible constituency under a barrage of accusations ranging from dictatorial tactics and abuse of the Diet to the galling charge that he had toadied to the United States at the expense of Japan's sovereign integrity.[9] In this respect, his legacy to the conservative cause was the contradictory one of hegemony on the one hand and factionalism on the other. Through the course of his postwar decade in the sun, Yoshida continued to play the role of "One Man," and as in the prewar period this added to both his colorfulness and the ranks of his enemies. As also in that earlier period, however, such idiosyncrasies of personality should not detract from recognition of the broad interests and causes he served.

Yoshida's postwar activities naturally were responsive to the pressing demands of the day—defeat, economic collapse, control by an alien force—but although the specific responses called for were new, ultimate goals remained consistent with objectives he had pursued prior to 1945. This was apparent in the tasks Yoshida set for himself in the immediate post-surrender period, which in broad outline were these: (1) preservation of the emperor and national polity; (2) repression of the revolutionary potential within Japan, particularly at the mass level; (3) restoration of the old guard and traditional levers of elite rule, a task of structural reconsolidation rather than simply overturning the occupation's purge of personnel; (4) economic reconstruction along capitalist lines, and in the *zaibatsu*-dominated mold of the prewar era; and (5) Japan's return to international stature as a partner of the Western powers.[10] Such an agenda reflected the outlook of the elitist and diplomatist, and in defending it Yoshida soberly and frequently made reference to those theories of history and explanations of disaster he had attempted to hammer into the minds of his Western counterparts in the past. Japan's surrender became the occasion to swing the pendulum *back* and return to the "traditional diplomacy" and, essentially, the traditional power structures of Meiji and Taishō. Expressed figuratively, Yoshida longed to return to the time of Versailles.

To his chagrin and alarm, the United States initially endorsed a radically different view of Japan's modern history—one that called for repudiating the Meiji legacy itself. Where Yoshida dismissed the recent catastrophe as an aberration, a "historic stumble," a militarist-communist conspiracy,[11] those who planned the occupation offered deeper, structural explanations. They looked less to the stumble than to the root, and Assistant Secretary of State Dean Acheson succinctly conveyed this line of analysis in September 1945, when he stated that "the present economic and social system in Japan which makes for a will to war will be changed so that the will to war will not continue."[12] The inimitable hyperboles of the supreme commander of the occupation force, General Douglas

MacArthur, carried this same message: that there was no viable past to which Japan might return. Even after his recall from the Far East in 1951, West Point's most famous soldier-pontificator was still gravely explaining that "tucked away there in the North Pacific, the Japanese had little or no realization of how the rest of the world lived. They had evolved a feudalistic system of totalitarianism which had produced results which were almost like reading the pages of mythology."[13]

The political significance of such historical explanations (leaving aside their ethnocentricity) was unmistakable, and received concrete embodiment in the "U.S. Initial Post-Surrender Policy for Japan" sent to MacArthur in September 1945. Japan was to be "democratized" as well as "demilitarized," and the former mission would entail far-reaching renovation of virtually the entire presurrender state. In the view of Yoshida and the old guard, this meant that the traditional state was now challenged by a new threat of "revolution from above," and thus to their basic priorities and objectives they inevitably, and almost desperately, added a further, overriding goal: to oppose, temper, and eviscerate these early "excesses" of the alien overlords.

In examining this transition from Imperial Japan to the occupation and the "Yoshida era," it is profitable first to reconsider the Konoe Memorial and the questions concerning war, polity, and "revolution" this document raised.

WAR, POLITY, AND REVOLUTION

The Konoe Memorial seems at first glance a curious and even capricious document, and it is reasonable to ask whether its vision of radicalism and revolution was overstated to encourage the emperor's intervention on behalf of the Kōdō-ha and against the war. The interpretation that this was merely a calculated evocation of the apocalypse, however, or a wayward view best relegated to history's curiosity shop, must be weighed against a number of considerations. These warrant separate study, and can only be suggested in passing here.[14]

There is, to begin with, a wealth of evidence that those who contributed to the memorial believed what they said, and that many other Japanese within the ruling class held similar views. Following the February 26th Incident, "Red" infiltration of the army and bureaucracy became a subject of frequent discussion among the elites, and an object of concerted investigation by the police. By the middle of the Pacific War, the parallel question of whether Japan was moving structurally in the direction of a socialist state had become a matter of intense debate. And even before the United States initiated systematic terror bombing of Japan's civilian population, deterioration of morale and the possibility of popular upheaval drew the attention of both proponents and opponents of surrender.

The communist-conspiracy thesis of the Konoe Memorial is untenable as a causal explanation of the events of the 1930s and early 1940s, but repudiation of this fatuous argument does not render the document valueless. At the most general level, the memorial reflects attitudes which carried over to shape old-guard perceptions of the immediate post-surrender situation: both what should be done in the way of "reform," and what was actually taking place. Since the old guard, as personified by Yoshida, neatly bridged the pre-surrender and post-surrender epochs, these attitudes are noteworthy. In addition, the tortured but almost breath-taking "logic" of the conspiracy thesis exposes the ideological ambiguities of developments that appear deceptively monolithic when compressed under conventional categories such as "ultranationalism" or "fascism" or "Japanism" (*Nipponshugi*). Most important, the Konoe Memorial was not a product of abstract, hysterical rationalization. It addressed concrete developments both outside and inside Japan. It concluded that these developments constituted a threat to the established order unprecedented since the Meiji Restoration—possibly unprecedented since time before history, in that the imperial institution itself seemed imperiled. And these perceptions were not without foundation.

War is most commonly and dramatically perceived through its

toll of misery and devastation, but it is also a profound catalyst of structural transformation, accelerated social change, and alteration of popular consciousness. This was what the Yoshida-Konoe group, in the final analysis, perceived and feared. World War Two was without parallel in Japanese history. It was also, for Japan and China, the final chapter of what is now known as the "fifteen-year war," beginning with the Manchurian Incident. In essence, the Konoe Memorial stated that the ultimate significance of the world war lay not in the struggle between the "democracies" and "fascists," not in the clash between blocs of nation states, but rather in the release of radical forces which prolonged war had triggered.

Such visions of profound political and economic crisis—of impending revolution, or of a more ponderous structural transformation in the direction of socialism—were not confined to Japanese with a vested interest in preservation of the bourgeois status quo. One man's fear was another man's hope, and throughout the 1930s and early 1940s, the police continued to ferret out clandestine "radicals" and communists who embraced comparable visions. The most sensational such case involved the brilliant Ozaki Hotsumi, arrested in connection with the Sorge spy ring two months before Pearl Harbor. Prior to his execution in November 1944, Ozaki conveyed his views freely to his interrogators. He described his vision of a "New Order of Society in East Asia" which would emerge from the ashes of war and form "one link in the world revolution,"[15] and he faced death with a sense of accomplishment:

> My hair has gone white from the struggle to carry out my hidden activities under false pretenses. But my campaign to make a "Red" Japan has succeeded. Japan is plunged in the Great War, the country is in chaos, and revolution is just around the corner. Nine-tenths of my work is done and my only regret is that I shall not live to see its completion.

Ozaki was regarded as one of Japan's most astute political analysts, and it is hardly surprising to learn that his confession made Konoe "shudder."[16]

Nor were such views, in the broadest sense, peculiar to Japan or the Japanese. In the postwar period, Yoshida was described as a "pocket Churchill"—an apt description in terms of size, cigars, arrogance, and imperialist ardor. And also with regard to the point in question, for during World War Two Churchill also decried the "slithering to the left" occurring on a global scale.[17] Ozaki too had counterparts among non-Japanese Marxist theoreticians. Beginning as early as 1933, for example, Trotsky emphasized the similarities between contemporary Japan and Russia in World War One, on the eve of the Bolshevik Revolution. Japan's war, he predicted, would push the contradictions within Japanese society to the point of explosion.[18] Mao Tse-tung predicted to Edgar Snow in 1936 that the strain of prolonged war would foment revolution in Japan, and his 1944 essay "On Coalition Government" contained a vision of post-defeat struggle and upheaval in the vanquished countries which the Yoshida group, then developing their own forecast, would have found chillingly persuasive.[19]

Had the Konoe Memorial been rendered iconographic by a political cartoonist, it might have been presented as a three-armed monster, each arm extending "the evil hand of communism": from outside, above, below. The gloss: bourgeois society and the emperor system were threatened from three directions, which meshed—or could potentially mesh—with communism. Iconography lacks the fourth dimension, but in the consciousness of Yoshida and his ilk, these three arms were to reach, tentacle-like, into the early years of occupied Japan.

The Japanese had been obsessed with international communism, the threat of revolution-from-outside, ever since the Bolshevik Revolution. Their collusion with White Russians during the Siberian Intervention was testimony to the immediacy of the fear, and this became more sharply focused with the consolidation of the Russian revolution, the creation of the Comintern, and Soviet intrigues in China in the 1920s. When Yoshida described anti-Japanese demonstrations in Mukden in 1927 as communist-inspired, he was reciting an accepted equation not entirely devoid of truth.[20] The defense of the Manchurian Incident and creation of

Manchukuo which Japan submitted to the League of Nations in 1932 reeked of references to the pernicious "influence of the Third International."[21] The Anti-Comintern Pact with Nazi Germany in 1936 represented an intensified commitment to the mission of "combating bolshevism," and the "New Order" in Asia proclaimed by Konoe in November 1938 was presented as a bulwark against the new menace of communism as well as the older menace of Western imperialism. Over six years prior to the Konoe Memorial, Konoe justified the war against China on the grounds that the Kuomintang had failed to prevent the "steady bolshevization and colonization" of the Asian mainland, and explained that creation of a Japan-Manchukuo-China bloc was necessary "to perfect the joint defense against Communism."[22] The list could be expanded almost indefinitely, again with complementary statements by Westerners who also believed that Japan's real and desirable destiny was to emerge as the anti-communist "stabilizing force" in Asia. Japanese such as Yoshida who were saturated in the prewar rhetoric of the international Red peril thus found the postwar ideology of cold-war America familiar, comfortable, easy to exploit.

By the time of the Konoe Memorial, the "joint defense against Communism" was in shambles and the threat of revolution-from-outside had taken on a new dimension of urgency. This derived from awareness of Soviet and communist successes in Europe; from recognition that Japan's 1941 neutrality pact with the Soviet Union was a marriage of convenience which Stalin would dissolve when the European conflict was resolved; and from knowledge of the organization of a Japanese fifth column.

According to Ogata Shōji, a Soviet specialist in the Foreign Ministry, Japanese leaders became preoccupied with global Soviet activities as the war progressed, and beginning around 1944 he began to be called upon to lecture about "world communism" before the House of Peers and senior statesmen. The first such occasion was sponsored by the Thought Policy Committee of the House of Peers and attended by some one-hundred persons. Ogata joined representatives of the Home and Justice ministries in discussion of the communist problem, and displayed a map of the world on which he had marked "communist areas" in red; the impact was sufficiently dramatic to get him invited back by the same group a month later. A copy of his discussion made its way into the hands of Hatoyama, and presumedly through him to Konoe, following which Ogata was invited to present his views to Konoe alone, and then shortly thereafter to the assembled senior statesmen, including Hiranuma, Wakatsuki, Okada, and again Konoe. Ogata later learned from Konoe's secretary that the prince used this latter talk as the basis for those sections of his memorial that dealt with the rising global strength of communism. Apart from these sessions with the cream of the civilian elite, Ogata also was consulted on a regular basis by representatives of the army and navy concerning Soviet affairs. Judging at least from his own experience, he later suggested, Japanese officials showed greater concern over Soviet relations with the Chinese Communist Party than they did over the military crisis in the Philippines and Okinawa.

Even while acting as an official consultant, moreover, Ogata found himself viewed with suspicion by virtue of the very fact that he was a specialist in communist affairs. His office was visited by plain-clothes military police once or twice monthly, and in the summer of 1942 he actually was summoned to police headquarters to explain why he had a copy of Mao's "On the New Democracy" on his desk. It was related, of course, to his job as an intelligence expert, but nonetheless he was treated to an embarrassing "re-education" lecture before being released. His work also entailed study of the Soviet planned economy in conjunction with officers from the General Staff, and this too placed him under suspicion of being at least potentially Red. Even in retrospect, Ogata appeared to find it all a bit bewildering for a good bureaucrat, but concluded that, solely on the basis of his own personal experience, Japan's leaders clearly did fear "Reds" more than a prospective Allied occupation.[23]

On April 5, 1945, seven weeks after the Konoe Memorial, the Soviet Union notified Japan of its intention to terminate the neutrality pact in a year's time. This did not come as a surprise, for on November 5 of the previous year Stalin had publicly denounced Japan as an aggressor cut of the same cloth as Nazi Germany, and this was recognized as an indication of intent to open an eastern offensive when the time was opportune. The prospect was frankly discussed in an Imperial Conference on June 8, 1945, at which the emperor was informed that the Soviet Union might "resort to the use of military power at a comparatively early date, with the objective of checking America's advancement in Asia."[24] The actual Soviet declaration of war in August was thus not unexpected, but it was no less shocking because of this. In a florid statement again suggestive of the language of the Konoe Memorial, the war minister described this as a Kremlin plot to "subjugate and rule all of East Asia."[25]

Stalin's November 1944 speech coincided almost to the day with the execution of Richard Sorge and Ozaki Hotsumi in Sugamo prison, a grim coincidental reminder that the Kremlin's plots were reinforced by Japanese agents. Exposure of the Sorge-Ozaki spy ring in 1941 actually placed the communist conspiracy in Konoe's own lap, for Ozaki had been a respected member of the Shōwa Kenkyūkai (Shōwa Research Association), one of Konoe's brain trusts. Officials were also acutely aware of the activities of the Japan Emancipation League, organized under the Japanese communist Nosaka Sanzō in Yenan in the beginning of 1944. Referred to in the Konoe Memorial by his pseudonym (Okano), Nosaka was engaged in indoctrination of Japanese prisoners of war. The League was a popular-front organization, and Nosaka's own theoretical projections for creation of a communist Japan envisioned a long process of post-defeat transition and adaptation. It was estimated that by early 1945 he had gained the firm allegiance of some two-hundred Japanese prisoners, who would return to a defeated Japan as dedicated cadres. In Japan, they could be expected to join the solid core of communists then languishing in jail, many of whom had been incarcerated since the late 1920s and early 1930s.[26]

Westerners also anticipated this. In *Dilemma in Japan*, an

influential book published in early 1945, the leftist American journalist Andrew Roth hopefully predicted that "Yenan will be able to supply hundreds of Japanese antifascist organizers," who in the future Japan would join disillusioned veterans, small shopkeepers, peasants, industrial workers, students, intellectuals, and "a reservoir of determined anti-militarist and pro-democratic leadership" which could be expected to emerge from among "the many thousands of 'dangerous thoughts' inmates of Japanese political prisons."[27]

The threat of international communism assumed awesome proportions in the eyes of the Yoshida-Konoe group because it appeared to be supported by domestic trends at the levels of both officialdom and the citizenry. Where revolution-from-above was concerned, the group again was not evoking disembodied shades. They could cite a long roster of radical military officers and reform-oriented bureaucrats, and couple this with a list of concrete policy enactments which promoted increasing central–and, in their view, socialistic–control.

In Japan as in the United States, war (and depression) fostered centralization and bureaucratization, thrust the state into hitherto relatively privatized realms. And in Japan, this *was* in many cases accompanied, on the part of the central planners, by disenchantment with the decadence, avarice, and inefficiency of bourgeois society and private capital. The very name of the arch villain in the YOHANSEN thesis–the Tōsei-ha, or "Control Faction"–exemplified the threat as perceived by the conservative war opponents. Although the name was originally adopted by army officers who desired to "control" the intemperate direct-actionist element in the military (associated with the Kōdō-ha), it gradually assumed connotations of controlled planning, controlled economy, control of the bureaucratic state by a tight and reformist vanguard clique.[28] The civilian bureaucrats who cooperated with these officers represented a generation that had come into prominence in the 1930s, and had acquired a similarly evocative label: they were commonly known as the reform, or renovationist, bureaucrats (*kakushin kanryō).*[29] The most spectacular exposure of

"Reds" at the highest level of government occurred in the Cabinet Planning Board Incident of 1941, when seventeen key bureaucrats were purged after lengthy investigation on grounds that they were attempting to turn the exigencies of war into an opportunity for creating a socialist state.[30]

This issue taps a deep stream in the history of Imperial Japan, and of twentieth-century Europe as well. It involves the problem of "right radicalism," or "national socialism," and the question of where the weight resides: on the rightist (national) or the radical (socialist) side? The problem is familiar to students of Italy and Germany, although in these countries there was little doubt, by the time of the war, as to how the scales were balanced. Established interpretations, including those of more radical historians, would hold this to be true of Japan as well: here the problem is defined largely in terms of right-wing, ultranationalistic, militaristic fascism. This was not, however, the impression held in the upper-class circles in which Yoshida moved. "There is no country which is so thorough in its communism as our country today," Admiral Nomura observed in 1944, in a conversation concerning bolshevism as the wave of the future.[31] Prince Takamatsu described the "Red tendency" as "distressing."[32]

If these were jokes, they were grim jokes, conveyed with hollow laughter; if paranoia, this was paranoia on a grand and collective scale, and with a lunatic genius for detail. The implication of "Red" or "communism" may have varied with the user, but it was most often evoked in a concrete context: specific individuals; specific cliques; specific ministries or agencies; specific laws, plans, and policies. Ironically, it was structural renovation set in motion under Konoe's own "New Structure" *(Shin Taisei)* program prior to Pearl Harbor that convinced many critics that Japan was moving toward the Soviet rather than Nazi model. As early as August 1940, for example, Yoshida informed Harada that certain "extremists" were criticizing Konoe's consolidation of political parties under the Imperial Rule Assistance Association (formally inaugurated October 1940) on the grounds that "instead of this being a combination of the Nazi or Führer system and the Kyōwakai ["Concordia Association" of Manchukuo], it bears an extremely close resemblance to the transitional period of Kerensky in the Soviet Union."[33] Ozaki Hotsumi, who had contributed to the planning of the New Structure as a member of the Shōwa Kenkyūkai, confessed after his arrest that he had hoped this political consolidation would become the basis for a Leninist party in Japan.[34]

The image of Konoe as a transitional figure and a dupe, outfoxed by wily communists, gained a certain currency; and the most natural comparison was to the transition from Tzarist to Soviet Russia. Yoshida mentioned Kerensky. Mazaki Katsuji, a peripheral figure in the YOHANSEN group, later drew the comparison between Konoe and Lvov.[35] The Konoe Memorial itself can be read as a personal confession by Konoe that he had indeed been used and misled, and that his own cabinets bore grave responsibility for opening the gates to the socialist and communist threat. And if this were true of the "New Political Structure" (*Shin Seiji Taisei*), it seemed even more ominously apparent in trends accelerated under the "New Economic Structure" (*Shin Keizai Taisei*).

These latter developments are too complex to be discussed here, for they open a major new area of inquiry: the respective roles of the state and monopoly capital in Japanese imperialism and the "total-war economy," or "national-defense state."[36] The crisis of the imperialist order promoted significant changes in the capitalist structure and economic role of the state, beginning in the early 1930s. Legislatively, this was defined by the evolution from the Major Industries Control Law of 1931 to the General Mobilization Law of 1938 to the Major Industries Association Ordinance of 1941, culminating in the Munitions Company Act of October 1943. The war economy and quest for autarky gave rise to an immense proliferation of "national-policy companies" (*kokusaku kaisha*), "special companies" (*tokushu kaisha*), industrial control associations (*tōsei kai* and *tōsei kumiai*), financial control companies (*kinyū tōsei kai*), special corporations (*eidan*), and the like. Extensive mergers of industrial and financial enterprises, especially banks, were promoted and supported by the state.

In retrospect, it is clear that these trends, which the conservative war opponents decried as "socialistic" or "communistic," actually strengthened the monopoly control of the great *zaibatsu*.[37] This can be interpreted as a classic case of collaboration and collusion between monopoly capital and the "fascist" managers of the state; private capital in Japan, as everywhere, readily spawned merchants of death. To terminate the analysis at this point, however, is to ignore the crisis of Japanese capitalism in the midst of the death throes of the old imperialism, and to ignore also the extent to which collusion in the war effort masked a power struggle between big capitalists and "reformist" military and civilian bureaucrats. The Konoe Memorial was correct in its perception that at least a portion of the central planners promoted these trends for reasons beyond and apart from the demands of the war economy: they welcomed the opportunity to accelerate the process of transformation from monopoly capitalism to state-monopoly capitalism. Even irrespective of deliberate intent, the question inevitably arose as to whether prolonged war was preparing the ground for ultimate expropriation of the expropriators—whether, given the nature of its war collaboration, the bourgeoisie was not producing "its own grave-diggers."

It should be emphasized that Marxist ideology was a significant component in Japanese thought during the pre-surrender period. As investigation of the Cabinet Planning Board Incident had vividly revealed, renovationist officials were widely read in Marxist literature. From the 1920s, the slogans and programs of so-called "right-wing radicals"—from systematic ideologues such as Kita Ikki to the terrorists impatient with mere words—reflected Marxist influence even while advancing the rallying cry of anti-communism. The elites represented by the Yoshida group were also conversant with the general categories of Marxism, and it is a striking aspect of their position that, in attempting to thwart the threat from the left, they implicitly accepted the logic and correctness of central concepts and auguries in the Marxist analysis. Their "Marxism" was naturally hodgepodge and vulgarized, but this did not diminish the potency of those key notions they seized upon.

This was again apparent in the third dimension of the communist threat as portrayed in the Konoe Memorial: revolution-from-below, the potential for a revolutionary upsurge of the Japanese people. In the end, it was this that colored the various apprehensions of the "anti-war group" fully Red. In pre-surrender as in early post-surrender Japan, loyalists and patriots such as Yoshida personified the contradiction of the orthodoxy. They affirmed the "polity" to be ineffable and eternal—and feared that the masses were fully capable of casting it into the rubble of their bombed-out homes. Police reports seemed to give credence to such fears. From the bitterness of bereaved parents to mounting absenteeism in factories, from "seditious" writings on the walls of public lavatories to the wildfire spread of "malicious and sensational rumors" (*ryūgen higo; zōgen higo*), trends were discerned that pointed to growing disrespect for authority, increasingly articulate consciousness of "haves" and "have-nots"—and even to inclinations toward *lèse majesté.*[38]

The network of upper-class gossip embraced such reports, and the queasy elites were not assuaged by official propaganda of one-hundred-million hearts beating as one. They were more receptive to alarmist opinions conveyed privately by their contacts within the domestic intelligence apparatus—the view, as Konoe was informed in June 1944 by an official of the Special Higher Police (Tokkō), that "the present situation is like a stack of hay, ready to burst into flame at the touch of a match."[39] Concrete examples of popular discontent were numerous—and who could know for sure what those who seemed silent and stoic really thought? Hosokawa Morisada, Prince Takamatsu's aide and one of the busiest gossip collectors connected with the Yoshida group, unfortunately had had a personal glimpse. Riding on the trolley on December 20, 1943, he had encountered an "intellectual-looking" man, drunk, and loudly improvising this song:

They started a war
they were bound to lose
saying we'll win, we'll win,
the big fools.
Look, we're sure to lose.

The war is lost
and Europe's turned Red.
Turning Asia Red
can be done before breakfast.

And when that time comes,
out I'll come.

The other passengers, Hosokawa noted, seemed uninterested. But perhaps there is no better glimpse of the sensitivities of the upper class on this score than the vignette of the aristocratic Hosokawa rushing home, mumbling the ditty over to himself, to record it in his diary for his prince, his friends, and history.[40]

Fear of insurrection was thus present even prior to late 1944, when the ferocious rain of death from the sky began. The brutal bombing of civilians by the United States was intended to bring about the destruction of Japanese morale, and the Yoshida group was ready to believe that this could succeed, and succeed beyond America's intention. Even an exceptionally loyal populace could be bombed into a new consciousness which went beyond mere defeatism. In part, this fear was proven correct. At least, the vigor and radicalism of popular movements in immediate post-surrender Japan seemed evidence of such alteration of consciousness.

The endeavor of the Yoshida-Konoe group to confront the tangled skein of war, polity, and revolution was, in sum, both ambitious and ambiguous, provocative and perverse. This reflected the disorder of the times and uncertainty of the future, a consideration of no little moment when it comes to addressing the immediate post-surrender period. The old guard believed that the foundations of the state had been profoundly shaken, and the potential for radical and even revolutionary change was immense.

The capitalist system, the class structure, and the imperial house all appeared in jeopardy.

At the same time, however, the ambiguity of the analysis also reflected the resiliency, complexity, and adaptability of the "national polity" itself. "Defense of the *kokutai*" could be evoked by both those who desired to preserve the status quo and those committed to overthrowing the present; by spokesmen for the elites as well as purported spokesmen for the masses; by the guardians as well as would-be destroyers of bourgeois society. The ideology seemed capable of embracing, or absorbing, such contradictions as "Red fascism" and "emperor communism"—at least at a certain stage. "Radical reformers" were still in practice little more than "social chauvinists," who slept in the same bed as the capitalists, even while dreaming their different dreams. Private monopoly control increased apace with state control, and if this was a potentially explosive antagonism, the capitalists had nonetheless been extremely adroit in postponing the explosion. The respect of the masses for established authority may have been severely eroded, but this had not yet advanced to the level of revolutionary class consciousness and capacity for mass action in opposition to the existing situation.

Such "contained elasticity" was not necessarily unique to the state and ideology in Japan. Whatever position may be taken on this question of cultural distinctiveness, however, the capacity for accommodation the Konoe Memorial implicitly revealed is as critical to an understanding of post-surrender Japan as is the obsessive fear of left-wing radicalism which was the memorial's explicit message. The question was whether such contradictions, at both the material and ideational levels, could be contained indefinitely—and, contrary to the bleakest visions of the Yoshida group, Japan's postwar experience answered this in the affirmative. Both despite and because of the nature of the American occupation, the *kokutai* was preserved, in a manner that simultaneously accommodated and restricted notable change.

This did not become clear immediately, however, and during

the opening stages of the occupation Yoshida and the old guard continued to fear that history had again delivered Japan a malicious and devastating cut.

REVOLUTION TRANSMOGRIFIED: THE AMERICAN OCCUPATION OF JAPAN

E. H. Norman once wrote that Clio loves her little jokes,[41] and she had a rather good one in immediate post-surrender Japan. The early stages of the American occupation not only seemed to confirm some of the unnerving visions of the Konoe Memorial, but also to replicate, or reincarnate, others. "Red fascists," "reform bureaucrats," "emperor communists"—all presumedly were removed by defeat. And replaced by what? A renovationist American military dictatorship, vigorously assisted by civilian reformers, determinedly trumpeting the mission of revolution from above, ostensibly committed to drastic restructuring of social and economic relations, radical enough in its initial policies to be labeled "communistic" by some, and possessing even an ambiguous emperor figure of its own in its imperious supreme commander, Douglas MacArthur.

Early occupation authorities themselves used the concepts of reform and revolution interchangeably, and to many observers MacArthur exemplified, in Japan, the paradox of the right-wing radical. And if his own goals were ultimately limited to bringing about a tightly controlled "democratic revolution," it nonetheless could be argued that his staff contained many planners whose conceptualization of desirable political, social, and economic change was more ambitious, more truly subversive of the "traditional polity." The military Control Faction and civilian reform bureaucrats who had been seen as Reds manipulating the situation from above in pre-surrender Japan thus had their regenesis, in this view, in the military reformers and "New Dealers" who set the clockwork for much of the occupation's early reform program.

Such revolution from above, moreover, seemed to intersect with and abet a surging revolutionary potential from below. Surrender spared the Japanese people the terror of the air raids, but apart from this it by no means led to immediate betterment of their lot. Living conditions deteriorated further, and soon assumed crisis proportions. A ravaged land, whose urban dwellers lived amidst rubble, was shorn of the resources of empire and normal trade, inundated by some six-million pathetic civilian repatriates and returned servicemen, plagued by food shortages of staggering complexity, and gutted by a runaway inflation. The ranks of the unemployed, swollen by those who returned from overseas, were estimated to have surpassed thirteen million in 1946; at the same time, disastrous harvests reduced both the rice and wheat crops to roughly sixty percent of the yield of previous years. In the months following surrender, newspapers carried reports of death by starvation.

In this situation, popular unrest mounted in the cities, workers organized with dramatic speed, and the labor movement became politicized and radicalized. Left-wing and Communist Party leadership gained wide support in the early unions, and strikes in a number of enterprises adopted the tactic of "production control" (*seisan kanri*), amounting to nascent soviets, whereby workers took over managerial functions and kept production going. On May Day 1946, an estimated 500,000 persons demonstrated before the imperial palace in Tokyo, and similar rallies took place throughout Japan; the press, Yoshida noted in his memoirs, "reported that Japan had been submerged under a sea of red flags." A second massive wave of protests took place on May 19, which had been designated "Food May Day." The first Yoshida cabinet was formed three days later—"to the accompaniment," Yoshida recalled, "of revolutionary songs chanted by a mob massed around my headquarters."[42] In early 1947, only MacArthur's intervention prevented a nationwide general strike, the most radical demonstration of worker solidarity and activism in Japanese history.

The specter of revolution thus remained very much alive in the early post-surrender period, and was intensified by apparent materialization of the third aspect of the wartime Yoshida group's analysis: Soviet-supported "revolution from outside." With the release of political prisoners, legalization of the Communist Party, and return of indoctrinated prisoners of war from Yenan and the Soviet Union, the old guard could easily conclude that surrender had exacerbated rather than thwarted the Soviet menace to Japan. When Nosaka returned from China in January 1946 and persuaded the Communist Party to abandon temporarily its uncompromising stand against the emperor system, "emperor communism" merely seemed regenerated for the postwar era. Communist organization, in addition, was complemented by socialist activity in labor and politics, and by the vigorous revival of Marxist methodology among an intelligentsia granted civil liberties.

Although the Yoshida group had anticipated that the United States would endeavor to promote "democratization" in defeated Japan, in the short-term view they had overestimated the moderating influence of their erstwhile benefactor in Washington, Joseph Grew. U.S. policy for post-surrender Japan was subjected to conflicting pressures within the State Department, and by war's end Yoshida's old *bête noire*, Stanley Hornbeck and the "China Crowd," had in certain respects overridden the more conciliatory proposals of the "Japan Crowd."[43] The conceptualization of "democratization" with which Yoshida and the old guard were confronted was thus unexpectedly thorough and wide-ranging, and the extent to which they responded to this much as they had responded to the war crisis is quite striking. They concluded that the drafters of policy in Washington were misguided; that the implementers of this policy within the occupation force itself included a hard core of "Red" Americans; and that more unwitting "idealistic" reformers within SCAP were being duped by this hard core, as well as by advice tendered them by the communistic elements within the Japanese scene.[44] At one point, Yoshida reportedly asked MacArthur directly if his intention was to turn Japan Red.[45] The familiar appraisal prompted a familiar reaction: the post-surrender Yoshida group endeavored to overturn these early and threatening "excesses" by resorting, among other tactics, to factional politics similar to those which YOHANSEN had tried to employ against the Tōsei-ha and reform bureaucrats.

Clio thus ventured further jests within her joke, one of these being the insinuation that contradictions and antagonisms within U.S. policy and among U.S. policy-makers were not all that dissimilar to Japan's recent experience. Right-wing officers of the 1930s and early 1940s such as Mazaki and Obata, who had coupled "Imperial Way" sentiments with plans to attack the Soviet Union, had their counterparts in the anti-Soviet ideologues within SCAP's own military bureaucracy, such as Major General Charles Willoughby and his Counter-Intelligence Section (G-2), and Lieutenant General Robert Eichelberger, commander of the Eighth Army. Yoshida evoked a favorite vocabulary from the days of the empire to describe this faction; he called them the "realists," as opposed (in his most charitable label) to the "idealists" centering around Brigadier General Courtney Whitney and Colonel Charles Kades in Government Section (GS). He and his colleagues recognized the potency of the "Soviet menace" and "Red subversives" arguments from the outset, and enlisted the support of SCAP's fanatic anti-communists against its "New Dealers" much in the manner in which YOHANSEN had attempted to use the Kōdō-ha against the Tōsei-ha, only this time with greater eventual success. By 1947–1948, SCAP had conducted its own internal purge of "Reds"; by 1949, SCAP had ordered the third Yoshida cabinet to purge the Japanese civil service of communists and fellow travelers; and by 1950, the "Red Purge" had been extended to the private sector as a weapon against the radical labor movement.[46]

In grand policy, official Washington had come to regard Japan from much the same anti-communist perspective as the Yoshida group by 1948, at which time the famous "reverse course" in occupation policy was accelerated. During the early stages of the occupation, however, anti-communism—much like the pre-surrender *kokutai* ideology—proved to be a double-edged sword which could also cut against the interests of the Japanese elites. In October 1945, for example, in one of the more eerie echoes of these early years, Konoe was granted an audience with MacArthur and delivered to Japan's "new Mikado" what amounted to an updated version of the threat-of-communism memorial he had presented to Hirohito eight months previously.[47] MacArthur's specific response to this is unclear, but the context of the meeting suggests the discrepancy between the supreme commander's appraisal of the situation in Japan and that of the Japanese old guard. The meeting was prompted by SCAP's famous "civil liberties" directive of October 4, which among other things called for the release of political prisoners and abrogation of "dangerous thoughts" legislation, and paved the way for legalization of the Communist Party. Such apparent equanimity concerning potential radical activity was profoundly shocking to Japan's leaders, and the October 4 directive actually precipitated the immediate resignation of the Higashikuni cabinet. Yet MacArthur's own anti-communist credentials were never in question. On the contrary, he also, and explicitly, regarded combating communism as a primary mission of the occupation—but interpreted the nature of the communist threat to Japan in a manner that justified some of the very reformist policies the Yoshida group regarded as excessive, and even virtually "communistic" themselves.

That such contradictory conclusions could be drawn from a seemingly common vocabulary ("anti-communism") can be partially explained by the contrasting stumble and root theses. The Yoshida group's emphasis upon conspiracy indicated that they regarded the communist menace largely in terms of infiltration and agitation, subversive individuals and groups. The more structurally oriented analysis that SCAP initially adopted, on the other hand, led individuals such as MacArthur to argue that the "roots" of Japanese militarism and aggression were simultaneously the potential roots of communism in Japan. The early occupation objective of "democratization" was thus construed as being simultaneously anti-fascist and anti-communist, and in various key areas it was anticipated that structural reform would eliminate the dual menace with a single stroke. This rationale was expressed with particular clarity in connection with two major reforms opposed by

Yoshida and the old guard: economic deconcentration and land reform.

Although Japanese conservatives had expressed alarm over trends toward state monopoly capitalism under the total-war economy, they were not opposed to monopoly capital or extensive economic concentration per se. In their eyes, the threat of socialism would be removed once the "controlled economy theorists" were purged. Thus, addressing a press conference of foreign correspondents shortly after the surrender, Yoshida sought to undercut SCAP's impending policies of *zaibatsu* dissolution and economic deconcentration with what became a well-known defense of the old financial and industrial cliques:

> It is a great mistake to judge the *zaibatsu* as having done only bad things. Japan's economic structure today was built by such old *zaibatsu (kyū zaibatsu)* as Mitsui and Mitsubishi. It can be said that the prosperity of the Japanese people has depended in great part upon the effort of these *zaibatsu.* Thus, it is doubtful that the dissolution of these old *zaibatsu* will really benefit the people. The various *zaibatsu* did not always work solely for their own profit and interest. During the war, for instance, they continued to manage various of their enterprises at a loss. The government ordered the manufacture of ships and planes, disregarding these losses by the *zaibatsu.* On the contrary, it was the new *zaibatsu (shinkō zaibatsu)* which reaped great profits in collaboration with the military clique. The military clique did not permit the old *zaibatsu* to operate in the occupied areas such as Manchuria, but rather gave special rights to the new *zaibatsu.* The old *zaibatsu* built up their property in time of peace, and they were the ones who were most happy when the war ended.[48]

The observation was vulnerable on its own terms, misleading in suggesting that the *zaibatsu* had not benefited from the war, and completely insensitive to the repressive social consequences of the *zaibatsu*-dominated dual economy. In contrast to this view, early U.S. economic policy for Japan was premised upon the conclusion that the *zaibatsu* represented an "excessive concentration of economic power" which kept wages low, repressed the domestic market, thwarted the development of a middle class, and fueled both economic imperialism and military aggression. "It is in this sense," the important Edwards Report of 1946 began, "that the zaibatsu—that is, the money clique—are to be regarded as among the groups principally responsible for the war and as a principal factor in the Japanese war potential. The responsibility is primarily institutional rather than personal."[49]

In itself, this argument exemplified the roots-of-aggression thesis which underlay early occupation reformism and contrasted so sharply with the Yoshida group's perception of a mere "historic stumble." MacArthur's public explanations of the decartelization and deconcentration policies, however, went further and succinctly equated such roots of aggression with the roots of potential communism or socialism. He described the pre-surrender *zaibatsu* system as "so complete a monopoly as to be in effect a form of socialism in private hands." "So long as it remains undisturbed," he declared on another occasion, "it is a standing bid for State ownership, and a fruitful target for Communist propaganda and collectivist purposes."[50]

Such pronouncements can be taken as a reflection of the classic laissez-faire ideal of petit bourgeois capitalism.[51] At the same time, however, at one level MacArthur in effect was calling attention to what Marxist-Leninists would refer to as the socialization of production under monopoly capitalism. Such a resonance of perceptions from purportedly opposite ends of the political spectrum was reminiscent of the ideological dilemma Japanese conservatives grappled with during the war years, and one might have expected the authors of the Konoe Memorial to applaud this line of analysis. Obviously, they did not do so. From their perspective, the dismantling of the war economy and elimination of the Tōsei-ha and renovationist bureaucrats had removed the threat of a "bid for State ownership." To go further was to imperil the very basis of the capitalist economy and modern state.

SCAP also evoked a threat-of-communism rationale in attacking the second pillar of the prewar economic structure: rural landlordism. Here the declared danger lay in the possibility of genuine agrarian revolution if the existing system of exploitative tenancy were allowed to continue. By eliminating "the feudalistic system of land ownership," MacArthur explained, "there will emerge in Japan, from a field heretofore fertile to the spread of communism, a new class of small capitalistic landowners which itself will stand firm against efforts to destroy the system of capitalistic economy of which it will then form an integral part."[52] In the words of Wolf Ladejinsky, a major adviser on the land reform, the twofold purpose of SCAP's initial directive in this area (December 1945) was to "multiply the number of freeholders and prevent the Communists from making political capital by posing as advocates of peasant interests."[53]

Again, this concern was consistent with one of the broad themes of the Konoe Memorial, in this case the potential for revolution from below, and in retrospect Yoshida did acknowledge the efficacy of the land reform. It contributed to improvement of agricultural productivity and rural living standards, and probably did defuse the countryside: "If at that time the farmers in the local areas had begun to raise a clamor simultaneously with the turbulent elements in the cities, there is no telling where it might have ended. And again, if the conservative parties at that time had lacked the courage to promote a thorough land reform, probably this would have provoked the strong discontent of the farmers and fomented political unrest from this direction as well."[54]

The land reform was initiated during Yoshida's first cabinet after SCAP had rejected proposals drafted by the Shidehara cabinet. And Yoshida carried out SCAP's directives faithfully, even to the extent of appointing a socialist and former reform bureaucrat, Wada Hiroo, as his minister of agriculture and forestry. Yet his compliance was reluctant, and Yoshida would never have supported such a program on his own initiative. He informed Wada at the time, for example, that "as a conservative, I am opposed to this in principle."[55] And in his memoirs, even while citing the positive consequences of land reform, Yoshida remained unable to acknowledge the legitimacy of prewar rural grievances or existence of a parasitic landlord class. As discussed further in the following chapter, his position on this issue was vivid testimony to the extent to which consistency in political ideology entailed sentimentality and inconsistency in socio-economic analysis.[56]

The concept of revolution was transmogrified in even more convoluted ways during the months following surrender. Many of the occupation's basic reforms, for example, were described as eliminating "feudalistic" patterns and structures. This was a favorite American pejorative for prewar Japanese society, and bore a resemblance to the orthodox (*Kōza*) line of the Japanese Communist Party, in which "feudal remnants" or "feudal vestiges" or "semi-feudalistic relationships" were regarded as determining characteristics of prewar society.[57] On the basis of this analysis, the mainstream communist position called for a two-stage revolution in Japan, and early occupation reformism was deemed consistent with this agenda insofar as it amounted to bringing about a peaceful bourgeois revolution. Yoshida regarded this similarity of vocabulary as revealing, and the "feudalistic" characterization itself as grossly misleading. From his perspective, Japan was already well on its way as a bourgeois, capitalist power when the "historic stumble" occurred and this normal and admirable process of modernization was interrupted. The breakdown of a stable world order created the situation in which unrest, conspiracy, and plain diplomatic ineptitude occurred in Japan, and the task for the future was to pick up the pieces.

This interpretation had obvious bearing upon concepts of necessary (or unnecessary) post-surrender reform. Less obviously, it also accounted in part for the differing ways in which the Japanese conservatives and SCAP evaluated and responded to the threat of communism and revolution. The Yoshida group regarded the threat as a cancer in a fundamentally sound and modern society, and addressed it largely in terms of conspiracy, agitation, subversion, and propaganda. Where socio-economic conditions may have aggravated the threat, these were aberrant conditions, temporary dislocations, the growing pains of any modern society, the bastard progeny of the international crisis and ultimately the war. The antidote to the threat lay largely abroad, in the establishment of sound global relations which would promote economic growth and well-being. Domestically, the Japanese elites appear to have believed that the threat could be contained by essentially the same methods resorted to in the prewar era: restrictive legislation, police control, and indoctrination—a reassertion, in short, of traditional authority.

To a degree, the manner in which U.S. planners emphasized the feudalistic nature of Japanese society imparted an ethnocentric cast to their early reformist policies. Authoritarianism, repression, immense disparities of wealth and social class, militarism, aggression—all became regarded as atavistic and more or less peculiar to Japan. Had the planners retained their sensitivity to structural dynamics but been more receptive to Yoshida's notion of Japan's *modernity*, and the global context of its crisis, they might have been forced to confront embarrassing questions concerning bourgeois society, capitalism, and imperialism more directly; and perhaps they would have found it more difficult to mete out victor's justice. As it was, they were able to direct their energies toward bringing about a controlled bourgeois revolution in Japan.

Although this seemed to coincide with the official Communist Party agenda, there was, as usual, a twist to the situation. Where the leftist analysis saw the bourgeois revolution as a precondition for the eventual socialist revolution, in SCAP's usage the liberalizing reforms of the occupation were designed to *prevent* a transition, virtually a leap, from "feudalism" to socialism or communism. There were two peculiarities to this notion. First, the democratic revolution was perceived in SCAP's own eyes as one-stage and *final*-stage. And second, the communist threat, in this analysis, resided in the possibility of a *direct* transition from feudalistic to communistic patterns. Japan's very socio-economic backwardness, that is, was conducive to communistic takeover.

Loose synonyms abounded in this line of analysis: feudalistic, traditionalistic, collectivistic, authoritarian, totalitarian, repressive, exploitative, and so on. In brief, it was assumed that the conditions that had given rise to the prewar crisis made Japan as vulnerable to "communism" as it had proven to be to "fascism."

The threat was a dual one: the authoritarian structure of the society would facilitate an easy transition to communist totalitarianism, while the repressive nature of the society posed a threat of revolutionary upheaval. Thus, to use the two previous examples, MacArthur did not hesitate to characterize both the *zaibatsu* and landlord systems as feudalistic, even while declaring that the first posed a standing bid for communist control while the second was a fertile field for revolutionary violence.

Such views had numerous ramifications. They illustrate once again how "anti-communism" could be elicited as a rationale for the reform program the Japanese anti-communists so strenuously opposed. They also suggest the contrary interpretations and objectives that underlay SCAP's "democratic revolution" and the early support given this by Japanese radicals. Implicit in the American perspective, moreover, was a model of controlled "revolution" which at a certain point would inevitably become, by more conventional radical criteria, anti-radical and counterrevolutionary.

On the theoretical level, it would appear that the anti-communist reformers were discarding the Marxist theory of stages by projecting the possibility of leapfrogging from "feudalism" to "communism." If this was indeed a revision of the Marxist augury, so also was the Russian Revolution.[58] This was an analogy to which the Yoshida group and Japanese elites had given painful attention during the war years—but which, again, they did not dwell upon once the extraordinary circumstances of the war had been terminated. On the contrary, in yet another turn of this kaleidoscopic preoccupation with reform and revolution, the post-surrender Japanese elites in effect tended to accept, with trepidation, the communist appraisal of the situation. They feared, that is, precisely what the communists and leftists hoped: that SCAP's "democratic revolution" would prepare the ground for an ongoing and genuinely radical transformation of society and the state.

The threat of revolution was felt most keenly by the Japanese conservatives during the first year-and-a-half of the occupation. SCAP's prohibition of the general strike, scheduled to begin on

February 1, 1947, signaled the long awaited swing of the pendulum, and the subsequent reverse course directed from Washington soon tempered those early reformist excesses which threatened the old guard. The bizarre pre-surrender spectacle of "old liberals" such as Yoshida attacking "rightists" such as Tōjō for leading Japan in the direction of "communism" reappeared in the American context in early 1948, when "liberals" such as George Kennan began to criticize MacArthur, the darling of the American conservatives, for paving the way for the communization of postwar Japan.[59] By 1949, the U.S. National Security Council was warning that if either the Japanese left *or* the virulently anti-communist (at home) extreme right gained political control in Japan, they would move the country into alliance with the Soviet Union.[60] And after June 1950, the ironies became more barbed, as Japan's newest military reformers began to gear the Japanese economy for war-related production, to plan for "co-prosperity" between Japan and southeast Asia, and to prepare Japan for possible war against the Soviet Union and China. Those who relish poetic balance in their history would perhaps round out the circle with a 1951 article in the journal of one of America's own vintage rightist-leftist amalgams, the American Federation of Labor; it was entitled, "Are We Rebuilding Tojo's 'Red' Army?"[61]

History's muse, it seems, can sometimes overdo her little jokes.

NINE

Imperial Japan and the "New Japan"

Both wittingly and unwittingly, Yoshida lent himself to political symbolism. In a most deliberate manner, he flaunted his traditionalism and sought by doing this to reinspire popular pride in the more positive accomplishments of Japan's recent history. The corollary to this naturally would be renewed acceptance of traditional patterns of authority. He also reaffirmed the liveness of the past in more bizarre ways. In 1946, for example, Yoshida rented Konoe's former house and proceeded to sleep in the very room in which the prince had committed suicide in December 1945. Yes, Yoshida blandly informed an uncomfortable guest, "I thought that if I slept here, Konoe might appear."[1]

There was always the characteristic touch of "One Man" in these gestures, cultivated with a certain relish. The nickname itself, Yoshida once facetiously explained, came from the fact that he snapped and barked like a dog (*wan-wan*, or "one-one") at others.[2] He spoke his piece more vividly than many, although it is possible to overdo the unusualness of this in Japan; neither before nor after the surrender were the Japanese as a whole timid sheep, although that impression has been reinforced by calculated evocations of "harmony" and attracted many observers. Still, Yoshida did come *and go* with undeniably conspicuous style. He took care to patronize Shinto shrines in the post-surrender period, for example, when the native religion was tainted for its alleged succor of militarism. Then, when he died, he was baptized Joseph Thomas More and buried with a Catholic service.[3]

As the first postwar decade unfolded, "reform" gave way to "reconstruction" and the "Yoshida era" evolved out of the occupation's "revolution from above." It became apparent that Yoshida was something more than a colorful relic. His survival symbolized not only the passage-through of the old guard, but also the persistence of certain traditional patterns of power, and the resilience and contemporaneity of aspects of the imperial consciousness. It has been suggested in previous chapters that the *kokutai* or national polity was an ambiguous concept capable of accommodating change and even inspiring criticism of the status quo. Yoshida and his compeers concurred that the polity was dynamic and flexible—within limits. Of course, they acknowledged neither the logical contribution of *kokutai* ideology to bald aggression abroad and institutionalized repression at home, nor the legitimacy of the ideology's radical right-wing progeny. At the same time, however, they also did not see the *kokutai* as incompatible with a paternalistic or elitist "democracy," any more than they saw it as inconsistent with a careful and cooperative imperialist policy.

This suggests some of the levels of congruence between Imperial Japan and the "new Japan." The positive content of the *kokutai* may have been ambiguous, but it did exist as an orthodoxy through negative enforcement. In the broadest sense, this was conveyed in the legislation against "dangerous thoughts" enacted and enforced from the era of "Taishō democracy," in which deviance was tested against the polestars of respect for the emperor and for private property. The Yoshida group certainly subscribed to this, and for all practical purposes so also did the occupation authorities, although for a while the latter appeared to be charting a wandering and perilous course. Preservation of the emperor and private capital thus came to link the reformers and the reluctant reformed, and inevitably the prewar and postwar epochs. The result was a new stage of bourgeois society under the emperor, rather than a radically new Japan.

The reconciliation between the Yoshida conservatives and one-time U.S. reformers was abetted by a further strain of thought Yoshida had sedulously cultivated in the prewar period. In his own vocabulary, this was the principle of traditional or cooperative diplomacy. More precisely, it was the thesis that Japan was as "Western" as it was Asian, that its destiny was to be a global power, and that the expansion as well as security of the state was best guaranteed by close alliance with the dominant Western power in Asia and the Pacific. The model here was a very obvious one, the Anglo-Japanese Alliance of 1902–1922, and Yoshida welcomed the eventual bilateral alliance with the United States as a new version of this "traditional diplomacy." Both alliances were directed primarily against Russia, with the U.S.-Japan security pact further cemented by another strong legacy from the prewar era: anti-communism. By the end of the occupation, these trends had meshed. The global anti-communist settlement had its essential counterpart in the pro-capitalist and anti-radical domestic settlement. If the early reformist ardor of the occupation had appeared as revolution transmogrified in conservative eyes, the succeeding Yoshida era could be seen, from a non-conservative perspective, as tradition transmogrified. The changes, both domestic and global, were undeniably great; but so also were the survivals.

Again, small examples suggest the larger reconciliation of past and present. By 1951, U.S. policy concerning Japanese capitalism had passed from "economic demilitarization and democratization" through "self-sufficiency" to a concept of "U.S.-Japan economic cooperation," in which the Japanese economy was to be tightly integrated with the economies of the United States and southeast Asia. This entailed the revival of both military-related production and the old *zaibatsu* oligopolies, and the new triangular relationship was often, and ironically, described with the old rhetoric of an anti-communist "co-prosperity sphere" in Asia. Yoshida's highest advisors for this new capitalism also evoked shades of the past. His three-man Supreme Economic Council, which has been characterized as "without any question, the most powerful advisory body in the postwar period," was comprised of top officials from Mitsui, Mitsubishi, and Sumitomo.[4]

The wedding of Imperial Japan and the new Japan was betokened with even greater succinctness and flair in the wake of the San Francisco Peace Conference of September 1951, at which Japan was promised both sovereignty and military embrace by the United States. Yoshida immediately arranged for the auspicious event to be reported to the emperor's ancestors enshrined in the hallowed imperial sanctuary at Ise Shrine.[5] And a year later, even while being criticized from both left and right for being unduly slavish toward the United States, Yoshida savored a quintessential moment of defiant loyalism. After reading a statement to the emperor in his capacity as prime minister in November 1952, he concluded, in lieu of his signature, by referring to himself as *Shin Shigeru*, "Your Loyal Servant Shigeru."[6] The phrase, redolent with the obsequiousness of traditional loyalism, was also indicative of the continuing tradition of bureaucratic hauteur. It was an expression of scarcely disguised contempt for the occupation endeavor to clarify the responsibility of the bureaucracy and government as "public servants" rather than "servants of the emperor"—a reaffirmation, in effect, of non-accountability to the public.[7]

In Yoshida's Japan, the emperor was an integral part of bourgeois ideology, the new capitalism was dominated by the old capitalists, and "democracy" remained patronizing and paternalistic. Yet this was not a simple return to the past. The emperor had been stripped of that de jure authority which, more than permitting him to rule, had enabled others to grasp at power in his name. The military establishment had been eliminated as a powerful faction within the ruling groups. Political parties and organized labor had greater voice, and a broader constituency. Civil liberties were more strongly protected by law. And, given the nature of the peace and military settlement of 1950–1952, "patriotism" had become bilateral.

YOSHIDA AND THE NEW CONSERVATIVE HEGEMONY

Chance, personality, and decimation of the ranks of his colleagues and contemporaries paved the way for Yoshida's emergence as the dominant Japanese figure in the postwar scene. He became foreign minister in the Higashikuni cabinet in September 1945 after SCAP's disapproval forced Shigemitsu Mamoru to resign from this post. Yoshida continued in this position under the Shidehara cabinet, while Shigemitsu, whom he had successfully supported as his successor in London in 1938, became indicted as a war criminal.[8]

The foreign minister's position gave Yoshida a certain measure of influence, since as head of the Central Liaison Office he functioned as a key intermediary between the Japanese government and SCAP. His responsibilities were numerous and he appears to have been instrumental in arranging one of the signal events of the immediate post-surrender period, the emperor's successful meeting with MacArthur in September 1945.[9] Even the official history of Yoshida's later cabinets, however, refers to his early activities with a tone of slight embarrassment. "Yoshida's objectives as foreign minister were to protect the imperial family and the conservative power centering on the *zaibatsu* and bureaucracy from the occupation force," it is noted, and he pursued these goals so single-mindedly that even some of his erstwhile conservative supporters expressed dismay. Iwabuchi Tatsuo, who had been Yoshida's close collaborator in the wartime YOHANSEN group and played an active role in promoting his appointment as foreign minister in 1945, became so disillusioned that he later lobbied behind the scenes against Yoshida's ascension to the premiership.[10]

Yoshida remained relatively aloof from the jockeying for power within the political parties during these early months. By April 1946 Shidehara's party had been repudiated at the polls, and it was widely assumed that Hatoyama, head of the rival conservative party, was the rising star in Japanese politics; Hatoyama's party had won a plurality in the general election. Again, SCAP's winnowing hand shaped Yoshida's destiny. Hatoyama was purged on the eve of assuming the premiership and, after various exchanges of the after-you-Alphonse variety, Yoshida accepted Hatoyama's invitation to take over the presidency of the revived Seiyūkai. He did so after many of his most intimate confidants, including Makino, advised him that he was entirely unsuitable for the job, and then proceeded to threaten to resign several times before he had even been formally designated premier. Yoshida's elevation to the highest office in the land took place with all the dignity of carnival and comic opera. Hundreds of thousands of demonstrators denounced him in the streets. Friends as well as foes urged him to withdraw, and both supporters and detractors scaled the walls around his residence to press their case upon him. There were secret agreements, bellowing confrontations, temporary disappearing acts, solitary and fuming pacings in the garden in the dark of night.[11]

These gracious beginnings were apt prelude to the performance of the first Yoshida cabinet, which survived for one year and impressed no one including Yoshida himself. In his memoirs, he all but disregarded this interlude on the grounds that he did not recall the cabinet doing anything tangible enough to merit recording in detail.[12] In fact, this cabinet did do a great deal, but mostly against the conservative grain in the form of enacting SCAP's reformist directives. While SCAP proclaimed the democratic revolution, Yoshida conveyed transparent scorn for "revolution for the sake of revolution" (*kakumei no tame no kakumei*). The proper concerns of the immediate post-surrender period, as he later described them, were alleviation of popular anxiety, restoration of law and order, and economic reconstruction.[13] If Yoshida had had his way, post-surrender Japan would have been subjected to little more than a mild purge and a lengthy lecture on "diplomatic sense."

There was little in Yoshida's performance or position during these early years to suggest that he, together with MacArthur, would become a symbol of Japan's first postwar decade. Even persons such as Joseph Ballantine, commonly associated with the

State Department's "Japan Crowd," agreed that Yoshida was an anachronism and his emergence as premier was due to the unsettled and extraordinary circumstances of the time. "People like Yoshida are throwbacks from the Old School," Ballantine observed in a public discussion in mid-1946, "and I doubt whether any popular election among people trained to express their thoughts would return such people."[14] The miserable performance of the first Yoshida cabinet did result in an electoral setback in April 1947, and Yoshida was no more inspiring as an opposition leader than he had been as premier. In early 1948, MacArthur privately characterized Yoshida as "monumentally lazy and politically inept."[15] Yet within a year this lazy and inept throwback from the Old School had won a smashing victory at the polls and become the man of the day.

Both Yoshida's high office during the key interlude of reformism and his remarkable comeback were symbolic of the nature of the occupation itself, which simultaneously represented a great epoch of reform and one of history's impressive holding operations. When the occupation ended in April 1952, after six-and-a-half years, the "New Dealers" were gone, MacArthur was gone, significant portions of the early reformist agenda had been jettisoned, and it was the political slogan of "reformism" itself that had become anachronistic. Yoshida presided at the pinnacle of political power, with an absolute majority in the House of Representatives, and the watchwords of the ruling groups were "reverse course" and "rectification of excesses." While the crusty old premier still caused chagrin in Washington, by 1952 this had little to do with his once condemned reactionary proclivities. Yoshida's perceived deficiencies now lay rather in being cautious about Japanese rearmament and unenthusiastic about containment of Communist China.

Such an accomplishment did not reflect successful adherence to a detailed blueprint of opposition, but rather the correctness of a pragmatic assumption: that the indigenous old guard could outlast the zealous alien reformers. During the long years of the prewar crisis, Yoshida had maintained a dogged conviction that history could be rolled back, the pendulum returned to an approximation of earlier times. Such optimism sustained him during the new postwar crisis, and he expressed this shortly after forming his first cabinet when he observed that "history provides examples of winning by diplomacy after losing in war."[16] The overriding objective was to win the peace, and in this respect the occupation represented a new stage in an old struggle on two fronts. Internationally, the goal was Japan's restoration as a great power, strong in the East, supported and *needed* by the dominant Western powers. Domestically, the years following defeat constituted a continuation of the threat to the "traditional polity" which Yoshida had remarked upon in his correspondence with Makino as early as 1921.[17] Beyond exorcising the dream of autarky and the aberrant scourge of "militarism," Yoshida regarded himself as standing in an essentially adversary relationship to the occupation authorities. Yet national pride called for grace in defeat, and plain common sense dictated the necessity of biding one's time. In a passage written a number of years after his retirement, Yoshida characterized his guiding philosophy during the occupation as to fulfill the obligations of a "good loser"—while preparing, once sovereignty had been regained, to overturn the work of the conquerors:

> When I became Foreign Minister in September 1945, I went to see Admiral Kantaro Suzuki who had been one of my masters in the Peers' School, and asked him what policy I should pursue. The Admiral answered that it was important after a victorious war to wind everything up properly, but that, after losing a war, one had to know how to be a good loser.
>
> I thought this very true; but, at the same time, I realized that it would not by any means be an easy task. I decided at any rate not to oppose everything that the Occupation said, nor to say yes to everything; since neither seemed to me in keeping with being a good loser. This meant that I was going to say all that I felt needed saying but that I would co-operate at the same time with the Occupation Forces to the best of my power. Whatever harm was done through the Occupation Forces not listening to what I had to say could be remedied after we had regained our independence.

> I acted on these principles, and faithfully carried out all that the Occupation Forces directed us to do without cavilling, wishing thereby to show them that we could be good losers. There was this idea at the back of my mind that, whatever needed to be revised after we regained our independence could be revised then.
>
> But once a thing has been decided on, it is not so easy to have it altered. . . .[18]

This observation fails to indicate the extent to which the reform agenda was both obstructed and modified prior to as well as after the restoration of sovereignty, but it does call attention to the complex power relationship that existed during the occupation. The implementation of reforms was entrusted to Japanese bureaucrats and politicians who by and large disapproved of them, among whom the Yoshida group was the most prominent. Although in some cases it proved possible to delay, dilute, or subvert SCAP's directives, in a number of significant areas the reforms were faithfully implemented. And although the conservative forces in Japan had reconsolidated and assumed the offensive well before the occupation ended, even after independence it proved impossible simply to revise "whatever needed to be revised." The occupation legacy was a new conservatism, but within a restructured state in which progressive and reformist ideals, and laws, retained a substantial constituency among the Japanese people themselves.

In Yoshida's appraisal, SCAP did not begin to come to its senses until the threatened general strike of early 1947. Business leaders and other opponents of the early reform agenda also commonly cite SCAP's prohibition of the strike as the first unequivocal step in the abandonment of reformism.[19] The inauguration of the reverse course coincided with the collapse of the first Yoshida cabinet, however, and for a year and a half—during which the decisive shift from "reform" to "reconstruction" was directed from Washington—Yoshida's party remained out of power, and his own future continued to appear uncertain. As it turned out, this interlude as the major opposition party proved a blessing in disguise, for the succeeding coalition cabinets organized by the major rival parties proved as incompetent as the first Yoshida cabinet. Katayama Tetsu, the only avowedly socialist prime minister in Japanese history, resigned in March 1948, after ten months of non-socialist debacle. The succeeding "centrist" government of Ashida Hitoshi was forced to resign in disgrace after seven months, due to exposure of massive graft and corruption in the labyrinthine Shōwa Denkō scandal. Thus in October 1948 Yoshida quelled mutinous mutterings within his own party and sidled back into the premiership. Three months later, he gambled on a general election and won a stunning absolute majority in the crucial House of Representatives.[20] The real inauguration of the "Yoshida era" occurred at this juncture, shortly after the old diplomat's seventieth birthday.

The political party Yoshida led during Japan's first postwar decade underwent numerous splits and mergers and changed its name several times: from Liberal (November 1945 to March 1948) to Democratic Liberal (March 1948 to March 1950) and back to Liberal (March 1950 to November 1955). It never changed its political coloring, which was to the right of center, and at certain inspired moments it even attempted to pre-empt some of the rhetorical razzle-dazzle SCAP had initially directed against the conservative constitutency itself. When the Democrat Liberal Party was formed in March 1948, at the time of the collapse of the Katayama cabinet, for example, its initial proclamation declared that "the cancer within Japan's recovery lies in the rampancy of socialistic ideas and the remnants of feudalistic bureaucratism which are camouflaged by socialism."[21] In 1950, when the original name of Liberal Party was restored, Yoshida himself proposed to no avail to call a spade a spade and formally adopt the designation Conservative Party (Hoshutō).[22] Whatever the name, the electoral victory of January 1949 symbolized the emergence of the new conservative hegemony. This was only the fifth time in Japan's sixty-year parliamentary history that a single party had gained an absolute majority in the lower house, and the victory set a pattern of conservative domination of government that remained unchallenged over the ensuing decades.[23]

The composition of Yoshida's party in 1949 revealed its essential role as the spokesman of business. Of 261 representatives in the lower house, 158 (61 percent) were identified as "business presidents, auditors, or members of boards of directors."[24] At the same time, the party had also been "bureaucratized" by recruitment of a skilled core of former high civil servants. Forty-four (17 percent) of the party members elected to the lower house in 1949 were ex-officials. As experienced technocrats, versed in law and legislation and intimate with both the personnel and procedures of the bureaucracy, their influence was disproportionately great.[25]

This dramatic recovery was facilitated by the default of the socialist and "centrist" opposition, but it also revealed that Yoshida had made good use of his interlude out of power. To some extent he had laid the groundwork for the conservative comeback during the final weeks of his first cabinet, when he succeeded in revising the electoral system in a manner detrimental to the leftist parties.[26] At the same time, he was able during this period to take advantage of the decimation of party ranks caused by the purge and create his own inner-party power base—to efface the impression of being a proxy leader of "Hatoyama's party," that is, and recast the party in his own image. This materialized in late 1948 and early 1949 in the form of the so-called "Yoshida School" (*Yoshida gakkō*).

The "Yoshida School" referred to the inner circle of Yoshida's supporters and reflected the new bureaucratization of the party, for it included a number of the former officials who entered politics at this time. Yoshida once dismissed a query concerning the size of the "Yoshida School" with a typical riposte to the effect that, since his pupils didn't pay tuition, he had no idea how many there were.[27] Actually, the core group was relatively small—a score or so individuals are commonly cited—but it provided the key lieutenants of the Yoshida era. These included Ikeda Hayato, Yoshida's most influential economic adviser; Satō Eisaku, a key broker in internal party affairs; and Okazaki Katsuo and Ōhashi Takeo, upon whom Yoshida relied in matters involving foreign relations, remilitarization, and domestic law and order.[28]

At the same time, there emerged a broader and more amorphous "Yoshida faction" within the ruling party. This derived in good part from the new blood which successfully entered electoral politics in the wake of the purges and had no personal ties with the prewar party cliques. The personal allegiance of many of these individuals was nurtured by Yoshida's practice of frequently reshuffling his ministerial rosters; over the course of his premierships, Yoshida appointed seventy-nine different individuals to cabinet posts.[29] The origins of postwar conservative factional politics reside in this period, and became pronounced after 1952, when scores of depurged old-line politicians returned to challenge Yoshida's "usurpation" of influence. In October 1952, it was estimated that roughly 140 of the ruling party's representatives in the lower house belonged to the "Yoshida faction."[30] Although this support was whittled away over the ensuing two years, during the bitter internecine struggle which marked Hatoyama's comeback, the Yoshida faction was eventually divided and inherited by Yoshida's two most famous protégés, Ikeda and Satō. The substantiality of Yoshida's contribution to factional politics is apparent in the fact that both Ikeda and Satō used this inheritance to attain the premiership themselves.

The third Yoshida cabinet, which remained in power from February 1949 to October 1952, has been described as "the strongest cabinet in Japanese history since the Meiji era."[31] In longevity (44 months), it was surpassed only by the second Itō cabinet of 1892–1896 (49 months) and the first Katsura cabinet of 1901–1906 (55 months). Much of this strength derived from external factors. The third cabinet was the beneficiary of SCAP's gradual transfer of formal political power to Japanese authorities; the beneficiary of the cold war and U.S. reordering of strategic and economic priorities; and the beneficiary of the Korean War, which Yoshida described as "a gift of the gods."[32] During the final two years of the occupation, this cabinet carried out the Dodge stabilization program; directed or encouraged the Red Purge in the public and private sectors; rode the windfall stimulus of the Korean war boom; processed the depurge of approximately 200,000 individuals; negotiated the indefinite post-occupation presence of U.S. military bases in Japan; set the pattern of "moderate" Japanese rearmament; committed Japan, albeit reluctantly, to containment of the People's Republic of China and optimum economic integration with the United States and the counterrevolutionary regimes of southeast Asia; and gained for Japan—at a price of inflexibility in the cold war, heightened domestic polarization, and the taint of "subordinate independence"—a non-restrictive peace settlement.

Between October 1948 and December 1954, the second through fifth Yoshida cabinets also presided over the unraveling of much of the original reform agenda, and these years can be seen as a period during which a kind of *modus vivendi* was worked out between the old imperial consciousness and patterns of authority and the purported original ideals of SCAP's "democratic revolution." Yoshida's rueful discovery that "once a thing has been decided on, it is not so easy to have it altered" points to the obvious fact that SCAP's early commitment to reformism did leave a positive legacy. In the final analysis, however, that legacy fell considerably short of original objectives and projections; some reforms were abandoned, others were stillborn, and yet others were revised both before and after the restoration of sovereignty in 1952. The paradox of Japan's first postwar decade is exemplified by Yoshida himself, and the fact that, in the broadest view, the anti-reformist Yoshida era was the major legacy of the occupation "revolution."

This was not a simple contradiction. The nature of America's liberal reformism, together with the crises and dynamics of both U.S. and Japanese capitalism, made the reformist endeavor itself inherently susceptible to accommodation and outright reaction. And at the same time, the "imperial consciousness" as exemplified by Yoshida embraced dimensions of adaptability and bourgeois modernity which permitted him to accede to certain postwar reforms "without cavilling," however unnecessary he originally may have believed such reforms to be. A general impression of this tension and congruence between the imperial consciousness and the "new Japan" can perhaps be conveyed by a brief resumé of the position taken by Yoshida and the conservatives on various key occupation reforms, and the status of these reforms at the end of the Yoshida era.

CONSTITUTION, EMPEROR, AND NATIONAL POLITY

Almost immediately after the formation of the Shidehara cabinet, two separate constitutional-revision projects were initiated by the government with an eye toward precluding SCAP initiative in this area, which bore directly upon the future status of the emperor. The first was undertaken by the hapless Konoe with SCAP encouragement in October 1945, disingenuously repudiated by SCAP on November 1, and had become a dead letter before Konoe's suicide on December 16. On October 19, Yoshida expressed the personal view that Konoe was "more or less the central figure in state affairs," but be this as it may, in both public and private statements on his proposed constitution Konoe gave no indication that he envisioned anything but the most tokenistic of changes in the Meiji charter. There is, however, some indication that Konoe did consider having Hirohito personally resign as sovereign—a possibility Yoshida gave no indication of considering.[33]

The more substantial Japanese endeavor to pre-empt SCAP action on the constitutional, and thus imperial, issue came with the announcement on October 13 of an official constitutional-revision committee under the direction of minister without portfolio Matsumoto Jōji. Yoshida made his own position clear within the week when he declared that the existing constitution was itself fundamentally democratic, and provided ample basis for government of, by, and for the people; only minor revision would be necessary, he indicated, to provide guarantees against abuse by militarists and the like such as had occurred in the recent past.[34] This was an argument Yoshida was to evoke again on later occasions, and fully consistent with his faith in the noble spirit of Meiji. The seventy-year-old Matsumoto shared such views, and these were endorsed by the Shidehara cabinet. As a result, the "Matsumoto draft" of early 1946 retained the emperor as "supreme and inviolable" (rather than "sacred and inviolable" as in the Meiji constitution), and proposed no substantial change in the de jure authority of the sovereign. The thrust of the Matsumoto committee's proposed revisions as a whole was comparably tokenistic.

SCAP rejected the Matsumoto draft and submitted its own proposed revision to Yoshida for transmission to the cabinet in a dramatic meeting on February 13, 1946. Yoshida and his colleagues responded to this famous "MacArthur draft," in which the emperor was deprived of formal authority, with shock and indignation. Yoshida characterized it as "revolutionary" and "outrageous" (*tondemonai*), and there followed an intense debate on the Japanese side in which he found himself supporting the most conservative position among his compeers–found himself, as it turned out, less willing to compromise on the emperor's position than was the emperor himself. SCAP officials at the time, and with good cause, regarded Yoshida as among the most reactionary and hidebound defenders of the Matsumoto draft. In the internal Japanese deliberations that followed, Yoshida sided with Matsumoto in opposing compromise; Shidehara advocated a more conciliatory position; and the issue appears to have been resolved only when the emperor personally endorsed the American draft.[35]

Ironically, the new constitution was introduced to the Diet as the Japanese government's own draft one month after the formation of the first Yoshida cabinet. Consequently, the most urgent immediate task Yoshida faced as prime minister was the critical one of defending the new charter and interpreting it to the legislature. Interpellations on this "government draft" began on June 23, 1946, and continued for a week; the final, slightly amended draft was reported out of committee two months later. The interpellations conveyed a lively atmosphere of parliamentary liberation which contrasted sharply with that of the war years, and which was interpreted by SCAP as evidence of rapid strides along the path of democratization. And although the Yoshida government resorted to various linguistic obfuscations and scarcely endeared itself to the draft's real authors in Government Section, it can be argued that it really only exploited openings which SCAP itself had provided.[36]

The government's overriding concern was to establish the interpretation that the new charter preserved the *kokutai* and in no fundamental way diminished the stature of the emperor or altered the nature of the traditional tie between the sovereign and his subjects. In addressing the House of Peers on June 23, for example, Yoshida emphasized that the draft had not been drawn up from a constitutional or legal point of view alone, but also out of consideration as to "how to save the country and how to keep the imperial family in safety."[37] This was the very heart of the conservatives' concern. It was also, however, a reasonably fair rendering of the understanding Yoshida and his colleagues had reached with SCAP. Viewed negatively, the new constitution dramatically altered the emperor's political authority. Viewed positively, however, it guaranteed the future of the throne. The SCAP draft which became the basis of the new constitution actually had been drawn up on the basis of three guiding principles submitted by MacArthur on February 3, the first of which was that "the emperor system would be preserved, though modified to bring it within constitutional limitations and subject to the ultimate will of the people"; the second and third principles concerned repudiation of war and abolition of feudal vestiges.

In effect, MacArthur and Government Section were guaranteeing the secure perpetuation of the imperial system, but only in the context of a more liberal national charter which removed the political prerogatives of the throne. At the same time, moreover, it was understood that if the Japanese conservatives rejected this, they would do so at the peril of jeopardizing both the emperor system in its entirety and their own fragile position of authority. Continued procrastination by the Japanese government would permit the constitutional-revision issue to be taken up by the newly-formed eleven-nation Far Eastern Commission, where less charitable and generous attitudes toward the emperor could be anticipated. In addition, it was made clear that if the Government Section draft was rejected, SCAP was prepared to by-pass the Japanese government entirely and present its constitutional principles *directly* to the Japanese people—a chilling prospect indeed to the defensive old guard.

General Whitney, a firm believer in the "psychological shaft," presented this latter alternative to the Yoshida group in the memorable meeting of February 13, and observed it strike home with considerable satisfaction: "The effect of this statement upon the Japanese representatives was immediately visible. Mr. Shirasu straightened up as if he had sat on something. Dr. Matsumoto sucked in his breath. Mr. Yoshida's face was a black cloud." Thus, well before the formation of the first Yoshida cabinet, it had become apparent to the conservatives that their own future, as well as that of the imperial house, was best guaranteed by adopting SCAP's constitutional draft as their own.[38] Indeed, Yoshida internalized this argument to the extent that he consistently thereafter argued that MacArthur's major *purpose* in revising the constitution was to preserve the emperor. It was largely for this act, he later argued, that MacArthur must be regarded as one of Japan's "great benefactors" (*dai onjin*).[39]

Although Diet discussion of the new constitution was wide-ranging, it focused upon two compelling issues: the status of the emperor (had the *kokutai* been altered?), and the intent of the renunciation-of-war clause (had Japan renounced even the right of armament for "self-defense"?).[40] While the government staunchly avowed its commitment to "democracy and pacifism," Yoshida and his spokesman on the constitution, State Minister Kanamori Tokujirō, were primarily concerned with establishing the continuity between the pre- and post-surrender periods. At the same time, they emphasized the international pressure which necessitated hasty enactment of a new charter, while explaining that such pressure derived in good part from foreign "misunderstanding" that the prewar Japanese state had been by both nature and law feudalistic, authoritarian, ultranationalistic, and militaristic. In a manner which calls to mind Yoshida's great hero Itō Hirobumi and the introduction of the Meiji constitution over a half-century earlier, Yoshida repeatedly indicated that constitutional reform was desirable not on its intrinsic merits alone, but also as a necessary step by which Japan might regain, "both in name and substance," a place of stature in the world community.[41]

Reference to foreign misunderstandings, and emphasis upon the positive continuities between prewar Japan and the new era of "democracy," were of course consistent with Yoshida's unshakable conviction that Japan's interwar breakdown had been a betrayal rather than consequence of the Meiji legacy. In the Diet sessions of June 1946 he buttressed this familiar argument by referring to the "democratic" nature of both the Charter Oath of 1868 and the constitution of 1889, arguing from this premise that the new draft constitution did not reflect "the slightest intention to transform the political life hitherto pursued by the Japanese people." Here again the language creaked with the ghostly voice of Itō Hirobumi, for the keynote to Itō's famous 1889 commentary on the Meiji constitution had been that "the original national policy is by no means changed by [the new constitution], but is more strongly confirmed than ever."[42]

It is inconceivable that Yoshida and his designated experts on the new constitution were not acutely conscious of replaying Itō's role. Like Itō, they were concerned with curbing progressive and potentially populist trends; they were defining the very fabric of the state by explaining its national charter; and they had but a single emperor-centered political fiction which would serve their conservative ends. Since Itō's version of that fiction had worn thin, the challenge was to rephrase, remold, remanipulate the potent imperial symbol. Thus where Itō had stressed the right of the throne from earliest times "to reign over and govern the State," the postwar conservatives emphasized the innately democratic qualities of the emperor-centered national life. The Charter Oath, in this view, was the pure embodiment of the "democracy" of the traditional polity, whether expressed in Japanese or borrowed-English phraseology (*minshushugi, demokurashii*),[43] while the Meiji constitution represented a fuller exposition of the principles expressed in the Charter Oath, and thus the very antithesis of feudalism, militarism, and authoritarianism as asserted by the critics of that document:

> The principles of the Japanese constitution have been distorted and misunderstood as if it were a feudalistic constitution, as if it were an oppressive constitution, as if it were a militaristic constitution. But the constitution authorized by Emperor Meiji is based on the so-called Charter Oath of Five Articles of early Meiji, and embodies the very principles of this Oath. Thus it is by no means oppressive in nature, nor is it a militaristic constitution. Indeed, I have no hesitation whatsoever in declaring that the political character of Japan as shaped by the constitution authorized by Emperor Meiji is, in the language of the present day, pre-eminently democratic, pre-eminently unmilitaristic. Therefore, I do not think that there is a hair's breadth of variance between this and the intent of the new constitution. Such being the case, I cannot for a moment think that, because of the enactment of the new constitution, there would occur a transformation of the political character of the Japanese people.[44]

Despite the admirable "spirit and significance" of the Meiji charter, Yoshida acknowledged that this had been distorted, or perverted, in actual practice, thus contributing to Japan's humiliating defeat.[45] Because of this—and given in particular the misunderstanding of other nations on this matter—constitutional revision was appropriate.

By far the most extended discussion focused directly on the nature of the emperor system under the new charter. In early Diet appearances (June 24 and 26), Yoshida argued that Japan had accepted the Potsdam Declaration only upon assurance that the national polity would be preserved intact. On June 27, presumedly upon instructions from SCAP, he corrected this and acknowledged that the Allied Powers had not committed themselves on this crucial matter; on the contrary, Japan's surrender had been unconditional, and the relationship between the Japanese government and occupying authorities did not rest on a contractual basis.[46] Despite this retraction, Yoshida and his ministers consistently did maintain that, *in essence*, the new constitution in no way altered the *kokutai*. In defending this position, they de-emphasized the significance of the constitutional change in the emperor's de jure status and dwelt instead upon the unchanged nature of the *spiritual* bond between emperor and populace, which had constituted the unique character of the Japanese state since time before history.

Inevitably, this raised the question of the precise locus of sovereignty under the new constitution, and in their initial explanations in particular both Yoshida and Kanamori attempted to argue, in Kanamori's words, that "sovereignty (*shuken*), or 'the right to rule' (*tōchiken*), if the phrase can be used in that sense, resides in the whole of the people, including the emperor."[47] Critics within the Diet labeled this sophistry, and the final report of the House of Representatives did explicitly acknowledge that the right of rule which accrued to the emperor under the Meiji constitution was denied by his designation as "symbol" under the new draft.[48] It was strongly emphasized at the same time, however, that this "politico-structural" change in no way reflected any basic transformation of the national polity. The prevailing conservative argument here was often subtle and illusive, and invariably intensely emotional. The corporate nature of the Japanese state, it was suggested, did not conform to the "dualistic" concepts of sovereignty that prevailed in the West. Sovereignty and *kokutai* were separate concerns; but the latter, implicitly, both transcended and subsumed the former.[49] Since this traditional *kokutai* was innately democratic, as Yoshida would have it, there was simply nothing to worry about; and the question of sovereignty was essentially academic. Although his responses to Diet interpellators were often brief, and frequently castigated as supercilious, on this issue Yoshida made no attempt to restrain his feelings or maintain his customary detachment:

> The Charter Oath is merely the reflection in words of the history of Japan, the national character of Japan. In the spirit of the Oath we find Japan's national polity (*kokutai*)—indeed, Japan itself. By looking at this Oath, it is clear that Japan is democratic, is democracy itself, and the national polity has never been one of autocratic government or oppressive government. Again, by looking at the august poems of the emperors through the ages, or by looking at the verse and songs and the like of the enlightened rulers and wise ministers, we can see that there

> has never been in Japan as in other countries a tyrannical government or a government which ignored the people's will. It is the national polity of Japan that they have taken the people's heart as their own heart. Thus democratic government is not being established for the first time by the new constitution, which does no more than simply express again in different words what the country has always had. . . . There is no distinction between the imperial house and the people. Sovereign and subject are one, as the saying goes. Sovereign and subject are one family. That there exists no antagonistic relationship between the sovereign and his subjects goes without saying. Thus the question of where sovereignty resides is transparent in Japan, and is not a matter on which one needs to waste words. . . . The national polity will not be altered in the slightest degree by the new constitution. It is simply that the old spirit and thoughts of Japan are being expressed in different words in the new constitution.[50]

Thus, on the evidence of court poetry and a five-line edict, Japan had enjoyed two millennia or so of democracy. In this area, the avowed old realist certainly had no difficulty in turning the adage that deeds speak louder than words inside out.

Kanamori, ostensibly the Yoshida cabinet's legal expert, was no less emotional when it came to discussion of the emperor and polity. There was no rupture, no conflict whatsoever, between democracy and the Japanese monarchy, he argued at one point. And again: "The water flows, but the river stays. In this point lies our basic conception concerning the draft constitution."[51] In a significant explanation to the House of Representatives, Kanamori succinctly summarized the government's basic position: nothing in the new draft constitution could be construed as setting the people and emperor "in contradistinction to each other"; the term "people" (*kokumin*) as it appeared in the draft was to be understood as including the emperor (for sovereign and subject were one); and the fact that the new constitution denied political prerogative to the sovereign by no means meant that the emperor had been relegated to a position "below the people" or "below the Diet."[52] Education Minister Tanaka Kōtarō, tapping a strain of thought that had been vividly conveyed in the Konoe Memorial—and that indeed had been articulated in almost identical words in the debate that preceded the Meiji constitution six decades earlier—argued that, should the emperor system be abolished and replaced by a republican form of government, Japan would inevitably fall into the maw of anarchy, revolution, and despotism.[53] Ashida Hitoshi (later prime minister from March to October, 1948), as chairman of the Constitutional Amendments Committee of the lower house, concluded the committee's report on the place of the emperor under the new constitution with these words:

> The first Chapter of the Revised Constitution expressly provides that the Emperor of one line unbroken through ages is assured of his position as a Monarch who on the basis of the sovereign will of the people unifies them coevally with Heaven and Earth, from eternity to eternity. Thus, it has been possible to confirm the solemn fact that the Emperor, while being in the midst of the people, stands outside the pale of actual politics, and still maintains his authority as the center of the life of the people and as the source of their spiritual guidance. This accomplishment the absolute majority of the committee have received with the utmost joy and satisfaction.[54]

These emotional affirmations that the "new" Japan was inseparably wedded to the old—that the Japanese had not been shorn of history and tradition, but retained deep roots in a unique, immutable (and certainly roseate) *kokutai* in which sovereign and subject were one—gave great solace to the majority of representatives in this last session of the Diet to be held under the Meiji constitution. To critics, this fundamental failure to overthrow history portended the seed of future nationalism, jingoism, and repression. Although MacArthur's own statements on the occupation "revolution" were bejeweled with references to the overthrow of "feudalism" and Japan's liberation from myth and mysticism, SCAP made no attempt to intervene in this *kokutai* debate of 1946. Privately, however, the more liberal officers viewed the whole business sourly, and General Whitney expressed this concern in no uncertain terms in a memorandum of July 17 to MacArthur. His own interpretation of the *kokutai* was rather less misty than that of the Yoshida group:

> Kanamori's statements that the new Constitution means no change in "national polity" is laying the foundation for the undermining of the

> democratic spirit of the new Constitution and is paving the way for the return to the old system of authoritarian government. The term was usually surrounded with an aura of mysticism but in reality "national polity" summarizes briefly and completely the chauvinistic and militaristic political philosophy of the old regime in Japan. It is generally understood to mean a state centering around the Emperor; a people obedient to and subservient to the authority of the executive agencies charged by the Emperor with the responsibility of governing the country; the "uniqueness" and, therefore, superiority of the Japanese as a race because they are the only ones to possess this "national polity"; the negation of the principles of domestic democracy and international cooperation toward which the Japanese are supposed to be striving.
>
> If Kanamori is successful in establishing the idea that the new Constitution is based on this unchanged concept of "national polity," it will be possible to defeat the democratic letter of the new Constitution by interpreting it in terms of this spirit, which will have been established as being the philosophical basis of the Constitution. The will of the people will be constantly subjugated to the mystic concept of the "national polity" which is considered to be something inclusive of, but at the same time above and beyond the will of the people.

Whitney prefaced his comments by expressing his appreciation of MacArthur's "desire to refrain from any open interference in matters relating to the Constitution and your view that much weasel-worded explanation is offered to persuade the two-thirds majority required by the Government for its adoption." MacArthur also refrained from responding to the memorandum. Whitney's file copy concludes with the brief handwritten notation: "read by C in C. no comment."[55]

Under the circumstances, Yoshida accomplished as much as anyone could in minimizing the progressive departures of the new national charter, and he lost no occasion thereafter to reinforce his position. He rather audaciously endeavored to have the new constitution promulgated on February 11, National Foundation Day (Kigensetsu)—in prewar years the most nationalistic of Japanese holidays, which celebrated the pseudohistoric "founding" of the Imperial Sun Line in Japan by Emperor Jimmu in 660 B.C. Although this was rejected by SCAP, which later abolished celebration of Kigensetsu, Yoshida then proceeded to win a gratifying and rather surprising compromise victory by having the new document promulgated on the Emperor Meiji's birthday (November 3)—a nice touch indeed in the game of symbolic politics.[56]

He was less successful in another bold gambit in the closing days of 1946 when, in connection with the revision of the criminal code, he appealed to MacArthur to reverse his opposition to those articles which dealt with the crime of high treason:

> In the first place, the fact that even under the new Constitution the Emperor's position is that of "Symbol of the State and of the unity of the people" accords with the traditional faith which has been held firmly by the Japanese nation ever since the foundation of Japan. It is truly a high and lofty position. Moreover, it is undeniable that the Emperor is ethically the center of national veneration. That an act of violence against the person of the Emperor, occupying such a position, should be considered as of a character subversive of the State and deserving of severer moral censure and a severer punishment than any act of violence against the person of an ordinary individual is quite natural from the standpoint of Japanese national ethics. . . .
>
> Secondly the same is true of the members of the Imperial Family. As long as acts of violence against the person of the Emperor are to be punished with special consideration as above, it follows that a member of the Imperial Family, occupying an important place in respect of succession to the Throne, should be placed in a position different from ordinary individuals.[57]

MacArthur did not reply until two months later, and rejected the appeal as a violation of "the fundamental concept, clearly and unequivocably expressed in the new Constitution, that all men are equal before the law."[58]

Despite the fact that the new constitution was one of SCAP's most controversial reforms, and that as foreign minister Yoshida had been one of the most intractable critics of the MacArthur draft, the new charter survived the later rectification campaign and became one of the occupation's most enduring legacies. Yoshida's personal position on the issue also appears to have undergone a subtle change, for he did not subsequently give active support to the conservative campaign for constitutional revision. In a personal letter to Makino shortly before the constitution became effective in 1947, Yoshida went so far as to express the view that, in becoming detached from direct political responsibility, the emperor's "position within"—presumedly meaning his symbolic and spiritual role—"will be that much more enlarged, and his position will increase in importance and delicacy."[59]

Makino was then in his mid-eighties, close to death's door, and these words may have been merely intended to comfort the old loyalist; but it is possible that Yoshida had come to believe what he said. Although in 1953 he did agree to the formation of an internal party committee to study the possibility of revision, this reflected a concession to his conservative opponents more than an initiative or commitment on his own part.[60] In his memoirs, published in 1957, as well as in later writings, Yoshida actually went out of his way to refute the argument that the constitution had been "forced" upon the Japanese. On the contrary, he emphasized the give-and-take both between SCAP and the government and within the Diet, and went on to indicate that, "in my opinion, there is little that we are debarred from doing that is important enough for us to feel impelled to demand any change." He appears to have concluded that the relegation of the emperor to symbolic status was indeed a desirable safeguard of the throne—a formal insulation of the sovereign, as it were, from any possible future taint of autocracy. In this area, Yoshida was willing to play the role of the sage old populist. Revision might come, he argued, but only when the populace itself deemed the time to be ripe.[61]

LAND REFORM

The land reform carried out under SCAP's orders beginning in 1946 was a classic product of the structural critique of presurrender Japanese society and the recognition by occupation authorities—as by Marxists—of a correlation between domestic repression and external expansion and aggression. Since the turn of the century, approximately 45 percent of the arable land in Japan had been cultivated under tenancy arrangements (a larger percentage than in the early Meiji period), and the miserable plight of small owner-cultivators was scarcely better than that of tenant farmers. Agrarian poverty constricted the domestic market and necessitated aggressive economic expansion abroad. And it fostered a collective psychology of potential violence and rage—one which threatened to turn inward, but prior to 1945 was largely deflected outward, in the form of ultranationalism, militarism, and "transfer of oppression."

Within the framework of this sort of "root" analysis, SCAP's objectives reflected a familiar combination of progressive idealism, counterrevolutionary alarm, and pragmatic self-interest. Through elimination of the repressive landlord class and creation of a relatively equitable pattern of private land ownership, the countryside would be democratized and grievances conducive to peasant revolution would be eliminated. In addition, the economic betterment of the agrarian population (along with parallel material advances for the urban working class) would enlarge the domestic market and thereby reduce the possibility of Japan's reemerging as a ruthless competitor internationally.

As noted in Chapter 8, Yoshida opposed the land reform "in principle" but supported it in practice. Obviously he could not accept the socio-economic premises behind the reform, for such structural concerns subverted his cherished notions of conspiracy or an historic "stumble" or the "democratic" nature of the Restoration or the "healthy" progress of the Meiji and Taishō periods. The reformist premises also entailed a flat assertion of stark class oppression and antagonism in Japan, and this was hardly compatible with the thesis of a harmonious traditional polity, which was so crucial to the old guard at that juncture. Even when it had become apparent that the land reform resulted in both greater productivity and higher living standards in the countryside, Yoshida's sympathies remained with the dispossessed landlords. They had been maligned, he said, and here as elsewhere SCAP acted on the basis of propagandist stereotypes. In Yoshida's appraisal, the vast majority of prewar landlords had been innovative rather than feudalistic, paternalistic rather than exploitative or parasitic, generous rather than oppressive. Indeed, "the manner in which they bowed out of existence as landlords was worthy of their past achievements."[62]

According to one inside account, Yoshida was distraught when he was shown the final government version of the land-reform legislation and berated his minister of agriculture and forestry, Wada Hiroo, to whom he had entrusted the program. Be that as it may, the fact remains that Yoshida himself had appointed Wada, an extremely controversial agrarian economist with decidedly leftist inclinations, in the face of strong opposition from his own conservative supporters; and by Wada's own account, the prime minister gave him a free hand in implementing the land reform. Furthermore, the land reform was excluded from the broad "rectification" agenda to which the conservatives devoted their energies from the time of the third Yoshida cabinet. Together with the constitutional revision, this was one of the most noteworthy survivals of the early era of occupation reformism.[63]

Two general observations may help clarify why the Yoshida group did not struggle more vigorously on behalf of the old landlord class, and why the landlords themselves, unlike the monopoly capitalists, failed to withstand the early occupation assault. First, as already noted, Yoshida was deeply sensitive to the counterrevolutionary dimension of the land reform. He may have rued the passing of the landlords, but in the immediate post-surrender period he was ready to believe that their demise might otherwise be effected (naturally, without legitimate reason) in a bloodbath of rural insurrection, which could in turn spill over into revolutionary upheaval in the cities. Second, one must keep in mind the relative weakness of the landlords' position at the time of Japan's defeat. Yoshida's defense of the *zaibatsu* was practical; of the landlords, more sentimental. After World War One, the strength of the Japanese state resided largely in the industrial and financial sector; and while the monopoly control of the *zaibatsu* expanded under the exigencies of economic mobilization for war, during these same years the position of the landlords became weaker. They lacked the cohesion and structural complexity which enabled the industrial and financial sector to resist the occupation assault;

and they were, by this date, regarded as expendable by the bureaucratic and urban elites whom Yoshida represented. Once the die was cast, however reluctantly, moreover, it would have been folly to try to dispossess the new class of *petit* rural landowners who had benefited from the land reform—and who had become, in fact, the electoral backbone of the new conservative hegemony.

THE PURGE

Yoshida did not oppose the purge per se, and in several instances he was accused of using it to remove political rivals.[64] He was, however, extremely critical of its breadth and scope. In 1946, for example, Yoshida warned MacArthur that extension of the purge to officials at the local level posed the threat of "anarchy, chaos, and communism."[65] When his finance minister, Ishibashi Tanzan, was belatedly purged in early 1947, Yoshida told him to just imagine he had been bitten by a mad dog.[66] When the rather minimal purge of economic personnel was extended to relatives to the third degree, Yoshida suggested to MacArthur that this was an archaic practice of guilt by association which he thought civilized nations had abandoned. The supreme commander responded with a blistering critique of the Japanese family system.[67] In a similar manner, Yoshida's criticism of the purge on the local level provoked an angry analysis of the *roots* of Japanese totalitarianism by General Whitney.[68]

As suggested by such exchanges, to some extent the categorical nature of the purge again reflected the early antithesis between SCAP's more structural approach and the conspiracy or "stumble" thesis of the old guard. In any case, the Potsdam Declaration had indicated a purge "for all time." By early 1948, however, the United States publicly expressed its recognition that "the men who were the most active in building up and running Japan's war machine—militarily and industrially—were often the ablest and most successful business leaders of that country, and their services would in many instances contribute to the economic recovery of Japan."[69] The process of depurge began in earnest in 1949 (at which time the existing purge mechanism was turned against leftist public employees in the Red Purge). By the time the occupation ended, all but a handful of the 200,000 individuals originally purged for contributing to the war effort had been permitted to return to public activity; those remaining under designation were depurged immediately following formal restoration of sovereignty. Several depurgees were immediately recruited by Yoshida to high economic advisory positions, while many were reabsorbed into the new police and military establishments.

In the general election of October 1952, 139 depurgees were elected to the lower house of the Diet—a testimony to the durability of old political networks, but a source of discomfort and ultimate disaster for old "One Man" himself. Yoshida was eventually unseated by a coalition led by these former purgees.[70]

LABOR

The rapturous language Yoshida evoked on behalf of the emperor, the immutable "national polity," and the beneficent old *zaibatsu* was almost perfectly counterbalanced by a vocabulary of contempt where organized labor was concerned. He regarded SCAP's early encouragement of labor as probably the most irresponsible and destructive of all occupation "excesses," and he commonly charged the unions with prime responsibility for Japan's miserable economic performance prior to the Korean War. In Yoshida's telling, organized labor in post-surrender Japan was little more than a pawn of the communists. Its demands were rarely reasonable. Its activism in a time of crisis and general social dislocation was at best irresponsible, at worst malicious. Its goals were selfish, negative, destructive.

In practiced disclaimers, Yoshida declared that he respected labor's legitimate right to organize, bargain collectively, and strike. In practice itself, he does not appear to have ever discerned an occasion when resort to dispute tactics was justified—certainly not during Japan's first postwar decade. The proper activity of the working class, Yoshida indicated in an essay in his later years, was not to struggle for an increased share, but to increase the production from which shares are taken. The irresponsibility and *selfishness* of organized labor in Japan, he observed shortly after retiring to his country estate, was revealed in the very fact that it thought in terms of class rather than national objectives. In this respect, the postwar Japanese worker compared poorly indeed to his patriotic counterpart in West Germany, Yoshida said, or to the "pragmatic and utilitarian" British workers he had observed while ambassador to London in the 1930s.[71]

In the prewar period, Yoshida had had little occasion to comment upon organized labor. This was due partly to the fact that as a diplomat he had other concerns, but mostly to the fact that the prewar labor movement had been small, weak, legally vulnerable, and soon co-opted or repressed—none of which Yoshida is known to have regretted or criticized at the time. Staggering defeat merely presented a new nationalistic rationale for keeping the workers quiescent and exhorting them to bear the unbearable. It was fine to speak as General MacArthur did of clothing the worker with dignity and giving him influence over his material life, Yoshida observed, but such ideals were inappropriate in a time of shortage and confusion, and only raised unreasonable hopes and succored unscrupulous radicals. Even after SCAP demanded action in this area, Yoshida and his colleagues (then in the Shidehara cabinet) assumed it would be sufficient to take the "healthy, democratic" unions of prewar Japan as their model.[72]

"Old liberals" of the Shidehara and Yoshida ilk tendered such phrases quite soberly. The early SCAP reformers, when not weeping, found them amusing, and in this area as in many others rejected the Japanese proposals and demanded tough new legislation protective of labor. In this setting of SCAP support and old-guard vulnerability, the web of constraints was sundered and the civilian elites were confronted by a serious working-class challenge. Yoshida's passionately hostile response to this new level of labor organization and activism reflected two pressing considerations. Labor's agitation could be made scapegoat for the ineptitude of the government and big capitalists in effecting economic recovery (contrary to Yoshida's charges, the total number of work days lost because of resort to dispute tactics during the occupation was low).[73] More important, prior to early 1947 Yoshida and the interests he represented genuinely feared that Japan was in a potentially revolutionary situation; and this fear, while diminishing, was never entirely dispelled. The major threat to the "traditional national polity," it appeared, had passed from radicalized militarists to an unshackled and radicalized proletariat.

It may be argued in retrospect that this threat was exaggerated, but the conservatives at the time took it very seriously indeed, and for good reason. The working class not only organized rapidly, but also was rapidly politicized. Communist influence *was* strong in the early labor movement, alongside a spectrum of social-democratic thought. And what this signified in the broadest sense was the *open* appeal—now with an organized and "orthodox" (that is, proletarian) constituency—of an ideological frame of reference antithetical to the bourgeois and emperor-centered values so essential to perpetuation of traditional bureaucratic and capitalist control. From the outset, the first Yoshida cabinet, like the Shidehara cabinet before it, was attacked by labor as a tool of the capitalists. By May 1946, when the first Yoshida government was formed, moreover, there had emerged *at the grass-roots level* the disconnected but dynamic practice of "production control," in which local workers took over managerial functions and kept their plants or mines running—in some cases with greater productivity than had been attained under the ousted managerial elites. The tactic graphically undercut the argument that activist workers were bent on disrupting production, and simultaneously discredited the mystique of capitalist relations of production.

Production control was a chilling portent to the groups represented by the Shidehara and Yoshida cabinets, and a specific target of some of their early alarmist declarations. On May 24, 1946, only two days after the formation of the first Yoshida cabinet, the government released a statement condemning the practice. On June 13, it issued a broader and more famous "Proclamation on the Preservation of Social Order" castigating the inflammatory words and deeds of "a portion of the populace, borrowing the name of democracy"; deploring the encouragement of lawless acts by irresponsible mass demonstrations; and observing in particular that while production control in some instances admittedly had led to increased output, this pernicious form of labor dispute threatened "to destroy the industrial structure and plunge the national economy into chaos." These early official denunciations of labor activism and mass demonstrations, it will be noted, coincided with the peaking of the constitutional-revision issue in mid-1946 and the concerted campaign to protect the emperor and reaffirm the unchanged *and harmonious* nature of the national polity. They also followed on the heels of a SCAP statement on May 20 criticizing the abuse of democratic rights by a "disorderly minority"—one of the earliest explicit signs that the occupation authorities themselves were beginning to reconsider their encouragement of a truly active role for labor.[74]

In marshaling his guns for the attack on labor activism and agitation, Yoshida as usual reached into an old arsenal. One of the rhetorical weapons he emerged with was a reworking of the conspiracy thesis he had adopted previously vis-à-vis the military, and he pursued this analogy in impressive and ingenious detail. An aspect of this already has been noted: on the side of SCAP, the early reformist legislation pertaining to labor was attributed to the clique of Red or fellow-traveling "New Dealers" within General Headquarters. In the extended analogy, however, organized labor in postwar Japan was neatly inserted in the slot just vacated by the irresponsible, conspiratorial, and (as the Konoe Memorial explained) radical military.

Yoshida belabored this theme in his memoirs. The excesses of postwar organized labor were comparable to the excesses of the prewar military. Labor strikes and demonstrations (aimed at "revolution") had merely replaced military incidents (aimed at war). The union leadership was the counterpart of the military cliques. "Youth action groups" (*seinen kōdōtai*) within the labor movement called to mind the radical "young officers" of the 1930s. The rank-and-file had become the dupe of communist agitators in the same way that the non-commissioned officers and enlisted men had been manipulated by conspiratorial military leaders.

On both sides of the equation, Yoshida endeavored to draw a distinction between the naive whole (the working class, the troops) and the radical, undemocratic part (the extremist cadre), and in both cases he indicated that the conspiratorial leadership was motivated by largely personal and selfish objectives. Indeed, with admirable aplomb for someone who spent much of his time addressing a conservative parliament overwhelmingly dominated by businessmen and ex-bureaucrats, he even declared that the reprehensible selfishness and insincerity of the labor leaders was revealed in the fact that some aspired to a seat in the Diet. With a familiar left-right combination, old "One Man" also hit the point that the autocratic manner in which the unions were run reflected not merely the realities of communism, but also "the feudalistic atmosphere which remains in our country."[75]

The most notorious of Yoshida's anti-labor epithets was delivered on the first day of 1947, as the broad movement for a general strike was coming to a head. On this occasion, the prime minister caused an uproar by describing activist labor leaders as "lawless elements" (*futei no yakara*), a phrase associated with the repressions of the Tanaka era. This was a careless choice of words, and indeed Yoshida was prone to such lapses into the prewar vocabulary; in 1948, for example, he threw the Diet into brief turmoil by inadvertently referring to the state by its heady old designation *Dai Nippon Teikoku*, the Great Empire of Japan. While the *futei no yakara* epithet captured Yoshida's truly visceral vituperation where labor activism was concerned, moreover, it was also an indirect commentary on conservative double standards, for the other side of this coin was essential silence where the lawlessness of the ruling classes was concerned. Yoshida had almost nothing to say concerning the immense looting and hoarding of industrial stores which the big capitalists carried out after the surrender, for example, and his criticisms of black-marketeering or heel-dragging by the capitalists were perfunctory. Again, in the gigantic "shipbuilding scandal" of 1954, which like the Shōwa Denkō scandal of 1948 temporarily lifted the lid off the cesspool of conservative money politics, he endeavored to influence the public prosecutors and succeeded in preventing the arrest of Satō Eisaku, one of the "honor pupils" of the Yoshida School. "Bribery," Yoshida declared at this time, "is just a groundless rumor. . . . I can't help but wonder about the ability of the investigating authorities if they are unable to collect evidence without making an arrest. The result of this is the destruction of democracy." It was foolish, he declared in this connection, to expect political parties to keep honest and open bookkeeping: "Party government would come to an end if it abided by the Political Funds Control Law."[76] Law was flexible, and where organized labor was concerned Yoshida was equally eager to see it bent the other way.

In part, although not in full, he saw his desires realized. Several laws were central to the confrontation between organized labor and the conservative elites, and the history of this legislation could be developed as the story writ small of the changing course of the occupation. By 1950, a substantial part of what had been granted labor had been withdrawn, and the taker was the original giver: SCAP. To the conservatives, this turnabout was late and incomplete, but a source of smug satisfaction nonetheless.[77]

Three laws constituted the heart of the occupation's labor reforms–the Trade Union Law (passed December 1945), Labor Relations Adjustment Law (passed September 1946), and Labor Standards Law (passed April 1947)–and all were opposed by Yoshida, although his own first cabinet had been forced to sponsor the latter two. When Yoshida returned to power in late 1948, however, SCAP already had moved decisively to weaken and drastically curtail the province of the first two laws (which established broad rights of organization, collective bargaining, and dispute tactics). MacArthur's ban of the general strike in 1947 had blunted the radical thrust of the labor movement, and in July 1948 the supreme commander moved to remove public employees from the full protection of the Trade Union Law and Labor Relations Adjustment Law. In December 1948, under the second

Yoshida cabinet, this culminated in legislation which denied civil servants the right to bargain collectively or strike (the revised National Public Service Law), and denied the right to strike to workers in public enterprises (the Public Corporation Labor Relations Law). This severe blow to employees of the national government was subsequently extended to local civil servants (in the Local Public Service Law of December 1950) and workers in local government-owned enterprises (the Local Public Enterprise Labor Relations Law of July 1952).

In June 1949, the Yoshida government also sponsored a major revision of the basic Trade Union Law, which SCAP itself had been preparing before Yoshida returned to power. Although ostensibly designed to strengthen the autonomy and "democratic" character of the unions, this revision increased governmental influence over the unions through more stringent "qualifications" requirements, and in practice also created financial problems for many of the smaller, more vulnerable unions. In Yoshida's own summation, where the original Trade Union Law had stressed workers' rights, the significance of the 1949 revision lay in limiting these rights and strengthening the hand of employers in responding to unionization and collective bargaining. This extensive revision of the Trade Union Law was accompanied by a less drastic revision of the companion Labor Relations Adjustment Law, which expanded the definition of "public utilities industries" required to submit to a thirty-day "cooling-off" period prior to resorting to dispute tactics. Beginning in 1949, SCAP followed up on this legislative assault upon organized labor by informally ordering the cabinet to purge "Reds" in the public employ, and immediately after the outbreak of the Korean War in June 1950, the Red Purge was extended to the private sector and used to fire thousands of additional activist union members. In his memoirs, Yoshida frankly characterized these various measures sponsored by SCAP as "coercive restraints," made necessary by organized labor's abuse of the rights originally granted and its failure to develop in a "healthy" manner.[78]

Between 1951 and 1954, Yoshida endeavored to carry the attack on labor further, but was only partially successful. His government failed to enact an all-embracing "anti-general-strike law," and settled in July 1952 for an amendment to the Labor Relations Adjustment Law that sanctioned government intervention in critical strikes which remained unsettled after fifty days (the so-called "right of emergency adjustment"). Other controversial legislation passed in August 1953 placed restrictions on dispute tactics in the coal and electric-power industries (the Law Concerning Control of Methods of Acts of Dispute in Electric and Coal-Mining Industry, popularly known as the "Strike Control Law"). A major conservative objective was to eviscerate the Labor Standards Law, which governed conditions in the work place, to permit more "rational" utilization of labor in smaller enterprises. Although this law was amended six times between August 1947 and July 1954, with the most concerted endeavor occurring in mid-1952, a combination of domestic and international opposition prevented the proponents of revision from effecting the substantial mitigation of protective standards they deemed rational and realistic.

At the end of the Yoshida era, the conservatives were confronted with a labor movement that still demonstrated an unsettling level of radical consciousness. This was expressed through the dominant Sōhyō federation, which had been formed as an anti-communist confederation in 1950, but rapidly moved to the left in response to the separate peace, the remilitarization of Japan, and the unabashedly pro-capital policy of SCAP and the Yoshida government.[79] Yet the working class was also by this time fragmented and vulnerable, and organized labor, although far stronger than in the prewar era, remained outside the realm of decisive political power. The reasons for this were numerous. They included the mitigation of the initial labor laws, as well as constraints within organized labor itself (ideological schism, enterprise unionism, worker hierarchies and elitism, and so forth). Beyond this, however, labor remained weak because the capitalist structure itself, with all its immense resources and levers of control, had survived the brief interlude of reformism relatively unscathed. Under the joint U.S.-Japanese slogans of the Yoshida era—"economic self-sufficiency" and "U.S.-Japan economic cooperation"—finance and big business again assumed the initiative, and labor was driven to a defensive and even ritualistic posture.

ECONOMIC DECONCENTRATION

The campaign to contain working-class radicalism was accompanied by retreat from reform of the capitalist structure. Although the great *zaibatsu* holding companies were dissolved and shareholding was somewhat diversified, the basic program of decartelization and economic deconcentration was essentially abandoned. The old *zaibatsu* Yoshida had defended in 1945, seemingly against the stream, still dominated the modern economy in 1954; and, although there was variation depending on the specific sector, overall levels of economic concentration in 1954 remained fairly close to those that prevailed in 1937.[80] This is not to imply that the structure of the Japanese economy remained unchanged, or that—even during the period after 1948, when both the Japanese and U.S. governments were committed to economic reconstruction—there was not considerable disagreement between the two governments concerning appropriate priorities and policies.[81] Nevertheless, both by early default and subsequent deliberate intent, SCAP's policies ultimately served big business and perpetuated gross economic dualism.

The economic crisis caused by war destruction and the dislocations of defeat was compounded by the failure of occupation authorities to swiftly define and implement two fundamental programs: deconcentration and reparations. In both cases, the delay reflected, beyond technical obstacles, conflict among U.S. policy-makers; the reparations issue also involved disagreements among the Allied nations. Japanese capitalists understandably had no desire to rebuild or invest in enterprises that might subsequently be designated for breakup and reorganization, or for removal as reparations. They were inclined to play a waiting game until assured their interests would be protected.

At the same time, the economic disorder of the first three years of the occupation also reflected deliberate acts on the part of the government and large capitalists. The latter displayed a capacity for obstruction and "negative sabotage" which posed a telling contrast to the lack of comparable resistance during the war years. Although in the pre-surrender period the *zaibatsu* had been engaged in a struggle with the "controlled-economy theorists" over ultimate control of the economy, their objectives had been obtained through skillful cooperation with the war effort; adroitly manipulated, mobilization for total war accelerated the concentration of capital in private hands. Alien occupation dangled no such prospects of reward for collusion, and in the weeks immediately following the surrender, the government and capitalists engaged in an almost frantic disposal of industrial stockpiles, accompanied by massive governmental payoffs to the large war contractors. The industrial materials remained hoarded or else were diverted to the black market, and this, together with the payoffs, helped set off a vicious inflationary spiral which soon became the symbol of the post-surrender "economic crisis." Actually, the inflation proved functional to many major enterprises, to the extent that it effectively canceled existing debts.[82]

Under Finance Minister Ishibashi Tanzan, moreover, deliberately inflationary pump-priming was promoted by the first Yoshida cabinet as essential to getting key sectors back on their feet. The economic policy adopted by this cabinet–and perpetuated by the succeeding Katayama and Ashida cabinets–was eventually designated "priority production" or "weighted production" (*keisha seisan*), and was strongly implemented by the Reconstruction Finance Bank that began operating in January 1947. Prior to implementation of the Dodge Line in early 1949, loans from this bank accounted for roughly three-quarters of investment in all industries. Eighty-four percent of these loans were directed to the coal, iron and steel, fertilizer, electric, shipbuilding, and textile industries–and sixty percent of the loans were received by a mere ninety-seven firms.[83]

Although Joseph Dodge was critical of the Japanese government's lending practices and inflationary proclivities, and privately even voiced concern over its pro-monopoly bias, the Dodge policy of "disinflation," "rationalization," tight credit, and export-oriented production also favored the larger enterprises. The Korean War boom stimulated small as well as large enterprise, but profit rates as a whole were higher among the latter, and many smaller firms which had flourished under the boom failed to adjust to the burst of the war bubble in 1951.[84] Simultaneously with these developments, big business took giant strides in the consolidation of its *political* base. Business associations, led by Keidanren, re-emerged as immensely powerful lobbies during the third Yoshida cabinet. And within the central bureaucracy, big business received an exceptionally potent ally through creation of the Ministry of International Trade and Industry (MITI) in mid-1949. This occurred, of course, in direct counterpoint to the attack on organized labor and denunciation of labor's inappropriate "politicization." It is also noteworthy that consolidation of the relationship between the bureaucracy and big business, and the real recovery of the latter, took place after June 1950 in a context of war—as in the 1930s, only in this case with the United States as a third partner in the promotion of war-related industrial production in Japan.[85]

Legislatively, the original policy of economic deconcentration was defined by a number of laws promoted by SCAP, of which two were especially important: the Anti-Monopoly Law (Law Relating to Prohibition of Private Monopoly and Methods of Preserving Fair Trade) of April 1947; and the Deconcentration Law (Law for the Elimination of Excessive Concentrations of Economic Power) of December 1947. The first of these laws fell within the general tradition of anti-trust legislation. The second was more drastic and unorthodox, and has been described as "the surgical procedure necessary for the economy, in order for it to be turned over to the safekeeping of the Antimonopoly Law." The Deconcentration Law called for the designation and breakup of companies deemed to possess an excessive concentration of economic power in any of the four areas of industry, distribution and services, insurance, and banking or finance.

Almost before it had even come into effect, the Deconcentration Law became the object rather than vehicle of drastic surgery. The late date of the law itself reflected indecision and backstage fighting within U.S. ruling circles, and passage of the law triggered the open attack upon occupation reform policy—and the end, in effect, of "the MacArthur era." The polemics inspired by the Deconcentration Law were in themselves a case study in the ambiguities of ideology. Conservative U.S. critics declared, much in tune with the Japanese conservatives, that the deconcentration program amounted virtually to a policy "to promote socialism or a controlled economy." MacArthur responded that, on the contrary, this was designed "to reshape the Japanese life toward [a] capitalist economy," and "if this concentration of economic power is not torn down and redistributed peacefully and in due order under the Occupation, there is not the slightest doubt that its cleansing will eventually occur through a blood bath and revolutionary violence." The Communist Party of Japan joined the chorus by denouncing the deconcentration program as a plot to colonize Japan through introduction of foreign capital, "a scheme of the traitorous, monopolistic capitalists."

MacArthur lost, and the Communist Party surely did not win. The Deconcentration Law became virtually a dead letter. Banks and fiscal organizations were almost immediately declared exempt from its purview, and the vaunted program of economic deconcentration was terminated in 1949 with only nineteen companies being ordered to reorganize (of 325 companies originally designated in early 1948).[86] Logic followed farce. The Anti-Monopoly Law was amended in mid-1949, and then subjected to extensive revision under the fifth Yoshida cabinet in August 1953. An official of the Fair Trade Commission (formed under the 1947 Anti-Monopoly Law) later described the 1953 revision as a "death blow" to the original spirit and intent of the law, and post-Yoshida cabinets proceeded to pursue what has been described as an outright "pro-monopoly policy" without substantial modification of the 1953 legislation.[87] Other legislation pertaining to cartelization, stockholding, corporate taxes and depreciation allowances, import and export regulation, credit, economic associations, and the like was also revised, or newly enacted, during the Yoshida era, almost invariably to the advantage of big business.[88]

As originally conceived, economic deconcentration necessarily entailed (1) drastically weakening the domination of the old *zaibatsu*; (2) prevention of cartel activities; (3) prevention of trust-building; and (4) optimum melioration of the gross disadvantages to which small and medium enterprises were subjected under the dualistic economy. By the end of the Yoshida era, the tide was running strongly against this "economic democratization" philosophy on all counts.

(1) The old *zaibatsu*, led by Mitsui, Mitsubishi, and Sumitomo, still maintained dominant positions in coal and metal mining, metal manufacture, engineering and shipbuilding, electric machinery and appliances, chemicals, glass, chemical fibers, and warehousing. They held a strong if not dominant position in trade, shipping, and construction.[89]

(2) Cartel-type arrangements emerged in various sectors, especially from around mid-1951 when the specter of a post-war-boom recession arose. One form of these was the so-called "underground cartels," which first appeared in the coal industry as early as September 1949. Another manifestation was the practice of collaborative production curtailment (*sōtan*), and in early 1952 MITI stepped in to sponsor production quotas and price arrangements in the guise of "recommended production curtailment" (*kankoku sōtan*) in certain precarious industrial sectors. Despite criticism from the Fair Trade Commission, MITI was able to enforce its "recommendations" by virtue of its control over foreign currencies and access to raw materials; the Bank of Japan reinforced this through selective extension of credit.[90]

(3) The immense industrial-financial groups which dominated the Japanese economy during the later high-growth period also had their genesis in trust-building trends of the final years of the Yoshida era. These trends began to emerge around 1952, and were accelerated by legislative revisions in 1953 pertaining to mergers, interlocking directorships, and stockholding. This process of

"lining-up" (*keiretsuka*) entailed the agglomeration of companies embracing a full cycle of financing, production, and sales. It involved the emergence of city banks (banks having survived the occupation virtually untouched) as the pivot of new "enterprise groups," and led eventually to the creation of a powerful "new *zaibatsu*" structure—in which, however, the old *zaibatsu* continued to play a leading role.[91]

(4) In the "new" Japan as in the old, economic concentration entailed industrial dualism, and the economic giants depended upon highly advantageous subcontracting arrangements with small enterprises. Early occupation policy had emphasized the relationship between economic dualism and both external aggression and domestic repression, but dualism remained a conspicuous legacy of the occupation. Although the Fair Trade Commission called attention to the vulnerability of the smaller enterprises, and their conspicuous lack of protection vis-à-vis the large contracting firms in matters involving payments, orders, and guaranteed prices, the Yoshida government essentially ignored the commission's proposed remedial policies.[92] Its general attitude was revealed in another notorious *gaffe* of the Yoshida era, in this case by Yoshida's economic czar, Ikeda Hayato. In March 1950, in response to a reporter who brought up recent press accounts of suicide among bankrupted small businessmen, Ikeda observed that this was unfortunate, "but it can't be helped if one or two businessmen commit suicide."[93] The comment was interpreted as a reflection of the government's callous disregard of the more disadvantaged economic strata, and Ikeda was forced to resign as minister of trade and industry after a no-confidence motion was successfully introduced in the lower house. The incident, of course, had no effect upon the government's policy or Ikeda's career.

THE POLICE

A major part of the early reform program involved dismantling of the Home Ministry and extensive decentralization of police control. These reforms were effected between the first and second

Yoshida cabinets, and the decentralization of the police was extensive: cities, towns, and villages of over 5,000 population were assigned responsibility for and control over their own autonomous police forces.[94] Conservatives attacked this as contributing to inefficiency in maintaining law and order and impeding response to "large-scale" domestic threats, while small communities chafed under the fiscal burden of supporting their own constabulary. In a succession of legislative revisions beginning in 1951 and culminating in 1954, the Yoshida government succeeded in recentralizing the police system, although certain checks upon central authority were preserved.

This was not at the outset an unpopular policy, and the fact that it was not told a simple and central lesson: authority, influence, and political power followed money. The first revision of the Police Law, in 1951, gave local communities the right to reject maintenance of an autonomous police force by popular vote—and most communities below the city level quickly did so for financial reasons. In March 1948, when the new Police Law went into effect, there were 1,386 local autonomous forces at the town and village (*chō-son*) level. Within a matter of months after the 1951 revision of the law, approximately eighty percent of these communities voted to terminate their support of an independent police, and by the beginning of 1954 only 129 towns and villages still maintained their own forces. The number of cities (*shi*) maintaining independent police, however, increased from 219 in October 1948 to 277 in early 1954.[95] Non-autonomous forces were not subject to direct national control under this revision, but rather to a more flexible hierarchy of "public safety commissions."

The goal of the Yoshida government, expressed openly in 1951, was creation of a central "Security Ministry" (Hoanshō).[96] Although this was not realized, the government came close to attaining its objectives before the end of the Yoshida era. In 1952, the Police Law was revised in a manner that gave the prime minister somewhat greater influence over the system, and in 1954 the system itself was drastically reorganized. The National Public Safety Commission was placed under the jurisdiction of the prime minister; the head of this commission was given the status of state minister; a national Police Agency (Keisatsuchō) was created, with regional branches throughout the country; local police administration was concentrated at the prefectural or equivalent (*to-dō-fu-ken*) level rather than the city-town-village level; financing of local police was borne primarily by the prefectural or comparable governments and the majority of police personnel were classified as local public servants, but the higher ranks at this level were designated national public servants; and so forth. The 1954 revision of the Police Law provoked riots in the Diet which were quelled by the summoning of 200 police into the legislative chambers, symbolic midwives indeed to the birth of a recentralized police apparatus.[97]

Yoshida personally regarded the original police reform as another of SCAP's more spectacular inanities, and remained dissatisfied with even the considerable recentralization effected under his own government. He later vented his feelings on the subject in commenting upon the popular demonstrations which occurred in 1960 and involved jostling the auto in which President Eisenhower's personal emissary, James Hagerty, was riding:

> The U.S. Occupation Forces came to Japan and declared that, because Japan was a militaristic state with a completely militaristic social system, everything in Japan had to be overturned if peace was to be maintained in the Pacific. They proceeded to do so from the position of our Emperor on down to such things as our educational system and our police system. Our police system before the war had achieved quite a high standard; but now it was what is called "democratized" and must think twice before even laying hands on a thief. So, one could not expect it to become suddenly efficient in protecting Mr. Hagerty. We had only the Occupation Forces to thank for that.[98]

EDUCATION

Democratization of the educational system was assigned high priority in the early reform agenda, with "democratization" itself being addressed from several perspectives. The prewar educational system was perceived as having played a central role in the indoctrination of the populace, fostering not only ultranationalism and militarism, but also acquiescence to a highly stratified and oppressive class society. The immense authority of the Ministry of Education both reflected and buttressed the authoritarian state. In addition, the system itself was elitist, and perpetuated social inequalities. Compulsory education ended at six years of elementary schooling; thereafter, those who continued on were shunted into a diversified and extremely determinative tracking system. At the apex of the educational ladder were a small number of prestigious universities.

The attack on this system was embodied in several directives and laws.[99] Courses in morals (*shūshin*) as well as Japanese history and geography were suspended in December 1945, with emphasis subsequently placed upon a liberal presentation of civics and social studies. Student participation and "problem solving" were encouraged, in contrast to prior emphasis upon memorization and rote. In March 1947, the Diet passed a Fundamental Law of Education which set forth ideals consistent with the new constitution. The aim of education was here defined as "the full development of personality, striving for the rearing of the people, sound in mind and body, who shall love truth and justice, esteem individual value, respect labor and have a deep sense of responsibility, and be imbued with an independent spirit, as builders of a peaceful state and society."[100] At the same time, the Diet also enacted the complementary School Education Law, establishing the famous 6-3-3 (or 6-3-3-4) system. Compulsory education was extended to include six years of elementary school and three years of junior high school (middle school); from this, one could proceed to three years of senior high school and, if qualified, four years of college. This caused considerable disruption, as schools that had been devoted to more specialized forms of training were hastily retooled to conform to the new and more uniform educational ladder.

In 1947, the authority of the Ministry of Education was curtailed by abolition of state-authorized textbooks, although the ministry continued to provide non-binding teaching guides. Under the "Textbook Law" (Law Governing Provisional Measures on

Publication of Textbooks) of July 1948, determination of curricula and selection of texts were formally assigned to the individual schools. The major blow against central control through the ministry also occurred in July 1948, in the form of the Boards of Education Law. This called for immediate establishment of elective boards of education in the 46 prefectures and 5 major cities, with local elective boards at the city, town, and village level to be established in two years' time (in earlier drafts of the law, the local boards also were to be established in 1948). This attack on the Ministry of Education and agenda for extensive decentralization of educational administrative responsibility paralleled the dismantling of the Home Ministry and decentralization of police administration. In May 1949, the essentially technical and advisory role of the central ministry was formally set forth in the Ministry of Education Establishment Law.

Yoshida opposed the abolition of ethics courses and courses devoted to Japanese history, but indicated that he was in general agreement with the democratic and egalitarian ideals expressed in both of the basic laws passed during his first cabinet.[101] Although the Fundamental Law of Education did encounter criticism similar to that leveled against the new constitution, it did not become a major target of the later rectification campaign.[102] Yet the conservatives did not initially see a need for this law, and many again argued that the "spirit of democracy" was fully embodied in the old Meiji prescriptions. Maeda Tamon, education minister in the Shidehara cabinet and a respected adviser to Yoshida later, in October 1945 urged teachers to seek the democratic qualities latent in the traditional national polity, and to inculcate "spiritual composure" by reading the 1890 Imperial Rescript on Education at student assemblies.[103] Tanaka Kōtarō, education minister in the first Yoshida cabinet, similarly informed the Diet in 1946 that the rescript constituted "the foundation of human morality infallible for all ages and true in all places." Since it retained its meaning "in this age of democracy," Tanaka urged that the rescript be maintained as a basis for future ethical and civic education, supplemented where appropriate by the religious and moral teachings of other countries and other times.[104] Such avowed faith in the innate "democracy" of the Imperial Rescript on Education was a classic expression of the imperial consciousness, and had an almost exact parallel in Yoshida's own endeavors to elicit the essential democratism of the Charter Oath and Meiji constitution. SCAP, on the other hand, regarded the 1890 rescript as another example of the feudalistic legacy, and required that it be abrogated; this was done through the Diet in June 1948.

In practice, moreover, Yoshida believed that these educational ideals were impractical, and he opposed the immediate introduction of the 6-3-3 system on the grounds that it placed an insupportable financial burden on the populace. Japan could not *afford* this, he argued unsuccessfully during his first cabinet. The country could still not afford nine years of uniform compulsory education, in his view, during the later Yoshida era. Revision of the 6-3-3 system became one of the objectives of the rectification campaign, and in late 1951 one of Yoshida's major advisory groups publicly advocated a return to a more rigid tracking system beginning at the middle-school level.[105] Although the 6-3-3 system was modified in some particulars, however, the conservatives failed to revise it substantially.

Other features of the occupation's educational reforms survived less well, and the basic principle of decentralization embodied in the Boards of Education Law was a notable casualty of the rectification campaign. Elective boards were established in the prefectures and large municipalities in late 1948, as scheduled. Their institution at the city, town, and village level was postponed from 1950 to October 1952, however; this purportedly fundamental reform, that is, was not even instituted until after the occupation ended. By this time, the political implications of elective grassroots boards of education had become greatly altered. Radicals and progressives who initially supported the concept now opposed it on the grounds that the political situation was such that they could influence the prefectural boards, but would fare poorly in elections at the sub-prefectural level. The conservatives themselves were in disarray on this issue, but recommendations of several important advisory groups to the Yoshida government, notably in November 1951 and October 1953, quite accurately foreshadowed the future thrust of government policy: authority was to be concentrated at the level of the prefectures and five large cities, with boards of education at this level being made appointive rather than elective and the Ministry of Education given greater influence in policy and administration.[106]

The issue was resolved two years after Yoshida's retirement by what amounted to repudiation of the Boards of Education Law. In the Law Concerning the Organization and Management of Local Educational Administration (1956), elective boards of education were abolished at all levels and replaced with boards appointed by the local executive, subject to approval by the local assembly. School superintendents at the prefectural level became appointees of the governor, subject to the approval of the minister of education, while sub-prefectural school superintendents required the approval of the prefectural board of education. The hiring and firing of teachers were removed from local boards and transferred to prefectural boards. Emphasis was placed upon the authority of the prefectural boards to give "guidance, advice, and assistance" to the sub-prefectural boards, and the minister of education was accorded similar authority vis-à-vis both prefectural and sub-prefectural boards. The size of the boards was reduced, and they were also deprived of what had hitherto been regarded as a meaningful prerogative, namely, the preparation of their own draft budgets for submission to local assemblies. Like the revision of the Police Law two years earlier, this legislation provoked riots in the Diet, in this case in the upper house, which were subdued only by police intervention.[107]

These revisions did not restore central authority of a formal and binding nature to the Ministry of Education, but rather increased the influence of the central ministry in a more subtle manner. The philosophy of sub-prefectural educational autonomy was vitiated; the principle of elective boards was discarded; and the "advisory" role of higher authority, culminating ultimately in the education minister, was reinculcated in a manner in which the line between "advice" and "directive" was in practice frequently obscured. This subtle tactic of de facto recentralization had actually been foreshadowed in the revision of the Ministry of Education Establishment Law in August 1952, in which it was stipulated that "The Ministry has the duty to promote school education, social education (adult), and culture, and assumes responsibility to carry out the administrative business concerning the above."[108]

Control over course content—curricula and textbooks—was the ultimate prize in the struggle over control of the educational system, and the Yoshida group fell short of its objectives in this regard. The very meaning of "democratic education" became a predictable focal point of controversy, and polarization on this issue was extreme: the conservatives were pitted here against the Japan Teachers Union, one of the most radical of the postwar unions. What emerged from this prolonged debate was not only a vivid impression of the strength of leftist ideology among a group that had been regarded as the drill sergeants of nationalistic orthodoxy in the prewar period, but also another confirmation of the fragility of "traditional values" as these were perceived by the old guard. The conservatives decried the "confusion of liberty with license"—or what Yoshida once cursed as "mad-dog liberty"[109]—and came to regard the lack of "patriotism" in the country with an alarm that often bordered on hysteria.[110]

This sensitivity to the necessity of vigilant defense and constant resuscitation of traditional values had been expressed in terms of "preservation of the throne" in 1945 and 1946. By 1950, when a vigorous popular movement arose against rearmament and in support of permanent Japanese neutrality in the cold war, the leadership had become convinced that "love of the country" itself had been eroded by SCAP's reformist excesses—and nowhere was the corrosion more extensive, or threatening to the future, than in the classroom. The situation was reminiscent of the ideological crisis Yoshida's heroes, the Meiji leaders, confronted in the early 1880s after a decade of intense Westernization. And the response was likewise similar, in that the conservative leadership again ransacked the past for an ethical code that could be adapted to present circumstances. They naturally desired reinstitution of moral teachings in the curricula, but the question remained: what *were* the moral and ethical values of the "new" Japan?

For numerous reasons, there was no simple answer to this. While the conservatives inevitably reaffirmed the applicability of Confucian virtues to the present day, they were neither so impractical nor reactionary as to believe that this in itself would suffice. By the early 1950s they also confronted a peculiar problem, in that the future defense of the country was construed in rigid cold-war terms. The Yoshida government by this time had cast its lot firmly with the United States, and in this respect "patriotism" had become bilateral. In the eyes of the ruling groups, education was a "security concern" of overriding importance, the arena in which decisive ideological battles could be won or lost. The paternalistic "democracy" of the new conservative hegemony required a supportive ethical structure, but one that would simultaneously foster popular support for the decision to pursue Japanese rearmament within the global anti-communist camp, and in an unusually intimate embrace with the United States. The Yoshida government found itself in the anomalous situation of championing "patriotism" and "love of the country" at a time when it was being attacked itself, by many conservatives as well as progressives, for selling Japan to Washington.

The "moral battle of Shōwa," as one commentator labeled it, was joined in earnest during the third Yoshida cabinet. It reached a peak in November 1951, when the press leaked an "Outline of Ethical Practice for the Japanese People" prepared by Yoshida's minister of education, Amano Teiyū. Amano was a Kantian philosopher who, like Yoshida, enjoyed an imprecise reputation as an "old liberalist"; it was later confirmed that his "unofficial draft" was to be published on the day the peace treaty with Japan came into effect. In the early post-surrender period, Amano had supported recision of the Imperial Rescript on Education; by 1951, he had concluded that the country required, not a code to memorize as in the case of the old rescript, but a general moral guideline that could be contemplated in times of crisis. In Yoshida's characterization, "since the termination of the Pacific conflict, the individual had become everything and the State nothing," and Amano's endeavors, which he wholeheartedly supported, were designed to emphasize (in nice Confucian phraseology) "the importance of the middle way." The education minister's draft code thus constituted "a sort of moral minimum," in Yoshida's view, although it was not received as such by the general populace. Amano's text interwove Confucian homilies with recognition of "the dignity of the individual personality," but its overall tone was traditionalistic. The outline proceeded, in succession, from individual to family to society to the state, culminating in all-too-familiar abstract allusion to the emperor. "The State," Amano wrote, "is the parent body of the individual; without the State there would be no individuals." And the emperor, in turn, was "a symbol of the State, wherein lies the peculiar nature of our national polity":

> It is a special characteristic of our country that there has always been an Emperor throughout its long history. The position of the Emperor partakes of the nature of a moral focus as the symbol of the State. . . . Morality is the lifeblood of the State. The State, in essence, is founded more deeply on its moral than on its political or economic character. The Emperor possesses an objective moral quality. Thus the position of the Emperor symbolizes the fundamental character of the State.[111]

Public reaction to the Amano outline was cynical and hostile, and the government was forced to abandon temporarily its endeavors to recodify public ethics and reintroduce this to the classroom. The major "rectification" in this area did not occur until 1958, when ethics courses were revived and greater central control was also imposed over textbooks and curricula. At the same time, however, the Yoshida government did sponsor various measures to curb the influence of the teachers' union. General revision of the labor laws to restrict dispute tactics by public employees had direct bearing upon the teachers, and the Red Purge was used to fire leftist instructors. In 1953, when he formed his fifth cabinet, Yoshida accelerated the campaign against the union by selecting a new minister of education from the ranks of the old watchdogs of Imperial Japan. His controversial appointment, Ōdachi Shigeo, was a prewar career bureaucrat in the Home Ministry who had been purged by SCAP. As part of his crusade against the left, Ōdachi brought two of his former Home Ministry colleagues with him to high positions, and restaffed the Ministry of Education with a number of its prewar officials who, like the new minister, had been purged after the war.[112]

Legislatively, this blatant politicization of the ministry was reflected in two "education neutrality laws" rammed through the Diet in June 1954 and designed to tighten the restrictions upon political activity by the nation's half-million public school teachers. Revision of the 1949 Special Education Public Service Law prohibited all political activity during or after school hours with the exception of voting; national civil servants were already subject to these restrictions under the National Public Service Law. The Temporary Law to Ensure Observance of Political Neutrality in Compulsory Education Schools provided that "no one or no organization may instigate or incite teachers to support or oppose a political party or activity." This was intended to undercut the decidedly political influence of the Japan Teachers Union, but did not in practice do so.[113]

While the teachers remained politically articulate through the union, however, succeeding conservative governments continued to advance the trend toward greater de facto central control over educational policy and administration which was initiated during the Yoshida era. Thus, looking back from the vantage point of 1975, an American participant in the early reforms concluded that "The *Mombusho* [Ministry of Education] today has recovered all of its authority and again controls the standards of schools, the courses of study, the authorization of all textbooks used in elementary and secondary schools. . . . The intent of the Occupation policy was clearly not achieved."[114]

LOCAL AUTONOMY

The early police and educational reforms were part of a broader program aimed at destroying the authoritarianism of the prewar state by promoting extensive decentralization and local autonomy. The guiding philosophy, in a phrase, was creation of genuine "grass-roots democracy." Subsequent recentralization of the police and educational systems was symbolic of the failure of the decentralization policy as a whole, and the cause of this failure transcended mere maneuver and statist inclinations on the part of the old guard. First, there was an inherent paradox in SCAP's sponsorship of "decentralization" while maintaining control over the situation through its own highly centralized organization; this was compounded by SCAP's practical reliance upon the existing Japanese administrative apparatus. Second, genuine local autonomy was unrealizable without creation of a firm and independent structure of local finance. Financial crisis at the local level gave decided impetus to recentralization of the educational as well as police systems, and ultimately vitiated local governmental independence in general. And third, the inexorable demands of modern technocracy and administration fostered interdependence and increasing reassertion of hierarchic lines of command.[115]

At the same time, the central government and bureaucracy did resist, both actively and passively, directly and obliquely, this threat to their traditional control. Following the surrender, for example, the various central ministries actually engaged in a concerted and relatively successful endeavor to strengthen their penetration of the local scene through establishment of a plethora of "branch offices" (*desaki kikan*) and the like.[116] SCAP's *modus operandi* of indirect governance through Japanese bureaucratic channels abetted this, and local officials who protested against these developments to occupation authorities saw their pleas founder on the unyielding rationale of "efficiency."[117] In January 1947, SCAP characterized the Yoshida Liberals as a coterie that "preferred to return to former methods of administration,"[118] but although legislation purportedly establishing local autonomy was introduced within the first year and a half of the occupation, SCAP itself did not seriously address the critical problem of local finance until 1949–1950, in a rather pathetic gesture of too little too late. By this time, the resurrected Yoshida group was strong enough to gut the program through a combination of neglect and legislative revision. Thus an American participant in the early local reforms concluded, in mid-1954, that "it may well be disputed whether anything more than the trappings of local self-government existed when the Occupation ended. Certainly, there was no excess of decentralization in actuality."[119] By the end of the Yoshida era, the bureaucratic apparatus through which central authority over the localities had been exercised prior to surrender had been partially reconstructed, and in certain respects, such as the reliance of local governments upon national disbursements, local dependency upon the central government was actually far greater than it had been in the prewar period.[120]

As in other areas, "rectification" of the local-autonomy program was carried further by the conservative cabinets that followed the Yoshida era; it frequently was accomplished in subtle form, in the manner of the previously noted "advisory" prerogatives given to the Ministry of Education; it involved acts of omission as well as commission; and the emergent structure of control naturally did not exactly replicate prewar structures. The complexity of these developments is suggested by the fate of the Local Autonomy Law, one of the basic pieces of legislation in this area, which became effective in 1947 simultaneously with the promulgation of the new constitution. This law rested upon revisions in local governance initiated in the latter part of 1946, and between 1946 and 1955 the core legislation underwent over forty revisions; Japanese scholars describe seven of these changes as major, of which five occurred during the occupation and one in its immediate aftermath.[121] Other pertinent legislation concerning taxes and subsidies, administrative renovation, and the like underwent comparable revision, and the general trends can only be suggested in brief outline here.

(1) As seen in the police and educational reforms, the early decentralization policy aimed at destroying the pyramidal control structure not only by reducing national authority, but also by elevating the autonomy of cities, towns, and villages vis-à-vis the prefectural governments. Theoretically, the 1947 Local Autonomy

Law placed the former entities (*shi-chō-son*) at the same level as the prefectures and major metropolitan areas (*to-dō-fu-ken*). The principle was violated in practice from the outset, and the greater authority of the prefectural entities was implicit in the 1952 revision of the Local Autonomy Law and more formally recognized two years after the Yoshida era, in the 1956 revision of the law.[122]

(2) In certain respects, the Japanese conservatives were more iconoclastic than the American reformers. SCAP, that is, accepted the existing administrative boundaries of prefectures, cities, towns, and villages, although in many cases these were already out of phase with demographic realities by the time of the surrender. Admittedly, there were both practical and ideal reasons for doing this: the system existed, and beyond this embraced innumerable small communities which seemed appropriate seed-beds for the implanting of "town-meeting" democracy. In any case, the Yoshida government was entirely willing to destroy traditional boundaries, and virtually to destroy in the process the small town and village as independent administrative entities. This was accomplished by passage of the Law for the Promotion of Amalgamation of Towns and Villages in September 1953, which set up a three-year plan for "rationalization" of local administrative units. Amalgamation was carried out as planned, and by 1956 the number of independent towns and villages in Japan had been reduced by two-thirds.[123] The Yoshida government also desired to promote administrative consolidation at the opposite end of the spectrum, by creating a supra-prefectural "regional" structure. This was seriously broached beginning around 1953, but did not materialize.[124]

(3) A central aspect of the recentralization process involved piecing together the dismembered parts of the Home Ministry, which had been formally abolished in December 1947. This powerful organ had controlled the prewar police and, through its Local Affairs Section, the local governments; its various functions were widely dispersed during the reformist phase of the occupation. Reconsolidation was partially accomplished in piecemeal fashion under the later Yoshida cabinets, invariably under the

rubric of "efficiency" and with the stated noble intent of ensuring local governments a voice at the highest level. Police recentralization was one aspect of this. The process also involved removing the spine from some of the "independent administrative commissions" (*gyōsei iinkai*) created by the occupation. This development was most visible in "administrative readjustments" effected in the central bureaucracy from 1949, in which the government gradually assumed increasing responsibility for local affairs. The transition was manifest in the progression from the Local Autonomy Section under the prime minister (1948) to the Local Autonomy Agency (Chihō Jichichō, 1949) to the Autonomy Agency (Jichichō, 1952). By 1953, Yoshida's advisers were proposing recreation of a ministry-level "Internal Affairs Ministry" (Naiseishō) or "Popular Affairs Ministry" (Minseishō), but this did not materialize until 1960, when the Autonomy Ministry (Jichishō) was created.[125]

(4) The Home Ministry was not reconstructed as such, and the reconsolidation of central authority should rather be seen as a process in which effective influence over the periphery was reabsorbed by the cabinet and central bureaucracy as a whole. In police control, this involved the Ministry of Justice (created in 1952). In education, local autonomy was vitiated by the increasing de facto authority of the Ministry of Education. Less obviously, but no less significantly, the authority of the state was ensured by the fact that local governments became deeply dependent upon fiscal subsidies from virtually every single ministry in the central bureaucracy. The most serious endeavor to sever this noose, these puppet's strings, occurred in 1949 and 1950, in the form of the wide-ranging recommendations of the U.S. tax mission to Japan headed by Professor Carl Shoup. Apart from its specific tax and fiscal recommendations, the Shoup mission insisted that establishment of a firm economic base for local autonomy necessitated creation of a powerful Local Finance Commission that fully represented local interests.[126]

Ostensibly, Yoshida responded positively to these recommendations. In practice, he was hostile to the very concept of a powerful quasi-autonomous commission. The Shoup proposals were instituted partially and eclectically; the follow-up recommendations by the Japanese committee entrusted with fleshing out the Shoup program were essentially ignored by the Yoshida government (the reports of the "Kambe committee" in December 1950 and September 1951); and Yoshida effectively killed the Local Finance Commission by the most elemental of oppositional tactics: he did not appoint sufficient personnel to render it workable. The commission was digested by the central Autonomy Agency created in 1952, and the *quid pro quo* system of national subsidies Shoup had endeavored to weaken remained a powerful source of national control over local governments.[127] In 1954, it was estimated that local executives spent approximately fifty percent of their time in affairs directly involving the national government.[128]

(5) Under the prewar system, prefectural governors were appointed by the Home Ministry. The position was made elective in late 1946, to the chagrin of the conservatives. During the final years of the Yoshida era, the possibility of returning to the appointive system was seriously considered, and Yoshida lent his voice to the chorus in 1954 when he publicly observed that "the administration takes the stand that the relations between the central and local governments are likely to be hampered by the present system, under which Socialists could serve as prefectural governors while the Liberal Party is in power."[129] Like the plan to create a supra-prefectural regional system (in which, as the conservatives proposed it, the regional executive would also be appointed rather than elected), the desire to return to appointed governors was not realized.

DOMESTIC PEACE-KEEPING AND THE POLITICAL LEFT

Yoshida's attitude toward the political left was somewhat more ambivalent than might be expected. He opposed the repeal of the Peace Preservation Law and legalization of the Communist Party, and after he had returned to the premiership his government considered declaring the party illegal again, but concluded that this was not feasible.[130] He certainly regarded the Communists as enemies of the state, but in his later years enhanced his reputation for predictable unpredictability by declaring his personal respect for one of the most fiery and radical of the Japanese Communist leaders, Tokuda Kyūichi. Tokuda, an elected representative to the postwar Diet, was purged from public activity by SCAP and the Yoshida government on June 6, 1950, along with twenty-three other members of the party's Central Committee. He went underground and eventually made his way to China, where he died in 1953.[131]

This esteem for Tokuda can be taken as the frank respect of one strong personality for another, and at times Yoshida also seemed capable of drawing similar personal distinctions within the non-Communist left. Prior to his purge in 1946, Hatoyama had been seriously exploring the possibility of a coalition with the right-wing Socialists. When Yoshida replaced Hatoyama as party president, he rejected this possibility out of hand and aligned instead with Shidehara's conservative party.[132] Yet at the same time, Yoshida did solicit the advice and assistance of a number of prominent "progressive intellectuals" during the first cabinet. His initial choice as minister of agriculture and forestry was a well-known progressive agrarian economist, Tōhata Seiichi. When Tōhata declined, Yoshida turned to Wada Hiroo, who had been purged as a "Red" in the 1941 Cabinet Planning Board Incident and later joined the Socialist Party. Hatoyama's overtures to the Socialists may have been too adventurous for Yoshida, but Wada's appointment in turn shocked the Hatoyama group and was reluctantly accepted by them only when Yoshida threatened to step down if his choice was not approved.[133]

While Wada handled the land reform, the early economic policy of "priority production" also was developed by a group of ostensibly leftist scholars, centering around Arizawa Hiromi. Several participants in this so-called "professors' group" had been purged from the university during the war years, but Yoshida solicited their counsel and even met fairly regularly with them for a while.[134] Ōuchi Hyōe, an eminent neo-Marxist economist, also participated in the "professors' group" and was enlisted by Yoshida at an early date to help untangle the government's woeful statistical procedures, and in the early post-surrender period Yoshida also sought advice from Nambara Shigeru, another leader of the non-conservative intellectual community.[135] Prior to the threatened general strike of early 1947, Yoshida retreated from his early opposition to cooperation with the Socialist Party and endeavored to stabilize his political position by offering several cabinet positions to the Socialists; negotiations to this end extended over a substantial period, were handled by Yoshida personally, and broke down on issues of detail rather than principle.[136] On numerous occasions, including his private correspondence with MacArthur, he spoke of the desirability of creating a genuine two-party system in Japan, with the Socialists as the second party.[137]

Yet Yoshida's more lasting image is that of the master of the Red smear and vitriolic anti-leftist invective. Among close colleagues, he was known to despise the "liberal men of culture" (*bunkajin*), while he dismissed Marxism as at best anachronistic and "nothing more than a system of thought to be relegated to museums."[138] His notion of a legitimate "socialist" opposition clearly accommodated only those who abstained from serious endeavor to create a socialist state, and who shared his own vigilant anti-communism. This became clearer in the wake of the first Yoshida cabinet. When the right-wing Socialist Katayama Tetsu succeeded Yoshida as prime minister in May 1947, Yoshida's conditions for participating in Katayama's coalition cabinet included the demands that the Socialist Party purge its left wing and not do anything that might raise fears of "social unrest." Katayama's refusal to make such a commitment prompted Yoshida to observe that, after all, "it is absolutely impossible to cooperate with persons of a different ideological persuasion."[139] For the left-wing Socialists, he coined a malodorous metaphor: they "may be likened to mermaids. Their faces suggest that they are beautiful maidens, but their bodies are like fish. Yes, they smell of fish." The world would be divided into two camps, Yoshida declared at this time, and it behooved the Liberal Party "to identify itself with the anti-Communist camp without swerving."[140] There was nothing fishy there. Although the Socialist Party split into independent left and right factions in 1951 over the issue of whether or not to support the peace treaty, both factions opposed rearmament and the bilateral security treaty with the United States. This infuriated Yoshida, and he later contrasted it to the support of NATO by German socialists.[141] Thus the non-communist left as a whole came increasingly to be depicted as "bookish" dupes: unrealistic, irrational, ignorant of the realities of communism, "raving like persons suffering from hallucinations."[142] In 1950, Yoshida caused a minor sensation by castigating Nambara in particular and the intellectual spokesmen for the peace movement in general as "literary sycophants"; he was here exhuming the classical epithet he had used privately in 1921 when telling Makino that modern Japan could profitably emulate the feudal sponsorship of ideological orthodoxy.[143]

Acerbic ridicule of the leftist and even liberal opposition thus became a conspicuous feature of the Yoshida style, counterpoint to his cultivation of the image of a doughty and "realistic" warrior in the wedded causes of traditional practices and contemporary cold-war "democracy." In his later years, Yoshida wrote with some passion of the "two Japans in the heart of the Japanese people." One of the tragic legacies of the occupation, in his view, was the ideological and political cleavage within the country. While postwar Japan had been spared the ordeal of physical partition, as occurred elsewhere, the populace itself had become divided; a "thirty-eighth parallel" had been drawn among the people themselves. And it was this great fissure that international communism sought to exploit.[144] Invective alone would hardly suffice to discredit those sycophants and "fifth columnists"[145] who had rendered Japan so vulnerable, and the campaigns to depoliticize the labor movement, recentralize the police, and reassert central control over the educational system all represented integral parts of the conservative counter-offensive. The Yoshida group also supported other direct policies of control and repression.

Critics of these measures commonly compared them to the peace-preservation measures of the prewar state. The comparison was a natural one, but Yoshida also had more current and non-Japanese models in mind. During his second and third cabinets, he proposed the creation of an "Un-Japanese Activities Committee" in the lower house of the Diet.[146] The U.S. Congress was his obvious inspiration here, and although this did not materialize, in June 1949 the government did create an internal intelligence apparatus devoted to investigation of communists and leftists. Somewhat symbolically, this emerged within the Special Investigation Bureau (SIB) of the Attorney General's Office (reorganized as the Ministry of Justice in 1952); SIB was originally established in early 1948 to oversee the activities of individuals purged for pre-surrender militaristic and ultranationalistic activities. At the time of its formation, SIB had a staff of 150; this had increased to 537 in May 1950, was enlarged to 1,200 in August 1950, and was further expanded to a staff of over 1,700 in August 1952. The bureau was completely reorganized in August 1950, and by 1951 its activities were almost exclusively directed to investigation of "communist" activities. This agency, often compared to the American F.B.I., was headed during this period by Yoshikawa Mitsusada, who had been involved in the investigation of the Sorge-Ozaki case in 1941–1942, and who became known to Americans in 1951 when he testified before the Senate Subcommittee on Internal Security (the McCarran committee) in the inquisition of the Institute of Pacific Relations. Many of the personnel who joined the bureau after the Korean War broke out were depurgees formerly associated with the prewar Home Ministry and Special Higher Police. SIB was the pendulum theory in microcosm.[147]

The open campaign against "communists" and "fellow travelers" was initiated prior to the Korean War, however—and prior also to the famous Cominform attack upon Nosaka and the strategy of the "lovable Communist Party," which occurred on January 6, 1950.[148] The Red Purge began in the public sector at the end of 1949, was diverted to the private sector shortly after the outbreak of war in Korea, and did not subside until the end of 1950. Approximately 22,000 public and private employees were fired during this campaign, a roughly equal number in each sector.[149] This was a coordinated assault involving SCAP, the Yoshida government, and private enterprise, and its swiftness revealed the thoroughness with which both SIB and General Willoughby's Counter-Intelligence Section had compiled their dossiers. In the context in which these events took place, there was no need for the Japanese conservatives to turn to the Tanaka era for inspiration. Readier models were at hand in SCAP, and in Washington.

SCAP provided, in fact, an even more systematic model. Although occupation authorities had required the Japanese to abrogate the repressive peace-preservation legislation of the pre-surrender era, they themselves had ensured law and order through issuance of a web of their own peace-keeping edicts and ordinances. These were formulated in terms of furthering the aims of the occupation, however, and did not exist as Japanese law. As the occupation drew to a close, the conservative government thus faced the prospect that sovereign Japan would be bereft of legislation against domestic "subversion." And it was SCAP's peace-preservation ordinances, rather than the comparable legislation of prewar Japan, that became the major model for the Yoshida government. The cabinet began to address this matter seriously in early 1951, and publicly announced its intentions in the fall of that year, almost simultaneously with the convening of the San Francisco Peace Conference. In mid-September, Attorney General Ōhashi Takeo, a key member of the "Yoshida School," revealed that the cabinet desired, "if possible, to submit to the Diet session which ratifies the peace and security treaties a public peace-protection law, prohibition of general strikes, regulations governing meetings and demonstrations, a press code, and also a draft anti-espionage law."[150] Public protest against this agenda was swift, vociferous, broadly based, and in the end partially successful.

This controversy forced the government to extend its timetable and reduce its ambitions. Its major accomplishment in this area was the Subversive Activities Prevention Law, which underwent a reported twenty-three revisions and four name changes before the government even submitted it to the Diet in April 1952. The draft was subjected to further revision in the House of Councillors, where Yoshida's party did not hold an absolute majority, and finally passed by both houses in July.[151] On July 1, as the debate reached a climax, Yoshida declared in the upper house that it was "cowardly" (*hikyō*) to compare the new legislation with the prewar Peace Preservation Law, for the law did not aim at violating free speech or human rights and was merely directed against forms of violence not covered by other laws. "Those who oppose this," he went on, were thus "those who succor and instigate violent groups." Then, in a sentence never completed, the prime minister stated: "There appears to be concern that the Subversive Activities Prevention Law goes too far, but even if it does go too far, the voice of the citizens who desire the immediate establishment of this law. . . ." The sentence was drowned in an uproar from the floor of the house.[152] Neither subtlety nor civil liberties were ever Yoshida's métier.

Prior to submission of the draft bill to the Diet, the government had been forced to delete numerous items providing, for example, for emergency detention, "compulsory investigation," restrictions on employment, obligatory reports from political organizations, and confiscation of the property of dissolved organizations.[153] Final revision in the Diet eliminated sections that made persons who even possessed "seditious" literature liable to prosecution, and tightened guarantees of due process. The revisions did not address a third major area of public protest: the application of the law to the grey realm of acts of "agitation" or "instigation" as well as actual commitment of "violent and destructive activities."[154] Complementary legislation to the main bill also set up investigative agencies which struck many observers as the opening wedge for recreation of a new Tokkō, or thought police.[155]

In the months immediately following passage of the Subversive Activities Prevention Law, the government did endeavor to apply it in several ominously petty cases, which subsequently dragged on in the courts. The law did not prove to be the effective weapon against the left which the Yoshida group had originally hoped, however, and was applied sparingly thereafter—although the threat of abuse remained ever present. Other aspects of the government's original peace-preservation agenda met even less success. The cabinet submitted a "Demonstration Control Draft Law" to the Diet in May 1952, but this died without action in the House of Councillors after being passed by the lower house.[156] The proposed anti-general-strike bill, as previously noted, was also vitiated.

In 1952, and again in 1954, however, the government did succeed in passing legislation reminiscent of prewar laws designed to protect the military; the later of these was the more controversial. Where the Subversive Activities Prevention Law was often compared to the prewar Peace Preservation Law, the 1954 Defense Secrets Protection Law evoked immediate comparison to the prewar Military Secrets Protection Law—under which Yoshida himself had been arrested in 1945. This also provoked broadly-based public opposition. Its terminology was characteristically ambiguous, and perceived as a threat to the public's "right to know" in matters pertaining to military affairs. It was feared it would lead to resurrection of the old Kempeitai, or military police, as well as necessitate a system of secret trials. And it was, moreover, vulnerable to nationalistic resentment. Here Yoshida caught the backlash of his own bilateral patriotism, for the law was directed primarily to the protection of *American* military secrets.[157]

TEN

The Separate Peace, Rearmament, and "Subordinate Independence"

The reconsolidation and recentralization of conservative authority which occurred during the Yoshida era was inseparable from the strategic settlement reached between Japan and the United States: the restoration of sovereignty within a framework of rearmament and rigid cold-war partisanship. The domestic "reverse course" meshed with changing perceptions of Japan's future global role, both strategically and economically, and controversy concerning revision of early reformist policies invariably reflected this broader setting. Well before the occupation ended, political alignments had turned topsy-turvy. The United States was closely identified with its one-time severest critics, the anti-reformist circles exemplified by the Yoshida group, while its current critics spoke on behalf of the reformist ideals the United States itself had originally propounded for Japan.

These early ideals had been encapsuled in the slogan "demilitarization and democratization," and in a general sense the non-conservative opposition continued to affirm the integrity of this conceptualization. As U.S. policy came to focus on Japan's strategic importance—as "workshop," as critical military base in the "forward line of defense," as source of industrial war potential, as potential participant in "regional self-defense"—the slogan was sundered, and "democratization" alone retained as a rhetorical staple. The opposition argued that this was but the withered leaf of the original and vital ideal; the reverse course and subsequent "rectification of excesses" seemed ample proof that, once Japan was made a strategic pawn, "democratization" would be tempered accordingly. The strong state would take precedence over the autonomous entity and liberated individual. And the very nature of post-occupation sovereignty would be such that the state itself would be denied full autonomy within the community of nations.

The capping of these developments, both real and symbolic, appropriately took place in the United States. In September 1951, in San Francisco, a Japanese delegation headed by Yoshida signed a peace treaty with forty-eight nations and a military agreement with one. The latter, the bilateral security pact with the United States, was *quid pro quo* for the former. And while the peace treaty was generous and non-restrictive, the security pact was not an agreement among equals. It committed Japan to rearmament and the indefinite stationing of U.S. forces in Japan, and as Secretary of State Christian Herter later observed when this came up for revision in 1960, "There were a number of provisions in the 1951–1952 Security Treaty that were pretty extreme from the point of view of an agreement between two sovereign nations."[1]

Because the peace treaty was linked to the bilateral military agreement, it was not endorsed by the Soviet Union and its allies; and because of disagreement concerning the legitimate government of China (especially between the United States and Britain), China was not represented at the San Francisco Conference, and India abstained from participation.[2] Thus the San Francisco settlement represented a peace for Asia that excluded the communist nations and the most populous countries of Asia: in the phrase of the day, it was a "separate peace." In addition, by the end of 1951 Yoshida had been forced to agree to a further condition to ensure U.S. ratification of the "generous" peace, namely, recognition of the Nationalist Chinese regime under Chiang Kai-shek and commitment to the containment of the People's Republic of China. Economically as well as militarily, Japan was incorporated into the *Pax*

Americana. It could not be said that sovereignty brought with it the capability of pursuing an independent foreign policy.

Once the status of the emperor had been settled, Yoshida devoted more personal energy to the restoration of sovereignty than he did to any other single area of concern. As a former career diplomat, he regarded this as his forte, his area of special expertise. It was in any case his old bailiwick, and until the end of the occupation he himself assumed the post of foreign minister concurrently with that of prime minister. There is no question that he was the dominant Japanese figure in shaping the "San Francisco system," and he regarded this as a great personal triumph. His critics were willing to acknowledge his responsibility, but they viewed the accomplishment as anything but a triumphant one. Yoshida was accused of selling the country to the United States by bartering true independence for nominal sovereignty, and in Japanese parlance the settlement he gained for Japan became widely characterized as "dependent independence" or "subordinate independence." The phrase was infuriating to the old patriot, and also effective in undermining his political authority, for its appropriateness was accepted by a wide range of Japanese across the political spectrum from left to right.

A majority of the more radical opposition endorsed a clear alternative to the San Francisco system in the form of the so-called "four peace principles": no rearmament, no post-treaty U.S. military forces in Japan, an overall as opposed to separate peace, and permanent neutrality in the cold war. To Yoshida, espousal of neutralism for Japan was the height of irrational idealism, and bordered closely on subversion; the Yoshida group drew no clear line between the two categories.[3] To seek permanent neutrality for Japan, Yoshida later wrote, was like trying to pluck a flower from a mirror; the neutralism thesis resembled "the babbling of a sleepwalker," and neutralism itself was "a cowardly attitude, the opportunism of the weak."[4] Yoshida's bitter vexation concerning the four peace principles triggered his characterization of the progressive intellectuals as "literary sycophants" in May 1950, and it was this, more than any other issue, that prompted his solemn later observations concerning a "thirty-eighth parallel" in the heart of the Japanese people. For the leftist critique did have an unmistakable appeal within the populace as a whole, even to those who did not necessarily endorse the leftist agenda. Yoshida's political opponents within the conservative ranks also did not hesitate to level against him the charge of relegating Japan to a status of subordinate independence; this line was successfully used by both Hatoyama Ichirō and Ishibashi Tanzan, for example, who successively assumed the premiership after Yoshida.[5]

Several public opinion polls during the period of transition from occupied to sovereign Japan suggest the tepid and qualified response of the general public to the nature of the peace settlement. According to a poll released by the *Asahi* newspaper on September 20, 1951, over a quarter of the populace did not bother to follow the proceedings of the San Francisco Conference by press or radio, and only 41 percent expressed a "good feeling" over the conclusion of a peace treaty; 23 percent were "relieved, but with mixed feelings," 9 percent felt unease concerning the future, and 21 percent had no opinion.[6] In May 1952, immediately following the formal end of the occupation, only 41 percent of an *Asahi* polling sample felt that Japan had become an "independent country"; 32 percent accepted the characterization of "independent in form only, semi-independent, etc.," while 8 percent believed Japan was "not independent" and 19 percent had no opinion.[7] In September 1952, this question was asked: "Japan has become independent, but are there things which make you think it cannot be called an independent country?" Only 18 percent of the sample answered in the negative, while 39 percent responded affirmatively and 43 percent did not know.[8] Avowed popular support of the Yoshida cabinet actually lofted to an ephemeral high point of 58 percent at the time of the San Francisco Peace Conference; a year later, as the price of peace continued to be fiercely debated, this had plumeted to 20 percent.[9]

THE DECISION ON POST-TREATY U.S. MILITARY BASES

The accusation that he was a lackey of the American cold-warriors was galling to Yoshida for many reasons. He had studied Japan's options carefully. He believed he had gained independence at a reasonable and necessary price, given the country's vulnerability and the pressures upon it. And he had bargained hard.

Even before his first term as prime minister, while serving as foreign minister in the Shidehara cabinet, Yoshida had initiated within the bureaucracy a comprehensive and ongoing study of strategic options for the future Japan. The inquiry was detailed and wide-ranging, and led to the conclusion that Japan had no realistic option other than to rely upon a bilateral military agreement with the United States. This coincided with Yoshida's own traditional view of balance of power and his long-standing idealization of the era of the Anglo-Japanese Alliance; the *Pax Americana* had replaced the *Pax Britannica*, and the old model seemed relevant to the new circumstances. There was also involved here, however, a close reading of U.S. policy, and the conclusion that the United States had no intention of relinquishing its advantageous military position in Japan.

This conclusion was reached, *and acted upon*, prior to the outbreak of war in Korea. The internal strategic studies initiated by Yoshida in 1946 and pursued under subsequent cabinets including his own had examined the options of neutrality, of guarantees of international military protection through the United Nations or a great-power agreement, of primary reliance upon the United States, and so forth.[10] By 1949, Yoshida had become convinced that the feasible alternatives were stark: a bilateral military agreement with the United States (and thus, inevitably, a "separate peace"), or indefinite prolongation of the occupation.[11] As early as April 1949, he publicly described the prospect for permanent neutrality as dubious, and in a provocative statement to the Diet in November of that year, he quite frankly indicated that the options were a separate peace or no treaty at all.[12] This was presented as the official government position in a Foreign Ministry white paper on June 1, 1950.[13]

As late as November 1949, however, the security task force within the Foreign Ministry still held as its primary objective the negotiation of a bilateral agreement whereby post-occupation Japanese security would be guaranteed by U.S. forces stationed *outside* Japan proper.[14] Shortly thereafter, Yoshida personally canceled this option, although it is not clear precisely when he concluded that this too was unrealizable. By April 1950, in any case, he had decided that the alternatives were now narrowed to sovereignty with continued U.S. military presence *in* Japan, or no sovereignty at all. And he then proceeded to take the initiative in formally broaching the possibility of post-treaty bases to U.S. policy-makers. This was done secretly in early May 1950 through an economic mission to Washington headed by Ikeda Hayato.

According to Miyazawa Kiichi, an intimate participant in these events, Yoshida did not confide his thoughts on the matter even to his closest associates, such as Ikeda, and it was only on the eve of his departure for the United States that Ikeda was summoned by the prime minister and instructed to tender the offer to U.S. officials. This was done on May 3 in a confidential meeting attended by Ikeda, Miyazawa, Dodge, and Ralph Reid of the Department of the Army (one of Dodge's major aides on Japan affairs). Ikeda began by observing that the desire for an early peace had become a major issue in Japan, and opposition parties in the Diet—led by the Communists and to a lesser extent the Socialists—were clamoring for an overall peace and strongly opposed any alternative settlement involving U.S. bases.[15] The Yoshida government, on the other hand, believed that it would be emotionally difficult for the Japanese to endure an indefinite continuation of the occupation until such time as an overall peace, however desirable, became feasible. There was no road to Japanese independence other than making an optimum arrangement under prevailing conditions, and the recent general election for the House of Councillors indicated that most Japanese supported this alternative.

The opposition parties were also arguing that SCAP was interfering unnecessarily in the minutest aspects of Japanese political and economic affairs, and thereby thwarting the development of Japan's democratic rights and prerogatives. Whether or not this was MacArthur's intention was unclear, but the fact that the Japanese government acquiesced in this policy had made it vulnerable to accusations of servility and obsequiousness.[16] It was further intimated that U.S. commitment to the defense of Asia seemed irresolute to the public—not only concerning Japan, but also Formosa, Indochina, and South Korea. In this uneasy situation, the Japanese people looked for American resolve and an early peace; and, while the Yoshida government now enjoyed majority support, should the peace issue remain unsettled it could be anticipated that Japanese politics would once again be plagued by unrest. The Yoshida offer was presented in this context, and read as follows:

> The Japanese Government desires to conclude a peace treaty at the earliest possible opportunity. Even after such a treaty is made, however, it will probably be necessary to allow U.S. forces to remain stationed in Japan in order to guarantee the future security of Japan and the Asian region. If it is difficult for this desire to be tendered from the American side, the Japanese Government is willing to study the manner in which it might be offered from the Japanese side. Concerning this point, we are consulting the studies of various constitutional scholars, and these scholars indicate that there would be few constitutional problems if an article pertaining to the stationing of American forces were included within the peace treaty itself. Even if the Japanese side tenders a request for the stationing of troops in another form, however, that also will not violate the Japanese constitution.[17]

The approach was both direct and subtle, for the unequivocal offer was obviously girded with intimations of increasing radicalism and anti-Americanism in Japan, and mildly barbed aspersions concerning American resolve. Dodge, frank and unruffled, responded in an unofficial capacity by observing that military and strategic considerations had recently taken precedence over purely diplomatic concerns in Washington. While the United States was not opposed to a peace treaty, it greatly feared any arrangement whereby its military posture vis-à-vis the Soviet Union would be weakened. As Dodge informed MacArthur on May 8, he attempted "to modify any unfortunate and unrealistic overoptimism" on the part of the Japanese concerning prospects for an early peace. Army policy concerning occupied areas still remained unclear at this juncture, he explained, and attention was currently being given to proposals whereby future U.S. military aid would be integrated with policies directed toward rectification of the international dollar-gap crisis. There was, as of May 1950, as yet "no clear definition of the issues."[18]

Ikeda's secret offer in Washington coincided almost to the day with Yoshida's denunciation of the "literary sycophants" in Tokyo (and in the larger context of the Dodge retrenchment and wave of Red Purges among public employees). It was made purely on Yoshida's initiative, and reflected his penchant for both secret diplomacy and "one-man" operation (as well as his dissembling attitude toward the Diet, before which he constantly and piously avowed that his government would not engage in secret diplomacy).[19] To some extent, the initiative calls to mind the secret "Yoshida plan" in London on the eve of the China Incident thirteen years earlier—with the great exceptions that "One Man" was now premier, that the ensuing conflagration in Korea redounded to Japan's benefit, and that his private proposal was indeed adopted. Dodge was correct in indicating that official Washington had not reached a clear decision concerning Japan at the time of the Ikeda mission; since the end of 1949, there had existed an acrimonious deadlock between the State Department and Department of Defense on this issue. This was resolved shortly thereafter, however, and post-treaty U.S. bases in Japan became a central feature of the San Francisco system.[20]

It can be argued that Yoshida and his security advisers underestimated their potential leverage vis-à-vis the United States, which was indeed committed to continued military presence in Japan, but which was also sensitive to the potentially counterproductive consequences of prolonged occupation. The Ikeda mission had indeed plucked this string, but the question remains whether the Yoshida government could have played it to greater advantage (a less "unequal" security treaty, a less extensive post-treaty U.S. presence in Japan, even a security agreement involving U.S. forces outside the main islands, as initially desired). The Korean War, on the other hand, dramatically heightened Japan's significance in U.S. military planning and made Yoshida's secret offer appear a prescient one. At the same time, it enabled the conservatives to argue more vigorously that continued U.S. military presence in Japan was desirable to ensure Japan's own territorial security against the Soviet and communist menace.

The latter argument—U.S. bases as a deterrent to aggression against Japan—was expedient and somewhat deceptive. As will be seen, Yoshida personally did *not* lay undue emphasis upon the direct communist threat to Japan, even after the outbreak of the war. The Yoshida government desired the bilateral alliance and assurance of U.S. military protection, but does not appear to have been genuinely convinced that such protection required the large-scale and indefinite *in situ* physical presence of U.S. forces. Phrased differently, Japan needed U.S. bases within the country not so much to guarantee its security as to regain its sovereignty. The *dominant* consideration was not communist policy, but the nature of Washington's anti-communist policy—not the imminent threat of Soviet aggression against Japan, but the threat of protracted American occupation of Japan. The "realist" position thus held that the bases were a *sine qua non* for sovereignty; that they were purely defensive in nature, and an effective (although probably excessive) guarantee of Japan's security. To critics, on the other hand, the bases were symbolic of Japan's lack of autonomy, evidence of the Yoshida government's participation in the global counterrevolutionary crusade, and a lightning rod which might well invite aggression or retaliation upon "military-base Japan."[21]

ARMS IN EDEN

The military-base issue soon became inseparable from the issue of rearmament, and this was made a matter of open record in September 1951: the U.S.-Japan security agreement signed in San

Francisco was prefaced with the understanding that Japan would gradually assume responsibility for its own self-defense. From the perspective of the Yoshida government, however, the two policies were not initially integrated. As in the case of post-treaty bases, the prospect of Japanese remilitarization was broached at the official level prior to the outbreak of war in Korea, with the initiative in this instance coming from the American side. This took place following the Japanese offer concerning military bases, but as of this date the Yoshida government does not appear to have drafted contingency plans of its own for creating a new military. Yoshida opposed the initial U.S. proposal, although his opposition was quickly eroded: recreation of a Japanese army actually began in July 1950, with the authorization of a 75,000-man "National Police Reserve" (Kokka Keisatsu Yobitai). For several years thereafter, however, Yoshida refused to acknowledge the military thrust of the new force. He played a sophist's game, but at the same time felt a certain understandable chagrin. While critics lambasted his remilitarization of the country, American policy-makers denounced his timidity in promoting remilitarization. Japan rearmed under Yoshida, but at a more moderate pace than Washington desired and had anticipated.

The story is well known, but has some less familiar embellishments. Early occupation policy called for dissolution of the military establishment, and this was by and large accomplished—although the nucleus for a future army and navy remained in such forms as the demobilization boards, former officers recruited by General Willoughby's Counter-Intelligence Section, retention of naval forces for repatriation and mine sweeping, and so forth.[22] The new constitution, moreover, included the famous and unprecedented Article Nine, which prohibited maintenance of war potential. The initial draft constitutional revisions prepared by the Shidehara cabinet in late 1945 and early 1946 had retained the military, and it will be recalled that Yoshida was an outspoken supporter of the basic "Matsumoto draft." Nonetheless, when it fell upon Yoshida as prime minister to present the "MacArthur draft" to the Diet in 1946, he personally delivered one of the most unqualified interpretations of the intent of Article Nine. The strongest assertion that Article Nine precluded all Japanese armament whatsoever, *even for self-defense*, was presented by Yoshida himself. In another of Clio's little jokes, his major critics on this point of interpretation at the time were Nambara Shigeru—who later became a leading spokesman of the Japanese peace movement, and a target of the "literary sycophants" invective—and Nosaka Sanzō, a leading spokesman for the Communist Party.[23]

The expressed position of the first Yoshida cabinet was unequivocal. On June 26, 1946, Yoshida informed the House of Representatives that the right of self-defense as well as of belligerency was renounced. Recent aggressive wars such as the Manchurian Incident and Greater East Asian War, he pointed out—and this was not an argument one would necessarily have expected him to pursue—had all been waged in the name of self-defense.[24] Nosaka challenged this in the Diet two days later on the grounds that it was necessary to distinguish between just and unjust wars. Japan's recent aggression had indeed belonged to the latter category, but the Allied Powers and China had been compelled to take up arms in a legitimate war of self-defense. On behalf of the Communist Party, Nosaka called for denunciation of war of aggression instead of "war in general." Yoshida's reply is worth quoting, since his own government's later repudiation of this original interpretation was to become not only one of the great legal controversies of postwar Japan, but also a major factor in exacerbating the political polarization which became one of the major legacies of the occupation period:

> With regard to the provisions of the draft constitution relating to the renunciation of war, it has been suggested that war may be justified by a nation's right of legitimate self-defense (*seitō bōeiken*), but I think that the very recognition of such a thing is harmful. It is an obvious fact that most modern wars have been waged in the name of the right of self-defense of the nation. Thus, I believe that to recognize a right of legitimate self-defense is, however unintentionally, to provide a rationale for provoking war. Also, the expectation behind the provisions in the draft relating to the renunciation of the right of belligerence is the establishment of an international peace organization.

> By establishing an international peace organization, it is intended to prevent all wars aimed at aggression. If there is to be a war of legitimate self-defense, however, this inevitably presupposes a country bent on a war aimed at aggression. Therefore, to recognize legitimate self-defense—a war in accordance with the right of self-defense of the nation—is a harmful thought which will provoke war, however unintentionally. Furthermore, I believe that in the event that a peace organization, an international organization, is established, the very idea of recognizing the legitimate right of self-defense is in itself harmful. I think that your [Nosaka Sanzō's] opinion is an argument which does more harm than good (*yūgai mueki no giron*).[25]

Less than two months later, on the first anniversary of Japan's surrender, Yoshida repeated this interpretation in a radio broadcast to the nation and indicated that, in its hour of trial and humiliation, Japan could find a rare source of pride—possibly even a sense of national superiority—in this unqualified demilitarization. He referred to the "reckless war waged under perverted leadership," and acknowledged that "the building up of Japan as a new nation of culture and a new democratic state remains a task yet to be accomplished." In the midst of hardship and uncertainty, he called for optimism and dedication in the building of a new Japan, and offered the renunciation of war as a major step in the direction of Japan's future contribution to a world of peace:

> The new constitution provides for renunciation of war, in which regard Japan leads the rest of the world. "But you are," some may say, "[a] beaten nation without a single soldier and without the power to wage wars." The truth is we do not want to repeat the calamitous experience of war even after we have become an independent nation both in name and in fact. Now that we have been beaten, and we haven't got a single soldier left on our hands, it is a fine opportunity of renouncing war for all time.[26]

Yoshida adhered to this position through 1949; and even thereafter, when his interpretation became more ambiguous, he did not at any point prior to the Korean War indicate support for Japanese rearmament. His administrative policy speech to the Diet on November 8, 1949, for example, contained this passage:

> Recently, in connection with the problem of atomic energy, there has arisen deep concern among the people regarding our national security. There is, however, but a single path for guaranteeing the security of our country. As is solemnly declared in the new constitution, our country stands before other countries as an unarmed nation, having voluntarily renounced war and abandoned armaments. Backed by world opinion devoted to peace, let us increasingly strengthen the resolve of our people to contribute to the civilization and peace and prosperity of the world, so that the civilized world more and more will understand and appreciate our country. This, I believe, is the only way to expedite a peace treaty. We need but consider the scars of defeat to be reminded that in the past our lack of sufficient knowledge concerning international conditions and trends, our overestimation of the armaments of our own country, and our unscrupulous destruction of world peace ultimately stained our history, disrupted the rise of our national fortunes, caused our people to lose their children, to lose their husbands, to lose their parents, made the whole world our enemy, and led to unprecedented disaster. It is my belief that the very absence of armaments is a guarantee of the security and happiness of our people, and will gain for us the confidence of the world, and will enable us as a peaceful nation to take pride before the world in our national polity. I therefore hope that this idea will be thoroughly taken to heart by all our countrymen.[27]

In response to an interpellation on this address, Yoshida re-emphasized Japan's solemn determination to abide by the principles of disarmament and renunciation of war, and again evoked the vision of Japan as a pioneer in world peace, setting an example that might hopefully lead to eventual global disarmament.[28] Such statements were noble and numerous—and also invariably paired with the observation that such an affirmation of pacifism was essential to dispel the suspicions of other powers, gain universal confidence, and thereby hasten the early conclusion of a peace treaty.[29]

In the view of most Japanese critics, Yoshida departed significantly from this position in his next administrative policy speech, delivered on January 23, one year after the formation of the third Yoshida cabinet. The often-quoted statement was this: "To abide fully by the renunciation of war does not mean renunciation of the right of self-defense"; this closely paralleled a similar statement by

MacArthur in his New Year's address several weeks earlier. Taken in context, however, the statement actually appears to have been intended as a subtle opening toward the separate peace, rather than toward future Japanese rearmament. The fuller passage reads as follows:

> All of us, of course, would like to see an overall peace. But the matter depends solely upon the objective international situation, which is utterly beyond our control in the present condition of our country. Quite naturally, great interest has arisen domestically and internationally concerning the future security of our country. The core of our security lies in the very determination of our people to persistently contribute to the peace, civilization, and prosperity of the world, abiding fully by the renunciation of war and armaments which is solemnly declared in our constitution, and backed by the public opinion of the peace-loving world. To abide fully by the renunciation of war does not mean renunciation of the right of self-defense. When our national policies are dedicated to peace and democracy, and when our people's resolution to adhere to these aims constantly ensures the trust of the peace-loving and democratic nations, then this very mutual trust will be the security which protects our country. It is such mutual trust that will lead to international cooperation to ensure the security of our country in the mutual interest of all the democratic nations.[30]

The sensitive phrase concerning Japan's "right of self-defense" was predictably challenged, and in responding Yoshida argued that "the nation naturally possesses the right of self-defense, excluding force of arms (*buryoku o nozoku jieiken*)"; or again, "the right of self-defense in Japan's case will be the right of self-defense without resorting to force of arms (*buryoku ni yorazaru jieiken*)."[31] At one point he evoked the image of the Tokugawa samurai: "I mean by the right of self-defense without force of arms the right of self-defense which does not employ even two swords."[32] Before the House of Councillors on January 30, Yoshida gave an extemporaneous speech on the realism of "security without armaments (*gunbi o motanai anzen hoshō*)" which could hardly have been surpassed by the "idealists" themselves. A simple reading of history, he declared, revealed the fatuousness of the argument that armaments were a guarantee of peace. "If we hold somewhere in the back of our minds the idea of protecting ourselves by armaments, or the idea of protecting ourselves by force of arms in case of war," he concluded, "then we ourselves will impede the security of Japan." The best security measure available to Japan was to defend itself by gaining the confidence of the rest of the world.[33]

The private test of Yoshida's public pronouncements occurred on June 22, 1950, three days before the Korean War began, when John Foster Dulles met Yoshida for the first time in Tokyo and urged Japan's remilitarization. With greater vigor than coherence, Yoshida declared that this was out of the question: Japan could afford neither the economic costs nor popular outcry rearmament would surely entail. Dulles found the encounter unnerving; he felt, he later said, like Alice in Wonderland. William Sebald, the State Department's representative in Japan who was present at the interview, described Yoshida's performance as "Puckish" and more or less asinine: "Smiling and with chuckles, he spoke with circumlocutory indirectness, with vagueness, and with an astute use of parables."[34] The circumlocutions apparently included, in addition to the economic and social-unrest arguments, a reiteration of the same "self-defense without resort to arms" thesis Yoshida had been presenting to the Japanese public—and, as Puck himself recounted, Alice became visibly disturbed. At that point Yoshida suggested that the issue be brought directly to MacArthur, to which Dulles agreed. MacArthur expressed full sympathy for Yoshida's concerns, and seemed prepared for the confrontation. He immediately produced a thick dossier listing idle military factories of the former imperial government and handed this to Dulles. There were many such plants in Japan, MacArthur observed, and he proposed that Dulles consider reactivating these "to assist in the reconstruction of American armaments." Dulles, for the time being, accepted this compromise proposal.[35]

Prior to the Korean War, the United States and Japan had thus addressed the *three* constituent aspects of Japan's subsequent participation in cold-war military activity: U.S. bases in Japan, industrial remilitarization, and Japanese rearmament. Yoshida supported the first two items of this agenda, but initially opposed the third. The outbreak of war on June 25 changed the picture while accelerating the process, and with creation of the nominally camouflaged National Police Reserve Japan took the first steps toward rebuilding a bona-fide military. Yet even thereafter, Yoshida endeavored to reaffirm his opposition to rearmament—both by publicly denying it was occurring and privately holding a lid on rapid military expansion.

Until the beginning of 1952, Yoshida endeavored to present Japan's new military as Gertrude Stein had presented her rose. A police reserve is a police reserve is a police reserve, he in effect argued, and not to be confused with an army. It was an energetic but unconvincing performance. Although the Japanese side *was* somewhat confused at first as to what they had agreed to create, and although the primary mission of the National Police Reserve *nominally* was suppression of domestic insurrection, it was quickly made clear that the new paramilitary was, as its U.S. planners declared from the outset, "the beginning of the Japanese Army."[36] Yoshida himself relied for advice in these matters upon a coterie of former imperial military officers, and in the fall of 1951 he was personally instrumental in arranging for former captains, majors, and lieutenant colonels of the Imperial Army to be depurged and recruited at the staff level of the National Police Reserve.[37] By the end of the occupation, these "police" had been incrementally equipped with pistols, carbines, M-1 rifles, 30-caliber and 50-caliber machine guns, 60-mm. and 81-mm. mortars, bazookas, flamethrowers, artillery, and tanks (alias "special vehicles"), and were on the verge of receiving aircraft.[38] As characterized by Colonel Frank Kowalski, who was intimately involved in training the new force between 1950 and 1952, both organizationally and technologically this paramilitary unit had become "a little American Army." To describe this as consistent with Article Nine—as Yoshida himself had originally interpreted the famous no-war clause, and as with increasingly strained logic he still sought to affirm—was, in Kowalski's words, "pure sophistry."[39] The Japanese public was more or less inclined to agree. In a poll conducted in February 1952, 48 percent answered that Yoshida was lying when he said Japan was not rearming; 40 percent were not sure, and only 12 percent believed what the prime minister said.[40]

Sophistry was, to Yoshida, the better part of "diplomatic sense" at this juncture. Diplomats dissemble as a matter of routine, and Yoshida clearly believed that, until Japanese sovereignty was actually a virtual *fait accompli*, there was little to be gained either domestically or internationally by an open affirmation of Japanese rearmament. Neither the Korean War nor the entry of the People's Republic of China into that war in December 1950 caused him to alter this opinion. Throughout 1951, while giving ample indication that he anticipated Japan would assume responsibility for defense against external aggression in the indefinite future, he continued to insist that the country was not presently rearming, and would not do so "under the present situation."[41] It was not until March 6, 1952, that he significantly altered this refrain when, in testifying concerning a proposed expansion of the National Police Reserve before the Budget Committee of the House of Councillors, he stated that the constitution did not prohibit "war potential for self-defense." When this caused an uproar in Japan, Yoshida returned to the Budget Committee four days later to suggest that "when Japan gains strength, acquires enough economic assets, and foreign powers acknowledge Japan's right to self-defense, we may then resort to a referendum for constitutional revision in order to possess fighting potential." This left Japan, Kowalski later suggested, "in a kind of twilight zone of rearmament. The Prime Minister had acknowledged that the Constitution would have to be revised before the nation could acquire 'fighting potentiality,' but the NPR, in the meantime, continued to be equipped with artillery, tanks and aircraft."[42]

In his own way, Yoshida gave a bravura performance on the rearmament issue during this period. On the one hand, he blandly argued that Japan was not rearming, in the very midst of both concrete developments and less than subtle indications to the contrary from the U.S. side; but, at the same time, he did seriously intend to limit the speed and scope of rearmament, and unquestionably succeeded in doing so. After September 1950, the United

States made no attempt to conceal its expectation that a remilitarized Japan would contribute actively to future "free-world" collective security; Dulles, for example, stated this publicly on September 15, and frequently thereafter.[43] The U.S.-Japan mutual security treaty initialed in September 1951, moreover, explicitly referred to the "expectation that Japan will increasingly assume responsibility for its own defense against direct and indirect aggression."

While Yoshida was naturally fully aware that his National Police Reserve was being trained and equipped as an embryonic infantry force, and personally encouraged the depurge and enlistment of former imperial officers in late 1951, the measure of his accomplishment in restraining this remilitarization lies in the fact that he, more than any other single individual, was responsible for the relatively slow growth in personnel of the NPR. The land force remained at a strength of 75,000 for the duration of the occupation, and was increased to 110,000 in October 1952, and this was hardly for want of candidates: 382,000 applicants applied for the initial 75,000 positions, and at the staff level 800 former military officers were selected from an available pool of over 10,000.[44] During Dulles's second visit to Tokyo in January 1951, Truman's starchy envoy and Japan's crusty prime minister engaged in an exchange on the rearmament issue reminiscent of that seven months earlier—in which Yoshida did eventually agree to the clause later incorporated in the mutual security treaty, but at the same time resisted Dulles's pressure for more rapid and open remilitarization. On this occasion, Yoshida once again was supported in his stance by MacArthur.[45]

American projections at this time for the future Japanese military establishment were far in excess of what Yoshida believed either feasible or necessary. At the San Francisco Peace Conference, Dulles endeavored unsuccessfully to persuade Yoshida to draft plans for a force of 300,000 men, and, as discussed in the following chapter, during the next several years U.S. policy-makers accepted a standard target figure of 325,000 to 350,000 Japanese ground troops—and, indeed, initially assumed this could and would be quickly achieved.[46] Pressures from the Japanese side were hardly less ambitious. In March 1951, former vice admiral Takagi Sōkichi called for creation of an air force of five fighter divisions (with 350–370 fighters per division) and four medium-bomber divisions (160–180 bombers per division); a three-flotilla navy (with one cruiser and 32 destroyers per flotilla); and a highly mechanized army of 150,000 to 200,000 men.[47] Also in 1951, Hattori Takushirō—a former member of Tōjō's General Staff, whom General Willoughby had been grooming for precisely this moment of military resuscitation—submitted a proposal to SCAP for the immediate organization of twenty infantry divisions. It was a further measure of Yoshida's comparatively moderate stance that, in addition to resisting such proposals for large-scale rearmament, he also took care to prevent the "Hattori clique," which embraced some 400 ex-military men, from gaining positions of influence in his own, more modest, force.[48]

Yoshida's position in brief was that Japanese rearmament had to be slow and camouflaged, and the rationale behind this included more concrete considerations than perhaps are generally recognized. On the more familiar side, he continued to argue that the Japanese economy, even under the war boom, could not stand the strain of massive rearmament; the populace, and especially the "tender sex," would not tolerate it; the constitution did not allow it; the left could exploit it; and a good part of the world would be appalled at the sudden spectacle. The latter concern, it should be noted, involved considerations beyond the immediate and compelling desire to gain wide international support for an early peace treaty. Should the countries of south and southeast Asia in particular conclude that Japan was returning to the path of militarism, Yoshida believed, this would also impede the restoration of long-term economic relations with the area—relations already being promoted under the occupation at that very time. The delicacy of this situation can be suggested by considerations regarding China and India. As indicated below, the Yoshida government desired eventual expansion of economic relations with the People's Republic of China, a cause that would be undermined by creating an impression of Japanese revanchism. At the same time, however, Japanese trade relations with China were placed under mounting restrictions as the Korean War progressed, and consequently the development of substitute markets in Asia assumed increasing importance. India was regarded at this juncture as one such important alternative for future Japanese economic expansion, but India was at the same time guided by Nehru's principles of neutralism, and looked with open disfavor upon American plans for a remilitarized Japan. Other prospective markets of the area, including Australia and New Zealand, shared comparable apprehensions.

Yoshida's unwillingness to rearm more rapidly was also motivated by a number of additional, pragmatic considerations. First, he believed that if Japan followed the U.S. blueprint, it would be subject to immense pressure from Washington to deploy troops to Korea. Second, he did not accept the Dulles thesis of monolithic communism, nor did he believe that Japan was in imminent danger of communist attack. And third, he did not trust his own new military.

Viewed from Yoshida's perspective, the Korean War had bearing on Japanese rearmament in two contradictory ways. The war gave the United States the opportunity to activate its plans for remilitarizing Japan. At the same time, it gave Yoshida further good reason for opposing rapid rearmament. His reasoning was well captured by Kowalski, who recalled this conversation with a Japanese official at the time:

> "I can't understand," I began, "why the Prime Minister refuses to increase the defense forces of your country when we are willing to assume the costly burden of supplying weapons and equipment. Surely, this is all to the advantage of Japan. All you're asked to furnish is manpower and you have a lot of that."
>
> "Ah so," responded my friend. "We will strengthen our forces, but not until 1955."
>
> "Why 1955?" I asked.
>
> "By then the Korean War will be over."
>
> "But why must you wait until the war is ended?" I persisted.
>
> "Because Mr. Yoshida does not want Japan to become involved in the Korean War. If we organize 300,000 troops as your Mr. Dulles

wanted us to do, your government will insist that we send some of these troops to Korea. That is why the Prime Minister agreed to expand our forces only to 110,000.

"Mr. Yoshida shudders every time he recalls how the Japanese army was bogged down in China. In that the people share his fears. Should Japan have 300,000 ground troops, a strong argument would be made that we don't need that many to defend Japan from attack and the United Nations, under your influence, would ask us to cooperate by sending at least a hundred thousand to Korea. Once these troops are dispatched, there is no telling when they will be withdrawn."

It has been suggested, in connection with this issue, that mounting American disenchantment with the fighting qualities of the South Korean troops impressed many U.S. planners all the more with the desirability of accelerating Japan's remilitarization.[49]

If the Korean War was, as many claimed, the first step in a Soviet-directed campaign for world conquest—or, indeed, for conquest of Asia's great workshop, Japan—then Yoshida's position might seem casual, if not irresponsible. Despite his own undeniable concern with the "communist menace," however, Yoshida did not stand with Dulles on the giddier heights of cold-war hysteria.[50] This was exemplified in his expressed detachment from *both* arguments as to why the Korean War threatened Japan and made rapid rearmament imperative—the "internal" argument that communist actions in Korea would inspire communist agitation in Japan; and the "external" argument that the Korean conflict threatened to engulf all Asia.

In a memorable press conference slightly more than two weeks after the war began, the prime minister was asked whether he thought the Korean incident had caused the Japanese people to become agitated and disturbed. There was no reason for disquiet, Yoshida replied, and then proceeded to offer a rather extraordinary, jumbled metaphor in which he depicted Japan as a poor but peaceful paradise in which interlopers ("thieves" or "bomb-throwers") "will be punished by the heavens, just as they were punished when they ate the apple in the Garden of Eden." The Japanese people, he concluded, needed only to set their minds at rest and work for peace.[51] By November 1950, the combined influences of the war boom, Red Purge, and reverse course permitted him to declare with apparent equanimity, and certainly with simpler sentences, that the combination of the regular police and newly created National Police Reserve made it "not at all difficult to maintain public peace at the present time." Yoshida dwelt upon this point at some length in an article prepared for Western readers and published in *Foreign Affairs* in January 1951, in which he wrote that "As far as the Japanese skies are concerned, the Red star is receding."[52] He consistently endeavored to project himself as a guardian against the communist menace who was ever vigilant but at the same time ever objective, and thus unswayed by the alarmism and global-war scares of popular discourse.

Interestingly, some of his strongest public statements in this regard were delivered in conjunction with Dulles's second and third visits to Japan, in January and April 1951. In his administrative-policy speech to the tenth session of the Diet on January 26, one day after Dulles had arrived, Yoshida began by speaking of the intensification of the cold war and noting with some pride that "international circumstances are now such that we are expected, as a bastion of democracy, to become a force in gaining ascendancy over communism in the Far East." He immediately coupled this, however, with reference to the decline of communist influence in Japan and the "internal peace and tranquility" now enjoyed by the country, and with a familiar warning:

> Our debates on rearmament have already caused needless misgivings at home and abroad, and moreover it is obvious that in reality any significant rearmament is beyond the capability of our defeated country. The security and independence of a nation is not merely a question of armaments and military strength. What we must rely upon is a passion for liberty and independence by the populace—a proper sense and understanding of the spirit of independence, liberty, and patriotism. That armament without this passion and proper sense leads to aggression abroad and militaristic government at home is made eminently clear by looking at the recent actual course of our own country. I hope that all our countrymen will be extremely prudent concerning rearmament.[53]

These views naturally were challenged by the advocates of disarmed neutrality, who fully recognized that Yoshida was now couching the rearmament issue as a matter of timing, rather than an absolute principle. The more effective opposition, however, came from within the conservative political ranks, and especially from spokesmen of the rival Democratic Party, which under the leadership of Ashida Hitoshi had taken a position in favor of constitutional revision and more open and rapid Japanese armament. In responding to this criticism from the conservatives, Yoshida most explicitly revealed his relative distance from the Dulles line. Thus in reply to an interpellation by Miki Takeo in the lower house on January 27, he offered this unexpectedly serene observation:

> We do not have the slightest expectation that the communist countries will invade Japan. Therefore, I believe that in addressing the security problem it is necessary to first consider the concrete questions of from which direction the danger comes and how imminent the danger is to Japan. Insofar as the threat of communism within the country is concerned, I think that at the present time even the members of the Communist Party do not believe that such a threat exists. Where the concrete problem of Japan's security is concerned, one must first grasp the concrete realities of the threat to Japan and then discuss this, but there can be no discussion, as if for the sport of it, on imaginary themes along the lines of a threat being imminent.

In the House of Councillors on the same day, he explicitly rejected the argument that a communist invasion of Japan was imminent, and argued that the real challenge lay not in girding for "World War Three," but in responding soberly to groundless rumors and the communist "war of nerves."[54] Two days later, when Yoshida's "optimism" was challenged in the upper house by another representative of the Democratic Party, he enlarged upon his view in this manner:

> The views and opinions I express in this Diet are frankly expressed, and most certainly do not convey optimism out of some political strategy or ulterior motive; my outlook is based on the objective situation. I too do not think that the present objective situation permits optimism or is

> not serious. As can be seen from my administrative-policy speech and other statements, I have frankly recognized that the present situation is by no means simple. I am only saying that, if asked whether the Korean disturbance will lead directly to World War Three, the answer is: No. If World War Three did break out, it could lead to the destruction of civilization and the human race . . . but I say with confidence that World War Three will not break out so simply. Although I would agree the present situation is not simple, it is not so acute as to lead directly to World War Three, for the United Nations and others are doing their utmost to prevent World War Three. . . . I have no hesitation in declaring that the Korean problem will not suddenly develop into World War Three. This is not an optimistic view; in fact, I am simply stating the actual situation. But if World War Three does not break out, what will happen? What I call the war of nerves will intensify throughout the world. In our country too at the present time there are naturally all sorts of wild rumors as a result of the war of nerves, and views much more pessimistic than my own are spreading concerning the objective situation. I believe this is the import of your question, and thus I wish to state my own view frankly: we are not on the verge of World War Three, but the war of nerves will become more intense, and therefore our people must take care not to lose their bearings and be led astray by this war of nerves.

Yoshida then proceeded to take issue with a recent statement by MacArthur urging the Japanese people to undertake their own self-defense, and went on to reiterate the legal and economic arguments against rearmament, the waning of subversive activities by communists (and Koreans) in Japan, and the adequacy of the existing police organization.[55]

On February 13, Yoshida gave a brief report to the Diet concerning his recent talks with Dulles, and indicated that domestic security was adequate, and would be maintained by "repletion" of Japan's own police force, while for the present Japan would rely upon the United States for security against foreign aggression. While it was to be expected that eventually Japan would also assume responsibility against external threats, "both the content and scope of the role to be played by Japan shall be settled in the future in accordance with the degree of rehabilitation of our national strength, after Japan has recovered its independence and joined the society of free nations on an equal footing." In May, Yoshida reported on his talks with Dulles the previous month—when Dulles had made an urgent visit to Tokyo in the wake of MacArthur's dismissal, to assure the Japanese that the peace treaty would be unaffected by this dramatic event—and again responded to criticism from the Democratic Party by reiterating his opposition to rearmament and belief that there was no present threat of "World War Three."[56]

Yoshida did not ingratiate himself with American policy-makers by diminishing the communist threat in this manner. To some degree, his position coincided with that held by the more maverick figures in U.S. ruling circles, such as MacArthur (on occasion) and George Kennan (whose comparatively moderate views made him *persona non grata* in Washington around this time). Both these men also minimized the direct external threat to Japan; as MacArthur observed in the congressional hearings that followed his dismissal, the Soviet Union and China simply lacked the amphibious capacity to invade Japan.[57] Colonel Kowalski, who dealt with the cabinet on a regular basis in conjunction with Japan's clandestine rearmament, later suggested that, as of 1950 at any rate (prior to China's entry into the war), Yoshida's evaluation of the strategic situation was based upon respect for America's preponderance of military power, recognition of the Soviet Union's pressing domestic problems, and an element of disdain for the Chinese Communists. The prime minister "was convinced that the Russians were too deeply involved in rebuilding their disrupted country to challenge directly the technologically advanced, highly industrialized Americans. He further regarded Red Chinese military power as composed of primitive coolie armies. Under these circumstances, he concluded that neither the Soviet Union nor Red China nor a combination of both would dare to confront the United States in direct combat. Under the protective American umbrella, therefore, there was no need for any hurried rearmament in Japan."[58]

The vision of combined Soviet and Chinese power which fueled the concept of "monolithic communism" constituted a further critical area in which Yoshida found himself at variance with the more hysterical premises of U.S. strategic planners—even after the Chinese had dispelled the belief that they would not dare to challenge American power. Yoshida prided himself upon his expertise concerning China and the Chinese, and in later years his supporters took satisfaction in pointing out that he never subscribed to the concept of the monolith, and had anticipated the later Sino-Soviet split. This is essentially correct, although the reasoning by which Yoshida reached this conclusion does not unequivocally enhance his stature as a China expert. He did point out that, given China's long history and racial pride, it was inconceivable that the country would remain tightly linked with and subordinate to the Soviet Union; failure to exploit this inherent tension by adopting a positive policy toward the People's Republic, Yoshida wrote in later years, was one of the tragic shortcomings of postwar U.S. policy. At the same time, however, he also assumed that the character of the Chinese people was too pragmatic, individualistic, and materialistic to provide fertile soil for the communist ideology. "The Chinese are basically individualists," he argued, and thus one could not believe that "Chinese peasants are happy in the loss of their lands without compensation."[59]

However shaky the sociology, the conclusion was that China would go its own way; that it did not pose a direct threat to Japan; and that, whatever its present political coloration, the country remained a natural market and source of raw materials for Japan. One of his advisers reportedly summarized Yoshida's thinking in this way:

> It is Mr. Yoshida's view, and many Japanese agree with him, that China should be left alone. China may turn Red or Black—all the same. Be it the people's revolution of Dr. Sun Yat-sen or Mao Tse-tung's communist revolution, leave this to China. What is an affair of China should be left to the Chinese. It will all settle down in the long run. That is the history of China, and it is not a business in which other people should interfere, Mr. Yoshida thinks.

No matter how things might "settle down" in China, mutually beneficial relations between the two countries were natural and ultimately unavoidable. Thus, with but a different coloration to the antithesis of being Red, Yoshida emphasized in the 1951 *Foreign Affairs* article that, "Red or white, China remains our next-door neighbor. Geography and economic laws will, I believe, prevail in the long run over any ideological differences and artificial trade barriers."[60] Neither militant brinksmanship, nor fanatical economic containment, nor belief in the necessity of massive Japanese rearmament followed from such premises.

Yoshida's final consideration in opposing rapid rearmament was articulated less openly, but was suggested by John Allison, Dulles's aide during the peace-treaty and security-treaty negotiations and later U.S. ambassador to Japan:

> During this second visit to Tokyo [January 1951] Mr. Dulles had, at first, again found Prime Minister Yoshida reluctant to discuss the security problem in detail. While Mr. Yoshida was a firm anti-Communist and was much more realistic than the Socialists, he nevertheless had a genuine fear of re-establishing a Japanese military machine. He had been imprisoned for a time by the Japanese army during the war. Later, when I was Ambassador to Japan and got to know Mr. Yoshida well, I often would discuss this problem with him. I pointed out that in the new Japan the military had none of the special powers they had in prewar Japan and that with civilian control the military could be the servant, not the master of Japan. Mr. Yoshida would look up at me with twinkling eyes and an impish grin and say, "Yes, but they have guns, haven't they?"[61]

Allison assumed that Yoshida feared a resurgence of militarism of the prewar sort in Japan, and this may be correct. But it must be recalled that in the pre-surrender period Yoshida was profoundly suspicious of the ideological inclinations of the military. In the postwar period, such apprehensions had hardly abated; the National Police Reserve had been created, after all, only a little more than five years after the Konoe Memorial. When contrasted to the dramatic surge of radicalism in early occupied Japan, the perceived threat of communism may have receded by the time the NPR was formed. Yoshida's portrayal of Japan as a tranquil Eden was poetic license, however, for this was also the period when the conservatives began to speak more openly about the crisis of morals and values in Japan, the lack of "patriotism" and "love of the country." It was in this context that Amano Teiyū felt compelled to prepare his "Outline of Ethical Practice for the Japanese People" –and saw it ridiculed and repudiated; that recentralization of education and the regular police began; and that the government turned attention to creation of a new corpus of "peace-preservation" legislation. Official histories and personal recollections concerning the new military, as well as speeches at the time, strongly indicate that the major problem was seen to be that of *morale*, rather than technology or economics or organization. Yoshida could not trust his military partly because he was not sure *on whom* they might turn their guns; and until the crisis of ideology and morale had been surmounted, it seemed folly to plunge headlong into massive recruitment.[62]

Certainly some of Yoshida's key advisers did not believe that the Red star over Japan was receding, and this was nowhere more vividly expressed than by Kimura Tokutarō. Kimura served as attorney general in the first Yoshida cabinet, before being purged; upon being depurged, he returned to Yoshida's side. His ties with the right-wing underground were extensive, and his vision of the situation in Japan in the early 1950s was almost an update of the Konoe Memorial. Kimura believed that a communist-led insurrection was imminent in Japan, and that "the Reds have even penetrated the National Police Reserve, and in the eventuality of a revolution the reserve cannot be depended upon." His proposed solution to this crisis was the creation of a clandestine "Patriotic Anti-Communist Drawn-Sword Militia" (Aikoku Hankyō Battōtai), to consist of some 200,000 vigilantes, mobilized within the traditional right-wing strata of gangsters, gamblers, and small vendors (*tekiya*). Kimura went so far as to promise government support for such a project, and his projected front group, the Japanese Youth Guidance Association (Nihon Seishōnen Zendō Kyōkai), was inaugurated in early 1951. The plan for a paramilitary of patriotic thugs was aborted when Yoshida refused even to consider the idea. This did not prevent the prime minister from appointing Kimura to his major advisory board on the "adaptation of democracy to actual conditions" shortly thereafter, however, and in 1952 Kimura was given the opportunity personally to eradicate "Red" thought in the new military. When the National Police Reserve was enlarged and reorganized as the National Safety Force, Yoshida appointed his vigilant colleague head of the new National Safety Agency.[63]

Yoshida's postwar policy of "go-slow rearmament" was reminiscent in some ways of his prewar philosophy of "go-slow imperialism." How he adhered to this after Japan regained its sovereignty is discussed in the following chapter, but several general observations may be appropriate here. To begin with, the policy was "moderate" primarily in comparison with Washington's reckless demands. By the end of the Yoshida era in 1954, Japan had an army, a small navy, and had just begun to create a separate air force. The designated overall personnel strength was 180,000, and the technology and training were sophisticated, because they were, of course, American. Under Yoshida, principles of civilian control and gradual expansion were emphasized, but this does not gainsay the fact that it was under Yoshida that Japan committed itself to remilitarization.

The question remains whether he had intended to do this from the start—whether he initially practiced an expedient "pacifism," all the while regarding disarmament and demilitarization as another occupation excess to be rectified when the time was ripe. In his later writings, Yoshida suggested that he had indeed manipulated the sorrows and hopes of a war-ravaged people and played a crafty game with Article Nine. His original position, he explained, had been dictated by political expediency: he deemed it necessary to erase the image of Japanese militarism in order to hasten Japan's return to the international community, and never envisioned "eternal" disarmament. Reliance upon others for one's own national security was "selfish"—and, once Japan had been restored to great-power status, could only be construed as a "deformity."[64] Article Nine thus simply offered a dramatic device through which to fashion a new image, and Yoshida's manipulation of this can be seen as the reverse side of his invitation of post-treaty U.S. bases. In considerable part, both endeavors originated as tactical approaches to attainment of an early peace: the bases to gain American support, professions of fidelity to Article Nine to encourage international as well as domestic support.

Retrospectively, it is possible to cite hedges in Yoshida's statements on disarmament. His early pronouncements, for example, were usually qualified by reference to a guarantee of future Japanese security through an international peace-keeping organization. In 1946 and early 1947, this coincided with the position of the Allied powers, who were then ostensibly considering the establishment of an internationally supervised twenty-five-year disarmament plan for Japan.[65] When the United Nations revealed itself to be scarcely less incohesive and ineffective than the League of Nations had been, and when intensification of the cold war eliminated even the remotest prospects of Great-Power cooperation in overseeing the security of a disarmed Japan, the escape clauses could be evoked. This provided the rationale for the bases agreement, and could be similarly applied to Japanese rearmament. In addition, Yoshida's resistance to Washington's rearmament proposals was couched, from the first confrontation just prior to the Korean War, in a temporal frame. He argued, first, that the Japanese economy could not *at that stage* withstand the strain of defense expenditures; and second, that while the Japanese people could be persuaded to accept American bases, however reluctantly, *blatant and all-out* rearmament would prove an irreparably divisive issue.[66]

Yet it is still possible that Yoshida was later overly generous in garnishing his early position with such cool calculation. There can be no doubt that he was deeply concerned with dispelling that simplistic belief in Japan's innate militarism of which MacArthur himself was a supreme exponent: the view that, "for centuries the Japanese people, unlike their neighbors in the Pacific basin—the Chinese, the Malayans, the Indians and the Whites—have been students and idolaters of the art of war and the warrior caste."[67] While Yoshida seized upon Article Nine to repudiate this peculiar variant of condescending culturalism, however, to all outward appearances he also imbibed some of the more idealistic draughts of MacArthur's perspective. It may be worth recalling that Yoshida's prewar career imbued him with no particular love for the military establishment as a whole, and well before the Manchurian Incident he had criticized the military's transgression into policy-making and contribution to the scourge of "double and triple diplomacy." At the same time, he had displayed a selective susceptibility to military charisma, and it may not be unreasonable to conjecture that MacArthur's lofty early visions of a pacifist Japan had some influence on Yoshida. The ideal of permament disarmament did receive some positive support within conservative circles at an early stage of the occupation, among others from another military figure Yoshida greatly esteemed. In early 1946, former admiral Suzuki Kantarō, who negotiated the Japanese surrender as prime minister and had been Yoshida's teacher at the Gakushūin four decades earlier, evoked traditional wisdom, here with a strong Taoist imprint, to express the realism of idealism: "There are many who are concerned about the renunciation of war in Article Nine," Suzuki declared, "but since ancient times there is a saying that softness overcomes hardness, gentleness is the correct path, toughness is the road to death. Article Nine expresses that point, and I hold it in great respect."[68]

In his public statements prior to 1950, Yoshida expressed this sentiment as strongly as any other Japanese figure. And this was not necessarily incompatible with his idealization of the era of the Anglo-Japanese alliance—not, that is, if one accepts the fact that prior to the Korean War Yoshida seems to have believed that he could have his new bilateral alliance without rearming. If this was a game of deception, it was skillfully and cynically played. If not, then the early ideals proved tragically illusive. For, whatever his initial intentions and expectations, Yoshida came to exemplify both the hope and denigration of a noble ideal.

The impression that remains is a curious combination of decisiveness and ambiguity. Yoshida was neither a suave nor an eloquent man, and in his professional dealings with Westerners he often conveyed a bewildering image of whimsy, frivolity, and mulishness. Ambassador Grew never quite managed to pin Yoshida down even after a decade of acquaintance prior to Pearl Harbor, and the

British expressed similar vexation during the protracted "secret Yoshida-Eden talks" of 1936 and 1937. In the postwar period, American officials such as Dulles, Sebald, and a variety of military officers were treated to the same distracting experience, and on no occasions more vividly than those where the rearmament issue was concerned. Public courtesies aside, it is doubtful if any of these men would have described Yoshida in private as a sophisticated negotiator, but once the die was cast, after June 25, 1950, he knew his own mind and, where Japanese rearmament was concerned, more or less had his way. In Kowalski's very knowledgeable opinion, Yoshida's influence was decisive in restraining the pressures for more rapid remilitarization which emanated from both American civilian and military officials and some of his own Japanese military advisers.[69] The issue, in Yoshida's view, was no longer rearmament per se, but the *pace and appearance* of rearmament, and if his style of exposition lacked the legalistic finesse of a Dulles, his personal confidence was probably comparable and his premises were less fanatic. The result was moderate rearmament—but also creeping rearmament, mendacity in the Diet, and a perversion of the constitution. "Realism" to some, but to others a tragic prelude to sovereignty.

CHINA AND THE GHOSTED LETTER

It has been suggested here, among other things, that Yoshida viewed the present partly through the past. This was natural, and done in a selective and flexible manner. Where Japan in the international political economy was concerned, there were two sides to the lesson Yoshida drew from recent history, however, and only one of these was accommodated in the postwar settlement. Thus, the postwar relationship with the United States could be welcomed as a kind of reinvocation of the relatively prosperous period of early twentieth-century imperialism, when Japan had enjoyed the military guarantee of the alliance with Great Britain. The separate peace, on the other hand, did violence to the crucial other side of "traditional diplomacy" by forcing Japan to become isolated from continental Asia. Prior to Japan's defeat, it was simply unthinkable that Japan could prosper without an intimate relationship with China, and Yoshida continued to believe this until the end of his premiership. Until close to the very end of the occupation, he and his colleagues looked forward to the resumption of meaningful Sino-Japanese relations—only to find this beyond their reach. The old historical relationship could not be resuscitated in however benign a form, and in the eyes of the Yoshida conservatives this was due more to political myopia in Washington than to the political radicalization of China itself.

On the eve of the San Francisco Peace Conference, Yoshida met Secretary of State Dean Acheson for the first time. "Responding to a question about Japan's future relations with China," Acheson recalled, "I urged that the Prime Minister relegate a matter of such importance to Japan to deliberate study and careful decision after the conference and conclusion of the treaty, with which he agreed."[70] Yoshida agreed readily, for he strongly desired to keep his options open concerning future ties with China; and, as Acheson's statement indicates, he was led to believe he would be allowed to do so.

This hope and expectation were quickly dispelled. The secretary of state's personal views on China were not shared by the congressional majority in McCarthyist America, and within a week after the peace conference the Senate informally expressed its expectation that Japan would pledge opposition to Communist China; the Senate, of course, was entrusted with ratifying the treaty of peace. In December 1951, the options were closed with the penning of the famous "Yoshida Letter," whereby the prime minister gave assurances that his government had "no intention to conclude a bilateral treaty with the Communist regime of China." The Yoshida Letter was made public in mid-January 1952, shortly before Senate committee hearings on the peace and security treaties were convened. During the same month, the Yoshida government also formally confirmed its intention to adhere to the rigid embargo lists prescribed by the United States for China and the communist countries under the Battle Act of 1951.[71] In February, peace negotiations were initiated with the Nationalist government in Taiwan, and on April 18, the same day the general peace treaty came into effect, Japan signed a separate treaty with Chiang Kai-shek's routed regime. This commitment to the containment and isolation of the People's Republic was to persist for two decades.

The circumstances surrounding the Yoshida Letter involved domestic politics as well as foreign policies in both the United States and Japan, and reflected tensions not only between these two countries, but also between the United States and Great Britain. The problem naturally originated in the existence of Communist and Nationalist regimes, each claiming to be the sole legitimate government of China, and had come to the fore—but been left ostensibly unresolved—prior to the San Francisco Conference. In drafting the peace treaty, the United States included the Kuomintang regime in its consultations, and the final treaty reportedly was viewed favorably by the Nationalist government.[72] As early as November 1950, however, Dulles reported to MacArthur that the Allies were "almost equally divided as between Communist and Nationalist Chinese participation" in the forthcoming conference,[73] and disagreement on this matter was especially vigorous between Washington and London, which had recognized the People's Republic early in 1950. In June 1951, after a meeting between Dulles and Foreign Secretary Herbert Morrison failed to resolve the impasse over Chinese representation, it was announced that neither Chinese government would be invited to the San Francisco Conference. It was Britain's understanding at this time that Japan would make no move toward either Peking or Taipei until after the peace treaty came into effect. In the months following the September conference, the British representative in Tokyo, Sir Esler Dening, endeavored to press the case for recognition of Peking upon Yoshida. The Yoshida Letter of December closed the door on the British position, and was attacked in London as a gross breach of faith on the part of the United States, which was correctly seen as having pressured Yoshida to take this action.[74]

Yoshida was no stranger to the problem of friction within the

Anglo-American camp. His activities as ambassador to London in 1936–1938 had been plagued by disagreements between the two powers. And, within a general "pro-Western" orientation, his own sympathies and proclivities still tended toward Anglophilism. As a good "realist," Yoshida played to the strongest hand, which after 1945 was unmistakably American—but the irritation this caused Britain disturbed him, and beyond this he believed that British policy concerning China was simply wiser than that of the United States. He expressed this with frankness (and a good measure of old imperial arrogance) in his memoirs, published in 1957:

> It is the British and Japanese, with many years of accumulated experience in the problems of China, who best understand the psychology of the Chinese people. To tell the truth, America has not reached the point of truly knowing China. It can be said that the policies which America has adopted toward China in the postwar period have been almost a total failure.[75]

Yoshida's disenchantment with U.S. China policy and his greater esteem for the British perspective are well known. Yet the situation was more complex than a matter of "accumulated experience" and "knowing China." Great Britain's motives in urging Japanese recognition of Peking rested less on abstract historical and psychological rumination than on solid considerations of self-interest. And, while Yoshida was more sympathetic to the British position than to the American, there is no evidence that prior to the Yoshida Letter he actually intended to recognize Peking as the sole legitimate government of China once Japan had attained sovereignty.

The undercurrent of tension and disagreement that existed between the United States and Britain concerning the future role of Japan in Asia is one of the interesting sub-themes in the study of occupied Japan. Its wellspring was economic: in British eyes, American projections concerning Japan's reconstruction and major role in a new, anti-communist co-prosperity sphere in Asia threatened Britain's own trade interests, particularly in the subcontinent. The U.S. policy after 1950 of encouraging Japan's economic integration with south and southeast Asia posed a serious challenge to the sterling bloc; and, if Japan were isolated from China, and thereby forced into an even more intensified economic drive to the south, the commercial threat to Britain would become correspondingly greater.[76]

Such premonitions had historical echoes Yoshida could not have failed to perceive, for his own dismal term as ambassador to London had been preoccupied with bloc economies and savage commercial conflicts of a comparable sort (with the notable difference that on the earlier occasion the British goal had been to get Japan less, rather than more, entrenched in China). While his belief that Japan could not survive economically without substantial relations with the Asian mainland was quite apparent, however, Yoshida's actual plans concerning future relations with China in the months immediately preceding and following the San Francisco Conference are not entirely clear—most probably because he had not resolved his position in his own mind.

Dulles, Okazaki Katsuo, and others subsequently argued that even prior to the peace conference the Yoshida cabinet was inclined to establish relations with the Kuomintang regime. A basic summation of the Sino-Japanese problem prepared by Dulles in January 1952, for example, emphasizes that, on August 6, 1951, Yoshida assured Dulles by letter that Japan had no intention of concluding a bilateral treaty with the Communists.[77] Yet Dulles's own files contain an apparent contradiction to this in the form of a letter from Yoshida, dated August 4, requesting a minor revision of the draft peace treaty on the grounds that the San Francisco settlement might become the model "in the event Japan should conclude a bilateral treaty" with Communist China or the Soviet Union. The point in question concerned repatriation, and Yoshida explained his request in these terms:

> They [families, relatives, and friends of unrepatriated Japanese] are apprehensive that if the Soviet Union and Communist China, with both of whom the repatriation question is involved, should propose to conclude a bilateral treaty which is identical with the present treaty with no provision for the repatriation of prisoners of war and civilian detainees, Japan might be obligated to accept it unconditionally, being

> in no position to insist upon the inclusion of provisions concerning the return of prisoners of war and civilian detainees still held by these countries.

Dulles accepted Yoshida's proposed revision, which appeared in the San Francisco Treaty as Chapter III, Article 6, Section (b), and on August 18 received a letter from Yoshida warmly thanking him for his understanding of Japan's concerns.[78]

The ink was scarcely dry on the San Francisco Treaty before Yoshida was made aware that in the American political game there were in fact no genuine options where China was concerned. On September 12, four days after the conclusion of the conference, Japan was sucked into the sodden bog of McCarthyism and the "loss of China" frenzy. This took the form of a brief letter to the president drafted by William Knowland (who had also spearheaded the congressional attack on the economic-deconcentration program in 1947–1948), and signed by fifty-six senators within a whirlwind 24-hour period of circulation. The letter declared that "prior to the admission of the Japanese Treaty to the Senate, we desire to make it clear that we would consider the recognition of Communist China by Japan or the negotiating of a bilateral treaty with the Communist regime to be adverse to the best interests of the people of both Japan and the United States." The letter was signed by senators such as Wayne Morse and Paul Douglas as well as the more familiar supporters of McCarthyism and the China Lobby, and Knowland later observed that the number of signatures would have been far greater had more time been spent in solicitation. He was undoubtedly correct, as testified by the Senate vote of 91–0 against admission of the People's Republic to the United Nations.[79]

Yoshida's talent in self-contradiction was not slight, and since the creation of the National Police Reserve in 1950 he had been having a field day with Article Nine and the rearmament issue. The China quandary inspired him to new heights. In late October 1951, he informed the lower house that Japan desired relations with the Kuomintang, and diplomatic relations with the communist countries were impossible. And he informed the upper house that his government was willing to deal with the communists; if Peking so desired, Japan would even consider setting up an Overseas Agency, the highest form of diplomatic mission possible under the occupation, in Shanghai.[80] The following month, Yoshida conveyed word to the Kuomintang ambassador to the United States that Japan would be willing to enter into "limited friendly" relations with the Nationalists.[81]

These statements caused confusion in Japan and consternation in Washington, where they were taken as an indication that Yoshida had not appreciated the import of the Knowland petition. The message that he had no genuine choice in the matter was thus conveyed to him personally in mid-December by a formidable mission consisting of Dulles and Senators John Sparkman and H. Alexander Smith. The two senators, Democrat and Republican respectively, carried particular prestige because they sat on the Far Eastern subcommittee of the Senate Committee on Foreign Relations, which was to consider the peace and security treaties before they were submitted to the full Senate for ratification. This grim troika chastized Yoshida for his recent ambiguous statements, and Dulles later made this third-person capsule summary of the rather one-sided conversation:

> They called the attention of Prime Minister Yoshida to the fact that the statements of intention which he had made before the Diet were ambiguous in certain respects and that the United States Senate, particularly in considering the United States-Japan Security Treaty, would doubtless want to have a clarification of Japan's attitude. They pointed out that if the Security Treaty were ratified the United States would assume a certain responsibility for Japan's security; that the threat to that security came largely from Communist China, already convicted of military aggressor [*sic*] in nearby Korea, and that the Senate, before ratifying, would doubtless want to know whether or not Japan contemplated giving moral, political or economic support to the aggressor regime against which the United States would be expected to defend Japan. They also pointed out that the defense of Japan was related to that of Formosa which, with Japan, formed part of the strategic "offshore island chain."[82]

As subsequent Senate discussion indicated, the real import of the confrontation with Yoshida concerned U.S. ratification of the peace treaty, and thus Japanese sovereignty itself, rather than just the security treaty. Yoshida, Dulles recorded, accepted the "propriety, indeed the inevitability, of these inquiries," and the Yoshida Letter ostensibly represented his own formal clarification of Japan's position. Dated December 24, four days after Dulles had departed, it read as follows:

> Dear Ambassador Dulles:
>
> While the Japanese Peace Treaty and the United States-Japan Security Treaty were being debated in the House of Representatives and the House of Councillors of the Diet, a number of questions were put and statements made relative to Japan's future policy toward China. Some of the statements, separated from their context and background, gave rise to misapprehensions which I should like to clear up.
>
> The Japanese Government desires ultimately to have a full measure of political peace and commercial intercourse with China which is Japan's close neighbor.
>
> At the present time it is, we hope, possible to develop that kind of relationship with the National Government of the Republic of China, which has the seat, voice and vote of China in the United Nations, which exercises actual governmental authority over certain territory, and which maintains diplomatic relations with most of the members of the United Nations. To that end my Government on November 17, 1951, established a Japanese Government Overseas Agency in Formosa, with the consent of the National Government of China. This is the highest form of relationship with other countries which is now permitted to Japan, pending the coming into force of the multilateral treaty of peace. The Japanese Government Overseas Agency in Formosa is important in its personnel, reflecting the importance which my Government attaches to relations with the National Government of the Republic of China. My Government is prepared as soon as legally possible to conclude with the National Government of China, if that Government so desires, a treaty which will reestablish normal relations between the two Governments in conformity with the principles set out in the multilateral treaty of peace. The terms of such bilateral treaty shall, in respect of the Republic of China, be applicable to all territories which are now, or which may hereafter be, under the control of the National Government of the Republic of China. We will promptly explore this subject with the National Government of China.
>
> As regards the Chinese Communist regime, that regime stands actually condemned by the United Nations of being an aggressor and in consequence, the United Nations has recommended certain measures against

> that regime, in which Japan is now concurring and expects to continue to concur when the multilateral treaty of peace comes into force pursuant to the provisions of article 5 (a)(iii), whereby Japan has undertaken "to give the United Nations every assistance in any action it takes in accordance with the Charter and to refrain from giving assistance to any state against which the United Nations may take preventive or enforcement action". Furthermore, the Sino-Soviet Treaty of Friendship, Alliance and Mutual Assistance concluded in Moscow in 1950 is virtually a military alliance aimed against Japan. In fact there are many reasons to believe that the Communist regime in China is backing the Japan Communist Party in its program of seeking violently to overthrow the constitutional system and the present Government of Japan. In view of these considerations, I can assure you that the Japanese Government has no intention to conclude a bilateral treaty with the Communist regime of China.
>
> Yours sincerely,
> SHIGERU YOSHIDA[83]

Dulles received this by diplomatic pouch on January 7, 1952, and it was released to the public on January 16. On January 21, brief committee hearings on ratification of the treaties were initiated in the Senate; final Senate approval came on March 20, by a vote of 66–10. In the interim, on February 20, formal peace negotiations between Japan and the Kuomintang were begun in Taipei.

Although the Yoshida Letter was not legally binding upon the Japanese government,[84] it is regarded as one of the major documents of the Yoshida era and is certainly one of the best known of Yoshida's personal statements. This is ironic, for the letter was actually written mostly by Dulles rather than Yoshida. The original draft was composed by the American emissary on December 17 and 18, and the next draft, following consultation with Yoshida, was again Dulles's own—hastily polished in the airport in Tokyo in the hour before Dulles's departure on December 20.[85] Dulles was, on this occasion, Yoshida's ghost—a not unprecedented experience for old "One Man," since his speech at the San Francisco Conference three months earlier had also been substantially rewritten by the Americans.[86] While Yoshida signed the letter with no outward show of protest, and even suggested toughening the language by reference to the purportedly threatening nature of the February

1950 Sino-Soviet pact, his concurrence was essentially a pragmatic and uncomfortable one. It placed Japan in an awkward position vis-à-vis Britain, aroused protest from virtually all sectors within Japan, and exposed an inherent contradiction between Yoshida's own watchwords of "pragmatism" and "diplomatic sense."

While Yoshida's apparent irresolution was the major spur behind the December confrontation, the persuasiveness of his American visitors was enhanced by two developments that occurred in November. The British Parliament ratified the peace treaty with Japan at the end of that month, permitting the United States to press for a Japan-Kuomintang accommodation without fear that this would adversely affect British deliberations on the treaty. And the United Nations rejected a Soviet proposal to discuss seating the People's Republic of China, which meant that the Kuomintang remained the nominal representative of China in the United Nations and, by virtue of its seat on the Security Council, could veto any later petition of Japan for admission to the international body. Yoshida's immediate priorities were clarified in this context: to gain U.S. ratification of the peace and security treaties, as well as later Nationalist Chinese support for admission to the United Nations, there seemed no choice but to enter into an agreement with the Kuomintang. But at the same time—and on this Yoshida remained adamant—he was not willing to recognize the Kuomintang as the sole legitimate government of China. He spelled this out before the House of Councillors on January 26, as preparations for formal talks with Taipei were getting underway: "To conclude a treaty with Taiwan does not mean that [the Kuomintang] will enter into a peace treaty with Japan as the representative of China. The Government of Taiwan holds actual authority of governance over a certain area, and we are bringing about a good-neighbor relationship with that area."[87]

When the treaty with the Chinese Nationalists was submitted to the Diet for ratification in May and June 1952, the Yoshida cabinet, not for the first time, proved incapable of speaking with one voice concerning exactly how it was to be interpreted. Several of the government's spokesmen argued that this constituted a total termination of the legal state of war with China, which ipso facto would imply that the Kuomintang constituted the sole legitimate government of China. On June 26, however, Yoshida himself reaffirmed in unmistakable terms that the scope of the treaty was limited:

> As a matter of principle, our government desires to establish a total good-neighbor relationship with China in the future. We concluded the treaty with the Nationalist Government as a first step in this direction, and in this sense the spirit of the Yoshida Letter has materialized. In essence, this treaty is a treaty with the government which presently rules Taiwan and the Pescadores, and in the future we desire to conclude an overall treaty. What kind of relationship we will enter into with the Communists hereafter must depend upon future developments. But unless Communist China changes its present ways, it will not be possible to enter into a treaty relationship.

The treaty was ratified in early July, and Yoshida appointed Yoshizawa Kenkichi, an old China hand from the days when Yoshida himself had been a diplomat in China, as ambassador to Taipei.[88] In theory—if not, as it turned out, in actual practice—Yoshida was still keeping his options open for future relations with the People's Republic.

The latter point was substantive, or seemed so at the time, and on this Yoshida was fortunate that Dulles was not in complete accord with the China Lobby. American pressure took the form of demanding Japanese relations with Taiwan and indefinite suspension of relations with the mainland, but it did not go so far as to require that the Yoshida government recognize the Kuomintang as the de jure government of all China. The possibility of future relations with Peking was vaguely suggested in the second paragraph of the ghosted letter, while the explicit qualification of Japan's recognition of the Nationalists was contained in the phrase stating that any bilateral treaty between Tokyo and Taipei would be "applicable to all territories which are now, or which may hereafter be, under the control of the Nationalist Government of China." The Japanese insisted upon incorporating this phrasing in the actual treaty between the two governments, and this became a focus of acrimonious debate in the negotiations which began in Taipei in February. On several occasions when his chief negotiator, Kawada Isao, appeared to be giving ground, Yoshida interceded to reaffirm the Japanese position of limited recognition. The bargaining position of the Nationalists was actually undercut by a development comparable to that which had helped pave the way for negotiations in the first place, that is, the prior British ratification of the San Francisco Treaty. When the U.S. Senate ratified the treaty on March 20, Chiang Kai-shek and the China Lobby had nothing more with which to threaten Japan.[89]

This success in theoretically preserving an option to establish relations with the mainland regime at some future date accorded with Yoshida's conviction that communism could not survive indefinitely in the Chinese setting, and this is often cited as an illustration of fundamental difference between Yoshida's outlook and that held by the United States and exemplified in the concept of monolithic communism. While Dulles did indeed stress "the impossibility of separating the Chinese and Soviet communist, at least for the predictable future," however, his professed vision of China's course in the more *indefinite* future actually was very similar to Yoshida's analysis. Testifying before the Senate Committee on Foreign Relations in January 1952, Dulles acknowledged that "it is obviously abnormal that Japan should be permanently divorced from the raw materials and the markets which are close at hand," and on several occasions stressed that "we should assume the impermanence, not the permanence, of the present Moscow-oriented rule of China." Indeed, Dulles argued this case in historical and psychological terms very similar to those employed by Yoshida:

> I can say to you with complete assurance that the best informed Japanese are totally convinced, as I think we are, that the alien doctrine of communism cannot permanently conquer the Chinese spirit or liquidate the innate individualism of the Chinese race. The Chinese nation will not permanently suffer the imposition of a tyranny which places it in the service of alien master.

Elsewhere, again like Yoshida, he called attention to the traditional dedication of the Chinese "to their families as the unit of highest value," and their historically demonstrated capacity to "absorb these alien doctrines that come, and are imposed on them from without." Churchill, Dulles noted, also shared these views.[90] Yoshida, in the final analysis, had very little to say about China, and communism in China, that was original or unacceptable to Dulles.

In theory, the Chinese *quid pro quo* through which Yoshida ensured American ratification of the peace and security treaties did not lock the door to future relations with Peking. In practice, it did. The limited treaty with Taipei in effect placed Japan in the position of accepting a "two-China" policy, which was anathema to the Peking regime until almost two decades later. More important, despite Dulles's sanguine anticipations concerning the inevitable dilution of communism in China, where immediate policy was concerned his position and that of the U.S. government was premised upon the belief that "we cannot expect that this change in China will take place automatically."[91] Isolation and economic strangulation were to be directed against the People's Republic by the capitalist countries in order to help the family system, innate individualism, and the Chinese spirit along. Japan was naturally expected to participate fully in this, and the concept of "U.S.-Japan economic cooperation" which was so heavily emphasized beginning in 1951 was in fact synonymous with economic containment of China. Where Yoshida differed from Dulles was in his belief that China could best be weaned from the communist attachment by being eased into, rather than excluded from, the international community.

This raises the question of the cards in the deck. If the Yoshida Letter was not legally binding, if Yoshida and indeed most Japanese believed that British policy toward China was more realistic than American, and if the imperatives of Japanese trade with the mainland were as compelling as many observers believed—then why did the Japanese government fail to adopt a more independent China policy once sovereignty had been restored? During the vigorous debate that took place on the floor of the U.S. Senate in mid-

March, there was in fact speculation that Japan, either under or after Yoshida, might venture to do precisely this.[92]

Several factors, however, worked against adoption of an independent or even quasi-independent Japanese China policy. The conservative Japanese governments professed a sense of obligation to the Kuomintang regime, which under Chiang Kai-shek had adopted an exceptionally conciliatory policy toward Japan on such critical issues as reparations, war criminals, and maintenance of the emperor. Under prevailing circumstances, moreover, the Peking regime on its part did not greatly encourage Japanese overtures. In addition, Japan eventually did develop adequate alternatives to the continental resources and market. And, most decisively, the United States rather than China held the key to Japanese economic growth in the form of special military procurements, investment capital, "international" loans, military aid, access to the most modern industrial technology, access to essential raw materials, support in such critical international agreements as GATT (General Agreement on Trade and Tariffs), and so forth. Much of this pressure–isolation from China as a *precondition* for economic favors from the United States–was formally prescribed and structured by the 1951 Battle Act (Mutual Defense Assistance Control Act), under which an embargo was imposed upon shipment of "strategic" items to the "Soviet bloc." This act was frequently evoked in Senate discussions of the Japanese peace and security treaties, and its bearing upon Japan's future relations with China was spelled out clearly by Dulles at this time:

> Some people seem to think that [the Yoshida] letter is determinative on the trade between China and Japan. Nothing could be more false than that assumption. The question of trade between Japan and China is governed by the provisions of the [Battle] act which are the conditions under which the United States gives the military, financial, and economic aid which Japan will be receiving. . . . [T]rade with the Communist area . . . is foreclosed not by Japan's policy in regard to Formosa, but by the provisions of the Battle Act.[93]

Subsequently, Japan was forced to adhere to the even more

extensive embargo list prescribed for China under the secret "CHINCOM" mechanism, first established in September 1952.[94] Thus, while the limited treaty with Taipei may have been the price paid for sovereignty, Japan's continued isolation from the People's Republic of China became the ongoing price demanded for continued access to the bounty of the global capitalist system dominated by the United States. This had little to do with whether or not Peking "changed its ways," and much to do with whether or not the United States changed its obsessive policy of containment, which did not occur until 1971.

The fear that Japan could not prosper without close relations with China proved ephemeral. The impression of subordinate independence which Yoshida's China policy symbolized endured, for the issue was as political and psychological as it was economic. In a poll conducted in May 1952, only 11 percent of those questioned approved of the failure to have relations with Communist China, while 57 percent agreed the situation should be rectified.[95] The inability of Yoshida and his successors to alter this situation became an inescapable symbol of Japan's inability to pursue an autonomous foreign policy. Under later cabinets this led to the so-called principle of separating "economics" and "politics" in international affairs (*seikei bunri*)—a deceptive phrase, since economic expansion is hardly apolitical, and since the arena of such activity remained largely defined by the containment policy. One consequence of this legacy, in any case—and an ironic one for an avowed "diplomatist" such as Yoshida—was to diminish the role and prestige of the Foreign Ministry. For the next several decades the diplomats of Kasumigaseki remained the translators, paraphrasers, and technicians of grand and gross strategies emanating from Washington, while decisions of consequence concerning the precise nature of Japan's "economic diplomacy" more often bore the seal of the Ministry of International Trade and Industry, the bureaucratic ally of big business in Japan.

ELEVEN

Cooperation and Conflict in the New Imperium

Slogans and idioms were signposts to the changing course of the occupation, although these varied with the speaker and were often wittingly or unwittingly misleading. In official U.S. parlance, occupation priorities turned from "reform" to "reconstruction" around 1948; the latter was described as necessary to preserve the accomplishments of the reformist phase. The Japanese more often used a different vocabulary: here early "democratization" was succeeded by a "reverse course" beginning around 1947–1948, which gave way to an even more coordinated "rectification-of-excesses" campaign from 1951.

The latter phrase was coined by the Yoshida conservatives and amounted, as they explained it, to "adapting democracy to actual conditions." Professor Tanaka Jirō, a specialist in administrative law appointed to Yoshida's first important advisory commission to review the gamut of occupation reforms in 1951, conveyed the realities of such adaptation in a later reminiscence. Tanaka was placed in charge of a subcommittee on administrative reform, and sincerely endorsed the proposed slogan of "democracy, economy, efficiency." When he naively raised the question of where the weight should be placed among these, his fellow committeemen told him there was no time for abstract discussion, and such matters could only be addressed as concrete cases arose. "But in the course of discussion," Tanaka recounted, "the demands of democracy were almost ignored, everything was economy, everything was efficiency. . . ."[1]

A comparable progression of slogans marked the process of remilitarization. Early ideals of "demilitarization" and "total and permanent disarmament" gave way to official expressions of the "right of self-defense" by early 1950, and by late 1952 to affirmation of the right to possess a "military without war potential." Concretely, the movement was from total disarmament to a nascent infantry disguised as "police" in 1950; to an army and navy under the rubric of "national safety forces" in 1952; and to an army, navy, and air force designated "self-defense forces" in 1954. There were no Japanese military personnel prior to August 1950, at which time the National Police Reserve was established with a complement of 75,000 men. This was increased to 117,590 military personnel in August 1952, and to 152,115 (with a larger *designated* complement) in July 1954.[2] Throughout all this, Article Nine, the no-war clause of the new constitution, remained unrevised.

These developments were inseparable from far-reaching changes in economic planning, and it was in this area that the interrelationship of domestic and global policy was most fully revealed. The vocabulary here moved from early professed ideals of "industrial demilitarization" and "economic democratization" to the vision of Japan as the "workshop" of Asia, as Dean Acheson phrased it as early as May 1947.[3] "Stabilization" and "reconstruction," "self-support" and "self-sufficiency" were the watchwords of the day from 1948, and these objectives became overriding after Joseph Dodge arrived in Japan at the beginning of 1949. As Finance Minister Ikeda Hayato informed the Diet, the "Dodge Line" was the first step to linking Japan to the international economy.[4]

There could be no disputing this, but it was hardly the whole of the story. Dodge's objectives were to curb Japan's rampant inflation and gear its industry to production for export, and the domestic political and economic implications of this were great. The Dodge Line demanded austerity in domestic consumption, curtailment of public works and services, sacrifice of "unrationalized" small and medium enterprises, restrictions on wage increases, extensive layoffs of workers, and repression of labor activism. What

Tanaka Jirō had perceived in his particular area of concern held true across the board: "democracy" remained a rhetorical staple, but "economy" and "efficiency" were the real touchstones of policy.

As it turned out, many of the slogans, policies, and projections of the Dodge Line also proved ephemeral, and the future structure of Japan's integration with the international economy did not really emerge until 1951. The new conceptualization was christened "U.S.-Japan economic cooperation," and was more militaristic and inflexible than Dodge or most observers had foreseen prior to the Korean War. In the postwar imperium as in the prewar empire, economic expansion and militarization were intertwined, with the notable difference that the United States played an exceptionally great role in shaping the contours of the new imperium. The blueprint of "U.S.-Japan economic cooperation" originated in Washington and projected a new capitalist bloc economy in Asia. It was accompanied by continued U.S. pressure for rapid Japanese rearmament, as well as for Japan's *industrial* remilitarization, and such pressure was partially structured and formalized under the Mutual Security Assistance (MSA) agreement concluded between the two countries in 1954. On the Japanese side, the MSA arrangement was accompanied by passage of two basic "defense" laws which were to remain the legislative basis of Japanese remilitarization over the ensuing decades.

Yoshida staked his reputation, and indeed his political life, on the emerging structure of military and economic cooperation. In the end, it cost him the premiership, but the legacy survived. If this was contradictory, it was then all the more apt as a symbol of the U.S.–Japan relationship itself, for until the end of the Yoshida era the cooperative framework remained riddled with tensions. To a great extent, these were a continuation of disagreements concerning economic and military priorities which had emerged between the two countries during the latter stages of the occupation. If anything, Yoshida's skeptical appraisal of American "diplomatic sense" grew stronger during his final years as prime minister of a sovereign Japan—yet never to the point of threatening to disrupt the basic structure of the alliance. The critical areas of disagreement, as well as agreement, between the two powers emerged with particular clarity in the autumn of 1953, during the "Ikeda-Robertson" talks in Washington, and again during the final months of 1954, when Yoshida personally journeyed to the United States in a vain endeavor to encourage a less overbearing and militaristic U.S. foreign policy and thereby to shore up his own plummeting political prestige at home.

These somewhat gingerly endeavors to handle the nettle of subordinate independence coincided with the comeback of the Hatoyama group and return of former purgees to all walks of Japanese life. Yoshida was a busy man indeed during these years, bouncing like a ball in a game dominated by conservative players positioned in both Washington and Tokyo. His most effective critics at home represented big business and conservative political rivals to the "Yoshida School" and "Yoshida faction," and personified ideological paradoxes as convoluted as those that had plagued Yoshida on the Japanese side during the war years, and on the American side during the early occupation. The anti-Yoshida coalition was led by figures from America's old discarded list of Japanese warmongers–ex-purgees and former indicted war criminals–who sided with the United States in criticizing Yoshida's policy of go-slow rearmament, while at the same time joining the Japanese left in criticizing Yoshida's relegation of Japan to subordinate independence. Domestic tensions thus meshed with international tensions, for Yoshida was forced to compromise with the domestic right not merely to stave off the wolves at the prime minister's door, but also in order to be able to present at least the appearance of conservative unity when confronting the United States. By December 1954, the personal game was over. Yoshida had been essentially repudiated in Washington, and totally repudiated at home.

"STABILIZATION," "ECONOMIC COOPERATION," AND THE NEW BLOC ECONOMY

From the outset it was generally clear for whom the workshop was to work, and it was not for Japan alone. In mid-1949, Dodge spoke of "a growing realization that Japan is an important border area in the world-wide clash between Communism and Democracy, and that only a self-supporting and democratic Japan can stand fast against the Communists,"[5] and in January 1950 he informed the National Advisory Council in Washington that "it is probable that the development of our future Far Eastern policy will require the use of Japan as a springboard and source of supply for the extension of further aid to the Far Eastern areas."[6] Before the Korean War—as the meeting among Yoshida, Dulles, and MacArthur on June 22, 1950 revealed—it had been proposed that Japanese industry be remilitarized for the cold war.[7] Yet economic remilitarization was not part of the original Dodge Line, and Dodge himself initially did not envision locking Japan to the dollar. He acknowledged that the occupation had tied Japan almost exclusively to the U.S. economy, but regarded this as abnormal. "That is not the historical pattern of Japanese foreign trade and may not and probably should not be the pattern of the longer term future," he stated in his first major public pronouncement in March 1949.[8] On another occasion, he declared that "the question is where can goods be sold abroad and where can necessary food and other materials be found, other than in the United States. This means more imports from sources other than from the United States and new markets for exports other than to the United States."[9] Prior to 1950, Dodge does not appear to have excluded the possibility, even necessity, of substantial Japanese trade with China—and this of course was in accord with the perceptions of the Japanese.[10]

The Dodge "disinflation" did not survive the Korean War boom in Japan, nor did the slogan of Japanese economic self-sufficiency. By 1951, under the new rubric of "U.S.-Japan economic cooperation," Japan's economic growth was tied to U.S. economic and military programs, and its external economic expansion was diverted away from continental Asia—away from China—and toward a triangular integration with the United States and southeast Asia.[11] Coincident with these developments, the Japanese government reached a clear and seemingly tardy understanding that future Japanese economic growth would require promotion of the machine and chemical industries rather than the light-industrial sector. This was revealed in January 1951, when the government rejected a report prepared by the Deliberation Committee for a Self-Sufficient Economy (Jiritsu Keizai Shingikai), an advisory board created by Yoshida in August 1950 and composed of some forty-five representatives from both bureaucratic and private circles. The report emphasized expansion of textile production, and was immediately discarded by the government as bearing "little relation to reality."[12] It also became understood that, for the foreseeable future, and irrespective of the situation in Korea, a major portion of Japan's industrial production would be military-related—serving the United States, Japan's own new military, and eventually the other counterrevolutionary regimes of Asia. As a matter of policy rather than fortuitous war boom now, the workshop was to maintain the characteristics of an arsenal.[13]

Where post-treaty U.S. bases in Japan symbolized the military aspect of subordinate independence, the dollar nexus of "U.S.-Japan economic cooperation" symbolized its economic dimension —or, more accurately, the inseparability of military and economic subordination. This was the argument advanced by progressive and leftist critics of the ruling groups, and the confidential papers of the architects of "U.S.-Japan economic cooperation" confirm the accuracy of the critique. This can be seen in a negative way in the fact that the slogan of "self-sufficiency" virtually disappeared from official documents after early 1951, but the evidence is positive as well. In November 1951, even while Yoshida continued to deny that Japan itself was rearming, Ichimada Hisato, governor of the Bank of Japan, reported to the Americans that "the economic position of Japan is fundamentally one of rearmament."[14] During the same month, Dodge bluntly informed representatives of the Ministry of International Trade and Industry that "Japan can be independent politically but dependent economically."[15] U.S. memoranda from this period contain innumerable references to the necessity of fully persuading the Yoshida group that Japan had no choice but to *fit in* with the American program. Autarky in the traditional sense may have been repudiated for Japan. Bloc economies, weighted toward potential war, obviously had not.

Like post-treaty bases, like rearmament, and like industrial remilitarization, the concept of triangular integration was on the boards before war occurred in Korea; the war ensured and hastened its finalization as policy.[16] In cold-war terminology, this was described as Japan's integration into the "free world," its democratic commitment to the "containment" of communism. The old roots of this new imperium, however, were revealed in the ease with which jargon from the era of Imperial Japan became fashionable once more. Japan again became described as the "stabilizing power" in Asia, and its projected arena of economic expansion and integration to the south was again accorded the felicitous label of a "co-prosperity" sphere.

These developments contributed to the progressive strengthening of big business and the conservative hegemony in Japan, and to Japan's gradual integration into the global capitalist economy. As such, they accorded with conservative goals. Yet, at virtually each stage in the unfolding of economic policy, the Japanese side voiced substantial criticism of U.S. policies and priorities, and the eventual conceptualization of "U.S.-Japan economic cooperation" proved no exception to this. The economic contours of the "new Japan," and of the new imperium, thus revealed in various ways the contradiction of conflict and cooperation within the emerging "Pacific partnership." This was a phenomenon natural to any power relationship, and it cannot be denied that the dimension of cooperation with the United States matured and solidified in the decades following the Yoshida era. The strains within the alliance nonetheless deserve attention, for they also persisted in various and changing form. They also were an occupation legacy to the postwar world.

Such disagreement was transparent during the first two years of the occupation. Although SCAP did address the problem of inflation and economic recovery in numerous papers and policies, it remains true that greater attention was given to "economic democratization"; stabilization and reconstruction took second place to this, and were not achieved. The thrust of conservative Japanese criticism of such reformist priorities is self-evident. In the succeeding period, disagreement over economic policy was more deliberately contained and camouflaged.

There was no political constituency in Japan, whether of left or right, that did not desire economic recovery. The issue lay rather in the manner, structure, and control of reconstruction, and the direction charted by the United States from 1948 most certainly served conservative capitalist interests; this was evident in the abandonment of economic deconcentration and parallel repression of labor. The *nature* of the "stabilization" program imposed by the United States, however, was in considerable part both politically and economically unpalatable to Japan's leaders. Thus, in 1949 Yoshida solemnly and dutifully stated that he and his party endorsed the Dodge Line "from the bottom of our heart,"[17] while his lieutenants were simultaneously informing Dodge that the severity of his cure threatened to kill the patient. While welcoming the restoration of trade and further restraints on labor and the left, the ruling party was acutely sensitive to the political liabilities of a policy of general austerity.[18] Beyond this, Japan's own economic planners believed that Dodge's exceptionally conservative fiscal policies of "disinflation" through tight credit and immediate creation of a balanced budget threatened to plunge the country into severe recession.

These internal criticisms emerged immediately after Dodge's arrival in early 1949 and grew in strength until the Korean War. The Economic Stabilization Board (ESB), for example, conveyed its critique of the Dodge Line in lengthy reports and pithy images. It argued that severe and immediate "stabilization" was incompatible with simultaneous reconstruction, and that what Dodge called "disinflation" threatened to turn into outright and crippling deflation. At one point Dodge was accused of asking Japan to make a suit without providing enough fabric to do so. More colorfully, the ESB compared the stabilization program to asking "a juggler to take out a rabbit before the audience while furnishing him with a top-hat which has room only for containing a rat."[19] By spring of 1950, most observers in Japan including business and the conservative government were convinced that their worst fears were being realized. While Dodge and his supporters in SCAP's Economic and Scientific Section naturally discerned positive trends in the economy, the more prevailing view of the situation was aptly summarized in the respected "Asahi Yearbook" (*Asahi Nenkan*) for 1950:

> Under the drastic methods of the Dodge Line, the majority of enterprises, centering on the basic industries, were virtually strangled. Trade was the last resort, but foreign demand for commodities was also affected by the global recession, and thus bankruptcy occurred throughout middle and small enterprises as a result of rapid increases in inventories, accumulated goods, and unpaid accounts. Industry was being driven into an historic recession. More specifically, the shock was especially severe on those key industries in the Japanese economy such as heavy industry, machinery, and chemicals, which carried the burden for the future. Personnel readjustment and rationalization on the labor front for the purpose of strengthening labor had reached its ultimate limits. The only remaining possibility whereby Japan could meet international price levels lay in the improvement of plant and equipment and introduction of technology, but with the exception of certain enterprises, there was little progress in this direction for both financial and international reasons. By June 1950, among the holdings in these sectors on the Tokyo and Osaka stock exchanges there were scarcely any which exceeded par value, thus presenting a pitiable spectacle.[20]

In the briefer summation of a later commentator, "the over-all economic outlook for Japan was dismal, to put it mildly; industries were collapsing one after another and unemployed workers were roaming the streets."[21] By March 1950, the government reported that almost one-million persons were applying to its various public employment agencies, and the great majority could not be accommodated. In April, it was calculated that minor incidents of violence deriving from the economic crisis had increased eighteen times over the number reported in December 1949. The official history of the Yoshida cabinets described the situation as portending the emergence of a "lumpen proletariat."[22] Thus, on the eve of the Korean War, it appeared that the vaunted program of stabilization and reconstruction was producing results entirely the opposite of those intended: the capitalist economy remained in crisis, while the working class seemed, once again, on the verge of radicalization. These developments coincided, of course, with the controversy over the separate peace.

It was in this setting that Finance Minister Ikeda led a delegation to Washington in May 1950 to convey Japanese opinions on the Dodge Line, and used the occasion to tender the offer of post-treaty U.S. military bases.[23] Before the test of fiscal conservatism could be played out, however, the Korean War began, rendering the Dodge Line passé and ushering in the real beginning of Japan's postwar economic recovery. As previously noted, Yoshida described the war as "a gift of the gods," and it was indeed the sort of tainted boon to imperial destiny with which he was well familiar. One is reminded of the opening sentence of his 1928 memorandum: "During the holy Meiji period, whenever there was financial depression or severe political struggle, there invariably arose momentous incidents involving the outside world. . . ."[24] The ensuing war boom derived almost entirely from Japanese military-related production for the United States—fostering industrial remilitarization and heightening the pattern of dollar dependency, while at the same time, to Dodge's chagrin, enabling the Japanese to revert to the more inflationary policies they had always supported.[25]

If the symbiosis of war and economic spurt was a recurrent phenomenon in the history of Japanese capitalism, however, this also had a complementary and negative side. Invariably, the bubble burst. Recessions followed the war booms, and popular unrest commonly accompanied the recessions. By early 1951, the Yoshida government was already anticipating an armistice in Korea and again viewing Japan's economic future with apprehension and great uncertainty. They looked for a bold solution from Washington, and were given, with minimal voice in the matter, the new concept of "U.S.-Japan economic cooperation." This program was intricate, and subject to refinement over a period of time, but in brief it linked Japan's future economic growth to two dubious and controversial policies: integration with southeast Asia and dependence upon U.S. aid, trade, and procurements programs that were overwhelmingly weighted toward military concerns.

"U.S.-Japan economic cooperation" was a misleading slogan on several accounts. It entailed "cooperation" on a blueprint drawn in Washington. It was inseparable from U.S. military policies. And it involved more than the two countries, being an endeavor to create an anti-communist capitalist bloc in Asia. On this latter point, it will be noted that there was an initial period of some ambiguity on the Japanese side insofar as future possibilities for trade with China were concerned. The general outline of the trilateral nexus emerged at the beginning of 1951, and was presented as an open and relatively coherent program in mid-year, shortly before the San Francisco Conference.[26] It was not until the end of 1951, however, that the Yoshida government really acknowledged that Japan would be severely and indefinitely restricted in future economic relations with China. Thus, during the early discussions of "U.S.-Japan economic cooperation" it was accepted that southeast Asia was to be of proportionately greater importance to Japan's external economic position than had been the case in the prewar years, but the fact that the subcontinent was in effect to take the place of China does not seem to have been faced squarely.

In the early post-occupation period, this among other issues became a source of friction between the Yoshida government and Washington, but the conclusion that southeast Asia was a poor substitute indeed for China was not reached idly or hastily by the Japanese. Ideally, it could be and was argued that the Japanese and southeast Asian economies seemed complementary: Japan could supply capital goods and investment capital to the subcontinent and receive critical raw materials in return, with U.S. aid and trade adjusted to boost and balance off the exchange. The first Japanese economic mission to southeast Asia took place under SCAP leadership in mid-1951, and trade between the two areas was vigorously promoted during the final phase of the occupation. The Ministry of International Trade and Industry devoted a great portion of its energies to exploring the possibilities of long-range economic integration with southeast Asia, and in January 1952 Yoshida appointed a top-level Supreme Council on Economic Cooperation (Keizai

Kyōryoku Saikōkai) with the charge of studying the triangular nexus.[27] On the U.S. side, the matter was given high priority by both SCAP's Economic and Scientific Section and policy-makers in Washington. The result of these intense endeavors was an outpouring of studies ranging from grand overviews to detailed investigative reports on the specific, usually extractive, enterprises in south and southeast Asia in which Japan was most interested.[28] For a while, the Yoshida group also explored the possibility of penetrating the subcontinent obliquely, with the assistance of the Chiang Kai-shek regime, by operating through the Overseas Chinese community. The stratagem collapsed when the Overseas Chinese proved more sympathetic to the People's Republic of China.[29]

When the occupation ended in April 1952, Japan was still riding the tide of the war boom, and still hopeful that the economic-cooperation program held the key to future economic growth. The Yoshida government repressed its chagrin concerning the China solution and proclaimed allegiance to the American scenario for a new co-prosperity sphere; and it well understood what this was to entail. Two confidential documents prepared in February 1952 make this clear. On February 1, Joseph Dodge finalized a much belabored memorandum for the U.S. government entitled "United States-Japan Economic Cooperation in the Post-Treaty Era," which contained this summation of Washington's expectations of Japan:

> There will be substantial reliance on Japan in the post-treaty period for
> a. Production of goods and services important to the United States and the economic stability of non-Communist Asia
> b. Cooperation with the United States in the development of the raw material resources of Asia
> c. Production of low cost military material in volume for use in Japan and non-Communist Asia
> d. Development of Japan's appropriate military forces as a defensive shield and to permit the redeployment of United States forces.[30]

In this same memorandum, Dodge also referred critically to the Yoshida government's expectations of American generosity, and implicitly underscored what critics of the "economic-cooperation" policy had in mind when they spoke of subordinate independence.

The Japanese approach to the problem, Dodge stated, "is inclined to be an expectation that the United States will plan and blueprint the needs of Japan and then fit the economy of the United States into those needs—instead of the reverse." Be that as it may, by this date the Yoshida government was under few illusions as to how it was expected to conform to the needs of the American economy. On February 12, Sutō Hideo, head of the ESB and one of the six members of the Supreme Council on Economic Cooperation, submitted a report entitled "Establishment of a Viable Economy and Promotion of Economic Cooperation" to the U.S. government. This was prefaced with the following general statement:

> 1. Japan shall establish a viable economy as quickly as possible by
>   a. Increasing production by utilizing her labor force and unutilized industrial capacity,
>   b. Promoting and tightening her economic cooperation with the United States, South East Asian countries and other democratic countries in order to contribute to their defense production and economic development and,
>   c. Assuring at the same time the volume of imports necessary for Japan.
>   d. Raising living standard,
>   e. Strengthening progressively her self-defense power.
> 2. Japan will vigorously implement the following measures along the lines mentioned above:
>   a. Japan will contribute to the rearmament plan of the United States, supplying military goods and strategic materials by repairing and establishing defense industries with the technical and financial assistance from the United States, and thereby assure and increase a stable dollar receipt.
>   b. Japan will cooperate more actively with the economic development of South East Asia along the lines of the economic assistance programs of the United States and the economic development of South East Asian countries and thereby increase the imports of goods and materials from this area and thereby improve the balance of sterling trade.
>   c. Japan will promptly increase the electric power supply, the shortage of which is proving to be the biggest bottleneck of the production increase necessary for such economic cooperation, with financial assistance from the United States.[31]

POST-OCCUPATION CONFLICT WITHIN THE COOPERATIVE FRAMEWORK

Stripped to barest bones, the U.S.-Japan relationship upon which Yoshida staked his reputation had two broad components: remilitarization under the security alliance and integration with the capitalist economies of the United States and south and southeast Asia. In the years following the occupation, it became apparent that the Yoshida government and the Eisenhower administration, while attentive to both dimensions, appraised and weighed them differently. As a consequence, the bilateral relationship developed in a manner that satisfied neither side.

The overriding concern of the Yoshida group was the shallowness of the Japanese economy, and from this perspective the basic problem of the alliance lay in the unfulfilled promises of "economic cooperation." "Normal" trade with the United States was grossly unbalanced and the Asian subcontinent remained unstable and underdeveloped. Japan continued to be heavily dependent upon U.S. procurement of war-related goods and services, and the government was deeply concerned that this critical dollar income might taper off before the trilateral nexus had been consolidated. In dealing with the United States, Yoshida's aides thus endeavored to focus discussions upon economic assistance to Japan and southeast Asia, rectification of overall trade mechanisms, and, for the interim at least, a guaranteed perpetuation of the procurements program. The key to stabilization of the Japanese economy, in this view, lay more in the international than domestic arena. And for the foreseeable future, Japan remained dependent not merely upon the good offices and good will of the United States, but upon America's extensive economic contribution to non-communist Asia.

Such reliance upon U.S. dollars as well as policy was one legacy of the occupation. In early 1951, Dulles's aide John Allison reported to the Far Eastern Commission that "there were those in Tokyo so concerned about the future of their economy that they tried to persuade Mr. Dulles to give a written agreement to underwrite Japan for an indefinite period." Dulles responded that

"Japan would have to stand on its own feet," but in the eyes of American policy-makers the Yoshida government until the end remained inclined to look to U.S. subsidy and largesse instead of adopting essential, if politically uncomfortable, austerity measures.[32] Thus when Ikeda journeyed to Washington in late 1953 to plead for understanding of the problems of Japan's "shallow economy," Joseph Dodge subjected him to essentially the same lectures on fiscal responsibility he had first delivered in 1949. A year later, Yoshida's spokesmen returned with a similar morose portrayal of the structural weaknesses of Japan's "semi-synthetic prosperity," and again the Americans responded with admonitions concerning the virtues of austere domestic housekeeping.[33]

Throughout this period, American officials continued to give vigorous vocal support to Japan's integration with non-communist Asia. The economic importance of southeast Asia to Japan, and Japan to southeast Asia, became a policy staple of the Eisenhower administration, and the fatal U.S. commitment to counterrevolution in the subcontinent frequently was justified in terms of preventing a situation in which Japan would be forced to "accommodate" to communism.[34] Yet Yoshida and his supporters came to entertain grave misgivings concerning the actual nature of America's contribution in this area. They criticized both the scope and mechanisms of U.S. aid and trade policies, and raised dire warnings about the consequences of Washington's unwillingness to mount an economic offensive in Asia comparable to that which had been directed toward Western Europe. Such criticism was conveyed on numerous occasions, most formally in the Ikeda-Robertson talks of October 1953 and in conjunction with Yoshida's personal visit to Washington in late 1954. On the latter occasion, the Japanese graphically revealed the extent to which they regarded U.S. economic policies as virtually tokenistic by proposing, to little avail, a "minimal" developmental program for non-communist Asia which would have entailed an annual dollar commitment ten times greater than that currently in effect.

U.S. policy-makers responded impatiently and sometimes peevishly to the "economics-first" policy of the Yoshida government, coupled as this was with what they regarded as prodigal practices and a supplicant's demeanor. The root of such irritation was not far to seek. Yoshida's priorities impeded progress in the area Washington regarded, above all others, as the pivot of the relationship: Japan's rapid military buildup and assumption of a forward role in Asian collective security. Allison, who became ambassador to Japan in April 1953, was more sympathetic to the Japanese government's position and trod an uneasy path between public apologetics and private remonstrance in this situation. "There was little to show that Washington read our messages very carefully," he wrote in reference to the situation in 1954, "or was seriously considering what Japan's future position in Asia should be other than as a safe base for American military activity. During the Dulles period economic and purely political activity took second place to the building up of a strong military base, which it was believed would deter further Communist expansion in Asia."[35]

The situation was easily susceptible to caricature. While the Japanese shuttled to Washington with armloads of economic position papers, Dulles regularly descended upon Asia like Mars to deliver statements concerning Japan's military responsibility as "the key country of Southeast Asia" [*sic*], or to bruit the possibility of a security pact "covering Japan, Korea, and Nationalist China."[36] Under the Eisenhower administration, which came into office in the wake of the cease-fire in Korea, strategies of "rollback" and "using Asians to fight Asians" were elucidated, and military-aid programs were revamped to give higher priority to Asia through the encouragement of indigenous anti-communist military establishments. This was pursued with conspicuous vigor in Korea, Indochina, and Taiwan, and the Japanese government was placed under immense pressure to undertake commensurate large-scale remilitarization. The prospect of a new Japanese military establishment, emerging full-blown from the brain of Washington, was alarming even to those Asian countries that were collaborating in the new U.S. strategy, although Dulles and his lugubrious chorus of American supporters tended to ignore this.[37] To critics on both the right and left in Japan, representing nationalistic as well as pacifistic outlooks, the new U.S. strategy could be construed as an attempt to develop Asian mercenaries to fight America's wars. During the final years of the Yoshida cabinets the phrase "war-loving America" gained currency in Japan, and even Yoshida's own aides acknowledged that this was more than groundless propaganda from the progressive camp.[38]

Yoshida was essentially satisfied with the military relationship as it stood; he regarded the security treaty as a guarantee of American protection under which industrial recovery could be pursued, with Japan slowly assuming a greater portion of the defense burden as economic and political conditions permitted. Even here, rearmament was still viewed less as an urgent military need than as a political and economic necessity. Only through expansion of the Japanese military could the political and social friction inevitable in maintenance of a huge foreign garrison on native soil be removed; thus bilateral discussions of remilitarization were always accompanied by Japanese requests for assurance that this would be coordinated with systematic withdrawal of U.S. forces from Japan. And only through rearmament could Japan gain the U.S. economic assistance it desired—a fact of life confirmed in the 1954 Mutual Security Assistance (MSA) agreement, which was the outstanding formal agreement enacted between the two countries in Yoshida's final years as premier. The MSA arrangement exemplified the full symbiosis of U.S. aid, trade, and military policies, for it placed agreements concerning such areas as foreign investment, patents and licenses, purchase of U.S. agricultural commodities, and "triangular trade transactions" under the roof of an aid program explicitly directed to the expansion of indigenous military forces.

To the Truman and Eisenhower administrations, the military status quo was anything but satisfactory. Just as Dodge's fiscal medicines continued to be prescribed for Japan's post-occupation economic maladies, so also the bloated Japanese military establishment Dulles had envisioned in 1950 remained the magic number for U.S. planners over the ensuing years. At the time Japan regained sovereignty, Washington actually hoped and expected that this could be attained quickly, and U.S. plans assumed a standing

Japanese army of between 325,000 and 350,000 men by March 1954—a fourfold expansion of pre-sovereignty strength in ground forces alone, with naval and air forces to be introduced alongside this. In December 1952, the State Department still calculated that this goal could be attained by March 1955.[39] The general public was made aware of these projections in July 1953, when Dulles stated in congressional testimony that the United States hoped Japan would eventually maintain ground forces of 350,000 men in ten divisions.[40]

In this situation, the prime minister was caught in a double bind. If U.S. bases in Japan posed a social irritant, indigenous remilitarization was even more politically volatile. While rearmament was a precondition for economic favors from Washington, moreover, Yoshida continued to believe that rapid and extensive rearmament would disrupt and distort Japan's fiscal and economic stabilization. General Matthew Ridgway later claimed that prior to termination of the occupation he had reached a personal agreement with Yoshida on the projected force level of a third of a million men.[41] In its concrete defense calculations, however, the Yoshida government never seriously considered this figure, and when Yoshida departed from the scene in December 1954, the *designated* overall military complement for ground forces stood at 180,000.

Yoshida's success in continuing to resist U.S. pressure for a larger force can be calculated as a personal victory in the exchanges between Tokyo and Washington. In the Japanese context, the expanded and reorganized defense structure was nonetheless a notable step in remilitarization, one Allison personally applauded as being "far ahead of Japanese public opinion."[42] At the end of the Yoshida era, the new forces were over twice as large as those existing when sovereignty was regained. They had been expanded to include naval and air branches. Their "mission" had been redefined in a manner that amounted to the formal christening of a bona-fide military establishment. Military expenditures had been established as a routine part of the annual budget, amounting to an impressive 19.3 percent of total expenditures in the transitional year of 1952, followed by 12 percent in 1953 and 13.3 percent in

1954.[43] The creation of a Safety Agency (Hoanchō) in 1952, moreover, was accompanied by initiation of an indigenous defense-production sector, with initial concentration upon production in such areas as military vessels, aircraft, small weapons, and parts of tanks.[44]

These developments left several problematic legacies to the post-Yoshida period. The constitution was subjected to further tortured reinterpretation, exacerbating political bipolarization (and, temporarily, conservative schism) and providing a symbolic focal point for subsequent political struggle. The legal framework for future military expansion was established in the "two defense laws" of 1954, which remained unrevised over the ensuing decades. The subordination of Japanese military policy to U.S. grand strategy—as well as to American hardware and technology—was consolidated. And, at the same time, a pattern of mild defiance of the United States in the military numbers game was staked out as virtually the only area in which Japan could lay feeble claim to pursuit of an "independent" policy. Although many of Yoshida's conservative opponents criticized his go-slow approach to rearmament, they themselves did not subsequently accelerate the pace of military personnel expansion in any dramatic way. The magic number remained unattained under the post-Yoshida conservative cabinets, and the alliance never ceased to be accompanied thereafter by a gnashing of teeth in Washington on this score.

What this revealed, however, was not so much the legacy of Yoshida's policy as the confirmation of his appraisal of the objective situation in Japan. It was his basic position that Japan *could* not remilitarize rapidly, and the ultimate impediment to rearmament—beyond economic capacity—was always popular sentiment. "Re-education" to instill a "defense consciousness" remained an obsession long after the Yoshida era, precisely because such indoctrination was not very effective. The belief that more precipitous rearmament would provoke popular upheaval continued to govern the Yoshida group, and as a matter of course this involved reconsideration of the constitutional inhibitions upon extensive remilitarization. In the Ikeda-Robertson talks of 1953, for example,

Ikeda informed the Americans that their projected force levels simply could not be implemented without constitutional revision, and this was politically out of the question for the foreseeable future. The constitution could be bent and distorted; breaking it entirely was another matter. In the final analysis, the force that ultimately restrained constitutional revision and remilitarization to the extent desired by Washington was not Yoshida, not the ruling conservatives, but the resistance of the Japanese people themselves to this extremity of "re-education" and "rectification of excesses."

While disagreements on economic and military priorities did not seriously jeopardize the alliance or weaken Yoshida's personal commitment to the San Francisco system, they did produce a relationship that was more frayed and frustrating than had been anticipated, and the resulting compromises left a sour aftertaste on both sides. This was compounded by the poorly disguised propensity among many Americans to continue to regard Japan as a subject state. This inability to shuck the condescending attitude of the occupation overlord gave a kind of visceral credence to the argument that the alliance relegated Japan to a subordinate status; it reinforced the vivid metaphors employed by the Chinese Communists, for example—that Japan had become the lackey, the running dog, the "fugleman" of American imperialism.[45] In public, American and Japanese spokesmen denounced this as pure propaganda. Privately, many squirmed under its element of truth. Allison, for example, painfully recalled planning for a festivity by the American community in Tokyo at which it was suggested that some "foreigners" —that is, Japanese—might even be invited. His own memoirs convey a sense of persistent frustration with both military and civilian policy-makers in Washington, who "seemed to think it would be possible to make Japan into a forward bastion of American strategic strength with the Americans calling the tune and the Japanese meekly accepting their secondary role." More pointedly, Allison acknowledged that the U.S. government continued to refuse to take Japan into its confidence in the discussion of overall Asian policy, and was less frank in dealing with Japanese officials that it was in its relations with such countries as the Philippines and the Republic of Korea.[46]

High Japanese officials such as Ikeda, Aichi Kiichi, and Miyazawa Kiichi rarely failed to evoke the sensitivity of the Japanese populace to such treatment when negotiating with the Americans, and themselves personally chafed under the tight harness of the alliance. This emerged in discussions of a variety of military and economic matters, and nowhere more sharply than in their criticism of the manner in which Japan was compelled to adhere to the U.S. containment of China. The Japanese *themselves* felt "contained" by the Dulles policy, and it is a token of their junior-partner status in the alliance that despite this they were unable to adopt a more independent stance toward Peking, as, for example, Great Britain had done. Mildly in 1953, and more vigorously in 1954, the Japanese missions to Washington unsuccessfully endeavored to persuade the Eisenhower administration to modify its China policy even slightly, and shortly before the last Yoshida cabinet resigned, Ikeda sent a tremor through the American embassy by declaring to leaders of the Liberal Party that it was time to loosen the tie with the United States and adopt a more flexible and independent policy between East and West.[47] This sentiment that under Yoshida Japan was indeed kowtowing to Washington became an increasingly effective argument among the *conservative* opposition which eventually unseated the prime minister.

After his retirement, Yoshida in time became invested with the aura of an elder statesman, and received homage as the grand old man of Japanese politics. As Japan began to enjoy a high economic growth rate under the alliance with the United States, Yoshida's conception of "diplomatic sense" was reinvoked in conservative circles as a standard to follow with complacency and a measure of pride. This amounted, as it were, to old One-Man's second rebirth—the first having occurred in 1946 when he was lifted from obscurity to the premiership—for the later image of a sagacious elder contrasted sharply with the general disesteem in which both Yoshida's style and policies were held during the final years of his premiership. He was hounded from office under a hail of brickbats from both conservatives and progressives, who agreed, if on little else, that the prime minister was an autocrat who had bartered true independence for U.S. security guarantees. His last grand gesture as premier, an official tour of Western capitals, sputtered to an almost symbolically unimpressive end in Washington, where pleas for a less militant and more economically intensive U.S. "counter-offensive" against communism in Asia were turned aside. As the discussion which follows suggests, neither the alliance, nor the economy, nor the domestic political scene could be regarded as stabilized in December 1954, when the Yoshida era finally came to an end.

REMILITARIZATION AND THE DOMESTIC CONSERVATIVE CONFLICT

Post-occupation tensions within the bilateral alliance were imperfectly replicated, as in a distorting mirror, by tensions within the domestic conservative camp. And here also the issues of contention tended to emerge most dramatically in polemics on the rearmament question.

After sovereignty had been restored, military expansion and reorganization were effected in two stages under Yoshida. In August 1952, following introduction of a separate maritime force earlier in the year, the land and sea forces were placed under the new Safety Agency. In July 1954, an air force was established, and the three military branches were designated the Self-Defense Forces (Jieitai) and placed under a Defense Agency (Bōeichō). The successive new central organs were attached as external agencies to the Prime Minister's Office, and the legislation creating the Self-Defense Forces and Defense Agency, known as the "two defense laws," remained the legal basis of Japan's military organization thereafter.

While this expansion was accompanied by public equivocation concerning the nature and mission of the new forces, ultimate objectives were never in doubt on America's part, and were quickly made clear to key Japanese officials. Just as U.S. Army officers assigned to train the National Police Reserve (NPR) in 1950 had been briefed that this was the nucleus of Japan's "new army," so the American naval officer assigned in late 1951 to assist in planning for the separate "maritime police" (Kaijō Keibitai) was immediately told that a new navy was being born.[48] Masuhara Keikichi, the first civilian head of the NPR, recalled that to the Americans who planned and trained the initial force, "whatever may be said, the clear and obvious threat was the Soviet Union." Contrary to official pronouncements, contingency planning for response to domestic insurgency apparently remained not only secondary but incomplete from the very beginning of remilitarization in 1950.[49]

Although the actual training received by the NPR was kept secret, the intention eventually to maintain a bona-fide military was acknowledged at an early date. The mutual security treaty initialed in September 1951 expressed the expectation that Japan would increasingly assume responsibility "against direct and indirect aggression," an understanding Yoshida had reached with Dulles around January 1951 and almost immediately conveyed to the public. Japan had "a right and obligation to defend its own security," he stated in February, and the creation of such "self-defense power" necessarily would entail armaments. The manner in which this was to be pursued, he indicated then, was to be decided by the populace once independence had been regained.[50] In an address delivered on the first day of sovereignty, Yoshida emphasized that the security arrangement with the United States "cannot be continued indefinitely. That is why we must undertake to build up a self-defense power of our own gradually according as circumstances and resources permit, and go a step further to defend world peace and freedom in collaboration with other free nations."[51]

Despite these clear objectives, Yoshida and his spokesmen continued to have difficulty in determining when to call a spade a spade. Even after the occupation, they found it easier to handle the flame-throwers, rockets, missiles, tanks, and war vessels that America supplied them than to handle the word "rearmament" itself. The latter tended to remain couched in the future tense until around 1953, while the spade was presented as teaspoon, tablespoon, trowel–but not as the substantial tool it already was. In 1950, when the NPR was formed, Yoshida had emphasized that this was "not aimed at rearmament . . . not an Army."[52] In the month following the San Francisco Conference, Attorney General Ōhashi Takeo endeavored to defend the constitutionality of U.S. bases in Japan by emphasizing that, while Article Nine clearly prohibited Japan from possessing armaments, it did not prohibit military reliance upon another power. The security treaty, Ōhashi also insisted at this time, did not place an obligation of rearmament upon Japan.[53] Even after depurged ex-military officers began to replace former Home Ministry officials in staffing the new forces, and after the 1952 creation of a navy and expansion of ground forces, it was maintained that the mission of the forces remained defense against internal aggression.

This dissemblance was conveyed in Yoshida's statements upon the creation of the Safety Agency in 1952. On August 4, he described this expansion and reorganization as "groundwork" for a new military, while illogically suggesting that it did not itself constitute rearmament since the "national power" did not yet permit this. The future military he himself envisioned, he went on, must derive from the will of the people themselves to defend their own country.[54] Two months later, when the Safety Agency was formally inaugurated, Yoshida characterized the duty of the new forces as "to assist the ordinary police forces in the event of a coup d'etat, riot, disturbance or large-scale natural calamity with which the strength of the latter is unable fully to cope. . . . Although the National Safety Force is not an army, it is a Force which possesses great strength for the purpose of maintaining peace and order of our country."[55] It was not until enactment of the two defense laws in 1954 that the mission was formally redefined as "to defend the peace and independence of the country" (rather than "to maintain peace and order of the country" as hitherto), and it was explicitly stated that this entailed defense "against direct or indirect aggression."[56]

These word games occurred partly because of the constitutional dilemma, and taxed the imagination of the government almost as much as they infuriated the opponents of rearmament. In April 1951, the impartial jurist John Foster Dulles had met with the chief justice of the Japanese Supreme Court and gained his concurrence that "a considerable degree of rearmament was possible within the existing framework of the Constitution."[57] The issue was not placed before the court, but instead subjected to prolonged circus proceedings in the public arena, in which Yoshida himself was virtually a one-man show: now the sword swallower, now the contortionist, now the Houdini who made elephants appear and disappear. Until 1950, he had been the most prominent exponent of the literal interpretation of Article Nine: that Japanese armament in any form was prohibited. Henceforth, under his government, Article Nine was blown up like a balloon, twisted like a pretzel, kneaded like plasticene. In the end, however, it still remained unamended, and its survival was as significant as its mutilation. Even while bending the law to its purposes, the Yoshida group remained acutely sensitive to its ultimate constraints.

The constitutional debate focused on the second paragraph of Article Nine (". . . land, sea, and air forces, as well as other war potential, will never be maintained. The right of belligerency of the state will not be recognized"), and the official reinterpretation evolved in an awkward and piecemeal manner. Initially the government seemed to argue that Japan possessed the right of self-defense but not of rearmament. The attorney general's statement of October 1951 reflected this, and the non-military names of the early forces ("police reserve," "safety force"), along with their pronounced mission of protection against "internal" disturbance, were designed to bolster the argument that Japan was not rearming. By 1952, in conjunction with creation of the Safety Agency, the anomaly of self-defense without rearmament was elevated to a higher level of contradiction focusing upon the meaning of "war potential." The Diet record for a single day in March 1952 preserved a nice picture of Yoshida in mid-flight from the first legal shadow to the second. "When it comes to rearming," he responded to one interpellator, "the constitution probably must be revised in accordance with the will of the people." And to another: "Although the constitution prohibits war potential as a tool in international disputes, it does not prohibit war potential as a means of self-defense."[58]

As usual, the looseness of Yoshida's phrasing had to be straightened out, but his statements illustrated the manner in which the focus of debate was shifted from "self-defense" to "war potential." The government's eventual reinterpretation of Article Nine by and large abandoned the "right of self-defense" argument and attempted to skirt the pitfalls involved in venturing to draw distinctions between this-as-opposed-to-that kind of "war potential." Instead, "war potential" was defined in an absolute manner as possession of a scale of weaponry, personnel, and organization that would enable a country to wage modern war effectively, and it was acknowledged that the constitution did prohibit this. The line of reasoning was then simply inverted to read: this—and only this—is what the constitution prohibits. The crux of this interpretation lay in the argument that "potential" meant full capacity and effectiveness in any modern war situation—the assurance, virtually, of victory—and, by defining the phrase so severely, the government also rendered it permissive: militarization short of this ideal level was not "war potential" and therefore not unconstitutional.[59] This received its consummate expression after the Safety Agency had been established, in the following legal brief issued by the Justice Ministry in November 1952:

- Article Nine, paragraph two of the constitution prohibits the maintenance of "war potential" regardless of whether this has aggression or self-defense as its objective.
- Such "war potential" means a degree of equipment and organization which can be utilized in the waging of modern war.
- The standard of "war potential" must be judged concretely, in accordance with the time and circumstances in which the country is placed.
- "Land, sea, and air forces" refer to an organization formed and equipped for war objectives; "other war potential" refers to that which, while not originally having war objectives, nonetheless possesses actual power which can be useful in reality.

*"War potential" is the consolidated power of both personnel and materiel. Therefore, weaponry alone does not in itself constitute "war potential." Naturally this applies also to factories which manufacture weapons.

·It goes without saying that "be maintained" in Article Nine, paragraph two, takes our own country as the subject of such maintenance. Since U.S. forces stationed here constitute a military maintained by the United States to protect our country, they have no relevance to Article Nine.

·To maintain a level of actual power which does not reach "war potential," and to use this for defense against direct aggression, does not violate the constitution. In theory this is identical with national police forces engaging in defense in times of emergency.

·The land and maritime Safety Forces are not "war potential." They are, as is made clear in Article Four of the Safety Agency Law, "forces which will act in cases of special necessity to maintain the peace and order of our country and protect life and property." Essentially they are police organizations. Consequently, not being organized for war purposes, it is clear that they are not a military. Also, viewed objectively, the equipment and organization of the Safety Forces is certainly not at a level which would permit the effective execution of modern warfare. Thus they do not approximate the "war potential" of the constitution.[60]

In popular shorthand, this became known as the concept of a "military without war potential" (*senryoku o motanai guntai*; *senryoku-naki guntai*), a phrase Yoshida himself later endorsed in one of his skittish performances on the hot floor of Diet interpellations.[61] This provided the government with a flexible formula which could be evoked, to different ends, domestically and in negotiating with the United States. Domestically, the permissive aspect of the "war potential" interpretation was cited to legitimize the next stage of limited rearmament in 1954. At the same time, in the bilateral exchanges culminating in the MSA agreement, Yoshida's spokesmen evoked the restrictive aspect of the formula to argue that the force levels urged by the United States would constitute war potential and thus require constitutional revision. As Ikeda explained to the Americans in 1953, "It is not the intention of the Japanese representatives to propose any defense program that might infringe upon the Japanese Constitution." Furthermore, "the cautions taken by the original drafters of this Constitution have made the amendment procedure extraordinarily difficult. An amendment does not seem feasible in the foreseeable future even if the national leaders should be convinced that such a step is advisable."[62] The Americans found the argument vexing, and some attempted to dismiss it as fatuous. Shortly before the Ikeda visit, the assistant secretary of defense derided the constitutional limitation as "an excuse for not doing something rather than the real obstacle that prevents our going and doing it."[63] In actuality, the legal constraint could not be so easily dismissed.

As a domestic policy, there was no expectation that the reinterpretation of Article Nine would be persuasive to the critics of rearmament. Such legitimization of gradual remilitarization was rather meant to win the support of the dubious general populace and, more particularly, of Yoshida's conservative critics. The issue within the conservative camp as a whole was the pace of rearmament rather than the ostensibly agreed-upon ultimate goal of military self-sufficiency, and Yoshida's critics on the right were in fact not appeased by the "war potential" solution. All parties agreed that the Yoshida policy was one of creeping rearmament. Where the left opposed this because it was rearmament, the conservative critics opposed it because it was creeping, because it reaffirmed that Japan could not constitutionally develop an autonomous defense capability, and because consequently Japan could not look forward to the early withdrawal of U.S. troops. They supported more rapid development of war potential, couched this in appeals to "true" independence, and called for outright constitutional revision to facilitate this. In the broadest perspective, the general policy of remilitarization did pit Japanese conservatives and their American patrons against the more progressive and pacifist forces in Japan. Disagreements over the pace and tactics of remilitarization, however, produced tensions and confrontations which were anything but simple, and exposed some paradoxical dilemmas within the San Francisco system. In part, these dilemmas derived from differing interpretations of nationalism, independence, self-interest, and self-sufficiency among the Japanese conservatives. They most certainly revealed that Yoshida did not represent a monolithic conservative outlook.

In sovereignty, as under the occupation, Yoshida preserved in the eyes of some the image of being "one of the staunchest anti-militarist conservatives in Japan."[64] This characterization rested upon certain fairly well-known positions maintained even after the occupation ended: the measure of restraint Yoshida continued to impose upon personnel expansion; his support of civilian control; his public criticism of the prewar "prerogatives of the Supreme Command," and repeated emphasis upon the necessity of ensuring that the new forces be "truly . . . for the people and of the people";[65] the priority he placed upon civilian rather than military-related industrial expansion; and, in the end, even his labored endeavor to affirm the constitutionality of moderate rearmament, rather than hastily open the Pandora's box of constitutional revision.

It is more accurate, however, to describe Yoshida's position as one of wary rearmament rather than staunch anti-militarism. While he did insist upon civilian control of the new military, so also did most other responsible Japanese and Americans. On the other hand, Yoshida not only supported staffing the new forces with depurged former military officers, even before SCAP itself had come around to this position, but also succeeded in extending the category of eligible ex-officers to include those who had held the rank of full colonel—a decision strongly opposed by the two Japanese he himself had appointed to head the NPR, Masuhara Keikichi and Hayashi Keizō. In practice, Yoshida was willing to carry this even further, as seen in his endeavor to make former lieutenant general Tatsumi Eiichi the uniformed head of the NPR.[66]

Similarly, while Yoshida did not accept the recommendations of the more aggressive rearmament lobbies—such as the interpenetrating "Hattori clique," the coterie surrounding former admiral Nomura, and Watanabe Tetsuzō's "Economic Research Institute"—he nonetheless encouraged them, even, as has been seen, to the point of funding some of their activities.[67] One can speculate that the prime minister's motives in financing such ostensible critics of his own policies extended beyond mere interest in their "research" findings, for the propagandizing of such right-wing spokesmen served an end he himself deemed urgent: to instill a "defense consciousness" among the populace. Yoshida also had few qualms in endorsing the re-creation of a top-level central military organ, for, although it did not in fact come to pass, in 1952 he spoke openly of future establishment of a "Defense Ministry."[68] At the same time, he accepted the advice of his military rather than civilian advisers in supporting a separate command and administrative structure for the new navy established in 1952, another decision opposed by Masuhara and Hayashi.[69] Yoshida's choice as civilian head of the new Safety Forces in 1952 also could hardly be construed as a serious endeavor to ensure moderation in the guiding of the enlarged forces. His appointee was none other than Kimura Tokutarō, whose fanatic plan for a clandestine vigilante "Patriotic Anti-Communist Drawn-Sword Militia" had been rebuffed by Yoshida only a short time earlier.[70]

Where expansion of Japan's military capacity per se was concerned, Yoshida tended to urge restraint concerning personnel rather than hardware—so long as the latter was supplied by the United States. In contrast to his convoluted public explanations, his private approach to concrete matters of rearmament appears from the outset to have been a model of cryptic clarity. Concerning the possession of "self-defense power," he told officials in the NPR: "Build it up." When informed the United States was offering artillery, or tanks, to the "police reserve," his response was reportedly a standard and brief: "Good, we'll take them."[71] But when, following the peace conference, the United States urged that Japan immediately expand its forces by almost 150 percent, from 75,000 to 180,000, Yoshida balked, and in January 1952 he persuaded Ridgway to support his own more moderate timetable. The 110,000-man ground force authorized in 1952 thus represented an increase of only one-third what Washington had proposed.[72]

The discrepancy between Yoshida's attitude toward rearmament and remilitarization and that of influential segments of the conservative business and political community became clearer after the creation of the Safety Agency. In addition to more rapid and extensive personnel expansion, the conservative critics envisioned a new and sustained boom in military-related industrial production, which would recapture the momentum of the Korean War boom but in an altered direction: production would now include direct military end products, and such products would be utilized by Japan itself. To accomplish such objectives, it was deemed necessary to affirm the military nature of the defense establishment by both revising the constitution and redefining the formal "mission" of the forces.

Judged by their military policies, Yoshida's conservative opponents seemed closer to Washington's line than he was. Yet for both personal and ideological reasons, they constituted at this time an uncertain element within the San Francisco system. Contrary to Yoshida's good fortune, the careers of many of his critics had been drastically disrupted by the occupation. The leading political spokesmen for rearmament included depurgees such as Hatoyama, Ishibashi, Miki Bukichi, Kōno Ichirō, and Ōno Bamboku, as well as accused war criminals such as Shigemitsu and Kishi Nobusuke, and there was no reason to expect such men to harbor special affection for the United States. In addition, while these critics shared the sense of expediency that underlay the U.S.-Japan alliance, they also espoused a brand of nationalism in which Yoshida's exclusive reliance upon the alliance was depicted as excessive to the point of slavishness.[73] To Washington, they were a discomforting reminder of the divergent strains in Japanese geopolitical thought which had existed in the prewar period—a reminder that Yoshida's exceptionally close identification with the Anglo-American powers did not represent the only appealing tradition in Japan's modern diplomatic history.

Yoshida, almost like the stereotyped character who protests too much, rarely overlooked an opportunity to portray himself as representing the mainstream tradition of post-Restoration foreign policy. His postwar policies were in effect a mutated continuation of views he had espoused as a representative of the prewar "pro-Anglo-American clique," and he regarded that post-World War One faction within the Foreign Ministry as the legitimate heir of the Meiji oligarchs. Given the nature of Japan's modern development, Yoshida argued, his country was more Western than Asian. And he maintained, virtually as an article of faith, that "the great principle that the keynote of Japanese diplomacy is friendship with the United States will not and must not be changed in the future. This is not simply the momentum of temporary postwar circumstances; it is preserving the main road of Japanese diplomacy since Meiji."[74] In their polemics as well as their own personal histories, however, the conservative opposition drew attention to the correctives to this gospel. They were resuscitated reminders of the tradition of antagonism with the United States and the West; of the comparable cycles of conflict and cooperation that had characterized Japanese relations with Russia since the late Meiji; and of the powerful ideological current that insisted Japan's destiny lay ultimately in Asia rather than in primary identification with the dominant Western powers.

From the perspective of U.S.-Japan relations, the paradox of conservative factionalism in the final years of the Yoshida era resided here, for many of the advocates of more rapid rearmament viewed their position as a nationalistic assertion which would hasten Japan's emancipation from the American embrace and the yoke of "dependent independence" to which Yoshida had relegated the country. Like two implacable enemies temporarily united by their common animosity toward a third foe, the pro-rearmament conservatives found themselves reaching into the same rock pile of anti-Yoshida epithets as the anti-remilitarization forces on the left. The government's approach to MSA aid, declared a spokesman for Shigemitsu's Progressive Party in a typical attack, for example, was interpreted by the public as a commitment to create "mercenary troops" for the United States.[75]

Similarly, at one level the debate concerning remilitarization of Japanese industry could be viewed as essentially a matter of differing economic analyses. Where Yoshida, viewing the situation largely from the perspective of the national budget, concluded that

Japan could not afford extensive domestic rearmament, business leaders, who thought more in terms of technological and industrial stimulation, as well as the potential export market for Japanese military products, argued that Japan could not afford *not* to move rapidly into military production. But this also had a deeper dimension, for to some conservatives independent rearmament also offered a potential escape from some of the more stifling aspects of "U.S.-Japan economic cooperation." They viewed MSA aid as attractive, for example, insofar as it stimulated the development of an independent industrial defense sector in Japan; but at the same time they expressed apprehension that such military aid might be structured in a manner that relegated Japan indefinitely to the role of being a military assemblage and repair shop for the products of the U.S. military-industrial complex.[76] This attitude extended to questions pertaining to trade with the communist bloc. Thus, while Yoshida pointed to "U.S.-Japan economic cooperation" as the main road to creating a viable economy, he in turn was pointed to by some businessmen as being little more than a comprador serving American interests.[77]

Yoshida's pro-rearmament opponents were not in unanimity on foreign policy issues, but a large percentage were outspoken critics of the diplomatic isolation incurred under the separate peace. They called for closer relations with the People's Republic of China—a cause Yoshida ostensibly shared, but conspicuously failed to promote. Many, led by the Hatoyama-Kōno group, also demanded normalization of relations with Moscow, an initiative definitely not on Yoshida's own agenda. Normalization was in fact realized under the Hatoyama cabinet in 1956, and Yoshida stuck to his guns even as this was in the process of being finalized. "Let me say boldly and in all sincerity," he proclaimed before the America-Japan Society in Tokyo, "that, with the cold war still on, this is no time for us to flirt with Moscow while making pious protestations of friendship for America; no time for us to debate this or that Article of the San Francisco Treaty. It is high time Japan and America got together and worked freely and heartily together without reservation."[78] Such cold-war Manichaeism, especially where the Soviet Union was concerned, did not mellow with the passage of time. It became, if anything, crisper. "Speaking frankly," Yoshida opined some ten years later, "the Soviet Union is not a country to make friends with."[79]

Such disagreements among the conservatives had several implications for the bilateral alliance. From Yoshida's perspective, by 1953 it had become imperative to create at least the appearance of general conservative support of his own rearmament policy in lieu of the impending MSA negotiations. To official Washington, the conservative camp offered unsettling prospects no matter in which direction one looked: fidelity but inadequate remilitarization under Yoshida; more rapid rearmament but coupled with threats of rapprochement with the communist powers under Yoshida's opponents. The latter sobering prospect actually had been addressed by the National Security Council even before the Korean War and the depurges, in stark and quite perceptive terms. "Even if totalitarian patterns in Japan were to reassert themselves in the form of extreme right-wing rather than Communist domination," it was stated in NSC 48/1 of December 1949, "the prospect would remain that Japan would find more compelling the political and economic factors moving it toward accommodation to the Soviet orbit internationally, however anti-communist its internal policies, than those that move it toward military alliance with the United States."[80]

By 1953, this dilemma had, to all outward appearances, come closer home. The rearmament controversy was only one index of this, but a revealing one that pointed to a basic question which remained latent within the alliance system over the ensuing decades: whether the inequitable nature of the military relationship was not itself a major factor holding Japan in the U.S. orbit. Was true Japanese military self-sufficiency—any more than genuine economic self-sufficiency—actually compatible with the *Pax Americana*? Although both the Safety Agency of 1952 and Defense Agency of 1954 were endorsed by conservatives as steps toward the assertion of greater Japanese control over planning, training, and weaponry,[81] these remained rudimentary assertions of independence when contrasted to the constraints and influence the United States continued to exert over a wide range of Japanese policy through the very nature and mechanisms of the security relationship. The alliance was finely tuned, and taut with tensions.

THE IKEDA-ROBERTSON TALKS AND THE SHALLOW ECONOMY

The debate over the pace of remilitarization simmered into the summer of 1953, when the heat upon the government was intensified by both Washington and the anti-Yoshida conservatives. This occurred in conjunction with the initiation of informal talks concerning Japan's participation in the MSA program, which began in late April and advanced to the stage of formal negotiations in July. Until June, Yoshida refused to comment on these conversations, leading to charges of "secret diplomacy"; he did not publicly commit himself to support of the MSA program until late June, following a public exchange of notes on the subject between the two governments. Even then, the government remained noncommital on its plans for future military expansion.

It was the American understanding as of mid-summer that the cabinet had set a tentative target of increasing ground forces to a total complement of 150,000 in the next stage of personnel expansion.[82] This was totally inadequate in Washington's view, as Dulles made eminently clear in early August when he visited Tokyo after concluding a security pact with the Republic of Korea. Not for the first time, Dulles engaged in a tense exchange on the subject with Yoshida, and surely did his cause little good by contrasting the Japanese defense effort unfavorably to the heroic remilitarization being undertaken in Italy and Korea.[83]

The dangling lucre of MSA together with the bullying of Dulles fed both the opportunistic and nationalistic concerns of the conservative opposition, which stepped up its criticisms of Yoshida's continued hesitancy on such matters as war potential and creation of an independent military capacity. Dulles's unveiled attacks on the cabinet's defense policy had also prompted general speculation that Yoshida had lost the support of the United States and was consequently at the end of his political string.[84] In response, the cabinet was compelled to clarify its position. On August 28, the first explicit indication of an imminent troop expansion was made by Vice Prime Minister Ogata Taketora, who announced that an increase in ground forces of between 20,000 and 40,000 men was contemplated for 1954. This was prelude to a more significant action. On September 6, the Safety Agency released a draft of its own tentative five-year defense plan, which projected the following military establishment by 1958: ground forces of 210,000 men (150,000 in 1954); a naval force of approximately 170 vessels (145,000 tons); and an air force of 1,400 aircraft.[85] This did not reflect official policy, however, which as it turned out was somewhat more modest.

While the five-year draft plan did not still the rearmament debate among the conservatives, it prepared the ground for a momentary truce between Yoshida's ruling Liberals and the opposition Progressive Party under Shigemitsu. Through the mediation of several prominent business leaders, the two men met on September 27 and agreed upon the following joint statement:

> Taking into consideration the present international situation as well as the spirit of national independence (*minzoku dokuritsu*) which is rising within the country, we take this opportunity to clarify the policy of increasing self-defense power, and agree to establish a long-term defense plan which accords with our national capabilities and the gradual reduction of foreign forces. Along with this, we agree in the interim to quickly revise the Safety Agency Law, change the Safety Forces into Self-Defense Forces, and add defense against direct aggression to their mission.[86]

This agreement prompted speculation that the Liberals might establish a more formal working relationship with the Progressives, possibly with Shigemitsu being appointed vice prime minister. This did not materialize. Closer relations were opposed by most members of the Progressive Party for a variety of reasons, not the least of these being that the September 27 statement had skirted the issue of constitutional revision.

While the communiqué marked only a temporary lull in the

conservative imbroglio, it was nonetheless of major importance to Yoshida's foreign policy plans, for it enabled the government to present itself to the United States as representing an essentially unified position on rearmament within the conservative camp. The relationship between the domestic reconciliation and MSA issue was demonstrated immediately. Two days after the Yoshida-Shigemitsu statement, Ikeda left for Washington at the head of a small delegation. It was emphasized that his mission was informal and exploratory, and that he went not in an official capacity, but as a personal representative of the prime minister. The talks, however "unofficial," were significant. They were pursued through the month of October, and culminated in the well-known "Ikeda-Robertson communiqué" of October 30.

Ikeda was chairman of the Liberal Party's Policy Committee at this time. He was accompanied by Aichi Kiichi, parliamentary vice minister of finance; Suzuki Gengo of the Ministry of Finance; Watanabe Takeshi of the Japanese embassy in Washington, who had been a key Finance Ministry aide in the implementation of the Dodge Line; and Miyazawa Kiichi of the House of Councillors.[87] Ikeda's counterpart on the U.S. side was Walter S. Robertson, assistant secretary of state for Far Eastern affairs, who was assisted by officials from the Defense, Treasury, Commerce, and State departments and from the Foreign Operations Administration. Joseph Dodge also participated in the discussions.

From the outset, the "Ikeda-Robertson talks" revealed the differing priorities of the two countries. The U.S. side regarded the main purpose of the meetings as being to decide the extent of Japan's participation in the MSA program, which was directed primarily toward equipping and training foreign military forces. As such, they were most concerned with Japan's military build-up. It was the Japanese position that the defense issue was inseparable from broader economic and social problems, and Ikeda, as Yoshida's personal spokesman, had several pressing objectives in mind: to restate the case for a relatively moderate program of Japanese remilitarization, and to solicit U.S. assistance in forms that were not so exclusively military-oriented.[88] The Japanese side largely determined the general format for the discussions, however, by submitting a number of general position papers as the talks progressed, to which the American side responded.

The Japanese argued that, although their government was committed to increasing Japan's defense power, such expansion remained subject to "four restrictions"–legal, political or social, economic, and physical. Within this context, Ikeda and his aides lingered longest upon economic constraints. On October 5, the first day of serious discussion, they presented two memoranda which dealt only in passing with defense and dwelt instead upon the problems of Japan's "shallow economy." One of these documents was already familiar to the Americans, being a version of a statement Yoshida had submitted to Dulles on August 11.[89]

While striking recovery had occurred in such sectors as mining, heavy and chemical industry, and gas and electric utilities, it was maintained, the shallowness of the economy was revealed in export decline, low living standards, and low real consumption levels. Current economic growth was depicted as resting largely upon a minor "consumption boom" in luxury items, plus an "uncertain special procurements demand." The export slump was attributed to the end of the war boom, intensification of international competition, high prices in Japan deriving from outmoded and unrationalized production, import restrictions in the Sterling and Open Account areas, and denial of the China market. A catalog of heavy impending expenditures was presented, which in addition to industrial modernization included routine capital expansion, repairs and replacements, land reclamation to increase domestic food production, natural-disaster relief, public works, war pensions, salary increases, reparations, and so forth. Military expansion, the Japanese argued, could only be discussed in the broader context of these problems.

The potential tinderbox of popular sentiment in Japan was a bargainer's point Ikeda was already versed in from the years of the Dodge Line, and this was also insinuated in the Yoshida memorandum to Dulles reintroduced on October 5. Although most Japanese supported government policy and did not harbor "any ill feeling against the United States," it was noted, "it should also be borne in mind that the fact that the Japanese national standard of living is still lower than pre-war level, together with Japan's geographical relations seems to make Japan critically sensitive of indirect aggression by communism. Under such circumstances, it is of great importance to guide the national feelings in a proper way. If any mistakes are carelessly committed, both domestic politics and foreign relations of Japan would fall into irretrievable difficulties." This was intended to persuade U.S. officials not merely that rapid remilitarization could be socially disruptive, but also that it was in America's own interest to woo popular support in Japan by largesse beyond that envisioned in the MSA program. In a written interim summary of proceedings to date, for example, Ikeda emphasized that external assistance would help to develop a "spirit of self defense" in Japan, and pursued this almost haughtily: "To the people who are poverty-stricken but nevertheless proud the most effective of such external assistances is the demonstration of generous friendship. They are a people who know how to respond to magnanimity, and how not to respond to compulsion."[90] In a résumé submitted at the end of the talks, the Japanese stated that they had "agreed that the Japanese people should feel primarily responsible for the defense of their own country, but they also added that the U.S. military as well as economic assistance would greatly help create such climate in Japan that the Japanese people would be more encouraged to develop their own defense forces in a shorter period."[91]

Mechanisms for guiding popular sentiment "in a proper way" were of course fundamental to the domestic rectification program which was underway at this time. In the Ikeda-Robertson talks, Yoshida's spokesmen were emphasizing that this could not be divorced from resolution of Japan's precarious position in the international economy. Thus, the Yoshida memorandum to Dulles went on to list specific economic areas in which American understanding and support was desired to "help eliminate the doubt or misunderstanding" the Japanese people held concerning U.S. policy toward Japan. These points were pursued throughout the talks and involved settlement of reparations problems with southeast Asia, Japanese participation in the reconstruction of South Korea, trade with mainland China, introduction of "capital funds from the United States," guarantees of continued U.S. offshore procurements in Japan, provision of pure economic aid to Japan, and Japan's obligation to repay the GARIOA funds expended during the occupation. The American response to requests in these areas ranged from negative to qualified.

The Yoshida government itself was not in unanimity on all these issues, and Miyazawa later revealed that Yoshida's own position on debt repayment and solicitation of foreign capital in particular was more conciliatory than that of his chief advisers. Repayment of GARIOA "aid," which amounted to some two-billion dollars, for example, became a stickly sub-theme of the Ikeda-Robertson talks. While the Japanese went to Washington seeking U.S. assistance in alleviating Japan's economic problems, the Americans were stubbornly insistent upon gaining a firm Japanese timetable for repaying this huge sum. There was strong feeling in Japan that the GARIOA funds were more properly regarded as a grant rather than loan, and the Finance Ministry had urged Yoshida to avoid any commitment on this issue whatsoever. The prime minister, however, regarded this as a matter of honor, and prior to the October talks personally promised Dulles that the obligation would be met. His idiom of fiscal honor was an interesting one. "After all," he remarked to Dulles, "Japan is a samurai country."[92]

The position finally adopted was that the Japanese government intended to repay this aid "as far as possible," but "in view of the present ability of Japanese economy . . . it seems very difficult for Japan to meet the obligation." The Americans contrasted this attitude unfavorably with that of West Germany—a comparison the Japanese dismissed as inappropriate, on the grounds that Germany had received Marshall Plan aid as well as GARIOA support and was consequently in a better economic position than Japan to repay its debts. It was finally agreed that the GARIOA issue would be addressed in subsequent talks.[93]

Yoshida's position concerning foreign capital was somewhat

puzzling. In a later venture as an historian of modern Japan, he emphasized that one of the great accomplishments of the Meiji oligarchs had been that they created a strong state without relying upon, and thereby becoming subordinate to, foreign capital. In the early 1950s, however, he was apparently very keen on introducing U.S. capital into Japan, although advisers such as Ikeda and Aichi entertained strong reservations.[94] In the Ikeda-Robertson talks, the Japanese indicated that "the furnishing of more capital to Japan, either in the way of direct investment, loan or credit, will be welcome."[95] Their emphasis tended to be on major developmental loans, and simultaneously with the conclusion of the October talks it was announced that a $40-million loan for thermoelectric power development had been granted by the World Bank and a $60-million cotton credit extended by the Export-Import Bank. The U.S. side, however, led by Dodge, cautioned against reliance upon large outside loans and emphasized instead the liberalization of Japanese laws and regulations governing private foreign investment, coupled with the creation of a domestic economic climate conducive to such investment. A recent study, the Americans reported, indicated four obstacles to direct private investment in Japan: weakness of the economic base, governmental restrictions, "apprehensions concerning a possible return by Japan to prewar business organizations" (a reference to the trend toward recartelization, presumedly), and "physical insecurity," referring to Japan's strategic vulnerabilities.[96] The Japanese promised liberalization of investment restrictions, and in late October Ikeda spent several days in New York discussing this among other matters with American businessmen.[97]

In the Yoshida memorandum to Dulles which was reintroduced on October 5, the Japanese also criticized the "discriminatory treatment" by which they were forced to adhere to exceptionally severe restrictions in trade with mainland China. It was presented as a "nation-wide wish" that Japan be permitted to follow an embargo list as lenient as that observed by the United Kingdom. Although this was repeated throughout the talks, Ikeda did not vigorously pursue the issue. Neither the "COCOM" or "CHINCOM" mechanisms nor specific items of trade were mentioned, and the China issue seems to have been on this occasion little more than another bargainer's point, by which Japan staked out a position in one area in the hopes of gaining concessions elsewhere. The Americans did express vague agreement with Japan's request "in principle," but made it clear that such principles would remain abstract at least until the situation in Korea had been resolved. In discussion of the October 5 position papers, Ikeda meekly agreed with Robertson that it was "appropriate" that Japan's trade restrictions were exceeded only by the United States and Canada. Ikeda himself volunteered that, since trade was managed under the Chinese Communist regime, its potential was restricted, and consequently Japan preferred to place emphasis upon southeast Asia. "Keep up pressure upon Red China," Robertson is quoted as saying in the cryptic minutes of this meeting kept by the Japanese side, to which Ikeda responded: "We understand it—that's why we want to explore market in South East Asia."[98] In 1954, the China issue was reinvoked by the Japanese in a more vigorous, but no more successful, manner.

By 1953, the Yoshida government had concluded that the new economic bloc envisioned under "U.S.-Japan economic cooperation" was developing poorly indeed, however, and this was nowhere more conspicuous than in the failure of the southeast Asian side of the trilateral nexus to develop as projected. In part this was attributed to economic backwardness and social and political instability. But beyond this, the leaders of the countries to the south still remembered—and indeed still suffered from—a chapter of history that had ended less than a decade previously, but seemed already forgotten by officials in Washington: Japanese rapacity and atrocity. They were less than eager to embrace Japan, and certainly unwilling to do so before the accounts of the recent war had been settled in the form of agreements concerning Japanese reparations—an issue suspended by the occupation to hasten the stabilization and reconstruction programs. Originally it had been hoped by both U.S. and Japanese officials, and with no little cynicism, that the reparations agreements would become an entering wedge for economic penetration.[99] Instead, bilateral negotiations with the various countries were proving bitter and protracted. The sums being demanded were "an enormous amount," in the words of the Ikeda delegation, and violated Japan's own understanding of the reparations provisions included in the San Francisco Peace Treaty. At the time of the Ikeda-Robertson talks, Japan had not succeeded in concluding a single agreement on this issue, and consequently the major countries involved—Burma, Indonesia, the Philippines, and South Vietnam—had not ratified the treaty of peace.

With the exception of Burma, these matters were not in fact resolved until after the Yoshida era,[100] but in the Ikeda-Robertson talks the Japanese made a strenuous effort to solicit concrete U.S. assistance in breaking the deadlock. On October 8, the Ikeda group submitted a paper in which the reparations problem was cited as the major impediment to formulation of a long-range defense plan, and it was proposed that U.S. aid to southeast Asia be coordinated with the reparations problem in the following manner:

> i) That the U.S. assistance to the free nations in the Southeast Asian area, either in the way of MSA or otherwise, be tied with the reparation payment of Japan, both in its planning and administration.
> ii) That if and when the U.S. plans a development program for one of these nations, full consideration be taken to call supply of capital goods and technical know-how from Japan.
> iii) That an assistance, both financially and otherwise, be considered by the United States if and when an agreement is to be made between Japan and one of these nations on a joint undertaking of developing such a nation.[101]

The U.S. response to this, conveyed in later meetings, was sympathetic but noncommittal. The United States promised its good offices where appropriate, but Robertson informed Ikeda that the southeast Asian countries involved had primary responsibility in such matters, and the United States could not make a general commitment to Japan. So long as Japan's prices remained competitive, however, it would be given full consideration in matters of supply and procurement for southeast Asia.[102]

The Japanese also requested maximum consideration in any programs introduced for the reconstruction of South Korea, and again received a discouragingly vague response. U.S. assistance to Korea, they were told, aimed at rebuilding the country by procurement within Korea itself to the extent possible. Where outside procurements were made, Japan would be given the opportunity to bid, but "at this stage," Robertson indicated, "we can not say how much procurement we can do in Japan."[103]

Hard guarantees concerning future procurements from Japan were a major objective of the Ikeda mission. This had been made clear in the Yoshida memorandum to Dulles, where it was observed that Japan could not attain a balance of payments through normal trade in the foreseeable future. Consequently the program of U.S. military-related purchases remained a critical source of foreign exchange, and it was requested that "MSA aid would not be limited to the military assistance but be carried out with a view of strengthening . . . Japan's national strength in whole by such measures as defense support financing and the off-shore procurement in Japan." In Washington, Ikeda carried this further with a plea for aid to Japan along the lines of the non-military assistance given Europe under the Marshall Plan. "The present status of Japan is exactly the same as those European nations in an early stage of ECA," he argued, "and there is good reason to believe that the effect accomplished in Europe can be repeated in Japan to the same or even a greater extent, if such an aid, under whatever name, is given her."[104]

This notion of a belated Marshall Plan for Japan was summarily dismissed on the grounds that there was "no justification for economic assistance."[105] What the United States was prepared to offer in the form of "aid" was: (1) equipping and training of Japanese army, navy, and air forces under the MSA program; (2) offshore procurements for an estimated $100-million for the coming fiscal year; (3) technological information and training in sectors pertaining to defense production; and (4) information services concerning investment opportunities in the United States and abroad which were available under the MSA program (the

Contact Clearing House Service and Investment Guaranty Program).[106] A year later, the Japanese returned to Washington with an agenda which placed high priority upon a more broadly conceived Marshall Plan "for Asia."

The target figure of $100-million in guaranteed offshore procurements (a fraction of total "special dollar income" from military-related U.S. spending in Japan) included Japan's participation in a significant feature of the MSA program, "Section 550," whereby U.S. agricultural products were funneled into an international digestive track that turned grain into grenades, bread into bullets. Local currency from such sales was used by the United States for military purchases within the same country. Since it was required that Section-550 sales be "in addition to usual marketings," the procedure tended to stimulate the militarization of foreign economies at the expense of development of indigenous self-sufficiency in foodstuffs. In the Ikeda-Robertson talks it was tentatively decided that Japan should receive $50-million of such commodities in the coming fiscal year, with the yen proceeds to be directed into development of Japanese munitions production and an "industrial mobilization base."[107] This complex mechanism whereby U.S. aid and trade policies were integrated with disposal of the American agricultural surplus was shortly thereafter revised under "Public Law 480," and became yet another area of disagreement between the two countries a year later.

Ikeda was thus unable to claim any great economic favors as a result of his October talks. He received no more than America had intended to offer from the start, and this all wrapped in military bunting. Had he chosen to do so, however, he could have reported some animated discussions pertaining to Japan's defense projections, and here the tables were turned. The Americans were able to extract little more in the way of promised remilitarization than the Yoshida group had decided to permit.

In Washington, Ikeda produced a tentative five-year military plan which differed from that released by the Safety Agency a month previously. This was described as a "personal study" which reflected the "up-to-date thinking" of the Japanese government.

According to this, by 1958 Japan would maintain ground forces of 180,000 men; a 156,550-ton navy, consisting of 210 vessels and 31,330 men; and an air force and "air base force" of 518 aircraft and 20,700 combat and maintenance personnel. Personnel expansion of the ground forces was to be completed within three years, with the troops organized into ten divisions; the "division slice" involved fewer personnel than the figure adopted in U.S. projections, which also called for ten divisions. Expansion of the maritime force, which then consisted of 68 vessels loaned by the United States, would entail transfer of 39 more American vessels plus construction of 103 new ships in Japan. The immediate objective of the navy was to ensure the security of Japanese ports and coastal transportation, while its broader mission was to protect Japan's trade routes; at that time, the government was thinking in terms of escort or convoy capability in the area up to 600 or 700 miles from Japan's coastline. The envisioned new air force would concentrate on pilot training in the first three years, and require 300 training aircraft. In 1957–1958 it would add 218 "first line combat planes," including 150 jet fighter-bombers. The estimated total cost of this five-year plan was $2,503-million, of which it was projected that $1,725-million would be paid by Japan and $778-million by the United States. Expansion of Japanese forces was to be accompanied by U.S. withdrawal, with the assumption that by the end of fiscal 1958 "all the United States forces except a part of the air and naval forces" would be removed from Japan.[108]

The American reception of this plan was typified by the informal comments of the Pentagon representative: "All low—rather disappointingly low—regrettable that this is what you can do."[109] The United States was most concerned at this stage with expansion of Japanese ground forces, its usual immediate target figure being 325,000; in some presentations, the figure of 350,000 was used. Minimum air force requirements were set by the Pentagon at 800 planes, although this was left to future discussion.[110] In a criticism which was to become the leitmotif in U.S. pressure for Japanese remilitarization thereafter, it was emphasized that projected defense outlays did not exceed 2.5 percent of GNP, and at one point the Americans expressed the opinion that Japan's defense spending could be doubled.[111] Even Dodge, the apostle of the balanced budget, fumed that the FY 1953 budget had been balanced only by cutting defense appropriations, which could and should be "substantially larger." As stern and forbidding as ever, Dodge delivered his usual denunciation of the Japanese government's "hardly outstanding" economic practices, and concluded that these indicated "inadequate justification of requests for military assistance, in view of inability to demonstrate that the Japanese Government is making maximum feasible effort to secure its own defense."[112]

The American position was premised upon preparation for World War Three. The Japanese were informed by the assistant secretary of defense that the Korean War represented a Soviet "invasion . . . to approach Japan," and that Japan was clearly "the most desired prize" for the Russians, "a natural target for the desire to dominate the Far East." "Time is running very fast," they were told in a presentation which was rather breathless itself, and if and when a communist offensive against Japan took place, 500,000 combined Soviet and Chinese forces would "come into Japan with lightning attack." The Japanese, to judge by Miyazawa's account, did not take this very seriously.[113]

Ikeda's rejoinder was strongly argued. Apart from the economic infeasibility of rearmament to the extent urged by the United States, neither the constitution nor popular sentiment permitted this. Such expansion would, moreover, force Japan to resort to conscription, which was politically unthinkable. As indicated in the preceding discussion of the "war potential" issue, Ikeda's private argument to the Americans was actually quite close to the position publicly taken by the Liberal Party, that is, that the Yoshida government's own plan remained defensive in nature and thus within the constitution, whereas fulfillment of U.S. proposals would require constitutional revision.

In the final analysis, Ikeda went on, it rested with the Japanese people themselves to decide whether or not to amend the constitution, and this required "education and publicity . . . so that the patriotism and voluntary spirit of self defense may be stirred up in Japan." The lack of such a spirit constituted the "political or social restriction" upon rapid remilitarization, and for this as for the constitutional constraint, the Americans really had no one to blame but themselves:

> Japanese were educated in the eight years of occupation not to take up guns no matter what may happen. And the ones who were mostly affected by this education are these youngsters who are first to be called into service. Besides, there are women, "the intellectuals," and the bereaved families who are least amenable to persuasion otherwise.

To this was added the so-called "physical restriction" of recruitment, in which Yoshida's emissaries went to far as to confess openly their fear of a "Red" army if personnel expansion were not carefully controlled:

> Unless the people are firmly held in conviction that nobody but themselves will defend them, which is a matter of education or rather of re-orientation in the case of Japan, and which accordingly will take a considerable time to accomplish, a hasty recruitment of a large number of youths will merely create a force of mob; the infiltration policy of the Communists is such that there is no assurance that they will not direct their guns toward Japan. All this means that a speedy recruitment of relatively a large number of youths is either impossible or very dangerous in Japan—that is short of a military draft which our Constitution clearly denounces.[114]

It was on these several grounds that the Japanese requested patience and good offices, hardware and procurements, economic as well as military aid. The Americans, while applauding all references to government-sponsored "re-education" in Japan, responded that the legal and political constraints were internal Japanese problems—a point the Ikeda group endeavored to qualify by reiterating that American largesse would go far to help rekindle a spirit of patriotism and self-defense. At the same time, the U.S. side requested that the conferees agree upon the tentative goal of a standing army of 325,000 to 350,000 men, and urged that Japan's defense budgets for fiscal 1954 and 1955 be substantially raised above present projections. The United States did not intend to provide aid to "shadow forces," it was stated at one point. If "popular sentiment" was the major bargaining card of the Japanese, "congressional opinion" was the conventional American counterplay to this, as the Japanese were all too well aware from their earlier experience concerning China and the peace treaty. Military assistance to Japan could not be defended before Congress, it was emphasized, if Japan did not display more vigorous commitment to remilitarization, and the immediate Japanese budgetary appropriations suggested as desirable were $556-million for 1954 and $653 million for 1955. The Japanese replied they did not know where the money would come from. Ikeda's projections of ground forces numbering 180,000 were accepted for the time being, but it was urged that the timetable be accelerated to accomplish this within two years—which the Japanese declared to be impossible.[115]

Public summary of the Ikeda-Robertson talks was made in a communiqué released on October 30. This was frank enough to provoke controversy in Japan, for it stated that, while recognizing "constitutional, economic, budgetary and other limitations," both parties had agreed to expedite Japan's military build-up to the extent possible within these constraints. The target figure of $50-million in agricultural commodities "to help develop the defense production and the industrial potential of Japan through offshore procurement and investment" was cited. The necessity of maintaining a high level of control over trade with Communist China was reiterated. It was noted that the U.S. side "attached great importance to an early settlement for GARIOA aid." And Japan's willingness to liberalize foreign investment laws and improve the economic climate for such investment was made known.[116]

MSA AND THE TWO DEFENSE LAWS

Having declared that "re-education" and constitutional revision were domestic problems to be resolved by the Japanese themselves, the United States proceeded to plunge directly into the fray. In mid-November, Vice President Richard Nixon came to Japan on a mission prefaced with the demand that his august visit be enclosed on both ends with Japanese schoolchildren, like living bookends. On both his arrival and departure, Nixon required that the fifteen-mile route between the airport and U.S. embassy be lined with children waving American and Japanese flags. This was dutifully arranged, although upon departure the vice president was miffed to find his conscripted young worshipers obediently standing on the wrong side of the road.[117] He may almost, one can imagine, have suspected subversion, for grand plots were uppermost in his mind.

Nixon's visit to Tokyo was part of a 72-day Asian tour which took him to fifteen countries, and his message was simpler than his itinerary: Soviet global ambitions were now directed more to Asia than Europe, and the necessity of mounting a collective Asian defense was urgent. This was the central theme in unpublicized letters from President Eisenhower which Nixon presented to both Yoshida and the emperor. In these letters, it was emphasized that the direct threat to Japan was formidable, and rapid rearmament of course essential. In his private conversations with Yoshida, Nixon virtually ignored Ikeda's labored presentation in Washington a few weeks earlier, and urged the prime minister to adhere to the latest version of the U.S. timetable: Japan should increase its ground forces to ten divisions comprising a minimum of 320,000 men within three years, that is, by 1956. Yoshida demurred, and in his counterargument cited the constitutional restriction.

This set the stage for an historic speech by the vice president. After conferring by phone with Washington, Nixon told some 700 guests at a luncheon of the America-Japan Society on November 19 that Article Nine was a mistake. With this statement, the United States in effect officially threw its hand in with the advocates of rapid rearmament through constitutional revision and, contrary to its pious proclamations, openly intervened in one of the most sensitive domestic issues in Japan. The intervention was hardly oblique, for on November 19, the day before his departure, Nixon also met with Shigemitsu, providing Yoshida's rival with the opportunity to proclaim that his own views were almost completely in accord with those of official Washington.[118]

The Nixon visit, following upon the flirtations between Yoshida and Shigemitsu which had been revealed in the September 27 joint statement by the two party leaders, prompted a further shift among the conservative factions which temporarily served Yoshida's interests. On November 29, Hatoyama led 25 of his supporters in the House of Representatives back into the Liberal Party fold (three others formally rejoined the Liberals in the upper house), thereby bringing the lower-house strength of the ruling party back to close to a majority.[119] As one condition for his return, Hatoyama demanded the creation of a Constitutional Revision Investigation Committee (Kempō Kaisei Chōsakai) within the Liberal Party, and Yoshida complied with this on December 15. As chairman he appointed Kishi Nobusuke, the former war criminal and future prime minister, who still bore the old prewar label of "renovationist" which had driven the wartime Yoshida group to distraction.

The creation of this committee was consequential in several respects, for while temporarily defusing the attack on Yoshida which had focused on revision of Article Nine, it simultaneously opened the general discussion of constitutional revision to the full gamut of controversial constitutional provisions, which extended far beyond the "no-war" clause. This included such matters as budget procedures, emergency proclamations, civil liberties, and the status of the emperor. At the same time, Yoshida endeavored to reaffirm his own personal opposition to hasty revision of the national charter. "The Constitution Investigation Committee [*sic*] is not an organ for revision," he stated; "the party holds deep respect for the constitution, which is the basic law of the land, and this has been created within the party as an organ to deepen our understanding through broad examination." Having opened the door in response to Nixon's battering ram and Hatoyama's bugle call, Yoshida now devoted himself to urging: go everywhere, but go slow. Despite the prime minister's disclaimers, the creation of the committee fused the issues of remilitarization and a broader conservative attack upon the liberal guarantees of the constitution, and immediately prompted the organization of popular umbrella groups devoted to "defense of the constitution."[120]

These gestures and realignments did not dissipate the general opposition to Yoshida within the conservative camp, but they did prepare the ground for capping the military dimension of the San Francisco system the following year. The MSA agreement was initialed by the two governments on March 8, 1954, after eight months of negotiation marked by infighting among American bureaucrats and a number of technical compromises between the United States and Japan. The agreement was approved by the Diet, becoming effective on May 1, and was accompanied by passage of the "two defense laws," effective July 1.[121]

On the American side, internal disagreements were reminiscent of 1949–1950, when Pentagon intransigence threatened to abort the restoration of sovereignty. Although the Pentagon was persuaded to temper its position, the issues evoked revealed the central role accorded Japan in U.S. military strategy for Asia. Thus, even as the Japanese government presented plans for indigenous military expansion with the understanding that this would be accompanied by withdrawal of U.S. troops, the Pentagon was introducing plans, ultimately repudiated, to increase the U.S. garrison in Japan.[122] With regards to the proviso that MSA aid be administered *in situ* by an American Military Assistance Advisory Group (MAAG), the Pentagon endeavored to treat Japan differently from other MSA recipients in two ways: first, by placing the advisory group under military rather than embassy control; and second, by assigning 1,489 men to the Japan MAAG, which would have made it the largest such contingent in the world. After some struggle, embassy control was affirmed and the initial MAAG delegation designated at 944 men, with the understanding it would be reduced to 500 at the end of 1954. These figures were still larger than desired by the Japanese government, and this was one of the major issues that prolonged the negotiations. The Pentagon also endeavored, again unsuccessfully, to maintain sole control of military procurements in Japan rather than cooperate with the embassy.[123]

Receipt of MSA aid placed some fifteen "obligations" upon Japan, and much of the Japanese effort in the negotiations was directed to tempering these and relegating some to annexes rather than the formal text of the agreement. The major obligations assumed were increase of defense capability and control of trade with the communist bloc, and these revealed the extent to which, in the final analysis, MSA represented the natural capstone of the separate peace Yoshida had agreed upon over three years previously. At the same time, Japan gained several concessions in the negotiations: (1) it was stated in the preamble to the agreement that promotion of defense industry rested upon the precondition of economic stability; (2) it was explicitly noted that military expansion must be in accord with the constitution; (3) the obligation to restrict trade with communist countries, which was viewed primarily in terms of China, was relegated to an annex; (4) a provision supported by the United States that would have prohibited Japan from receiving aid from a third country was withdrawn; and (5) the expenses to be borne by the Japanese government for support of MAAG were reduced. The first two of these items were unique to the agreement with Japan and not found in the standard MSA agreements enacted by the United States with other countries. The agreement also departed from the norm in that it did not delineate a specific force level which Japan was expected to maintain.

The approximate value of weapons and military equipment the United States agreed to supply for the coming year was $150-million. Japan was also to receive roughly $100-million in the form of offshore procurements and the agricultural commodities transaction. In addition, the United States agreed to promote Japanese defense industry by providing technical information and training. Complementary agreements dealt with foreign investments, U.S. agricultural commodities, and patents and licenses.[124]

Between December 3, 1953, and the beginning of March, Liberal Party leaders met with their conservative opponents on ten occasions to reconcile their views on the framing of new domestic military legislation. The cabinet's final drafts of the Defense Agency Law and Self-Defense Forces Law were completed almost simultaneously with the initialing of the MSA agreement, submitted to the Diet on March 11, and subsequently passed without amendment after heated debate. Under the two defense laws, the organizational structure was revamped, designated personnel complements increased, and a separate air force established. In creating an air force, Japan assumed responsibility for participating in defense of its air space, which hitherto had been entrusted entirely to the United States; immediate plans to this end concentrated upon the training of Japanese pilots by the United States. In accordance with the Yoshida-Shigemitsu agreement of September 1953, the mission of the forces was reformulated explicitly to include defense against direct, or external, aggression.[125]

The reorganization and redefinitions of 1954 thus enlarged the legal parameters under which future physical military expansion could be justified as well as the circumstances under which forces might be deployed. This was abetted by introduction of those ambiguities that also characterized so much of the rectification campaign in domestic legislation. Article 76 of the new Self-Defense Forces Law, for example, stated that external aggression "includes circumstances in which there is a threat of military attack from outside."[126] In Diet debate prior to passage of the laws, a cabinet spokesman intimated that defense against external aggression could in certain circumstances necessitate the dispatch of forces outside of the national territory. Although the House of Councillors successfully introduced a supplementary resolution prohibiting this, the inevitable logic of military expansion had been briefly unveiled.[127] To many critics, Japan had now unequivocally entered the garden gate which had been unlocked in 1950 and pushed ajar in 1952. It was set upon the path all military planners eventually march along, where the signposts point in a single direction and read: the best defense is a good offense—keep moving, keep moving.

Because of the peculiar circumstances of Article Nine, however, and the government's own definition of "war potential" and insistence that the constitutional restriction be formally acknowledged in such agreements as MSA, this remained a constricted portal. Conscription or overseas deployment, for example, would almost certainly provoke a constitutional crisis. The settlement of 1954 thus set a tactically subtle and legally ambivalent pattern for future remilitarization, in which Japan concentrated upon creation of a relatively small but sophisticated military establishment, rather than the mass of manpower envisioned by the United States; pursued this in piecemeal fashion; drew its contingency plans, as before, in secret and in collusion with the United States; and awaited the day when patient ministration of the night soil of "re-education" made possible the harvesting of a new patriotism.

As a step in the definition of Japan's global policy, the 1954 military settlement clarified the U.S.-Japan security relationship and confirmed: (1) Japan's indefinite dependency upon U.S. grand strategy, U.S. military technology, and major end products of U.S. defense industry; (2) Japan's economic as well as military commitment to containment and counterrevolution in Asia; and (3) Japan's commitment to incremental remilitarization, with the assumption that at some point in the future this would necessarily require constitutional revision. At the same time, MSA and the two defense laws meshed with the domestic rectification-of-excesses campaign and were inseparable from the consolidation of a conservative power base, although merger of the conservative parties and routinization of the relationship with big business awaited Yoshida's personal departure from the scene. It was during this same session of the Diet that the Defense Secrets Protection Law was enacted in accordance with one of the obligations incurred in receiving MSA aid, that the police were recentralized, and that the first legislative attacks upon the reformed educational system were effected.

As a step toward the resolution of Japan's economic crisis, however, the new military arrangements were of dubious value, and in the eyes of the Yoshida group Japan's place within the San Francisco system remained precarious. MSA was America's military response to Japan's request for economic assistance; the two defense laws were Japan's qualified response, in part, to U.S. pressure for remilitarization. With these issues resolved for the time being, Yoshida mustered his energies for one final, futile endeavor to persuade the United States to adopt a more flexible and economically-oriented policy toward Japan and non-communist Asia.

TWELVE

The 1954 Yoshida Mission and the End of an Era

> . . . action less noble, less decisive than that which I have outlined will not be enough to tip the scales. There is not much time. Let us act, now.
>
> –Yoshida to National Press Club
> November 8, 1954[1]

"WAR-LOVING AMERICA"

On September 26, 1954, Yoshida left Japan on a global tour which lasted for close to eight weeks. This enabled him to escape the heat of domestic politics. It did not, in the end, enhance his stature at home as he had hoped, or prevent him from being roasted by his political opponents.

Yoshida's peregrination took him to Rome, Bonn, Paris, London, and Ottawa, and culminated in Washington. It provided him with thin material for some later essays,[2] but none of the political ammunition he had hoped to collect to defend his tottering premiership. The journey was partly a symbolic affirmation of Yoshida's belief that in global affairs Japan was fundamentally a "Western" nation, and as such was intended to highlight his own significance in furthering bonds between Japan and the West. But it went further than this. By 1954 the U.S.-Japan relationship, touchstone of the Yoshida policy, seemed imperiled, as Miyazawa observed, by mounting acceptance of the image of "war-loving America."[3] And more than abstract rhetoric had come to reinforce the impression that the United States was myopically preoccupied with military solutions. The consciousness of the Japanese people had been seared by the "*Lucky Dragon* Incident" of March 1, 1954, when twenty-three Japanese fishermen were exposed to radiation from an American atomic-bomb test on the Bikini atoll. On September 23, three days before Yoshida left Japan, the nation was stunned by the death of one of the fishermen from radiation sickness. Between these tragic dates, the United States had turned its back on the Geneva Accords pertaining to a peace settlement in Indochina.

Disenchantment with "war-loving America" was exploited by both conservative and progressive critics of the government, and shared by some of Yoshida's own aides. He himself was not immune to milder versions of such heresy, and thus the "world" tour can be seen as cloak for a pressing mission to Washington. The goal was to encourage certain substantive changes in U.S. policy toward Asia and Japan, and by so doing simultaneously enhance the attractiveness of the alliance and prolong Yoshida's own political life. As with the Ikeda mission one year earlier, America's response to these entreaties was tepid.

This equation between official diplomacy and Yoshida's personal fortunes was obliquely intoned in a memorandum sent to Japanese officials in Washington who were laying the groundwork for the prime minister's visit. Support of the "conservative force" in Japan was essential to maintenance of friendly relations between the two countries, this instructed, and thus "at the present stage it is necessary that the United States give unqualified support to Prime Minister Yoshida."[4] Yoshida's major negotiator on this occasion was Aichi Kiichi, then minister of international trade and industry, who softened his own criticism of U.S. military fixations with a minimum of diplomatic nicety. In a preliminary statement, Aichi not only invoked the conventional premonition of anti-Americanism and popular discontent in Japan, but also conveyed that the Japanese government recognized that such sentiments were not entirely groundless. Indirectly, for example, Aichi suggested that such recent American progeny as SEATO (Southeast

Asia Treaty Organization) were but proof of the pudding that Washington viewed Asia through lenses ground by military technicians.[5] "The test of strength in fighting communism lies as much, if not more, in the political and economic fields as in the military," the Japanese declared in an early position paper—an indirect but deliberate rebuke to the policies of confrontation exemplified by Secretary of State Dulles.[6]

Although Yoshida's stay in the United States was brief (November 2 to 11), the preparations were substantial. The visit culminated in an "Eisenhower-Yoshida communiqué" on November 10, and the measure of the futility of the mission can be seen in the discrepancy between this bland and *pro forma* statement and the private proposals of the Japanese. Specifically, the United States was unreceptive to Japanese proposals concerning a more concerted economic offensive in Asia, and the communiqué glossed over the three major areas of concern that dominated the Japanese presentation at this time: intensive development of southeast Asia in a trilateral linkage with the United States and Japan; restructuring of U.S. trade and aid mechanisms, particularly as these involved disposal of American agricultural commodities; and relaxation of the economic containment of China.

THE WISTFUL "MARSHALL PLAN FOR ASIA"

The Japanese rested their arguments upon a presentation of "the stark facts of our economy" which was familiar fare to the Americans: the stark facts differed little from what Ikeda had conveyed a year earlier, enlivened only occasionally by a felicitous new phrase. Japan's economic growth since the outbreak of the Korean War was described as in good part "fortuitous and temporary in nature"—a "semi-synthetic prosperity" stimulated by "god-sends incidental to the Korean war." Unlike Ikeda's earlier mission, however, relatively little time was devoted to discussion of Japan's defense policy per se. The Japanese reported that their defense outlay for 1955 would amount to slightly more than $400-million (as opposed to the target figure of $653-million which the United

States had declared to be minimal at the time of the Ikeda-Robertson talks), and then focused the conversations upon problems and prospects within the global capitalist economy. While Aichi and his team pursued this in confidential negotiations in Washington, Yoshida carried the message publicly to such audiences as the National Press Club and New York Chamber of Commerce.

The Yoshida government was attempting, in these final months of its existence, to revitalize "U.S.-Japan economic cooperation" by encouraging an intensive capitalist offensive to integrate Japan, the United States, and south and southeast Asia. This concept had received the rhetorical blessing of U.S. officials ever since its inception in Washington in 1950–1951. Having made this their own policy, the Yoshida group found themselves, in 1954, holding an unexpectedly frayed and porous bag and being in the position of urging America to follow through on its rhetoric with a *serious* material commitment, one which would have involved reconsideration of basic aid and trade policies.

In the Japanese view, the triangular relationship was problematic at all corners, as reflected most notably in "the tremendous imbalance in dollar trade." Japan's trade deficit in 1953, not including procurements income, amounted to over $1.1-billion, and the greatest part of this ($670-million) derived from trade with the dollar area. Income from special procurements was calculated to have been $760-million in 1953. When other considerations were taken into account, the Japanese estimated their deficit at approximately $400-million. The critical annual income from special procurements was already on the decline, however, and while the Japanese acknowledged certain encouraging economic indices, their general prognosis was gloomy. "There seem to be hardly any grounds for optimism for the future," they noted at one point, "since all these god-sends incidental to the Korean war are bound to taper off while exports are expected to become more and more difficult because of the increasingly severe international competition."

What the Japanese desired was a fairly firm guarantee of

substantial military purchases in the immediate future, coupled with creation of a secure groundwork for future exports to the United States and southeast Asia, which in time would more than compensate for the anticipated loss of dollar-income from procurements. In addition, they looked forward to an increase in non-strategic trade with China, and requested America's good offices in helping normalize Japan's relations with other countries, where economic discrimination was reflected in tariff and customs barriers, denial of full membership in the General Agreement on Trade and Tariffs, and failure to conclude treaties of friendship, commerce, and navigation with any country besides the United States and Canada.[7]

The U.S. and southeast Asian markets held the key to export expansion, but in their current state neither was appraised with confidence. U.S. exports to Japan exceeded imports from Japan by $430-million in 1952 and $531-million in 1953, and the Japanese discerned trends that threatened to perpetuate this imbalance, such as discriminatory tariffs and mounting "Buy American" sentiment. Japan's export industries, it was noted in a prepared statement, "consider the United States market as an unstable one." In response to such complaints, the U.S. side minimized the extent of its protective tariffs and called attention to the grievances of American businessmen concerning Japan's own import restrictions, infringements upon industrial property rights, and unfair pricing practices. American spokesmen also countered that, despite their expectations following the Ikeda-Robertson talks, Japan had not substantially removed impediments to foreign capital investment.[8]

The Japanese were even less sanguine concerning the prospects of their critical Asian markets. Although between 30 and 40 percent of Japanese exports were directed to south and southeast Asia, the market here too was regarded as ominously vulnerable. The backwardness of local non-communist economies forced Japan into extension of long-term credits, and the current slow rate of economic growth offered meager promise of a durable and expanding outlet for Japanese capital goods.

Although these conversations with the United States dwelt heavily upon the problems of developing non-communist Asia as a market for Japanese machinery and manufactured products, the Yoshida government was no less concerned with the prospects of the area as a source of basic raw materials. Import of primary products from south and southeast Asia was deemed essential not merely in lieu of the inaccessibility of the area under Communist Chinese control, but also to avoid overdependence upon U.S. exports of raw materials, which entailed higher transportation costs and also exacerbated Japan's dollar shortage. The introduction of the "economic cooperation" concept in 1951 had encouraged Japan to investigate a wide range of prospective projects in the subcontinent, and in the immediate aftermath of the occupation these were pursued on a grand and ambitious scale. Capital export, together with provision of technology from Japan, was construed as part and parcel of the relentless cycle of survival through trade: the subcontinent was to provide Japan a steadily increasing supply of primary products, which in turn would ensure the steady growth of Japanese production for export.

Due to the economic backwardness of most of non-communist Asia, however, coupled with unresolved reparations negotiations, lingering nationalistic suspicion of Japan's ulterior objectives, and Japan's own paucity of capital, most of the ambitious overseas developmental schemes advanced between 1951 and 1954 failed to materialize. By the time of the last Yoshida cabinet, the sense of failure and frustration in this area was immense, and the projects that had actually been arranged numbered only a handful: iron ore in Goa, copper and non-ferrous metal in the Philippines, staple fiber in Taiwan, and so forth. Although such central agencies as MITI, the Japan Export-Import Bank, and the Japan Development Bank had drafted detailed plans for joint overseas development of such resources as iron ore, coal, magnesium, bauxite, copper, nickel, chrome, petroleum, rubber, salt, timber, sugar, tea, and various other agricultural products—and dispatched missions to such countries as India, Pakistan, Malaya, Indonesia, the Philippines, Thailand, and Taiwan—most of these schemes remained on the drawing boards, if they had not already been abandoned.[9]

As the Japanese attempted to portray the crisis to Washington in 1954, much of the subcontinent was ripe for communism, but this was the ripeness not of military vulnerability but of economic stagnancy and default. There were stylistic differences in approach to this crisis between Yoshida and the Aichi delegation, with the prime minister being more given to bombast concerning "the strong but specious appeal that Communism has for the poverty-stricken and the politically immature," and the manner in which economic development under communist regimes was accomplished only by "terror, forced labor, confiscation of property and wealth, and inhuman demands on the populace." What emerged most strikingly from their presentations at this time, however, was the grudging respect with which the Japanese, including Yoshida, viewed the effectiveness of economic policies in Communist China, and the alarming contrast they drew between this and the bleak outlook for capitalist development among China's neighbors to the south. In Yoshida's words, "If China's economic progress is such that she outstrips her neighbors substantially in the years ahead, the gravitational pull will be too much to resist, and Southeast Asia will fall to the Communists without a struggle."[10] In a confidential paper, the Japanese phrased this slightly differently, *sans* Newton, by suggesting that if capitalism faltered, "Communist China and the U.S.S.R. might appear more attractive partners to Southeast Asian countries." Or again, with more specific reference to China: "Economics represents a vital element in determining the political future of Southeast Asia. If China under Communist control makes rapid economic progress, leaving the comparatively slow Southeast Asian countries far behind, there will develop a great margin between Communist and non-Communist areas of Asia, enabling Communist China to place the whole of Southeast Asia under her influence without resorting to arms."[11]

The repercussions of this upon Japan would be profound, and the Japanese negotiators did not hesitate to extend to their own country the "domino theory" which was then coming into vogue in the Eisenhower administration. "It is not too much to say that self-sufficiency and development of our economy depend largely upon whether and to what extent our trade with Southeast Asia may be expanded," they declared. "From the political point of view, if a greater part of Southeast Asia should be placed under Communist sphere of influence, Japan will find it impossible to stand out of it alone."[12]

The Japanese did not rest with dire forecasts, but went on to suggest a concrete and ambitious "counteroffensive," in which their rule of thumb was explicitly China. The Americans were politely informed that their faith in private capital investment was naive, a reliance upon "negative methods," and that just to maintain a level of economic growth in the subcontinent at least equal to that of the People's Republic an influx of $4-billion annually was essential. This sum, frequently cited, was ten times larger than current aid commitments to southeast Asia, which at the time involved approximately $400-million annually, administered through such organs as the World Bank, the U.S. Foreign Operations Administration, and the new Colombo Plan.

In the Ikeda-Robertson talks, Ikeda had informally broached the idea of a Marshall Plan "for Japan." By the time of the Yoshida visit, this had been reformulated as a major developmental program for non-communist Asia and assigned high priority. The scope was more ambitious, sense of urgency keener, emphasis upon southeast Asia rather than Japan per se more pronounced. Little could be expected from the World Bank, since that institution's loans, "instead of being used to raise the economic level of poverty-stricken areas, inevitably go to areas of comparatively advantageous conditions with firm standing from a commercial point of view." In addition, the backwardness of the subcontinent was such that the proposed developmental program would in many instances have to entail outright grants rather than loans. "In any case," the Aichi group commented in its lengthy general statement on this subject,

> most of the funds for the development of Southeast Asia would be expected to come from the United States. The most desirable form in which this supply could be made would be in dollars which could be

> used freely by the recipient countries for purchases from other countries. In this case Japan would be enabled to obtain dollars by her exports to Southeast Asia, and thus to acquire an important source of income to compensate for decreases in offshore procurement orders in Japan.

Both the Aichi delegation and Yoshida argued the case for a Marshall Plan for Asia strongly, and the latter made it the basic theme of his address to the National Press Club: "Will this plan work? The fact is, it *has* worked. I refer you to the Organization for European Economic Cooperation. Such an organization in Southeast Asia would mean the difference between chaos and healthy, steady progress toward solid democratic achievement." The Japanese suggested that the Colombo Plan could become the organizational nucleus for such a regional development program, or alternatively it might be administered through establishment of an "Asian Payment Union" or an "Asian Development Fund."[13]

In the context in which it was presented, this proposal was, if not audacious, at least spunky. The Japanese, two years out of formal tutelage, were saying: here is high policy—you carry it out. They were proposing for south and southeast Asia an American outlay of dollars which amounted to twice as much annually as had been expended for the entire six-and-a-half-year occupation of Japan, and this at a time when Congress was balking at foreign aid and the U.S. government was nagging Japan itself for repayment of the GARIOA debt. Whatever the merits of the proposal, its presentation by Japan at this time was quixotic, and its interest lies in its revelation of the Yoshida government's perceptions of both the inadequacy of U.S. policy and the notable economic accomplishments under communist policy in China.

The private American response to this grand scheme was courteously non-committal. It had been read, it was said, "with great interest"; the United States was "deeply interested" in the economic development of the subcontinent; and Japanese references to utilization of the Colombo Plan had been noted "with particular interest."[14] What was most interesting about this interest was that it did not, from the perspective of the Yoshida group, bear fruit.

In their own proposed draft of a joint statement to be issued by Eisenhower and Yoshida, the Japanese endeavored to convey their sense of urgency with an effusive, if unspecific, declaration:

> . . . in the light of the present world situation, we deem the political and social development of the Asian area to be a key vital to the maintenance of world peace and the preservation of the stability and security of the nations in the area against Communist aggression, both direct and indirect. Such development shall be assisted in every feasible way, with full regard and respect for the national independence and aspirations of the nations involved, and in a manner that will conform with the indigenous social and political life of the peoples concerned.
>
> We are agreed that Japan's participation in the Colombo Plan represents substantial progress toward the goal embodied in the above declaration and that further study will be conducted jointly with interested nations as to all other conceivable measures which might accelerate the accomplishment of the above purposes.

The final communiqué, as sifted through American hands, contained little more than a shopworn recognition of "the mutual benefits which might arise from Japan's participation with the other free nations of South and Southeast Asia in the economic development of that area," and a pledge to maintain and promote the peace and prosperity of non-communist Asia. No reference was made to the Colombo Plan.[15]

AID, TRADE, AND THE U.S. AGRICULTURAL SURPLUS

It was understood that aid, trade, and military policy were inseparable, but the Japanese took the position that in American hands this linkage had become too intimate, too military, too cumbersome, and in certain respects too self-serving. They were critical of the mechanisms as well as scope of American "economic" diplomacy, and this emerged with particular sharpness in discussions concerning the U.S. endeavor to integrate military aid and the surplus agricultural commodities program within a structured pattern of triangular trade.

In 1954, the "Section 550" mechanism for disposing of the

U.S. agricultural surplus was refashioned under the well-known Public Law 480 (PL-480) and assigned a central place in U.S. military-economic strategy. Japan, which was the principal foreign market for U.S. wheat, cotton, and other agricultural products, was slated to be a major participant in this program. Congressional drafters of the PL-480 legislation such as Walter Judd, moreover, envisioned that a large portion of yen proceeds from the sale of agricultural commodities provided to Japan would be directed to the furtherance of trade between Japan and "the SEATO area."[16]

Public Law 480, like "Section 550," provided for aid in the form of agricultural commodities above the "normal" import or "usual marketings" of such products by the recipient country. While the Yoshida government acknowledged that the influx of such large quantities of farm products posed difficult domestic problems, it was in general principle supportive of "the noble policy enunciated in Public Law 480." In fact, the Japanese submitted proposals for a larger amount of commodities to be received under PL-480 than the United States was prepared to offer—with the expectation that the yen proceeds from sale of these products "would, in large measure, be placed at the disposal of the Japanese Government, either by loan or grant, to be used in the strengthening of the Japanese economy and the economic development of Southeast Asia." That assumption was betrayed by the minute conditions attached to disposal of yen proceeds by the United States, which the Aichi delegation described as "disconcerting" and "most disappointing." "The contrast between the reported prior declarations of United States officials at the policy-making level and the suggested program arrived at by officials at the working level is rather striking," the Japanese complained, and went so far as to suggest that the PL-480 mechanism threatened to become "purely a United States disposal program with only incidental effects upon Japan's urgent need for economic support."

The PL-480 program posed an intrinsically sensitive problem. From the domestic American perspective, its objective was to simultaneously conserve dollars while resolving the crisis of agricultural overproduction. For the recipient country, this could easily not only lead to a decline in dollar receipts, but also foster agricultural *underproduction* and a consequent deterioration of self-sufficiency in foodstuffs. In criticizing the concrete mechanisms of PL-480, the Aichi team was quick to point this out and relate it to their ever-ready theme of the delicacy of Japanese public opinion and popular support for the U.S.-Japan alliance. In this case, they drew attention to the rural constituency upon which conservative electoral power rested:

> It should be recognized that, from the viewpoint of a recipient nation, the purchase of surplus farm products does not, in and of itself, provide economic assistance, since the law stipulates that the procurement must be in excess of "usual marketings." For Japan, in particular, where rural communities constitute half the population, such a program is apt to arouse resentment among the farmers unless they are convinced that the sales proceeds will be used for the overall benefit of their country. And, let there be no doubt about it, the farmers represent the backbone of support for the present conservative government, which wholeheartedly favors a policy of full cooperation with the free world against the neutralist sentiments espoused by the opposition.

In harping upon the manner in which the agricultural commodities program was "not necessarily advantageous to Japan," Yoshida's spokesmen raised the following points: (1) By committing itself to the purchase of PL-480 commodities above normal import requirements, Japan was forced to reduce its import of such products from countries other than the United States, thus prejudicing Japanese exports to these third countries. (2) The system also required Japan to make prior commitments to the United States concerning its "normal" imports of agricultural products from that country, which tended to consolidate the existing trade imbalance between the two countries. (3) The potential stimulation the program might give to Japanese shipping was vitiated by the requirement that 50 percent of all PL-480 products be transported in American vessels. (4) Technical procedures were "vastly more complicated" than normal open-account commercial transactions, and often resulted in Japan receiving products of undesirable quality and price. (5) Since the program operated with yen rather than dollars, it could easily be used in a manner that disrupted rather than helped to rectify Japan's dollar earnings and balance-of-payments position–for example, by the United States directing these yen funds toward procurements that it otherwise might have made with dollars.

The Japanese also expressed reservations concerning "triangular trade transactions" as conceived by the United States and integrated with disposal of the agricultural surplus. Under this formula, for example, the Philippines would agree to buy cement from Japan over and above normal imports of this commodity from Japan; the Philippines would then sell a corresponding amount of, say, chromite, to the United States; and the United States in turn would sell Japan a corresponding amount of surplus agricultural commodities. To the Japanese, this pattern was flawed in several ways. It did not improve Japan's balance-of-payments situation, since additional exports to, in this case, the Philippines would be offset by the necessity of increasing agricultural imports from the United States; this simply worsened Japan's trade deficit with the United States. The economic situation in Asia was in such a state of flux, moreover, that it was difficult to establish meaningful figures for "normal" imports. Thus, in the case of the Philippines, the actual demand for cement could easily be underestimated. Japanese cement which would have been imported on a straight trade basis anyway (and paid for in dollars) would then be shunted to the triangular-trade arrangement, forcing Japan to receive unwanted imports rather than badly wanted dollars. This American-sponsored mechanism was described as complicated, cumbersome, and "against the common aim of the free nations to encourage a more liberal international trade."

Aichi and his aides did not recommend that these procedures be entirely abandoned, but urged that they be restricted to rather exceptional commodities, and that the requirement to import from the United States be modified. Numerous technical proposals were submitted concerning Japan's proposed use of yen proceeds from the sale of U.S. farm products, but the fundamental principle which was repeated again and again was simple, and almost plaintive: Yoshida's spokesmen pleaded that such yen funds "be invested in their entirety in projects designed to strengthen the nation," and that the United States recognize that it was "essential that actual disbursement of the funds be at the free discretion of the Japanese Government."

In the final outcome, the Japanese request for 1955 of $133-million in unencumbered "aid" tied to agricultural commodities was reduced to $85-million, and of this amount the United States initially offered the Japanese government free use of only $39-million of the yen accruing from the sale of these commodities in Japan. The Aichi delegation described this as "far from satisfactory," and in a written response stated that this "would seem to suggest that approximately 55 percent of the Japanese currency generated by sales of surplus commodities should be used for purposes which could be of no benefit to Japan and which, in fact, might prove to be detrimental to our general objective of strengthening our country so that it might be an effective partner in the free world alliance." They requested that, at a minimum, 80 percent of PL-480 yen proceeds (approximately $70-million) be devoted to projects such as those the Japanese government itself had proposed. In the face of this expression of "great indignation," as Miyazawa described it, the United States raised the sum of relatively unencumbered proceeds to $50-million on the day before Yoshida's departure.[17]

In addition to aid available under the PL-480 program, the Aichi group also submitted a request for "an additional increment of dollar aid" to be used in the strengthening of Japan's industrial defense base. This would have involved $29-million over a three-year period, allocated under the MSA program, to be used largely for the purchase of machinery for defense industries. It was noted that the rehabilitation of Japan's defense industries still relied primarily upon U.S. offshore purchases, and was currently limited mostly to bullets, shells, light guns, aircraft parts, and aircraft repairs. The objective was to move away from this "into balanced production of all defense items," and to stimulate certain sectors by supplying military items to "friendly nations in Asia." In part, these ends were to be obtained by a combination of domestic capital, "physical aid" (machinery and machine tools) under the MSA program, and application of a portion of the proceeds from sale of agricultural commodities to defense production. Beyond this, the Japanese also desired that the United States begin to shift from supplying military "end items" to the Japanese forces to a policy of contracting for production of such end items within Japan itself. As during the Ikeda-Robertson talks a year earlier, the request for outright dollar aid was flatly rejected on the grounds that it "does not appear to be justified by Japan's current economic situation."[18]

THE ABORTIVE CHINA CAPER

During these exchanges of late 1954, the Japanese focused upon the trilateral relationship and gave ample lip service to denunciation of "International Communism." Some of the latter rhetoric appears to have been intended to appease that staunch opponent of appeasement, John Foster Dulles, and the most hackneyed of such statements came from Yoshida himself. Following a meeting with the secretary of state on November 9, for example, Yoshida summarized his position in an *aide-mémoire* which concluded with the language Dulles found so gratifying: "Communists are talking peace while they go about busily as ever with their secret maneuvers and underground intrigues to prepare for open and armed aggression at the place and time of their own choosing. . . ."[19]

In actuality, there appears to have been relatively little discussion of communist military aggression—or Japanese defense policies—in these conversations. The communist threat was presented largely as an economic one, and even here lay primarily in the attractive and positive *example* of economic success that China in particular seemed in the process of presenting to the underdeveloped countries of Asia. Moreover, the Japanese at this time made a more concerted effort than they had a year earlier to persuade the United States to allow Japan to engage in more extensive non-strategic economic relations with the People's Republic of China.

The Japanese side was at some variance on this issue, with Yoshida taking a more cautious approach than the Aichi group. In his speech to the National Press Club, Yoshida described Communist China as "a bleak fact of life in Asia that occupies our minds constantly," and before the Chamber of Commerce in New York he assured his audience that "the government and majority of the people of Japan have no intention to enter into closer relations with Communist China, at the expense of their friendly ties with the United States and other free countries." At the same time, however, he noted that "it is desirable that restrictions upon trade with Communist China be eased insofar as compatible with the unity and security of the free countries. We must bear in our minds the possibility that if these restrictions are too tight, proposal for more trade by the Communists as a means of peace offensive sounds so inviting that people come to complain [about] such restrictions." On other occasions, Yoshida indulged in his conviction that communism in China was merely a "temporary phenomenon."[20]

The Aichi delegation was less impressed than Yoshida with the temporary-phenomenon argument, and at the same time less timid than the prime minister in directly challenging the U.S. containment policy. Thus, without first consulting Yoshida, they submitted a draft "joint statement" to the State Department which contained this forthright declaration immediately following their proposed introductory clichés:

> . . . We [Eisenhower and Yoshida] consider that the interests of the free world in the Far East would better be served by a properly regulated intercourse between the peoples of Japan and China than by the interposition of an impenetrable wall designed to cut off all relationships. The efforts of the United States and Japanese Governments in this regard shall be directed, not to the maintenance of an impossible vacuum, but to a channelling of the inevitable forces leading to a greater understanding between China and Japan into a road open to friendship and trade but resolutely barred to Communist ideological influence.

Aichi and his aides assumed that Yoshida himself would reject this, and entertained no expectations that it would be approved by the U.S. government. It was construed as a wedge that might open the way for a milder statement, which at the second stage of drafting was presented in the following form: "The wellbeing and security of Southeast Asia will be realized only when aggressive tendencies are ceased and free association among the various peoples of Asia achieved." Yoshida was shown this version, and approved it after long deliberation. It was also accepted by the American drafters representing the State Department, giving the Aichi group a momentary feeling of elation that they had smuggled in a subtle but significant point that could be exploited in Japan's future dealings with China. On November 10, however, the very day on which the joint communiqué was to be released, Dulles personally intervened to express his opposition to the clause, and succeeded in persuading Yoshida to agree to its deletion. It was, Miyazawa ruefully observed, a nice revelation of the secretary of state's eagle eye.[21]

It was also a revelation of Yoshida's ultimate obsequiousness on the China issue. Although he endeavored to portray himself as a serious critic of U.S. policy toward China, on the two major occasions when he was actually confronted with a concrete decision —in December 1951 and November 1954—he bowed with scarcely a murmur before the messiah of containment, John Foster Dulles. Unlike conservative opponents such as Ishibashi, Hatoyama, Shigemitsu, and Ogata, Yoshida seems never to have even seriously entertained the thought that Japan should or could undertake to develop an independent policy toward China (or the Soviet Union). While willing to adopt a relatively firm, albeit essentially tactical, critical position on matters pertaining to Japanese remilitarization, he accepted the necessity of obedience to Washington's dictates where basic issues of diplomatic or economic alignment were concerned. This may have reflected his "realism"—but if so, it was implicitly at the same time a reflection of his, and Japan's, lack of independence. On this major foreign-policy challenge to sovereign Japan, Yoshida's actual practice of "diplomatic sense," and his style of "opposition," conveyed an aura of burlesque. He emerged at intervals between main acts to voice a mumbled complaint, drop a random and wooly proposal, execute a short soft-shoe, and disappear again behind the curtain of allegiance to the United States. Yoshida's position on China in the early 1950s was characterized by much the same flummery and irrelevance he had displayed in the pre-surrender era in his insubstantial criticism of Japanese aggression against China, his erratic imperialistic proposals while ambassador to London, and his sporadic and ineffectual tactical maneuvers against the Tōjō cabinet. On this particular occasion in late 1954, moreover, it is even remotely possible that a truly firm and serious representation concerning China policy by Yoshida personally might have had some effect—for President Eisenhower was not in fact in accord with Dulles on this issue. Eisenhower actually had supported the promotion of closer Sino-Japanese economic relations privately in a cabinet meeting several months earlier, but there is no evidence that Yoshida ever gave serious thought to playing personal and factional politics on this issue, as he had done previously with the Americans in attempting to circumvent SCAP's reformers.[22]

The China issue, proposed Marshall Plan for Asia, and problems relating to aid and agricultural commodities were the major points of discussion between the Aichi delegation and its American counterpart, although a variety of other matters were also considered. Among these, two appear to have carried Yoshida's special imprimatur. They concerned release of Japanese war criminals and solicitation of material American support for Japanese emigration, and both were singled out for special attention in the prime minister's *aide-mémoire* to Dulles of November 10.

In speaking before the American public, Yoshida did not hesitate to try to bell the cat in its own backyard by relating Japan's current problems to America's own earlier occupation policies. "Some of the difficulties now confronting us, in connection with government, economy, and education," he told the Chamber of Commerce, "originated in excesses which sometimes occurred under the occupation." As examples he cited the labor laws, Deconcentration Law and Anti-Monopoly Law, and "systems of education and local autonomy which are not adapted to the actual situation in Japan." He asserted that "the majority of the Japanese people do not believe that these excesses should remain as they are," and urged that Americans take these matters into consideration when evaluating Japan's politics and economy. He did not go so far as to publicly criticize the "excess" of war criminals still serving sentences in Sugamo prison, but conveyed this privately to Dulles in these words:

> The continued incarceration of war criminals is to the Japanese public a highly emotional issue as well as a social and political problem. To the families and relatives of these prisoners it is a tragic matter. To leave this problem unsolved serves only to perpetuate the bitter memories of war. Speedy action is requested.

Of some 755 war criminals in Sugamo at the time, approximately 300 were serving sentences meted out by U.S. military courts; the remainder had been sentenced by Britain, Australia, and the Netherlands. It was argued in a formal presentation that "these long-imprisoned men have had enough punishment and gone through a period of complete reorientation," and that "the Japanese public has manifested extraordinary sympathy and solicitude toward these men and their families, many of whom are destitute." The appeal was made "from the standpoint of humanitarianism," baited on a political hook: continued incarceration was "a stigma to Japanese prestige which impedes our people from a great willingness to take with pride a more active role in the efforts of the Free World." If the United States took the lead in abrogating these sentences, it was anticipated that the other powers involved would feel compelled to follow suit.[23] The joint communiqué merely stated that this subject had been "reviewed."

In the 1930s, Yoshida had endorsed the argument that "overpopulation" was one of Japan's basic economic problems, and he resurrected this in 1954 by soliciting U.S. capital support for a modest emigration program. As broached, this would involve 10,000 families over the ensuing five or six years, relocating mostly in South America. It was estimated that this would require the backing of $30-million in loans. Although this was formally included on the Japanese agenda in Washington, Aichi and his U.S. counterparts gave it but cursory attention. To the embarrassment of his aides, however, Yoshida endeavored to pursue the matter in conversations with bankers in New York.[24] The subject was not mentioned in the final joint communiqué.

The joint Eisenhower-Yoshida statement was released on November 10 and consisted of four brief sections. The first stressed the peaceful goals of the two governments and their commitment to cooperate with the "free nations of Asia." The second and lengthiest section referred to Japan's economic situation and the importance of its well-being "to the entire free world." The United States had agreed, it was noted, to cooperate with Japan's endeavor to rectify its balance of payments through export expansion, and to sell Japan agricultural commodities with "a substantial portion of the proceeds" to be used for domestic economic improvement, defense support, and regional economic development. In the following brief section, the United States expressed regret over the Bikini incident, and the two governments "emphasized their belief that the peaceful uses of atomic energy would be steadily developed and would eventually become of great value to Japan and other friendly nations throughout the world." The concluding section referred to other subjects reviewed in the conversations: disposition of Japanese assets in the United States, "communist efforts to weaken and discredit the operations of free governments of Asia," Japan's request for "expedited consideration of the cases of war criminals," the status of the Ryukyu and Bonin islands, and Japan's request that former inhabitants be allowed to return to the Bonins. The communiqué made no mention of military matters.

ERA'S END

On his previous departure from the United States three years earlier, following the San Francisco Peace Conference, Yoshida had been euphoric. He had guided Japan to sovereignty. His personal popularity was at a peak. His pre-eminence within the ruling conservative party was not yet seriously challenged. This was the Indian summer of his political career, followed by a prolonged winter of tribulation and discontent. Now, as he left American shores this second time, in November 1954, he was in every political respect at journey's end.

The contrast to 1951 was striking. Then he had carried with him a document, the peace treaty, which he regarded as his crowning achievement; and a majority of Japanese applauded him for it. Now he held, in the joint statement with Eisenhower, a scrap of paper which said nothing new and impressed no one including himself; and he returned to a Japan in which he was cast as a political liability by conservative politicians and businessmen as well as his perennial foes on the left. On the day the perfunctory Yoshida-Eisenhower statement was released, the prime minister read in *The New York Times* that Hatoyama and Shigemitsu had announced plans to form an anti-Yoshida conservative party.[25]

On November 24, Hatoyama formally executed a by now well-rehearsed exit from the Liberal Party and allied his coterie with Shigemitsu's Progressives to form the Japan Democratic Party; he traveled on well-greased skids. Four days later, a palace coup within the Liberal Party unseated Yoshida as president. He was replaced in that position by Vice Prime Minister Ogata Taketora, who supported a more aggressive rearmament policy and was endorsed by big business.[26] Yoshida, however, still maintained the premiership.

On December 6, the opposition parties, including the Left and Right Socialists as well as the new Democratic Party, introduced a no-confidence vote against Yoshida in the lower house, and Yoshida's cabinet members decided on their own initiative to resign en masse. Yoshida's immediate response was to propose dissolving the Diet—as he had done on a previous occasion—thereby forcing another general election. He also attempted to dismiss Ogata, who personally conveyed the unhappy tidings that, in those days of shipbuilding scandal and overseas journeys, Yoshida was now a captain without a ship. Only when Yoshida found himself in virtual isolation within his own party did he resign—reportedly in a rage. The Yoshida era ended on December 7, as Hatoyama tasted the doubly sweet fruits of revenge and command, while Yoshida returned to his beloved estate in Ōiso, there to sulk and fume.

Notes

Bibliography

Index

Abbreviations Used in the Notes

CJN Jichichō (Autonomy Agency). *Chihō Jichi Nenkan* (Local Autonomy Yearbook), 1954 (vols. I and II) and 1955 (vol. III).

CPM Correspondence with Prime Minister. Three folders of letters exchanged between Japanese prime ministers and SCAP, located among Government Section materials in Record Group 331, National Records Center, Suitland, Maryland. The specific titles are: "Correspondence between MacArthur, Whitney and Prime Minister" (Box 2974); "Correspondence between General Whitney and Prime Ministers" (Box 2974); "Prime Minister [1946–1951]" (Box 2993). These materials were declassified upon request in June 1970.

ESBP Economic Stabilization Board (Keizai Antei Honbu) papers. These materials are presently maintained in the archives of the National Planning Agency in Tokyo. Citations are to the multi-volume collection of English-language reports prepared by the ESB.

FO Foreign Office of Great Britain. Diplomatic records maintained in the Public Record Office, London. Where the notes refer to the internal Foreign Office "minutes" on a cable or memorandum, the date given is that of the basic cable/memorandum.

FRUS *Foreign Relations of the United States* (U.S. Department of State series).

JFDP John Foster Dulles papers, Princeton University. Transcripts of interviews concerning Dulles in the Princeton collection are cited as *JFDP-Oral.*

JFMA Japanese Foreign Ministry archives. Citations follow the standard microfilm designation of these captured Japanese documents, with the sub-designation *PVM* referring to materials from the Parliamentary Vice Minister files.

JGP Joseph Grew papers, Houghton Library, Harvard University.

JJS Bōeichō (National Defense Agency). *Jieitai Jūnen Shi* (Ten Year History of the Self-Defense Forces). 1961.

JMDP Joseph M. Dodge papers, Detroit Public Library.

JSPIJ *Journal of Social and Political Ideas in Japan,* 1.3 (December 1963).

KG *Kampō Gogai* (Official Gazette–Extra Number). Verbatim transcript of speeches, interpellations, and the like in the plenary sessions of both houses of the Diet (not to be confused with *Kampō*, the legislative record of the Diet). Includes both *Teikoku Gikai Gijiroku* (Proceedings of the Imperial Diet of Japan) and *Kokkai Kaigiroku* (Proceedings of the National Diet of Japan). Pagination begins on page 1 for each house at the beginning of each new session of the Diet. The *Kampō Gogai* is dated the day following the session transcribed. These records are available on microfilm (Yushodo Film Publications, 1966). For most of the occupation period, they are also available in English translation; see *OGE* below. Citation of this source is cumbersome, and the following key has been used:

HR Shūgiin (House of Representatives)

HC Sangiin (House of Councillors)

HP Kizokuin (House of Peers—the pre-1947 predecessor of the House of Councillors under the old constitution).

A sample citation would be: *KG-HR-10*, January 28, 1951 (p. 51). This refers to page 51 of the *Kampō Gogai* for the House of Representatives in the Tenth Session of the Diet. The publication is dated January 28; the session took place January 27. Although the *OGE* translation contains some infelicities, it is generally accurate and thus a most convenient reference source for the Western reader. All of the quotations in this present manuscript, however, have been checked against the original Japanese in *KG*. While some of the *OGE* phraseology is retained, the majority of direct quotations have been, in varying degrees, revised and recast. Both the *KG* and *OGE* versions are cited in the notes. (Each issue of *OGE* begins at page 1. Occasional issues of *OGE* are dated one day later than the counterpart *KG* issue; where no date follows a citation to *OGE*, this means that the *KG* and *OGE* dates are the same.)

KJ Yoshida Shigeru. *Kaisō Jūnen* (Recollections of Ten Years), 4 volumes. Shinchōsha, 1957–1958. Yoshida's autobiography. As the title indicates, this concentrates on the postwar period, but some of the more personal, anecdotal, and interesting reminiscences deal with the prewar period. Considerable portions of the "autobiography," especially the drier factual accounts, were reportedly drafted by a committee under Okazaki Katsuo. A partial English translation is available under the title *The Yoshida Memoirs* (see *YM* below).

KK *Kasekikai Kaihō*. An internal monthly newsletter issued by the Kasekikai, an organization of former Japanese Foreign Ministry officials. See the note to the Introduction on p. 499.

KTI Kōsei Torihiki Iinkai (Fair Trade Commission). *Dokusen Shihon Seisaku Nijūnen Shi* (A History of Two Decades of Policy Toward Monopoly Capital). Ōkurashō, 1968.

OGE Official Gazette Extra. English translation of *Kampō Gogai*, prepared under the auspices of the Supreme Commander for the Allied Powers, Japan. See the explanation under *KG* above.

PRJ Supreme Commander Allied Powers, Government Section, *Political Reorientation of Japan: September 1945 to September 1948.* Government Printing Office, 1949.

SGP Suzuki Gengo papers, archives of the Ministry of Finance, Tokyo.

SN Yoshida Shigeru. *Sekai to Nihon* (The World and Japan). Banchō Shobō, 1962.

SSNS *Shiryō: Sengo Nijūnen Shi* (Documents: A History of the Two Postwar Decades). 6 volumes. Nihon Hyōronsha, 1966. The separate volumes in this major collection are: I, Politics; II, Economics; III, Law; IV, Labor; V, Education, Society; VI, Chronology.

YM Yoshida, Shigeru. *The Yoshida Memoirs.* Houghton Mifflin, 1962. An abridged translation, largely by Yoshida's son Kenichi, of *Kaisō Jūnen.* The translation, although generally faithful and felicitous, is occasionally free. It omits most of the reminiscences concerning presurrender Japan which appear in the original Japanese edition, and compresses passages or chapters in a number of places. See *KJ* above.

YN Yoshida Naikaku Kankōkai (Yoshida Cabinets Publication Association). *Yoshida Naikaku* (The Yoshida Cabinets). 1954. The massive "official" history of the Yoshida cabinets.

YST "Yoshida Shigeru no Tegami," letters from Yoshida to his father-in-law, Makino Nobuaki, included among the Makino papers in the National Diet Library, Tokyo. See note 19 in Chapter 2 here for an explanation of the citations to this valuable but vexing collection.

*

Periodicals, where appropriate, are identified as follows: volume.number:pages (date). Thus, 7.4:624–625 (December 1965) refers to volume 7, number 4, pages 624–625 in the December 1965 issue of the periodical cited.

NOTES TO THE PREFACE TO THE PAPERBACK EDITION

1. See, for example, Andrew Gordon, *The Evolution of Labor Relations in Japan: Heavy Industry, 1853–1955* (Council on East Asian Studies, Harvard University, 1985); Chalmers Johnson, *MITI and the Japanese Miracle: The Growth of Industrial Policy, 1925–1975* (Stanford, 1982); Takafusa Nakamura, *The Postwar Japanese Economy: Its Development and Structure* (University of Tokyo, 1981).
2. For a suggestive analysis of Nakasone and the "Yoshida doctrine," see Kenneth B. Pyle, "In Pursuit of a Grand Design: Nakasone Betwixt the Past and the Future," *Journal of Japanese Studies* 13.2:243–270 (Summer 1987).
3. Inoki Masamichi's authorized and generally laudatory three-volume biography of Yoshida was published by Yomiuri Shimbunsha between 1978 and 1981 under the title *Hyōden Yoshida Shigeru* (A critical biography of Yoshida Shigeru). New and recently declassified U.S. archival materials pertaining to the Occupation in U.S. cold-war policy are closely analyzed in William S. Borden, *The Pacific Alliance: United States Foreign Economic Policy and Japanese Trade Recovery, 1947–1955* (University of Wisconsin, 1984) and Michael Schaller, *The American Occupation of Japan: The Origins of the Cold War in Asia* (Oxford, 1985). For bibliographic materials in English through 1985, see John W. Dower, *Japanese History & Culture from Ancient to Modern Times: Seven Basic Bibliographies* (Markus Wiener, 1986), pp. 199–222.
4. Takeshi Igarashi, "Peace-Making and Party Politics: The Formation of the Domestic Foreign-Policy System in Postwar Japan," *Journal of Japanese Studies* 11.2:323–356 (Summer 1985), esp. p. 350. The Yoshida letters are contained in "VIP File, Yoshida, Shigeru," in the MacArthur Memorial in Norfolk, Virginia (RG 10, box 11).
5. *FRUS* 1950, 6:1166. The official *Foreign Relations of the United States* volumes covering U.S. policy toward Japan between 1950 and 1954 which have become available since *Empire and Aftermath* was written contain a wealth of documentation (and pithy comment) that reinforces the general themes presented here.

Notes

INTRODUCTION

1. The campaign to promote Yoshida for the Nobel Peace Prize was initiated around 1964–1965 by some of his colleagues in Japan—with support from the Foreign Ministry and with an eye to winning the November 1967 prize. As part of the campaign, a lengthy article surveying Japan's modern history was published in English under Yoshida's name in the 1967 *Britannica Book of the Year*, and issued in book form by Praeger the same year, under the title *Japan's Decisive Century, 1867–1967*. A slightly revised Japanese version, *Nihon o Kettei Shita Hyakunen*, was published by Nihon Keizai Shimbunsha at approximately the same time. This survey is of some interest as an example of the general interpretation of modern Japanese history endorsed by the Yoshida group, although it is not clear how much of the manuscript Yoshida actually wrote himself. He died in October 1967, shortly before that year's recipient of the peace prize was decided. These activities are briefly discussed by Kitazawa Naokichi, one of the participants in the endeavor, in *Kasekikai Kaihō*, number 267 (May 1968), pp. 10–11. This is an internal monthly newsletter of the "Kasekikai," an organization of former Foreign Ministry officials. Reminiscences about Yoshida appear in almost every issue between October 1967 and April 1971. The newsletter is cited hereafter as *KK*.

1. YOUNG GENTLEMAN OF MEIJI

1. Kōsaka Masataka, *Saishō Yoshida Shigeru* (Chūō Kōronsha, 1968), p. 18; Asahi Shimbunsha, ed., *Yoshida Shigeru* (Asahi Shimbunsha, 1967), p. 126; Fujiwara Hirotatsu, *Yoshida Shigeru: sono Hito sono Seiji* (Yomiuri Shimbunsha, 1964), pp. 23–35; Abe Shinnosuke, *Gendai*

Seijika Ron (Bungei Shunjūsha, 1954), p. 207. The family register (*koseki*) in which Yoshida's mother is indicated as "unknown" is reproduced in "Kinkyū Tokushū: Yoshida Shigeru no Shōgai," *Asahi Gurafu*, November 5, 1967, pp. 82–83.

2. Kase Toshikazu, "Yoshida Shigeru: sono Kyūjūsai no Nenrin," *Bungei Shunjū*, November 1967, p. 136; Shinobu Seizaburō, *Sengo Nihon Seiji Shi*, I, 323; Asahi Shimbunsha, p. 126; Abe, p. 205. Among Yoshida Shigeru's own writings, see *Sekai to Nihon* (Banchō Shobō, 1962; cited hereafter as *SN*), p. 249; "Ōiso no Shōrai," *Chūō Kōron*, December 1965, p. 203; and (with Yoshida Kenichi) *Ōiso Seidan* (Bungei Shunjū Shinsha, 1956), p. 25. On the 1877 relationship between the party movement and the Satsuma rebellion, see Robert Scalapino, *Democracy and the Party Movement in Prewar Japan* (California, 1953), p. 61; also Peter Duus, *Party Rivalry and Political Change in Taishō Japan* (Harvard, 1968), p. 74. Although the leaders of the Risshisha plot were Mutsu Munemitsu and Hayashi Yuzō, Takeuchi personally seems to have conspired more closely with Kataoka Kankichi and Ōe Taku. Mutsu later became foreign minister; Hayashi was Takeuchi's cousin and the father of Hayashi Jōji, a well-known politician in the later Meiji period. Most sources describe Takeuchi as a Jiyūtō leader, and one claims he was one of "nine prominent secretaries" of the party; *Contemporary Japan*, 14.4–12:195 (April-December 1945). Both Takeuchi and Yoshida Kenzō are commonly described as *shishi* ("men of high purpose"), those impulsive and attractive actors in the Restoration drama who are well described by Marius B. Jansen in *Sakamoto Ryōma and the Meiji Restoration* (Princeton, 1961).
3. Shinobu, I, 323. Cf. Yoshida's own versions in *Ōiso Seidan*, pp. 98–99, and "Chichi to Haha: Oitachi no Koto Nado," *Kaizō*, January 1950, p. 104.
4. Shinobu, I, 323.
5. Itagaki's comment might be described as not only scornful, but also disingenuous. The occasion of his derision was Takeuchi's acceptance of money from Itō Hirobumi to be used by Itagaki.
6. Asahi Shimbunsha, p. 126. Workers in the Takashima mine at this time, according to one account, "were recruited or kidnapped from far and wide and labored under conditions close to outright slavery"; Koji Taira, *Economic Development and the Labor Market in Japan* (Columbia, 1970), p. 106. Interestingly, Yoshida's daughter Kazuko later married a Kyushu coal-mine owner, Asō Tagakichi, who became one of Yoshida's financial backers in the postwar period.
7. Shinobu, I, 323.
8. Kase, pp. 136, 142–143; Asahi Shimbunsha, p. 126; Bijutsu Shuppansha,

ed., *Rokuon Yoshida Shigeru* (Bijutsu Shuppansha, 1968), p. 32; *SN*, pp. 245–248 (on Itō's mortuary temple), 249–252, 259. Yoshida's reflections on the *Hoan Jōrei* of 1887 appear in "Chichi to Haha," pp. 104–105. He offers a slightly different version of Takeuchi's comments on presenting the sword in "Ōiso no Shōrai," p. 204; Takeuchi was thinking of bureaucratic graft and bribery. Yamagata Aritomo, it will be noted, was not included among those venerated. It would be a mistake, however, to overemphasize the differences between the oligarchs and the early political opposition with which Takeuchi was associated. Both were strongly motivated by the feelings of nationalism and loyalism that Yoshida later came to exemplify.

9. Asahi Shimbunsha, p. 127. The conversion, based on comparative rice prices, is made by Shibata Toshio.
10. Asahi Shimbunsha, p. 126; Kōsaka, p. 18; Abe, p. 206.
11. Yoshida, "Chichi to Haha," p. 106; *SN*, pp. 253–255.
12. Kōsaka, p. 19. Yoshida Kenichi, Yoshida Shigeru's son, describes Yoshida Kotoko as a "child of Edo" in Asahi Shimbunsha, p. 79.
13. *SN*, pp. 258–259.
14. *SN*, pp. 256–259; "Chichi to Haha," p. 108; "Ōiso no Shōrai," p. 203; Asahi Shimbunsha, p. 79. Critics of Yoshida also associate his upbringing as both adopted child and only child with a basic "coldness" in his relationships with others; cf. Fujiwara, pp. 23–24; Abe, p. 207. On *amae*, see Takeo Doi, *The Anatomy of Dependence* (Kodansha International, 1973).
15. *SN*, p. 257. On Satō, cf. Harry D. Harootunian, *Toward Restoration: The Growth of Political Consciousness in Tokugawa Japan* (California, 1970), pp. 124–125, 260, 330; also Tetsuo Najita, "Ōshio Heihachirō," in Albert M. Craig and Donald H. Shively, eds., *Personality in Japanese History* (California, 1970), pp. 158–159. On iconoclasm in the Japanese intellectual tradition, see Najita's *Japan* (Prentice-Hall, 1974).
16. On the various schools, see Abe, p. 211; Asahi Shimbunsha, p. 126; Kōsaka, p. 22. On Chinese thought, see "Chichi to Haha," p. 108.
17. Kase, p. 144; Abe, p. 208.
18. Yoshida, *Ōiso Seidan*, pp. 109–115. Yoshida entered the Fujisawa school with the aid of Nakajima Nobuyuki, then governor of Kanagawa and later speaker of the lower house; ibid., pp. 98–99.
19. Ibid., pp. 109–115. This would have been around 1890–1891, when the new Meiji constitution had just been promulgated and the first Diet convened.
20. Cf. Earl Kinmonth, "The Self-Made Man in Meiji Japanese Thought," Ph.D. dissertation, University of Wisconsin, Madison, 1975.
21. *Asahi Gurafu*, November 5, 1967, p. 193.

22. Yoshida Shigeru, *Kaisō Jūnen* (Shinchōsha, 1957–1958), IV, 90. The English version of these memoirs, *The Yoshida Memoirs* (Houghton Mifflin, 1962), omits a large part of those sections of the original which deal with Yoshida's early life and career. These sources are cited hereafter as *KJ* and *YM*. See also "Ōiso no Shōrai," p. 204.

23. The emergence in middle and late Meiji (from the 1880s) of muscular nationalism, emperor worship, and the mystique of the family state (*kazoku kokka*) involves, among other scholarly controversies, the issues of Meiji "absolutism," the state and ideology, and the revivification as opposed to simple continuity of "traditional cultural values." The new nationalism and statism were not monolithic, and naturally reflected international pressures and stimuli and, indeed, models (notably German) —as well as complex dynamics within the popular culture. But they were in any case assiduously suckled by the state, and part and parcel of the consolidated state structure exemplified in the emperor-centered constitution (1889), the Imperial Rescript on Education (1890) and subsequent strengthening of ethical indoctrination in the schools (reaching a first peak in 1910), and the paternalistic and family-centered revised civil code (1898). In English, the following sources may serve as an introduction to aspects of the problem: Marlene Mayo, ed., *The Emergence of Imperial Japan: Self-Defense or Calculated Aggression?* (Heath, 1970); Masaaki Kosaka, ed., *Japanese Thought in the Meiji Era*, vol. VIII of *Japanese Culture in the Meiji Era* (Toyo Bunko, 1958), especially Part 5; Kenneth B. Pyle, *The New Generation in Meiji Japan: Problems of Cultural Identity, 1885–1895* (Stanford, 1969), especially Chapter 9; Donald H. Shively, "The Japanization of the Middle Meiji," in Donald H. Shively, ed. *Tradition and Modernization in Japanese Culture* (Princeton, 1971), pp. 77–119; "A Symposium on Japanese Nationalism," *Journal of Asian Studies* 31.1:5–62 (November 1971); Wilbur M. Fridell, "Government Ethics Textbooks in Late Meiji Japan," ibid., 29.4:823–833 (August 1970); Joseph Pittau, *Political Thought in Early Meiji Japan, 1868–1889* (Harvard, 1967), especially p. 125 on *tennō*.

24. On the early Gakushūin curriculum and objectives, see David Anson Titus, *Palace and Politics in Prewar Japan* (Columbia, 1974), pp. 72–73. On Konoe Atsumaro, see Yabe Teiji, *Konoe Fumimaro* (Jiji Tsūshinsha, 1958), p. 5; *Dai Hyakka Jiten* (Heibonsha, 1932–1939), X(1), 7–8. Cf. Shumpei Okamoto, *The Japanese Oligarchy and the Russo-Japanese War* (Columbia, 1970), pp. 58ff., 82, 246; Marius B. Jansen, *The Japanese and Sun Yat-sen* (Harvard, 1954), p. 52.

25. *Dai Hyakka Jiten*, XXIV(2), 362; F. Hilary Conroy, *The Japanese Seizure of Korea, 1868–1910: A Study of Realism and Idealism in International Relations* (Pennsylvania, 1960), pp. 306–321; Yoshida,

"Ōiso no Shōrai," p. 204. Following the murder of Queen Min, Miura and his co-conspirators were tried and acquitted in Japan.

26. Abe, pp. 211–212; Yoshida, "Chichi to Haha," p. 109.
27. Robert M. Spaulding, *Imperial Japan's Higher Civil Service Exams* (Princeton, 1967), p. 225. Hirota also entered the foreign service at this time; Asahi Shimbunsha, p. 127. Yoshida's first appointment was really to Tientsin in late 1906, but he never actually assumed this post; *SN*, pp. 250–251.
28. *KJ*, IV, 130–131.
29. Comments on the marriage derive from conversations with individuals familiar with Yoshida. He was thirty, and his wife nineteen, at the time of their marriage.
30. Cf. Kase, p. 139.
31. In April 1906, Makino delivered a speech calling for development of patriotism among youth. Two months later, the Ministry of Education issued an "Instruction on Thought Control of Students," and shortly thereafter the ministry helped sponsor student tours of the battlefields of the recent Russo-Japanese War; *The Japan Weekly Chronicle*, June 12 and July 19, 1906, and Itō Takeo, *Mantetsu ni Ikite* (Keisō Shobō, 1964), p. 38. I am indebted to Herbert Bix for these references, which appear in the first chapter of his Ph.D. dissertation, "Japanese Imperialism and Manchuria, 1890–1931," Harvard University, 1972.
32. Scalapino, pp. 358–359. See Chapter 7, notes 49–51 below.
33. Masao Maruyama, *Thought and Behaviour in Modern Japanese Politics* (Oxford, 1963), pp. 12–13.

2. "TRADITIONAL DIPLOMACY," 1906–1922

1. *KJ*, IV, 92–93.
2. Sumimoto Toshio, *Senryō Hiroku* (Mainichi Shimbunsha, 1952), I, 119.
3. Cf. the following documents in the archives of the British Foreign Office (*FO*) in the Public Record Office, London: *FO* 371/20279 (December 17, 1936), pp. 244–247; ibid., (December 4, 1936), pp. 231–232; *FO* 371/20277 (July 30, 1936), p. 86. These arguments are documented in fuller detail in Chapter 4 below.
4. Yoshida Shigeru, *Ōiso Zuisō* (Sekkasha, 1962), pp. 48–49.
5. Yoshida, *Nihon o Kettei Shita Hyakunen*, p. 64. These "special feelings" had been nurtured by Yoshida's father-in-law, among others. As education minister in 1906, Makino helped organize patriotic tours for secondary-school students to visit Manchuria and the battlefield sites of the recent war; see the citation in Chapter 1, note 31.
6. Cf. *YM*, p. 1, and *Ōiso Seidan*, pp. 45–48, 63–64.

7. See Chapters 4 and 5.
8. See notes 32 and 37 in Chapter 2; 52 in Chapter 3; 18 and 88 in Chapter 5; 23 and 30 in Chapter 6; 4 in Chapter 8; and 75 in Chapter 10.
9. See Chapter 10.
10. *SN*, pp. 250–251.
11. *SN*, p. 251, and "Ōiso no Shōrai, p. 204. Tamura Kōsaku, "Wakai Hi no Yoshida-san no Tsuikai," in *KK* 261:9 (November 1967).
12. The Japanese position in Antung was established by the Sino-Japanese Treaty of December 1905, in which Japan acquired the right to construct a military railway between Mukden and Antung; John V. A. MacMurray, ed., *Treaties and Agreements With and Concerning China* (Carnegie Endowment for International Peace, 1921), I, 552. On Terauchi, see Okamoto, pp. 73, 75; Marius B. Jansen, *Japan and China: From War to Peace* (Rand McNally, 1975), pp. 205, 219–222; and (for a blistering critique), Takayoshi Matsuo, "The Development of Democracy in Japan," *The Developing Economies,* 4.4:624–625 (December 1966).
13. *KJ*, IV, 133–135.
14. *KJ*, I, 109–110; ibid., IV, 134–135: *YM*, pp. 54–55. Yoshida's relationship with Tanaka is developed here in Chapter 3; with Mazaki and Obata in Chapter 7; and with the Willoughby group in Chapter 8.
15. Tamura, *KK* 261:8.
16. Cf. *SN*, pp. 148–152.
17. Tamura, *KK* 261:8.
18. As postwar premier, Yoshida threw the Diet into an uproar by calling an interpellator a "stupid fool" (*bakayarō*). According to one old acquaintance, this was a label Yoshida bestowed freely throughout his career; Miyake Kijirō, "Yoshida-san o Shinobite Omou Kotodomo," *KK* 285: 12–13 (November 1969).
19. *YST*, July 27 [1916?], pp. 289–297. An extensive and almost entirely neglected collection of letters written by Yoshida is included among the papers of Makino Nobuaki maintained in the National Diet Library in Tokyo. These cover a period of roughly four decades, from shortly after Yoshida's marriage to Makino's daughter in 1909 to around 1947. The majority of letters are personal communications from Yoshida to Makino; some handwritten copies of important letters from Yoshida to prominent officials are also included. Most of the letters are written by brush, and are in considerable part indecipherable to even the average educated Japanese reader; I am indebted to Fujii Jōji of Kyoto University for rendering these materials into legible script. The Yoshida letters *in toto* number in the neighborhood of 450 pages, and are available on microfilm from the Diet Library. They follow no chronological order whatsoever, and although most bear a notation of month and day, almost

none give the year in which they were written. It is thus necessary to conjecture the year of composition from the contents. It is virtually impossible to give an exact "pagination" of the letters, especially when working from the microfilm, as has been done here. Some of the letters are on a single roll of paper, and there is considerable overlap of content on the microfilm frames. In the citations to this collection hereafter, the letters are identified as *YST* (*Yoshida Shigeru no Tegami*, or "Yoshida Shigeru Letters"); the pagination cited is an *approximate* pagination, based on working copies made from the microfilm; and the year of composition is given in brackets to indicate that it is the assumed year, based on internal evidence, with a question mark inserted where the date is especially problematic. Unless otherwise noted, the letters cited are from Yoshida to Makino.

20. Tamura, *KK* 261:8; Miyake, *KK* 285:12.
21. *YST* [1916; no month or day given], pp. 84–94.
22. Yoshida refers to his opposition to the Twenty-One Demands in passing in *KJ*, IV, p. 94, and most Japanese secondary sources appear to rely upon this cryptic reference; cf. Kōsaka, p. 9; Asahi Shimbunsha, p. 127; Kase, p. 137. Yoshida mentioned the incident to Ambassador Joseph Grew in 1933, but again in general terms; see the Joseph Grew Papers (cited hereafter as *JGP*) in the Houghton Library at Harvard University, vol. 65, p. 792 (November 27, 1933). It is conceivable that Yoshida's opposition to the Demands also may have been influenced by the political configuration within Japan itself. In the clash between Prime Minister Ōkuma Shigenobu and Foreign Minister Katō Kōmei, who presented the Demands, and Hara Kei plus the *genrō* led by Yamagata, who opposed them, Makino was close to Hara and the *genrō*. Yoshida's position may well have been partly shaped by these more personal associations. In general, however, it can be assumed that his opposition was fundamentally pragmatic and tactical. It was not Yoshida's style to take positions on the basis of "humane" or "liberal" concern for the well-being of China, nor would this have been in keeping with the spirit of Japanese imperialism which characterized this period. Moreover, many of the Japanese "rights" in continental Asia which Yoshida staunchly defended derived from the Twenty-One Demands; cf. Paul Clyde, *The Far East* (Prentice-Hall, 1948), p. 385: "The Manchurian demands in Group 2 were thus designed to make permanent Japan's control of Kwantung, Darien, Port Arthur, the zones of the South Manchurian Railway, the Antung-Mukden Railway, and the Kirin-Changchun Railway. . . ." At the Eastern Conference of 1927, Yoshida referred to the tactical blunder of the Demands; in the standard microfilm records of the Japanese Foreign Ministry archives (*JFMA*), see

JFMA PVM 41, pp. 353–354. As discussed in Chapter 5 below, in 1936 and 1937 he also essentially resurrected some of the notorious "wishes and desires" in "group five" of the Demands in attempting to promote an Anglo-Japanese agreement concerning China. For some of his brief later comments on the Demands, see, in addition to note 37 in this chapter, *KJ*, I, 27–28; *YM*, p. 5; *Nihon o Kettei Shita Hyakunen*, p. 60; *Japan's Decisive Century*, p. 36; "Ōiso no Shōrai," p. 205.

23. For letters to Makino on the subject of the *Shina rōnin*, see *YST*, January 15 [1916], pp. 348–357, and *YST* [1916; no month or day given], pp. 84–94. The letter concerning Terauchi's views appears in *YST*, June 9 [1916?], pp. 382–390. Yoshida's memorandum to the foreign minister on the subject, dated March 16, 1916, is reproduced in *KK* 300:19 (February 1971), together with an illuminating brief background discussion by Kurihara Ken.
24. "Ōiso no Shōrai," p. 205.
25. *KJ*, IV, 94.
26. "Ōiso no Shōrai," p. 205; *KJ*, IV, 148–149. Yoshida offers a nice vignette of the diligent Shidehara polishing his English-language skills during an early assignment in London by first translating editorials from the London *Times* into Japanese, then translating this Japanese back into English and comparing his version with the original; ibid., pp. 111–112.
27. *YST*, October 31 [1918], pp. 95–98.
28. *KJ*, IV, 108. Although there was an interesting "young Turk" movement within the Japanese delegation to Versailles, Yoshida does not appear to have participated actively in this; cf. Horiuchi Kensuke, "Berusaiyu Kōwa Kaigi no Kaisō," *Kingu*, January 1951, pp. 78–91.
29. *KJ*, IV, 96–98.
30. *Japan's Decisive Century*, pp. 31–32. The Japanese version, published after the English, omits this sentence; *Nihon o Kettei Shita Hyakunen*, pp. 56–57.
31. Ibid.
32. *JFMA PVM* 41, p. 39 (June 10, 1927); cf. Kōsaka, p. 15. Akira Iriye regards Makino as a leading spokesman for Wilson's "new diplomacy"; see "The Failure of Economic Expansion: 1918–1931," in Bernard S. Silberman and H. D. Harootunian, eds., *Japan in Crisis: Essays on Taisho Democracy* (Princeton, 1974), pp. 237–269. On the split between advocates of the "old" and "new" diplomacies within the Japanese Foreign Ministry during the 1920s, see James B. Crowley, *Japan's Quest for Autonomy* (Princeton, 1968), p. 110.
33. *KJ*, IV, 95.
34. Konoe, like Yoshida, had used his personal connections (with Saionji) to gain a position in the Japanese delegation to the Paris Peace Conference.

For his early, cynical, and almost prophetic views concerning the war and its settlement as simply another stage in the expansion of Western imperialism, see Yabe (1958), pp. 16–22.

35. Dulles was thirty-one at the time of the Paris Peace Conference, while Yoshida was forty-one. In defending the relatively generous peace settlement proposed for Japan after World War Two, both men frequently relied on the negative example of the Versailles precedent. This point is made in a number of the transcripts in the Dulles Oral History Project at Princeton University; see, for example, the interviews with William J. Sebald, Sir Percy Spender, and C. Stanton Babcock. It might be noted that prior to World War Two Dulles showed no great concern for this particular "lesson" of Versailles, and was most recalcitrant in speaking out against German revanchism; cf. Hans Morgenthau's essay in Norman Graebner, ed., *An Uncertain Tradition: American Secretaries of State in the Twentieth Century* (McGraw-Hill, 1961). For an example of Yoshida's later elicitation of the harsh settlement with Germany as a *positive* model for the imperialists in China, see Chapter 3, note 55 below. A general comment on the "lessons of Versailles" is given by Professor Crowley in James B. Crowley, ed., *Modern East Asia: Essays in in Interpretation* (Harcourt, Brace & World, 1970), pp. 238–240.
36. Tamura, *KK* 261:9.
37. M. Soko, "Japan's Far Eastern Policy," *The Fortnightly Review*, New Series, 109:267–270 (February 1, 1921). Yoshida indicated that he was the author of this article in a letter to Makino; *YST*, June 10 [1921], pp. 321–329.
38. Tamura, *KK* 261:9.
39. Osanagi Kanroji, *Hirohito: An Intimate Portrait of the Japanese Emperor* (Gateway, 1975), pp. 79–98, especially pp. 79–84.
40. Cf. Harry D. Harootunian, "Introduction," in Silberman and Harootunian, pp. 6–8.
41. *YST*, June 10 [1921], pp. 321–329.
42. It is difficult to say whether Yoshida's "ecstasy" led him to exaggerate the crown prince's poise, or whether Hirohito himself later became more timid and withdrawn. It has been suggested that Hirohito held himself at least partially responsible for the apparent (although well-concealed) suicide of former prime minister Tanaka Giichi in 1928, since he had reprimanded Tanaka shortly before on the handling of the assassination of Chang Tso-lin. The emperor's shock at the suicide, in this view, was profound. This is suggested by Miyake in *KK* 290:8–11 (April 1970). For a contemporaneous report on the crown prince's visit similar to Yoshida's account to Makino, see the letter from Kobayashi Seizō quoted in Kanroji, pp. 85–87.

43. See Chapter 9, note 143 below. The contemptuous phrase "literary sycophant" derives from the Chinese classic *Shih-chi*, which has been translated into English by Burton Watson as *Records of the Grand Historian of China* (Columbia, 1961). It is the type of set phrase with which most Japanese of Yoshida's generation, with a background in classical Chinese, would be familiar—although he did not in fact reproduce it accurately in the 1921 letter. His variant rendering was ***kyokugaku amin*** 曲學阿民; the original phrase, in Japanese reading, is ***kyokugaku asei*** 曲學阿世. An alternative English equivalent is "prostitute of learning."

3. MANAGING THE EMPIRE, 1922–1930

1. *YST*, [ca. mid-1923], pp. 272–281.
2. *YST*, January 3 [1923], pp. 50–69.
3. *YST*, [ca. mid-1923], pp. 272–281.
4. Yoshida, "Ōiso no Shōrai," p. 205.
5. This fascination with personality, and undisguised delight in Yoshida's idiosyncrasies and less conventional pronouncements and escapades, emerges strongly in the long series of reminiscences concerning Yoshida sponsored by the Kasekikai (see Introduction, note 1). For extended examples of this personality-oriented approach, see Kase Toshikazu, *Yoshida Shigeru no Yuigon* (Yomiuri Shimbunsha, 1967), and Kon Hidemi, *Yoshida Shigeru* (Kodansha, 1967).
6. *KJ*, IV, 101.
7. On the general problems confronting Yoshida in Mukden, see Morishima Morito, *Imbō, Ansatsu, Guntō: Ichi Gaikōkan no Kaisō* (Iwanami Shinsho, 1950), pp. 14–18. The most detailed English-language study of Japanese policy in the Three Eastern Provinces in the 1920s is Gavan McCormack, *Chang Tso-lin in Northeast China, 1911–1928: China, Japan, and the Manchurian Idea* (Stanford, 1977). McCormack emphasizes the "positively imperialistic overtones" of the word "Manchuria" as used in much Western and Japanese writing, in that it has tended to reinforce the notion of the separateness of China's northeastern provinces (p. 4). For the configuration of power among leaders in the Three Eastern Provinces, I have also drawn upon an unpublished paper by Thomas Engelhardt.
8. Morishima, p. 18. Kodama Hideo was the eldest son of Kodama Gentarō, a Chōshū-clique general who held several prominent positions prior to his death in 1906, among them governor general of Taiwan, Army minister in several cabinets, education minister, and commander of one force in the Russo-Japanese War. Yoshida used the "double and triple diplomacy" phrase in a dispatch of September 30, 1927; *JFMA PVM* 23,

pp. 543, 544. The phrase is sometimes rendered as "triple and quadruple diplomacy"; cf. *KK* 266:2–4.

9. *JFMA PVM* 41, pp. 33, 34 (June 10, 1937).
10. See the references to Chang in Allen S. Whiting, *Soviet Policies in China, 1917–1924* (Stanford University edition, 1968), and Stuart Schram, *Mao Tse-tung* (Penguin, 1966).
11. Akira Iriye, *After Imperialism: The Search for a New Order in the Far East, 1921–1931* (Harvard, 1965), p. 162.
12. A further consideration in the Japanese attempts to persuade Chang to abandon his activities south of the Great Wall was the hope that, by causing his withdrawal, Chiang Kai-shek would be better able to suppress the radical wing of the Kuomintang, which at that time still included the Communists; Iriye, pp. 144, 164.
13. *KJ*, IV, 147.
14. Morishima, pp. 15–16. The Japanese editors were Sahara Tokusuke and Kikuchi Teiji.
15. Ibid., pp. 16–17. In advocating this vintage imperialist tactic of loans-with-concessions, Yoshida was in tune with the sentiment of the Foreign Ministry; cf. Iriye, p. 113.
16. This recurs throughout his dispatches; cf. *JFMA PVM* 23, pp. 22–24 (April 21, 1927). McCormack deals with these matters in considerable detail.
17. In addition to McCormack and Iriye, see Nobuya Bamba, *Japanese Diplomacy in a Dilemma: New Light on Japan's China Policy, 1924–1929* (British Columbia, 1973).
18. *FO* 371/13167 (1928), p. 54.
19. Cf. *JFMA PVM* 23, p. 22 (April 21, 1927).
20. Ibid., pp. 22–24.
21. *YST*, May 9 [1927?], pp. 177–183.
22. *JFMA PVM* 41, pp. 351–354.
23. *YST*, July 2 [1926], pp. 417–431.
24. Iriye, p. 154.
25. Ibid., pp. 110, 114.
26. *JFMA PVM* 23, p. 162 (August 3, 1927).
27. Ibid., p. 34 (June 12, 1927).
28. Ibid., p. 160 (August 3, 1927).
29. Ibid., p. 724 (April 27, 1928).
30. Ibid., p. 36 (June 12, 1927).
31. Ibid., p. 34.
32. Ibid., p. 160 (August 3, 1927).
33. Ibid., p. 34 (June 12, 1927).
34. Ibid., p. 195 (August 5, 1927).

35. Ibid., p. 130 (July 26, 1927).
36. Ibid., p. 123 (July 23, 1927).
37. *Contemporary Japan* 14.4–12:196 (April-December 1945).
38. *JFMA PVM* 23, pp. 22–24; McCormack, p. 233.
39. McCormack stresses the sweeping purview of the first clause in Yoshida's memorandum of April 21, and states that this proposal "appears to have been the first serious recommendation from a senior Japanese official, civil or military, for an effective takeover of Northeast China"; pp. 233 and 307 (n. 151).
40. *JFMA PVM* 41, pp. 29–30, 33–34 (June 9 and 10, 1927).
41. *JFMA PVM* 23, pp. 144–145 (August 1, 1927).
42. Ibid., p. 175 (August 4, 1927).
43. Ibid., pp. 209–210 (August 6, 1927).
44. Iriye, p. 178.
45. *JFMA PVM* 23, p. 665 (January 1, 1928).
46. Particularly Tanaka's cable of July 20, 1927; cf. Iriye, pp. 173–174.
47. *JFMA PVM* 23, pp. 171–174 (August 4, 1927).
48. Ibid., pp. 182–186 (August 1, 1927) and pp. 310–312 (August 12, 1927).
49. Ibid., p. 191 (August 5, 1927).
50. Ibid., pp. 191–197 (August 5, 1927); p. 664 (January 1, 1928).
51. Cf. Iriye, pp. 118, 184.
52. *JFMA PVM* 41, p. 39 (June 10, 1927).
53. Ibid., pp. 27–39 (June 9 and 10, 1927). Cf. *YST*, May 9 [1927?], pp. 177–183, and *YST*, September 17 [1927?], pp. 169–172.
54. *JFMA PVM* 41, pp. 35–37 (June 10, 1927).
55. Ibid., p. 38. On the occupation of the Rhine, cf. A. J. P. Taylor, *The Origins of the Second World War* (Fawcett/Premier, 1963), pp. 27–28, 31, 48.
56. *FO* 371/13167 (1928), pp. 54–56; cf. pp. 76–78.
57. In a letter to Makino dated "September 17," Yoshida noted that he was preparing a paper on "management of Manchuria." This was presumedly in 1927, and it is possible that the memorandum of April 27, 1928 represented culmination of this same project. There is no way of proving this, but the April document does bear the earmarks of being a carefully considered composition, as opposed to the memoranda of everyday business. *YST*, September 17 [1927?], pp. 169–172.
58. *JFMA PVM* 23, pp. 713–727 (April 27, 1928).
59. See, for example, Bamba (note 17 above).
60. *KJ*, IV, 152–153.
61. As the Pacific War entered its final stage, Owen Lattimore conveyed this

general argument crisply and pungently in *Solution in Asia* (Little, Brown, 1945); see especially pp. 5, 45–48, 190–191.

62. In Japanese terminology, the quotation was that it was all right to wear a *maedare* toward China proper, but for Manchuria it was necessary to wear a *haori*; Miyake, *KK* 289:11 (March 1970).
63. Tsutsui Kiyoshi, "Mori Kaku no Seikaku," *KK* 289:7–10 (March 1970), especially p. 9; also Tsutsui's "Mori Kaku to wa Donna Hito," *KK* 288: 8–10 (February 1970).
64. *YST*, January 12 [1928?], pp. 301–309.
65. Tsutsui, *KK* 289:9. This was apparently only the second time in his entire diplomatic career that Yoshida personally solicited a position, the first being inclusion in the delegation to the Paris Peace Conference (and subsequent posting to London). He approached Tanaka directly, declared he was the most appropriate man for the job, and delivered an impromptu speech on the policy he would pursue toward the continent if he were foreign minister; *KJ*, IV, 145.
66. Tsutsui, *KK* 289:9; Miyake, *KK* 289:12.
67. Miyake, *KK* 289:12.
68. On Tanaka's downfall, see Titus, pp. 144–147. Tsutsui discusses these events, culminating in Tanaka's suicide, in "Nani ga Tanaka Taishō o Jisatsu ni Oikonda ka," *KK* 290:8–11 (April 1970).
69. *KJ*, IV, 102, 143–146. It might be noted in passing that Makino apparently played an important role in both Tanaka's appointment to the premiership and his ouster. On the ascent, see Duus, p. 232. On the descent, see Titus, p. 147.
70. See Bamba, especially Chapters 3 and 7, for Tanaka's views and activities prior to as well as during his premiership.
71. On the Peace Preservation Law, see the following general sources: Richard H. Mitchell, *Thought Control in Prewar Japan* (Cornell, 1976), and "Chian Ijihō Taisei: sono Jittai to Dōtai," a special issue of *Gendai Shi*, June 1976. The Tanaka quote appears in *Trans-Pacific*, April 21, 1928, and is quoted in Donald Trowbridge Roden, "The Pre-war Japanese Student Movement: Some Observations and Comparisons," M.A. thesis, University of Wisconsin, Madison, 1969, p. 41.
72. These matters are discussed in Chapters 7 and 9 below.
73. Kobayashi had been naval attaché in the embassy in London in the early 1920s when Yoshida served there as first secretary.
74. *KJ*, IV, 135–137.
75. Harada Kumao, *Saionji Kō to Seikyoku* (Iwanami Shoten, 1951–1952), I, 235–237. The incident is also known as the Wanpaoshan Incident.
76. Ibid., II, 404.

4. *EXPLAINING THE NEW IMPERIALISM, 1931–1937*

1. *KJ*, IV, 103. Mazaki Ryū, "Ko Yoshida Shigeru-san o Shinobu," *KK* 271: 13 (September 1968); "Yoshida Shigeru-san o Shinobu," *KK* 276:11 (February 1969).
2. Sawada Setsuzō, "Yoshida-san no Omoide," *KK* 274:15 (December 1968).
3. Cf. *YST*, March 22 [1932], pp. 162–168; June 7 [1932], pp. 225–233; August 2 [1932], pp. 340–342.
4. *FO* 371/16163 (April 9, 1932), p. 179.
5. Mazaki, *KK* 271:14.
6. *FO* 371/13167 (April 2, 1928), p. 56.
7. *FO* 371/16163 (April 9, 1932), p. 179.
8. *FO* 371/20279 (November 6, 1936), p. 145 [sub-page 3].
9. *YST*, March 22 [1932], pp. 162–168.
10. Ibid.; *YST*, June 7 [1932], pp. 225–233.
11. *YST*, June 7 [1932], pp. 225–233. Cf. Yoshida's earlier undated letter to Makino in *YST* [1927–1928?], pp. 272–281.
12. *YST*, March 22 [1932], pp. 162–168.
13. *YST*, June 7 [1932], pp. 225–233.
14. William Roger Louis, *British Strategy in the Far East, 1919–1939* (Oxford, 1971), Chapter 6, especially pp. 185–188.
15. *YST*, August 2 [1932], pp. 340–342. He had requested permission to return via England and the United States.
16. *KJ*, IV, 129–130.
17. Harada, II, 365–366. Some nine years later, after a conversation with Matsuoka on May 14, 1941, Grew also reached the conclusion that Matsuoka was mentally ill; *JGP*, "Personal Notes, 1941," pp. 5097–5098. According to his memoirs, Yoshida again met with Matsuoka shortly before the latter's departure for Geneva, and, upon expressing his case against withdrawal, received Matsuoka's firm concurrence. When newspaper reports from Geneva indicated that Japan was indeed moving in the direction of withdrawal, Yoshida visited Saionji to urge his intercession in preventing this, and met an enigmatic response from the old Genrō. "I agree with what you say in the abstract," Saionji told Yoshida after listening to his views, "but oppose it in the concrete." When Yoshida indicated he did not understand what that meant, Saionji grew angry and exclaimed: "In discussing such important affairs of the nation one must be determined enough to put his life on the line. Do you have that determination?" As a matter of fact, Yoshida noted in the memoirs, he did not—not in the slightest. *KJ*, IV, 129–130; cf. Kōsaka, pp. 52–53.
18. Harada, III, 20–26.

19. *YST*, August 2 [1932], pp. 340–342.
20. Harada, II, 341, 374–375; Kase, *Bungei Shunjū*, p. 136. Actually, the refusal did not reflect disinterest in the prestigious U.S. post. A year or so later, in December 1933, for example, Grew noted in his diary that Yoshida seemed disappointed that he was not appointed ambassador to Washington when his old classmate Hirota became foreign minister; *JGP* 65:821.
21. Howard Schonberger, "The Japan Lobby in American Diplomacy, 1947–1952," *Pacific Historical Review* 46.3:327–359 (August 1977).
22. Transcript of interview with Eugene Dooman in the Columbia University oral history project dealing with the occupation of Japan, pp. 79–80. William Castle was a former U.S. ambassador to Japan, and personal friend of Makino, who advocated appeasement toward Japan until a very late date; cf. his article "A Monroe Doctrine for Japan," *The Atlantic Monthly*, October 1940, pp. 445–452. In the post-1945 period, Castle was also associated with the informal "Japan lobby," the American Council on Japan, which opposed the extensiveness of initial occupation reforms in Japan (see note 21 above). For Yoshida, one of the most memorable events of this trip was his conversation with Colonel Edward House, who warned him of the dangerous path Japan was treading and compared this to developments in Germany which culminated in World War One. Yoshida was so impressed with this conversation that, over two decades later, he opened his four-volume memoirs with an account of House's advice; *KJ*, I, 22–24; *YM*, pp. 1–2.
23. *KJ*, IV, 103; Kōsaka, p. 17; *JGP* 59:281; *JGP* 65:824; *JGP* 72:2010; *JGP*, "Conversations I," pp. 145–146; *FO* 371/18195 (December 20, 1934), pp. 373–376. The itinerary included the Middle East; Kitazawa Naokichi, "Kitazawa Naokichi Tsuioku-Dan," *KK* 267:9 (May 1968). See also U.S. Department of State, *Foreign Relations of the United States*, 1934, I, 306–307, 309–311; hereafter this source is cited as *FRUS*.
24. Harada, IV, 94.
25. *JGP* 72:2010, 2013–2015, 2021–2022.
26. *FRUS*, 1935, III, 840–841, 854.
27. *JGP* 79:2799, 2801–2802; *FRUS*, 1936, IV, 222.
28. *FRUS*, 1935, III, 853–854; *JGP* 75:2275.
29. *YST*, March 29 [1934?], pp. 99–106.
30. *JGP*, "Conversations I," pp. 71–72.
31. *JGP* 65:716; also unpaginated "Conversation No. 1" of October 2, 1933 in this same volume.
32. *FRUS*, 1934, I, 310.
33. *JGP* 65:826.

34. *JGP* 65:550; cf. *JGP* 58:281–284, 296. Waldo Heinrichs, Jr., also discusses this in *American Ambassador: Joseph C. Grew and the Development of the United States Diplomatic Tradition* (Little, Brown, 1966).
35. *JGP* 72:end matter. When Grew was on leave between May and October 1939, he delivered a standard speech on the lecture circuit in which he referred indirectly to the importance of these Japanese acquaintances to himself and his wife: "As I once wrote to Stanley Hornbeck, if we weren't surrounded in Tokyo with Japanese who have the finest instincts, quite apart from their good manners, and who themselves deplore what is going on in China today, we would find it very difficult to remain at our present post." *JGP* 94:4082.
36. Cf. *JGP* 65:820; *JGP* 71:1192–1194; *JGP* 75:2435.
37. *JGP*, "Personal Notes, 1941," pp. 5830–5831, 5860. The cultured sensitivity of Yoshida's wife, Yukiko, emerges in a small book she published in English several years before her death: *Whispering Leaves in Grosvenor Square, 1936–37* (Longmans, Green, 1938). She used here a shorter form of her given name, Yuki.
38. *JGP* 79:2689; *JGP* 65:716.
39. *JGP* 65:761.
40. *JGP* 79:2802. The question of Yoshida's English-language facility is somewhat intriguing. As early as 1928, Cecil Dormer of the British embassy in Tokyo reported that "Mr. Yoshida speaks excellent English"; *FO* 371/13167 (April 2, 1928), p. 56. On more than one occasion, however, Grew made reference to Yoshida's faltering command of English, and intimations of this occur in the British Foreign Office records pertaining to Yoshida's activities as ambassador to London in 1936–1938. Miyake claims that Yoshida's English was good in conversation but poor in more formal speeches; *KK* 287:14 (January 1970). Kase Toshikazu, who was assigned to the Japanese embassy in London during Yoshida's ambassadorship, indicates that he often took over the conversation when the going got tough; "Kōen: Yoshida Shigeru o Kataru," *KK* 282:12 (August 1969). See also Kase's *Yoshida Shigeru no Yuigon*, pp. 15, 27. Available letters in English which Yoshida clearly wrote himself reveal an adequate command of the language, although with occasional grammatical lapses.
41. *JGP* 75:2435–2436.
42. Cf. *JGP* 71:1018; *JGP* 75:2493.
43. Grew summarized the discussion about the emperor in U.S. governing circles prior to Japan's surrender at length in his *Turbulent Era: A Diplomatic Record of Forty Years, 1904–1945* (Houghton Mifflin, 1952), II, 1406–1442. The credit Japanese such as Yoshida gave to

Grew's influence on this critical issue is noted in *KJ*, I, 53; *YM*, p. 21. See also Chapter 7, notes 75, 87, and 90.

44. Harada, V, 16–18. One of the charges leveled against both Makino and Yoshida by the militarists at this time and later was their alleged involvement in the "Castle Incident." This harked back to the naval controversy of 1930, when William Castle visited Tokyo just prior to the London Naval Conference and gave the impression that he had already received Makino's approval of the 10:6 cruiser ratio proposed by the United States. Cf. Harada, VIII, 304–305; *KJ*, I, 40–41; *YM*, p. 13; Asahi Shimbunsha, p. 128; Scalapino, p. 384.
45. Hayashi Shigeru, *Taiheiyō Sensō*, vol. 25 of *Nihon no Rekishi* (Chūō Kōronsha, 1967), pp. 12–14; *KJ*, I, 40–41; *YM*, pp. 13–14; Kōsaka, p. 17.
46. Mamoru Shigemitsu, *Japan and Her Destiny* (Dutton, 1958), p. 108.
47. Cf. Kase, *Bungei Shunjū* p. 136.
48. *JGP* 79:2688–2690; Joseph C. Grew, *Ten Years in Japan* (Simon & Schuster, 1944), pp. 178–179.
49. *JGP* 79:2729.
50. *JGP* 79:2768.
51. Cf. Harada, V, 16–18; Maruyama, pp. 66–67.
52. *KJ*, I, 41; *YM*, p. 14.
53. Harada, V, 32–33.
54. *FO* 371/20287 (November 23, 1936), p. 283.
55. The bracketed sentence appears in Grew's original account of the conversation but was omitted by Hornbeck in making his summary. With this exception, the Hornbeck summary follows Grew's account closely and thoroughly. See *JGP* 79:2768–2770, 2798–2802; also *JGP*, "Conversations I," pp. 217–223.
56. *FRUS*, 1936, IV, 220–222.
57. Hull's record of his conversation with Yoshida appears in *FRUS*, *Japan 1931–1941*, I, 241–244; also U.S. Department of State, *Peace and War: United States Foreign Policy, 1931–1941*, pp. 40–41, 319–322. See also Dorothy Borg, *The United States and the Far Eastern Crisis of 1933–1938* (Harvard, 1964), pp. 180, 243, 529.
58. *FRUS*, 1936, IV, 222–223.
59. *KJ*, IV, 105–106; *Contemporary Japan* 15.5–8:167 (May-August 1946); Kase, *KK* 280:17.
60. *KJ*, I, 44–46; this is an essay by Tatsumi included in Yoshida's memoirs.
61. Harada, VIII, 328.
62. See Chapter 7, pp. 229–231. Yoshida was not alone in his opposition to rapprochement with Germany. Until the very end, a substantial body of opinion within the Foreign Ministry opposed the Axis Alliance, and

similar sentiment could be found in navy and court circles as well as in the Japanese business world. Yoshida himself saw his position in this regard as essentially a majority position. See, for example, *KJ*, I, 29; *YM*, p. 6; Shigemitsu, p. 168; Heinrichs, p. 297; *JGP* 101:4530, 4564, 4715, 4865–4866. At the same time, it would appear that Yoshida's appraisal of the military situation in Europe was more accurate than that of the Japanese high command, which had anticipated a German victory in Europe; see Jerome B. Cohen, *Japan's Economy in War and Reconstruction* (Minnesota, 1949), p. 50n. It should be noted that the 1936 Anti-Comintern Pact and the 1940 Axis Alliance were brought about during the premierships of Hirota and Konoe, two of the "moderates" in whom Grew and the Japanese advocates of the "pendulum theory" placed great hope. As indicated in Chapter 7, Konoe continued to remain one of Yoshida's main hopes for the resolution of Japan's dilemma. Konoe's interesting rationale for promoting the Axis Alliance can be found in the opening sections of his "memoirs," translated in 1946 for the International Military Tribunal, Far East.

63. Mazaki, *KK* 271:14.
64. *FO* 371/20285 (November 16, 1936), p. 380.
65. *JGP*, "Conversations I," p. 257; *FRUS*, 1937, III, 976.
66. Harada, V, 193.
67. *FO* 371/20279 (May 21, 1936), pp. 65–66.
68. Ibid. (September 23, 1936), pp. 111–112.
69. *FO* 371/20281 (November 17, 1936), pp. 246–249.
70. *FO* 371/21029 (January 21, 1937), pp. 4–7; ibid. (January 27, 1937), pp. 23–25.
71. Ibid. (February 5, 1937), p. 35.
72. Ibid. (March 15, 1937), p. 58.
73. As reported by Cadogan to Norman Davis; *FRUS*, 1937, III, 975–976.
74. *FO* 371/16163 (April 9, 1932), pp. 178–180.
75. *FO* 371/20279 (April 30, 1936), p. 55.
76. Ibid., pp. 66, 95, 113.
77. Ibid. (November 6, 1936), pp. 177–187. Piggott, who spoke Japanese, had only recently been reposted to Tokyo after a lengthy absence. He dwells upon the "favourable breeze" of 1936 in his autobiography, which identifies his Japanese military contacts in some detail; *Broken Thread: An Autobiography* (Gale & Polden, 1950), Chapter 10, especially pp. 263–272.
78. *FO* 371/20279 (November 6, 1936), pp. 168–176.
79. Ibid., pp. 188–189. Sansom's comments were made on September 22.
80. Ibid. (April 30, 1936), p. 53.

81. Ibid. (July 17, 1936), p. 95; (September 23, 1936), p. 113; (December 4, 1936), p. 233.
82. *FO* 371/22054 (April 29, 1938), p. 213; (May 6, 1938), p. 204; (July 28, 1938), p. 271.
83. *FO* 371/22181 (September 10, 1938), pp. 266–267.
84. *FO* 371/20279 (December 4, 1936), p. 229.
85. Ibid. (December 17, 1936), p. 243.
86. *FO* 371/20254 (April 5, 1938), p. 133.
87. *FO* 371/20279 (December 17, 1936), pp. 244–247. On December 4, Sir Robert Craigie recorded a conversation with Yoshida along similar lines: "He then proceeded to give a survey of the principal events in Sino-Japanese and Anglo-Japanese relations since the termination of the Anglo-Japanese alliance. The main conclusion he appeared to draw from this survey was that, with the disappearance of the Anglo-Japanese alliance, Japan's foreign policy had lost its former orientation and, not to put too fine a point on it, had been devoid of any orientation at all. The military element had steadily taken more and more control of policy on the ground that, since Japan no longer had any friends, it was necessary to increase armaments to the limit. As a further justification of this policy it was necessary to have an enemy. For this role Soviet Russia was cast, at a time when Russian power in the Far East was relatively weak. The only result of this policy had been the strengthening of Russia's Far Eastern defenses to such an extent that her position was now completely impregnable. Another serious result was that Japanese trade had found itself cut off progressively from China as a result of political boycotts, and had sought compensation for this by increasing Japanese exports to the British Dominions and Colonies. This in turn had led to a commercial controversy with the British Empire. In Japanese eyes our policy also had not been blameless in bringing about the progressive decline in Anglo-Japanese relations, for we had appeared to be only too ready to benefit by any deterioration in Sino-Japanese relations. In other words, it was felt by some in Japan that we had endeavoured to exploit the situation to our own advantage (At this I, of course, protested and tried to put the matter in its proper perspective)." Ibid., pp. 231–232. Cf. *FO* 371/20277 (July 30, 1936), p. 86.
88. *FO* 371/22054 (April 29, 1938), p. 212.
89. See note 87 above.
90. *FO* 371/20277 (July 30, 1936), p. 86 [sub-page 2].
91. Ibid. (August 7, 1936), pp. 110–111.
92. Ibid. (October 7, 1936), p. 118. Cf. the January 22, 1938 speech by

Foreign Minister Hirota submitted to the British Foreign Office by Yoshida; *FO* 371/22107 (February 4, 1938), pp. 155ff.

93. *FO* 371/20279 (January 22, 1936), p. 23.
94. Ibid. (April 30, 1936), p. 53.
95. Ibid. Cf. *FO* 371/21029 (January 15, 1937), p. 258.
96. *FO* 371/20277 (August 7, 1936), p. 106.
97. *FO* 371/20279 (October 26, 1936), p. 125. Cf. ibid. (December 11, 1936), p. 251; *FO* 371/20277 (October 7, 1936), p. 121.
98. *FO* 371/20279 (December 8, 1936), p. 198. Cf. ibid. (December 11, 1936), p. 251; *FO* 371/21029 (June 2, 1937), p. 150.
99. *FO* 371/20279 (December 4, 1936), p. 233.
100. *FO* 371/20288 (August 7, 1936), pp. 50ff. Sansom's report referred to the economic situation in Japan as of June 1936.
101. *FO* 371/20297 (November 6, 1936), p. 190. The comments were actually written on September 22 as a rebuttal to the Piggott memorandum (note 77 above). Sansom began to express these pessimistic and almost fatalistic views at an earlier date, and naturally continued them later; cf. Louis (note 14 above), and Peter Lowe, *Great Britain and the Origins of the Pacific War: A Study of British Policy in East Asia, 1937–1941* (Oxford, 1977). Although now best known as an eminent social and cultural historian of Japan prior to the twentieth century, Sansom was actually one of the most experienced and esteemed Western experts on Japanese economic affairs in the decades prior to the China and Pacific wars. A collection of some of his major internal reports to the Foreign Office over this critical period, carefully edited and introduced, could still be an illuminating scholarly contribution.

5. The Secret Yoshida-Eden Plan of 1936–1937

1. *KJ*, IV, 104.
2. *FO* 371/20288 (February 17, 1936), p. 215 [sub-page 38]. Cf. Chapter 4, note 40.
3. *FO* 371/20277 (August 7, 1936), p. 108.
4. *FO* 371/10179 (May 21, 1936), p. 67; *FO* 371/20277 (August 7, 1936), p. 109.
5. *FO* 371/20279 (January 22, 1936), p. 22. For general studies of British policy toward the Far East during the interwar years, see Louis; Lowe; Ann Trotter, *Britain and East Asia, 1933–1937* (Cambridge, 1975); Stephen Lyon Endicott, *Diplomacy and Enterprise: British China Policy 1933–1937* (British Columbia, 1975); Nicholas Clifford, *Retreat from China: British Policy in the Far East, 1937–1941* (Washington, 1967); Bradford A. Lee, *Britain and the Sino-Japanese War, 1937–1939: A*

Study in the Dilemmas of British Decline (Stanford and Oxford, 1973); Malcolm Kennedy, *The Estrangement of Great Britain and Japan, 1917–35* (California, 1969).

6. Kennedy, p. 334.
7. Cf. *YST*, August 7 [1936], pp. 330–339. A glimpse of the social life and contacts enjoyed by the ambassador and his wife in London at this time is conveyed in Yoshida Yukiko's short and impressionistic "memoir," *Whispering Leaves in Grosvenor Square, 1936–37.*
8. In 1936, for example, the empire and United States together supplied seventy percent of Japan's imports while taking sixty-five percent of Japan's exports; *FO* 371/22054 (April 13, 1938), pp. 158–159. See also the draft letter to Yoshida of July 1939, after his return, in *FO* 371/23459, pp. 317–319.
9. Cf. notes 82, 86, 87 below.
10. *FO* 371/20232 (November 10, 1936), p. 489.
11. Ibid., pp. 491ff.
12. Cf. note 92 below.
13. Harada, V, 176; ibid., VI, 317–318; Kase, *Bungei Shunjū*, p. 139; Asahi Shimbunsha, p. 128. On Chamberlain's Far Eastern policy, see Clifford, pp. 2, 12, 26, 33, 78, and especially p. 89.
14. *FO* 371/20279, pp. 19ff. Cf. *FO* 371/21029 (March 10, 1937), p. 61.
15. *YST*, August 7 [1936], pp. 330–339.
16. *YST*, April 10 [1937], pp. 260–264. See note 91 below.
17. See Chapter 4, notes 93–95.
18. Cf. Chapter 3, note 52; also note 88 below.
19. See the discussion of the "Hornbeck memorandum" in the final section of this chapter.
20. *FO* 371/20279 (May 22, 1936), pp. 70–78.
21. *FRUS*, 1937, III, 291.
22. E. L. Woodward and Rohan Butler, eds. *Documents on British Foreign Policy, 1919–1939*, Third Series (London, 1955), IX, 509–510, 522. For general treatments of the Yoshida initiatives, see Trotter, Chapter 11, and Endicott, especially pp. 145–149.
23. *FO* 371/20277 (July 30, 1936), p. 85–86, 93–105 (especially p. 99).
24. *FO* 371/20279 (October 26, 1936), p. 120b; ibid. (November 6, 1936), p. 145b.
25. *FO* 371/20279 (September 23, 1936), p. 112; ibid. (November 6, 1936), p. 145; *FO* 371/20277 (July 30, 1936), p. 86. Cf. *FO* 371/20279 (November 3, 1936), p. 139.
26. *FO* 371/20277 (October 7, 1936), pp. 120–121; cf. *FO* 371/20279 (October 26, 1936), p. 125.
27. *FO* 371/20279 (December 4, 1936), p. 229. Cf. ibid. (October

26, 1936), pp. 122b and 123b; also *FO* 371/20286 (December 4, 1936), p. 87.

28. *FO* 371/20279 (October 26, 1936), p. 129 [sub-pages 1–3].
29. *FO* 371/20279 (October 26, 1936), p. 120; ibid., (November 3, 1936), pp. 137–142.
30. *FO* 371/20279 (October 26, 1936), pp. 122b, 125.
31. *FO* 371/20279 (December 4, 1936), p. 229; cf. *FO* 371/20286 (December 17, 1936), p. 115.
32. *FO* 371/20279 (November 3, 1936), p. 143.
33. Ibid. (December 11, 1936), p. 248b.
34. Ibid. (December 24, 1936), p. 270.
35. Ibid. (October 26, 1936), pp. 123, 125; *FO* 371/21029 (March 13, 1937), p. 62; ibid. (June 2, 1937), pp. 145b, 146.
36. Cf. *FO* 371/20279 (October 26, 1936), p. 125; ibid. (November 27, 1936), 163b; ibid. (December 11, 1936), pp. 248–249.
37. *FO* 371/20277 (July 30, 1936), p. 93.
38. *FO* 371/20279 (October 26, 1936), p. 120b.
39. Ibid. (November 24, 1936), p. 163.
40. Ibid. (October 26, 1936), pp. 123, 124b.
41. Ibid., p. 124b.
42. *FO* 371/22181 (July 27, 1938), pp 231–232.
43. Cf. George Sansom's comments, *FO* 371/20279 (November 6, 1936), p. 190.
44. *FO* 371/20279 (October 26, 1936), pp. 121, 123.
45. See below, pp. 183–188.
46. *FO* 371/20279 (November 6, 1936), pp. 145ff.
47. Ibid. (October 26, 1936), pp. 120b, 121b, 124b; *FO* 371/21029 (January 23, 1937), p. 253.
48. *FO* 371/20279 (November 27, 1936), p. 163; ibid. (December 11, 1936), pp. 248–249.
49. Ibid. (November 27, 1936), pp. 162–163.
50. Ibid. (December 8, 1936), p. 198.
51. *FO* 371/20232; see various entries from October 29 through December 11, 1936, pp. 470–524.
52. Ibid., pp. 480, 522; *FO* 371/20281 (November 17, 1936), p. 248.
53. *FO* 371/20286 (December 4, 1936), pp. 86–90.
54. *FO* 371/20279 (December 21, 1936), pp. 261–265.
55. *FO* 371/21029 (January 7, 1937), pp. 241–248.
56. Ibid. (January 13 and 15, 1937), pp. 252–259, 267–274.
57. Ibid. (January 15, 1937), p. 258.
58. See *FO* 371/21029 (January 15, 1937), p. 270, sub-pages 1–10, plus pp. 273–274, for a marked draft and explanation of the British *aide-*

mémoire; this appears to be the closest approximation to the final version given Yoshida which is available in the Foreign Office archives. An earlier draft appears in ibid. (January 7, 1937), pp. 241–248. The record of the actual presentation of the British response to Yoshida appears in ibid. (January 18, 1937), pp. 1–3. The response to item (f) read as follows: "His Majesty's Government are fully alive to the importance of ensuring a fair market for Japanese exports and the desirability, if it is feasible, of reaching an agreement mutually satisfactory to both countries. His Majesty's Government for their part have never desired to impose any unfair restrictions on Japanese exports and they regret that any ill-feeling should have been caused by the imposition of import quotas on certain textiles in the Colonial Empire. His Majesty's Government were forced to adopt this method in order to prevent the disastrous effects on their industries of the excessive and unregulated competition then taking place, and they only took action after negotiations between the industries of the two countries had failed to achieve results. These negotiations broke down because the Japanese industrial representatives were only prepared to discuss a limitation of exports to the United Kingdom and British Colonies, whereas the British representatives did not consider that such a limited agreement would be of any substantial value and their desire was to obtain an agreed allocation of markets generally between the industries of the two countries. His Majesty's Government fear that, if the Ambassador's suggestion is to limit Japanese exports only to the United Kingdom and Colonies, it would not appear any more attractive to the British manufacturing industries now than in 1934; and before expressing any definite view on the precise proposal as to the amount of Japanese exports which would be permitted (viz. the 1935 level of exports less 20 per cent) they would be glad to learn (1) which are the classes of textile goods which would be covered by the proposal; and (2) whether the Japanese Government would undertake to give effect to any agreement by an effective control of their export trade. On receipt of further information on these points, His Majesty's Government would be ready to sound the U.K. industries as to the possibility of a negotiation on this basis; but His Majesty's Government would again urge the Japanese Government to consider whether it would not be in the best interests of the producers in both countries to negotiate an agreed allocation of their respective exports to all markets." Ibid. (January 15, 1937), p. 270, subpages 7–8. On the "communist threat" issue, see also *FO* 371/20279 (December 11, 1936), p. 264.

59. *FO* 371/21029 (January 21, 1937), pp. 5, 6.
60. Ibid., pp. 4–10. Kase Toshikazu indicated that he generally took over

talks in London when the linguistic difficulties became formidable, but this obviously did not occur in key conversations; *KK* 282:12 (August 1969).

61. Ibid. (January 23, 1937), pp. 13–19.
62. Ibid. (January 25, 1937), pp. 20–22.
63. Ibid. (January 27, 1937), pp. 23–25. The critical "blunder" section read as follows: "I am afraid that Mr. Yoshida is not taken very seriously in Japan and I do not understand his persistent desire to return here nor do I see what he hopes to accomplish. He was sent to London to save his face when the military refused to have him as Minister for Foreign Affairs in the Government which has now resigned. He has made two blunders which have much annoyed the Court. (1) He told journalists before leaving that he had a letter to the King besides his credentials. Questions were to have been asked in the Diet about this letter. (2) He had no personal message to communicate from the Emperor. . . . He had misread his instructions which were merely that the Emperor wished to be kept fully informed about British constitutional crisis as His Majesty deeply sympathized with unprecedented difficulties of the situation. Mr. Matsudaira told me this himself."
64. Ibid., pp. 23, 23b.
65. Ibid. (January 28, 1937), pp. 26–32. In his diary, Cadogan described what Yoshida was requesting at this point as a piece of paper to say "we should like to kiss and be friends. Quite easy but useless." It is this diary that identifies Cadogan as the essential author of Yoshida's January 28 statement: "That ridiculous Yoshida sent me round his aide-memoire (which he had written at my dictation). This process of negotiations, whereby I have to draft his communications as well as ours, is both laborious and embarrassing, and likely to prove unfruitful." Cited in Endicott, p. 147.
66. *FO* 371/21029 (February 5, 1937), pp. 33–35.
67. Cf. *FO* 371/20279 (December 11, 1936), p. 252.
68. *FO* 371/21029 (June 2, 1937), p. 148; but cf. ibid. (June 3, 1937), p. 141.
69. Ibid. (June 3, 1937), p. 144.
70. Ibid. (April 23, 1937), p. 90; cf. ibid. (June 19, 1937), pp. 143–144.
71. *Parliamentary Debates, House of Commons,* Fifth Series, 323:253.
72. *FRUS* 1937, III, 82–83.
73. Ibid. pp. 83, 95–96; *FO* 371/21029 (April 23, 1937), pp. 92–93.
74. *FRUS*, 1937, IV, 602–603.
75. *FO* 371/20129 (February 17, 1937), p. 43; ibid. (March 3, 1937), p. 61; ibid. (April 23, 1937), p. 90.
76. Ibid. (June 2, 1937), p. 146b.

77. Ibid., pp. 150–155; Foreign Office commentaries are on pp. 145–149.
78. *FRUS* 1937, III, 115–116.
79. Ibid., p. 126.
80. *FO* 371/20279 (December 11, 1936), p. 252.
81. Harada, V, 238.
82. *JFMA PVM* 32, pp. 589–600.
83. Ibid., pp. 597–600.
84. On the Sian incident, see Lyman P. Van Slyke, ed., *The Chinese Communist Movement: A Report of the United States War Department, July 1945* (Stanford, 1968), pp. 39–44; Immanuel C. Y. Hsu, *The Rise of Modern China* (Oxford, 1970), pp. 661–663; and Schram, pp. 198–199.
85. Cf. Clyde, p. 263.
86. *JFMA PVM* 32, pp. 601–607. Unfortunately there is little material with which to document Yoshida's changing impressions of the internal situation in China, and Japan's proper response to it, during this crucial decade. At the same time, however, there is nothing to indicate that, whatever tactical adjustments he may have espoused, he ever departed from the fundamental attitude that China existed primarily as an arena in which Japan was destined to act, and to act in a commanding role.
87. Ibid., pp. 602–604.
88. Ibid., p. 607.
89. Ibid., pp. 608–621. Satō's very vague recollection of this is conveyed in *KK* 265:2–3 (March 1968).
90. *JFMA PVM* 32, pp. 608–609.
91. Ibid., p. 610.
92. Ibid., pp. 611–612.
93. Ibid., pp. 613–614.
94. Ibid., pp. 614–616.
95. Ibid., pp. 617–619.
96. Ibid., pp. 619–621.
97. Ibid., pp. 654–661.
98. Ibid., pp. 654–655.
99. Ibid., pp. 656–658.
100. Ibid., pp. 658–660.
101. *FO* 371/22053 (January 5, 1938), pp. 22–30.
102. Ibid., pp. 25–29.
103. Ibid., p. 30, subpages 1–9.
104. Ibid., (February 14, 1938), pp. 33–39.
105. Cf. ibid., p. 30, subpages 1–2. Pratt observed that a Japanese attack on Canton, and establishment of a puppet government there, "may render Hong Kong worthless as a British colony."
106. *FO* 371/22054 (April 13, 1938), pp. 163–165, including subpages

1–26; the lengthy Foreign Office commentary appears on pp. 156–162.

107. Ibid., p. 156.
108. Ibid., pp. 157b, 156b.
109. Ibid., pp. 157, 156b.
110. Ibid., p. 160b.

6. PURSUING RAINBOWS, 1937–1941

1. *FRUS*, 1937, IV, 128. Cf. *FRUS*, 1937, III, 976.
2. *FRUS*, 1937, IV, 134. Cf. *JGP*, "Conversations IV," pp. 235–236.
3. *FO* 371/22054 (May 7, 1938), p. 207-A. On October 26, 1938, Halifax similarly referred to Yoshida as being "out of touch with developments in his own country"; Woodward and Butler, VII, 163–164.
4. Woodward and Butler, VI, 528–529.
5. *JGP* 94:4056.
6. *JGP* 100:4368–4369.
7. *JGP*, "Personal Notes, 1941," pp. 5863–5864.
8. Ibid., p. 6145.
9. Clifford, p. 30.
10. Kase, *Bungei Shunjū*, p. 139.
11. *FO* 371/20249 (July 12, 1937), pp. 81–83; *FO* 371/21029 (July 18, 1937), p. 167.
12. *YST*, September 21 [1937], pp. 310–320.
13. See note 11 above.
14. *FRUS*, 1937, IV, 126–129.
15. Contrast the view of Herbert Feis in *The Road to Pearl Harbor* (Princeton, 1950), pp. 15–16. He describes the failure of the Western powers to take a firm stand following the China Incident as "the last, lost good chance" for peace in Asia, concluding that "the only way in which the war in China could have been well ended was by firm collective action, action which would have offered Japan an inducement for peace and met refusal with compulsion."
16. *FRUS*, 1937, IV, 126–129.
17. Woodward and Butler, VIII, 528–529. As of August 1937, Craigie, the new British ambassador to Japan, was expressing views remarkably similar to Yoshida's. Passing through Canada on his way to assume his new post in Tokyo, Craigie cited the "steady progress" of the "moderate" elements in Japan and pointed out that the military campaign in China would increase taxes and thereby bring about an unfavorable reaction against the Japanese military. To what extent Craigie based these opinions upon views he heard from Yoshida is not clear, but

Yoshida did have occasion to deal directly with Craigie before the latter's departure for Japan; Borg, p. 451. See also Clifford, pp. 27–28; Grew, *Turbulent Era*, II, 1019; Chapter 4, note 81 above; notes 61 and 65 below.

18. Borg, pp. 452–453.
19. Grew, *Turbulent Era*, II, 1186.
20. *FRUS*, 1937, IV, 134–135; Grew, *Turbulent Era,* II, 1187–1189.
21. Clifford, p. 40.
22. *FRUS*, 1937, III, 687–689, 699–701.
23. *FO* 371/22107 (February 4, 1938), pp. 143–146. Cf. *FRUS*, 1938, III, 139–140; also *FRUS, Japan 1931–1941*, I, 463–464.
24. *FO* 371/22107 (February 4, 1938), pp. 155ff; ibid., (February 16, 1938), p. 221.
25. *FO* 371/22053 (February 9, 1938), pp. 67–68; ibid., (February 16, 1938), pp. 74–75; ibid., (February 23, 1938), pp. 79–80.
26. *FO* 371/22053 (February 15, 1938), pp. 69–72.
27. Ibid. (February 16, 1938), pp. 73–75; ibid. (February 22, 1938), pp. 76, 78.
28. Ibid. (February 22, 1938), pp. 76–78.
29. *FO* 371/22054 (February 25, 1938), pp. 88–92.
30. Yoshida's conversation with Hankey prompted a lengthy internal response by the Foreign Office, including a draft critique of Japan's avowed grievances against Great Britain; *FO* 371/22054 (April 5, 1938), pp. 125–134. With Cadogan on April 29, Yoshida referred to Soviet-Japanese relations and "said that on the whole, although there had been incidents on the frontier, the Japanese Government would favour an improvement of relations with the Soviet"; *FO* 371/22188 (May 6, 1938), pp. 442–444. To the secretary of dominion affairs, he urged British mediation on the grounds that soon "both sides would become war weary"; *FO* 371/22054 (April 29, 1938), pp. 211–213. Clive reported meeting with Yoshida at Brussels, where the latter "admitted in a roundabout way that breaking off relations with Chiang Kai Shek had been a great mistake, and he could only see an end to the war namely that Chiang Kai Shek should temporarily abdicate power to enable some other Chinese statesman to make peace. Chiang Kai Shek could then more sinico [*sic*] stage a comeback and resume power"; ibid. (May 1, 1938), pp. 196–198. Hore-Belisha reported Yoshida's complaint that "we always seemed inclined to drag in America, and we had now a far better chance of getting on without America. He added that if we did not arbitrate, Germany or some other power would." The British secretary of war went on to note that Yoshida "asked if he might explain to me on a map exactly what was involved, and show how easy it

would be to achieve a settlement"; ibid. (May 6, 1938), pp. 203–206.

31. *FO* 371/22054 (May 6, 1938), p. 204.
32. Ibid., pp. 207–208.
33. Ibid. (May 30, 1938), pp. 217–221.
34. Foreign Office materials pertaining to Yoshida's resignation as ambassador are cited in Great Britain, Foreign Office, *Index to General Correspondence, 1938*, IV (S–Z), p. 538, and include reference to "question of British decoration on termination of appointment; decision against." These archives, however, are no longer maintained by the Public Record Office, and were apparently destroyed.
35. Cf. *FO* 371/22054 (April 7, 1938), pp. 128–131.
36. Harada, VI, 317–318.
37. Ibid.
38. *Parliamentary Debates, House of Commons*, Fifth Series, 337:905–906; *North China Herald*, June 29, 1938 (cited in Clifford, p. 78).
39. Borg, p. 446; the argument is developed at length in Chapter 15. See also Heinrichs, pp. 248–254, 354.
40. Harada, VI, 220, 245; Borg, pp. 456ff.
41. Crowley, *Japan's Quest for Autonomy*, p. 367. Chapter 6 of this work draws together some of the most interesting material available concerning the decision-making process of the immediate post-China Incident period. In Japanese, the Harada diary provides an excellent inside source.
42. Crowley, pp. 338, 340–341.
43. Ibid., p. 353.
44. Ibid., p. 357.
45. Harada, VI, 192–193; Crowley, pp. 372–376.
46. Harada, VI, 192; Crowley, pp. 357, 366, 393.
47. Harada, VI, 208, 203; cf. Crowley, p. 374.
48. Professor Maruyama observes that Konoe's "political career certainly provides a wealth of examples of how fatally a weakness of character can operate at important moments," and goes on to find this character "debility" characteristic of most Japanese wartime leaders; pp. 97–98. A recent work by Ian Nish reiterates this interpretation of Konoe: "While he was flexible and open-minded, he was to prove weak and indecisive"; *Japanese Foreign Policy 1869–1942: Kasumigaseki to Miyakezawa* (Routledge & Kegan Paul, 1977), p. 219. Crowley and more recently Gordon M. Berger assess Konoe quite differently. In Berger's view, "There is no evidence to suggest that Konoe was coerced into supporting the Army's foreign and military policies, or that he was unwittingly made a 'robot' of military interests, as he and historians have often

lamented after the fact." *Parties Out of Power in Japan, 1931–1941* (Princeton, 1977), pp. 269–270.

49. Crowley, p. 349; *FRUS, Japan 1931–1941*, pp. 392–393, 368.
50. *FO* 371/22107 (February 4, 1938), pp. 155ff.
51. Harada, VI, 192–194, 201ff; Crowley, p. 353.
52. Harada, VI, 208–209.
53. Ibid., p. 67.
54. *FO* 371/22054 (May 1, 1938), pp. 196–198; see note 30 above.
55. Cf. *FO* 371/22054 (May 30, 1938), pp. 217–221.
56. *FO* 371/22181 (July 27, 1938), pp. 231–232.
57. *FO* 371/23459 (July, 1939), pp. 317–320. Yoshida's original letter to Wilson is unavailable, and it is not clear whether the reply was actually sent to Yoshida.
58. *FO* 371/22181 (September 9, 1938), pp. 261–267; Woodward and Butler, VIII, 78–79, 83.
59. Kase, *Bungei Shunjū*, pp. 138–139; Woodward and Butler, IX, 509–510.
60. *JGP* 94:3996–3997.
61. Woodward and Butler, VIII, 528–529.
62. *JGP* 94:4043, 4056. On Yoshida's English, see Chapter 4, note 40 above.
63. *JGP* 94:4118, 4240.
64. *JGP* 94:4178, 4181, 4240.
65. *JGP* 100:4368–4369.
66. *JGP* 100:4381–4385.
67. *JGP* 100:4430–4439.
68. *JGP*, "Personal Notes, 1941," pp. 5863–5864.
69. Ibid., p. 5865.
70. Cf. *YST* letters from Yoshida to Makino, obviously in 1941, of the following dates: September 6 (pp. 343–347); November 1 (pp. 212–218); November 14 (pp. 26–32); November 22 (pp. 219–224); December 1 (pp. 447–450). Kido Kōichi was apparently one of Yoshida's important sources for information on the progress of the Hull-Nomura talks; Kido Kōichi, *Kido Kōichi Nikki* (Tokyo Daigaku, 1966), II, 920–921 (entries for October 31, November 1 and 2, 1941).
71. Nobutake Ike, ed. and trans., *Japan's Decision for War: Records of the 1941 Policy Conferences* (Stanford, 1967), pp. 129–163.
72. *YST*, September 6 [1941], pp. 343–347. Yoshida went on to note that the army and navy had fallen under the influence of "the youthful group," and the Home Ministry was so apprehensive of the right-wing movement that it could not be expected to take a stand against the anti-U.S. tide. The only hope for reversing the trend toward war lay in the finance minister.

73. *YST*, September 17 [1941], pp. 459–464. This is a copy of the actual letter to Konoe, which Yoshida prepared for Makino. See *YST*, September 20 [1941], pp. 465–466, for the covering note to Makino.
74. Ike, pp. 196–199.
75. Ibid., pp. 199–207.
76. *YST*, November 1 [1941], pp. 212–218; November 2 [1941], pp. 42–49.
77. Hayashi, *Taiheiyō Sensō*, p. 255; *KJ*, I, 47; *YM*, p. 16.
78. Ike, p. 267.
79. Ibid., p. 204.
80. Ibid., pp. 204–207.
81. Ibid., pp. 205, 210.
82. Feis, p. 309. For the final version of Proposal B, see Ike, pp. 210–211. For the official English-language version handed to Hull by Ambassador Nomura on November 20, see *FRUS, Japan 1931–1941*, II, 755. Cf. also Roberta Wohlstetter, *Pearl Harbor: Warning and Decision* (Stanford, 1962), pp. 233–234.
83. Nihon Kokusai Seiji Gakkai, *Taiheiyō Sensō e no Michi* (1963), VII, 320; cited in Ike, p. 208.
84. Ike, pp. 207–227.
85. Ibid., pp. 214, 231–232, 240, 245.
86. *FRUS*, *Japan 1931–1941*, II, 753–757; Cordell Hull, *The Memoirs of Cordell Hull* (Macmillan, 1948), II, 1069–1071.
87. Wohlstetter, pp. 233–235.
88. For a critical appraisal of Hull's role in the Japanese-American negotiations, see Paul Schroeder, *The Axis Alliance and Japanese-American Relations* (Cornell, 1958).
89. Heinrichs, pp. 355–356. On November 7, Grew had a conversation with an unidentified Japanese who might have been Yoshida. In his calendar for that date he noted simply "Yoshida." The diary entries proper for the same day make no mention of a meeting with Yoshida, but separately, under "Conversations" for November 7, Grew included a three-page memorandum of a conversation with "a leading Japanese and reliable informant." This informant expressed the view that it was essential that the conversations in Washington continue; that in his personal view the situation in Japan was intolerable and the Japanese government might have to go along with American views; and that the Japanese military was becoming "frightened" and the United States would do well to treat the Japanese as children rather than adults. Grew regarded the conversation as significant, but later came to suspect its accuracy; *JGP*, "Personal Notes, 1941," pp. 5989–5991, 6009. The emphasis upon a firm position on the part of the United States, however,

is not consistent with Yoshida's general stress upon the necessity of conciliation and compromise on the part of the Anglo-American powers.

90. *KJ*, I, 48; *YM*, p. 17.
91. *YST*, November 14 [1941], pp. 26–32; November 22 [1941], pp. 219–224.
92. *KJ*, I, 49; *YM*, p. 18.
93. *KJ*, I, 50–52; *YM*, pp. 18–20.
94. Ike, pp. 264–271. Roberta Wohlstetter, for example, whose account of the events leading to Pearl Harbor is generally regarded as one of the most authoritative studies of the English-language record, observes that "the tone and content of the note were on the whole so drastic that it is easy to understand why this document was characterized immediately by the Japanese as an ultimatum"; Wohlstetter, p. 245.
95. *KJ*, I, 52; *YM*, p. 20.
96. *KJ*, I, 50–51; *YM*, pp. 18–19.
97. *KJ*, I, 50, 52; *YM*, pp. 18, 20. Cf. *YST*, December 1 [1941], pp. 447–450.
98. *JGP*, "Personal Notes, 1941," p. 6145. The letter conveys a personal touch very characteristic of Yoshida, and offers an interesting contrast to the more polished and correct letter Grew received from Shigemitsu at this same time.

7. THE "YOSHIDA ANTI-WAR GROUP" AND THE KONOE MEMORIAL, 1942–1945

1. *YST*, December 8 [wartime], pp. 257–259.
2. This is developed below, but cf. also *YST* [no month or day; 1943?], pp. 375–382.
3. Abe, p. 221. Hatakeyama Seikō, *Mitsuroku Rikugun Nakano Gakkō* (Banchō Shobō, 1971), pp. 203–253; this popular account of secret activities of the Japanese army contains several chapters of rather gossipy detail pertaining to Yoshida during the war years.
4. Mukoyama Hiroo, "Minkan ni Okeru Shūsen Kōsaku," in Nihon Gaikō Gakkai, ed., *Taiheiyō Sensō Shūketsu Ron* (Tokyo Daigaku, 1958), p. 100. The section of Mukoyama's essay which deals with the Yoshida group (pp. 100–117) is the best straightforward account of the group's activities available in Japanese. Mukoyama, however, tends to give less emphasis than others to the importance of the role played by Ueda Shunkichi in articulating the "Red conspiracy" thesis which came to underlay the group's activities.
5. *KJ*, I, 61; *YM*, p. 27; Kase, *Bungei Shunjū*, p. 140; *JGP*, "Personal Notes, 1941," p. 6145.

6. *KJ*, I, 54–55; *YM*, p. 22; Hayashi Shigeru, et al., *Nihon Shūsen Shi* (Yomiuri Shimbunsha, 1962), II, 13; Kase, *Bungei Shunjū*, pp. 140–141.
7. Cf. Shinobu, I, 23.
8. *KJ*, I, 55–56; *YM*, pp. 22–23.
9. *Kido Kōichi Nikki*, II, 967–968.
10. Mukoyama, p. 102; Hayashi, II, 60; *KJ*, I, 56; *YM*, pp. 22–23; Robert J. C. Butow, *Japan's Decision to Surrender* (Stanford, 1954), pp. 14–15.
11. See, for example, Butow, p. 18; also the appeal Konoe had for "liberal" Japanese which emerges in Chalmers Johnson's account of the Ozaki-Sorge spy ring, *An Instance of Treason: Ozaki Hotsumi and the Sorge Spy Ring* (Stanford, 1964). Cf. Chapter 8, note 29 below.
12. Mukoyama, p. 100; Ōtani Keijirō, "Yoshida Shigeru Taiho no Shinsō," in Ōtani's *Kempei Mitsuroku* (Hara Shobō, 1965), pp. 12–14, 29, 37; this same essay appears in an earlier work by Ōtani, *Nikumare Kempei* (Nihon Shuhōsha, 1957), pp. 13–73. See also *Kido Kōichi Nikki*, II, 992, 1005; Gaimushō [Foreign Ministry], ed., *Shūsen Shiroku* (Shimbun Gekkansha, 1952), pp. 121–122; Abe, pp. 215–218; Kōsaka, p. 21; Hayashi, *Taiheiyō Sensō*, p. 419; Yoshida Naikaku Kankōkai, ed., *Yoshida Naikaku* (1954), pp. 4–5. The last work, the "official history" of the Yoshida cabinets, is cited hereafter as *YN*.
13. Abe, p. 221.
14. Mukoyama, p. 110.
15. Hosokawa Morisada, *Jōhō Tennō ni Tassezu* (Isobe Shobō, 1953), II, 292–293. See Chapter 8, note 31 below concerning this valuable source.
16. Iwabuchi Tatsuo, "Konoe Kō no Jōsōbun," *Sekai Bunka* 3.8:38 (August 1, 1948); Mukoyama, p. 110; *KJ*, I, 59; *YM*, p. 26.
17. See, for example, Konoe's prewar essay "Genrō, Jūshin to Yo," reprinted in Yabe Teiji, *Konoe Fumimaro* (Jiji Tsūshinsha, 1958), pp. 48–56; this also appears in Yabe's earlier two-volume work of the same title (Kōbundō, 1952), pp. 220ff.
18. Hosokawa, pp. 162–163, 173–174.
19. Yabe (1958), pp. 168–169.
20. Hosokawa, p. 187. Konoe made this comment to Rear Admiral Takagi Sōkichi, who was himself associated with various peace considerations and regarded the Yoshida group's reliance on the Kōdō-ha as ill-conceived; cf. Mukoyama, p. 111. In the post-surrender period, Takagi again found himself at odds with Yoshida's policies; see Chapter 10, note 47 below.
21. See, for example, the next-to-last paragraph of the Konoe Memorial on p. 264 below.
22. See note 42 below.
23. Hosokawa, pp. 150, 162–163, 222–225, 279–283; Mukoyama, p. 111.

24. Hosokawa, pp. 339–341.
25. Cf. Shigemitsu, pp. 146–147, 199; Crowley, *Japan's Quest for Autonomy*, pp. 203–206, 275, 393; Hayashi, *Nihon Shūsen Shi*, II, 20; Abe, p. 220; Butow, p. 50. Konoe's relationship with Obata began around 1931, when he asked Mori Kaku to recommend a "good man" in the military, and the ubiquitous Mori introduced him to Obata; Yabe (1958), p. 31.
26. Cited in Crowley, p. 248. The original source is Konoe's *Ushinawareshi Seiji* (Asahi Shimbunsha, 1946).
27. See the Konoe essay cited in note 17 above and Gordon Berger's portrayal of the prince in *Parties Out of Power* and "Japan's Young Prince: Konoe Fumimaro's Early Political Career, 1916–1931," *Monumenta Nipponica* 29.4:451–475 (Winter 1974).
28. Mukoyama, p. 103.
29. Harada, IV, 418–420.
30. Cf. Crowley, pp. 258–259, 260ff. Makino, and presumedly Yoshida, were known to be supporters of Minobe's theory of constitutional monarchy; Titus, pp. 111–112.
31. Harada, III, 21–24. See Chapter 4, note 18 above.
32. Crowley, pp. 183–184, 204–205.
33. Cf. Crowley, pp. 30, 87, 90; Scalapino, pp. 371, 378, 386; Clifford, pp. 83–85.
34. Crowley, pp. 87, 89, 97ff.
35. Iriye, *After Imperialism*, pp. 51, 66.
36. *JGP* 100:4314.
37. Crowley, p. 88.
38. Gaimushō, *Shūsen*, pp. 121–122.
39. Mukoyama, pp. 102–103. According to Miyake Kijirō, Yoshida took no pains to disguise his personal dislike of Tōjō; *KK* 293:14 (July 1970).
40. Mukoyama, pp. 101–102, 112.
41. Ueda Shunkichi, "Shōwa Demokurashii no Zasetsu," *Jiyū*, October and November, 1960. Ueda died just before this two-part essay was published. Part One is subtitled "Manshū Jihen Zengo" (October issue, pp. 81–94); Part Two is subtitled "Gunbu, Kakushinha Kanryō no Nihon Kyōsanka Puran" (November issue, pp. 89–99). In the first of these articles, Ueda describes his discovery of the plot in some detail, drawing attention to the activities of a research group named the Ni-Man Zaisei Keizai Kenkyūkai (Japan-Manchuria Finance and Economy Research Association), half of whose twenty-odd members, he claimed, were "apostates" (*tenkōsha*) from communism. The mastermind behind the group, in his view, was Miyazaki Masayoshi, an officer with extensive experience in the Soviet Union and linguistic competence in Russian (as well,

reportedly, as German, English, and French). Through Miyazaki, Ueda traced a complex web of relations involving Ayukawa's Nissan interests, the South Manchurian Railway, Ishiwara Kanji and the Kwantung Army, and the high-level Cabinet Planning Board. The plan received from Ayukawa (probably around the end of 1936) was reportedly destroyed in the wartime air raids. Cf. Abe, pp. 215ff. I am indebted to Professor Matsuo Takayoshi for providing me with copies of the *Jiyū* articles. For the context of the planning which so alarmed Ueda, see Berger's *Parties Out of Power* and Mark R. Peattie, *Ishiwara Kanji and Japan's Confrontation with the West* (Princeton, 1975).

42. Ueda Shunkichi, "Nihon Badorio Jiken Tenmatsu," *Bungei Shunjū*, December 1, 1949; Mukoyama, p. 113; Gaimushō, *Shūsen*, pp. 121–122. Former prime minister Wakatsuki's response to the "secret plan" shown him by Ueda is reprinted from his memoirs in Gaimushō, pp. 125–126. Yoshida's early comments to the British concerning "communistic" intrigue behind the February 26th Incident and within the Japanese military in Manchuria are cited in Chapter 4, notes 90 and 91 above.

In December 1945, E. H. Norman prepared a report for the Counter-Intelligence Section of SCAP based largely on information derived from Ueda, of whom Norman wrote: "UEDA Shunkichi was formerly an official of the Ministry of Overseas. He served in the Governor-General's office in Formosa and in the Finance Ministry. He was private secretary to the late General TANAKA, who died in 1929. Since that time he has been in private business, but has had intimate contact with important Japanese political leaders. His knowledge of political personalities had made him a valuable source of information although his political judgment need not be accepted uncritically. He would be described as a rather rare type of Japanese who is conservative in politics but quite genuinely non-militarist. He has a Boswellian curiosity and a searching mind which makes him refreshingly objective and uninhibited in his approach to high politics." The Norman memorandum, dated December 17 and entitled "A Japanese *Eminence Grise*: Izawa Takiwo," was sent to the U.S. Department of State under a covering letter by George Atcheson, Jr. on January 7, 1946. It was declassified upon request in March 1974; file 740.00119/1–746.

43. Cf. Duus, pp. 205–206; Mitchell, pp. 55–68.

44. Butow, p. 46.

45. Maruyama, pp. 92, 301.

46. Scalapino, p. 360. An informative study of Ikeda by Arthur Tiedemann, "Big Business and Politics in Prewar Japan," appears in James W. Morley, ed., *Dilemmas of Growth in Prewar Japan* (Princeton, 1971), pp. 267–316.

47. Yamagata Kiyoshi, "Yoshida-san no Omoide," *KK* 272:9 (October 1968); Shinobu, I, 55, 61.
48. *KJ*, IV, 130–132.
49. Scalapino, pp. 358–359; cf. *Kido Kōichi Nikki*, II, 1057.
50. Harada, II, 114.
51. Harada, III, 5, 213–214, 238, 304–305. Cf. Heinrichs, pp. 194–195.
52. The account of Hatoyama is based primarily on the files pertaining to him in RG 331 of the SCAP archives in the Washington National Records Center at Suitland, Maryland. The SCAP investigation of Hatoyama in early 1946 led to his dramatic last-minute purge, thus paving the way for Yoshida's postwar rise to political influence as Hatoyama's replacement in the party structure. Hatoyama's overall record in both domestic and foreign policy matters was deemed by SCAP officers in Government Section to have "aided the forces of obscurantism, reaction and militarism," his commitment to democracy to have been but "lip service," his political skills to have been those of "a backstage political trafficker," his political philosophy to have reflected nothing more than "a thin veneer of liberalism." For some appraisals of Hatoyama and his purge by Western observers, see Mark Gayn, *Japan Diary* (Sloane, 1948); W. MacMahon Ball, *Japan: Enemy or Ally?*, revised edition (John Day, 1949); and Harry Emerson Wildes, *Typhoon in Tokyo: The Occupation and Its Aftermath* (Macmillan, 1954). Gayn was personally involved in instigating the investigation and purge of Hatoyama. Wildes, an officer in SCAP and enthusiastic delineator of SCAP foibles, takes a more critical view of SCAP's actions in this case. For a brief comparison of the personality, background, and upbringing of Hatoyama and Yoshida, see Abe, p. 200.
53. Hatoyama regarded universal suffrage as potentially a "fuse for dangerous thought" which would exacerbate class conflict and "the labor problem" in Japan. See quotations from his speeches at the time in Shinobu Seizaburō, *Taishō Seiji Shi* (Kawade Shobō, 1954), especially p. 919; also Marius Jansen's review of an earlier edition of this work in *Far Eastern Quarterly*, 14, 1:74, 79 (November 1954).
54. Cf. Hosokawa, p. 442.
55. By one account, he tried to strike a hopeful note at this time with an old cliché that has a close English equivalent: If winter comes, spring cannot be far behind (*fuyu kitarinaraba haru tōkaraji*); Miyake, *KK* 292:17 (June 1970).
56. *Kido Kōichi Nikki*, II, 992–993 (November 7, 1942) and 1005 (January 6, 1943); Mukoyama, pp. 103–104. Mukoyama's discussion of the various "plans" advanced by the Yoshida group provides the major source for this section. If a criticism is to be made concerning his

excellent presentation, it would probably be that he imposes more order upon the group, its thoughts, and the progression of its activities than actually prevailed. It should be kept in mind that YOHANSEN was loosely structured to an extreme, that its activities consisted primarily of talk, and that, even while pushing one candidate for the premiership at a given moment, other possible candidates were not thereby excluded from consideration. A massive "fictionalized" biography of Konoe by Tateno Nobuyuki provides vivid but unfortunately unreliable detail on this and other episodes; *Taiyō wa Mata Noboru: Kōshaku Konoe Fumimaro* (Rokkō, 1952), III, 28–38.

57. *YST*, March 2 [1943?], pp. 441–446.
58. Mukoyama, pp. 104–105; Hosokawa, pp. 153–154, 195–196. Much of the activity at this time took place in Karuizawa, where Konoe, Ugaki, and Hatoyama had residences. Hayashi Shigeru's account of this flurry of anti-Tōjō activity in Karuizawa notes that, in addition to Hatoyama, Yoshida, Ueda, and Iwabuchi, those who were "running around" in support of the Ugaki or Kobayashi plans included Tomita Kenji, Sakai Kōji, and Nakano Seigō; *Nihon Shūsen Shi*, II, 19–20.
59. Mukoyama, pp. 105–106.
60. The Koiso cabinet had previously said that, if the Allies set foot on Leyte, that would determine the outcome of the Pacific War; Gaimushō, *Shūsen*, p. 198.
61. For a concise résumé of various Japanese individuals and groups who opposed the war and at least engaged in some form of passive resistance, see Ienaga Saburō, *Taiheiyō Sensō* (Iwanami Shoten, 1968), Chapter 12; also *Taiheiyō Sensō Shūketsu Ron* (note 4 above).
62. Mukoyama, pp. 106–107.
63. Kōmura Sakahiko, *Shinjitsu no ue ni Tachite: Sensō to Senryō Jidai* (Hakubundō, 1954), p. 79.
64. Ibid., p. 80.
65. "I was in complete agreement with these opinions of the prince," Yoshida noted in his memoirs in discussing this meeting, "and together we cooperated in revising the draft"; *KJ*, I, 58; *YM*, p. 25.
66. See citations in Chapter 8, especially note 36.
67. Kido Kōichi Kenkyūkai, ed., *Kido Kōichi Kankei Bunshō* (Tokyo Daigaku, 1966), pp. 591–593. The various Konoe statements concerning a Red conspiracy are summarized in Oka Yoshitake, *Konoe Fumimaro* (Iwanami Shinsho, 1972), pp. 200–209.
68. Konoe Fumimaro, *Konoe Nikki* (Kyōdō Tsūshinsha, 1968), pp. 36–37.
69. Ibid., pp. 92–93. See also *Kido Kōichi Kankei Bunshō*, p. 1125; *Kido Kōichi Nikki*, II, 1125 (July 18, 1944); Gaimushō, *Shūsen*, pp. 135–140 (especially 138); Butow, p. 31.

70. Mukoyama, pp. 111–112. Almost all sources stress Ogata's reports, but it should be noted that Konoe and the Yoshida group derived their intelligence on global affairs from many channels. It has been noted that Yoshida had access to shortwave radio reports. Hosokawa's diary, to cite but one example, reveals that evaluations of the international scene were solicited from a variety of persons, among them Itō Nobufumi (a former intelligence chief under Konoe), Kase Toshikazu, Shigemitsu Mamoru, Yabe Teiji (later Konoe's biographer), and others; cf. Hosokawa, pp. 18–19, 41, 173–174, 292–293, 312–313, 323–325. This is discussed further, especially with regard to Ogata's reports, in the following chapter.
71. The Konoe Memorial can be found in numerous Japanese sources, including: Iwabuchi (note 16 above), pp. 32–35; Gaimushō, *Shūsen*, pp. 195–198; Nihon Gaikō Gakkai, ed. (note 4 above), pp. 107–110; Yabe (1952; note 17 above), II, 529–533; Ōtani Keijirō, *Gunbatsu: Ni-ni-roku Jiken kara Haisen made* (Tosho, 1971), Preface. An English translation of the greater part of the memorial is included in Butow, pp. 47–50; this has been reproduced in Arthur Tiedemann, *Modern Japan: A Brief History*, revised edition (Van Nostrand, 1955), pp. 152–156. There seems little doubt that the actual first draft of the memorial was written by Konoe himself; cf. Hosokawa, pp. 342–344, and Kōmura, pp. 79–80.
72. Pseudonym of Nosaka Sanzō.
73. This sentence is not included in the Iwabuchi version of the memorial, which is generally used as the standard text. Mukoyama includes it, however, as does Butow, who had access to an English translation of the memorial held by Ushiba Tomohiko, one of Konoe's former aides; Butow, pp. 47, 48. The problem of "emperor communism" is worthy of separate study in itself. In brief, it involved both a sociological appraisal of "communalism" in traditional Japanese society, as well as the perception of implicitly socialistic ideals in the emperor-system, or *kokutai*, ideology. This line of thought can be discerned in the writings of right-wing ideologues such as Kita Ikki, for example, as well as in the statements of certain Japanese apostates from communism, who defended their recantations on the grounds that they had come to realize that a socialist revolution (in effect, a Japanese version of "socialism in one country") could be best brought about under the emperor; cf. the famous recantation of Communist leaders Sano Manabu and Nabeyama Sadachika as quoted by George M. Beckmann, "The Radical Left and the Failure of Communism," in Morley, *Dilemmas of Growth in Prewar Japan*, p. 167. During the final stages of the Pacific War, Prince Takamatsu ruminated on this problem and observed that the

popular saying "everything belongs to the emperor" amounted, in his words, to "thorough-going communism." In fact, he continued, it seemed that "there is not the slightest difference between communism and the way of the gods (*kaminagara no michi*)"; Hosokawa, pp. 196–197. In June 1944, Konoe actually felt constrained to lecture Takamatsu on the dangerous fallacy of such a line of thought; Hosokawa, p. 223. Somewhat along the same lines, as early as July 1936, Harada had expressed concern over Prince Higashikuni's receptivity to Soviet techniques of organization and economic control; Harada, V, 115.

74. Konoe actually formed three cabinets. The third, however, was essentially a shake-up of the second, designed primarily to get rid of Foreign Minister Matsuoka Yōsuke; cf. the SCAP translation of Konoe's "memoirs," RG 331, Suitland, Maryland, pp. 38–41.

75. Iwabuchi, pp. 36–38. Both Gaimushō (*Shūsen*, p. 200) and Mukoyama (p. 110) follow Iwabuchi's presentation, and indicate that Konoe recommended only Ugaki and Mazaki. Butow, drawing on other sources, states that Konoe suggested at least six other military figures as well: Ishiwara, Kōzuki, Obata, Anami, Yamashita, and Minami; p. 50n. Hosokawa offers yet another version; in his diary for February 16, 1945, he recorded that Konoe had suggested Ugaki, Obata, Ishiwara, and Anami; pp. 342–344. Ōtani, head of the military police in Tokyo at the time, follows Hosokawa's version; *Kempei Mitsuroku*, p. 16.

The impression that the United States would not act to destroy Japan's *kokutai* had been voiced by a number of Konoe's informants over the course of the preceding months. In April 1944, Itō Nobufumi expressed the view that America would go no further than the possible removal of the present emperor from the throne. In August 1944, the diplomat Kase Toshikazu described American public opinion as being quite favorable to the emperor. Konoe himself indicated that his optimism concerning U.S. intentions in this regard was based to a considerable extent upon his knowledge of the view held by former ambassador Grew. See Hosokawa, pp. 173–174, 292–293, 342–344; Ōtani, *Kempei Mitsuroku*, p. 7.

76. Mukoyama, p. 111; Iwabuchi, p. 38; Oka, *Konoe Fumimaro*, p. 209.

77. Gaimushō, *Shūsen*, pp. 121–122; Abe, pp. 219–220; Butow, pp. 60ff. As early as January 10, 1945, Hosokawa recorded that Yoshida and Obata were backing Konoe for the premiership. Two-and-one-half months later, on March 30, he also made cryptic reference to the fact that Koiso was interested in reshuffling his cabinet and bringing Yoshida in as foreign minister "representing the Konoe line." Hosokawa, pp. 331, 363; Ōtani, *Kempei Mitsuroku*, p. 37.

78. *KJ*, I, 57; *YM*, p. 24. Akizuki was more sanguine about Yoshida's

appropriateness as an envoy than Prince Takamatsu. On July 10, 1944, Hirota proposed that Yoshida be sent to Switzerland, where he might engage in peace negotiations with British representatives. Takamatsu rejected the suggestion on the grounds that Yoshida's style was too blunt; Hosokawa, pp. 261–262.

79. Ōtani, *Kempei Mitsuroku*, pp. 8–11. Ōtani notes that Yoshida, Harada, Kabayama, and Ikeda Seihin all had estates in Ōiso, and were known to the Kempeitai as the "Ōiso group"; pp. 40–41. Hatakeyama gives 1940 as the date surveillance of Yoshida began; pp. 237–238. On "leaks" to ambassadors Grew and Craigie through Yoshida, see Kase, *Yoshida Shigeru no Yuigon*, p. 36. The bulk of the account in Hatakeyama deals with the actual spy operation.
80. Ōtani, *Kempei Mitsuroku*, pp. 2–3, 11–23.
81. Ibid., pp. 28–29. The second group consisted of Obata, Harada, Kabayama, Yanagigawa Heisuke, and Sakai Kōji. Sakai was a reserve general associated with Konoe (and with the Kōdō-ha) who came to the Kempeitai's attention around 1944, when he prepared a translation of Clemenceau's memoirs. The translation enjoyed a certain popularity among some middle-echelon officers, and was regarded as potentially subversive because of sections dealing with Clemenceau's purge of the French military establishment during World War One; ibid., pp. 12–13. Obata, Harada, and Kabayama were briefly interrogated and placed under surveillance in their homes near the end of April; ibid., pp. 51–52. Konoe and Makino comprised the third and most sensitive level of suspects, and were not apprehended or approached.
82. Ibid., pp. 21–24.
83. Ibid., pp. 3–4, 28, 39, Ōtani's version is inconsistent. At one point (p. 28) he indicates that part of Yoshida's original copy of the memorial was obtained at Ōiso, but elsewhere (p. 39) he states that the original copy was not found. There was some controversy at the time and in the immediate postwar years as to whether the contents of the memorial were actually revealed to the Kempeitai by Kido, who was present during the audience and is harshly dealt with as a pro-militarist in most Japanese sources. In his memoirs, however, Yoshida offers only the version that the memorial was made available through a spy within his household. Kase elaborates the latter version with an anecdote that belongs among the vintage Yoshida stories. According to this, the "spy" involved was a student working part-time in the Yoshida house who had been bought off by the Kempeitai. After the war the young man needed a letter of recommendation from his previous employer, that is, Yoshida, and got a good one. He was, Yoshida allegedly wrote, a youth who pursued his assigned tasks diligently and thoroughly. Cf. Mukoyama,

p. 113; Iwabuchi, pp. 39–40; *KJ*, I, 60; Kase, *Bungei Shunjū*, p. 141; Hatakeyama, pp. 241–243.

84. Mukoyama, pp. 97–99, 113–115; Ōtani, *Kempei Mitsuroku*, p. 30. Butow (p. 75) indicates a much broader wave of arrests took place at this time, but the YOHANSEN members appear in any case to have been treated as a special problem.

85. Ōtani, *Kempei Mitsuroku*, pp. 35–37.

86. Ibid., p. 41. Ōtani cited the line in question as being this: "The army has already lost its confidence in pursuing this war; the decline of fighting spirit cannot be disguised, and I think defeat is inevitable."

87. Ibid., pp. 37–40.

88. Iwabuchi, p. 40; Ueda (note 42); *KJ*, I, 60–61. The perceived parallel between Konoe and Badoglio is interesting. Marshal Pietro Badoglio had supported Mussolini and commanded the conquest of Ethiopia. He was closely associated with the fascists and monarchists, but became the rallying point of those who saw the war as lost, and who deposed Mussolini on July 25, 1943. And he used the specter of communism to gain support for his conservative cause. Immediately after its formation, the Badoglio government sent secret agents to negotiate a settlement with the Allies. They passed the word to Churchill, who relayed it to Roosevelt on August 5, that "there is nothing between the King, with the patriots who have rallied round him . . . and rampant Bolshevism." Neither Badoglio's background, his monarchist associations, nor on the other hand the desires of Italy's anti-fascists was of primary concern to the Anglo-American leaders in this situation. As Churchill had already made clear to Roosevelt on July 31, "My position is that once Mussolini and the Fascists are gone, I will deal with any Italian authority which can deliver the goods. . . . Those purposes would certainly be hindered by chaos, Bolshevisation, or civil war. . . . I should deprecate any pronouncement about self-determination at the present time"; cited in Gabriel Kolko, *The Politics of War* (Random House, 1968), p. 45. The extent to which the Japanese were aware of the situation in Italy and perceptive enough to see its similarities to the movement associated with Konoe reveals, among other things, one reason why Konoe and the Yoshida group may have been hopeful of the possibilities of arranging a fairly generous peace settlement with the Allies. They too might hope to "pull a Badoglio," and save the imperial institution by presenting it and themselves as Japan's best hope for a check against "chaos, Bolshevisation, or civil war." And indeed, although Konoe did not succeed in following Badoglio's precedent, the imperial institution *was* retained by the victors, festooned with the same rationale of being a bulwark against chaos and revolutionary upheaval. The parallels (and,

of course, differences) between the war and occupation experiences of Italy and Japan offer a virtually unexplored area for study relating to the politics and geopolitics of the 1940s.

89. Ōtani, *Kempei Mitsuroku*, pp. 46–47. The socialist influence, Ōtani argued, had been imparted largely through two admitted socialists, Asahara Kenzō and Miyazaki Masayoshi, who had penetrated the Kwantung Army group centering around Ishiwara Kanji. The influence was broken in the "Asahara Incident" of 1938. Cf. also p. 17 for Ōtani's critique of the YOHANSEN position, as well as his far more extended counter-argument in *Gunbatsu*. Concerning Miyazaki, see note 41 above. For an analysis of the Kyōwakai, see Hirano Kenichirō, "Manshūkoku Kyōwakai no Seijiteki Tenkai," in Nihon Seiji Gakkai, ed., *"Konoe Shintaisei" no Kenkyū* (Iwanami, 1972; this is a special annual issue of *Seijigaku*), pp. 231–283.

90. Ōtani, *Kempei Mitsuroku*, p. 36.

91. Ibid., p. 32.

92. Abe, p. 221; cf. Ōtani, *Kempei Mitsuroku*, p. 33. For a description of Yoshida in an actual interrogation session, see ibid., pp. 42–45, 49–50.

93. *KJ*, I, 62–63; *YM*, pp. 28–29.

8. "REVOLUTION"

1. Cf. Konoe's appraisal cited in Chapter 2, note 2; the comments on Yoshida by British and American diplomats in Chapters 4 and 5; Owen Lattimore's remarks on "go-slow" imperialists cited in Chapter 3, note 61; and Joseph Ballantine's appraisal of Yoshida in Chapter 9, note 14.

2. Kase, *Yoshida Shigeru no Yuigon*, pp. 10–11.

3. Cf. Chapter 9, note 20.

4. The valuable Joseph M. Dodge Papers (hereafter *JMDP*) contain numerous examples of such disagreement between the United States and Japan, as suggested in more detail here in Chapter 11. In August 1949, for example, Dodge flatly told the Yoshida government in writing that its attitude "suggests the possibility of a substantial effort to sabotage the program"; "Ikeda Letter" file, Box VI, *JMDP*, 1949. Yoshida's disagreements with Dulles over the rearmament issue are discussed in Chapter 10 below. His disesteem for the Dulles brand of diplomacy is frequently commented upon by Japanese intimate with him at the time. Cf. Kase, *Yoshida Shigeru no Yuigon*, p. 79, and interview with Shirasu Jirō in Andō Yoshio, ed. *Shōwa Seiji Keizai Shi e no Shōgen* (Mainichi Shimbunsha, 1966), III, 407. For a later sample of Yoshida's criticism of U.S. foreign policy, see his *Ōiso Zuisō*, pp. 10–11: "Irresolution seems to pervade United States' foreign aid policy as a whole. Many of the

actions taken by the United States give the impression that she is wanting in knowledge and assurance."

5. *KJ*, IV, 122–123.
6. Wildes, *Typhoon*, p. 107. Cf. *YN*, p. 26.
7. *Asahi Gurafu*, November 5, 1967, p. 88. He was notorious for curt responses to interpellations in the Diet, and for reading his policy addresses to the legislature in a rather diffident manner. On one occasion, he dropped a page from his prepared text, and critics sometimes cite this as symbolic of his general attitude; the incident is mentioned in Takahashi Seiichirō, "Yoshida Shigeru-shi Tsuisō," *KK* 270:5 (August 1968). Takahashi's phrase for Yoshida's attitude toward the Diet was *daitan fuson*, audacious, or bold and insolent. Yoshida's arrogance toward party and parliament was strongly criticized by the Hatoyama group during the power struggles of 1951–1954; a good sample appears in Kōno Ichirō's *Kōno Ichirō Jiden* (Tokuma Shoten, 1965), Chapter 10. There is another line of thought, however, which portrays Yoshida as a committed liberal or "liberalist"; this emerges quite strongly in Kase Toshikazu's various affectionate tributes. The official history of the Yoshida cabinets describes him as a political "idealist"; *YN*, p. 10. See also Chapter 9, note 137.
8. On funding, see citations in Chapter 9, note 28.
9. *YN*, p. 10. For samples of such criticism, see Kōno, Chapter 10, and Hatoyama Ichirō, "Ura kara Mita Jūnen," *Mainichi Shimbun*, August 15, 1955.
10. Yoshida's own version of his priorities at the time appears in his *Sekai to Nihon* (*SN*), pp. 85–87; cf. *YN*, p. 7.
11. The "historic stumble" phrase appears in *YM*, p. 7. It captures Yoshida's view nicely, although it is not an exact translation from the original; cf. *KJ*, I, 29. This theme has been illustrated at some length in the preceding chapters; for another capsule expression, see *SN*, pp. 123–127, 157. This was, of course, an orthodox conservative interpretation; cf. Shinobu, *Sengo Nihon Seiji Shi*, I, 174, 203.
12. Dean Acheson, *Present at the Creation: My Years in the State Department* (Norton, 1969), p. 126.
13. U.S. Senate, Committee on Armed Services and Committee on Foreign Relations, *Hearings to Conduct an Inquiry into the Military Situation in the Far East* (82nd Congress, 1st Session, 1951), p. 310.
14. In the draft manuscript for this present volume, four chapters were devoted to examining the various themes that emerge from the Konoe Memorial. This became virtually a separate inquiry in its own right, and has been deleted; the present section is thus intended merely as a suggestion of *some* of the questions the memorial raises for scholars of the

1930s and early 1940s. These are questions of "consciousness" at both the elite and popular levels, but questions that in turn demand reexamination of the concrete activities and dramatic structural changes that occurred in Japan during this period. Some illustration and documentation not included here appear in the Ph.D. dissertation which was the point of departure for this volume: "Yoshida Shigeru and the Great Empire of Japan, 1878–1945," Harvard University, 1972. I have also tried briefly to suggest the importance of the dynamics of this period to any understanding of early postwar Japan in "Occupied Japan as History and Occupation History as Politics," *Journal of Asian Studies* 34.2: 485–504 (February 1975).

15. Misuzu Shobō, ed., *Gendai Shi Shiryō: Zoruge Jiken* (Misuzu Shobō, 1962), II (2), 128. Cf. Johnson, *An Instance of Treason*, p. 191; also pp. 2, 5, 7, 120, 131, 160, 172. This was not a peripheral observation on Ozaki's part, but the very heart of his hopes and expectations.
16. Shigemitsu, pp. 244–245. Mukoyama singles out the Sorge-Ozaki affair above all other considerations in attempting to explain Konoe's almost "abnormal" suspicion of communism; p. 112. For a similar appraisal by a peripheral YOHANSEN figure, see Mazaki Katsuji, *Nihon wa Doko e Iku–Wana ni Kakatta Nihon* (Jitsugyō no Sekaisha, 1960), pp. 28–29, 37, 61.
17. Cited in Kolko, p. 142.
18. *Writings of Leon Trotsky*, second edition (Pathfinder Press, ca. 1971–1976), volumes for *1930–1931* (pp. 356–361), *1932–1933* (pp. 287–294), *1937–1938* (pp. 410–415); also pp. 101, 106, and 108 in the first edition of the volume for *1937–1938*. See also Mazaki, p. 31.
19. Edgar Snow, *Red Star Over China* (Grove edition, 1961), p. 95; U.S. Department of State, *United States Relations with China, with Special Reference to the Period 1944–1949* ("The China White Paper"), Department of State Publication 3573, Far Eastern Series 30, especially p. 711.
20. Cf. Chapter 3, note 38.
21. Government of Japan, *Document A–The Present Condition of China: With Reference to Circumstances Affecting International Relations and the Good Understanding between Nations upon which Peace Depends*, revised edition (July 1932; submitted to the League of Nations), especially pp. 16–18 and Appendix A-3, entitled "Communism in China" [47 pp.]. See also the companion volume: *Document B–Relations of Japan with Manchuria and Mongolia.*
22. *FRUS*, *Japan 1931–1941*, I, 477–481 (an English version of the New Order speech).
23. Ogata Shōji, "Shūsen no Hankyōteki Seikaku," "Geppō #3" (November 1953), a detached insert which appeared in the multi-volume publication

by Iwanami Shoten, *Nihon Shihonshugi Kōza: Sengo Nihon no Seiji to Keizai* (1953). See also Mazaki, pp. 42–46, for references to similar reports from other specialists.

24. Gaimushō, *Shūsen*, pp. 359–360.
25. Ibid., p. 614. Cf. Butow, p. 183.
26. Andrew Roth, *Dilemma in Japan* (Little, Brown, 1945), pp. 242–272. Nosaka's Yenan interlude is briefly discussed in Rodger Swearingen and Paul Langer, *Red Flag in Japan: International Communism in Action 1919–1951* (Harvard, 1952), Chapter 9; selections of his writings from this period appear in *Nosaka Sanzō Senshū: Senji-hen 1933–1945* (Shin Nihon, 1967).
27. Roth, p. 5. Following the surrender, some three-thousand political prisoners were in fact released from Japan's prisons.
28. For an illuminating memoir by one of the army founders of the Tōsei-ha, see Ikeda Sumihisa, *Nihon no Magari Kado: Gunbatsu no Higeki to Saigo no Gozen Kaigi* (Senjō, 1968). An extended analysis of the military cliques which is specifically devoted to refuting the thesis set forth in the Konoe Memorial is presented by Ōtani Keijirō, the prolific former Kempeitai official, in *Gunbatsu*.
29. Robert M. Spaulding has published two illuminating studies of the civilian reformers: "Japan's 'New Bureaucrats,' 1932–1945," in George Wilson, ed., *Crisis Politics in Prewar Japan* (Sophia, 1970); and "The Bureaucracy as a Political Force, 1920–1945," in James Morley, ed., *Dilemmas of Growth in Prewar Japan* (Princeton, 1971). The reform clique in the Foreign Ministry is briefly mentioned in Chihiro Hosoya, "Retrogression in Japan's Foreign-Policy Decision-Making Process," in Morley, pp. 86–93. A most useful article in Japanese is Hashigawa Bunzō, "Kakushin Kanryō," in Kamishima Jirō, ed., *Kenryoku no Shisō,* volume 10 in *Gendai Nihon Shisō Taikei* (Chikuma Shobō, 1965), pp. 251–273. This is particularly interesting because it includes a case study of Okumura Kiwao, a "reform bureaucrat" who is not well known, and who was associated with right-wing movements as a student. Okumura's retrospective reflections on the period appear in Andō, II, 198–209. Foreign diplomats were sensitive to these developments, and British ambassador Sir Robert Clive submitted a report on the subject in 1936; *FO* 371/21038 (December 17, 1936). E. H. Norman also touched on this in "A Japanese *Eminence Grise*: Izawa Takiwo" (Chapter 7, note 42 above).

The contribution of the intelligentsia to these developments can be effectively approached through the Shōwa Kenkyūkai (Konoe's "brain trust," with which Ozaki Hotsumi was associated). For an account by participants, see Shōwa Dōjin Kai [under the supervision of Gotō

Ryūnosuke], ed., *Shōwa Kenkyūkai* (Keizai Ōraisha, 1968); Gotō's interview in Andō, II, 210–229; and the discussion by Takehashi Kamekichi and Sakai Saburō in Tokyo Jūni Chanaru Hōdōbu, ed., *Shōgen: Watakushi no Shōwa Shi* (1969), II, 236–245. James Crowley deals with the subject in "Intellectuals as Visionaries of the New Asian Order," in Morley, pp. 319–373.

30. The detailed police report on this dramatic incident appears in Naimushō [Home Ministry], Keihokyoku Hoanbu, *Tokkō Geppō*, February 1942, pp. 4–38. *Tokkō Geppō* was the monthly internal report of the Special Higher Police, or "Thought Police." It is available in a multi-volume reprint edition covering the period from March 1930 through November 1944.

31. Hosokawa, pp. 189, 312–313. Hosokawa's two-volume *Jōhō Tennō ni Tassezu* is actually a diary for the period from October 30, 1943 to December 31, 1945, which he kept after becoming Prince Takamatsu's aide. He was recommended to Takamatsu by Konoe, his father-in-law, and his duties were to keep Takamatsu informed of the gossip and activities of Japan's ruling classes. Both directly and indirectly, the diary provides exceptional insight into the atmosphere in which YOHANSEN operated. Hosokawa kept its existence secret from Allied authorities, thus making it unavailable for use in the war-crimes trials, and only allowed it to be published after the occupation ended.

32. Ibid., p. 225.

33. Harada, VIII, 328.

34. Johnson, *An Instance of Treason*, pp. 6–7, 120–121. On June 7, 1940, Grew recorded a conversation with Ambassador Craigie, whose "informants said that Prince Konoye would head the new cabinet." Craigie was upset by this because, Grew explained, "he regarded such a development with some anxiety because Prince Konoye is surrounded by radical elements—a sort of brain trust he said—and is known to be weak and rather lazy"; *JGP* 100. The most detailed discussion of the New Structure in English appears in Berger, *Parties Out of Power.*

35. Mazaki, pp. 31–41, especially p. 31. George E. Lvov, a "liberal aristocrat," was premier and minister of the interior of the provisional government established in Russia on March 16, 1917. Like Konoe, he faced the problems of war, revolution, and controlling the military. He resigned on July 21, and Kerensky became premier of the coalition government on August 7, 1917.

36. In English, see the following sources: *Report of the Mission on Japanese Combines*, Part I (the famous "Edwards Report," submitted to the Department of State and the War Department in 1946); T. A. Bisson, *Japan's War Economy* (Macmillan, 1945); Bisson, *Zaibatsu Dissolution*

in Japan (California, 1954); Bisson, "Increase of Zaibatsu Predominance in Wartime Japan," in Jon Livingston, Joe Moore and Felicia Oldfather, eds., *The Japan Reader: Imperial Japan, 1800–1945* (Pantheon, 1974), pp. 456–464; Jerome B. Cohen, *Japan's Economy in War and Reconstruction*; Eleanor M. Hadley, *Antitrust in Japan* (Princeton, 1970). In Japanese, see the multi-volume survey by Kajinishi Mitsuhaya, Katō Toshihiko, Ōshima Kiyoshi and Ōuchi Tsutomu, *Nihon Shihonshugi no Botsuraku* (Tokyo Daigaku, 1960–1968), especially volumes 3 and 4.

37. Cf. statistics in Hadley, pp. 48–55; also in Mitsubishi Economic Research Institute, ed., *Mitsui-Mitsubishi-Sumitomo: Present Status of the Former Zaibatsu Enterprises* (Mitsubishi Economic Research Institute, 1955), p. 6.
38. *Tokkō Geppō* (note 30 above) is a fundamental primary source in this area. For an analysis of wartime "rumors," see Ikeuchi Hajime, "Taiheiyō Sensōchū no Senji Ryūgen," *Shakaigaku Hyōron*, June 1951, pp. 30–42. In English, see United States Strategic Bombing Survey, *The Effects of Strategic Bombing on Japanese Morale* (Morale Division, 1947); also Frederick S. Hulse, "Some Effects of the War upon Japanese Society," *Far Eastern Quarterly* 7.1:22–42 (November 1947).
39. Hosokawa, pp. 250–251; cf. 153–154, 164–167.
40. Ibid., pp. 73–74.
41. E. H. Norman, "On the Modesty of Clio," unpublished manuscript.
42. *YM*, pp. 75, 200, 228.
43. Hata Ikuhiko has examined pre-surrender U.S. planning (and factionalism) in detail in his contribution to the multi-volume Ministry of Finance project on the occupation period: *Amerika no Tai-Nichi Senryō Seisaku*, vol. 3 of Ōkurashō Zaisei Shi Shitsu, ed., *Shōwa Zaisei Shi: Shūsen kara Kōwa made* (Tōyō Keizai Shimpōsha, 1976). For an angry inside account, see the interview with Eugene Dooman in the Columbia University oral history project on the occupation (see Chapter 4, note 22 above).
44. Cf. Yoshida's *KJ*, II, 260; *YM*, pp. 225–226; *SN*, pp. 10–19, 86–87; and "Jūnen no Ayumi," *Mainichi Shimbun*, August 10, 1945. For similar comments by other Japanese conservatives concerning the "Reds" in SCAP, cf. the introductory pages of Kon Hideme, *Yoshida Shigeru*; the interview with Shirasu Jirō in Andō, III, 409; Kase, *Yoshida Shigeru no Yuigon*, p. 119; Hatoyama's view as noted in Sumimoto, II, 56. Hadley refers to a 1947 conversation with the head of the Mitsui family in which the Red-baiting appears to have clear anti-Semitic overtones; pp. 42–43.
45. Recounted by Kon Hideme in *KK* 271:4 (September 1968).
46. Yoshida discusses his affinity with SCAP's hard-line anti-communists, as opposed to "New Dealer" types, in *KJ*, I, 94–114; cf. *YM*, Chapter 5.

The conservative tactic of exploiting the factionalism between GS and G-2 is often commented upon by Japanese; see, for example, Kase, *Yoshida Shigeru no Yuigon*, p. 42. It deserves further detailed study, however, which will necessarily involve examination not only of the precise roles and influence of GS and G-2 (as well as Economic and Scientific Section), but also the activities of the Japanese government's Central Liaison Office, and the role of MacArthur himself. (Beyond this, of course, lie the further questions of factions in Washington, and tensions between Washington and SCAP.) In effect, Yoshida endeavored to counter early reformist policies by circumventing GS and appealing both to G-2 (and like-minded officers in other assignments) and *directly* to the supreme commander himself; for an example of successful resort to the latter, see Shirasu Jirō's recollections included in *KJ*, I, 114–116. MacArthur's response was not always favorable, but Yoshida concluded that in the final analysis the supreme commander's influence was conservative; see his appraisal of MacArthur in *SN*, pp. 83–103.

A systematic study of the purge of "radicals" within SCAP also remains to be undertaken; cf. passing references in Wildes, *Typhoon*, pp. 228, 276, 286. Almost certainly, this will reveal a link between the F.B.I. and political purges in the United States and Willoughby's Counter-Intelligence Section. The names of a number of former occupation personnel were evoked in the 1956–1957 investigations of *Scope of Soviet Activity in the United States* by the Senate (Committee on the Judiciary, Subcommittee to Investigate the Administration of the Internal Security Act and Other Internal Security Laws; 84th Congress, 2nd Session, and 85th Congress, 1st Session). On the Red Purge and overall SCAP campaign against communists and "fellow travelers," see the citations in Chapter 9, note 149.

47. James William Morley, "The First Seven Weeks," *The Japan Interpreter* 6.2:160–163 (September 1970).

48. *KJ*, II, 70. Cf. *YM*, pp. 150–151; Hadley, pp. 43–44; Bisson, *Zaibatsu Dissolution*, pp. 69–71; Sumimoto, I, 165–166. Yoshida reaffirmed this in May 1946 when he was forming his first cabinet; *YN*, p. 7.

49. "Edwards Report" (see note 36 above), pp. vii–viii. See also the famous "FEC-230" (SWNCC 302) of January 1947, reproduced in Hadley, pp. 495–514.

50. Supreme Commander Allied Powers, Government Section, *Political Reorientation of Japan: September 1945 to September 1948* (Government Printing Office, 1949), II, 776, 780; cited hereafter as *PRJ*. Cf. note 67 in Chapter 9.

51. This argument that the choice was between small-scale business or socialism was also expressed by U.S. officials in regard to occupied

Germany. On October 12, 1946, for example, General Lucius Clay informed his staff, in connection with the German decartelization program, that "your choice in Germany today is between free enterprise . . . of small business and socialism. We must have small ventures or we will find our ventures will be affected by influence of Communists, and the influence of the British Labor Party in the British Zone." See *Report of the Committee Appointed to Review the Decartelization Program in Germany to The Honorable Secretary of the Army*, April 15, 1949 (the "Ferguson Report"), pp. 102–103; in Records of Ferguson Committee, Record Group 335, National Archives, Box 1. Similarly, the chief of the Decartelization Branch in the U.S. zone observed that "It was almost impossible prior to the war to determine in the German social structure where government ended and private enterprise began." Consequently, "the program of the Decartelization Branch, while not conceived or primarily designed to prevent the advent of socialization in Germany, nevertheless does have a deterrent effect on the socialization of German finance and industry. It has this effect because it offers to the Germans a positive economic program which makes socialization unnecessary." Phillips Hawkins, *Digest of Report of the Decartelization Branch*, September 23, 1947, pp. 42–43; in ibid., Box 2. I am grateful to Professor Charles S. Maier for sharing materials on decartelization in occupied Germany with me.

52. *PRJ*, II, 780.

53. Quoted in Robert E. Ward and Frank Joseph Shulman, eds., *The Allied Occupation of Japan, 1945–1952: An Annotated Bibliography of Western-Language Materials* (American Library Association, 1974), entry 1719; see also entries 1415, 1699a, 1718, 1720, 1726a, 1727, and 1739.

54. *KJ*, II, 193; *YM*, pp. 200–201. Cf. Yoshida's *SN*, p. 18, and *Ōiso Zuisō*, p. 26. The anti-communist significance of the land reform was emphasized by many Japanese; see, for example, the interview with Ishikawa Ichirō in Andō, III, 206.

55. See the interview with Wada in Andō, III, especially p. 44. Wada was actually one of the reform bureaucrats purged in the 1941 Cabinet Planning Board Incident, and Yoshida overrode intense inner-party opposition in appointing him; see Chapter 9, note 133 below.

56. See Chapter 9, pp. 329–332.

57. See George M. Beckmann and Genji Okubo, *The Japanese Communist Party, 1922–1945* (Stanford, 1969), especially the Party theses included in the appendix. For a Japanese survey of the complex internal controversies among prewar Japanese Marxists, see Koyama Hirotake, *Nihon Shihonshugi Ronsō Shi* (Aoki Shoten, 1953), 2 volumes.

58. In the 1930s, Trotsky emphasized the similar *backwardness* of Japan

and Tzarist Russia in predicting imminent revolution in Japan; see note 18 above. Mao Tse-tung drew similar conclusions in what has been called his "timing theory"; cf. Richard Levy, "New Light on Mao: His Views on the Soviet Union's *Political Economy*," *China Quarterly*, 61:95–117 (March 1975), especially p. 108. From a very different methodological and ideological perspective, much the same point was also emphasized by Talcott Parsons in a 1946 essay on Japan in Douglas G. Haring, ed., *Japan's Prospect* (Harvard, 1946).

59. George Kennan, *Memoirs 1925–1950* (Little, Brown, 1967), Chapter 16.
60. U.S. Department of Defense, *United States-Vietnam Relations, 1945–1967*, Book 8, pp. 239–242; this is the official version of the "Pentagon Papers." A fuller treatment of this problem is given in John W. Dower, "The Superdomino in Postwar Asia: Japan In and Out of the Pentagon Papers," in Noam Chomsky and Howard Zinn, eds., *The Pentagon Papers: The Senator Gravel Edition* (Beacon, 1972), V, 101–142.
61. Richard L-G. Deverall, "Are We Rebuilding Tojo's 'Red' Army?", *The New Leader*, January 15, 1951, pp. 2–5.

9. *IMPERIAL JAPAN AND THE "NEW JAPAN"*

1. Yamagata Kiyoshi, "Yoshida-san no Omoide," *KK* 272:9–10 (October 1968).
2. "Ko Yoshida Gensōri Tsuitō Zadankai," *KK* 267:8 (May 1969). The "One Man" appellation was expressed in borrowed English (*Wan Man*). More precisely, Yoshida's joke was that the newspapers gave him the label because he barked like a dog at reporters.
3. On visiting shrines, see *SN*, pp. 219–226. A Catholic priest was summoned as Yoshida lay on his deathbed, but arrived and baptized him after he had passed away. Yoshida himself had expressed partiality to the name Joseph; his family, some of whom were practicing Catholics, chose Thomas More. The funeral service was held at the Catholic cathedral in Tokyo. This final act prompted a final cartoon of old One Man ascending to heaven; to the familiar kimono, white footwear, walking staff, cigar and pince-nez were now added a halo and wings. Photos of the funeral, a reproduction of the cartoon, and a brief account by the priest who baptized Yoshida appear in "Yoshida Shigeru no Shōgai," a special issue of *Asahi Gurafu*, November 5, 1967.
4. Chitoshi Yanaga, *Big Business in Japanese Politics* (Yale, 1968), p. 74.
5. *Nippon Times*, September 16, 1951.
6. A well-known photo of the imperial audience at which Yoshida delivered his famous *Shin Shigeru* statement is reproduced in *Asahi Gurafu*, November 5, 1967; also in Kase, *Yoshida Shigeru no Yuigon.*

7. Cf. *Jurisuto* 100:29 (February 15, 1956) on SCAP's reform concerning the concept of "public servant." Also *Jurisuto* 361:90 (January 1, 1967).
8. Yoshida was also considered as a possible successor to Higashikuni in October 1945; *Kido Kōichi Nikki*, II, 1240 (October 5, 1945). On his appointment as foreign minister under Higashikuni, see *YN*, pp. 6–7; Shinobu, I, 161–162; Sumimoto, I, 117–122. Both Obata Toshishirō and Konoe were ministers of state in the Higashikuni cabinet; with Yoshida, this gave the cabinet a notable representation from the YOHANSEN group. Higashikuni himself had had a fairly close if ambiguous relationship with the Kōdō-ha in the pre-surrender period; see Ben-Ami Shilloney, *Revolt in Japan: The Young Officers and the February Twenty-Six Incident* (Princeton, 1972), pp. 107–109, 180.
9. Shinobu, I, 170.
10. *YN*, p. 7; Sumimoto, I, 73, 118–122, 129–130. At one point Yoshida proposed that he personally resign as a gesture of responsibility, and protest, for SCAP having arrested Prince Nashimoto, one of the more swaggering members of the imperial family; Sumimoto, II, 39.
11. *YN*, pp. 17–28; Shinobu, I, 300–316; Sumimoto, II, 54–77.
12. *YM*, p. 78.
13. *SN*, pp. 85–87.
14. Quincy Wright, ed., *A Foreign Policy for the United States* (Chicago, 1947), p. 141; cf. p. 143.
15. As reported from Tokyo by E. H. Norman in memorandum No. 110, April 13, 1948; External Affairs archives, Ottawa, Canada. Norman went on to note that MacArthur "was surprised that [Yoshida's] party had not already chosen a more suitable chairman. Yoshida continually exaggerated his own popularity in the country and left the arduous task of campaigning to his lieutenants; he was not even a first-class parliamentarian. Perhaps when Japan returns to the commity [*sic*] of nations and has a greater access to the world, leaders might appear with greater imagination and energy, but in the meantime he feared that the Japanese would have to endure mediocre and uninspiring leaders." I am grateful to Ōkubo Genji for this document.
16. Kōsaka, p. 5; Kase, *Yoshida Shigeru no Yuigon*, p. 71; Uchida Kenzō, *Sengo Nihon no Hoshu Seiji* (Iwanami Shinsho, 1969), p. 44.
17. See Chapter 2, pp. 52–53 above.
18. Yoshida, *Ōiso Zuisō*, pp. 42–43; cf. his "Jūnen no Ayumi," *Mainichi Shimbun*, August 9, 1955.
19. *SN*, p. 19; cf. Keizai Dantai Rengōkai, ed. *Keidanren no Jūnen* (1956), p. 183.
20. *YN*, pp. 111–124, 165–172; *SN*, pp. 90–91; Shinobu, III, 851–855,

904–917; Sodei Rinjirō, *Makkaasaa no Nisen Nichi* (Chūō Kōronsha, 1974), pp. 257–263. The abortive inner-party attempt to unseat Yoshida involved a movement to replace him with Yamazaki Takashi, the speaker of the House of Representatives. In the Diet election to chose a successor to Ashida, Yoshida received 183 votes against 213 blank ballots; despite his lack of a majority, he proceeded to form the first single-party cabinet since the beginning of the occupation. In the general election of January 1949, Yoshida's party gained 264 seats (of a total of 466) in the lower house; the next most successful party, also conservative, gained 66.

21. *YN*, pp. 119–120; Shinobu, III, 760.
22. *YN*, pp. 177–178.
23. *YN*, p. 168; the four prior majority victories had been by the Kenseitō in 1898, Seiyūkai under Hara in 1920, Minseitō under Hamaguchi in 1930, and Seiyūkai under Inukai in 1932.
24. Robert A. Scalapino and Junnosuke Masumi, *Parties and Politics in Contemporary Japan* (California, 1962), p. 165. Haruhiro Fukui, using narrower criteria for "businessmen," gives the figure as 86 (31.8 percent); *Party in Power: The Japanese Liberal-Democrats and Policy-making* (California, 1970), p. 272.
25. Scalapino and Masumi, p. 165. Fukui gives the figure of 47 "public officials" (17.4 percent); p. 272.
26. *YN*, p. 93; Shinobu, II, 532–536; T. A. Bisson, *Prospects for Democracy in Japan* (Macmillan, 1949), pp. 50–60. Japanese newsmen estimated that the revision of the election law cost the Socialists at least 50 seats; Bisson, p. 59. SCAP permitted Yoshida to revise the electoral law with full awareness that this was to the advantage of the conservative parties. A memorandum of March 17, 1947, on "The Merits of the Electoral System Proposed by Mr. Yoshida," for example, concluded that "while there is nothing undemocratic about the proposed system it is, *in comparison to the existing system,* definitely advantageous to the parties now in power, and unfavorable to minority representation and to women." Box 2032, RG 331, National Archives, Suitland, Maryland; I am indebted to Kim Stege for this document.
27. Mazaki, *KK* 271:13.
28. Commentary on the "Yoshida School," "Yoshida faction," and bureaucratization of the party is rather widely dispersed. The following sources are of interest: *YN*, pp. 119–120, 124, 171, 179, 554, 565, 595; Watanabe Tsuneo, *Habatsu* (Kōbundō, 1958), especially pp. 19, 43, 51, 58–81, 108, 152–160; Watanabe Tsuneo, *Daijin* (Kōbundō, 1959), pp. 17–19, 245–254; Watanabe Tsuneo, "Yoshida Gakkō no Keifu," *Shūkan Yomiuri*, November 15, 1967, pp. 74–75; Sasaki Tōru, "Jimintō: Kikikan-naki Taihei Seitō," *Jiyū*, September 1967, pp. 88–90; Sasaki

Tōru, "Yoshida Shigeru no Shi to Hoshu Seiji no Meiun," *Gendai no Me*, December 1967, pp. 130–139; "Yoshida Gakkō no Jittai to Kongo," *Asahi Jyanaru*, November 5, 1967, pp. 105–107; Masumi Junnosuke, "Yoshida Shigeru," in Kamishima Jirō, ed., *Kenryoku no Shisō* (volume 10 in *Gendai Nihon Shisō Taikei*, Chikuma Shobō, 1965), especially pp. 375–385; Oka Yoshitake, ed., *Gendai Nihon no Seiji Katei* (Iwanami Shoten, 1958), pp. 74–81; Shinobu, III, 823; Fukui, pp. 40–53, 60–61, 271–273; Scalapino and Masumi, Chapter 3 and pp. 164–168.

Watanabe, who has written extensively on party factionalism, identifies the core of the "Yoshida School"—that is, Yoshida's most intimate supporters and "disciples"—as consisting of Ikeda Hayato, Satō Eisaku, Okazaki Katsuo, Kitazawa Naokichi, Nishimura Naoki, Maeo Shigesaburō, Yoshitake Keiichi, and Ōhashi Takeo. Ikeda and Satō, known as the "honor students" (*yūtōsei*) of the school, led the major subfactions of the broader "Yoshida faction" in the Diet, with other subfaction leaders being Masuda Kaneshichi, Hirokawa Kōzen, Inukai Takeru, Hori Shigeru, Fukunaga Kenji, Asō Tagakichi (Yoshida's son-in-law), and Tsubokawa Shinzō. Other key figures in the faction were Hayashi Jōji, Masutani Hideji, Kosaka Zentarō, Aichi Kiichi, Tanaka Kakuei, Hashimoto Ryūgō, Sutō Hideo, Kogane Yoshiteru, Nọda Uichi, Nemoto Ryutarō, Ohira Masayoshi, Miyazawa Kiichi, Matsuno Yorizō, Kurogane Yasumi, Niwa Kyoshirō, Minami Yoshio, and Setoyama Kazuo. See especially Watanabe's concise summary in *Shūkan Yomiuri.*

Funding of the conservative party under Yoshida was complex and a matter of considerable speculation by outsiders, for the formal financial linkage between the conservatives and big business was not established until 1955. For general discussions, see Shinobu Seizaburō, "Dokusen Shihon to Seiji," in Oka (above), pp. 207–252; Fukui, pp. 42–43, 51–52, and Chapter 6; Frank C. Langdon, "Japan," in Arnold J. Heidenheimer and Frank C. Langdon, *Business Associations and the Financing of Political Parties* (Martinus Nijhoff, 1968), pp. 140–205; Yanaga, especially pp. 19, 78–87, 93; Harry Emerson Wildes, "Underground Politics in Post-War Japan," *The American Political Science Review* 42.6:1149–1162 (December 1948); Wildes, *Typhoon*, especially pp. 108–109 and Chapter 6; Kenneth E. Colton, "Pre-war Political Influences in Post-war Conservative Parties," *The American Political Science Review*, 42.5:940–957 (October 1948).

Colton characterizes initial conservative funding as coming largely from construction companies, "dealers in scarce commodities," and "brokers for the sale and distribution of government stockpiles" (pp. 95–96); this is a genteel allusion to underground money politics by labor bosses, black-marketeers, and big capitalists involved in the hoarding or clandestine dispersal of vast material resources obtained at the time of the surrender. Wildes more specifically links Yoshida and his party with funds obtained through Ishibashi Shojirō (of Bridgestone Tyre Co.), former Diet member Terao Yutaka, banker and stockbroker Matsushima Kisaku, contractor Isumi Kenji, and "political manipulator" Tsuchiya Kameichi ("Underground," p. 1151). Yoshida's son-in-law, Asō Tagakichi, whose family fortune derived from coal interests in Fukuoka, was a source of personal funds to Yoshida. Cf. Shinobu, I, 325; Yanaga, p. 19; Wildes, *Typhoon*, p. 108. Yoshida also maintained links to the *zaibatsu* through his former classmate Miyajima Seijirō of Nisshin Spinning Co.; through Oya Shinzō of the Teikoku Rayon and Silk Co., who held the portfolios of both Industry and Commerce, and Finance, in the second Yoshida cabinet and maintained close ties with the financial world in Osaka; and through Hirokawa Kōzen, the so-called "political comet," who served as minister of agriculture and forestry in the third and fourth Yoshida cabinets. Cf. Yanaga, pp. 80, 93; Shinobu, I, 325; Watanabe, *Daijin*, p. 243; Watanabe, *Habatsu*, p. 19. John Roberts cites Miyajima, Shirasu Jirō, Mitsui's Mukai Tadaharu, and Mitsubishi's Katō Takeo as Yoshida's major early financial backers. From 1952, Roberts claims, he was strongly supported by the so-called "four heavenly kings" of finance: Kobayashi Ataru (head of Arabian Oil Co. and Yoshida's appointee as head of the Japan Development Bank in 1952) and the non-*zaibatsu* executives Sakurada Takeshi, Nagano Shigeo, and Mizuno Shigeo. See John G. Roberts, *Mitsui: Three Centuries of Japanese Business* (John Weatherhill, 1973), pp. 441–443. The officially acknowledged financial contributions received by the Liberal Party in the final year of the occupation (May 1951–April 1952) totaled 27.7-million yen. For a breakdown of these official figures, which are only a fraction of actual funds received, see Shinobu, "Dokusen," pp. 238–239.

29. In addition, during Yoshida's presidency from 1946 to 1954 the three key internal party positions (secretary general, chairman of the political research committee, and chairman of the executive committee) were shuffled among twenty men. All but three of these individuals, however, also were appointed to ministerial posts by Yoshida at one time or another. Cabinet and party-officer rosters are conveniently given in Asahi Shimbunsha, pp. 137–139.
30. Fukui, p. 45.
31. Kiyoaki Tsuji, "The Cabinet, Administrative Organization, and the Bureaucracy," *The Annals of the American Academy of Political and Social Science*, 308:10 (November 1956).
32. Maeda Riichi, "Yoshida-san to Kankoku," *KK* 295:16 (September 1970); Shinobu, IV, 1151.

33. Cf. Sumimoto, I, 131–133; also Higashikuni's recollections in *Mainichi Shimbun*, August 17, 1955. Sumimoto provides a detailed behind-the-scenes account of the revision issue: I, 73–115.
34. *New York Times*, October 20, 1945; cited in Harold S. Quigley and John E. Turner, *The New Japan: Government and Politics* (Minnesota, 1956), p. 115.
35. Sumimoto, I, 101–103; Yoshida, *Mainichi Shimbun*, August 16, 1955; Kōsaka, p. 22; Shinobu, I, 279; Quigley and Turner, p. 119; Courtney Whitney, *MacArthur: His Rendezvous with History* (Knopf, 1956), pp. 250–253; Charles A. Willoughby and John Chamberlain, *MacArthur, 1941–1951: Victory in the Pacific* (McGraw-Hill, 1954), p. 336. Yoshida's own account of the new constitution is conveyed in a letter he submitted to the Committee to Investigate the Constitution in 1957; Kempō Chosakai, *Kempō Chōsakai Dai-8-kai Sōkai Gijiroku* (December 18, 1957), pp. 1–11.
36. The controversy over appropriate renderings of English terms appears among documents included in the Alfred R. Hussey, Jr. Papers, University of Michigan.
37. *KG-HP-90*, June 23, 1946 (p. 17), and *OGE-HP*, June 24, 1946 (p. 21). These are the Japanese and English versions of the Diet record; see Abbreviations Used in the Notes (pp. 496, 497) for an explanation of the shorthand adopted for this cumbersome reference.
38. Whitney, pp. 246–251. Shirasu's account of the constitutional revision appears in Andō, III, 402–405. Ashida Hitoshi also indicated that SCAP's threat to take the issue directly to the people was decisive; *Mainichi Shimbun*, August 19, 1955.
39. *SN*, pp. 94–99; also Yoshida's letter cited in note 35 above. MacArthur's other great qualification as a benefactor to Japan, in Yoshida's account, was that he supposedly prevented the Soviet Union from establishing an occupation zone in Hokkaido. In general, Yoshida regarded MacArthur as a conservative and restraining force among the occupation reformers—despite the many head-on disagreements that occurred between the two men during the early years of the occupation; *SN*, pp. 83–103. Elsewhere he stressed MacArthur's role in solving the early postwar food crisis, effecting the repatriation of millions of Japanese, and later siding with him in opposing pressure from Washington for more rapid Japanese rearmament; "Ōiso no Shōrai," p. 209.
40. On the latter issue, see Chapter 10, pp. 377–380 below. Scholars consulted by Yoshida in preparing the defense of the emperor are noted by Miyake in *KK* 293:15–17 (July 1970).
41. *KG-HP-90*, June 21, 1946 (p. 6), and *OGE-HP* (p. 9). Cf. *KG-HP-90*, June 23, 1946 (p. 17), and *OGE-HP* (p. 21); *KG-HP-90*, August 28, 1946

(p. 254), and *OGE-HP* (p. 11); *KG-HR-90*, June 28, 1946 (p. 103), and *OGE-HR* (p. 11). Also *Shiryō: Sengo Nijūnen Shi* (Nihon Hyōronsha, 1966), I, 49; hereafter this 6-volume documentary collection is cited as *SSNS*.

42. *KG-HP-90*, June 25, 1946 (p. 35), and *OGE-HP* (p. 36). The Charter Oath is translated in Ryusaku Tsunoda, et al., *Sources of Japanese Tradition* (Columbia, 1958), pp. 643–644. English texts of both the Meiji and postwar constitutions appear in Quigley and Turner, pp. 407–421. Itō's "Commentaries on the Constitution of the Empire of Japan" is translated in Centre for East Asian Cultural Studies, ed., *Meiji Japan Through Contemporary Sources* (1969), I, 181–221.
43. *KG-HR-90*, June 26, 1946 (p. 75); the rendering in *OGE-HR* (p. 11) is very loose.
44. *KG-HP-90*, June 25, 1946 (p. 35), and *OGE-HP* (p. 36).
45. *KG-HR-90*, June 26, 1946 (p. 75), and *OGE-HR* (p. 11); *KG-HR-90*, June 25, 1946 (p. 50), and *OGE-HR* (p. 15).
46. *KG-HR-90*, June 25, 1946 (p. 42), and *OGE-HR* (p. 5); *KG-HR-90*, June 27, 1946 (p. 81), and *OGE-HR* (p. 3); *KG-HR-90*, June 28, 1946 (p. 97), and *OGE-HR* (p. 5); *KG-HR-90*, June 29, 1946 (p. 124), and *OGE-HR* (p. 15).
47. *KG-HR-90*, June 23, 1946 (p. 16), and *OGE-HR*, June 24, 1946 (p. 3). Cf. *KG-HR-90*, August 25, 1946 (p. 500), and *OGE-HR*, August 26, 1946 (p. 2). Matsumoto had taken this position earlier in internal government discussion of the revision; Sumimoto, I, 111–112.
48. *KG-HR-90*, August 25, 1946 (p. 501), and *OGE-HR*, August 26, 1946 (p. 3).
49. *KG-HR-90*, August 25, 1946 (pp. 500–501), and *OGE-HR*, August 26, 1946 (pp. 2–3). Excerpts from the committee report of the House of Representatives appear in *SSNS*, I, 51.
50. *KG-HR-90*, June 26, 1946 (p. 75), and *OGE-HR* (pp. 11–12). The first part of the quotation is excerpted in *SSNS*, I, 50.
51. *KG-HR-90*, June 26, 1946 (pp. 75–76), and *OGE-HR* (p. 12).
52. *KG-HR-90*, June 28, 1946 (p. 108), and *OGE-HR* (p. 16). Also *SSNS*, I, 50.
53. *KG-HP-90*, August 28, 1946 (p. 258), and *OGE-HP* (p. 16). Tanaka's specific negative example was "various countries of Latin America." A very similar vision of chaos was tendered officers in Government Section by Naruhashi Wataru in February 1946; Sumimoto, I, 98.
54. *KG-HR-90*, August 25, 1946 (p. 501), and *OGE-HR*, August 26, 1946 (p. 3).
55. Whitney to MacArthur, "Developments on Proposed Constitution for Japan," July 17, 1946. Hussey Papers.

56. The constitution became effective six months later, on May 3, 1947. Kigensetsu was reinstated as a national holiday in 1966, one year before Yoshida's death. His desire to have the new charter promulgated on this holiday is noted in an unpublished manuscript by T. A. Bisson.
57. Yoshida to MacArthur, December 27, 1946, *CPM*. See the explanation of this valuable "Correspondence with Prime Minister" on p. 495. This particular letter is reproduced in *PRJ*, II, 679, as well as in *Life* magazine, November 27, 1950.
58. *PRJ*, II, 679.
59. *YST*, March 24 [1947], pp. 252–256.
60. Cf. Fukui, pp. 205–206; also Chapter 11, p. 465 below.
61. Cf. Yoshida's letter to the Committee to Investigate the Constitution (note 35 above); *YM*, Chapter 14; Mazaki, *KK* 271:14.
62. *YM*, pp. 202–203; *KJ*, II, 196–197.
63. Mazaki, *KK* 271:14. Interview with Wada in Andō, III, 41–51. For general studies, see Ronald Dore, *Land Reform in Japan* (Oxford, 1959), and *The Developing Economies*, 4.2 (June 1966); the latter is a special issue devoted to critical assessment of the legacy of the land reform. An illuminating analysis of pre-surrender Japanese considerations concerning land reform is presented by Tsutomu Takigawa in "Historical Background of Agricultural Land Reform in Japan," *The Developing Economies* 10.3:290–310 (September 1972).
64. See the following general discussions of the purge: Sumimoto, vol. 2; Hans H. Baerwald, *The Purge of Japanese Leaders under the Occupation* (University of California Publications in Political Science, VIII, 1959); John D. Montgomery, "The Purge in Occupied Japan: A Study in the Use of Civilian Agencies under Military Government" (Operations Research Office, The Johns Hopkins University, 1953).
65. Yoshida to MacArthur, October 23, 1946; *CPM*. This was a cover letter to a formal memorandum from the Japanese government to SCAP which also emphasized that the extension of the purge "might well act as an impetus to extreme communists and the like"; see memorandum of October 22, 1946, in "Purge Background 1945–1946" file, Box 2134, RG 331, National Archives. Cf. Sumimoto, II, 80–81.
66. Sumimoto, II, 101. Ishibashi was actually emerging as a potential rival to Yoshida within the party, and himself argued that Yoshida "did not work too enthusiastically" to prevent his purge; cf. Sumimoto, II, 94–105, especially p. 103.
67. Yoshida to MacArthur, December 21, 1946, and MacArthur to Yoshida, December 26, 1946; *PRJ*, II, 499–500; also in *CPM*. MacArthur spoke of "that dangerous concentration of economic and political power which resides in the traditional family system," and raised the familiar specter

of "the private socialism of concentrated economic power. . . ." For prior exchanges on the economic purge, cf. Yoshida to MacArthur, November 8, 1946, and Whitney to President, Central Liaison Office, November 14, 1946; both in *CPM. Newsweek* magazine (the mouthpiece for U.S. critics of early occupation reform policies) attacked the economic purge in its issue of January 27, 1947, to which MacArthur responded in a revealing letter dated January 30; *PRJ*, II, 549.

68. Whitney to President, Central Liaison Office, October 23, 1946; *CPM*. In response, Yoshida typically by-passed Whitney and wrote directly to MacArthur on October 31, 1946. Officials on the local level "have always been the backbone of the peace loving people who hate and despise anarchy and chaos," he said, and concluded his letter with solemn hopes for "the future of democratic and uncommunist Japan"; *CPM*; also *PRJ*, II, 496–497.
69. From the famous speech of Secretary of the Army Kenneth C. Royall to the Commonwealth Club of San Francisco, January 6, 1948.
70. A total of 329 depurgees entered the 1952 general election for the lower house. These struggles are discussed in detail in numerous sources; cf. Masumi Junnosuke, *Gendai Nihon Seiji Taisei* (Iwanami Shoten, 1969), pp. 152–175. Also *YN*, pp. 553ff.
71. *KJ*, II, Chapter 16; *YM*, Chapters 21 and 22. *SN*, pp. 11–14.
72. *KJ*, II, 230–231. The startling notion of "healthy, democratic" unions in pre-surrender Japan emerges as "sensibly Socialist" in *YM*, p. 213.
73. Cf. Miriam Farley, *Aspects of Japan's Labor Problems* (John Day, 1950), pp. 44–49, 85, 97. Farley indicates that for the period up to June 1948, the number of "man-days" lost through strikes exceeded one percent of total man-days available only in one month (October 1946). For data from 1947 to 1954, see the official *Nihon Tōkei Nenkan, 1955–1956*, pp. 354–355.
74. Joe Baldwin Moore, "Production Control and the Postwar Crisis of Japanese Capitalism, 1945–1946," Ph.D. dissertation, University of Wisconsin, Madison, 1978. The June 13 proclamation is reproduced in *KJ*, II, 228–230 and translated in SCAP, General Headquarters, *Non-Military Activities in Japan, Summation No. 9* (June 1946), pp. 24–25. A résumé of these tensions is given in "A Brief Survey of the Growth of Japanese Labor Sentiment Against the Government," February 14, 1947, in the U.S. Delegation Subject Files of the Far Eastern Commission documents at the National Archives: "Labor File 1946–47," Box 228, RG 287. I am grateful to Joe Moore for this document.
75. Yoshida's diatribe against labor is strongly conveyed in *KJ*, II, 226–258, with the analogy to the prewar military appearing on pp. 252–255; see also pp. 237–238. The "translation" in *YM* conveys the spleen, but

omits some of the more detailed comparisons and invectives noted here.

76. Farley (p. 149) quotes the *Asahi* newspaper's commentary on the notorious *futei no yakara* phrase; see also Shinobu, II, 446. On the *Dai Nippon Teikoku* flap, cf. *OGE-HC*, December 8, 1948 (pp. 7–10), and December 9, 1948 (pp. 1–2); *OGE-HR*, December 15, 1948 (p. 5). Yoshida's comments in connection with the shipbuilding scandal appear in *Shūkan Sankei*, special issue, March 7, 1976, pp. 65–67, and Yanaga, p. 130. The major study of the scandal is probably Murobushi Tetsurō, *Sengo Gigoku* (Ushio, 1968); Murobushi gives a slightly different version of the "destruction of democracy" quotation (p. 173).

77. The summation that follows draws upon the following general sources: Yamazaki Gōrō, *Nihon Rōdō Undō Shi*, rev. ed. (Rōmu Gyōsei Kenkyūjo, 1961); Ōkochi Kazuo, *Sengo Nihon no Rōdō Undō*, rev. ed. (Iwanami Shinsho, 1961); surveys of labor legislation in *Jurisuto* 100:97–100 (February 15, 1956) and *Jurisuto* 361:234–259 (January 1, 1967); Solomon B. Levine, *Industrial Relations in Postwar Japan* (Illinois, 1958); Levine, "Labor Patterns and Trends," *The Annals of the American Academy of Political and Social Science* 308:102–112 (November 1956); Iwao F. Ayusawa, *A History of Labor in Modern Japan* (East-West, 1966); The Daily Labor Press, ed., *The Labor Union Movement in Postwar Japan* (1954).

78. *KJ*, II, 251. See also note 149 below.

79. Cf. Yamazaki's general discussion of Sōhyō; also Nihon Rōdō Kumiai Sōhyōgikai, *Sōhyō Jūnen Shi* (1964). An interesting interview with Takano Minoru, who led Sōhyō's turn to the left, appears in Andō, III, 242–252.

80. For general accounts, see Yanaga, *Big Business*, and the citations in Chapter 8, note 36, in addition to the following sources: SCAP, General Headquarters, Statistics and Reports Section, *History of the Non-Military Activities of the Occupation of Japan* (Tokyo, 1952), especially monographs 22, 24, 25, 26, 39, 40, and 50; Kōsei Torihiki Iinkai [Fair Trade Commission], *Dokusen Shihon Seisaku Nijūnen Shi* (Ōkurashō, 1968; cited below as *KTI*); Ōuchi Hyōe, "Keizai," in Yanaihara Tadao, ed., *Sengo Nihon Shōshi* (Tokyo Daigaku, 1958), I, 63–174; Kozo Yamamura, *Economic Policy in Postwar Japan: Growth Versus Economic Democracy* (California, 1967); Howard Schonberger, "Zaibatsu Dissolution and the American Restoration of Japan," *Bulletin of Concerned Asian Scholars*, 5.2:16–31 (September 1973). The discussion in volume 7 of Kajinishi (Chapter 8, note 36) is useful, and includes a table of levels of economic concentration in 1937, 1949, and 1955 (pp. 1906–1907).

81. In addition to the Joseph M. Dodge Papers, two Japanese archival collections contain intimate detail (much of it in English) on economic policy, discussion, and disagreement between the two countries: the voluminous papers of the Economic Stabilization Board (Keizai Antei Honbu) maintained in the National Planning Agency; and the working papers of Suzuki Gengo, a key Ministry of Finance official in bilateral discussions from 1952, maintained in the Ministry of Finance (see Chapter 11, note 88). The proposals and accomplishments of big business are discussed in detail in Keidanren's three-volume *Keizai Dantai Rengōkai Jūnenshi* (1962–1963), and the Ministry of International Trade and Industry published an economic history of the first postwar decade under the general editorship of Arizawa Hiromi: Tsūsan Daijin Kanbō Chōsakai, ed., *Sengo Keizai Jūnen Shi* (Sankō Kaikan, 1954). A Ministry of Finance official involved in the Dodge Line and final years of occupation economic policy, Watanabe Takeshi, kept a diary which is maintained at the Ministry of Finance and is especially useful for 1949–1951. On the basis of this diary, Watanabe published an illuminating memoir, *Senryōka no Nihon Zaisei Oboegaki* (Nihon Keizai Shimbunsha, 1966); an interview with Watanabe also appears in Andō, III, 312–331. Differences and disagreements on economic policy between the two countries naturally were also reflected in policy controversies within SCAP and between SCAP and Washington.
82. Cf. Martin Bronfenbrenner, "Monopoly and Inflation in Contemporary Japan," *Osaka Economic Papers* 3.2:41–48 (March 1955). The hoarding scandal was investigated during the Katayama cabinet, and one of the basic reports on the subject is published in *PRJ*, II, 728–733. See also Moore, Chapter 3.
83. Yamamura, pp. 27–28. Cf. Ishibashi's memoirs, *Tanzan Kaisō* (Mainichi Shimbunsha, 1951), and his published diary for 1945–1947, *Tanzan Nikki: Shōwa 20-22-nen* (Ishibashi Tanzan Kinen Zaidan, 1974). The origins of "priority production" are discussed by Arizawa Hiromi in in Andō, III, 274–293.
84. For some general statistics on the war boom, see Tsūsan Daijin (note 81 above), tables 33 (pp. 40–41) and 35 (pp. 42–43). On profit rates, see Industrial Bank of Japan estimates in ibid., table 84 (p. 116); different estimates are cited in *SSNS*, II, 155. Ministry of Finance estimates of profit rates in both large and medium-small enterprise appear in *SSNS*, II, 207.
85. The publications cited above all deal with this phenomenon. Valuable inside commentary on this subject appears in three formerly classified studies prepared by SCAP's Economic and Scientific Section (Programs and Statistics Division) under the title *Japan's Industrial Potential*

(February 1951, October 1951, and February 1952). For a simple impression of the significance of U.S. military-related "special procurements" in Japan, see the data on procurements and overall trade in George C. Allen, *Japan's Economic Recovery* (Oxford, 1958), pp. 197, 198, 203.

86. See Hadley, Chapters 6–9, especially pp. 113, 120, 140, 142, 180 for quotations and figures.
87. Yamamura, p. 60 and Chapter 5. The 1947 and 1953 texts of the Anti-Monopoly Law are included in ibid., pp. 196–216. The Fair Trade Commission's position on the 1953 revision was actually ambiguous; cf. *KTI*, pp. 122, 135, 140, 146–149, 151, 390–392.
88. See the general surveys of economic legislation in *Jurisuto* 100:111–114, and *Jurisuto* 361:270–279.
89. Mitsubishi Economic Research Institute, pp. 17–19; Kajinishi, VII, 1920–1938.
90. *KTI*, p. 123; Yamamura, pp. 44–45; Yanaga, p. 160; Daily Labor Press, p. 53; *Jurisuto* 100:113; *Jurisuto* 361:276; Kobayashi Yoshio, *Sengo Nihon Keizai Shi* (Nihon Hyōronsha, 1963), pp. 97–98.
91. *KTI*, p. 125.
92. Ibid.
93. A transcript of the exchange appears in Shioguchi Kiichi, *Monjo: Ikeda Hayato* (Asahi Shimbunsha, 1975), pp. 65–69; cf. pp. 83–84.
94. The following are useful on the decentralization and recentralization of the police: Kurt Steiner, *Local Government in Japan* (Stanford, 1965), pp. 90–94, 255–259; *Jurisuto* 100:48–50 and *Jurisuto* 361:127–130; *SSNS*, III, 147–158, 372–378.
95. *SSNS*, III, 372–374; *Asahi Nenkan, 1955*, p. 320.
96. *SSNS*, III, 348; *Asahi Nenkan, 1952*, p. 143; Steiner, p. 255.
97. See also *Asahi Nenkan, 1955*, pp. 319, 331–332 on the 1954 revision.
98. Yoshida, *Ōiso Zuisō*, p. 41; see also his general comments in *YM*, pp. 176–181.
99. For general discussions of the existing educational system and postwar developments, see: "Education in Japan, 1945–1963," special issue of *Journal of Social and Political Ideas in Japan*, 1.3 (December 1963), cited below as *JSPIJ*; Steiner, *Local Government*, pp. 94–97, 250–255; Daishiro Hidaka, "The Aftermath of Educational Reform," *The Annals of the American Academy of Political and Social Science* 308:140–155 (November 1956); Robert King Hall, "Education in the Development of Postwar Japan," *The Occupation of Japan: Proceedings of a Seminar on the Occupation of Japan and Its Legacy to the Postwar World* (The MacArthur Memorial Library and Archives, November 6 and 7, 1975), pp. 116–148; Hall, *Education for a New Japan* (Yale, 1949); Hall,

Shūshin: The Ethics of a Defeated Nation (Columbia, 1949); *Jurisuto* 100:60–62 and *Jurisuto* 361:110–114; *SSNS*, III, 158–160, 378–379 (for chronologies).

100. The full text is included in *JSPIJ*, pp. 122–124. An interesting comparison could be drawn between the early postwar reforms and the remarkably liberal and individualistic ideals espoused by Meiji educators in the 1870s; in both cases, conservative reaction and calculated reaffirmation of "traditional" values ensued.
101. *YM*, Chapter 16. Cf. Takahashi, *KK* 270:7.
102. *JSPIJ*, p. 18.
103. *JSPIJ*, p. 16; the text of the 1890 rescript is given in Tsunoda, pp. 646–647.
104. *KG-HR-90*, June 28, 1946 (p. 105), and *OGE-HR* (p. 13).
105. *SSNS*, V, 39–41 (the date given here appears to be incorrect, and should be November 16, 1951; cf. *SSNS*, III, 378, 380; also *JSPIJ*, p. 22). The advisory group was the Ordinance Review Commission (Seirei Shimon Iinkai, sometimes called Legislation Review Commission), formed by Yoshida in May 1951 as a *personal* task force. Its influence on the "rectification of excesses" campaign was extremely great, both symbolically and practically. Cf. *Asahi Nenkan, 1952*, pp. 141–142; Yoshida in *Mainichi Shimbun*, August 16, 1955; Shinobu, IV, 1269–1271, 1292–1293, 1369, 1404; *SSNS*, III, 348–350, 412, 450. In this connection, mention should also be made of an important letter from Yoshida to the Supreme Commander dated April 9, 1951, and included in *CPM*. In this, Yoshida urged that local boards of education be eliminated and replaced with prefectural committees, and that the entire 6-3-3-4 system as well as existing curricula be re-examined "with a view to adapting them to the actual conditions of the country." Out of consideration of space alone, the Ordinance Review Commission and wide-ranging April 9 letter have not been discussed here.
106. *SSNS*, V, 39–41; Jichichō [Autonomy Agency], *Chihō Jichi Nenkan* (1954), II, 40; Steiner, p. 97.
107. Steiner, pp. 250–255; *JSPIJ*, pp. 43–47 (also 3, 8, 23, 32, 38, 40); Hidaka, p. 154.
108. Benjamin C. Duke, *Japan's Militant Teachers: A History of the Left-Wing Teachers' Movement* (East-West, 1973), pp. 114–115.
109. Kase, *Yoshida Shigeru no Yuigon*, pp. 124, 128.
110. See Chapter 10, note 62.
111. Ronald P. Dore, "The Ethics of the New Japan," *Pacific Affairs* 25.2:147–159 (June 1952); a full translation of Amano's text is included in this article. The Japan Teachers Union responded with its own "Code of Ethics," reprinted in *JSPIJ*, pp. 129–131. Cf. also

YN, pp. 310–321; *YM*, p. 173; *SSNS*, 1, 102–103; *SSNS*, V, 38–39, 44, 168–179.

112. Duke, pp. 116–117. Among other important pre-surrender posts, Ōdachi had served in Manchukuo, as governor of occupied Singapore, and as home minister in the wartime Koiso cabinet.

113. For a general comment on the two 1954 laws, see Cecil Carter Brett, "Japan's New Education Laws," *Far Eastern Survey* 23.10:174–176 (November 1954).

114. Hall, "Education," p. 140.

115. Steiner's *Local Government in Japan* is detailed and excellent, and includes much data on the occupation period. A basic Japanese source for local developments during the Yoshida era is the three lengthy "yearbooks" published by the Autonomy Agency (Jichichō) for 1954 and 1955: *Chihō Jichi Nenkan.* These are somewhat confusingly titled; volumes I and II are the yearbook for 1954, and volume III, the last of the series, is for 1955. They contain extensive statistical, as well as descriptive and analytical, material, and are cited hereafter as *CJN*. A useful source for local financial statistics is the Autonomy Agency's *Chihō Zaisei Tōkei Nempō* series, of which the volume for 1956 is probably the most useful for the Yoshida period. Key documents appear in *SSNS*, III, 134–147 and 360–369. Surveys of legislation relevant to local autonomy (and local taxes) appear in *Jurisuto* 100:33–36 and 44–47; also *Jurisuto* 361:83–89 and 93–100. A useful survey of local problems and developments is Tanaka Jirō, Tawara Shizuo, and Hara Ryūnosuke, eds., *Chihō Jichi Nijūnen: sono Kaiko to Shōrai no Tenbō* (Hyōronsha, 1970; volume 6 in *Gendai Chihō Jichi Sōsho*). Tanaka, later a Supreme Court justice, was a member of the Ordinance Review Commission (note 105 above), with particular responsibility for local affairs, and his comments on the conservatism of his colleagues are often revealing.

116. Cf. Tanaka, pp. 16, 22, 71–73, 94–99; Steiner, pp. 318–321; *CJN*, I, 22; Ashida to Whitney, May 17, 1948, *CPM*; Gyōsei Kanrichō [Administration Control Agency], Kanribu, ed. *Gyōsei Kikō Nempō*, I (1950), 180–189, II (1951), 75–79, and III (1952), 195–197.

117. Whitney to Prime Minister, June 20, 1948, *CPM.*

118. Steiner, p. 487.

119. Kurt Steiner, "Local Government in Japan: Reform and Reaction," *Far Eastern Survey* 23.7:102 (July 1954).

120. On fiscal dependency, cf. data in *CJN*, III, statistical appendix pp. 22, 23, 25; and *Chihō Zaisei Tōkei Nempō, 1956*, pp. 42–43.

121. Cf. *Jurisuto* 100:33–35.

122. Cf. Steiner, *Local Government in Japan*, p. 235; *Jurisuto* 100:33–35.

123. *CJN*, I, 34–35; Steiner, *Local Government in Japan*, pp. 45–46; 186–194; also the table in *SSNS*, III, 367.
124. Cf. Steiner, *Local Government in Japan*, pp. 143–144, 152–153.
125. The Naiseishō and Minseishō proposals were introduced in 1953 by the Local System Investigation Committee with the customary caveat that this was not to be modeled on the former Home Ministry; *CJN*, II, 32.
126. Shoup's recommendations are discussed in Steiner, *Local Government in Japan*; *CJN* (especially I); and Saburo Shiomi, *Japan's Finance and Taxation, 1940–1956* (Columbia, 1957), especially pp. 82–92.
127. Yoshida's initial and ostensibly favorable response was conveyed in a letter of September 16, 1949 to MacArthur; *CPM*. His first attempts to water down the commission provoked a blistering response from MacArthur; letters of April 10 and 11, 1950 in *CPM*. The failure to adequately staff the commission is noted by Steiner, p. 110. In addition to Steiner, the government's neglect of the Kambe committee reports is acknowledged in the official, or insider, sources: *CJN*, I, 16; *CJN*, II, 23; Tanaka, pp. 26–27. The attack on the quasi-autonomous "administrative commissions" (*gyōsei iinkai*) was extremely important in the recentralization effort, and deserves separate study in itself. It was accomplished under the rubric of bureaucratic "retrenchment" or "rationalization," especially in 1949 and 1952.
128. *CJN*, I, 16.
129. *Nippon Times*, January 18, 1954; cited in Steiner, p. 144. It should be noted, however, that much de facto power at the prefectural level remained in the hands of the old guard despite the system of elected governors. Of 48 persons who served as vice-governors during the critical period between 1947 and 1950, for example, no more than 10 were former city officials or civilians with no bureaucratic background; the remainder were ex-bureaucrats, and 25 of these had been associated with the Home Ministry. Tsuji Kiyoaki and Oka Yoshitake, "Sengo Taisei no Seisaku to Kikō," in Nihon Seiji Gakkai, ed., *Sengo Nihon no Seiji Katei* (Iwanami Shoten, 1953), p. 44.
130. Shinobu, I, 177; Sumimoto notes the general opposition to dissolution of the Special Higher Police (Tokkō) by Japan's post-surrender leaders, who believed its retention to be essential to preservation of the imperial system (II, 42). The possibility of declaring the Communist Party illegal was discussed openly in 1951; Swearingen and Langer, pp. 249–250.
131. The tribute appears in "Ōiso no Shōrai," pp. 209–210; cf. Mazaki, *KK* 271:14–15. Yoshida's diatribes against the communists are too numerous to cite; for samples, see *SN*, pp. 9–22, 185–201; *KJ*, II, 259–290; *YM*, Chapter 23.
132. Hatoyama's interest in forming a coalition with the right-wing Socialists

was well known and dated from shortly after the surrender; cf. Hatoyama in *Mainichi Shimbun*, August 15, 1955; Sumimoto, II, 55–58, 74; Shinobu, I, 304–307.

133. Andō, III, 43–44; Sumimoto, II, 75–76.
134. Andō, III, 282–283, 342; Shinobu, II, 444.
135. Ōuchi Hyōe, "Yoshida-san to no En," *Sekai*, December 1967, pp. 158–159; Takahashi, *KK* 270:6–7.
136. Shinobu, II, 444–479; Sumimoto, II, 107–111; Nishio Suehiro, *Nishio Suehiro no Seiji Oboegaki* (Mainichi Shimbunsha, 1968), pp. 72–108; *YN*, p. 94.
137. Cf. *OGE-HR*, June 4, 1947 (p. 2); December 9, 1948 (p. 6); December 14, 1948 (p. 9); April 6, 1949 (p. 5). His comments to MacArthur concerning a two-party (socialist-conservative) system were expressed as late as 1949, and seemed quite unequivocal: "As a long-range program we must work out a sound and stable parliamentary government system on a two-major-party basis. In this regard, I myself hope for the growth of the Socialist Party in stature and strength so that it may play the role of an effective opposition to the now preponderant Conservatives. On the other hand, there are not a few who disagree with me in the light of what appears to be an unhappy denouement of British experiments in Socialism." Yoshida to MacArthur, August 9, 1949, *CPM*.
138. Kase, *KK* 282:13; Kase, *Yoshida Shigeru no Yuigon*, pp. 135–136; *SN*, pp. 21, 136.
139. *SSNS*, VI, 14. On June 21, 1948, Yoshida announced his party would respect the Katayama government and play the role of a cooperative but "healthy" and appropriately critical opposition party. By mid-August, in response to the cabinet's proposal to nationalize key industries (especially coal), the Yoshida Liberals announced that they were a "total opposition party"; *YN*, p. 118.
140. *Yomiuri Shimbun*, May 29, 1948; cited in Yukichi Kuroki, "Katayama's Coalition Cabinet Takes Over," *Contemporary Japan* 16.4–6:164 (April-June 1947); cf. Wildes, *Typhoon*, p. 107. In the June 21 speech, Yoshida similarly described the international scene as being divided between "class monopoly thought and democratic thought, pro-communist and anti-communist thought," and declared that "we raise the banner of anti-communism, and together with countries of like mind we contribute to the happiness of mankind, and under their assistance we shall complete the recovery of our fatherland." *YN*, p. 118.
141. *SN*, p. 24.
142. Ibid., pp. 10, 128–138, 186.
143. *SSNS*, VI, 100; see also Chapter 2, notes 41 and 43.
144. *SN*, pp. 186–187.

145. Swearingen and Langer, p. 252.

146. *YN*, pp. 158, 173.

147. Miyauchi Yutaka, *Sengo Chian Rippō no Kihonteki Seikaku* (Yushindō, 1960), pp. 40–42, 55–57. Swearingen and Langer, pp. 250–251. Miyauchi's study is exceptionally detailed and useful on the postwar peace-preservation structure, including both SCAP's apparatus and that of the Japanese government.

148. See Swearingen and Langer, Chapter 18.

149. There is discrepancy in statistics concerning the Red Purge in the public sector. The most detailed, itemized calculation appears to be given in a 1951 Government Section report entitled "Counter-Measures Against the Subversive Potential in Japan—1946 to 1951 Inclusive," which gives a total of 10,793 persons purged. I am indebted to Joe B. Moore for providing me with a copy of this report. There is greater agreement on the total of individuals fired in the Red Purge conducted in the private sector, largely between July and December 1950. This amounted to 10,972 individuals from 537 companies. Cf. *SSNS*, I, 77; and Furushima Toshio et al., ed., *Nihon Shihonshugi Kōza* (Iwanami Shoten, 1954), VII, 187.

150. *SSNS*, III, 407–408. For details on peace-preservation legislation under the occupation, see Miyauchi, pp. 27–35.

151. *YN*, pp. 284–294; *KJ*, II, 290–292; *SSNS*, I, 94–99; *SSNS*, III, 407–414; *SSNS*, IV, 190–197; *Asahi Nenkan, 1953*, especially pp. 144, 147, 159–61, 174–177; Shinobu, IV, 1349–1351, 1410–1412, 1431–1436; *Jurisuto*, 100:88–90; *Jurisuto* 361:226–228. The names by which the basic bill was known before emerging as the Subversive Activities Prevention Law were National Public Peace Protection Law, Organizations Control Law, and Special Peace Preservation Law. The figure of 23 revisions is given in *YN*, p. 489. An English translation of the law appears in *Contemporary Japan* 21.4–6:328–337 (April-June 1952).

152. *Asahi Shimbun*, July 2, 1952.

153. *YN*, p. 489.

154. *Asahi Shimbun*, July 4, 1952; *Asahi Nenkan, 1953*, pp. 174–176. The key section of the law here is section 4.

155. Such apprehensions were hardly irrational, for the serious depurge of former thought police and Home Ministry officials began around September and October 1951, simultaneously with the Yoshida government's open drive to create an extensive new peace-keeping apparatus. Cf. *SSNS*, I, 64; *SSNS*, III, 407; *Asahi Nenkan, 1952*, p. 143; Shinobu, IV, 1350. For a radical critique of these developments, see Inoue Kiyoshi, Kobiki Shinsaburō, and Suzuki Masashi, *Gendai Nihon no Rekishi* (Aoki Shoten, 1953), II, 569–574.

156. Summaries of the cases prosecuted under the law appear in *SSNS*, III, 413–414, and are extensively treated in Miyauchi. The Demonstration Control Draft Law is reproduced in *SSNS*, III, 223–225; cf. *Asahi Nenkan, 1953*, pp. 160–161. The official history of the Yoshida cabinets acknowledges that the public outcry thwarted the government in its intention to apply the Subversive Activities Prevention Law more vigorously against the left; *YN*, p. 493.
157. Cf. *SSNS*, III, 414–416 (especially the selection from the law journal *Hōritsu Jihō*); *Asahi Nenkan, 1953*, p. 159; *Asahi Nenkan, 1955*, pp. 317–318, 332–333.

10. THE SEPARATE PEACE, REARMAMENT, AND "SUBORDINATE INDEPENDENCE"

1. U.S. Senate, Committee of Foreign Relations, *Treaty of Mutual Cooperation and Security with Japan*, 86th Congress, 2nd Session (June 7, 1960), especially pp. 11–12, 27, 30–31.
2. India, however, did proceed to sign the treaty separately in June 1952; this became effective in August.
3. Cf. Nishimura Kumao, *San Furanshisuko Heiwa Jōyaku*, volume 27 in Kajima Heiwa Kenkyūjo, ed., *Nihon Gaikō Shi* (Kajima Kenkyūjo, 1971), p. 51. Nishimura was one of Yoshida's major aides in planning and negotiating the security treaty, and this study is a major inside account of strategic planning on the Japanese side from shortly after the surrender. See also Yoshida's comments to the Diet on February 7, 1950; *KG-HR-7*, February 8, 1950 (p. 216), and *OGE-HR* (p. 2).
4. *SN*, pp. 131–135, 137, 155, 161. Cf. Yoshida's comment on the cowardice of those who opposed the Subversive Activities Prevention Law in Chapter 9, note 152.
5. The Hatoyama cabinet supported normalization of relations with the Soviet Union, and Ishibashi emphasized closer relations with the People's Republic of China, but resigned after two months in office for reasons of health.
6. *SSNS*, V ("Shakai" section), 94. The remaining 6 percent had miscellaneous responses.
7. Ibid., pp. 113–114.
8. Ibid., p. 118.
9. Ibid., pp. 65, 76, 90, 92, 96, 117, 130, 150. Popularity was naturally affected by other factors as well.
10. Nishimura, pp. 18–53, is most illuminating on early Japanese planning. Much of volume 3 of *KJ* is devoted to the peace and security issues; see especially pp. 108–123, and Chapter 28 of *YM*. Cf. also Martin E.

Weinstein, *Japan's Postwar Defense Policy, 1946–1968* (Columbia, 1971), Chapter 2; Shunsaku Kato, "Postwar Japanese Security and Rearmament, with Special Reference to Japanese-American Relations," in D. C. S. Sissons, ed., *Papers on Modern Japan, 1968* (Australian National University), pp. 62–78; and, also in the latter publication, Masataka Koosaka [Kōsaka], "Japan's Postwar Foreign Policy," pp. 1–25.

11. *SN*, pp. 159–169.
12. *OGE-HC*, November 12, 1949 (p. 7).
13. Translated in *Contemporary Japan*, 19.4–6:314–319 (April-June, 1950).
14. Nishimura, p. 50.
15. The Socialist Party had adopted a position in favor of permanent neutrality in December 1949.
16. On May 1, 1950, the opposition parties had called for a vote of "no confidence" in the Yoshida cabinet in the lower house, charging among other things that "the Government has lost its autonomy altogether." The Communist spokesman characterized Yoshida personally as behaving like a dictator to the Japanese people, but "like a dog wagging its tail to its master" to the foreign powers. *KG-HR*-7, May 2, 1950 (pp. 1275–1289), and *OGE-HR* (pp. 1–21). The canine metaphor was excised from the Japanese transcript (p. 1276).
17. Miyazawa Kiichi, *Tokyo-Washington no Mitsudan* (Jitsugyō no Nihonsha, 1956), pp. 44–46, 52–56. This is a valuable inside account by a member of the "Yoshida faction" who was an intimate participant in some of the major bilateral talks that occurred between 1950 and 1954. It has been possible to compare Miyazawa's general account with internal documents for a slightly later period (notably the Suzuki Gengo papers for 1953–1954, described in Chapter 11, note 88), and he emerges as a frank and quite thorough purveyor of "secret history"—somewhat surprisingly so given the sensitivity of some of the issues and his own establishment position. Miyazawa served as foreign minister in the mid-1970s.
18. Miyazawa, pp. 56–57; Dodge to MacArthur, May 8, 1950, "Correspondence—Marquat" file, Box IV, *JMDP*, 1950.
19. Cf. *KG-HR*-7, January 26, 1950 (p. 159), and *OGE-HR* (p. 15).
20. For general accounts concerning the U.S. side, see Burton Sapin, "The Role of the Military in Formulating the Japanese Peace Treaty," in Gordon B. Turner, ed., *A History of Military Affairs in Western Society Since the Eighteenth Century* (Harcourt Brace, 1953), pp. 751–762; Frederick S. Dunn, *Peace-making and the Settlement with Japan* (Princeton, 1963); Dean Acheson, *Present at the Creation*, especially pp. 426–435, 539; George F. Kennan, *Memoirs 1925–1950* (Little, Brown, 1967), Chapter 16; Kennan, *Memoirs 1950–1963* (1972), Chapter 3.

21. This became the title of a popular book shortly after independence: Inomata Kōzō, Kimura Kihachirō, and Shimizu Ikutarō, *Kichi Nihon: Ushinaware Iku Sokoku no Sugata* (Wakōsha, 1953)—literally, "Military-Base Japan: The Condition of the Fatherland, Which Is Being Lost." The question whether Japan could have bargained harder on the precise nature of the post-occupation U.S. military presence entails consideration of not merely the mutual security treaty, but also the implementing Administrative Agreement signed on February 28, 1952, as well as the negotiations which continued until late June concerning the concrete number and location of U.S. bases and installations. Miyazawa Kiichi, for one, argued that Yoshida was unnecessarily acquiescent in this general area; Miyazawa, pp. 125–131.
22. Cf. John W. Dower, "The Eye of the Beholder: Background Notes on the U.S.-Japan Military Relationship," *Bulletin of Concerned Asian Scholars* 2.1:15–31 (October 1969). On the postwar Japanese navy, see James E. Auer, *The Postwar Rearmament of Japanese Maritime Forces, 1945–71* (Praeger, 1973); this first appeared in a Japanese translation, in two volumes, under the title *Yomigaeru Nihon Kaigun* (Jiji Tsūshinsha, 1972).
23. For Nambara, see *KG-HP-90*, August 27, 1946 (pp. 249–250), and *OGE-HP*, August 28, 1946 (pp. 6–7); for Nosaka, *KG-HR-90*, June 29, 1946 (pp. 124–125), and *OGE-HR* (p. 14).
24. *KG-HR-90*, June 27, 1946 (pp. 81–82), and *OGE-HR* (p. 4).
25. *KG-HR-90*, June 29, 1946 (pp. 124–125), and *OGE-HR* (pp. 14–15).
26. *Contemporary Japan*, 15.9–12:393–394 (September-December 1946).
27. *KG-HC-6*, November 9, 1949 (p. 60), and *OGE-HC* (pp. 3–4). A slightly variant version of this passage in the administrative-policy address appears in *KG-HR-6*, November 9, 1949 (p. 75), and *OGE-HR* (p. 1).
28. *KG-HC-6*, November 11, 1949 (p. 72), and *OGE-HC* (p. 10).
29. *KG–HC–6*, November 11, 1949 (p. 67), and *OGE–HC* (p. 5); *KG–HC–6*, November 17, 1949 (p. 121), and *OGE-HC* (p. 3); *KG-HC-6*, November 19, 1949 (p. 136), and *OGE-HC* (p. 2).
30. *KG-HR*-7, January 24, 1950 (pp. 131–132), and *OGE–HR* (p. 2). The key phrase reads in Japanese: Sensō hōki no shui ni tessuru koto wa, kesshite jieiken o hōki suru to iū koto o imi suru mono de wa nai no de arimasu.
31. *KG-HR*-7, January 26, 1950 (p. 150), and *OGE-HR* (p. 5); *KG-HR*-7, January 29, 1950 (p. 206), and *OGE-HR* (p. 5). Cf. *KG-HR*-7, January 27, 1950 (pp. 167, 172), and *OGE-HR* (pp. 5, 10); *KG-HR*-7, January 29, 1950 (p. 205), and *OGE-HR* (p. 3).
32. *KG-HR*-7, January 28, 1950 (p. 200), and *OGE-HR* (p. 15).
33. *KG-HC*-7, January 31, 1950 (pp. 169–170), and *OGE-HC* (pp. 3–4).

34. William J. Sebald with Russell Brines, *With MacArthur in Japan: A Personal History of the Occupation* (Norton, 1965), p. 257.
35. *SN*, pp. 99–103; *KJ*, II, 162.
36. Frank Kowalski, "An Inoffensive Rearmament," draft manuscript published in Japanese translation as *Nihon Saigunbi* (Simul, 1969). This is an extremely illuminating account of Japanese rearmament between 1950 and 1952, under the guise of the National Police Reserve, by a former U.S. Army colonel who was intimately involved in training the new Japanese force. I am indebted to Colonel Kowalski for permitting me to consult the original; citations hereafter are to this English draft, with the statement quoted here appearing on p. 33. On the Japanese side, early developments, missions, weapons, subterfuges, and confusions are revealed through a number of sources. Masuhara Keikichi, who was Yoshida's first appointee as head of the National Police Reserve, discusses this in Andō, III, 388–400. Okazaki Katsuo, a member of the "Yoshida School" and key aide in negotiating the peace and security treaties (as well as the 1952 Administrative Agreement) touches on these various general problems in several places: an interview in the oral history project associated with the John Foster Dulles Papers at Princeton University (cited hereafter as *JFDP* for the papers and *JFDP-Oral* for the interviews); a brief article ("Yoshida Naikaku no Shutsugen to Heiwa Jōyaku Teiketsu no Butai Ura") in *Gaikō Jihō*, April 1964 (pp. 56–62); and testimony before the Committee to Investigate the Constitution: *Kempō Chōsakai Dai-30-kai Sōkai Gijiroku* (May 6, 1959), pp. 1–43. Nishimura Kumao testifies in this same transcript. The Bōeichō [Defense Agency] later published several volumes which provide considerable insight into this early period of remilitarization: *Keisatsu Yōbitai Sōtai Shi* (1958); *Jieitai Jūnen Shi* (1961; cited below as *JJS*); and the first volume of the basic "defense yearbook," *Bōei Nenkan, 1955*. Other useful sources include *YN*, pp. 208–213, 378–459, 556–575 for the official version from the perspective of the Yoshida government; *SSNS*, I, 719–732, and *SSNS*, III, 55–58, 290–305, 414–416, for chronologics and basic statements, documents, etc. to 1954; *Jurisuto* 361:38–46 for military-related legislation; Masumi, *Gendai Nihon no Seiji Taisei*, pp. 107–112, for numerous quotations by government spokesmen concerning rearmament and "war potential."
37. Cf. Kowalski, pp. 33, 156–157; *SSNS*, I, 719. Yoshida's major advisors on military and security affairs included the following former officers: General Shimomura Sadashi; Lieutenant Generals Kawabe Torashirō, Tatsumi Eiichi, Iimura Yuzuru, and Kamitsuki Yoshio; Admiral Nomura Kichisaburō; Vice Admiral Hori Teikichi; Rear Admiral Yamamoto Yoshio; and Enomoto Shigeharu, a former instructor at the naval

academy. Cf. Shinobu, IV, 1158–1159, 1185–1187, 1228, 1311; Kowalski, pp. 101, 150–151, 160–161. Auer also touches on these matters, and reveals that Yoshida went against the advice of his civilian advisers in supporting the recruitment of former officers at the ex-colonel level. He also originally urged Tatsumi (cf. Chapter 4, note 60) to become the uniformed head of the NPR; Tatsumi himself convinced Yoshida of the folly of this. Auer, pp. 72–73.

38. Kowalski, pp. 156–157, 205. The Bōeichō publications cited in note 36 above contain considerable detail on both armaments and personnel.
39. Kowalski, pp. 61, 143–144.
40. *SSNS*, V, 109.
41. *KG-HR-10*, January 28, 1951 (p. 54), and *OGE-HR* (p. 10). Cf. *OGE-HR*, July 18, 1950 (p. 18), January 27, 1951 (pp. 1–2), February 15, 1951 (p. 6), May 11, 1951 (pp. 4–5). Also *OGE-HC*, July 18, 1950 (p. 3), November 29, 1950 (p. 12), January 28, 1951 (pp. 5–6), January 30, 1951 (pp. 4–5, 7), February 3, 1951 (p. 5).
42. Kowalski, pp. 212–213.
43. Cf. Dunn, p. 108; Sebald and Brines, p. 259; *YN*, p. 394; Gerald L. Curtis, "The Dulles-Yoshida Negotiations on the San Francisco Peace Treaty," in Andrew W. Cordier, ed., *Columbia Essays in International Affairs, the Dean's Papers* (Columbia, 1966), II, 47; and the illuminating meeting of Dulles with the Study Group on Japanese Peace Treaty Problems of the Council on Foreign Relations, October 23, 1950, *JFDP*.
44. Shinobu, IV, 1186; Masuhara in Andō, III, 391.
45. The most detailed account of Dulles's second visit (January 26 to February 11, 1951) appears in the interview with William Sebald in *JFDP-Oral*. John M. Allison, Dulles's aide at the time, touches on this more briefly in his autobiography, *Ambassador from the Prairie, or Allison Wonderland* (Houghton Mifflin, 1973; Tuttle edition, 1975), pp. 156–157 in the latter edition. See also *YN*, pp. 380–386; *KJ*, III, 28–30, 115–123; *YM*, pp. 250–251, 265–267; Sebald and Brines, p. 262; Curtis, pp. 50–55.
46. Kowalski, pp. 222–224. General Willoughby used the pages of *Reader's Digest* in February 1952 to call for a Japanese military of 250,000, considerably below the official U.S. target figure. See Chapter 11, notes 39–41, 110, 115, 118 below.
47. *Contemporary Japan* 20.1–3:92–95 (January-March 1951). Takagi's article originally appeared in the March 1951 issue of *Nippon Hyōron*. It should be noted that although Yoshida emerged as a proponent of "go-slow rearmament," he gave support, even to the extent of funding, to Japanese groups and individuals who were advocating rapid and

extensive rearmament. According to Auer, for example, Yoshida gave 250,000 yen to Watanabe Tetsuzō, whose "3-3-3 Plan" called for a 300,000-man army, 300,000-man navy, and air force of 3,000 planes; Auer, pp. 76, 276n.

48. Shinobu, IV, 1159; Kowalski, pp. 101, 234–237. Masuhara makes light of the Hattori issue, unduly so to judge by other evidence; Andō, III, 393.
49. Kowalski, pp. 223–224; cf. Shinobu, IV, 1185, 1220, 1230.
50. Dulles embraced the most dire scenarios in private as well as public. For example, a secret "Estimate of the Situation" he prepared for the secretary of state on November 30, 1950, begins as follows: "Developments in Asia confirm that there is a comprehensive program, in which the Soviet and Chinese communist [*sic*] are cooperating, designed as a present phase to eliminate all Western influence on the Asiatic mainland, and probably also in relation to the islands of Japan, Formosa, the Philippines, and Indonesia. It would be reckless not to assume that such a program has been carefully worked out and that steps are being prepared to implement all its various aspects." *JFDP*, Box 116.
51. Shinobu, IV, 1160.
52. *KG-HC-9*, November 29, 1950 (p. 35), and *OGE-HC* (p. 12). "Japan and the Crisis in Asia," *Foreign Affairs* 29.2:176–177 (January 1951).
53. *KG-HR-10*, January 27, 1951 (p. 35), and *OGE-HR* (p. 1).
54. *KG-HR-10*, January 28, 1951 (p. 51), and *OGE-HR* (p. 6). *KG-HC-10*, January 28, 1951 (p. 63), and *OGE-HC* (p. 8). Miki became prime minister in 1974. In a letter of August 9, 1949, to MacArthur, Yoshida had observed with comparable serenity that "it is a matter of history that political upheavals on the Continent have never menaced directly our island nation"; *CPM*.
55. *KG-HC-10*, January 30, 1951 (pp. 70–71), and *OGE-HC* (pp. 4–5). Cf. *KG-HR-9*, November 27, 1950 (p. 54), and *OGE-HR* (p. 5). MacArthur's statement was in his New Year's address.
56. *KG-HR-10*, February 14, 1951 (p. 133), and *OGE-HR* (pp. 1–2). Cf. *KG-HR-10*, May 10, 1951 (pp. 673–674), and *OGE-HR* (p. 1); *KG-HR-10,* May 11, 1951 (pp. 680, 683), and *OGE-HR* (pp. 4–5, 8).
57. U.S. Senate, *Military Situation in the Far East*, pp. 6–7, 254–255, 264. At other points, MacArthur was more equivocal on the Soviet threat to Japan; cf. pp. 274, 277, 480, 594. For General Marshall's repudiation of this argument, see pp. 647–648. Kennan's views can be found in his memoirs (note 20 above) and in his interview in *JFDP-Oral.* See also his article in *U.S. News and World Report*, June 29, 1956 (pp. 74–75), and "Japanese Security and American Policy," *Foreign Affairs* 43.1:14–28 (October 1964).

58. Kowalski, pp. 76–82, especially 79.
59. Yoshida, *SN*, pp. 45–47; *Ōiso Zuisō*, p. 6; cf. Kōsaka, pp. 60–64. As indicated in note 90 below, this was not *initially* a point of view that leading U.S. spokesmen, including Dulles, denied.
60. Kowalski, p. 224; *Foreign Affairs* (January 1951), p. 179. Cf. *KJ*, I, 270 and III, 72.
61. Allison, pp. 156–157.
62. See, for example, Masuhara in Andō, III, 395–396; Okazaki in *Gaikō Jihō*, pp. 61–62; Hayashi Keizō in *JJS*, p. 32; Kimura Tokutarō in *JJS*, pp. 60, 66; also *JJS*, p. 164. In the Ikeda-Robertson talks of October 1953, the Japanese frankly expressed their fear of Red infiltration of the new military; see Chapter 11, note 114.
63. *Ekonomisuto*, February 24, 1976, pp. 23–24. Prior to becoming head of the Safety Agency, Kimura served as attorney general in the third Yoshida cabinet and played an active role in enacting the Subversive Activities Prevention Law. The select advisory committee on which he served in 1951 was the Ordinance Review Commission noted in Chapter 9, note 105.
64. *SN*, pp. 202–209; Yoshida's initial position against rearmament is frankly summarized in ibid., pp. 23, 101, 133, 202—and in numerous other places. Kase suggests that Yoshida did not adopt a militant and unqualified position in support of rearmament until the mid-1960s, and this was motivated by alarm at the Chinese Cultural Revolution and China's development of nuclear weapons; *Yoshida Shigeru no Yuigon*, pp. 79–80. In this regard, it might be noted in passing that Yoshida appears to have become rather senile in his final years.
65. On the early discussions of a multi-power 25-year demilitarization and disarmament program for Japan, see *Department of State Bulletin*, June 30, 1946, pp. 1113 ff.; *FRUS*, 1946, VIII, 152–155, 326–329, 348–349; and the general discussion of a possible peace treaty with Japan in *FRUS*, 1947, VI, 446–595; also Dunn, pp. 58–59.
66. Even after Yoshida finally acknowledged that Japan was developing "war potential," he continued even in private to maintain that Japan's present economic and social conditions did not permit rapid rearmament. This emerges strongly, for example, in records of bilateral discussions in 1953 and 1954 among the Suzuki Gengo Papers. See Chapters 11 and 12 below.
67. *Contemporary Japan* 15.9–12:395 (September-December 1946). This statement by MacArthur does not appear in *PRJ*.
68. Sumimoto, I, 111–112.
69. Kowalski, p. 82.
70. Acheson, p. 545; cf. 540–541.

71. U.S. Senate, Committee on Foreign Relations, *Japanese Peace Treaty and Other Treaties Pertaining to Security in the Pacific* (January 1952; 82nd Congress, 2nd Session), pp. 10–11.
72. Cf. *Congressional Record,* vol. 98, part 2, pp. 2455, 2593.
73. Dulles to MacArthur, November 15, 1950, Box 142, *JFDP.*
74. Cf. Dulles's memorandum of January 11, 1952, Box 474, *JFDP*, and Morrison's remarks in *Parliamentary Debates, House of Commons*, Fifth Series, 496:945–952.
75. *KJ*, I, 270. The official history of the Yoshida cabinets also notes that Yoshida was more sympathetic to the British position; *YN*, p. 452.
76. In August 1954, Dulles summarized the British position in blunt terms at a meeting of the U.S. cabinet: "England looks upon Japan as one of her great competitors. The great battle I had with the British in drafting the Japanese treaty was on this very point. The British wanted sort of a Morgenthau plan for Japan. They wanted to keep Japan alive through what would amount to doles so that Japan would have no chance to compete with British goods in the world market." James Hagerty Diary, Box 1 (August 6, 1954), Dwight D. Eisenhower Library. I am grateful to William Borden for this document as well as the Whitman minutes cited in Chapter 12, note 22.
77. "Japan and China," January 9, 1952, Box 116, *JFDP*; the revised version of this memorandum, dated January 11, does not specifically give the August 6 date. Cf. transcript of interview with Okazaki in *JFDP-Oral.*
78. Yoshida to Dulles, August 4 and August 18, 1951, Box 143, *JFDP.*
79. *Congressional Record,* 98.2:2331, 2451.
80. Asahi Shimbunsha, ed., *Shiryō: Nihon to Chūkoku '45 - '71*, volume 8 of *Asahi Shimin Kyōshitsu: "Nihon to Chūkoku"* (1972), pp. 2–4. Cf. Dulles memorandum of March 6, 1952 in Box 116, *JFDP.*
81. *YN*, p. 454.
82. Dulles memorandum of March 6, 1952, Box 116, *JFDP.* The U.S. mission was in Japan from December 10 to December 20.
83. *Department of State Bulletin*, January 28, 1952, p. 120; *Japanese Peace Treaty . . .*, pp. 9–10.
84. *Congressional Record*, 98.2:2329, 2331, 2582.
85. Sebald, *JFDP-Oral.* This interesting account includes excerpts from Sebald's diary at the time.
86. Sebald and Brines, pp. 278–280; cf. interview with Shirasu Jirō in Andō, III, 409–410. Yoshida's proposed speech was written in English, and he intended to deliver it in this language until persuaded otherwise. The problem was larger than this, however. Sebald writes: "I do not know who wrote the speech, but it was not good. In fact, portions of it would unwittingly have undone much of the good will which had been

engendered by the conference, especially among some of the Asian nations. Something had to be done to change the tone and theme of the speech, and quickly. . . ."

87. *YN*, p. 454.
88. *YN*, pp. 456–457.
89. *YN*, p. 455.
90. *Japanese Peace Treaty* . . . , pp. 12, 28, 45–48. The comment on Sino-Soviet inseparability appears in Dulles's "Estimate of the Situation," November 30, 1950, *JFDP*, Box 116.
91. *Japanese Peace Treaty* . . . , p. 12.
92. Cf. *Congressional Record*, 98.2:2329, 2331, 2582.
93. *Japanese Peace Treaty* . . . , pp. 48–50. Cf. ibid., pp. 10–11, 19, 60, 112, 155–156; also *Congressional Record* 98.2:2360, 2453–2454, 2509, 2582–2583.
94 On "CHINCOM," see Gunnar Adler-Karlsson, *Western Economic Warfare 1947–1967: A Case Study in Foreign Economic Policy*, volume 9 in *Acta Universitatis Stockholmiensis, Stockholm Economic Studies*, New Series (1968), especially pp. 6–8 and Chapter 16. Almost immediately after the occupation ended, Japan was forced to agree to a more extensive embargo list on exports to China than that followed by European participants in the embargo; Fukui, pp. 228–230. Trade with mainland China did develop, but under continued severe restriction.
95. *SSNS*, V, 113–114.

11. COOPERATION AND CONFLICT IN THE NEW IMPERIUM

1. Tanaka, p. 119; cf. p. 31. The commission on which Tanaka served was the Ordinance Review Commission (see Chapter 9, note 115).
2. *JJS*, Chapter 7, especially pp. 254–255.
3. The phrase was included in Acheson's famous speech in Cleveland, Mississippi on May 8, 1947; for a full text, see Joseph Marion Jones, *The Fifteen Weeks* (Harcourt, Brace & World: Harbinger edition, 1964), pp. 274–281.
4. *OGE-HR*, April 5, 1949 (p. 8).
5. "The Role of Japan in Our Relations with the Orient." This draft speech by Dodge bears a State Department stamp dated July 7, 1949, and is included in the materials collected by the "Sengo Zaisei Shi" project, Ministry of Finance, Tokyo.
6. "Statement of Mr. Joseph M. Dodge for the National Advisory Council—Fiscal Year 1951 Appropriation for Economic Aid to Japan," January 19, 1950, "Appropriation" file, Box I, *JMDP* 1950.
7. See Chapter 10, note 35.

8. Gaimushō Tokubetsu Shiryōka, ed., *Nihon Senryō oyobi Kanri Jūyō Bunshōshū* (1949), III, 29–33.
9. The statement appears in an interesting brief catechism of the Dodge philosophy entitled "Comments on the Inflation Problem," no date, "Sengo Zaisei Shi" collection (note 5 above).
10. Cf. "Summary of Interview with Mr. Ikeda," April 28, 1949, "Program Material–Official Memos" file, Box IX, *JMDP* 1949; Dodge to Ikeda, February 1, 1950, "Correspondence–U.S. Govt." file, Box IV, *JMDP* 1950; "Personal Conferences of Mr. Dodge with Minister Ikeda," May 3, 1950, "Correspondence–Marquat" file, Box IV, *JMDP* 1950; "Japan: Foreign Trade and Economic Aid Requirements," July 6, 1950 [unofficial memorandum by Wilford Gavin, Dept. of the Army], p. 8, "Appropriations–U.S. Economic Aid" file, Box I, *JMDP* 1950, and also in "Korea–Relief Impact" file, ibid. In NSC 48/1 of December 23, 1949, the National Security Council assumed that a "middle-of-the-road" administration in Japan "would undoubtedly wish to maintain normal political and economic relations with the Communist bloc" (p. 241), and that "Japan's economy cannot possibly be restored to a self-sustaining basis without a considerable volume of trade with China" (p. 263). The same document, however, also stressed the importance of developing export markets for Japan in southeast Asia to lessen Japanese economic dependence on China (pp. 258–261). See Department of Defense citation in Chapter 8, note 60.
11. As used in official discussion at this time, "southeast Asia" commonly included south Asia (India, Pakistan, Goa) as well.
12. *YN*, pp. 345–347. An English version of the report appears under the title "Economic Self-supporting Program of Japan" in volume 26 of the extensive collection of English materials prepared by the Economic Stabilization Board and now maintained in the archives of the National Planning Agency, Tokyo. Hereafter these "papers" are cited as *ESBP*. Cf. Kyodo News Agency dispatch of February 19, 1951, in "Economic Cooperation–Japan-U.S." file, Box IV, *JMDP* 1951.
13. Cf. the E.S.S. reports cited in Chapter 9, note 85.
14. Dodge memorandum, November 9, 1951, "Memoranda Incident to 1951 Mission to Japan" file, Box I, *JMDP* 1951.
15. Dodge memorandum, November 19, 1951, "Foreign Trade" file, Box IV, *JMDP* 1951.
16. See especially the "Aid for S. E. Asia–West-Andrews Report" file, Box I, *JMDP* 1950; also Garvin-Marquat exchanges of May 29, 1950 in "Ikeda Visit to U.S." file, Box VII, *JMDP* 1950. The unfolding of this policy can also be studied through the reports of the Committee on Industry and Trade, Economic Commission for Asia and the Far East

[ECAFE], Economic and Social Council, United Nations. See in particular the numerous working papers emanating from ECAFE conferences in Singapore (October 1949), Bangkok (May 1950), Lahore (February 1951), and Rangoon (January 1952). Cf. also note 10 above.

17. Cf. *OGE-HR*, April 5, 1949 (pp. 1–9), April 6, 1949 (pp. 6, 14), and January 26, 1950 (p. 11).
18. Cf. "Summary of Meeting . . . ," March 24, 1949, "Budget, Ikeda Interviews" file, Box I, *JMDP* 1949.
19. "Stabilization As We See It," March 1, 1949, *ESBP*, volume 16.
20. *SSNS*, VI, 20–21.
21. Ayusawa, p. 298. Cf. *YN*, p. 337.
22. *YN*, pp. 221–222, 316. In mid-1949, personnel retrenchments announced in conjunction with the Dodge Line were associated with three spectacular, and still unresolved, incidents of violence on the railways: the famous Mitaka, Shimoyama, and Matsukawa incidents. Matsumoto Seichō's *Nihon no Kuroi Kiri* (volume 30 in *Matsumoto Seichō Zenshū*, Bungei Shunjū, 1972) includes a well-known and itself controversial account of the Shimoyama incident, involving the apparent murder of the president of the National Railways. The Matsukawa incident is examined in Chalmers Johnson's *Conspiracy at Matsukawa* (California, 1972). Johnson refers to layoffs involving approximately two-million workers in 1949; p. 69.
23. Key documents on the Ikeda visit appear in the "Correspondence–Marquat" file, Box IV, *JMDP* 1950, with additional materials in the "Ikeda Visit" and "Ikeda Visit to U.S." files, Box VII, ibid. The mission resulted on the Japanese side in an "Ikeda plan," submitted to MacArthur by Yoshida on May 22; this, together with MacArthur's reply of May 25, is also included in *CPM*. On the offer of bases, see Chapter 10.
24. See Chapter 9, p. 316, and Chapter 3, p. 78.
25. Cf. materials in the "Correspondence–Marquat" and "Correspondence–Economic and Scientific Section" files, Box III, *JMDP* 1951; also "Correspondence–Marquat" file, Box I, *JMDP* 1952.
26. *YN*, pp. 350–355. The so-called "Marquat Plan" of May 16, 1951 was the first relatively comprehensive public statement of the program; this is reproduced in full in *Nippon Times*, May 17, 1951, and *Contemporary Japan* 20.4–6:273–276 (April-June 1951). The government's formal response to the Marquat Plan was issued through the Ministry of Finance on June 23, and is reproduced in *SSNS*, II, 145. For other key statements and exchanges, see the "Wilson Plan" of July 21, reported in the *New York Times* of the following day; also materials in "Economic Cooperation–Japan-U.S." file, Box IV, *JMDP* 1951.
27. *YN*, pp. 355–356.

28. Extensive documentation of this appears in *JMDP, ESBP*, and the ECAFE reports (note 16 above).
29. *YN*, pp. 458–459.
30. "Government Loan" file, Box II, *JMDP* 1952. An earlier draft of this, dated January 17, 1952, is included in the "Economic Cooperation–Japan-U.S." file, Box IV, *JMDP* 1951 [*sic*].
31. "Economic Cooperation–Japan-U.S." file, Box IV, *JMDP* 1951 [*sic*].
32. Allison, pp. 162–163; cf. 209, 244–246.
33. These missions are discussed elsewhere in this and the following chapter.
34. Cf. Dower, "Superdomino." This theme appears with monotonous regularity in official speeches during this period; see, for example, the *Department of State Bulletin*.
35. Allison, pp. 267–268; cf. 239–244.
36. Miyazawa, pp. 192–193; Allison, p. 240.
37. Cf. *YN*, pp. 660–664.
38. See, for example, note 75 below and the section on "War-Loving America" in Chapter 12.
39. Allison, p. 215; Miyazawa, pp. 151, 191.
40. *YN*, p. 602.
41. Matthew B. Ridgway, *Soldier: The Memoirs of Matthew B. Ridgway* (Harper, 1956), p. 226.
42. Allison, pp. 247, 248.
43. *JJS*, pp. 114–131, especially 115; *Bōei Nenkan 1956*, pp. 283–293, especially 283. As a percentage of "national income," this amounted to 3.5 percent in 1952, 2.1 percent in 1953, and 2.2 percent in 1954.
44. *JJS*, pp. 222–244, especially 222; cf. p. 85. Masuhara in Andō, III, 395.
45. Cf. Chinese People's Institute of Foreign Affairs, ed., *Oppose the Revival of Japanese Militarism (A Selection of Important Documents and Commentaries)* (Foreign Language Press, Peking, 1960).
46. Allison, pp. 227–228, 236, 243, 257.
47. Ibid., p. 268.
48. Auer, p. 83.
49. Masuhara in Andō, III, 398–399. This inside account indicates that the "threat" from China was not strongly emphasized at this time, although U.S. records seem to contradict this; cf. Chapter 10, note 82.
50. *SSNS*, III, 298.
51. *Contemporary Japan*, 21.1-3:159–160 (January-March, 1952). For extensive quotations of official statements on this issue, see *SSNS*, III, 297–305; *YN*, pp. 556–575, 608–611; *JJS*, pp. 376–384; Masumi, *Gendai Nihon no Seiji Taisei*, pp. 105–112.
52. *SSNS*, III, 298 (July 30, 1950).
53. Ibid. (October 22 and 29, 1951).

54. Ibid., pp. 294–295.
55. Statement of October 15, 1952, in *Contemporary Japan* 21.10–12: 679–680 (October-December 1952). Cf. Kimura's statement of February 3, 1953, in Masumi, pp. 109–110.
56. Cf. *JJS*, pp. 53–54. 75–76.
57. Yanaga, p. 242.
58. Masumi, pp. 107, 109 (March 7, 1952); cf. Yoshida's statement of March 10 in ibid., p. 109.
59. Cf. *YN*, p. 609.
60. *SSNS*, III, 299.
61. *YN*, p. 610; Masumi, p. 111.
62. Suzuki Gengo Papers, vol. 1, entry 18 (see note 88 below).
63. Allison, p. 234.
64. Ivan Morris, *Nationalism and the Right-Wing in Japan: A Study of Post-war Trends* (Oxford, 1960), p. 207.
65. *Contemporary Japan* 21.10–12:679. See also *SSNS*, III, 294–295.
66. Masuhara in Andō, III, 391–392; Auer, pp. 72–73.
67. See Chapter 10, note 47.
68. *JJS*, p. 43.
69. Auer, p. 86.
70. See Chapter 10, note 63.
71. Masuhara in Andō, III, 395.
72. *JJS*, pp. 44, 64–65.
73. Cf. Kōno, p. 225.
74. *KJ*, I, 35–38; cf. Masumi, p. 144.
75. *YN*, p. 608.
76. Cf. Fujii Shōichi and Ōe Shinobu, *Sengo Nihon no Rekishi* (Aoki Shoten, 1970), I, 208–209; Keizai Dantai Rengōkai, ed., *Keidanren no Nijūnen* (1969), pp. 89–90, 97–98.
77. Yanaga, p. 65.
78. Allison, p. 290; cf. Kase, *Yoshida Shigeru no Yuigon*, pp. 84–85 for another of Yoshida's 1956 attacks on the Soviet Union.
79. Albert Axlebank, *Black Star Over Japan: Rising Forces of Militarism* (Tuttle, 1973), p. 191. The comment was made in 1966.
80. See Department of Defense citation in Chapter 8, note 60, pp. 240–241.
81. Cf. Masuhara in Andō, III, 397.
82. Allison, p. 239.
83. *YN*, pp. 604–605, 662.
84. *YN*, p. 662.
85. *YN*, p. 605.
86. *YN*, p. 674. Cf. *JJS*, pp. 51, 62, 65; Miyazawa, pp. 179–180. The joint statement was regarded as very significant at the time.

87. Both Aichi and Miyazawa later served as foreign minister, while Watanabe shortly thereafter became head of the Japan Development Bank. Suzuki played an intimate role in U.S.-Japan negotiations thereafter.
88. Miyazawa, pp. 204–205. The account that follows is based largely upon the working papers and minutes of the Ikeda-Robertson talks maintained in the archives of the Ministry of Finance. These appear in volumes 1 and 2 of the voluminous "Suzuki Gengo Papers," under the title *Ikeda-Robertson Kaidan*; they are cited below as SGP [followed by volume number and the internal entry or document number]. Miyazawa's account of these "secret" conversations, published in 1956, is lengthy and impressively frank on the actual exchanges that occurred. It is especially valuable as a supplement to the Suzuki papers for the peripheral comment and context it provides. For an official account of the "shallow economy" as of 1953, and the Japanese government's pessimistic appraisal of the accomplishments of the Ikeda-Robertson talks, see *YN*, pp. 669–672.
89. *SGP* 1:7 (October 5); Miyazawa, pp. 206–209. Yoshida's August memorandum to Dulles was drafted by Ikeda and Miyazawa. The English version presented on October 5, however, is more detailed than the Japanese version presented in Miyazawa's text, and has been utilized in this presentation.
90. *SGP* 1:18 (October 21). Cf. Ikeda's comments in *SGP* 2 (minutes for October 15).
91. *SGP* 1:25 (October 27).
92. Miyazawa, pp. 211–212.
93. *SGP* 1:20 (October 21), 23 (October 23), 25 (October 27); *SGP* 2 (minutes for October 5 and 15).
94. Yoshida, *Japan's Decisive Century*, pp. 15–16; Miyazawa, pp. 219–220.
95. *SGP* 1:10 (October 8).
96. *SGP* 1:23 (October 23).
97. Dodge quite firmly advised the Japanese to avoid "over-emphasis on the need for foreign investment and an under-emphasis on methods of providing greater investment from domestic sources." He also attacked the trend toward recartelization as promoting domestic inefficiency and dumping practices overseas; *SGP* 1:17 (October 14). See also *SGP* 1:7 (October 5), 18 (October 19), 20 (October 21), 25 (October 27); *SGP* 2 (minutes for October 5).
98. *SGP* 2 (minutes for October 5). Cf. *SGP* 1:18 (October 19), 20 (October 21), 23 (October 27).
99. Cf. the Ikeda-Dodge conversation in "Memorandum of Conversation," September 3, 1951, "San Francisco Conference" file, Box VII, *JMDP*

1951; Dodge to Kakitsubo, April 21, 1952, "Correspondence–Japanese Government" file, Box III, *JMDP* 1951 [*sic*]; and *YN*, pp. 133–136. Yanaga deals with the reparations problem in considerable detail in *Big Business.*

100. Reparations agreements were concluded with Burma in November 1954, the Philippines in May 1956, Indonesia in January 1958, and South Vietnam in May 1959. Burma initially demanded $10-billion, the Philippines $8-billion, and Indonesia $17-billion. Final settlements were drastically lower. See Yanaga, Chapter 8.
101. *SGP* 1:10 (October 8); Miyazawa, pp. 224–226. At one point the Japanese also ventured to suggest that the GARIOA obligation be somehow adapted in a manner that would further Japanese interests in southeast Asia, but this was not pursued.
102. *SGP* 2 (minutes of October 15); *SGP* 1:23 (October 23); Miyazawa, pp. 242–248.
103. *SGP* 1:10 (October 8) and 23 (October 23); *SGP* 2 (minutes for October 15).
104. *SGP* 1:18 (October 19).
105. *SGP* 1:20 (October 21); *SGP* 2 (minutes for October 10 and 15).
106. *SGP* 1:23 (October 23).
107. *SGP* 1:20 (October 21) and 25 (October 27).
108. *SGP* 1:14 (October 13). A more detailed but undated version of this plan is included in *SGP* 2, with total projected expenses amounting to $2,598-million, of which the U.S. share would be approximately $810-million. It was also acknowledged here that the Ikeda plan was more modest than that of the Safety Agency.
109. *SGP* 2 (minutes for October 15).
110. *SGP* 2 (minutes for October 12).
111. *SGP* 1:11 (October 8).
112. *SGP* 1:17 (October 14).
113. *SGP* 2 (minutes of October 8); Miyazawa, pp. 227–228. Cf. Allison, pp. 246–247.
114. *SGP* 1:18 (October 19); a variant version of this appears in *SGP* 2. Cf. Chapter 10, notes 61–63.
115. *SGP* 1:20 (October 21) and 25 (October 27); *SGP* 2 (minutes for October 23).
116. *SSNS*, I, 645.
117. Allison, pp. 251–256.
118. *YN*, pp. 607, 663–664.
119. Yoshida's majority in the lower house was undercut by the return of former purgees to the Diet and the in-again-out-again tactics of the

Hatoyama clique vis-à-vis the Liberal Party. In the general election of April 1953, for example, the "Yoshida Liberals" were calculated to hold 199 (42.7 percent) of the seats in the lower house, while the "Hatoyama Liberals" held 35 (7.5 percent). See the general election statistics in *SSNS*, I, 448, 450. Although Hatoyama's return to the fold strengthened the Liberals against Shigemitsu and his Progressive Party, it had actually been arranged in a meeting between Hatoyama and Yoshida on November 17, that is, before the Shigemitsu-Nixon meeting.

120. *YN*, pp. 675–677.
121. The MSA agreement was approved by the House of Representatives on March 31 and House of Councillors on April 18. The two defense laws passed the lower house on May 7 and upper house on June 2.
122. Allison, pp. 246–247.
123. Ibid., pp. 237–239.
124. *YN*, pp. 679–682.
125. For general accounts of these legal and structural changes, see *JJS*, pp. 62–78, 132–134; also *Jurisuto* 361:38–42.
126. *JJS*, p. 75.
127. *SSNS*, III, 299 (March 15, 1954); *JJS*, p. 65.

12. THE 1954 YOSHIDA MISSION AND THE END OF AN ERA

1. SGP 115. The discussion of the Yoshida mission which follows is based largely upon volumes 115 and 116 of the Suzuki Gengo papers, which bear the title *Sōri Tobei Kankei Shiryō.* These bilateral exchanges are again well summarized by Miyazawa, pp. 279–313. The text of this particular speech by Yoshida was printed in *The New York Times*, November 9, 1954.
2. Notably in *Sekai to Nihon* (1963).
3. Miyazawa, pp. 284–85.
4. *SGP* 115, undated and unnumbered memorandum.
5. Miyazawa, pp. 286–287.
6. SGP 115, untitled and undated position paper.
7. These problems and observations are most fully laid out in *SGP* 116, document 102311. See also documents 10223, 102515, and 102210 in the same volume, and the general untitled and undated position paper in *SGP* 115.
8. *SGP* 115, Yoshida address to N.Y. Chamber of Congress; also U.S. "Statement on U.S.-Japanese Economic Questions." *SGP* 116, "agenda" of October 25 and documents 10229 and 102311. Subsequent trends in U.S.-Japanese trade were more favorable than the Japanese anticipated;

Jerome B. Cohen, "Problems in Foreign Trade and Investment," *Annals of the American Academy of Political and Social Science*, 308:95–101 (November 1956).

9. *YN*, pp. 495–518 (especially 517–518), 666–667.
10. Yoshida to National Press Club; *SGP* 115, and *New York Times*, November 9, 1954.
11. *SGP* 116, document 10221.
12. Ibid.
13. Ibid. This document is dated October 12 and titled "A Survey of Elements Necessary to Facilitate the Economic Development of Southeast Asia." The problem is also addressed in *SGP* 116, document 10223. The concept of a "Marshall Plan for Asia" was by no means a new one and had been broached by the Yoshida government—in precisely the same words—at least as early as February 1949. See the memorandum entitled "Summary Observations on Some of the Most Important Problems of Present Day Japan" among the occupation documents released by the Foreign Ministry in mid-1976; microfilm no. 54, roll 2, pp. 37–38.
14. *SGP* 115, U.S. "Statement on U.S.-Japanese Economic Questions."
15. The early Japanese draft appears in *SGP* 115.
16. Cf. *SGP* 115, letter from Walter Judd to Walter Robertson, October 18, 1954.
17. The basic Japanese critique of the U.S. program, and detailed proposals, appear in *SGP* 116, especially documents 10224, 10225, 10246, and 10247. These were submitted to the U.S. government in the final week of October. The U.S. counterproposal, dated November 6, is also included in *SGP* 116. The Japanese expression of disappointment with the U.S. response was delivered on November 8 and appears in *SGP* 115, as does the public statement of November 13 concerning agreement on Japan's participation in the agricultural commodities program, largely on the lines proposed by the United States. An internal summary memorandum of agreements on the package, dated November 16, appears in *SGP* 116. Miyazawa's discussion of disagreements on these matters appears on pp. 288–291. The total amount of agricultural products offered by the United States was actually $100-million, of which $15-million was earmarked as an outright grant for support of a school lunch and clothing program in Japan.
18. *SGP* 115, U.S. "Statement on U.S.-Japanese Economic Questions"; *SGP* 116, documents 10225 and 102312.
19. *SGP* 115, Yoshida *aide-mémoire* to Dulles, November 10.
20. Miyazawa, p. 308.
21. The original draft communiqué prepared by the Japanese side is contained in *SGP* 115; the revised version is cited in discussion of the general exchange concerning China in Miyazawa, pp. 308–311.

22. In the cabinet meeting of August 6, 1954, Dulles made a strong presentation concerning Japan's economic crisis and the fact that, "If the free nations can't provide Japan with markets, Japan could very soon go bankrupt." As recorded by presidential aide James Hagerty, Eisenhower interrupted as follows: "It is an absolute fallacy to say that no free nation cannot [*sic*] trade with any Red nation. I have always believed that this kind of trade should not only be allowed but encouraged, particularly as far as Japan is concerned with the neighboring Red areas in Asia. I have always believed that this sort of trade would set up influences behind the Iron Curtain, particularly in China, which would work to the advantage of the free world. If China, for example, finds that it can buy cheap straw hats, cheap cotton shirts, sneakers, bicycles and all the rest of that sort of stuff from Japan, it would seem to me that that would set up the need within China for dependence upon Japan. In return for this trade Japan could get iron ore from Manchuria and coal from China. We will have to exercize [*sic*] great care and we will have to watch Japan very closely, but anyone who says that to trade with a Red country is in effect advocating a traitorous act just doesn't know what he is talking about. In the long run it may be the best for our country." Hagerty Diary, Box 1, Dwight D. Eisenhower Library. See also the more formal minutes of this cabinet meeting in the Ann Whitman Cabinet Series, Box 3, in the Eisenhower Library. Yoshida's close supporters tended to exaggerate the extent to which Yoshida seriously endeavored to persuade the United States to alter its China policy. In 1956, for example, former foreign minister Okazaki Katsuo wrote: "As a neighbor to the Chinese mainland and traditionally close to the ancient culture of China, Japan cannot be indifferent to the role of Communist China in the world, nor to the attitude of the free nations toward her. Former Prime Minister Yoshida brought up the question of divergent policies of the democratic nations with the leaders of the United States and Great Britain when abroad in 1954, in the hope of obtaining some fundamental common policy, but his attempt was not successful." "Japan's Foreign Relations," *Annals of the American Academy of Political and Social Science*, 308:160 (November 1956). Okazaki did not comment on the considerations which prevented Japan from diverging, like Britain, from the containment policy dictated in Washington.
23. *SGP* 115, undated and untitled position paper; *SGP* 116, "agenda" of October 19.
24. Miyazawa, p. 301; *SGP* 116, "agenda" of October 19 and document 10225.
25. Miyazawa, pp. 312–313.
26. Cf. Yanaga, p. 132.

Bibliography

Abe Shinnosuke. *Gendai Seijika Ron* (Essays on Contemporary Politicians). Bungei Shunjūsha, 1954.

Acheson, Dean. *Present at the Creation: My Years in the State Department.* Norton, 1969.

Adler-Karlsson, Gunnar. *Western Economic Warfare 1947–1967: A Case Study in Foreign Economic Policy*, volume 9 in *Acta Universitatis Stockholmiensis, Stockholm Economic Studies,* New Series. 1968.

Allen, George C. *Japan's Economic Recovery.* Oxford University, 1958.

Allison, John M. *Ambassador from the Prairie, or Allison Wonderland.* Tuttle, 1975 (originally Houghton Mifflin, 1973).

Andō Yoshio, ed. *Shōwa Seiji Keizai Shi e no Shōgen* (Testimonies Toward a Political and Economic History of Shōwa). 3 volumes. Mainichi Shimbunsha, 1966.

Asahi Gurafu. See "Yoshida Shigeru no Shōgai" below.

Asahi Nenkan (Asahi Yearbook).

Asahi Shimbunsha (Asahi Newspaper Company), ed. *Shiryō: Nihon to Chūkoku '45–'71* (Documents: Japan and China, 1945–1971), Volume 8 in *Asahi Shimin Kyōshitsu: "Nihon to Chūkoku"* (Asahi People's Classroom: "Japan and China"). 1972.

Asahi Shimbunsha, ed. *Yoshida Shigeru.* 1967.

Auer, James E. *The Postwar Rearmament of Japanese Maritime Forces, 1945–71.* Praeger, 1973. First published in Japanese translation as *Yomigaeru Nihon Kaigun*, 2 volumes, Jiji Tsūshinsha, 1972.

Ayusawa, Iwao F. *A History of Labor in Modern Japan.* East-West Center, University of Hawaii, 1966.

Baerwald, Hans H. *The Purge of Japanese Leaders under the Occupation*, volume 8 in University of California Publications in Political Science. 1959.

Ball, W. MacMahon. *Japan: Enemy or Ally?*, revised edition. John Day, 1949.

Ballantine, Joseph W. "The Far East," in Quincy Wright, ed. *A Foreign Policy for the United States*. University of Chicago, 1947, pp. 139–161.

Bamba, Nobuya. *Japanese Diplomacy in a Dilemma: New Light on Japan's China Policy, 1924–1929*. University of British Columbia, 1973.

Beckmann, George M. and Genji Okubo. *The Japanese Communist Party, 1922–1945*. Stanford University, 1969.

Beckmann, George M. "The Radical Left and the Failure of Communism," in James W. Morley, ed. *Dilemmas of Growth in Prewar Japan*, pp. 139–178.

Berger, Gordon M. "Japan's Young Prince: Konoe Fumimaro's Early Political Career, 1916–1931," *Monumenta Nipponica* 29.4:451–475 (Winter 1974).

——. *Parties Out of Power in Japan, 1931–1941*. Princeton University, 1977.

Bijutsu Shuppansha (Bijutsu Publishing Company), ed. *Rokuon Yoshida Shigeru* (Yoshida Shigeru Recorded). 1968.

Bisson, T. A. "Increase of Zaibatsu Predominance in Wartime Japan," in Jon Livingston, Joe Moore, and Felicia Oldfather, eds., *The Japan Reader: Imperial Japan, 1800–1945*. Pantheon, 1974, pp. 456–464.

——. *Japan's War Economy*. Macmillan, 1945.

——. *Prospects for Democracy in Japan*. Macmillan, 1949.

——. *Zaibatsu Dissolution in Japan*. University of California, 1954.

Bix, Herbert. "Japanese Imperialism and Manchuria, 1890–1931." Ph.D. dissertation, Harvard University, 1972.

Bōeichō (Defense Agency). *Bōei Nenkan* (Defense Yearbook). 1955.

——. *Jieitai Jūnen Shi* (Ten Year History of the Self-Defense Forces). 1961. Abbreviated in the notes as *JJS*.

——. *Keisatsu Yōbitai Sōtai Shi* (Complete Force History of the National Police Reserve). 1958.

Borg, Dorothy. *The United States and the Far Eastern Crisis of 1933–1938*. Harvard University, 1964.

Brett, Cecil Carter. "Japan's New Education Laws," *Far Eastern Survey* 23.10:174–176 (November 1954).

Bronfenbrenner, Martin. "Monopoly and Inflation in Contemporary Japan," *Osaka Economic Papers* 3.2:41–48 (March 1955).

Butow, Robert J. C. *Japan's Decision to Surrender*. Stanford University, 1954.

Centre for East Asian Cultural Studies, ed. *Meiji Japan Through Contemporary Sources*. 3 volumes. 1969–1972.

"Chian Ijihō Taisei: sono Jittai to Dōtai" (The Peace Preservation Law System: Its Essence and Dynamics). Special issue of *Gendai Shi*, June 1976.

Chinese People's Institute of Foreign Affairs, ed. *Oppose the Revival of Japanese Militarism (A Selection of Important Documents and Commentaries)*. Foreign Language Press, Peking, 1960.

Clifford, Nicholas. *Retreat from China: British Policy in the Far East, 1937–1941.* University of Washington, 1967.

Clyde, Paul. *The Far East: A History of the Impact of the West on Eastern Asia.* Prentice Hall, 1948.

Cohen, Jerome B. *Japan's Economy in War and Reconstruction.* University of Minnesota, 1949.

——. "Problems in Foreign Trade and Investment," *The Annals of the American Academy of Political and Social Science* 308:95–101 (November 1956).

Colton, Kenneth E. "Pre-war Political Influences in Post-war Conservative Parties," *The American Political Science Review* 42.5:940–957 (October 1948).

Congressional Record, Volume 98, part 2.

Conroy, F. Hilary. *The Japanese Seizure of Korea, 1868–1910: A Study of Realism and Idealism in International Relations.* University of Pennsylvania, 1960.

Contemporary Japan. Published quarterly by the Foreign Affairs Association of Japan.

Crowley, James. "Intellectuals as Visionaries of the New Asian Order," in James W. Morley, ed. *Dilemmas of Growth in Prewar Japan*, pp. 319–373.

——. *Japan's Quest for Autonomy: National Security and Foreign Policy, 1930–1938.* Princeton University, 1968.

——, ed. *Modern East Asia: Essays in Interpretation.* Harcourt, Brace and World, 1970.

Curtis, Gerald L. "The Dulles-Yoshida Negotiations on the San Francisco Peace Treaty," in Andrew W. Cordier, ed. *Columbia Essays in International Affairs, the Dean's Papers*, Volume 2. Columbia University, 1966.

Dai Hyakka Jiten (Great Encyclopedia). Heibonsha, 1932–1939.

The Daily Labor Press, Inc., ed. *The Labor Union Movement in Postwar Japan.* Tokyo, 1954.

Deverall, Richard L-G. "Are We Rebuilding Tojo's 'Red' Army?," *The New Leader*, January 15, 1951, pp. 2–5.

Dodge, Joseph M. Papers. Detroit Public Library. Abbreviated in the notes as *JMDP*.

Doi, Takeo. *The Anatomy of Dependence.* Kodansha International, 1973.

Dooman, Eugene. Interview. Columbia University oral history project on the occupation of Japan. Butler Library, Columbia University.

Dore, Ronald P. "The Ethics of the New Japan," *Pacific Affairs* 25.2:147–159 (June 1952).

——. *Land Reform in Japan.* Oxford University, 1959.

Dower, John W. "The Eye of the Beholder: Background Notes on the

U.S.-Japan Military Relationship," *Bulletin of Concerned Asian Scholars* 2.1:15–31 (October 1969).

——. "Occupied Japan as History and Occupation History as Politics," *Journal of Asian Studies* 34.2:485–504 (February 1975).

——. "The Superdomino in Postwar Asia: Japan In and Out of the Pentagon Papers," in Noam Chomsky and Howard Zinn, eds., *The Pentagon Papers: The Senator Gravel Edition*, Volume 5. Beacon, 1972, pp. 101–142.

——. "Yoshida Shigeru and the Great Empire of Japan, 1878–1945." Ph.D. dissertation, Harvard University, 1972.

Duke, Benjamin C. *Japan's Militant Teachers: A History of the Left-Wing Teachers' Movement*. East-West Center, University of Hawaii, 1973.

Dulles, John Foster. Papers and transcripts of interviews concerning Dulles. Princeton University. Abbreviated in the notes as *JFDP* and *JFDP-Oral*.

Dunn, Frederick S. *Peace-making and the Settlement with Japan*. Princeton University, 1963.

Duus, Peter. *Party Rivalry and Political Change in Taishō Japan*. Harvard University, 1968.

Economic Stabilization Board (Keizai Antei Honbu). Papers and reports in English. Maintained in the National Planning Agency, Tokyo. Abbreviated in the notes as *ESBP*.

"Education in Japan, 1945–1963," special issue of *Journal of Social and Political Ideas in Japan*, 1.3, December 1963. Abbreviated in the notes as *JSPIJ*.

Endicott, Stephen Lyon. *Diplomacy and Enterprise: British China Policy, 1933–1937*. University of British Columbia, 1975.

Farley, Miriam. *Aspects of Japan's Labor Problems*. John Day, 1950.

Feis, Herbert. *The Road to Pearl Harbor*. Princeton University, 1950.

Fridell, Wilbur M. "Government Ethics Textbooks in Late Meiji Japan," *Journal of Asian Studies* 29.4:823–833 (August 1970).

Fujii Shōichi and Ōe Shinobu. *Sengo Nihon no Rekishi* (History of Postwar Japan). Aoki Shoten, 1970.

Fujiwara Hirotatsu. *Yoshida Shigeru: sono Hito sono Seiji* (Yoshida Shigeru: The Man and His Politics). Yomiuri Shimbunsha, 1964.

Fukui, Haruhiro. *Party in Power: The Japanese Liberal-Democrats and Policy-making*. University of California, 1970.

Furushima Toshio et al., eds. *Nihon Shihonshugi Kōza* (Japanese Capitalism Series), Volume 7. Iwanami Shoten, 1954.

Gaimushō (Foreign Ministry), ed. *Shūsen Shiroku* (Historical Record of the End of the War). Shimbun Gekkansha, 1952.

Gayn, Mark. *Japan Diary*. William Sloane, 1948.

Graebner, Norman, ed. *An Uncertain Tradition: American Secretaries of State in the Twentieth Century*. McGraw Hill, 1961.

Great Britain, Foreign Office. Diplomatic records, maintained in the Public Record Office, London. Abbreviated in the notes as *FO*.

——. *Index to General Correspondence,* 1938. Volume 4.

Grew, Joseph C. Papers. Maintained in Houghton Library, Harvard University. Abbreviated in the notes as *JGP*.

——. *Ten Years in Japan: A Contemporary Record Drawn from the Diaries and Private and Official Papers of Joseph C. Grew, United States Ambassador to Japan.* Simon and Schuster, 1944.

——. *Turbulent Era: A Diplomatic Record of Forty Years, 1904–1945.* 2 volumes. Houghton Mifflin, 1952.

Gyōsei Kanrichō (Administration Control Agency), Kanribu (Bureau of Control). *Gyōsei Kikō Nempō* (Administrative System Annual Report). Volumes 1 (1950), 2 (1951), and 3 (1952).

Hadley, Eleanor M. *Antitrust in Japan.* Princeton University, 1970.

Hall, Robert King. *Education for a New Japan.* Yale University, 1949.

——. "Education in the Development of Postwar Japan," in *The Occupation of Japan: Proceedings of a Seminar on the Occupation of Japan and Its Legacy to the Postwar World.* The MacArthur Memorial Library and Archives, November 6 and 7, 1975.

——. *Shūshin: The Ethics of a Defeated Nation.* Columbia University, 1949.

Harada Kumao. *Saionji Kō to Seikyoku* (Prince Saionji and State Affairs). 8 volumes. Iwanami Shoten, 1951–1952.

Harootunian, Harry D. *Toward Restoration: The Growth of Political Consciousness in Tokugawa Japan.* University of California, 1970.

Hashigawa Bunzō, "Kakushin Kanryō" (Reform Bureaucrats), in Kamishima Jirō, ed. *Kenryoku no Shisō* (The Thought of Power-holders), Volume 10 in *Gendai Nihon Shisō Taikei* (Outline of Modern Japanese Thought). Chikuma Shobō, 1965, pp. 251–273.

Hata Ikuhiko. *Amerika no Tai-Nichi Senryō Seisaku* (U.S. Occupation Policy Toward Japan), Volume 3 of Ōkurashō Zaisei Shi Shitsu (Ministry of Finance Financial History Section), ed. *Shōwa Zaisei Shi: Shūsen kara Kōwa made* (A Financial History of the Shōwa Period: From Surrender to Sovereignty). Tōyō Keizai Shimpōsha, 1976.

Hatakeyama Seikō. *Mitsuroku Rikugun Nakano Gakkō* (Secret Account of the Army's "Nakano School"). Banchō Shobō, 1971.

Hatoyama Ichirō. "Ura kara Mita Jūnen" (Ten Years: A Backstage View). *Mainichi Shimbun*, August 15, 1955.

Hayashi Shigeru. *Nihon Shūsen Shi* (History of the End of the War in Japan). 3 volumes. Yomiuri Shimbunsha, 1962.

——. *Taiheiyō Sensō* (The Pacific War), Volume 25 in *Nihon no Rekishi* (History of Japan). Chūō Kōronsha, 1967.

Heinrichs, Waldo H., Jr. *American Ambassador: Joseph C. Grew and the Development of the United States Diplomatic Tradition.* Little, Brown, 1966.

Hidaka, Daishiro. "The Aftermath of Educational Reform," *The Annals of the American Academy of Political and Social Science* 308:140–155 (November 1956).

Hirano Kenichirō, "Manshūkoku Kyōwakai no Seijiteki Tenkai," (The Kyōwakai and the Political Stabilization of Manchukuo), in Nihon Seiji Gakkai (Japan Political Science Association), ed. *"Konoe Shintaisei" no Kenkyū* (Studies on Konoe's New Structure), special issue of *Seijigaku.* Iwanami Shoten, 1972, pp. 231–283.

Horiuchi Kensuke. "Berusaiyu Kōwa Kaigi no Kaisō" (Recollections of the Versailles Peace Conference), *Kingu,* January 1951, pp. 78–91.

Hosokawa Morisada. *Jōhō Tennō ni Tassezu* (Reports Do Not Reach the Emperor). 2 volumes. Isobe Shobō, 1953.

Hosoya, Chihiro. "Retrogression in Japan's Foreign-Policy Decision-Making Process," in James W. Morley, ed. *Dilemmas of Growth in Prewar Japan,* pp. 81–105.

Hsu, Immanuel C. Y. *The Rise of Modern China.* Oxford University, 1970.

Hull, Cordell. *The Memoirs of Cordell Hull.* 2 volumes. Macmillan, 1948.

Hulse, Frederick S. "Some Effects of the War Upon Japanese Society," *Far Eastern Quarterly* 7.1:22–42 (November 1947).

Hussey, Alfred R. Papers. University of Michigan.

Ienaga Saburō. *Taiheiyō Sensō* (The Pacific War). Iwanami Shoten, 1968.

Ike, Nobutake, ed. and transl. *Japan's Decision for War: Records of the 1941 Policy Conferences.* Stanford University, 1967.

Ikeda Sumihisa. *Nihon no Magari Kado: Gunbatsu no Higeki to Saigo no Gozen Kaigi.* (Japan's Turning-point: The Tragedy of the Military Cliques and the Last Imperial Conference). Senjō, 1968.

Ikeuchi Hajime. "Taiheiyō Sensōchū no Senji Ryūgen" (Wartime Rumors During the Pacific War), *Shakaigaku Hyōron,* June 1951, pp. 30–42.

Inomata Kōzō, Kimura Kihachirō, and Shimizu Ikutarō. *Kichi Nihon: Ushinaware Iku Sokoku no Sugata* (Military-Base Japan: The Condition of the Fatherland, Which Is Being Lost). Wakōsha, 1953.

Inoue Kiyoshi, Kobiki Shinsaburō, and Suzuki Masashi. *Gendai Nihon no Rekishi* (History of Modern Japan). 2 volumes. Aoki Shoten, 1953.

Iriye, Akira. *After Imperialism: The Search for a New Order in the Far East, 1921–1931.* Harvard University, 1965.

——. "The Failure of Economic Expansion, 1918–1931," in Bernard S. Silberman and H. D. Harootunian, eds. *Japan in Crisis: Essays on Taishō Democracy,* pp. 237–269.

Ishibashi Tanzan. *Tanzan Kaisō* (Recollections of Tanzan). Mainichi Shimbunsha, 1951.

——. *Tanzan Nikki: Shōwa 20-22-nen* (Tanzan Diary: 1945–1947). Ishibashi Tanzan Kinen Zaidan, 1974.

Iwabuchi Tatsuo. "Konoe Kō no Jōsōbun" (The Konoe Memorial), *Sekai Bunka*, 3.8:32–40 (August 1, 1948).

Jansen, Marius B. "From Hatoyama to Hatoyama," *Far Eastern Quarterly* 14.1:65–79 (November 1954).

——. *Japan and China: From War to Peace, 1894–1972*. Rand McNally, 1975.

——. *The Japanese and Sun Yat-sen*. Harvard University, 1954.

——. *Sakamoto Ryōma and the Meiji Restoration*. Princeton University, 1961.

The Japan Biographical Encyclopedia and Who's Who, third edition. Rengo Press, 1964–1965.

Japan, Government of. *Document A—The Present Condition of China: With References to Circumstances Affecting International Relations and the Good Understanding between Nations upon which Peace Depends.* Revised edition, July 1932. Submitted to the League of Nations.

——. *Document B—Relations of Japan with Manchuria and Mongolia.* July 1932. Submitted to the League of Nations.

Japan-Manchoukuo Year Book, 1940. The Japan-Manchoukuo Year Book Co.

"Japan Since Recovery of Independence." Special issue of *The Annals of the American Academy of Political Science* 308, November 1956.

Japanese Foreign Ministry. Archives. Abbreviated in the notes as *JFMA*.

Jichichō (Autonomy Agency). *Chihō Jichi Nenkan* (Local Autonomy Yearbook). Volumes 1 and 2 (1954), and Volume 3 (1955). Abbreviated in the notes as *CJN*.

——. *Chihō Zaisei Tōkei Nempō* (Local Finance Statistical Annual). 1956.

Johnson, Chalmers. *An Instance of Treason: Ozaki Hotsumi and the Sorge Spy Ring*. Stanford University, 1964.

——. *Conspiracy at Matsukawa*. University of California, 1972.

Jones, Joseph Marion. *The Fifteen Weeks (February 21–June 5, 1947).* Harcourt, Brace, and World, 1955.

"Jūnen no Ayumi," (Ten Years' Journey), 15 parts. *Mainichi Shimbun*, August 5–20, 1955. Recollections by Japan's post-surrender prime ministers: Higashikuni (1–3), Yoshida (4–11), Katayama (12–13), and Ashida (14–15).

Jurisuto (Jurist), 100, February 15, 1956. Special issue titled "Kaiko to Tembō: Sengo Hōsei no Hensen" (Retrospect and Prospect: Changes in Postwar Legislation).

——, 361, January 1, 1967. Special issue titled "Sengo Hōseido no Nijūnen" (Twenty Years of the Postwar Legal System).

Kajinishi Mitsuhaya, Katō Toshihiko, Ōshima Kiyoshi, and Ōuchi Tsutomu.

Nihon Shihonshugi no Botsuraku (The Collapse of Japanese Capitalism). 7 volumes. Tokyo Daigaku, 1960–1968.

Kampō Gogai (Official Gazette—Extra Number). Transcript of discussion in both houses of the Diet, under both the Meiji constitution and 1947 constitution. Abbreviated in the notes as *KG*.

Kanroji, Osanaga. *Hirohito: An Intimate Portrait of the Japanese Emperor*. Gateway, 1975. This appeared in Japanese under the title *Tennōsama*.

Kase, Toshikazu. "Kōen: Yoshida Shigeru o Kataru" (Lecture: On Yoshida Shigeru), 3 installments. *Kasekikai Kaihō* 280–282, June, July, and August 1969.

——. *Yoshida Shigeru no Yuigon* (Yoshida Shigeru's Testament). Yomiuri Shimbunsha, 1967.

——. "Yoshida Shigeru—sono Kyūjūsai no Nenrin" (Yoshida Shigeru—His Ninety Years), *Bungei Shunjū*, November 1967, pp. 134–144.

Kasekikai Kaihō (Kasekikai Newsletter). Internal monthly newsletter of former Foreign Ministry officials. Abbreviated in the notes as *KK*.

Kato, Shunsaku. "Postwar Japanese Security and Rearmament, with Special Reference to Japanese-American Relations," in D. C. S. Sissons, ed., *Papers on Modern Japan, 1968*, Australian National University, pp. 62–78.

Keizai Dantai Rengōkai (Federation of Economic Organizations). *Keidanren no Jūnen* (Ten Years of Keidanren). 1956.

——. *Keidanren no Nijūnen* (Twenty Years of Keidanren). 1969.

——. *Keizai Dantai Rengōkai Jūnenshi* (Ten-Year History of the Federation of Economic Organizations). 3 volumes. 1962–1963.

Kempō Chōsakai (Committee to Investigate the Constitution). *Dai-8-kai Sōkai Gijiroku* (Transcripts of the Eighth General Meeting), December 18, 1957. Yoshida Shigeru's account of the drafting of the postwar constitution appears on pp. 1–11.

Kennan, George F. "Japanese Security and American Policy," *Foreign Affairs* 43.1:14–28 (October 1964).

——. *Memoirs, 1925–1950*. Little, Brown, 1967.

——. *Memoirs, 1950–1963*. Little, Brown, 1972.

Kennedy, Malcolm. *The Estrangement of Great Britain and Japan, 1917–35*. University of California, 1969.

Kido Kōichi. *Kido Kōichi Nikki* (Kido Kōichi Diary). 2 volumes. Tokyo Daigaku, 1966.

Kido Kōichi Kenkyūkai (Kido Kōichi Research Association), ed. *Kido Kōichi Kankei Bunshō* (Documents Relating to Kido Kōichi). Tokyo Daigaku, 1966.

Kinmonth, Earl. "The Self-Made Man in Meiji Japanese Thought." Ph.D. dissertation, University of Wisconsin, Madison, 1975.

Kitazawa Naokichi. "Kitazawa Naokichi Tuioku-dan" (Kitazawa Naokichi's Recollections). *Kasekikai Kaihō* 267, May 1968.

Kobayashi Yoshio. *Sengo Nihon Keizai Shi* (Economic History of Postwar Japan). Nihon Hyōronsha, 1963.

Kokkai Kaigiroku (Proceedings of the National Diet of Japan). See *Kampō Gogai* above.

Kolko, Gabriel. *The Politics of War: The World and United States Foreign Policy, 1943–1945.* Random House, 1968.

Kōmura Sakahiko. *Shinjitsu no ue ni Tachite: Sensō to Senryō Jidai* (Standing on the Truth: The War and Occupation Period). Hakubundō, 1954.

Kon Hidemi. "Hito to shite no Yoshida Shigeru" (The Man Yoshida Shigeru). *Kasekikai Kaihō* 271, September 1968.

——. *Yoshida Shigeru.* Kodansha, 1967.

Kōno Ichirō. *Kōno Ichirō Jiden* (Autobiography of Kōno Ichirō). Tokuma Shoten, 1965.

Konoe Fumimaro. *Konoe Nikki* (Konoe Diary). Kyōdō Tsūshinsha, 1968.

——. *The Memoirs of Prince Fumimaro Konoye.* Translated from the *Asahi Shimbun,* December 20–30, 1945. Okuyama Service, Tokyo, 1946. Another translation is included in Record Group 331, National Archives. These "memoirs" were published in book form in Japanese as *Konoe Fumimaro-kō no Shuki: Ushinawareshi Seiji* (The Memoirs of Prince Konoe Fumimaro: Abortive Politics), Asahi Shimbunsha, 1946.

Konsaisu Jinmei Jiten: Nihon-hen (Concise Biographical Dictionary: Japan Volume). Sanshōdō, 1976.

Kosaka, Masaaki, ed. *Japanese Thought in the Meiji Era,* Volume 8 of *Japanese Culture in the Meiji Era.* Toyo Bunko, 1958.

Koosaka [Kōsaka], Masataka. "Japan's Postwar Foreign Policy," in D. C. S. Sissons, ed., *Papers on Modern Japan, 1968.* Australian National University, pp. 1–25.

Kōsaka Masataka. *Saishō Yoshida Shigeru* (Premier Yoshida Shigeru). Chūō Kōronsha, 1968.

Kosei Torihiki Iinkai (Fair Trade Commission). *Dokusen Shihon Seisaku Nijūnen Shi* (Twenty-Year History of Policy Toward Monopoly Capital). Ōkurashō, 1968. Abbreviated in the notes as *KTI.*

Kowalski, Frank. "An Inoffensive Rearmament," unpublished English manuscript which appeared in Japanese translation as *Nihon Saigunbi* (Rearmament of Japan). Simul, 1969.

Kurihara Ken. "Yoshida Shigeru Antō Ryōji no Iken-den" (Cable of Opinion of Yoshida Shigeru, Consul in Antung). *Kasekikai Kaihō* 300, February 1971.

Kuroki, Yukichi. "Katayama's Coalition Cabinet Takes Over," *Contemporary Japan* 16.4–6:159–167 (April-June 1947).

Langdon, Frank C. "Japan," in Arnold J. Heidenheimer and Frank C. Langdon, *Business Associations and the Financing of Political Parties.* Martinus Nijhoff, The Hague, 1968.

Lattimore, Owen. *Solution in Asia.* Little, Brown, 1945.

Lee, Bradford A. *Britain and the Sino-Japanese War, 1937–1939: A Study in the Dilemmas of British Decline.* Stanford University and Oxford University, 1973.

Levine, Solomon B. *Industrial Relations in Postwar Japan.* University of Illinois, 1958.

——. "Labor Patterns and Trends," *The Annals of the American Academy of Political and Social Science* 308:102–112 (November 1956).

Levy, Richard. "New Light on Mao: His Views on the Soviet Union's *Political Economy,*" *China Quarterly* 61:95–117 (March 1975).

Louis, William Roger. *British Strategy in the Far East, 1919–1939.* Oxford University, 1971.

Lowe, Peter. *Great Britain and the Origins of the Pacific War: A Study of British Policy in East Asia, 1937–1941.* Oxford University, 1977.

MacMurray, John Van Antwerp, comp. and ed. *Treaties and Agreements With and Concerning China, 1894–1919.* 2 volumes. Carnegie Endowment for International Peace, 1921.

Maeda Riichi. "Yoshida-san to Kankoku" (Yoshida and Korea). *Kasekikai Kaihō* 295, September 1970.

Maruyama, Masao. *Thought and Behaviour in Modern Japanese Politics.* Oxford University, 1963.

Masumi Junnosuke. *Gendai Nihon Seiji Taisei* (The Structure of Modern Japanese Politics). Iwanami Shoten, 1969.

——. "Yoshida Shigeru," in Kamishima Jirō, ed., *Kenryoku no Shisō* (The Thought of Power-holders), Volume 10 in *Gendai Nihon Shisō Taikei* (Outline of Modern Japanese Thought). Chikuma Shobō, 1965, pp. 367–391.

Matsumoto Seichō. *Nihon no Kuroi Kiri* (Japan's Black Mist). Bungei Shunjū, 1972.

Matsuo, Takayoshi. "The Development of Democracy in Japan," *The Developing Economies* 4.4:612–637 (December 1966).

Mayo, Marlene, ed. *The Emergence of Imperial Japan: Self-Defense or Calculated Aggression?* D. C. Heath, 1970.

Mazaki Katsuji. *Nihon wa Doko e Iku–Wana ni Kakatta Nihon* (Where Is Japan Going?–Japan Caught in the Snare). Jitsugyō no Sekaisha, 1960.

Mazaki Ryū. "Yoshida Shigeru-san o Shinobu" (Remembering Yoshida Shigeru), 5 installments, *Kasekikai Kaihō* 271, September 1968, and 275–278, January through April 1969.

McCormack, Gavan. *Chang Tso-lin in Northeast China, 1911–1928: China, Japan, and the Manchurian Idea.* Stanford University, 1977.

Misuzu Shobō (Misuzu Books), ed. *Gendai Shi Shiryō: Zoruge Jiken* (Documents on Modern History: The Sorge Case), Volume 2, part 2. Misuzu Shobō, 1962.

Mitchell, Richard H. *Thought Control in Prewar Japan.* Cornell University, 1976.

Mitsubishi Economic Research Institute, ed. *Mitsui-Mitsubishi-Sumitomo: Present Status of the Former Zaibatsu Enterprises.* 1955.

Miyake Kijirō. "Yoshida-san o Shinobite Omou Kotodomo," (Various Thoughts on Remembering Yoshida), 11 installments, *Kasekikai Kaihō* 284–294, October 1969 through August 1970.

Miyauchi Yutaka. *Sengo Chian Rippō no Kihonteki Seikaku* (Fundamental Nature of Postwar Peace-Preservation Legislation). Yushindō, 1960.

Miyazawa Kiichi. *Tokyo-Washinton no Mitsudan* (Secret Talks between Tokyo and Washington). Jitsugyō no Nihonsha, 1956.

Montgomery, John D. "The Purge in Occupied Japan: A Study in the Use of Civilian Agencies under Military Government." Technical Memorandum ORO-T-48 (FEC), Operations Research Office, The Johns Hopkins University, 1953.

Moore, Joe Baldwin. "Production Control and the Postwar Crisis of Japanese Capitalism, 1945–1946." Ph.D. dissertation, University of Wisconsin, Madison, 1978.

Morishima Morito. *Imbō, Ansatsu, Guntō: Ichi Gaikōkan no Kaisō* (Conspiracies, Assassinations, Sabers: Recollections of a Diplomat). Iwanami Shinsho, 1950.

Morley, James W., ed. *Dilemmas of Growth in Prewar Japan.* Princeton University, 1971.

——. "The First Seven Weeks," *The Japan Interpreter* 6.2:151–164 (September 1970).

Morris, Ivan. *Nationalism and the Right-Wing in Japan: A Study of Post-war Trends.* Oxford University, 1960.

Mukoyama Hiroo. "Minkan ni Okeru Shūsen Kōsaku" (Plans for Ending the War in the Civilian Sector), in Nihon Gaikō Gakkai (Japan International Relations Association), ed., *Taiheiyō Sensō Shūketsu Ron* (On the Termination of the Pacific War). Tokyo Daigaku, 1953, pp. 100–117.

Murobushi Tetsurō. *Sengo Gigoku* (Postwar Scandals). Ushio, 1968.

Naimushō (Home Ministry), Keihokyoku Hoanbu (Police Bureau, Peace Preservation Division). *Tokkō Geppō* (Monthly Gazette of the Special Higher Police). Covers from March 1930 to November 1944.

Najita, Tetsuo. *Japan.* Prentice-Hall, 1974.

——. "Ōshio Heihachirō (1793–1837)," in Albert M. Craig and Donald H. Shively, eds. *Personality in Japanese History*. University of California, 1970, pp. 155–179.

Nakamura Kikuo and Kamijō Sueo. *Sengo Nihon Seiji Shi* (Political History of Postwar Japan). Yushindō, 1973.

Nihon Gaikō Gakkai (Japan International Relations Association), ed. *Taiheiyō Sensō Shūketsu Ron* (On the Termination of the Pacific War). Tokyo Daigaku, 1958.

Nihon Rōdō Kumiai Sōhyōgikai (General Council of Trade Unions of Japan). *Sōhyō Jūnen Shi* (Ten-Year History of Sōhyō). 1964.

Nihon Seiji Gakkai (Japanese Political Science Association), ed. *Sengo Nihon no Seiji Katei* (The Political Process of Postwar Japan). Iwanami Shoten, 1953.

Nihon Tōkei Nenkan (Japan Statistical Yearbook). Annual publication of the Statistics Bureau under the Prime Minister's Office (Sōrifu Tōkeikyoku).

Nish, Ian. *Japanese Foreign Policy, 1869–1942: Kasumigaseki to Miyakezawa*. Routledge and Kegan Paul, 1977.

Nishimura Kumao. *San Furanshisuko Heiwa Jōyaku* (The San Francisco Peace Treaty), Volume 27 in Kajima Heiwa Kenkyūjo (Kajima Peace Research Institute), ed., *Nihon Gaikō Shi* (History of Japanese Diplomacy). Kajima Kenkyūjo, 1971.

Nishio Suehiro. *Nishio Suehiro no Seiji Oboegaki* (Political Recollections of Nishio Suehiro). Mainichi Shimbunsha, 1968.

Norman, E. H. "A Japanese *Eminence Grise*: Izawa Takiwo." Memorandum submitted to the U.S. Department of State on January 7, 1946. Department of State file 740.00119/1-746.

Nosaka Sanzō. *Nosaka Sanzō Senshū: Senji-hen 1933–1945* (Selected Writings of Nosaka Sanzō: Wartime, 1933–1945). Shin Nihon, 1967.

Ogata Shōji. "Shūsen no Hankyōteki Seikaku" (The Anti-Communist Character of the Termination of the War), "Geppō #3" (Newsletter #3), an insert included in the multi-volume series *Nihon Shihonshugi Kōza* (Japanese Capitalism Series). Iwanami Shoten, 1953.

Oka Yoshitake, ed. *Gendai Nihon no Seiji Katei* (The Political Process of Contemporary Japan). Iwanami Shoten, 1958.

——. *Konoe Fumimaro: "Unmei" no Seijika* (Konoe Fumimaro: "Fate's" Politician). Iwanami Shinsho, 1972.

Okamoto, Shumpei. *The Japanese Oligarchy and the Russo-Japanese War*. Columbia University, 1970.

Okazaki, Katsuo. "Japan's Foreign Relations," *The Annals of the American Academy of Political and Social Science* 308, November 1956, pp. 156–166.

——. "Yoshida Naikaku no Shutsugen to Heiwa Jōyaku Teiketsu no Butai

Ura" (Behind the Scenes of the Appearance of the Yoshida Cabinet and Conclusion of the Peace Treaty), *Gaikō Jihō*, April 1964, pp. 56–62.

Ōkochi Kazuo. *Sengo Nihon no Rōdō Undō* (The Labor Movement in Postwar Japan), revised edition. Iwanami Shinsho, 1961.

Osborne, John. "My Dear General–Letters of MacArthur and Prime Ministers Reveal How Occupied Japan is Ruled," *Life*, November 27, 1950, pp. 127–139.

Ōtani Keijirō. *Gunbatsu: Ni-ni-roku Jiken kara Haisen made* (Military Cliques: From the February 26th Incident to Surrender). Tosho, 1971.

——. "Yoshida Shigeru Taiho no Shinsō" (The Truth about Yoshida Shigeru's Arrest). Appears in Ōtani's *Nikumare Kempei* (The Despised Military Police), Nihon Shuhōsha, 1957, pp. 13–73; and also in his *Kempei Mitsuroku* (Secret Record of the Military Police), Hara Shobō, 1965, pp. 1–57.

Ōuchi Hyōe, "Keizai" (The Economy), in Yanaihara Tadao, ed. *Sengo Nihon Shōshi*, Volume 2, pp. 63–174.

——. "Yoshida-san to no En" (My Association with Yoshida). *Sekai*, December 1967, pp. 158–163.

Parliamentary Debates, House of Commons. Fifth Series, especially Volumes 323, 326, 337, 496.

Parsons, Talcott. "Population and Social Structure," in Douglas G. Haring, ed. *Japan's Prospect*. Harvard University, 1946, pp. 87–114.

Peattie, Mark R. *Ishiwara Kanji and Japan's Confrontation with the West.* Princeton University, 1975.

Piggott, F. S. G. *Broken Thread: An Autobiography*. Gale and Polden, 1950.

Pittau, Joseph. *Political Thought in Early Meiji Japan, 1868–1889.* Harvard University, 1967.

Pyle, Kenneth B. *The New Generation in Meiji Japan: Problems of Cultural Identity, 1885–1895.* Stanford University, 1969.

Quigley, Harold S. and John E. Turner. *The New Japan: Government and Politics.* University of Minnesota, 1956.

Ridgway, Matthew B. *Soldier: The Memoirs of Matthew B. Ridgway.* Harper and Brothers, 1956.

Roberts, John G. *Mitsui: Three Centuries of Japanese Business.* John Weatherhill, 1973.

Roden, Donald Trowbridge. "The Pre-war Japanese Student Movement: Some Observations and Comparisons." M.A. thesis, University of Wisconsin, Madison. 1969.

Roth, Andrew. *Dilemma in Japan.* Little, Brown, 1945.

Sapin, Burtin. "The Role of the Military in Formulating the Japanese Peace Treaty," in Gordon B. Turner, ed. *A History of Military Affairs in*

Western Society Since the Eighteenth Century. Harcourt-Brace, 1953, pp. 751–762.

Sasaki Tōru. "Jimintō: Kikikan-naki Taihei Seitō" (The Liberal Democratic Party: the Tranquil Party with No Sense of Crisis), *Jiyū*, September 1967, pp. 83–91.

——. "Yoshida Shigeru no Shi to Hoshu Seiji no Meiun" (Yoshida Shigeru's Death and the Fate of Conservative Politics), *Gendai no Me*, December 1967, pp. 130–139.

Satō Naotake. "Satō Naotake-shi Tsuioku-dan" (Satō Naotake's Recollections), *Kasekikai Kaihō* 265, March 1968.

Sawada Setsuzō. "Yoshida-san no Omoide" (Remembrances of Yoshida), *Kasekikai Kaihō* 274, December 1968.

Scalapino, Robert. *Democracy and the Party Movement in Prewar Japan*. University of California, 1953.

—— and Junnosuke Masumi. *Parties and Politics in Contemporary Japan*. University of California, 1962.

Schonberger, Howard. "The Japan Lobby in American Diplomacy, 1947–1952," *Pacific Historical Review* 46.3:327–359 (August 1977).

——. "Zaibatsu Dissolution and the American Restoration of Japan," *Bulletin of Concerned Asian Scholars*, 5.2:16–31 (September 1975).

Schram, Stuart. *Mao Tse-tung*. Penguin, 1966.

Schroeder, Paul. *The Axis Alliance and Japanese-American Relations*. Cornell University, 1958.

Sebald, William J. and Russell Brines. *With MacArthur in Japan: A Personal History of the Occupation*. Norton, 1965.

Shigemitsu, Mamoru. *Japan and Her Destiny: My Struggle for Peace*. Dutton, 1958.

Shilloney, Ben-Ami. *Revolt in Japan: The Young Officers and the February Twenty-Six Incident*. Princeton University, 1972.

Shinobu Seizaburō. "Dokusen Shihon to Seiji" (Monopoly Capital and Politics), in Oka Yoshitake, ed. *Gendai Nihon no Seiji Katei*, pp. 207–252.

——. *Sengo Nihon Seiji Shi, 1945–1952* (A Political History of Postwar Japan, 1945–1952). 4 volumes. Keisō Shobō, 1965–1967.

——. *Taishō Seiji Shi* (A Political History of the Taishō Period). Kawade Shobō, 1954.

Shioguchi Kiichi. *Monjo: Ikeda Hayato* (Transcripts: Ikeda Hayato). Asahi Shimbunsha, 1975.

Shiomi, Saburo. *Japan's Finance and Taxation, 1940–1956*. Columbia University, 1957.

Shiryō: Sengo Nijūnen Shi (Documents: A History of the Two Postwar Decades). 6 volumes. Nihon Hyōronsha, 1966. Abbreviated in the notes as *SSNS*.

Shively, Donald H. "The Japanization of the Middle Meiji," in Donald H. Shively, ed., *Tradition and Modernization in Japanese Culture.* Princeton University, 1971, pp. 77–119.

Shōwa Dōjin Kai (Shōwa Comrades Association), ed. *Shōwa Kenkyūkai* (The Shōwa Research Association). Keizai Ōraisha, 1968.

Silberman, Bernard S. and H. D. Harootunian, eds. *Japan in Crisis: Essays on Taishō Democracy.* Princeton University, 1974.

Snow, Edgar. *Red Star Over China.* Grove Edition, 1961.

Sodei Rinjirō. *Makkaasaa no Nisen Nichi* (MacArthur's Two-thousand Days). Chūō Kōronsha, 1974.

Soko, M. [pseudonym of Yoshida Shigeru]. "Japan's Far Eastern Policy," *The Fortnightly Review*, New Series, 109, February 1, 1921, pp. 267–270.

Spaulding, Robert M. "The Bureaucracy as a Political Force, 1920–1945," in James W. Morley, ed. *Dilemmas of Growth in Prewar Japan*, pp. 33–80.

——. *Imperial Japan's Higher Civil Service Exams.* Princeton University, 1967.

——. "Japan's 'New Bureaucrats,' 1932–1945," in George M. Wilson, ed. *Crisis Politics in Prewar Japan.* Sophia, 1970, pp. 51–70.

Steiner, Kurt. *Local Government in Japan.* Stanford University, 1965.

——. "Local Government in Japan: Reform and Reaction," *Far Eastern Survey* 23.7:97–102 (July 1954).

Sumimoto Toshio. *Senryō Hiroku* (Secret Record of the Occupation). 2 volumes. Mainichi Shimbunsha, 1952.

Supreme Commander for the Allied Powers, Japan. *Official Gazette Extra.* English translation of *Kampō Gogai.* Abbreviated in the notes as *OGE.*

——, Economic and Scientific Section, Programs and Statistics Division. "Japan's Industrial Potential," 3 unpublished volumes: February 1951, October 1951, and February 1952.

——, Government Section. *Political Reorientation of Japan: September 1945 to September 1948.* 2 volumes. Government Printing Office, 1949. Abbreviated in the notes as *PRJ.*

Suzuki Gengo. Papers. Ministry of Finance, Tokyo. Abbreviated in the notes as *SGP.*

Swearingen, Rodger and Paul Langer. *Red Flag in Japan: International Communism in Action, 1919–1951.* Harvard University, 1952.

"A Symposium on Japanese Nationalism," *Journal of Asian Studies* 31.1: 5–62 (November 1971).

Taira, Koji. *Economic Development and the Labor Market in Japan.* Columbia University, 1970.

Takahashi Seiichirō. "Yoshida Shigeru-shi Tsuisō" (Reminiscence of Yoshida Shigeru), *Kasekikai Kaihō* 270, August 1968.

Takigawa, Tsutomu. "Historical Background of Agricultural Land Reform in Japan," *The Developing Economies* 10.3:290–310 (September 1972).

Tamura Kōsaku. "Wakai Hi no Yoshida-san no Tsuikai" (Recollections of the Young Yoshida), *Kasekikai Kaihō* 261, November 1967.

Tanaka Jirō, Tawara Shizuo, and Hara Ryūnosuke, eds. *Chihō Jichi Nijūnen: sono Kaiko to Shōrai no Tenbō* (Twenty Years of Local Autonomy: Retrospect and Future Prospects), Volume 6 in *Gendai Chihō Jichi Sōsho* (Contemporary Local Autonomy Series). Hyōronsha, 1970.

Tateno Nobuyuki. *Taiyō wa Mata Noboru: Kōshaku Konoe Fumimaro* (The Sun Rises Again: Prince Konoe Fumimaro). 3 volumes. Rokkō, 1952.

Teikoku Gikai Gijiroku (Proceedings of the Imperial Diet of Japan). See *Kampō Gogai* above.

Tiedemann, Arthur. "Big Business and Politics in Prewar Japan," in James W. Morley, ed., *Dilemmas of Growth in Prewar Japan*, pp. 267–316.

Titus, David Anson. *Palace and Politics in Prewar Japan.* Columbia University, 1974.

Tokyo Jūni Chanaru Hōdōbu (Tokyo Channel 12 Broadcasting Bureau), ed. *Shōgen: Watakushi no Shōwa Shi* (Testimony: My Shōwa History). 1969.

Trotsky, Leon. *Writings of Leon Trotsky,* 2nd edition. Edited by George Breitman et al. 12 volumes. Pathfinder Press, ca. 1971–1976.

Trotter, Ann. *Britain and East Asia, 1933–1937.* Cambridge Unversity, 1975.

Tsuji, Kiyoaki. "The Cabinet, Administrative Organization, and the Bureaucracy," *The Annals of the American Academy of Political and Social Science* 308:10–17 (November 1956).

—— and Oka Yoshitake. "Sengo Taisei no Seisaku to Kikō" (The Organization and Policies of Postwar Administration), in Nihon Seiji Gakkai, ed. *Sengo Nihon no Seiji Katei,* pp. 29–52.

Tsunoda, Ryusaku, Wm. Theodore De Bary, and Donald Keene, eds. *Sources of Japanese Tradition.* Columbia University, 1958.

Tsūsan Daijin Kanbō Chōsakai (Research Association of the Minister's Secretariat, Ministry of International Trade and Industry), ed. *Sengo Keizai Jūnen Shi* (Economic History of the First Postwar Decade). Sankō Kaikan, 1954.

Tsutsui Kiyoshi. "Mori Kaku to wa Donna Hito" (What Sort of a Person Was Mori Kaku?), *Kasekikai Kaihō* 288, February 1970.

——. "Mori Kaku no Seikaku" (Mori Kaku's Personality), *Kasekikai Kaihō* 289, March 1970.

——. "Nani ga Tanaka Taishō o Jisatsu ni Oikonda ka" (What Drove General Tanaka to Suicide?), *Kasekikai Kaihō* 290, April 1970.

Uchida Kenzō. *Sengo Nihon no Hoshu Seiji* (Conservative Politics in Postwar Japan). Iwanami Shinsho, 1969.

Ueda Shunkichi. "Nihon Badorio Jiken Tenmatsu" (The Circumstances of Japan's Badoglio Incident), *Bungei Shunjū*, December 1, 1949, pp. 42–55.

——. "Shōwa Demokurashii no Zasetsu" (The Breakdown of Shōwa Democracy), in 2 parts: "Manshū Jiken Zengo" (Before and After the Manchurian Incident), *Jiyū*, October 1960, pp. 81–94; and "Gunbu, Kakushin-ha Kanryō no Nihon Kyōsanka Puran" (The Plan of the Military and Reformist Bureaucrats to Communize Japan), *Jiyū*, November 1960, pp. 89–99.

U.S. Department of Defense. *United States-Vietnam Relations, 1945–1967.* Book 8. [The "Pentagon Papers"].

U.S. Department of State. *Department of State Bulletin.*

——. *Foreign Relations of the United States.* Abbreviated in the notes as *FRUS.*

——. *Peace and War. United States Foreign Policy, 1931–1941.*

——. *Report of the Mission on Japanese Combines, Part I: Analytical and Technical Data. A Report to the Department of State and the War Department, March 1946.* Department of State Publication 2628, Far Eastern Series 14. [The "Edwards Report"].

——. *United States Relations with China, with Special Reference to the Period 1944–1949.* Department of State Publication 3573, Far Eastern Series 30. [The "China White Paper"].

U.S. Senate, Committee on Armed Services and Committee on Foreign Relations. *Hearings to Conduct an Inquiry into the Military Situation in the Far East.* 82nd Congress, 1st Session. 1951.

——, Committee on Foreign Relations. *Japanese Peace Treaty and Other Treaties Pertaining to Security in the Pacific.* 82nd Congress, 2nd Session. January 1952.

——, Committee on Foreign Relations. *Treaty of Mutual Cooperation and Security with Japan.* 86th Congress, 2nd Session. June 7, 1960.

——, Committee on the Judiciary, Subcommittee to Investigate the Administration of the Internal Security Act and Other Internal Security Laws. *Scope of Soviet Activity in the United States.* 84th Congress, 2nd Session, and 85th Congress, 1st Session. 1956–1957.

U.S. Strategic Bombing Survey, Morale Division. *The Effects of Strategic Bombing on Japanese Morale.* 1947.

Van Slyke, Lyman P., ed. *The Chinese Communist Movement: A Report of the United States War Department, July 1945.* Stanford University, 1968.

Ward, Robert E. and Frank Joseph Shulman, eds. *The Allied Occupation of Japan, 1945–1952: An Annotated Bibliography of Western-Language Materials.* American Library Association, 1974.

Watanabe Takeshi. *Senryōka no Nihon Zaisei Oboegaki* (Recollections of Japanese Finance under the Occupation). Nihon Keizai Shimbunsha, 1966.

Watanabe Tsuneo. *Daijin* (Ministers of State). Kōbundō, 1959.

——. *Habatsu* (Cliques). Kōbundō, 1958.

——. "Yoshida Gakkō no Keifu" (Geneology of the Yoshida School), *Shūkan Yomiuri*, November 15, 1967, pp. 74–75.

Weinstein, Martin E. *Japan's Postwar Defense Policy, 1946–1968*. Columbia University, 1971.

Whiting, Allen S. *Soviet Policies in China, 1917–1924*. Stanford University edition, 1968.

Whitney, Courtney. *MacArthur: His Rendezvous with History*. Knopf, 1956.

Who's Who in Japan, 1940–41, edited by Tsunesaburo Kamesaka. The Who's Who in Japan Publishing Office, 1941.

Wildes, Harry Emerson. *Typhoon in Tokyo: The Occupation and Its Aftermath*. Macmillan, 1954.

——. "Underground Politics in Post-War Japan," *The American Political Science Review* 42.6:1149–1162 (December 1948).

Willoughby, Charles A. and John Chamberlain. *MacArthur, 1941–1951: Victory in the Pacific*. McGraw-Hill, 1954.

Wohlstetter, Roberta. *Pearl Harbor: Warning and Decision*. Stanford University, 1962.

Woodward, E. L. and Rohan Butler, eds. *Documents on British Foreign Policy, 1919–1939*, Third Series, especially Volumes 8 and 9. H. M. Stationery Office, 1955.

Wright, Quincy, ed. *A Foreign Policy for the United States*. University of Chicago, 1947.

Yabe Teiji. *Konoe Fumimaro*. 2 volumes. Kōbundō, 1952.

——. *Konoe Fumimaro*. Jiji Tsūshinsha, 1958.

Yamagata Kiyoshi. "Yoshida-san no Omoide" (Remembrance of Yoshida), *Kasekikai Kaihō* 272, October 1968.

Yamamura, Kozo. *Economic Policy in Postwar Japan: Growth Versus Economic Democracy*. University of California, 1967.

Yamazaki Gōrō. *Nihon Rōdō Undō Shi* (History of the Japanese Labor Movement), revised edition. Rōmu Gyōsei Kenkyūjo, 1961.

Yanaga, Chitoshi. *Big Business in Japanese Politics*. Yale University, 1968.

Yanaihara Tadao, ed. *Sengo Nihon Shōshi* (A Short History of Postwar Japan). 2 volumes. Tokyo Daigaku, 1958.

Yoshida Naikaku Kankōkai (Yoshida Cabinets Publication Association). *Yoshida Naikaku* (The Yoshida Cabinets). 1954. Abbreviated in the notes as *YN*.

Yoshida Shigeru. "Chichi to Haha: Oitachi no Koto Nado" (Father and Mother: Matters of My Youth), *Kaizō*, January 1950, pp. 104–109.

——. "Japan and the Crisis in Asia," *Foreign Affairs* 29.2:171–181 (January 1951).

——. *Japan's Decisive Century, 1867–1967.* Praeger, 1967. Published in Japanese as *Nihon o Kettei Shita Hyakunen.*

——. "Jūnen no Ayumi" (Ten Years' Journey), 8 installments. *Mainichi Shimbun,* August 8–17, 1955.

——. *Kaisō Jūnen* (Recollections of Ten Years). 4 volumes. Shinchōsha, 1957–1958. Abbreviated in the notes as *KJ.*

——. Letters. Included among the papers of Makino Nobuaki in the National Diet Library, Tokyo, and abbreviated in the notes as *YST.*

——. *Nihon o Kettei Shita Hyakunen.* Nihon Keizai Shimbunsha, 1967. Japanese version of *Japan's Decisive Century.*

——. "Ōiso no Shōrai" (The Whispering of the Pines at Ōiso), *Chūō Kōron,* December 1965, pp. 203–210.

——. *Ōiso Seidan* (Ōiso Conversations). Okakura Shobō Shinsha, 1952.

——, with Yoshida Kenichi. *Ōiso Seidan* (Ōiso Conversations). Bungei Shunjū Shinsha, 1956.

——. *Ōiso Zuisō* (Random Thoughts from Ōiso). Sekkasha, 1962. A bilingual volume, containing articles previously published by Yoshida in the magazine *This Is Japan.*

——. *Sekai to Nihon* (The World and Japan). Banchō Shobō, 1963. Abbreviated in the notes as *SN.*

——. *The Yoshida Memoirs.* Houghton Mifflin, 1962. An abridged translation of *Kaisō Jūnen.* Abbreviated in the notes as *YM.*

"Yoshida Shigeru no Shōgai" (The Life of Yoshida Shigeru), special issue of *Asahi Gurafu,* November 5, 1967.

Yoshida, Yuki. *Whispering Leaves in Grosvenor Square, 1936–37.* Longmans, Green, 1938.

Index

This text is set in 12-point IBM Aldine Roman, with Garamond No. 3 Italic for display / Book design and typography by J. W. Dower / Composition by Horne Associates, Inc., Hanover, New Hampshire / Printing and binding by the Maple-Vail Book Manufacturing Group, Binghamton, New York.

Harvard East Asian Monographs

1. Liang Fang-chung, *The Single-Whip Method of Taxation in China*
2. Harold C. Hinton, *The Grain Tribute System of China, 1845–1911*
3. Ellsworth C. Carlson, *The Kaiping Mines, 1877–1912*
4. Chao Kuo-chün, *Agrarian Policies of Mainland China: A Documentary Study, 1949–1956*
5. Edgar Snow, *Random Notes on Red China, 1936–1945*
6. Edwin George Beal, Jr., *The Origin of Likin, 1835–1864*
7. Chao Kuo-chün, *Economic Planning and Organization in Mainland China: A Documentary Study, 1949–1957*
8. John K. Fairbank, *Ch'ing Documents: An Introductory Syllabus*
9. Helen Yin and Yi-chang Yin, *Economic Statistics of Mainland China, 1949–1957*
10. Wolfgang Franke, *The Reform and Abolition of the Traditional Chinese Examination System*
11. Albert Feuerwerker and S. Cheng, *Chinese Communist Studies of Modern Chinese History*
12. C. John Stanley, *Late Ch'ing Finance: Hu Kuang-yung as an Innovator*
13. S. M. Meng, *The Tsungli Yamen: Its Organization and Functions*
14. Ssu-yü Teng, *Historiography of the Taiping Rebellion*
15. Chun-Jo Liu, *Controversies in Modern Chinese Intellectual History: An Analytic Bibliography of Periodical Articles, Mainly of the May Fourth and Post-May Fourth Era*
16. Edward J. M. Rhoads, *The Chinese Red Army, 1927–1963: An Annotated Bibliography*
17. Andrew J. Nathan, *A History of the China International Famine Relief Commission*
18. Frank H. H. King (ed.) and Prescott Clarke, *A Research Guide to China-Coast Newspapers, 1822–1911*
19. Ellis Joffe, *Party and Army: Professionalism and Political Control in the Chinese Officer Corps, 1949–1964*
20. Toshio G. Tsukahira, *Feudal Control in Tokugawa Japan: The Sankin Kōtai System*

21. Kwang-Ching Liu, ed., *American Missionaries in China: Papers from Harvard Seminars*
22. George Moseley, *A Sino-Soviet Cultural Frontier: The Ili Kazakh Autonomous Chou*
23. Carl F. Nathan, *Plague Prevention and Politics in Manchuria, 1910–1931*
24. Adrian Arthur Bennett, *John Fryer: The Introduction of Western Science and Technology into Nineteenth-Century China*
25. Donald J. Friedman, *The Road from Isolation: The Campaign of the American Committee for Non-Participation in Japanese Aggression, 1938–1941*
26. Edward Le Fevour, *Western Enterprise in Late Ch'ing China: A Selective Survey of Jardine, Matheson and Company's Operations, 1842–1895*
27. Charles Neuhauser, *Third World Politics: China and the Afro-Asian People's Solidarity Organization, 1957–1967*
28. Kungtu C. Sun, assisted by Ralph W. Huenemann, *The Economic Development of Manchuria in the First Half of the Twentieth Century*
29. Shahid Javed Burki, *A Study of Chinese Communes, 1965*
30. John Carter Vincent, *The Extraterritorial System in China: Final Phase*
31. Madeleine Chi, *China Diplomacy, 1914–1918*
32. Clifton Jackson Phillips, *Protestant America and the Pagan World: The First Half Century of the American Board of Commissioners for Foreign Missions, 1810–1860*
33. James Pusey, *Wu Han: Attacking the Present through the Past*
34. Ying-wan Cheng, *Postal Communication in China and Its Modernization, 1860–1896*
35. Tuvia Blumenthal, *Saving in Postwar Japan*
36. Peter Frost, *The Bakumatsu Currency Crisis*
37. Stephen C. Lockwood, *Augustine Heard and Company, 1858–1862*
38. Robert R. Campbell, *James Duncan Campbell: A Memoir by His Son*
39. Jerome Alan Cohen, ed., *The Dynamics of China's Foreign Relations*
40. V. V. Vishnyakova-Akimova, *Two Years in Revolutionary China, 1925–1927*, tr. Steven I. Levine
41. Meron Medzini, *French Policy in Japan during the Closing Years of the Tokugawa Regime*
42. *The Cultural Revolution in the Provinces*
43. Sidney A. Forsythe, *An American Missionary Community in China, 1895–1905*
44. Benjamin I. Schwartz, ed., *Reflections on the May Fourth Movement: A Symposium*
45. Ching Young Choe, *The Rule of the Taewŏn'gun, 1864–1873: Restoration in Yi Korea*

46. W. P. J. Hall, *A Bibliographical Guide to Japanese Research on the Chinese Economy, 1958–1970*
47. Jack J. Gerson, *Horatio Nelson Lay and Sino-British Relations, 1854–1864*
48. Paul Richard Bohr, *Famine and the Missionary: Timothy Richard as Relief Administrator and Advocate of National Reform*
49. Endymion Wilkinson, *The History of Imperial China: A Research Guide*
50. Britten Dean, *China and Great Britain: The Diplomacy of Commerical Relations, 1860–1864*
51. Ellsworth C. Carlson, *The Foochow Missionaries, 1847–1880*
52. Yeh-chien Wang, *An Estimate of the Land-Tax Collection in China, 1753 and 1908*
53. Richard M. Pfeffer, *Understanding Business Contracts in China, 1949–1963*
54. Han-sheng Chuan and Richard Kraus, *Mid-Ch'ing Rice Markets and Trade, An Essay in Price History*
55. Ranbir Vohra, *Lao She and the Chinese Revolution*
56. Liang-lin Hsiao, *China's Foreign Trade Statistics, 1864–1949*
57. Lee-hsia Hsu Ting, *Government Control of the Press in Modern China, 1900–1949*
58. Edward W. Wagner, *The Literati Purges: Political Conflict in Early Yi Korea*
59. Joungwon A. Kim, *Divided Korea: The Politics of Development, 1945–1972*
60. Noriko Kamachi, John K. Fairbank, and Chūzō Ichiko, *Japanese Studies of Modern China Since 1953: A Bibliographical Guide to Historical and Social-Science Research on the Nineteenth and Twentieth Centuries, Supplementary Volume for 1953–1969*
61. Donald A. Gibbs and Yun-chen Li, *A Bibliography of Studies and Translations of Modern Chinese Literature, 1918–1942*
62. Robert H. Silin, *Leadership and Values: The Organization of Large-Scale Taiwanese Enterprises*
63. David Pong, *A Critical Guide to the Kwangtung Provincial Archives Deposited at the Public Record Office of London*
64. Fred W. Drake, *China Charts the World: Hsu Chi-yü and His Geography of 1848*
65. William A. Brown and Urgunge Onon, translators and annotators, *History of the Mongolian People's Republic*
66. Edward L. Farmer, *Early Ming Government: The Evolution of Dual Capitals*
67. Ralph C. Croizier, *Koxinga and Chinese Nationalism: History, Myth, and the Hero*
68. William J. Tyler, tr., *The Psychological World of Natsumi Sōseki*, by Doi Takeo

69. Eric Widmer, *The Russian Ecclesiastical Mission in Peking during the Eighteenth Century*
70. Charlton M. Lewis, *Prologue to the Chinese Revolution: The Transformation of Ideas and Institutions in Hunan Province, 1891–1907*
71. Preston Torbert, *The Ch'ing Imperial Household Department: A Study of its Organization and Principal Functions, 1662–1796*
72. Paul A. Cohen and John E. Schrecker, eds., *Reform in Nineteenth-Century China*
73. Jon Sigurdson, *Rural Industrialization in China*
74. Kang Chao, *The Development of Cotton Textile Production in China*
75. Valentin Rabe, *The Home Base of American China Missions, 1880–1920*
76. Sarasin Viraphol, *Tribute and Profit: Sino-Siamese Trade, 1652–1853*
77. Ch'i-ch'ing Hsiao, *The Military Establishment of the Yuan Dynasty*
78. Meishi Tsai, *Contemporary Chinese Novels and Short Stories, 1949–1974: An Annotated Bibliography*
79. Wellington K. K. Chan, *Merchants, Mandarins, and Modern Enterprise in Late Ch'ing China*
80. Endymion Wilkinson, *Landlord and Labor in Late Imperial China: Case Studies from Shandong by Jing Su and Luo Lun*
81. Barry Keenan, *The Dewey Experiment in China: Educational Reform and Political Power in the Early Republic*
82. George A. Hayden, *Crime and Punishment in Medieval Chinese Drama: Three Judge Pao Plays*
83. Sang-Chul Suh, *Growth and Structural Changes in the Korean Economy, 1910–1940*
84. J. W. Dower, *Empire and Aftermath: Yoshida Shigeru and the Japanese Experience, 1878–1954*

STUDIES IN THE MODERNIZATION OF THE REPUBLIC OF KOREA: 1945–1975

86. Kwang Suk Kim and Michael Roemer, *Growth and Structural Transformation*
87. Anne O. Krueger, *The Developmental Role of the Foreign Sector and Aid*
88. Edwin S. Mills and Byung-Nak Song, *Urbanization and Urban Problems*
89. Sung Hwan Ban, Pal Yong Moon, and Dwight H. Perkins, *Rural Development*
90. Noel F. McGinn, Donald R. Snodgrass, Yung Bong Kim, Shin-Bok Kim, and Quee-Young Kim, *Education and Development in Korea*

91. Leroy P. Jones and Il SaKong, *Government, Business, and Entrepreneurship in Economic Development: The Korean Case*

92. Edward S. Mason, Dwight H. Perkins, Kwang Suk Kim, David C. Cole, Mahn Je Kim, et al., *The Economic and Social Modernization of the Republic of Korea*